W9-AXV-001

KAPLAN

RELATED TITLES FOR COLLEGE-BOUND STUDENTS

The Procrastinator's Guide to the ACT 2006

SAT Premier Program 2006
SAT Comprehensive Program 2006
12 Practice Tests for the SAT
SAT Strategies for Super Busy Students
Inside the SAT: 10 Strategies to Help You Score Higher
SAT 2400, Second Edition
SAT Critical Reading Workbook
SAT Math Workbook
SAT Writing Workbook
SAT Vocabulary Flashcards Flip-O-Matic, Second Edition
Extreme SAT Vocabulary Flashcards Flip-O-Matic, Second Edition
The Ring of McAllister: A Score-Raising Mystery Featuring 1,046 Must-Know SAT Vocabulary Words
Frankenstein: A Kaplan New SAT Score-Raising Classic
The Tales of Edgar Allan Poe: A Kaplan New SAT Score-Raising Classic
Dr. Jekyll and Mr. Hyde: A Kaplan New SAT Score-Raising Classic
Wuthering Heights: A Kaplan New SAT Score-Raising Classic
Domina El SAT: Prepárate para Tomar el Examen para Ingresar a la Universidad

AP Biology
AP Calculus AB/BC
AP Chemistry
AP English Language & Composition
AP English Literature & Composition
AP Macroeconomics/Microeconomics
AP Physics B & C
AP Psychology
AP Statistics
AP U.S. Government & Politics
AP U.S. History
AP World History

SAT Subject Test: Biology E/M
SAT Subject Test: Chemistry
SAT Subject Test: Literature
SAT Subject Test: Mathematics Level 1
SAT Subject Test: Mathematics Level 2
SAT Subject Test: Physics
SAT Subject Test: Spanish
SAT Subject Test: U.S. History
SAT Subject Test: World History

Test Prep and Admissions

ACT®

2006 Edition
with CD-ROM

By the Staff of Kaplan Test Prep and Admissions

Simon & Schuster

NEW YORK · LONDON · SYDNEY · TORONTO

Kaplan Publishing
Published by SIMON & SCHUSTER
Rockefeller Center
1230 Avenue of the Americas
New York, New York 10020

Contributing Editor: Jon Zeitlin
Editorial Director: Jennifer Farthing
Project Editor: Anne Kemper
Production Manager: Michael Shevlin
Content Manager: Patrick Kennedy
Interior Page Layout: Jan Gladish
Cover Design: Mark Weaver

Manufactured in the United States of America
Published Simultaneously in Canada

January 2006

10 9 8 7 6 5 4 3
ISBN-13 978-0-7432-6574-4
ISBN-10 0-7432-6574-2

For information regarding special discounts for bulk purchases, please contact Simon & Schuster Special Sales at 1-800-456-6798 or business@simonandschuster.com.

Table of Contents

Available Online

FREE ADDITIONAL PRACTICE

kaptest.com/booksonline

As owner of this guide, you are entitled to get more ACT practice and help online. Log on to **kaptest.com/booksonline** to access a selection of ACT workshops and practice questions.

Access to this selection of online ACT practice material is free of charge to purchasers of this book. When you log on, you'll be asked to input the book's ISBN number (see the bar code on the back cover). And you'll be asked for a specific password derived from the text in this book, so have your book handy when you log on.

FOR ANY TEST CHANGES OR LATE-BREAKING DEVELOPMENTS

kaptest.com/publishing

The material in this book is up-to-date at the time of publication. However, ACT Inc. may have instituted changes in the test after this book was published. Be sure to carefully read the materials you receive when you register for the test. If there are any important late-breaking developments—or any changes or corrections to the Kaplan test preparation materials in this book—we will post that information online at **kaptest.com/publishing**.

FEEDBACK AND COMMENTS

kaplansurveys.com/books

We'd love to hear your comments and suggestions about this book. We invite you to fill out our online survey form at **kaplansurveys.com/books**. Your feedback is extremely helpful as we continue to develop high-quality resources to meet your needs.

How to Use This Book

Ideally, you should take a couple of months to work through this book, though it's certainly possible to work through in far less time. Here's how to go about training with it, assuming you have at least a month. If you have less than a month to prepare, read the Emergency Plan section that follows this one.

1. Read the User's Guide at the back of the book to learn how to use the *Higher Score on the ACT* CD-ROM for your training.
2. Read the section entitled **ACT Basics** to get a handle on the test, its format, and the basic Kaplan strategies for approaching the test.
3. Go on to the **Skill-Building Workouts**. These will prepare you in a more focused way for each type of ACT question, and teach you all sorts of test-taking strategies and techniques. If you find that you're weak in one of the knowledge-based areas (if, for instance, your geometry principles are a little rusty) refer to the **ACT Resources** at the back of the book.
4. When you've finished the Workouts, review what you've learned by going over the **Strategic Summaries**.
5. Take **Practice Test 1** *under strictly timed conditions*.
6. Go over the **Explanations for Practice Test 1**. Find out where you need help and then review the appropriate Workouts.
7. Take **Practice Test 2** under testlike conditions.
8. Go over the **Explanations for Practice Test 2**.
9. Read the **Last-Minute Tips** and review the **Strategic Summaries** once more before taking your actual ACT.
10. Give yourself a day of rest right before the real exam.

If you have time, do just two or three Workouts a week, and let it sink in slowly. Don't hesitate to take some time off from the ACT when you need to. Nobody can take this stuff day in and day out for weeks at a time without a break.

This book contains two complete practice tests written by our staff of Kaplan ACT gurus to provide you with real testlike practice. We have included explanations for these tests, so you can better understand your mistakes (and your successes) and use that information to shore up your weak points before Test Day.

You'll also find the most important points regarding the ACT and invaluable advice in Kaplan easy-to-read sidebars throughout the book.

ACT EMERGENCY PLAN

Maybe you have only two or three weeks. Or even less. Don't freak! This book has been designed to work for students in your situation, too. If you go through a Workout or two every day, you can finish this book in a couple of weeks. If you have very limited time to prepare for the ACT (fewer than two weeks), we suggest you do the following:

1. Take a slow, deep breath. Check out the CD-ROM User's Guide to find out how to use the software that accompanies this book.
2. Read the section of this book entitled **ACT Basics**.
3. Skip to the **Strategic Summaries** and go over them thoroughly.
4. Take **Practice Tests 1** and **2** under timed conditions.
5. Review your results, with special attention to the questions you missed. Then read the **Last-Minute Tips**.
6. Give yourself the day before the test off.

If you have more than a couple of weeks to prepare, read as many of the Workouts as you can, especially in areas you know will give you trouble. The English and Math subtests require specific knowledge of the rules of grammar and mathematics. If you have trouble with English or Math because you just don't know the material being tested, we suggest you use the **ACT Resources** section.

Scattered throughout the book you'll find sidebars that spotlight some very important test prep information. Sidebars also highlight key points, fun facts, and real-world stories.

ACT Emergency FAQs

Q: *It's two days before the ACT and I'm clueless. What should I do?*

A: First of all, don't panic. If you have only a day or two to prepare for the test, then you don't have time to prepare thoroughly. But that doesn't mean you should just give up. There's still a lot you can do to improve your potential score. First and foremost, you should become familiar with the test. Read the section called **ACT Basics.** And if you don't do anything else, take one of the full-length **Practice Tests** at the back of this book under reasonably testlike conditions. When you finish the practice test, check your answers and look at the explanations to the questions you didn't get right.

Q: *Math is my weak spot. What can I do to get better at math in a big hurry?*

A: Review the **Math Glossary** and the **100 Key Math Concepts for the ACT**, in **ACT Resources**. Then do as many of the **Math Workouts** as you have time for. If you don't have time to do the Workouts, just read the sidebars in those chapters. They contain really helpful facts and tips.

Q: *I'm great at math, but terrible at English. How can I improve my English score right away?*

A: Go straight to the **ACT Resources** and read through the **English Review for the ACT**. Then do as many of the **English Workouts** as you have time for. If you don't have time to do the Workouts, just read the sidebars in those chapters. The strategies can help boost your score. Remember the words "when in doubt, leave it out." This strategy will get you far in a pinch.

Q: *I'm not very good at science in school. How can I improve my Science score right now?*

A: Fortunately, the Science section of your ACT tests your ability to think critically and interpret data, and not your ability to memorize specific scientific facts and theories. Cutting through the jargon and not being intimidated by this section is the first, best step to a higher Science score.

Q: *I read very slowly. How can I boost my Reading score quickly?*

A: Remember that ACT Reading is all about getting the gist of the passage, and not focusing on the details. Focus on the first third of the passage, paraphrase, and skim past any confusing details so you can get to the questions quickly. You don't get any points for reading the passage: All your points on the Reading section will come from answering the questions. Get the gist of the passage, and skim the details, and you'll have extra time to handle the questions. For more ACT Reading tips, check out the **Reading Workouts**.

Q: *The ACT is tomorrow. Should I stay up all night studying geometry formulas?*

A: The best thing to do right now is to try to stay calm. Read the **Last-Minute Tips** chapter to find out the best way to survive the next couple of days. And get a good night's sleep.

Q: What's the most important thing I can do to get ready for the ACT?

A: Relax, stay calm, and know the basics of the test. Remember there is no penalty for wrong answers on the ACT. Take good guesses and manage your time so that you leave no questions unanswered. Focus on your strengths rather than your weaknesses, since that's where you'll earn the bulk of your points. Stay confident, and don't cram. The key to getting your best score possible is showing up on Test Day well rested, well fed, and confident.

Q. *So it's a good idea to panic, right? RIGHT?*

A. No! No matter how prepared you are for the ACT, stress will hurt your performance, and it's really no fun. Stay confident, and don't cram. So . . . breathe. Stay calm and remember, it's just a test.

Note for International Students

If you are an international student considering attending an American university, you are not alone. Over 586,323 international students pursued academic degrees at the undergraduate, graduate, or professional school level at U.S. universities during the 2002–2003 academic year, according to the Institute of International Education's Open Doors report. Almost 50 percent of these students were studying for a bachelor's or first university degree. This number of international students pursuing higher education in the United States is expected to continue to grow. Business, management, engineering, and the physical and life sciences are particularly popular majors for students coming to the United States from other countries.

If you are not a U.S. citizen and you are interested in attending college or university in the United States, here is what you'll need to get started.

- If English is not your first language, you'll probably need to take the TOEFL® (Test of English as a Foreign Language) or provide some other evidence that you are proficient in English. Colleges and universities in the United States will differ on what they consider to be an acceptable TOEFL score. Because American undergraduate programs require all students to take a certain number of general education courses, all students—even math and computer science students—need to be able to communicate well in spoken and written English.
- You may also need to take the SAT® or the ACT®. Many undergraduate institutions in the United States require both the SAT and TOEFL for international students.
- There are over 3,400 accredited colleges and universities in the United States, so selecting the correct undergraduate school can be a confusing task for anyone. You will need to get help from a good advisor or at least a good college guide that gives you detailed information on the different schools available. Since admission to many undergraduate programs is quite competitive, you may want to select three or four colleges and complete applications for each school.
- You should begin the application process at least a year in advance. An increasing number of schools accept applications year round. In any case, find out the application deadlines and plan accordingly. Although September (the fall semester) is the traditional time to begin university study in the United States, you can begin your studies at many schools in January (the spring semester).
- In addition, you will need to obtain an I-20 Certificate of Eligibility from the school you plan to attend if you intend to apply for an F-1 Student Visa to study in the United States.

KAPLAN ENGLISH PROGRAMS*

If you need more help navigating the complex process of university admissions, preparing for the SAT, ACT, or TOEFL, or building your English language skills in general, you may be interested in Kaplan's programs for international students.

Kaplan English Programs were designed to help students and professionals from outside the United States meet their educational and career goals. At locations throughout the United States, international students take advantage of Kaplan's programs to help them improve their academic and conversational English skills, raise their scores on the TOEFL, SAT, ACT, and other standardized exams, and gain admission to the schools of their choice. Our staff and instructors give international students the individualized attention they need to succeed. Here is a brief description of some of Kaplan's programs for international students:

General Intensive English

Kaplan's General Intensive English classes are designed to help you improve your skills in all areas of English and to increase your fluency in spoken and written English. Classes are available for beginning to advanced students, and the average class size is 12 students.

TOEFL and Academic English

This course provides you with the skills you need to improve your TOEFL score and succeed in an American university or graduate program. It includes advanced reading, writing, listening, grammar, and conversational English. You will also receive training for the TOEFL using Kaplan's exclusive computer-based practice materials.

OTHER KAPLAN PROGRAMS

Since 1938, more than 3 million students have come to Kaplan to advance their studies, prepare for entry to American universities, and further their careers. In addition to the above programs, Kaplan offers courses to prepare for the ACT, GMAT®, GRE®, MCAT®, DAT®, USMLE®, NCLEX-RN®, and other standardized exams at locations throughout the United States.

Applying to Kaplan English Programs

To get more information, or to apply for admission to any of Kaplan's programs for international students and professionals, contact us at:

Kaplan English Programs

700 South Flower, Suite 2900
Los Angeles, CA 90017, USA
Phone (if calling from within the United States): 800-818-9128
Phone (if calling from outside the United States): 213-452-5800
Fax: 213-892-1364
Website: www.kaplanenglish.com
Email: world@kaplan.com

*Kaplan is authorized under federal law to enroll nonimmigrant alien students. Kaplan is accredited by ACCET (Accrediting Council for Continuing Education and Training).

Chapter One: **Introduction to the ACT**

- **Three Keys to ACT Success**
- **What Is the ACT?**
- **Overview of the ACT**
- **ACT FAQs**
- **ACT Registration Overview**

Before you plunge into studying for the ACT, let's take a step back and look at the big picture. What's the ACT all about? How can you prepare for it? How's it scored? This chapter will answer these questions and more.

The ACT is an opportunity, not a barrier. In fact, you should be grateful that you have to take it. Really. Because a strong ACT score is one credential that doesn't depend on things you can't control. It doesn't depend on how good or bad your high school is. It doesn't depend on how many academic luminaries you know, or how rich and famous your family is, or whether any of your teachers are gullible enough to swear in a letter of recommendation that you're the greatest scientific mind since Isaac Newton. No, your ACT score depends on only you.

Granted, the ACT is a tough exam. It's probably one of the toughest exams you'll ever take. But you should be grateful for that too. Really. If the ACT were easy, everyone would do well. A good score wouldn't mean much. But because it's such a bear of a test, the ACT can be your single best opportunity to show what you can do, to prove to colleges that you are the candidate of choice—for admission, for advanced placement, for scholarships.

Emergency Plan

If you have two weeks or fewer to prep for the ACT, don't panic. The first thing you should do is become familiar with the test. This chapter is the place to start.

It's important, though, that you take the test in the right spirit. Don't be timid in the face of the ACT. Don't let it bully you. You've got to take control of the test. Our mission in this book is to show you exactly how to do that.

It helps to think of the ACT challenge as a contest—not only between you and the test, but also between you and that other person trying to get your spot in college. The ACT, after all, is meant to provide a way for all college applicants to compete on an even playing field. How do you compete successfully in a fair academic fight? You train—harder and smarter than the next person. First, you learn whatever knowledge and skills you need to know. But then, just as important, you learn how to show what you know, in ways that the test is designed to reward. You learn how to be a savvy test taker.

THREE KEYS TO ACT SUCCESS

There are three basic commandments for achieving ACT success. Following any of these by itself will improve your score. Following all three together will make you nothing less than awesome.

1. Thou Shalt Learn the Test

The ACT is very predictable. You'd think the test makers would get bored after a while, but they don't. The same kinds of questions, testing the same skills and concepts, appear every time the ACT is given.

Because the test specifications rarely change, you should know in advance what to expect on every section. Just a little familiarity can make an enormous difference on the ACT. Here are a few ways in which learning the test will boost your score:

- **You'll learn the directions.** Why waste valuable time reading directions when you can have them down pat beforehand? You need every second during the test to answer questions and get points.
- **You'll learn the difficulty range of questions.** It's a fact that a typical ACT test taker gets only about half the questions right. Knowing this will stop you from panicking when you hit an impossible science passage or trigonometry question. Relax! You can skip many tough questions on the ACT and still get a great score! And once you know that the questions aren't arranged in order of difficulty, you'll know that just beyond that awful question will be one, two, or even three easy questions that you can score on with no sweat at all.
- **You'll learn how to get extra points by guessing.** Unlike some other standardized tests, the ACT has no wrong-answer penalty. Knowing that simple fact can boost your score significantly. If you can't answer a question, guess.
- **You'll learn what makes a high-scoring essay.** If you are taking the optional Writing test, learning how it is scored will help you craft a good essay.

We'll help you get a better understanding of the ACT in the chapter following this one, entitled "The Subject Tests: A Preview."

2. Thou Shalt Learn the Strategies

The ACT isn't a normal exam. Most normal exams test your memory. The ACT isn't like that. The ACT tests problem-solving skills rather than memory, and it does so in a standardized-test format. That makes the test highly vulnerable to test-smart strategies and techniques.

Most students miss a lot of ACT questions for no good reason. They see a tough-looking question, say to themselves, "Uh-oh, I don't remember how to do that," and then they start to gnaw on their No. 2 pencils.

But many ACT questions can be answered without perfect knowledge of the material being tested. Often, all you need to do to succeed on the ACT is to think strategically and creatively. We call this kind of strategic, creative frame of mind "The ACT Mindset."

How do you put yourself into the ACT Mindset? You continually ask yourself questions like: "What does this mean? How can I put this into a form I can understand and use? How can I do this faster?" Once you develop some savvy test-taking skills, you'll find yourself capable of working out problems that at first reading might have scared you half to death! In fact, we'll show you how you can sometimes get right answers when you don't even understand the question or the passage it's attached to!

There are many, many specific strategies you can use to boost your score. For instance, here are just a couple of things you'll learn:

- **You'll learn the peculiarities of the ACT format.** Except for the Writing test, the ACT is a multiple-choice test. The correct answer is always right there in front of you. We'll show you how to develop specific tactics for each question type to maximize the chances of selecting the correct answer. The wrong answers are often predictable. For example, in English the shortest answer is the correct answer with surprising frequency. Strange, but true. Knowing statistical information like this can give you an important edge.
- **You'll learn a plan of attack for each subject test.** We'll show you some really useful ways of attacking each subject test. You'll learn how to do "question triage"—deciding which questions to do now and which to save for later. You'll learn a strategic method for each subject test designed to get you points quickly and systematically. You'll learn gridding techniques to avoid any answer-sheet disasters.
- **You'll learn "unofficial" ways of getting right answers fast.** On the ACT, nobody cares how you decide which choice to select. The only thing that matters is picking the right answer. That's different from the way it works on most high school tests, where you get credit for showing that you've done the questions the "right" way (that is, the way you were taught to do them by Mrs. Crabapple in high school). We'll show you how to find creative shortcuts to the correct answers—"unofficial" methods that will save you precious time and net you extra points.

The basic test-smart techniques and strategies for the whole test are covered in the chapter called "Taking Control: The Top Ten Strategies." General strategies for each subject test, plus specific hints, techniques, and strategies for individual question types, are found in the Skill-Building Workouts. These are then summarized in the Strategic Summaries.

3. Thou Shalt Learn the Material Tested

The ACT is designed to test skills and concepts learned in high school and needed for college. Familiarity with the test, coupled with smart test-taking strategies, will take you only so far. For your best score you need to sharpen up the skills and knowledge that the ACT rewards. Sometimes, in other words, you've just got to eat your spinach.

The good news is that most of the content on the ACT is pretty basic. You've probably already learned most of what the ACT expects you to know. But you may need help remembering. That's partly what this book is for—to remind you of the knowledge you already have and to build and refine the specific skills you've developed in high school. Here are just a few of the things we'll "remind" you of:

- **You'll learn how to read graphs and tables.** Many Science questions rely on your ability to use data presented in the form of graphs and tables. (We'll teach you how to read graphs and tables in Science Workout 1.)
- **You'll learn how to do trigonometry problems.** Do you remember exactly what a cotangent is? A cosine? We didn't think so. But there are four trig problems on every ACT. (You can learn about trigonometry problems in 100 Key Math Concepts for the ACT, items 96–100.)
- **You'll learn the difference between *lie* and *lay*.** Is it "I lay down on the couch" or "I lie down on the couch"? You may want to lie down yourself if you encounter such issues on the ACT. But don't fret. We'll remind you of the common grammar traps the test lays for you (or is it *lies* for you ???). (For a discussion of this conundrum, see Classic Grammar Error #9 in English Workout 3.)

Specifics like those mentioned above comprise what we call the ACT "knowledge base." The components of this knowledge base are reviewed along the way throughout this book. The ACT Resources section summarizes this information for the two sections of the ACT that explicitly test knowledge: English and Math.

In sum, then, follow these three commandments:

1. Thou shalt learn the test.
2. Thou shalt learn the strategies.
3. Thou shalt learn the material tested.

If you do, you'll find yourself just where you should be on test day: in full command of your ACT test-taking experience. Count on it.

WHAT IS THE ACT?

It was Attila the Hun who first coined this epigram: Knowing the enemy is the first step in conquering the enemy. Attila, of course, was talking about waging wars on the steppes of Central Asia, but his advice also works for taking standardized tests in central Illinois. In fact, that's probably why Attila got a Composite Score of 30 on the ACT.

Well, to be honest, we haven't fact-checked Attila the Hun's ACT score, but the point remains valid. To succeed on the ACT, you've got to know the ACT.

But is the ACT really your enemy? Only in a manner of speaking. The test is more like an adversary in a game of chess. If you know your adversary's entire repertoire of moves and clever stratagems, you'll find it that much easier to beat him. Myths about the ACT are common. Even high school teachers and guidance counselors sometimes give out inaccurate information (we know you're shocked to hear this). To earn your best score, you need to know how the ACT is really put together.

So, before anything, take some time and get to know this so-called adversary. Let's start with the basics. The ACT is a three-hour exam (three and a half hours if you take the optional Writing test) taken by high school juniors and seniors for admission to college. It is not an IQ test; it's a test of problem-solving skills—which means that you can improve your performance by preparing for it.

Speaking of myths, you may have heard that the ACT is really the only thing colleges look at when deciding whether to admit you. Untrue. Most admissions officers say the ACT is only one of several factors they take into consideration. But let's be realistic about ACT scores. Here's this neat and easy way of comparing all students numerically, no matter what their academic backgrounds and no matter how much grade inflation exists at their high schools. You know the admissions people are going to take a serious look at your test scores.

The ACT consists of four subject tests: English, Math, Reading, and Science, as well as the optional Writing test. All the subject tests are primarily designed to test skills rather than knowledge, though some knowledge is required—particularly in English, for which a familiarity with grammar and writing mechanics is important, and in Math, for which you need to know the basic math concepts taught in a regular high school curriculum. The Writing test tests your ability to communicate clearly your position on an issue.

OVERVIEW OF THE ACT

- The ACT is about three hours long (three and a half with the Writing test).
- There will be a short break between the second and third subtests.
- The ACT consists of a total of 215 scored multiple-choice questions, and 1 optional essay
- The exam is comprised of four subject tests and an optional Writing test:
  English (45 minutes, 75 questions)
  Math (60 minutes, 60 questions)
  Reading (35 minutes, 40 questions)
  Science (35 minutes, 40 questions)
  Writing (30 minutes, 1 essay question)

ACT FAQS

Here are some quick answers to the questions students ask most frequently about the ACT.

What's a Good ACT Score?

Most ACT test takers score between 17 and 23. A score below 17 will seriously limit your choice of colleges. But any score above 23 will be an asset in your quest for admission to a competitive college.

How Is the ACT Scored?

No, your ACT score is not merely the sum total of questions you get right. That would be too simple. Instead, what the test makers do is add up all of your correct answers to get what they call a "raw score." Then they put that raw score into a very large computer, which proceeds to shake, rattle, smoke, and wheeze before spitting out an official score at the other end. That score—which has been put through what they call a *scoring formula*—is your "scaled score."

ACT scaled scores range from 1 to 36. Nearly half of all test takers score within a much narrower range: 17–23. Tests at different dates vary slightly, but the following data are based on a recent administration of the test and can be considered typical.

ACT Approximate Percentile Rank*	Scaled (or Composite) Score	Percentage of Questions Correct
99%	31	90%
90%	26	75%
76%	23	63%
54%	20	53%
28%	17	43%

* Percentage of ACT takers scoring at or below given score

Notice that to earn a score of 20 (the national average), you need to answer only about 53 percent of the questions correctly. On most tests, getting only a bit more than half the questions right would be terrible. Not so on the ACT. Getting about half of the ACT questions correct and earning a score of 20 won't earn you a lifetime membership in the Academy of Arts and Sciences, maybe, but it's nothing to be ashamed of.

A Little Goes a Long Way

Just a few questions right or wrong on the ACT can make a big difference. Answering only five extra questions correctly on each subject test can move you from the bottom of the applicant pool into the middle, or from the middle up to the top.

The score data above includes two very strong scores: 26 and 31. Either score would impress almost any college admissions officer. A 26 would put you in the top ten percent of the students who take the exam, and a 31 would put you in the top one percent. Even a 31 requires getting only about 90 percent of the questions right. The best student in your high school will probably get at least a dozen questions wrong. There are questions that even your smartest teachers would get wrong.

If you earn a score of 23, you'll be in about the 76th percentile. That means that 76 percent of the test takers did as well as, or worse than, you did—in other words, that only 24 percent did better than you. It means you're in the "top quarter" of the people who take the ACT. That's a good score. But notice that to earn this score, you need only about 63 percent of the questions correct. On most tests, a score of 63 is probably a D or an F. But on the ACT, it's about a B+.

How Many ACT Scores Will You Get?

The "ACT scaled score" we've talked about so far is technically called the "composite score." It's the really important one. But when you take the ACT, you actually receive twelve (or thirteen) different scores: the composite score, four (or five) subject scores, and seven (or eight) subscores. Though the subject scores can play a role in decisions at some schools, the subscores usually aren't important for most people, so feel free to ignore the chart below if you don't feel like looking at it.

Here's the full battery of ACT scores (1–36) you'll receive. Few people (except your parents, maybe) will care about anything except your composite score for college admissions, though some schools use subscores for course placement.

English Score (1–36)	Usage/Mechanics subscore (1–18); Rhetorical Skills subscore (1–18); (Optional) Writing subscore (2–12)
Math Score (1–36)	Prealgebra/Elementary Algebra subscore (1–18); Algebra/Coordinate Geometry subscore (1–18); Plane Geometry/Trigonometry subscore (1–18)
Reading Score (1–36)	Social Sciences/Sciences subscore (1–18); Arts/Literature subscore (1–18)
Science Score (1–36)	There are no subscores in Science.
(Optional) Combined English-Writing Score (1–36)	Does not count towards your composite score, but colleges will see it.

How Do Colleges Use Your ACT Score?

The most important score for most test takers is the composite score (which is an average of the four major subject scores). This is the score used by most colleges and universities in the admissions process, and the one that you'll want to mention casually at parties during your freshman year of college. The subject scores and subscores may be used for advanced placement or occasionally for scholarships, but are primarily used by college advisors to help students select majors and first-year courses.

Answer Every Question

By the end of each subject test, you should have answered every question, even if you had to take a random guess on some. A lucky guess will raise your score, and an unlucky guess will leave you no worse off. There's no penalty for a wrong answer. None. Zippo.

Although many schools deny that they use benchmark scores as cutoffs, we're not sure we really believe them. Big Ten universities and colleges with similarly competitive admissions generally decline to accept students with composite scores below 22 or 23. For less competitive schools, the benchmark score may be lower than that; for some very selective schools, the cutoff may be higher.

To be fair, no school uses the ACT as an absolute bar to admission, no matter how low it is. But for most applicants, a low ACT score is decisive. As a rule, only students whose backgrounds are extremely unusual or who have overcome enormous disadvantages are accepted if their ACT scores are below the benchmark. It also sometimes helps if you can convince your parents to donate a gymnasium to the school you're aiming for.

Should You Take the Optional Writing Test?

You should decide whether to take the ACT Writing test based on the admissions policies of the schools you will apply to and on the advice of your high school guidance counselors. A list of colleges requiring the test is maintained on the ACT website, www.act.org/aap/writing. If you are unsure about what schools you will apply to, you should plan to take the Writing test. However, testing will be available later if you decide not to take the Writing test and discover later that you need it.

How Do Schools Use the Optional Writing Test?

The ACT Writing test may be used for either admissions or course placement purposes, or both. Students who take the Writing test will receive an English score, a Writing subscore, and a combined English-Writing score on a 1–36 scale. (The combined English-Writing score is not averaged into the composite score.) Copies of the essay (with the graders' comments) will also be available online for downloading. Schools that do not require the Writing test will also receive the Combined English-Writing score for students who have taken the Writing test, unless the school specifically asks *not* to receive those results.

Should You Guess on the ACT?

The short answer? Yes! The long answer? Yes, of course!

As we saw, ACT scores are based on the number of correct answers only. This means that questions that you leave blank and questions you answer incorrectly simply don't count. Unlike some other standardized tests, the ACT has no "wrong-answer penalty." That's why you should always take a guess on every ACT question you can't answer, even if you don't have time to read it. Though the questions vary enormously in difficulty, harder questions are worth exactly the same as easier ones, so it pays to guess on the really hard questions and spend your time breezing through the really easy ones. We'll show you just how to do this in the chapter called "Taking Control: The Top Ten Strategies."

Wait to Send Your Score

When you sign up for the ACT, you can choose colleges to receive your score. Unless time is of the essence, don't do it, even though the first four score reports are sent for free. Wait until you get your score, then send it out (for a small additional fee) if you're happy. If you hate your score, you can take the test again and send only the new, improved score.

Can You Retake the Test?

You can take the ACT as many times as you like. You can then select whichever test score you prefer to be sent to colleges when you apply. However, you cannot take advantage of this option if, at the time you register for the test, you designate certain colleges to receive your scores. Thus it is crucial that you not designate any colleges at the time you register for the test. You can (for a small additional fee) have ACT scores sent to colleges at any time you desire after the scores are reported.

Unless you don't have enough money for that small extra fee or if you're taking the ACT under the wire and you need your scores to reach the schools you're applying to ASAP, give yourself the freedom to retake the test. What this means, of course, is that even if you blow the ACT once, you can give yourself another chance without the schools of your choice knowing about it. The ACT is one of the few areas of your academic life in which you get a second chance.

ACT REGISTRATION OVERVIEW

- To get a registration packet, see your guidance counselor, or contact:

  ACT Registration
  P.O. Box 168
  Iowa City, IA 52243-0168
  Phone: (319) 337-1270
  Web: act.org

- Students with disabilities or with other special circumstances can call (319) 337-1332.
- The basic fee at press time for the ACT is $29.00 without the Writing test, and $43.00 with the Writing test, in the United States. (For students testing outside the fifty United States, the fee is $47.00. Call 319-337-1448 for more information on taking the test outside the United States.)

  This price includes reports for you, your high school, and up to four college choices. There are additional fees for late registration, standby testing, changing test centers or test dates, and for additional services and products.
- In the United States, the ACT is administered in October, December, February, April, and June. (The February date is not available in the state of New York.) In selected states, the ACT is also offered in late September. Register early to secure the time you want at the test center of your choice and to avoid late registration fees.
- You may take the ACT Assessment as often as you wish. Many students take it twice, once as a junior and again as a senior. There are no limitations on how many times you can take the ACT, but there are some restrictions on how often you can test. For example, you can test only once per national test date.
- Be sure you take your test center admission ticket and acceptable identification with you to the test center. Acceptable forms of identification are a photo ID or a recent published photo with your full name printed. Unacceptable forms of identification are a birth certificate, social security card, or any other ID without photo. You will not be admitted without acceptable identification.
- Check with ACT, Inc. for all the latest information on the test. Every effort is made to keep the information in this book up to date, but changes may occur after the book is published.
- You might be considering whether to take the ACT, the SAT, or both. For more information on the SAT, go to the College Board's website at collegeboard.com.

Chapter Two: **The Subject Tests: A Preview**

- **English**
- **Math**
- **Reading**
- **Science**
- **Writing**

Okay, you've seen how the ACT is set up. But to really know your adversary, you've got to know something about the ACT subject tests (which, by the way, always appear in the above order.)

As we'll see, the questions in every subject test vary widely in difficulty. Some are so easy that most elementary school students could answer them. Others would give even Einstein a little trouble. But, again: The questions are not arranged in order of difficulty. That's different from some other tests, in which easier questions come first. Skipping past hard questions is very important, since otherwise you may never reach easy ones toward the end of the exam.

Emergency Plan

If you have two weeks or fewer to prep for the ACT, you should spend time getting familiar with the test. Be sure to read this chapter. You'll learn the directions and how the tests are organized.

Here's a preview of the types of questions you'll see on the subject tests. We'll keep them toward the easy end of the difficulty scale here, but later, in the Skill-Building Workouts, we'll be less kind.

After we look at the four required subject tests, we'll give you a preview of the optional Writing Test.

ENGLISH

The English test lasts 45 minutes and includes 75 questions. That works out to about 30 seconds per question. When it comes down to it, though, you should spend less time on easier questions and more on harder questions. The test is divided into 5 passages, each with about 15 questions.

Note: You're not tested on spelling or vocabulary here. Rather, the ACT is designed to test your understanding of the conventions of English—punctuation, grammar, sentence structure—and of rhetorical skills. Rhetorical skills are more strategic things like organizing the text and making sure it's styled clearly.

Students nearly always get more questions correct in English than in any other section. That tends to make them think that English is a lot easier than the rest of the ACT. But, alas, it's not that simple. Because most students do well, the test makers have much higher expectations for English than for other parts of the test. They know that it's generally easier to get English questions right than, say, Science questions. They've got a whole department of little statistician elves who keep track of things like this. That's why, to earn an average English subscore (a 20, say), you have to get almost two-thirds of the questions right, while on the rest of the test you need to get only about half right.

Don't Get Bogged Down

ACT questions are not arranged in order of ascending difficulty. Theoretically, the first question you see could be the hardest on the test. Who needs that kind of aggravation? Not you. Skip past the tough questions and spend your first minutes on the test piling up some easy points.

The Format

Almost all of the English questions follow a standard format. A word, phrase, or sentence in a passage is underlined. You're given four options: to leave the underlined portion alone ("NO CHANGE," which is always the first choice), or to replace it with one of three alternatives.

Example

. . . Pike's Peak in Southwest Colorado is named before Zebulon Pike, an early explorer. (37) He traveled through the area, exploring . . .

37. **A.** NO CHANGE
B. before Zebulon Pike became an explorer,
C. after Zebulon Pike, when,
D. after Zebulon Pike.

The best answer for number 37 above is D. The other choices all have various problems: grammatical, stylistic, logical. They make the passage look and sound like it was written by your baby brother. Only D makes the sentence sensible and correct. That's why it's the answer.

Notice that a single question can test several kinds of writing errors. We find that about a third of the English questions test your ability to write concisely (we call them Economy Questions), about another third test for logic and sense (Sense Questions), and only the remaining third test hard-and-fast rules of grammar (Technicality Questions). There's a lot of overlap between these question types, so don't worry too much about categories. We provide them simply to give you an idea of the kinds of errors you'll be expected to correct.

To Omit or Not to Omit

Some English questions offer, as one of the alternatives, the chance to completely omit the underlined portion, usually as the last of the four choices.

Example

Later, Pike fell while valiantly defending America in the War of 1812. <u>It goes without saying that this took place after he discovered Pike's Peak.</u> [40] He actually died near York (now called Toronto) . . .

40. F. NO CHANGE
    G. Clearly, this must have occurred subsequent to his discovering Pike's Peak.
    H. This was after he found Pike's Peak.
    J. OMIT the underlined portion.

In this case, J is correct. The idea really does "go without saying." For that reason, it shouldn't be stated. On recent ACTs, when OMIT has appeared as an answer choice, it's been correct more than half of the time (As you can see, the ACT makers aren't the only ones with a department of little statistician elves . . .). This doesn't mean you should always select "OMIT," however, since it's also been wrong almost half of the time.

The Directions

The directions on the English test illustrate why there's an advantage to knowing the directions beforehand. The directions are long and complicated. Here's what they'll look like, but take our advice. Don't bother reading them. We'll show you what you'll need to do. Then, while everyone else is reading the directions on Test Day, you'll be racking up points.

> **Directions:** In the following five passages, certain words and phrases have been underlined and numbered. You will find alternatives for each underlined portion in the right-hand column. Select the one that best expresses the idea, that makes the statement acceptable in standard written English, or that is phrased most consistently with the style and tone of the entire passage. If you feel that the original version is best, select "NO CHANGE." You will also find questions asking about a section of the passage or about the entire passage. For these questions decide which choice gives the most appropriate response to the given question. For each question in the test, select the best choice and fill in the corresponding space on the answer folder. You may wish to read each passage through before you begin to answer the questions associated with it. Most answers cannot be determined without reading several sentences around the phrases in question. Make sure to read far enough ahead each time you choose an alternative.

Nonstandard-Format Questions

Some ACT English questions—usually about 10 per exam—don't follow this standard format. These items pose a question and offer four possible responses. In many cases, the responses are either "yes" or "no," with an explanation. Pay attention to the reasoning. Question 40 could have appeared in a nonstandard format as follows:

Example

. . . Later, Pike fell while valiantly defending America in the War of 1812. [40] He actually died near York (now called Toronto) . . .

40. Suppose the author considered adding the following sentence at this point "It goes without saying that this occurred after he discovered Pike's Peak." Given the overall purpose of the passage, would this sentence be appropriate?

- **F.** No, because the sentence adds nothing to the meaning of the passage.
- **G.** No, because the passage is not concerned with Pike's achievements.
- **H.** Yes, because otherwise the sequence of events would be unclear.
- **J.** Yes; though the sentence is not needed, the author recognizes this fact by using the phrase *it goes without saying*.

The correct answer for this question is F. Though G correctly states that the sentence doesn't belong in the passage, it offers a pretty inappropriate reason. The passage is concerned with Pike's achievements. Choices H and J are wrong because they recommend including a sentence that is clearly redundant.

Many of the nonstandard questions occur at the end of a passage. Some ask about the meaning, purpose, or tone of individual paragraphs or of the passage as a whole. Others ask you to evaluate the passage. And still others ask you to determine the proper order of words, sentences, or paragraphs that have been scrambled in the passage.

We think you'll like the English subject test. It can actually be fun, which is probably why the test makers put it first. We'll cover strategies for the English question types in the English Workouts.

MATH

The Math test is 60 minutes long and includes 60 questions. That works out to one minute per question, but you'll want to spend less time on easy questions and more on the tough ones.

The Format

All of the Math questions have the same basic multiple-choice format. They ask a question and offer five possible choices (unlike questions on the other subject tests, which have only four choices each). Why the Math test has five choices while the other tests have only four is one of those mysteries that only the ACT makers understand.

The questions cover a full range of math topics, from prealgebra and elementary algebra through intermediate algebra and coordinate geometry, to plane geometry and even a little bit of trigonometry. We'll tell you the exact number of questions in each area later, in Math Workout 1. If you have specific weaknesses in any of these areas, the 100 Key Math Concepts for the ACT section at the end of this book will help.

Although the Math questions, like those in other sections, aren't ordered in terms of difficulty, questions drawn from elementary school or junior high tend to come earlier in the section, while those from high school math curricula tend to come later. But this doesn't mean that the easy questions come first and the hardest ones come later. We've found that high school subjects tend to be fresher in most students' minds than things they were taught years ago, so you may actually find the later questions easier. (Do *you* remember the math you learned in seventh grade?)

The Directions

Here's what the Math directions will look like:

> **Directions:** Solve each of the following problems, select the correct answer, and then fill in the corresponding space on your answer sheet.
>
> Don't linger over problems that are too time-consuming. Do as many as you can, then come back to the others in the time you have remaining.
>
> Calculator use is permitted, but some problems can best be solved without a calculator.
>
> **Note:** Unless otherwise noted, all of the following should be assumed:
>
> **1.** Illustrative figures are *not* necessarily drawn to scale.
> **2.** All geometric figures lie in a plane.
> **3.** The term *line* indicates a straight line.
> **4.** The term *average* indicates arithmetic mean.

Again, when it comes to directions on the ACT, the golden rule is: *Don't read them on Test Day!* You'll already know what they say by the time you take the test.

The Math directions don't really tell you much anyway. Of the four special notes at the end of the Math directions, #2, #3, and #4 almost go without saying. Note #1—that figures are *not* necessarily drawn to scale—seems pretty scary, but in fact the vast majority of ACT figures *are* drawn to scale, a fact that, as we'll see, has significant implications for how to guess on geometry questions.

Reading and Drawing Diagrams

We find that about a third of the Math questions either give you a diagram or describe a situation that should be diagrammed. For these questions, the diagrams are crucial.

Example

1. The figure below contains five congruent triangles. The longest side of each triangle is 4 meters long. What is the area of the whole figure?

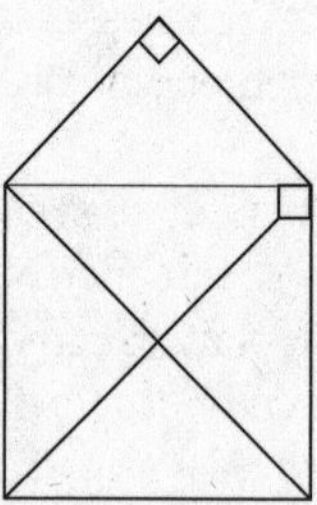

A. 12.5 square meters
B. 15 square meters
C. 20 square meters
D. 30 square meters
E. Cannot be determined from the given information

HINT

In ACT Math questions, the answer choice "cannot be determined" is rare. When it does appear, it's usually wrong. "Cannot be determined" is almost always wrong in a question that comes with a diagram or for which you can draw one.

The key to this question is to let the diagram tell you what you need to know: that each triangle represents one-quarter of the area of the square, and that the sides of the *square* are 4 meters (you can figure this out because the top side of the square is the hypotenuse—or longest side—of the triangle that makes the "roof"). Since the area of a square can be found by squaring the side, the area of the square is 16 square meters. Thus, each triangle has an area one-fourth as much—4 square meters. Since the whole figure consists of *five* triangles, each with area 4, the total area is $5 \times 4 = 20$. The answer is C.

How to Approach That Story

We find that about another third of the Math questions are story problems like the following:

Example

2. Evan drove halfway home at 20 miles per hour, then sped up and drove the rest of the way at 30 miles per hour. What was his average speed for the entire trip?

   F. 20 miles per hour
   G. 22 miles per hour
   H. 24 miles per hour
   J. 25 miles per hour
   K. 28 miles per hour

A good way to comprehend—and resolve—a story problem like this is to think of a real situation just like the one in the story. For example, what if Evan had 120 miles to drive? (You should pick a distance that's easily divisible by both rates). He would go 60 miles at 30 mph, then 60 miles at 20 mph. How long would it take? Well, 60 miles at 30 mph is 2 hours; 60 miles at 20 mph is 3 hours. That's a total of 120 miles in 5 hours; 120 divided by 5 gives an average speed of 24 mph. The correct answer is thus H. (Note: We'll show you alternative ways to answer questions like this later on.)

Getting the Concept

Finally, we find that about a third of the questions directly ask you to demonstrate your knowledge of specific math concepts.

Example

3. If angles A and B are supplementary, and the measure of angle A is 57°, what is the measure, in degrees, of angle B?

   A. 33
   B. 43
   C. 47
   D. 123
   E. 147

This question simply requires that you know the concept of "supplementary angles." Two angles are *supplementary* when they form a straight line—in other words, when they add up to 180°. Thus, question 3 boils down to this: What number, added to 57, makes 180? The answer is D.

These three types of Math questions, of course, will be discussed more fully in the Math Workouts.

READING

The Reading test is 35 minutes long and includes 40 questions. It contains four passages, each followed by 10 questions. When you factor in the amount of time you'll initially spend on the passages, this works out to about 30 seconds per question—again, more for the tough ones, less for the easy ones.

The Format

There are four categories of reading passages: Social Studies, Natural Sciences, Humanities, and Prose Fiction. You'll get one passage in each category. The passages are about 1,000 words long and are written at about the same difficulty level as college textbooks and readings. After each passage, you'll find 10 questions.

The Social Studies, Natural Sciences, and Humanities passages are usually well-organized essays. Each has a very specific theme. Questions expect you to recognize this theme, to comprehend specific facts contained in the passage, and to understand the structure of the essay. Prose Fiction passages require you to understand the thoughts, feelings, and motivations of fictional characters, even when these are not explicitly stated in the passage (we'll have a special section on Prose Fiction passages in Reading Workout 3).

There are really only three different categories of Reading questions:

- Specific Detail Questions
- Inference Questions
- Big Picture Questions

The Directions

Here's what the Reading directions will look like:

> **Directions:** This test contains four passages, each followed by several questions. After reading a passage, select the best answer to each question and fill in the corresponding oval on your answer sheet. You are allowed to refer to the passages while answering the questions.

Nothing stupefying here. But nothing very substantive either. We'll be a little more specific and strategic than the test makers when we suggest a plan of attack in the three Reading Workouts.

Nailing Down the Details

Specific Detail Questions ask about things stated explicitly in the passage. The challenge with these questions is, first, finding the proper place in the passage where the answer can be found (sometimes you'll be given a line reference, sometimes not), and second, being able to match up what you see in the passage with the correct answer, which will probably be worded differently. Many wrong choices will be designed to trip you up by including details from other parts of the passage, or by using the same wording as the passage while distorting the meaning.

Example

When we say "Bach" we almost always refer to Johann Sebastian Bach (1685–1750), but in fact the name "Bach" belongs to a whole family of Baroque German musicians . . .

(*7 paragraphs and 950 words omitted*)

The works of Johann Christian Bach, J. S. Bach's son, clearly prefigure the rich musical developments that followed the Baroque period. Thus, it is both surprising and unfortunate that the rest of J. S. Bach's family isn't more well known.

6. According to the author, J. S. Bach is the best-known:

- **F.** German Baroque musician.
- **G.** member of a musical family.
- **H.** organist in German history.
- **J.** composer of Lutheran hymns.

7. Johann Christian Bach was:

- **A.** born earlier than Johann Sebastian Bach.
- **B.** a composer of the "Romantic" school of music.
- **C.** a composer whose works are transitional in style.
- **D.** well known during his own lifetime.

The answer for question 6 is G. Both the first and last sentences in the passage refer to J. S. Bach as the most famous member of a whole family of musicians. You might think J. S. Bach is the best-known "German Baroque musician" (choice F), but that's not what the passage says, so it's wrong.

The answer for question 7 is C. At the end of the passage the author says that Johann Christian's work "prefigure[d]" the music that followed the Baroque. Thus, it must have had some Baroque characteristics and some new aspects. In other words, it was transitional.

Making an Inference

We find that most Reading passages also include a large number of Inference Questions, which require you to make an inference from the passage (to "read between the lines"). They differ somewhat from Specific Detail Questions. For one thing, students usually consider them harder. An example of each can be found on the next page.

Example

. . . though schizophrenia and multiple personality disorder (M.P.D.) may be related, and are often confused by laymen, the two terms have radically different meanings . . .

32. Which of the following best expresses the relationship between schizophrenia and multiple personality disorder?

F. They are two terms that describe essentially the same phenomenon.
G. The two disorders have nothing in common.
H. Though the two have some similarities, they are fundamentally different.
J. The two are not exactly alike, but are very close.

33. Suppose that a patient has been diagnosed with schizophrenia. Based on the passage, which of the following is least likely?

A. The patient's doctors immediately assume that the patient also suffers from M.P.D.
B. The patient is a layman.
C. The patient denies that he has M.P.D.
D. The patient is related to someone with M.P.D..

Note the differences between Specific Detail and Inference Questions: Question 32, a Specific Detail Question, requires that you understand the explicitly stated idea that schizophrenia and M.P.D. have some connection, but are not the same. That's what choice H says. Question 33, on the other hand, requires you to apply the idea that the two disorders are different. If they are, it's highly unlikely that doctors would simply assume that a patient suffering from one disorder must suffer from the other. Therefore, choice A is least likely—and therefore correct. The other choices may or may not be true, and nothing in the passage leads us to think one way or the other about them. Question 33 is what we'd call a garden-variety Inference Question.

Getting the Big Picture

Although the majority of Reading questions are Specific Detail and Inference Questions, the Reading subtest also includes another type of question that we call Big Picture Questions. Some Big Picture Questions ask about the passage as a whole, requiring you to find the theme, tone, or structure of the passage. Others ask you to evaluate the writing. Here's a typical Big Picture Question that might have appeared with the Bach family passage we talked about earlier.

Example

9. The author's main point in the passage is to:
   - A. show that many of the lesser-known members of the Bach family also influenced music history.
   - B. argue that J. C. Bach was actually a greater composer than his father, J. S. Bach.
   - C. demonstrate that musical talent always runs in families.
   - D. dispute the claim that the Bach family was the best-known family of German Baroque musicians.

In order to answer this kind of question, you've got to have a good sense of the Big Picture—of the shape and flow of the whole passage. Of course, we printed only a few selected lines from the passage, but that should have been enough to lead you to A as the answer. The first line definitely indicates that the subject of the passage is going to be the entire Bach family, with a focus on the ones who aren't as well known as the big cheese, J. S. himself.

SCIENCE

The Science test is 35 minutes long and includes 40 questions. It has seven passages, each with 5 to 7 questions. Factoring in the amount of time you'll initially spend on the passage, that will give you something over 30 seconds for each question.

No, you don't have to be a scientist to succeed on the ACT Science test. You don't have to know the atomic number of cadmium or the preferred mating habits of the monarch butterfly. All that's required is common sense (though a knowledge of standard scientific processes and procedures sure does help). You'll be given passages containing various kinds of scientific information—drawn from the fields of biology, chemistry, physics, geology, astronomy, and meteorology—which you'll have to understand and use as a basis for inferences.

The Format

On most Science subtests, there are six passages that present scientific data, often based on specific experiments. Also, there's usually one passage in which two scientists state opposing views on the same issue. Each passage will generate between five and seven questions. A warning: Some passages will be very difficult to understand, but they'll usually make up for that fact by having many easy questions attached to them. The test makers do show some mercy once in a while.

The Directions

Here's what the Science directions will look like:

> **Directions:** Each of the following seven passages is followed by several questions. After reading each passage, decide on the best answer to each question and fill in the corresponding oval on your answer sheet. You are allowed to refer to the passages while answering the questions.

Sounds a lot like the set of directions for Reading, doesn't it? Not much substance here, either. But don't worry. We'll show you the best strategic way to attack this subject test in the three Science Workouts.

Analyzing Data

About a third of the questions on the Science subtest require you to read data from graphs or tables. In easier questions, you need only report the information. In harder questions, you may need to draw inferences or note patterns in the data. For example:

Example

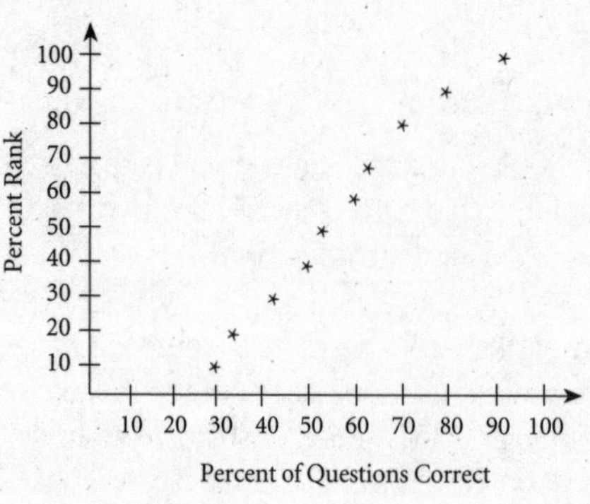

1. A test taker who scores in approximately the 40th percentile has correctly answered about what fraction of the questions?

A. $\frac{9}{10}$

B. $\frac{2}{3}$

C. $\frac{1}{2}$

D. $\frac{1}{5}$

2. Which of the following best describes the relationship between percentile rank and percent of questions correct?

F. As percentile rank increases, percent of correct questions also increases.

G. Percentile rank is inversely proportional to the percent of correct questions.

H. As percentile rank increases, the percent of correct questions decreases.

J. As percentile rank decreases, percent of correct questions usually, but not always, also decreases.

The correct answer to question 1 is C. The point for the 40th percentile is slightly above the 50 percent point on the horizontal axis (percent correct). 50 percent is the same as $\frac{1}{2}$. Note that this question involves a little simple arithmetic (translating a percent into a fraction)—not uncommon for Science questions.

In question 2, the correct answer is F. The points that are higher on the graph (higher percentile) are always farther to the right (higher percentage of correct questions). Note that answers G and H say essentially the same thing (we'll discuss direct and inverse proportionality in Science Workout 1), and thus are wrong for the same reason: they get the relationship backwards. J is wrong because it says that the percent of correct questions does not always decrease as percentile rank decreases.

Conducting Experiments

Other Science questions require that you understand the way experiments are designed and what they prove. For example, part of a passage might describe an experiment as follows:

Example

Experiment 1

A scientist adds one drop of nitric acid to Beakers A, B, and C. Each Beaker contains water from a different stream. The water in Beaker A came from Stream A, that in Beaker B came from Stream B, and that in Beaker C came from Stream C. Precipitates form in Beakers B and C, but not in Beaker A.

12. Which of the following could properly be inferred on the basis of Experiment 1?

F. Stream A is more polluted than Streams B and C.

G. Streams B and C are more polluted than A.

H. Stream A contains material that neutralizes nitric acid.

J. Streams B and C contain some substance that reacts in the presence of nitric acid.

The correct answer is J. Since a precipitate forms when nitric acid is added to Beakers B and C, which contain water from Streams B and C, something in these streams must be involved. However, we don't know that it is pollution, so answers F and G are unwarranted. We also don't know exactly *why* no precipitate formed in Beaker A, so H is also an unwarranted conclusion. Scientists *hate* unwarranted conclusions.

The Principle of the Thing

The remaining Science questions require you either to logically apply a principle or to identify ways of defending or attacking a principle. Often, the question will involve two scientists stating opposing views on the same subject. But this is not always the case. A passage might describe a theory of the process whereby most "V-shaped" valleys are typically formed on Earth—by water erosion through soft rock.

Example

16. Which of the following is most likely to be a V-shaped valley?

F. A valley formed by glaciers
G. A river valley which is cut into very hard basalt
H. A valley formed by wind erosion
J. A river valley in a region of soft shale rocks

17. Which of the following discoveries would most weaken the theory of V-shaped valley formation given in the passage?

A. Certain parts of many valleys formed by water that are U-shaped
B. A group of V-shaped valleys almost certainly formed by wind erosion
C. A group of U-shaped valleys formed by water erosion in hard rock
D. A group of valleys on Mars that appear to be V-shaped but that are not near any running water

In question 16, the correct answer is J, since this is consistent with the passage as described. The correct answer in question 17 is B. Finding V-shaped valleys not formed by water erosion would tend to weaken the theory that they are formed this way. The other answers do not offer evidence about V-shaped valleys on Earth, and thus are irrelevant to a theory about them.

We'll be showing you strategies for each kind of Science question in the three Science Workouts.

WRITING

The Writing test is 30 minutes long and includes one essay. You'll be given a topic or issue and expected to take a position on it, supporting your point of view with examples and evidence.

You don't have to be a great creative writer to succeed on the ACT Writing test. Instead, you have to show that you can focus on an issue and argue your point of view in a coherent, direct way with concrete examples. Furthermore, the essay graders are not primarily concerned with your grammar and punctuation skills. In terms of writing, clarity is what they are looking for. You are being tested on your ability to communicate in writing.

One of the biggest challenges of the Writing test is the time frame. With only 30 minutes to read about the issue, plan your response, draft the essay, and proofread it, you have to work quickly and efficiently. Coming up with a plan and sticking to it are key to succeeding on the Writing test.

The Format

The Writing test consists of one prompt that lays out the issue and gives directions for your response. There are no choices of topic; you have to respond to the topic that's there. Don't worry too much about not knowing anything about the issue you have to write about. Test makers try to craft topics that will be relevant to high school students and about which they can be expected to have a point of view.

The Directions

Here's what the Writing test directions will look like:

> In many high schools, the administration has provided guidelines for the publication of student newspapers. These guidelines often determine which topics can and cannot be discussed in the newspaper and prohibit what the administration deems inappropriate language. Many administrators and teachers feel that these restrictions enable them to provide a safe learning environment for students. Others feel that any restriction on the student newspaper is a violation of freedom of speech. In your opinion, should high schools place restrictions on student newspapers?
>
> In your essay, take a position on this question. You may write about either one of the two points of view given, or you may present a different point of view on this question. Use specific reasons and examples to support your position.

The first paragraph gives some background on the issue about which you must write. The final paragraph giving directions is always the same. Notice that there are two distinct parts to the assignment: (1) state a position and (2) provide support for your position.

That's not much guidance, is it? But don't worry. In the Writing Workout, we'll show you how to plan and draft a high-scoring essay. You'll learn what the essay readers will be looking for and how to give it to them.

Writing Test Skills

The readers realize you're writing under time pressure and expect you to make some mistakes. The content of your essay is not relevant; readers are not checking your facts. Nor will they judge you on your opinions. What they want is to see how well you can communicate a relevant, coherent point of view.

The test makers identify the following as the skills tested in the Writing test:

- **Stating a clear perspective on an issue.** This means answering the question in the prompt.
- **Providing supporting evidence and logical reasoning.** This means offering relevant support for your opinion, building an argument based on concrete details and examples.
- **Maintaining focus and organizing ideas logically.** You've got to be organized, avoid digressions, and tie all your ideas together in a sensible way.
- **Writing clearly.** This is the only skill addressing your ability to write directly, and it's limited to clarity.

The Writing test is not principally a test of your grammar and punctuation (which are tested in the English test)—colleges want a chance to see your reasoning and communication skills. To learn more about doing well on the Writing test, review the Writing Workout.

Chapter Three: **Taking Control: The Top Ten Strategies**

- The ACT Mindset
- Ten Strategies for Mastering the ACT
- Basic Strategy Reference Sheet

Now that you've got some idea of the kind of adversary you face in the ACT, it's time to start developing strategies for dealing with this adversary. In other words, you've got to start developing your ACT Mindset.

The ACT, as we've just seen, isn't a normal test. A normal test requires that you rely almost exclusively on your memory. On a normal test, you'd see questions like this:

The "golden spike," which joined the Union Pacific and Central Pacific Railroads, was driven in Ogden, Utah, in May 1869. Who was president of the United States at the time?

To answer this question, you have to resort to memory dredging. Either you know the answer is Ulysses S. Grant or else you don't. No matter how hard you think, you'll never be able to answer this question if you can't remember your history.

Emergency Plan

This chapter will help you to take control of the ACT. You should read this chapter even if you have two weeks or fewer to prep.

But the ACT doesn't test your long-term memory. The answer to every ACT question can be found in the test. Theoretically, if you read carefully and understand the words and concepts the test uses, you can get almost any ACT question right. Notice the difference between the regular-test question above and the ACT-type question below:

Example

1. What is the product of n and m^2, where n is an odd number and m is an even number?

A. An odd number
B. A multiple of four
C. A noninteger
D. An irrational number
E. The square of an integer

Aside from the obvious difference (this question has answer choices, while the other one does not), there's another difference: The ACT question mostly tests your ability to understand a situation rather than your ability to passively remember a fact. Nobody expects you to know off the top of your head what the product of an odd number and the square of an even number is. But the ACT test makers do expect you to be able to roll up your sleeves and figure it out (as we'll do below).

Be Creative

The mindset for the ACT is "creative problem-solving mode." Don't rely too heavily on your brain's memory cells. Instead, use your brain's creative thinking cells. The ACT mindset isn't too different from the one you'd use to play chess, work a crossword, or run a maze. (You run mazes all the time, don't you?)

THE ACT MINDSET

Most students take the ACT with the same mindset that they use for normal tests. Their brains are on "memory mode." Students often panic and give up because they can't seem to remember enough. But you don't need to remember a ton of picky little rules for the ACT. Don't give up on an ACT question just because your memory fails.

On the ACT, if you understand what a question is really asking on the test, you can almost always answer it. For instance, take the math problem above. You might have been thrown by the way it was phrased. "How can I solve this problem?" you may have asked yourself. "It doesn't even have numbers in it!"

The key here, as in all ACT questions, is taking control. Take the question (by the throat, if necessary) and wrestle it into a form you can understand. Ask yourself: What's really being asked here? What does it mean when they say something like "the product of n and m^2"?

Well, you might start by putting it into words you might use. You might say something like this: "I've got to take one number times another. One of the numbers is odd and the other is an even number squared. Then I've got to see what kind of number I get as an answer." Once you put the question in your own terms like this, it becomes much less intimidating—and much easier to get right. You'll realize that you don't have to do complex algebraic computations with variables. All you have to do is substitute numbers.

So do it! Try picking some easy-to-use numbers. Say that n is 3 (an odd number) and m is 2 (an even number). Then m^2 would be 4, because 2^2 is 4. And $n \times m^2$ would be 3×4, which is 12—a multiple of four, but not odd, not a noninteger, not an irrational number, and not a perfect square. The only answer that can be right, then, is B.

Figure It Out

ACT questions are puzzles to solve, not quizzes for which you must remember the answers. Don't think: "Can I remember?" Think: "Let me figure this thing out!"

See what we mean about figuring out the answer creatively rather than passively remembering it? True, there are some things you had to remember here—what even and odd numbers are, how variables and exponents work, and maybe what integers and irrational numbers are. But these are very basic concepts. Most of what you're expected to know on the ACT is like that: basic. (By the way, you'll find such concepts gathered together in the very attractive 100 Key Math Concepts for the ACT section at the end of this book.)

Of course, basic doesn't always mean easy. Many ACT questions are built on basic concepts, but are tough nonetheless. The problem above, for instance, is difficult because it requires some thought to figure out what's being asked. This isn't only true in Math. It's the same for every part of the ACT.

The creative, take-control kind of thinking we call the ACT Mindset is something you want to bring to virtually every ACT question you encounter. As we'll see, being in the ACT Mindset means reshaping the test-taking experience so that you are in the driver's seat.

It means:

- Answering questions if you want to (by guessing on the impossible questions rather than wasting time on them).
- Answering questions when you want to (by skipping tough but "doable" questions and coming back to them after you've gotten all of the easy questions done).
- Answering questions how you want to (by using "unofficial" ways of getting correct answers fast).

And that's really what the ACT Mindset boils down to: Taking control. Being creative. Solving specific problems to get points as quickly and easily as you can.

What follows are the top ten strategies you need to do just that.

TEN STRATEGIES FOR MASTERING THE ACT

1. Do Question Triage

In a hospital emergency room, the triage nurse is the person who evaluates each patient and decides which ones get attention first and which ones should be treated later. You should do the same thing on the ACT.

Practicing triage is one of the most important ways of controlling your test-taking experience. It's a fact that there are some questions on the ACT that most students could never answer correctly, no matter how much time or effort they spent on them.

Example

57. If $\sec^2 x = 4$, which of the following could be $\sin x$?

A. 1.73205
B. 3.14159
C. $\sqrt{3}$
D. $\frac{\sqrt{3}}{2}$
E. Cannot be determined from the given information.

Clearly, even if you could manage to come up with an answer to this question, it would take some time (if you insist on doing so, refer to the explanation below). But would it be worth the time? We think not.

This question clearly illustrates our point: Do question triage on the ACT. The first time you look at a question, make a quick decision about how hard and time-consuming it looks. Then decide whether to answer it now or skip it and do it later.

- If the question looks comprehensible and reasonably doable, do it right away.
- If the question looks tough and time-consuming, but ultimately doable, skip it, circle the question number in your test booklet, and come back to it later.
- If the question looks impossible, forget about it. Guess and move on, never to return.

Food for Thought

Let's say you took three minutes to get a tough question right. That might make you feel good, but you would actually be better off if you had skipped the tough question and, in the same amount of time, answered two or three easier questions correctly.

This triage method will ensure you spend the time needed to do all the easy questions before getting bogged down with a tough problem. Remember, every question on a subject test is worth the same number of points. You get no extra credit for test machismo.

Answering easier questions first has another benefit: It gives you confidence to answer harder ones later. Doing problems in the order you choose rather than in the order imposed by the test makers gives you control over the test. Most students don't have time to do all of the problems, so you've got to make sure you do all of the ones you can easily score on!

Do You Know Your Trig?

Okay, since you're reading this, it's obvious that you want to know the answer to the trig question we just looked at. The answer is D. Here's how we got it:

$\sec^2 x = 4$	given
$\sec x = 2$ or -2	square root both sides
$\cos x = \frac{1}{2}$ or $-\frac{1}{2}$	$\cos x = \frac{1}{\sec x}$
$\cos^2 x = \frac{1}{4}$	square both sides
$\sin^2 x = 1 - \frac{1}{4}$	$\sin^2 x + \cos^2 x = 1$ $\sin^2 x = 1 - \cos^2 x$
$\sin^2 x = \frac{3}{4}$	
$\sin x = \sqrt{\frac{3}{4}}$ or $-\sqrt{\frac{3}{4}}$	square root both sides
$\sin x = \frac{\sqrt{3}}{2}$ or $-\frac{\sqrt{3}}{2}$	$\sqrt{4} = 2$

So answer choice D is correct. But if you got it right, don't congratulate yourself quite yet. How long did it take you to get it right? So long that you could have gotten the answers to two easy questions in the same amount of time?

Develop a Plan of Attack

For the English, Reading, and Science sections, the best plan of attack is to do each passage as a block. Make a longish first pass through the questions (call it the "triage" pass), doing the easy ones, guessing on the impossible ones, and skipping any that look like they might cause trouble. Then, make a second pass (call it the "cleanup pass") and do those questions you think you can solve with some elbow grease.

For Math, you use the same two-pass strategy, except that you move through the whole subject test twice. Work through the doable questions first. Most of these will probably be toward the beginning, but not all. Then come back and attack the questions that look possible but tough or time-consuming.

No matter what subject test you're working on, you should take pains to grid your answers in the right place. It's easy to misgrid when you're skipping around, so be careful. And of course: *Make sure you have an answer gridded for every question by the time the subject test is over!*

2. Put the Material into a Form You Can Understand

ACT questions are rarely presented in the simplest, most helpful way. In fact, your main job for many questions is to figure out what the question means so you can solve it.

Since the material is presented in such an intimidating way, one of your best strategies for taking control is to recast (reword) the material into a form you can handle better. This is what we did in the math problem about "the product of n and m^2." We took the question and reworded it in a way we could understand.

Testing Tip

Write all over your test booklet. Crossing out wrong answers eliminates confusion and helps you to see clearly which answer is correct. Underlining key points when reading passages helps you to determine the main idea.

Mark Up Your Test Booklet

This strategy should be employed on all four subject tests. For example, in Reading, many students find the passages overwhelming: 85 to 90 lines of dense verbiage for each one! But the secret is to put the passages into a form you can understand and use. Circle or underline the main idea, for one thing. And make yourself a road map of the passage, labeling each paragraph so you understand how it all fits together. That way, you'll also know—later, when you're doing the questions—where in the passage to find certain types of information you need. (We'll show you how to do all of these things in the Skill-Building Workouts.)

Reword the Questions

You'll find that you also need to do some recasting of the *questions*. For instance, take this question from a Science passage.

Example

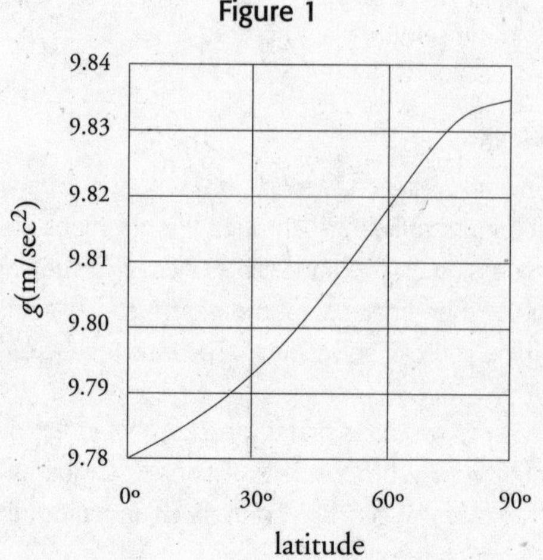

15. According to Figure 1, at approximately what latitude would calculations using an estimated value at sea level of $g = 9.80$ m/sec^2 produce the least error?

A. 0°
B. 20°
C. 40°
D. 80°

At what latitude would the calculations using a value of $g = 9.80$ m/sec^2 produce the least error? Yikes! What does that mean?

Take a deep breath. Ask yourself: Where would an estimate for g of 9.80 m/sec^2 produce the least error? In a latitude where 9.80 m/sec^2 is the real value of g. If you find the latitude at which the real value of g is 9.80 m/sec^2, then using 9.80 m/sec^2 as an estimate there would produce no error at all!

So, in other words, what this question is asking is: At what latitude does $g = 9.80$ m/sec^2? Now that's a form of the question you can understand. In that form, you can answer it easily: choice C, which you can get just by reading the chart.

Draw Diagrams

Sometimes, putting the material into usable form involves drawing with your pencil. For instance, take a look at the following math problem.

Example

2. Jason bought a painting with a frame 1 inch wide. If the dimensions of the outside of the frame are 5 inches by 7 inches, which of the following could be the length of one of the sides of the painting inside the frame?

   F. 3 inches
   G. 4 inches
   H. $5\frac{1}{2}$ inches
   J. $6\frac{1}{2}$ inches
   K. 7 inches

Just looking at the question the first time, you might be tempted simply to subtract 1 from the outside dimensions and think that the inside dimensions are 4 by 6 (and pick G). Why isn't this correct? Because the frame goes all the way around—both above and below the painting, both to the right and to the left. This would have been clear if you had put the problem in a form you could understand and use.

For instance, you might have made the situation graphic by actually sketching out the painting frame (who says you don't have to be an artist to succeed at the ACT?):

When you draw the picture frame like this, you realize that if the outside dimensions are 5 by 7, the inside dimensions must be 3 by 5. Thus, the correct answer is F.

So remember: On the ACT, you've got to put everything into a form that you can understand and use.

3. Ignore Irrelevant Issues

It's easy to waste time on ACT questions by considering irrelevant issues. Just because an issue looks interesting, or just because you're worried about something, doesn't make it important.

Example

...China was certainly one of the cradles of civilization. It's obvious that, China has a long history. (14) As is the case with other ancient cultures, the early history of China is lost in mythology...

14. **F.** NO CHANGE
G. It's obvious that China has a long history.
H. Obviously; China has a long history.
J. OMIT the underlined portion.

In this question, the test makers are counting on you to waste time worrying about punctuation. Does that comma belong? Can you use a semicolon here? These issues might be worrisome, but there's a bigger issue here—namely, does the sentence belong in the passage at all? No, it doesn't. If China has an ancient culture and was a cradle of civilization, it must have a long history, so the sentence really is "obvious." Redundancy is the relevant issue here, not punctuation. Choice J is correct.

Remember, you've got limited time, so don't get caught up in issues that won't get you a point.

4. Check Back

Remember, the ACT is not a test of your memory, so don't make it one. All of the information you need is in the test itself. Don't be afraid to refer to it. Much of the information is too complex to accurately remember anyway.

In Reading and Science, always refer to the place in the passage where the answer to a question can be found (the question stem will often contain a line reference or a reference to a specific table, graph, or experiment to help you out). Your chosen answer should match the passage—not in exact vocabulary or units of measurement, perhaps, but in meaning.

Example

Isaac Newton was born in 1642 in the hamlet of Woolsthorpe in Lincolnshire, England. But he is more famous as a man of Cambridge, where he studied and taught...

7. Which of the following does the author imply is a fact about Newton's birth?

A. It occurred in Lincoln, a small hamlet in England.
B. It took place in a part of England known for raising sheep.
C. It did not occur in a large metropolitan setting.
D. It caused Newton to seek his education at Cambridge.

You might expect the right answer to be that Newton was born in a hamlet, or in Woolsthorpe, or in Lincolnshire. But none of those is offered as a choice. Choice A is tempting, but wrong. Newton was born in Lincolnshire, not Lincoln. Choice B is actually true, but it's wrong here. As its name suggests, Woolsthorpe was once known for its wool—which comes from sheep. But the question asks for something implied in the passage.

The correct answer here is C, because a hamlet is a small village. That's not a large metropolitan setting. (It's also a famous play, but that's not among the choices.)

Checking back is especially important in Reading and Science, because the passages leave many people feeling adrift in a sea of details. Often, the wrong answers will be "misplaced details"—details taken from different parts of the passage. They are things that don't answer the question properly but that might sound good to you if you aren't careful. By checking back with the passage, you can avoid choosing such devilishly clever wrong choices.

There's another important lesson here: Don't pick a choice just because it contains "key words" you remember from the passage. Many wrong choices, like D in the question above, are distortions—they use the right words but say the wrong things about them. Look for answer choices that contain the same ideas you find in the passage.

One of the best ways to avoid choosing misplaced details and distortions is to check back with the passage.

5. Answer the Right Question

This strategy is a natural extension of the last. As we said, the ACT test makers often include among the wrong choices for a question the correct answer to a *different question*. Under time pressure, it's easy to fall for one of these red herrings, thinking that you know what's being asked for when really you don't.

Example

7. What is the value of $3x$ if $9x = 5y + 2$ and $y + 4 = 2y - 10$?

   A. 5
   B. 8
   C. 14
   D. 24
   E. 72

To solve this problem, we need to find y first, even though the question asks about x (because x here is given only in terms of y). You could solve the second equation like this:

$y + 4 = 2y - 10$	given
$4 = y - 10$	by subtracting y from both sides
$14 = y$	by adding 10 to both sides

But choice C, 14, isn't the right answer here, because the question doesn't ask for the value of y—it asks about x. We can use the value of y to find x, however, by plugging the calculated value of y into the first equation:

$9x = 5y + 2$	given
$9x = 5(14) + 2$	because $y = 14$
$9x = 70 + 2$	
$9x = 72$	

But E, 72, isn't the answer either, because the question doesn't ask for $9x$. It doesn't ask for x either, so if you picked B, 8, you'd be wrong as well. Remember to refer to the question! The question asks for $3x$. So we need to divide $9x$ by 3:

$9x = 72$	from above
$3x = 24$	dividing by 3

Thus, the answer is D.

Always check the question again before choosing your answer. Doing all the right work but then getting the wrong answer can be seriously depressing. So make sure you're answering the right question.

6. Look for the Hidden Answer

On many ACT questions, the right answer is hidden in one way or another. An answer can be hidden by being written in a way that you aren't likely to expect. For example, you might work out a problem and get .5 as your answer, but then find that .5 isn't among the answer choices. Then you notice that one choice reads "$\frac{1}{2}$." Congratulations, Sherlock. You've found the hidden answer.

Elimination Helps

If you guess blindly, you have one chance in four (or one in five, on the Math) of getting the question right. But if, before guessing, you can eliminate one or two choices as definitely wrong, you can improve those odds.

There's another way the ACT can hide answers. Many ACT questions have more than one possible right solution, though only one correct answer choice is given. The ACT will hide that answer by offering one of the less obvious possible answers to a question. For example:

Example

2. If $3x^2 + 5 = 17$, which of the following could be the value of x?

A. –3
B. –2
C. 0
D. 1
E. 4

You quickly solve this very straightforward problem like so:

$3x^2 + 5 = 17$	given
$3x^2 = 12$	by subtracting 5
$x^2 = 4$	dividing by 3
$x = 2$	taking square root of both sides

Having gotten an answer, you confidently look for it among the choices. But 2 isn't a choice. The explanation? This question has two possible solutions, not just one. The square root of 4 can be either 2 or −2. B is thus the answer.

Keep in mind that though there's only one right answer choice for each question, that right answer may not be the one that occurs to you first. A common mistake is to pick an answer that seems "sort of" like the answer you're looking for even when you know it's wrong. Don't settle for second best. If you don't find your answer, don't assume that you're wrong. Try to think of another right way to answer the question.

7. Guess Intelligently

An unanswered question is always wrong, but even a wild guess may be right. On the ACT, a guess can't hurt you, but it can help. In fact, smart guessing can make a big difference in your score. Always guess on every ACT question you can't answer. Never leave a question blank.

Smart Guessing

Make sure you get the points you deserve on the questions you can answer. But don't worry about the ones you have to guess on. Odds are good that you'll guess some correctly. And those correct guesses will increase your score just as much as if you'd figured out the answers.

You'll be doing two different kinds of guessing during your two sweeps through any subject test:

- Blind guessing (which you do mostly on questions you deem too hard or time-consuming even to try).
- Considered guessing (which you do mostly on questions that you do some work on, but can't make headway with).

When you guess blindly, you just choose any letter you feel like choosing (Many students like to choose B for Bart; few choose H for Homer). When you guess in a considered way, on the other hand, you've usually done enough work on a question to eliminate at least one or two choices. If you can eliminate any choices, you'll up the odds that you'll guess correctly.

Here are some fun facts about guessing: If you were to work on only half of the questions on the ACT but get them all right, then guess blindly on the other half of the questions, you would probably earn a composite ACT score of around 23 (assuming you had a statistically reasonable success rate on your guesses). A 23 would put you in roughly the top quarter of all those who take the ACT. It's a good score. And all you had to do was answer half the questions correctly.

On the other hand, if you were to hurry and finish all the questions, but get only half of them right, you'd probably earn only a 19, which is below average.

How? Why are you better off answering half and getting them all right instead of answering all and getting only half right?

Here's the trick. The student who answers half the questions right and skips the others can still take guesses on the unanswered questions—and odds are this student will have enough correct guesses to move up 4 points, from a 19 to a 23. But the student who answers all the questions and gets half wrong doesn't have the luxury of taking guesses.

In short: Guess if you can't figure out an answer for any question!

8. Be Careful with the Answer Grid

Your ACT score is based on the answers you select on your answer grid. Even if you work out every question correctly, you'll get a low score if you misgrid your answers. So be careful! Don't disdain the process of filling in those little "bubbles" on the grid. Sure, it's mindless, but under time pressure it's easy to lose control and make mistakes.

It's important to develop a disciplined strategy for filling in the answer grid. We find that it's smart to grid the answers in groups rather than one question at a time. What this means is this: As you figure out each question in the test booklet, circle the answer choice you come up with. Then transfer those answers to the answer grid in groups of five or more (until you get close to the end of the section, when you start gridding answers one by one).

Gridding in groups like this cuts down on errors because you can focus on this one task and do it right. It also saves time you'd otherwise spend moving papers around, finding your place, and redirecting your mind. Answering ACT questions takes deep, hard thinking. Filling out answer grids is easy, but you have to be careful, especially if you do a lot of skipping around. Shifting between "hard thinking" and "careful bookkeeping" takes time and effort.

Grid in Groups

You should, of course, circle the correct answers in your test booklet as you figure them out. But don't transfer those answers to the grid one by one. That takes too much time.

- In English, Reading, and Science, grid at the end of each passage.
- In Math, grid at the end of every page (or every two-page spread).

In English, Reading, and Science, the test is divided naturally into groups of questions—the passages. For most students, it makes sense to circle your answers in your test booklet as you work them out. Then, when you're finished with each passage and its questions, grid the answers as a group.

In Math, the strategy has to be different because the Math test isn't broken up into natural groups. Mark your answers in the test booklet and then grid them when you reach the end of each page or two. Since there are usually about five math questions per page, you'll probably be gridding five or ten math answers at a time.

No matter what subject test you're working on, though, if you're near the end of a subject test, start gridding your answers one at a time. You don't want to be caught with ungridded answers when time is called.

During the test, the proctor should warn you when you have about five minutes left on each subject test. But don't depend on proctors! Yes, they're usually nice people, but they can mess up once in a while. Rely on your own watch. When there's five minutes left in a subject test, start gridding your answers one by one. With a minute or two left, start filling in everything you've left blank. Remember: Even one question left blank could cut your score.

9. Use the Letters of the Choices to Stay on Track

One oddity about the ACT is that even-numbered questions have F, G, H, J (and, in Math, K) as answer choices, rather than A, B, C, D (and, again, E in Math). This might be confusing at first, but you can make it work for you. A common mistake with the answer grid is to accidentally enter an answer one row up or down. On the ACT, that won't happen if you pay attention to the letter in the answer. If you're looking for an A and you see only F, G, H, J, and K, you'll know you're in the wrong row on the answer grid.

Another advantage of having answers F through K for even-numbered questions is that it makes you less nervous about patterns in the answers. It's common to start worrying if you've picked the same letter twice or three times in a row. Since the questions have different letters, this can't happen on the ACT. Of course, you could pick the first choice (A or F) for several questions in a row. This shouldn't worry you. It's common for the answers in the same position to be correct three times in a row, and even four times in a row isn't unheard of.

10. Keep Track of Time

During each subject test, you really have to pace yourself. On average, English, Reading, and Science questions should take about 30 seconds each. Math questions should average less than one minute each. Remember to take into account the fact that you'll probably be taking two passes through the questions.

Set your watch to 12:00 at the beginning of each subject test, so it will be easy to check your time. Again, don't rely on proctors, even if they promise that they will dutifully call out the time every 15 minutes. Proctors get distracted once in a while.

For English, Reading, and Science questions, it's useful to check your timing as you grid the answers for each passage. English and Reading passages should take about nine minutes each. Science passages should average about five minutes.

More basic questions should take less time, and harder ones will probably take more. In Math, for instance, you need to go much faster than one per minute during your first sweep. But at the end, you may spend two or three minutes on each of the harder problems you work out.

Suggested Timings

The suggested times below are rough guidelines only!

English, Reading Passages:
About 9 minutes each (including questions)

Science Passages:
About 5 minutes each (including questions)

Math Questions:
About 30–60 seconds each, depending on the difficulty

Take Control

You are the master of the test-taking experience. A common thread in all ten strategies above is: Take control. That's Kaplan's ACT Mindset. Do the questions in the order you want and in the way you want. Don't get bogged down or agonize. Remember, you don't earn points for suffering, but you do earn points for moving on to the next question and getting it right.

BASIC STRATEGY REFERENCE SHEET

The Three Commandments

1. Thou Shalt Learn the Test

- Learn the directions before test day.
- Become familiar with all the subject tests.
- Get a sense of the range of difficulty of the questions.

2. Thou Shalt Learn the Strategies

- Develop a plan of attack for each subject test.
- Develop a guessing strategy that works for you.
- Find "unofficial" ways of finding answers fast.

3. Thou Shalt Learn the Material

- Bone up on weak areas.
- Find out what is and isn't part of the ACT knowledge base.
- Use the ACT Resources section to review important Math and English concepts.

The Top Ten Strategies

1. Do question triage.
2. Put the material into a form you can understand and use.
3. Ignore irrelevant issues.
4. Check back.
5. Answer the right question.
6. Look for the hidden answer.
7. Guess intelligently.
8. Be careful with the answer grid.
9. Use the letters of the choices to stay on track.
10. Keep track of time.

Chapter Four: **English Workout 1: When in Doubt, Take It Out**

- **Economy Questions**
- **When in Doubt...And Other Tips**
- **The Kaplan Three-Step Method for ACT English**

Think back to the last paper you had to write. Maybe your teacher assigned something like ten pages. You wrote and you wrote, and ended up with six pages. It was the night before the paper had to be turned in. You were out of research and ideas. But you knew what to do: pad it.

You're not alone. Almost all of us have padded papers at one time or another. The recipe for padding, in fact, is practically universal: You repeat yourself a few times. You trade short phrases for long-winded verbiage. You add a few offbeat ideas that don't really belong. And presto! Your six-page paper is transformed into a ten-page paper.

The ACT test makers know that most students pad. And they know how to punish you for it. In fact, almost a third of the English questions on the ACT are testing for the very same bad writing habits—long-windedness, repetitiousness, irrelevance—that padders tend to cultivate.

But there's hope. Once you know what ACT English is testing for, you can easily avoid making these common English mistakes. More than any other part of the exam, the ACT English subject test is predictable.

Question Breakdown

The ACT English test includes:

- 10 punctuation questions
- 12 grammar and usage questions
- 18 sentence structure questions
- 12 strategy questions
- 11 organization questions
- 12 style questions

Emergency Plan

If you don't have much time, learn the Kaplan Method for ACT English. Try the practice passage that follows. If you need more help, go back and read the whole chapter.

ECONOMY QUESTIONS

On the ACT, more than 20 questions—almost a third of all the English items—test your awareness of redundancy, verbosity, relevance, and similar issues. We call these Economy Questions. Take a look.

Example

On recent ACTs, the shortest answer has been correct, and absolutely right [1], for about half of all English questions. Because this is true [2], a student who knows no English at all could earn—and justly so— [3] an English subject score of about 15. Such a student could compare the choices carefully, and choose the single shortest one [4] every time. Where the answers are the same length, the student could pick at random. On recent published ACTs, guessing in this way would have yielded between 35 and 38 correct answers out of 75 questions. Of course, you're going to be doing [5] much better than that. You actually are capable of speaking the English language [6]. You may not know every little rule of English usage, but you certainly know something. Obviously, getting the question right because you know the right answer [7] is better than getting it right because you guessed well.

1. **A.** NO CHANGE
B. correct
C. right, that is, correct,
D. correct, absolutely, and right,

2. **F.** NO CHANGE
G. truthfully factual
H. factually correct
J. factual—and true too—

3. **A.** NO CHANGE
B. , and justly so,
C. and justify
D. OMIT the underlined portion.

4. **F.** NO CHANGE
G. singularly shortest one
H. uniquely short item
J. shortest one

5. **A.** NO CHANGE
B. do
C. achieve
D. be, achieving,

6. **F.** NO CHANGE
G. possess the capability of speaking that wonderful language called the language of England
H. possess the capability of speaking in the land called England
J. speak English

7. **A.** NO CHANGE
B. best choice to select
C. most correct answer of the choices given
D. answer considered as correct

But you should always remember that the ACT test
makers like the shortest answers. Why? Why should the
8
ACT make life so easy for you? Why can't History or
9
Science classes in high school be so easy? Because
9
usually, the best way to write something really is the
shortest way to write it. The ACT can't help that, any
10
more than you can help the fact that you must take the
10
ACT to get into college. Good writing is concise and
10
clear. There are many rules of English, but many of
11
them grow from one dominant principle: use only the
words you need to say what you mean. [12]

8. **F.** NO CHANGE
G. have a habit of liking
H. habitually tend to like
J. are in the habit of liking

9. **A.** NO CHANGE
B. Why isn't History or Science?
C. History and Science aren't so easy, either!
D. OMIT the underlined portion.

10. **F.** NO CHANGE
G. just as you are helpless to avoid the requirement of taking the ACT
H. whether or not they'd want to
J. OMIT the underlined portion and end the sentence with a period after "that."

11. **A.** NO CHANGE
B. clearly better
C. translucent, like clear water
D. clear. Thus it is short and to the point.

12. Suppose the author considers adding this final sentence: "Thus, if you can't say something nice, don't say anything at all." Would this be an effective conclusion for the paragraph?

F. Yes, because this concept is needed to explain the meaning of the previous sentence.
G. Yes, because it adds an uplifting moral tone to an otherwise depressing, amoral text.
H. Yes, because this thought is relevant to the next paragraph.
J. No, because the paragraph is not concerned with being nice.

Answers

1. B, 2. F, 3. D, 4. J, 5. B, 6. J, 7. A, 8. F, 9. D, 10. J, 11. A, 12. J

The shortest answer happens to be correct in all twelve of the questions above. Note that "OMIT," where it is an option, is the shortest answer, since taking the material out leaves a shorter text than leaving anything in. In question 12, answer J is the "shortest" answer, since it leaves the proposed final sentence off entirely.

Redundancy

In questions 1–4 above, the wrong (long) answers are redundant. This means that they make the passage say the same thing twice. The ACT is very strict about redundancy: Never let the text in a sentence repeat itself.

Verbosity

In questions 5–8, the wrong (long) answers are verbose. They force the reader to read more words, but they are no clearer than the short answers and don't add meaning. This is another rule the ACT is very strict about: The best way to write something is the shortest way, as long as it doesn't violate any rules of writing mechanics (like grammar or punctuation) or contain vulgarities inappropriate to civilized discourse.

Keep It Simple

On recent ACTs, the shortest answer has been correct on about half of all English questions.

Irrelevance

Questions 9–12 test relevance. The wrong (long) answers introduce irrelevant concepts. The paragraph is about ACT English questions and how to answer them—it's not about History or Science classes, the necessity of taking the ACT, or that lovely translucence of clear water. Omit the ideas that are not directly and logically tied in with the purpose of the passage.

WHEN IN DOUBT . . . AND OTHER TIPS

With Economy Questions, the shortest answer is correct with great frequency. What that means is:

- If you're not sure whether an idea is redundant, it probably is, so take it out.
- If you're not sure whether a certain way to say something is too verbose, it probably is, so take it out.
- If you're not sure whether an idea is relevant, it probably isn't, so take it out.

In other words: When in doubt, take it out.

Keep It Short—on All English Questions

Questions in which the lengths of the answers vary greatly, or questions that contain the answer choice "OMIT," are usually Economy Questions. For these questions, you should be especially inclined to choose the shortest choice. For the other questions, the shortest answer is not nearly as often correct.

As we'll see in later workouts, the other English questions mostly test your ability to spot nonsense, bad grammar, and bad punctuation. But even in these cases, the rule "when in doubt, take it out" still holds. Most grammatical mistakes can be solved by removing the offending words.

Because these issues of writing economy are so important to English questions of all kinds, we've made them the linchpin for our recommended approach to the English subject test. When approaching English questions, the very first question you should ask yourself is: "Does this stuff belong here? Can the passage or sentence work without it?"

Skimming English Questions

Before launching in to correct the prose on an ACT English passage, it usually pays to skim each paragraph to get a sense of how it's shaped and what it's about. This makes correcting the underlined portions a little easier, since you'll have a better sense of the context. The skimming technique is simple: You skim a paragraph, then do the questions it contains, then skim the next paragraph, do the questions that one contains, etcetera. Some students even find it helpful to skim the entire passage before starting on the questions.

In this preliminary step, you needn't read carefully—you'll be doing that when you tackle the questions—but you should at least get a sense of what the passage is about and, just as important, whether it's written in a formal or informal style (we'll talk more about the tone and style of passages in English Workout 2).

After your brief skim of a paragraph (it should only take a few seconds), it's time to start work on its questions.

THE KAPLAN THREE-STEP METHOD FOR ACT ENGLISH

Here's our three-step (or really, three-question) approach to ACT English questions. (Note: Steps 2 and 3 will be covered more thoroughly in English Workouts 2 and 3.)

Step 1. Does This Stuff Belong Here?

As we've seen, writing economy is very near to the hearts of ACT test makers. So ask yourself: Does the underlined section belong? Is it expressed as succinctly as possible? If the answer is no, choose the answer that gets rid of the stuff that doesn't belong. If the answer is yes, move on to . . .

Step 2. Does This Stuff Make Sense?

The ACT test makers want simple, easy-to-understand prose. They expect everything to fit together logically. Does the underlined part of the passage make logical sense? If the answer is no, select the choice that turns nonsense into sense. If the answer is yes, go on to . . .

Step 3. Does This Stuff Sound Like English?

Many grammar errors will sound wrong to your ear. Even the ones that don't will be recognizable to you if you study our nineteen Classic Grammar Errors in English Workout 3 and create a "flag list" of the ones you're shaky on. Choose the answer that corrects the error and makes the sentence sound right.

Most ACT English test takers are so worried about grammar and punctuation that they don't think about anything else. That's the wrong mindset. Don't think too much about technical rules. As indicated in the approach above, the first thing to think about is getting rid of unnecessary or irrelevant words. Only after you've decided that the underlined selection is concise and relevant do you go on to Steps 2 and 3. Note that this means you won't necessarily be going through all three steps on any English question. The answer can come at any point in the three-step method.

Practice Being Economical

Now try the next practice passage, keeping in mind the approach you just learned:

Example

The Phoenix Cardinals are the oldest, most long-established, longest-playing 1 football club in the National Football League (NFL). They began as the Racine Avenue Cardinals on Chicago's South Side sometime in the 1870s or 1880s, during the nineteenth century 2. At that time, the Cardinals were an amateur team that did not play for money 3.

There was nothing in the world which so much as resembled 4 pro football in those days. The Racine Avenue Cardinals played amateur ball all through the late 1800s and the game they played was football, no doubt about it 5.

1. **A.** NO CHANGE
   B. oldest
   C. most long-established
   D. longest-playing

2. **F.** NO CHANGE
   G. 1880s
   H. the nineteenth century
   J. during the 1880s

3. **A.** NO CHANGE
   B. that played for the pure joy of the sport
   C. that played on a nonprofessional level
   D. OMIT the underlined portion and end the sentence with a period.

4. **F.** NO CHANGE
   G. nothing anything like
   H. no such thing as
   J. not even a dream of

5. **A.** NO CHANGE
   B. no doubt about it
   C. to be assured it was football
   D. OMIT the underlined portion and end the sentence with a period.

None of the other clubs in the NFL was formed before the league itself was established in 1919. When the NFL was first established, the Cardinals remained <u>aloof and thumbed their noses at it</u>.[6] Professional football had a bad reputation, and the Cardinals were <u>greatly prideful</u>[7] of their record as amateurs. But in 1921, the Cardinals decided to join the NFL. They were required to play a "game to the death" with the Chicago Tigers <u>(the Detroit Tigers are a baseball team)</u>.[8] Whichever team won would be allowed to stay in Chicago; the other team would <u>have to move</u>.[9] The Cardinals won. The Tigers moved away and soon went bankrupt. The Cardinals are thus the only NFL team that won their franchise on the football field.

6. F. NO CHANGE
   G. aloof.
   H. aloof and tried to ignore it.
   J. off in their own corner.

7. A. NO CHANGE
   B. full of great pride
   C. proud
   D. gratefully proud

8. F. NO CHANGE
   G. (not to be confused with the Detroit Tigers, a baseball team)
   H. (not the more famous modern-day Detroit Tigers baseball team)
   J. OMIT the underlined portion and end the sentence with a period.

9. A. NO CHANGE
   B. be forced to move along
   C. be legally obliged, by injunction, to relocate their franchise
   D. be obligated to be moving out

Ironically, the team that fought to stay in Chicago eventually moved away. The Cardinals were rarely as <u>successfully able to win games or make money</u>[10] as the Chicago Bears, their crosstown rivals. Fans gradually deserted the Cardinals, so the team moved—to St. Louis in 1958 and to Phoenix in 1986, seeking a more profitable market. Maybe Phoenix <u>is the place in which</u>[11] the Cardinals are destined to stay. Some people say that the name "Cardinal" was a nineteenth-century

10. F. NO CHANGE
    G. successful at winning
    H. winning or profitable, a team,
    J. successful

11. A. NO CHANGE
    B. is the place at which
    C. is where
    D. OMIT the underlined portion.

name for a mythical bird that arose from its own ashes
in the fireplace, and that the Cardinals date back to
12
1871, the year of the great Chicago fire—which may
have begun on Racine Avenue (or maybe not). Chicago
13
was proud to rise from its ashes like the mythical
Cardinal. The name that is more common for that
14
mythical firebird is—the Phoenix. [15]

12. F. NO CHANGE
G. that had consumed it
H. created by the fire that had consumed it
J. OMIT the underlined portion.

13. A. NO CHANGE
B. according to ironic legend
C. resulting from violations of the fire code and a cow in a barn
D. OMIT the underlined portion and end the sentence with a period.

14. F. NO CHANGE
G. common name
H. name that is famous
J. common way of speaking

15. Suppose the author wishes to add a new paragraph at the end of the existing passage quickly summarizing the history of Canadian football. Would this be appropriate, in light of the content and style of the rest of the passage?
A. Yes, because it is only fair to mention Canadian football at least once in the passage.
B. Yes, because the Phoenix Cardinals now play Canadian football.
C. No, because the passage does not focus on sports history.
D. No, because the passage has nothing to do with Canadian football.

Did you see the point? On every regular format question except number 11, you shouldn't have gotten past the first step of the three-step method, because all of the questions test economy errors. In fact, the shortest answers are correct on every question here except that one. In 11, if you omit the phrase "is the place in which," the sentence doesn't make any sense, meaning that you'd correct it in Step 2 of the three-step approach. (Note: This passage is not typical—most ACT passages don't consist exclusively of Economy Questions—but we used this passage to drive home the point about choosing concise answers on the English subject test.)

Many students might object to answer J in question 10, because the word *successful* alone does not indicate the kind of success meant. But use common sense. What would make a professional football team successful? Winning, and making money. Thus, the concepts of "winning" and "profitability" are implicit in the notion that the Cardinals are (now) a successful team. The ACT expects you to cut anything that isn't absolutely needed.

Answers

1. B, 2. G, 3. D, 4. H, 5. D, 6. G, 7. C, 8. J, 9. A, 10. J, 11. C, 12. J, 13. D, 14. G, 15. D

HINT

Remember that "OMIT," when it is an option, is always the shortest answer. For instance, D is "shorter" than A and B in question 15 because not including a new paragraph makes the passage shorter than including it. (But notice that you still had to decide between C and D in that question.)

Chapter Five: **Math Workout 1: The End Justifies the Means**

- **The ACT Math Mindset**
- **The Kaplan Three-Step Method for ACT Math**
- **Kaplan's Two-Pass Plan for ACT Math**
- **To Calculate or Not to Calculate**

Your goal on the Math subject test is to get as many correct answers as you can in 60 minutes. It doesn't matter what you do (short of cheating, naturally) to get those correct answers.

You don't have to do every problem the way your math teacher would. Be open to clever and original solution methods. All that matters is that your methods be quick and that they get you a solid number of correct answers. How many correct answers you need depends on what kind of score you're aiming for, but chances are you don't have to get so many right as you might think to get a good score. Yes, it's a tough test, but it's graded "on a curve."

Emergency Plan

Here's how to use this chapter if you don't have much time. Learn the Kaplan Method for ACT Math, trying the sample questions that follow. Read the sidebars throughout the whole chapter for quick ACT strategy tips.

As we've pointed out, the ACT is different from the typical high school test. On a typical high school math test, you get a series of problems just like the ones you've been doing in class. Since you're being tested on a relatively narrow scope of topics, you're expected to get almost every question right.

ACT Math is different. The scope of what's tested is deliberately wide so that every student will get an opportunity to demonstrate his or her strengths, wherever they may lie.

Nobody needs to get all 60 questions right. The average ACT student gets fewer than half of the Math questions right. You need only about 40 correct answers to get your Math score over 25—just two right out of every three questions gets you a great score!

THE ACT MATH MINDSET

According to an old legend at M.I.T., a physics professor once asked the following question on a final exam: *How could a barometer be used to determine the height of a tower?*

Question Breakdown

The ACT Math test includes:

- 24 prealgebra and elementary algebra questions (corresponding roughly to the 100 Key Math Concepts for the ACT, #1–65)
- 10 intermediate algebra questions (100 Key Math Concepts for the ACT, #66–70)
- 8 coordinate geometry questions (100 Key Math Concepts for the ACT, #71–77)
- 14 plane geometry questions (100 Key Math Concepts for the ACT, #78–95)
- 4 trigonometry questions (100 Key Math Concepts for the ACT, #96–100)

To answer the question, most students worked out complex equations based on the fact that air pressure (which is what a barometer measures) decreases at higher altitudes. But one student made three suggestions instead:

1. Measure the length of the barometer, then use the barometer as a ruler and measure the tower.
2. Drop the barometer and time its fall, keeping in mind that the acceleration of falling objects is about 32 ft/sec^2.
3. Find the person who built the tower and say, "I'll give you a nice barometer if you tell me how tall your tower is."

Guess which student got an A . . .

On the ACT, as in college and beyond, you'll sometimes be called upon to do more than merely regurgitate memorized facts and unquestioningly follow prepackaged procedures. True, some ACT Math questions are straightforward: As soon as you understand what the question's asking, you know what to do. But more challenging—and more fun (really)—are the ACT Math questions that aren't what they seem at first glance. These are the questions that call for creative solutions.

Don't Be Obedient

Too often, high school math instruction degenerates into obedience training: You show your work on tests to prove that you did everything the way it was taught in class. If you show the "right" kind of work, you get partial or even full credit, regardless of whether your answers are correct. If you're lucky, your teacher might even give you a nice pat on the back.

On the ACT, though, there's no partial credit. All that matters is the right answer. It makes no difference how you find it. In fact, as we'll see, it's sometimes safer and faster if you don't do ACT problems the "right" way—the way you've been taught in school. For a lot of ACT Math problems there's more than one way to find the answer. And many of these other ways are faster than the so-called right way.

Of course, old habits die hard. For years you've been subjected to obedience-training math. You've learned to waste time writing everything out. You've learned to depend on remembering "how you're supposed to do it" instead of finding ways to do it faster and smarter. Maybe you've even learned not to care much about getting right answers. It'll take something pretty drastic to break away. The drastic step we recommend is: Don't show your work.

Don't Show Your Work

No, we don't mean that you should try to do every ACT Math problem in your head. Nobody could do that—though most people could and should do a lot less paper calculation than they do. Go ahead and use your pencil to calculate and organize. But don't put stuff down just for the sake of getting it on paper. Don't write out every step. Don't worry about whether you're being neat or whether anybody would be able to understand your notes. Jot things down for yourself.

If you do every problem the way your algebra teacher would want you to, you may earn his or her undying gratitude, but you won't achieve your goal of getting as many correct answers as possible. You don't have time to use the textbook approach on every question. You don't have time to write out every step.

Only the Bubbles Count

You will not get credit for anything you write under "DO YOUR FIGURING HERE." You get credit only for correct answers correctly gridded into the "bubbles" on your answer sheet.

Be a Thinker—Not a Number Cruncher

One reason you're given limited time for the Math subject test is that the ACT is testing your ability to think, not your willingness to do a lot of mindless calculations. So, one of your guiding principles for ACT Math should be: Work less, but think harder.

If you want to get the best score you can, be on the lookout for quicker ways to solve problems. Here's an example that could take a lot more time than it needs to.

Example

1. When $\frac{4}{11}$ is converted to a decimal, the 50th digit after the decimal point is

A. 2
B. 3
C. 4
D. 5
E. 6

Calculator Tip

Don't rely on your calculator for every operation. It's there to supplement your skills, not to replace them.

It seems that when you convert $\frac{4}{11}$ to a decimal, there are at least 50 digits after the decimal point. The question asks for the 50th. One way to answer this question would be to divide 11 into 4, carrying the division out to 50 decimal places. That method would work, but it would take forever. It's not worth spending that much time on one question.

No ACT Math question should take more than a minute to take care of, if you know what you're doing. There has to be a faster way to solve this problem. There must be some kind of pattern you can take advantage of. And what kind of pattern might there be with a decimal? How about a *repeating* decimal?!

In fact, that's exactly what you have here. The decimal equivalent of $\frac{4}{11}$ is a repeating decimal: $\frac{4}{11}$ = . 3636363636 . . .

The 1st, 3rd, 5th, 7th, and 9th digits are each 3. The 2nd, 4th, 6th, 8th, and 10th digits are each 6. Put simply, odd-numbered digits are 3s and even-numbered digits are 6s. The 50th digit is an even-numbered digit, so it's a 6 and the answer is E.

What looked at first glance like a "fractions and decimals" problem turned out to be something of an "odds and evens" problem. If you don't use creative shortcuts on problems like this one, you'll get bogged down, you'll run out of time, and you won't get a lot of correct answers.

Be Creative

Be creative in the process you use to solve problems, not in the answer choices you pick. Don't try to select answers that somehow "look good." The ACT is not a beauty contest.

Question 1 demonstrates how the ACT designs problems to reward clever thinking and to punish students who blindly "go through the motions." But how do you get yourself into a creative mindset on the Math test? For one thing, you have to take the time to understand thoroughly each problem you decide to work on. Most students are so nervous about time that they skim each math problem and almost immediately start computing with their pencils. But that's the wrong way of thinking. Sometimes you have to *take* time to *save* time. A few extra moments spent understanding a math problem can save many extra moments of computation or other drudgery.

THE KAPLAN THREE-STEP METHOD FOR ACT MATH

At Kaplan, we've developed this take-time-to-save-time philosophy into a three-step method for ACT Math problems. The approach is designed to help you find the fast, inventive solutions that the ACT rewards. The steps are:

Step 1. Understand

Focus first on the question stem (the part before the answer choices) and make sure you understand the problem. Sometimes you'll want to read the stem twice, or rephrase it in a way you can better understand. Think to yourself: "What kind of problem is this? What am I looking for? What am I given?" Don't pay too much attention to the answer choices yet, though you may want to give them a quick glance just to see what form they're in.

To understand an ACT Math problem, you first have to understand the language. Mathematicians are generally very precise in their use of language. They choose their words carefully and mean exactly what they say.

In everyday life we can be a little loose with math terminology. It doesn't really matter that Harvard Square is not a square or that a batting average is not an average.

In an ACT Math problem, however, words have precise meanings. You don't need to memorize definitions (you'll never have to recite one on the ACT) but you do need to understand what the question writer means.

Step 2. Analyze

Think for a moment and decide on a plan of attack. Don't start crunching numbers until you've given the problem a little thought. Ask: "What's a quick and reliable way to find the correct answer?" Look for patterns and shortcuts, using common sense and your knowledge of the test to find the creative solutions that will get you more right answers in less time. Try to solve the problem without focusing on the answer choices.

Once you're sure you've gotten a math problem into a form you can understand, you still have to know what to do with the problem. Sometimes you'll know what to do the moment you understand the problem.

Step 3. Select

Once you get an answer—or once you get stuck—check the answer choices. If you got an answer and it's listed as one of the choices, chances are it's right—fill in the appropriate bubble and move on. But if you didn't get an answer, narrow down the choices as best you can by process of elimination and then guess.

Each of these steps can happen in a matter of seconds. And it may not always be clear when you've finished with one step and moved on to the next. Sometimes you'll know how to attack a problem the instant you read and understand it.

Using the Kaplan Method

Here's how the Three-Step Method could be applied to Question 1 above.

Step 1: Understand

First, we made sure we understood what the problem was asking for: the 50th digit after the decimal point in the decimal equivalent of a certain fraction. Because we knew what digit and decimal equivalent mean, it took only a second to understand what the problem was asking.

Think

Most students hate it when they solve a problem and their answer isn't among the choices. But actually, not having the answer you want among the choices helps you if you've made a mistake, because it makes you realize that you did something wrong. You can then go back and do the problem right.

Step 2: Analyze

Second, and most crucially, we analyzed the situation and thought about a plan of attack before we tried to solve the problem. We realized that the "obvious" method would take too long, so we figured out a creative approach that got us an answer of 6 in just a few seconds.

Step 3: Select

Third, we looked at the answer choices, found 6, and selected choice E.

The Three-Step Method isn't a rigid procedure; it's a set of guidelines that will keep you on track, moving quickly, and evading pitfalls. Just remember to think before you solve: Focus on the question stem first and save the answer choices for later.

Example

2. If the sum of five consecutive even integers is equal to their product, what is the greatest of the five integers?

   F. 4
   G. 10
   H. 14
   J. 16
   K. 20

Step 1: Understand

Before you can begin to solve this problem, you have to figure out what it's asking, and to do that you need to know the meanings of *sum, product, consecutive, even,* and *integer*. Put the question stem into words you can understand. What the question stem is really saying here is that when you add up these five consecutive even integers you get the same thing as when you multiply them.

Step 2: Analyze

How are we going to figure out what these five numbers are? We could set up an equation:

$$x + (x - 2) + (x - 4) + (x - 6) + (x - 8) = x(x - 2)(x - 4)(x - 6)(x - 8)$$

But there's no way you'll have time to solve an equation like this! So don't even try. Come up with a better way.

Let's stop and think logically about this one for a moment. When we think about sums and products, it's natural to think mostly of positive integers. With positive integers, we would generally expect the product to be *greater* than the sum.

But what about negative integers? Hmm. Well, the sum of five negatives is negative, and the product of five negatives is also negative, and generally the product will be "more negative" than the sum, so with negative integers the product will be *less* than the sum.

So when will the product and sum be the same? How about right at the boundary of positive and negative—that is, around 0? The five consecutive even integers with equal product and sum are: –4, –2, 0, 2, and 4.

$$(-4) \times (-2) \times 0 \times 2 \times 4 = (-4) + (-2) + 0 + 2 + 4$$

The product and sum are both 0. Ha! We've done it!

Test Prep and Admissions

Step 3: Select

The question asks for the greatest of the five integers, which is 4, choice F.

You've probably encountered every math term that appears on the ACT sometime in your high school math career, but you may not remember exactly what every one of them means. The Math Glossary at the back of this book is a complete but compact list of the terminology you need for ACT Math problems. Look it over. Mark or jot down the ones you're not so sure of for future reference. And be sure to use the Glossary to look up any unfamiliar term you encounter while practicing with ACT Math questions.

Definition Alert

As you refresh your memory of key terminology, watch out for technicalities. Here are a few examples of such technicalities (by the way, these are great for stumping your know-it-all friends):

- *"Integers" include 0 and negative whole numbers.* If a question says "x and y are integers," it's not ruling out numbers like 0 and −1.
- *"Evens and odds" include 0 and negative whole numbers.* Zero and −2 are even numbers; −1 is an odd number.
- *"Prime numbers" do not include 1.* The technical definition of a prime number is: "a positive integer with exactly two distinct positive integer factors." Two is prime because it has exactly two positive factors: 1 and 2. Four is not prime because it has three positive factors (1, 2, and 4)—too many! And 1 is not prime because it has only one positive factor (1)—too few!
- *"Remainders" are integers.* If a question asks for the remainder when 15 is divided by 2, don't say "15 divided by 2 is 7.5, so the remainder is .5." What you should say is: "15 divided by 2 is 7 with a remainder of 1."
- *The $\sqrt{\ }$ symbol represents the positive square root only.* The equation $x^2 = 9$ has two solutions: 3 and −3. But when you see $\sqrt{9}$, it means positive 3 only.
- *"Rectangles" include squares.* The definition of a rectangle is a four-sided figure with four right angles. It doesn't matter if the length and width are the same or not—if it has four right angles, it's a rectangle. When a question refers to "rectangle ABCD," it's not ruling out a square.

Example

3. What is the value of $x^2 + 3x - 9$ when $x = -3$?

A. −27
B. −9
C. −6
D. 0
E. 9

Step 1: Understand

You've probably seen dozens of problems just like this. If so, then you realize right away that what it's asking is, "What do you get when you plug $x = -3$ into $x^2 + 3x - 9$?"

Step 2: Analyze

So that's what you do—plug it in and "solve":

$$\begin{aligned} x^2 + 3x - 9 &= (-3)^2 + 3(-3) - 9 \\ &= 9 + (-9) - 9 \\ &= -9 \end{aligned}$$

Step 3: Select

The answer is B.

So this is a case where you knew exactly what to do as soon as you understood what the question was asking. Sometimes you're not so lucky. Let's look at a case where the method of solution is not so obvious, even after you "understand" the stem:

Example

4. What is the greatest of the numbers 1^{50}, 50^1, 2^{25}, 25^2, 4^{10}?

F. 1^{50}
G. 50^1
H. 2^{25}
J. 25^2
K. 4^{10}

Step 1: Understand

It's not hard to figure out what the question is asking: Which of five numbers is the greatest? But the five numbers are all written as powers, some of which we don't have time to calculate. Yikes! How are we going to compare them?

Step 2: Analyze

If all the powers had the same base or the same exponent, or if they could all be rewritten with a common base or exponent, we could compare all five at once. As it is, though, we should take two at a time.

Analysis Is Where It's At

Step 2: "Analyze" is where you'll be doing most of your serious thinking. The other two Math Workouts will address this step in greater detail.

Compare 1^{50} and 50^1 to start: $1^{50} = 1$, while $50^1 = 50$, so there's no way choice F could be the biggest.

Next, compare 50^1 and 2^{25}. We don't have time to calculate 2^{25}, but we can see that it doesn't take anywhere near 25 factors of 2 to get over 50. In fact, 2^6 is 64, already more than 50, so 2^{25} is much more than 50. That eliminates G.

Choice J, 25^2, doesn't take too long to calculate: $25 \times 25 = 625$. How does that compare to 2^{25}? Once again, with a little thought, we realize that it doesn't take 25 factors of 2 to get over 625. That eliminates J.

The last comparison is easy because choice K, 4^{10}, can be rewritten as $(2^2)^{10} = 2^{20}$, in that form clearly less than 2^{25}. That eliminates K.

Step 3: Select

So the answer is H.

Know When to Skip

At any time during the Three-Step process you could choose to cut bait and skip the question. Almost everyone should skip at least some questions the first time through.

If you know your own strengths and weaknesses, you can sometimes choose to skip a question while still in Step 1: "Understand." For example, suppose you never studied trigonometry. Maybe you think that a secant is something that sailors sing while climbing up the yardarms. Well, the ACT includes exactly four trigonometry questions, and it's not hard to spot them. Why waste a second on such a question? Skip it! You don't need those four measly questions to get a great score. And since you know a second visit later won't help any, you might as well go ahead and make some random guesses.

It can be harder to decide when to skip a question if you understand it, but then get stuck in Step 2: "Analyze." Suppose you just don't see how to solve it. Don't give up too quickly. Sometimes it takes 30 seconds or so before you see the light. But don't get bogged down either. Never spend more than a minute on a question the first time through the section. No single question is worth it. Be prepared to leave a question and come back to it later. Often, on the second try, you'll see something you didn't see before. That old light bulb will light up over your head and you'll be on your way.

Of course, eventually you're going to grid in an answer choice for every question, even the ones you don't understand. The first time through the section, however, you should concentrate on the questions you understand.

Do the Ones You Can

Don't worry about the ones you can't do. Get your points where you can, and don't expect miracles in the hard problems. Guess and move on.

KAPLAN'S TWO-PASS PLAN FOR ACT MATH

We recommend that you plan two "passes" through the Math test.

- **First Pass:** Examine each problem in order. Do every problem you understand. Don't skip too hastily—sometimes it takes a few seconds of thought to see how to do something—but don't get bogged down. Never spend more than a minute on any question in the first pass. This first pass should take about 45 minutes.

- **Second Pass:** Use the last 15 minutes to go back to the questions that stumped you the first time. Sometimes a fresh look is all you need—after going away and then coming back you'll sometimes suddenly see what to do. In most cases, though, you'll still be stumped by the question stem, so it's time to give the answer choices a try. Work by process of elimination, and guess. Be sure to select an answer for every question, even if it's just a blind guess.

Don't plan on visiting a question a third time; it's inefficient to go back and forth that much. Every time you leave a question and come back to it, you have to take at least a few seconds to refamiliarize yourself with the problem. Always grid in an answer choice on the second pass—even if it's just a wild guess. At the end of the second pass, every question should be answered.

Don't worry if you don't work on every question in the section. The average ACT test taker gets fewer than half of the problems right. You can score in the top quarter of all ACT test takers if you can do just *half* of the problems on the test, get every single one of them right, and guess blindly on the other half. If you did just *one-third* of the problems and got every one right, then guessed blindly on the other 40 problems, you would still earn an average score.

Don't Make Careless Mistakes

Most students don't worry much about careless errors. Since in school (where you show your work) you can earn partial credit, many students think that careless errors somehow "don't count." Not so on the ACT. There are only so many problems you'll know how to do. Some of the problems will be impossible for you, so you'll make or break your score on the problems you can do. You can't afford to miss one easy problem!

Unless math is a very strong area for you, the best way to maximize your score is to work on the questions you deserve to get correct. Don't worry about getting to every problem (though, of course, you should mark an answer for every problem on your answer grid, even if it's a blind guess).

Even if math is a strong area for you, don't get complacent on easy problems—that causes careless errors. For strong students, the easy problems may be the most challenging. You have to find a way to answer them quickly and accurately in order to have time for the tougher ones. You won't have time for the hard problems unless you save some time on the easy ones.

Stuck? Try Guesstimates and Estimates

Sometimes when you understand a problem but can't figure out how to solve it, you can at least get a general idea of how big the answer is—what is sometimes called a "ballpark estimate," "guess-estimate," or "guesstimate." You may not know whether you are looking at something the size of an African elephant or the size of an Indian elephant, but you may be pretty sure it isn't the size of a mouse and it isn't the size of a battleship.

Here's a question that's not hard to understand but is hard to solve if you don't remember the rules for simplifying and adding radicals:

Example

5. $\frac{\sqrt{32}+\sqrt{24}}{\sqrt{8}} = ?$

 A. $\sqrt{7}$
 B. $\sqrt{2}+\sqrt{3}$
 C. $2+\sqrt{3}$
 D. $\sqrt{2}+3$
 E. 7

Guesstimating

Guesstimating is much cruder than the kind of estimating and rounding off you are usually taught to do in school. The purpose of using guesstimates is to quickly and easily find the smallest and largest that the answer could possibly be. Our advice: Don't bother to make a guesstimate if you can't think of an easy way to do it.

Step 1: Understand

The question wants you to simplify the given expression, which includes three radicals. In other words, turn the radicals into numbers you can use, then work out the fraction.

Step 2: Analyze

The best way to solve this problem would be to apply the rules of radicals—but what if you don't remember them? Don't give up; you can still guesstimate. In the question stem, the numbers under the radicals are not too far away from perfect squares. You could round $\sqrt{32}$ off to $\sqrt{36}$, which is 6. You could round $\sqrt{24}$ to $\sqrt{25}$, which is 5. And you could round $\sqrt{8}$ off to $\sqrt{9}$, which is 3. So the expression is now $\frac{6+5}{3}$, which is $3\frac{2}{3}$. That's just a guesstimate, of course—the actual value might be something a bit less or a bit more than that.

Step 3: Select

Now look at the answer choices. Choice A—$\sqrt{7}$—is less than 3, so it's too small. Choice B—$\sqrt{2}+\sqrt{3}$—is about 1.4 + 1.7, or just barely more than 3, so it seems a little small, too. Choice C—$2+\sqrt{3}$—is about 2 + 1.7, or about 3.7—that's very close to our guesstimate! We still have to check the other choices. Choice D—$\sqrt{2}+3$—is about 1.4 + 3, or 4.4—too big. And choice E, 7, is obviously way too big. Looks like our best bet is C—and C in fact is the correct answer.

NOTE: To review the traditional textbook methods for adding and simplifying radicals, see the 100 Key Math Concepts for the ACT section.

Stuck? Try Eyeballing

There is another simple but powerful strategy that should give you at least a fifty-fifty chance on almost any diagram question: When in doubt, use your eyes. Trust common sense and careful thinking; don't worry if you've forgotten most of the geometry you ever knew. For almost half of all diagram questions you can get a reasonable answer without solving anything: Just eyeball it.

The math directions say, "Illustrative figures are NOT necessarily drawn to scale," but in fact they almost always are. You're never really *supposed* to just eyeball the figure, but it makes a lot more sense than random guessing. Occasionally, eyeballing can help you narrow down the choices.

Learn Common Estimates

It pays to learn the approximate value of these three irrational numbers:

$\sqrt{2} \approx 1.4$

$\sqrt{3} \approx 1.7$

$\pi \approx 3.14$

Here's a difficult geometry question that you might just decide to eyeball:

Example

6. In the figure below, points A, B, and C lie on a circle centered at O. Triangle AOC is equilateral, and the length of OC is 3 inches. What is the length, in inches, of arc ABC?

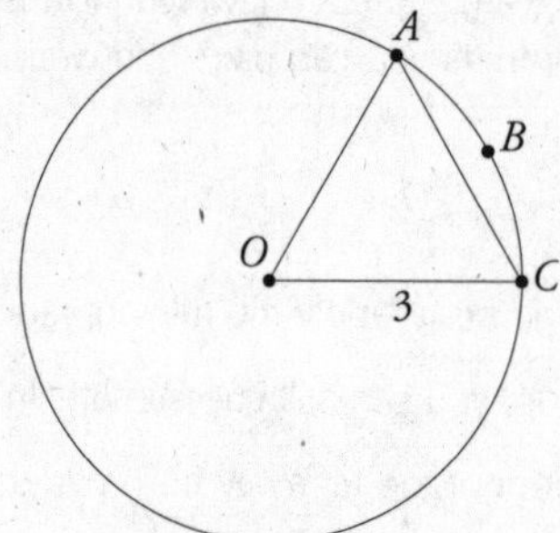

F. 3
G. π
H. 2π
J. 3π
K. 6π

Step 1: Understand

There's an "equilateral" triangle that connects the center and two points on the circumference of a circle. You're looking for the length of the arc that goes from A to C.

Step 2: Analyze

What you're "supposed" to do to answer this question is recall and apply the formula for the length of an arc. But suppose you don't remember that formula (most people don't). Should you give up and take a wild guess?

No. You can eyeball it. If you understand the question well enough to realize that "equilateral" means all sides are equal, then you know immediately that side $\overline{AC}$ is 3 inches long. Now look at arc *ABC* compared to side $\overline{AC}$. Suppose you were an ant, and you had to walk from *A* to *C*. If you walked along line segment $\overline{AC}$, it would be a 3-inch trip. About how long a walk would it be along arc *ABC*? Clearly more, but not much more, than 3 inches.

Step 3: Select

Now look at the answer choices. Choice F is no good: You know the arc is more than 3 inches. All the other choices are in terms of π. Just think of π as "a bit more than 3," and you will quickly see that only one answer choice is in the right ballpark. Choice G—π—would be "a bit more than 3," which sounds pretty good. Choice H—2π—would be "something more than 6." Already that's way too big. Choices J and K are even bigger. It sure looks like the answer has to be G—and it is.

Not many ACT students would be able to solve question 6 the textbook way. If you could, great! Solving the problem is always more reliable than eyeballing. But when you *don't* know how to solve a diagram problem, or if you think it would take forever to get an answer, eyeballing and eliminating answer choices sure beats wild guessing. Sometimes, as with question 6, you might even be able to narrow the choices down to the one that's probably correct.

Reminder

If you have forgotten any of the geometry terms discussed in this Workout, look them up in the Math Glossary!

TO CALCULATE OR NOT TO CALCULATE

You are permitted to use a calculator on the Math section. The good news is that you never *absolutely need* to use a calculator on the ACT. No Math question requires messy or tedious calculations. But while the calculator can't answer questions for you, it can keep you from making computational errors on questions you know how to solve. The bad news, however, is that a calculator can actually cost you time if you overuse it. Take a look at this example:

Example

7. The sum of all the integers from 1 to 44, inclusive, is subtracted from the sum of all the integers from 7 to 50, inclusive. What is the result?

A. 6
B. 44
C. 50
D. 264
E. 300

You could . . . add all the integers from 1 through 44, and then all the integers from 7 through 50, and then subtract the first sum from the second. And then punch in all the numbers into the calculator. And then hope you didn't hit any wrong buttons.

But that's the long way . . . and the wrong way. That way involves hitting over 250 keys on your calculator. It'll take too long, and you're too likely to make a mistake. The amount of computation involved in solving this problem tells you that there must be an easier way. Remember, no ACT problem absolutely requires the use of a calculator.

Think Before You Calculate

If a problem seems to involve a lot of calculation, look for a quicker way. Try to spot a pattern that will help you save some time.

Look at the problem again: A calculator *can* help you on this question, but you have to think first. Both sums contain the same number of consecutive integers, and each integer in the first sum has a corresponding integer 6 greater than it in the second sum. Here's the scratchwork:

```
 1     7
+2    +8
+3    +9
 .     .
 .     .
 .     .
+42   +48
+43   +49
+44   +50
```

This means there are 44 pairs of integers which are each 6 apart. So the total difference between the two sums will be the difference between each pair of integers, times the number of pairs. Now you can pull out your calculator, punch "6 × 44 =" and get the correct answer of 264 with little or no time wasted. Mark (D) in your test booklet and move on.

Here's another way to solve the problem. Both sets of integers contain the integers 7 through 44 inclusive. Think of $7 + 8 + 9 + 10 + \ldots + 50$ as $(7 + 8 + 9 + 10 + \ldots + 44) + (45 + 46 + 47 + 48 + 49 + 50)$. Now think of $1 + 2 + 3 + 4 + \ldots + 44$ as $(1 + 2 + 3 + 4 + 5 + 6) + (7 + 8 + 9 + 10 + \ldots + 44)$.

So $(7 + 8 + 9 + 10 + \ldots + 50) - (1 + 2 + 3 + 4 + \ldots + 44) =$

$(45 + 46 + 47 + 48 + 49 + 50) - (1 + 2 + 3 + 4 + 5 + 6) =$

$(45 - 1) + (46 - 2) + (47 - 3) + (48 - 4) + (49 - 5) + (50 - 6) =$

$44 + 44 + 44 + 44 + 44 + 44 = 6\,(44) = 264$

Of course, there will be many situations on the ACT in which using a calculator can save you time. Here's a trig question that's much easier with a calculator.

Example

8. sin 495° =

F. $-\frac{\sqrt{2}}{2}$

G. $-\frac{1}{2}$

H. $\frac{1}{2}$

J. $\frac{\sqrt{2}}{2}$

K. $\frac{3\sqrt{2}}{2}$

Without a calculator this is a very difficult problem. To find a trigonometric function of an angle greater than or equal to 90°, sketch a circle of radius 1 and centered at the origin of the coordinate grid. Start from the point (1, 0) and rotate the appropriate number of degrees counterclockwise. When you rotate counterclockwise 495°, you rotate 360° (which brings you back to where you started), and then an additional 135°. That puts you midway into the second quadrant. Now you need to know whether sine is positive or negative in the second quadrant. Pretty scary, huh?

With a calculator this problem becomes simple. Just punch in "sin 495°" and you get 0.7071067811865. Choices F and G are negative, so they're out, and 0.7071067811865 is clearly not equal to $\frac{1}{2}$, so H is also wrong. That leaves only J or K. Now, with respect to choice K: $\sqrt{2}$ is greater than 1, so if you multiply it by another number greater than 1 (namely $\frac{3}{2}$), the result is obviously greater than 1. So you can eliminate K, leaving J as the correct answer. With a calculator, you can get this question right without really understanding it.

The key to effective calculator use is practice, so don't run out the night before the test to buy a fancy new calculator. If you don't already have a calculator (and intend to use one on the test), buy one now. Unless you're studying math or science in college, you won't need anything more complex than trig functions. You're better off bringing a straightforward model you're familiar with than an esoteric model you don't know how to use.

Practicing with your calculator is the best way to get a sense of where it can help and save time. Here's a brief guide to spotting those calculator-friendly Math questions.

Calculators NOT Allowed on the Test

Pocket organizers, computers, models with writing pads, computers with QWERTY keyboards, paper tapes, power cords, wireless transmitters, calculators that are noisy, Kray supercomputers.

Example

9. $(7.3 + 0.8) - 3(1.98 + 0.69) =$

A. –0.99
B. –0.09
C. 0
D. 0.09
E. 0.99

This problem basically involves straightforward computation, so you'd be right if you reached for your calculator. However, if you just start punching the numbers in as they appear in the question, you will come up with the wrong answer. When you're performing a string of computations, you know that you need to follow the right order of operations. The problem is, your calculator might not know this. Some calculators have parentheses keys and do follow the order of operations, so it's important to know your calculator and what its capabilities are. See 100 Key Math Concepts for the ACT, #7 for further explanation of PEMDAS.

Know Your Calculator

Some calculators automatically follow the proper order of operations but others don't. Know before Test Day what your calculator can and cannot do.

If your calculator doesn't follow the order of operations, you'd need to perform the operations within parentheses separately and proceed carefully from there. You'd get 8.1 – 3(2.67). Multiplication comes before subtraction, so you'd get 8.1 – 8.01, and then finally 0.09, choice D.

Example

10. A certain bank issues 3-letter identification codes to its customers. If each letter can be used only once per code, how many different codes are possible?

F. 26
G. 78
H. 326
J. 15,600
K. 17,576

Just manipulating the numbers in this problem will get you nowhere, but once you arrive at the setup, a calculator is very useful.

For the first letter in the code you can choose any of the 26 letters in the alphabet. For the second letter, you can choose from all the letters in the alphabet except the one you used in the first spot, so there are 26 – 1 = 25 possibilities. For the third there are 26 – 2 = 24 possibilities. So the total number of different codes possible is equal to 26 × 25 × 24. Using your calculator you find that there are 15,600 codes—choice J.

Example

11. Which of the following fractions is greater than 0.68 and less than 0.72?

 A. $\frac{5}{9}$

 B. $\frac{3}{4}$

 C. $\frac{7}{11}$

 D. $\frac{2}{3}$

 E. $\frac{5}{7}$

Here you have to convert the fractions to decimals and see which one falls in the range of values given in the question. If you're familiar with common decimal/fraction conversions you might know that choice B, $\frac{3}{4}$, is equal to 0.75 (too large) and choice D, $\frac{2}{3}$, is approximately 0.67 (too small). But you'd still have to check out the other three choices. Your calculator can make short work of this, showing you that choice A, $\frac{5}{9}$, equals $0.5\overline{5}$, choice C, $\frac{7}{11}$, equals $.\overline{63}$, and choice E, $\frac{5}{7}$, is approximately 0.71. Only 0.71 falls between 0.68 and 0.72, so E is correct.

Chapter Six: **Reading Workout 1: Know Where You're Going**

- **The Key to Active ACT Reading**
- **The Kaplan Five-Step Method for ACT Reading**

Reading skills are crucial on every part of the ACT, not just on the Reading test. Savvy ACT-style reading is certainly useful for the English and Science tests, and even your work on many of the Math problems will benefit from the skills discussed below. So don't ignore the Reading Workouts, even if you think you're an ace reader.

The kind of reading rewarded by the ACT is special. You probably know how to do it already, but you may be reluctant to do it on a standardized test. You may think that success on a test like this requires that you read very slowly and deliberately, making sure you remember everything. Well, we at Kaplan have found that this kind of reading won't work on the ACT. In fact, it is a sure way to run out of time halfway through the Reading test.

Question Breakdown

The ACT Reading test includes:

- 1 Prose Fiction passage with 10 questions
- 1 Humanities passage with 10 questions
- 1 Social Sciences passage with 10 questions
- 1 Natural Sciences passage with 10 questions

THE KEY TO ACTIVE ACT READING

The real key to ACT reading is to read quickly but actively, getting a sense of the gist or "main idea" of the passage and seeing how everything fits together to support that main idea. You should constantly try to think ahead. Look for the general outline of the passage—determine how it's structured. Don't worry about the details. You'll come back for those later.

Emergency Plan

Here's how to use this chapter if you don't have much time. Learn the Kaplan Method for ACT Reading. Try the sample passage that follows. Check your answers. If you need more help, go back and read the whole chapter.

Fast, active reading, of course, requires a little more mental energy than slow, passive reading. But it pays off. Those who dwell on details—who passively let the passage reveal itself at its own pace—are sure to run out of time. Don't be that kind of reader! Make the passage reveal itself to you on your schedule, by skimming the passage with an eye to structure rather than detail. Look for key words that tell you what the author is doing so that you can save yourself time. For instance, read examples very quickly, just glancing over the words. When an author says "for example," you know that what follows is an example of a general point. Do you need to understand that specific example? Maybe, maybe not. If you do, you can come back and read the verbiage when you're attacking the questions. You'll know exactly where the author gave an example of general point *x* (or whatever). If you *don't* need to know the example for any of the questions, great! You haven't wasted much time on something that won't get you a point.

You actually do this kind of "reading" all the time, and not just when you're reading a book or newspaper. When you watch TV or see a movie, for instance, you can often figure out much of what's going to happen in advance. You see the bad guys run out of a bank with bags of money in their hands, and you can guess that the next thing they'll do is get into a car and drive away in excess of the speed limit. You see a character in an old sitcom bragging to his friends about how great a driver he is, and you know that he's bound to get into a fender bender before the next commercial. This ability to know where something is going is very valuable. Use it on the ACT.

Reminder

Read actively, with an eye toward where the author is going. Don't worry about remembering the details. You can (and should) always refer to them later.

To help you know where an author is going, pay careful attention to "structural clues." Words like *but, nevertheless,* and *moreover* help you get a sense of where a piece of writing is going. Look for signal phrases (like *clearly, as a result,* or *no one can deny that*) to determine the logic of the passage. The details, remember, you can come back for later, when you're doing the questions. What's important in reading the passage is getting a sense of how those details fit together to express the point or points of the passage.

Practice Knowing Where You're Going

In the following exercise, try to fill in the word or phrase that should come next. For most, there are many possible answers, so don't worry about getting the "right" answer.

1. You'd think that the recipe for a strawberry soufflé would be complicated, but my friend's version was _______.
2. I can't believe my good luck! The one time in my life I buy a lottery ticket, I _______.
3. A parked car burns no fuel and causes no pollution. Once the ignition is turned on, however, _______.
4. As their habitat is destroyed, wild animals _______.
5. The new word-processing program was far easier to use than the old one. Moreover, the accompanying instruction booklet explained the commands in a _______ way.
6. The new word-processing program was far easier to use than the old one. On the other hand, the accompanying instruction booklet explained the commands in a _______ way.

Answers

- In Sentence 1, the active reader would probably complete the sentence by saying that the friend's version was "actually quite simple" or something similar. How do you know what's coming next here? The structural clue *but* tips you off. *But* tells you that a contrast is coming up. You'd think the recipe would be complicated, *BUT* it's "actually quite simple."
- In Sentence 2, on the other hand, there's no real structural clue to help you out, but the *meaning* of the sentence should make clear what's coming up. The speaker here is marveling at his good luck, right? That means that he must have won some money. So, a likely completion would be something like: The one time in my life I buy a lottery ticket, I "win the jackpot."
- In Sentence 3, we have another contrast, signaled by the clue *however*. A parked car doesn't burn fuel or pollute. *HOWEVER*, once you turn on the ignition. . . . The answer has to be something like "the car starts burning gas and polluting." That's the clear contrast that was anticipated by the structural clue *however*.
- Sentence 4 demonstrates again that you don't need explicit structural clues to stay ahead. Sometimes all you need is common sense. What do you think would happen to animals whose habitat had been destroyed? Would they thrive? Celebrate? Buy a condo in Florida? No, they'd probably "start dying out." They might even "become extinct."
- Sentences 5 and 6 show clearly how you can use an author's language to anticipate what point he or she is going to make next. Here, we have identical sentences, except for one small (but very important) difference. In #5, the second sentence begins with the word *moreover*, indicating a continuation, an addition of similar information. In #6, the second sentence starts with *On the other hand*, indicating a contrast, the other side of the coin, something that stands in opposition to what has come before. The blank to #5 should be filled by a phrase like: in a "clear and easy-to-understand" way. That would allow the sentences to make sense together: The program was easy to use; moreover, the instructions were easy to understand. But the sentences in #6 make sense together only if you fill the blank with something like: in a "confusing and unclear" way (to carry out the sense of contrast). To drive the point home, try reversing the suggested completions we just gave you. #5: The program was easier to use; moreover, the instructions were confusing and unclear. Huh? That doesn't make sense. And #6: The program was easier to use; on the other hand, it was easy to understand. Again, that makes no sense.

Common Structural Clues

Indicating a contrast:
but, however, on the other hand, nevertheless

Indicating a continuation with a similar or complementary thought:
moreover, furthermore, ; (a semicolon)

Indicating a conclusion:
therefore, thus

Indicating reasons for a conclusion:
since, because of, due to

Indicating an example or illustration:
for instance, for example

THE KAPLAN FIVE-STEP METHOD FOR ACT READING

There are many ways to read, depending on your purpose. When you read your teacher's comments on a paper you wrote, you go very slowly and work out every word to make sure you know what you did right and what you did wrong. When you read for pleasure, you read what you like and skim what you don't. When you cram for most tests, you try to remember the facts you know you'll be asked to recall.

For the ACT, however, you have a special purpose: to answer specific multiple-choice questions. And we've found that the best way to do that is initially to read a passage quickly and actively for general understanding, then refer to the passage to answer individual questions. Not everybody should use the exact same strategy, but we find that almost every ACT test taker can succeed by following these basic steps:

1. Preread the passage
2. Consider the question stem
3. Refer to the passage (before looking at the choices)
4. Answer questions in your own words
5. Match your answer with one of the choices

For most students, these five tasks should together take up about nine minutes per passage. Less than three of those nine minutes should be spent prereading. The remaining time should be devoted to considering the questions and referring to the passage to check your answers. As we mentioned in the ACT Basics section, you'll probably want to take two sweeps through the questions for each passage, getting the doable ones the first time around, coming back for the harder ones.

Step 1: Preread the Passage

Prereading means quickly working through the passage before trying to answer the questions. Remember to "know where you're going," anticipating how the parts of the passage fit together. In this preread, the main goals are to:

- Understand the "gist" of the passage (the "main idea").
- Get an overall idea of how the passage is organized—a kind of road map—so that it will be easier to refer to later.

Draw a Road Map

Mark up the passages! Have a system worked out where you use different symbols to mean different things. For example, circle names, box numbers and dates, underline key sentences, and draw arrows to lists of details. Once you know your system, you can find the facts you are looking for faster.

You may want to underline key points, jot down notes, circle structural clues—whatever it takes to accomplish the two goals above. You may even want to label each paragraph, to fix in your mind how the paragraphs relate to one another and what aspect of the main idea is discussed in each. That could be your road map.

Two important reminders: *Don't* read slowly, and *don't* get bogged down in individual details. Most of the details in the passage aren't required for answering the questions, so why waste time worrying about them?

Step 2: Consider the Question Stem

Approaching the questions requires self-discipline in Reading. Most test takers have an almost irresistible urge to immediately jump to the answer choices to see what "looks okay." That's not a good idea. Don't let the answer choices direct your thinking. The test makers intentionally design the answers to confuse you. So, if you look at the answer choices hoping that they'll suggest something to you, you're just falling into one of their cleverly set traps.

In Reading, think about the question stem without looking at the choices. In most questions, you won't be able to remember exactly what the passage said about the matter in question. That's okay. In fact, even if you do think you remember, don't trust your memory. Instead . . .

Step 3: Refer to the Passage

You won't be rereading the whole passage, of course. But refer by finding the place where the answer to a question can be found (the question stem will sometimes contain a line reference to help you out; otherwise, rely on your road map of the passage). Your chosen answer should match the passage—not in exact vocabulary, perhaps, but in *meaning*.

Step 4: Answer the Question in Your Own Words

It's extremely important in Reading to make a habit of answering the question in your own words (based on your checking of the passage) *before* looking at the answer choices. Most students waste enormous amounts of time thinking about answer choices in Reading. If you do that, you'll never finish, and you'll get so confused you'll probably get many questions wrong.

Step 5: Match Your Answer with One of the Choices

When you look at answer choices in Reading, your mental process should be "matching." You've got an answer in your head based on what you've read and rechecked in the passage. You need to match it to one of the answer choices. Avoid trying to see if they "look right." You don't want to think very hard about the choices if you can help it. They're intended to confuse you, after all, so don't think about them any more than you absolutely have to.

Timing

Keep track of time. If you can, try to devote only 9 minutes to each passage and its questions.

Now practice the Kaplan method on the full-length ACT passage that follows. We're going to give you added incentive to use it by first showing you the questions *without* answer choices. That way you can't give in to the temptation to look at the choices before you think about the questions. The same questions in ACT style, *with* answer choices, will follow the passage. But try to answer them in "fill-in-the-blank" format first.

Example

Your Answers

Questions

1. The author states that "on many manors meadow land was even more valuable than the arable" (lines 75–76) because:

2. According to the passage, the fact that the peasants' individual strips of land were unfenced subdivisions of larger fields required each peasant to:

3. According to the second paragraph (lines 4–31), the fallow part of the arable had to be plowed a total of how many times in any given calendar year?

4. The passage suggests that the practice of peasants owning strips "scattered through the three fields in different parts" (lines 37–38) was instituted in order to:

5. On the basis of the information in the passage, it may be inferred that people in medieval times did not think of sowing hay because:

6. As it is used in line 53, the word "garnered" means:

7. According to the passage, if one of the arable's three great fields were left fallow one year, it would be:

8. Which of the following conclusions is suggested by the fourth paragraph (lines 41–58)?

9. According to the passage, a manor's value might be judged according to the number of its plows because:

10. According to the passage, summer pasture for a manor's geese would be provided:

Passage I

By the tenth century most of northern Europe was divided into farming units known as manors . . . .

Almost always a manor comprised four parts: arable, meadow, waste, and the village area itself. The arable was of course the land which grew the crops on which the inhabitants of the manor subsisted. To maintain fertility and keep down weeds it was necessary to fallow a part of the cultivated land each year. It was, therefore, usual (though not universal) to divide the arable into three fields. One such field was planted with winter grain, a second with spring grain, and the third left fallow; the following year, the fallow field would be planted with winter grain, the field in which winter grain had been raised was planted with spring grain, and the third field left fallow. By following such a rotation, the cycle was completed every three years. Since the fallow field had to be plowed twice in the year in order to keep down the weeds, and the others had to be plowed once, work for the plow teams extended almost throughout the year. Plowing stopped only at times when all hands were needed to bring in the harvest, or when the soil was too wet to be plowed, or was frozen. The amount of land that could be tilled was fixed fairly definitely by the number of plows and plow teams which the manor could muster; and official documents sometimes estimated the wealth and value of a manor in terms of the number of plows it possessed.

The three great fields lay open, without fences, but were subdivided into numerous small strips (often one acre in size, i.e., the amount of one day's plowing) which individual peasants "owned." The strips belonging to any one individual were scattered through the three fields in different parts, perhaps in order to assure that each peasant would have strips plowed early and late, in fertile and infertile parts of the arable land.

Custom severely restricted the individual's rights over his land. The time for plowing and planting was fixed by custom and each peasant had to conform, since he needed his neighbor's help to plow his strips and they needed his. Uniform cropping was imperative, since on a given day the village animals were turned into the fields to graze after the harvest had been gathered, and if some individual planted a crop which did not ripen as early as that of his neighbors, he had no means of defending his field from the hungry animals. If his crop ripened sooner, on the other hand, it could not be garnered without trampling neighboring fields. Moreover, the very idea of innovation was lacking: men did what custom prescribed, cooperated in the plowing and to some extent in the harvesting, and for many generations did not dream of trying to change.

The meadow was almost as important as the arable for the economy of the village. Hay from the meadow supported the indispensable draught animals through the winter. The idea that hay might be sown did not occur to men in medieval times; consequently they were compelled to rely on natural meadows alone. One result was that in many manors shortage of winter fodder for the plow teams was a constant danger. It was common practice to feed oxen on leaves picked from trees, and on straw from the grain harvest; but despite such supplements the draught animals often nearly starved in winter. In some cases oxen actually had to be carried out from their winter stalls to spring pastures until some of their strength was recovered and plowing could begin. Thus on many manors meadow land was even more valuable than the arable and was divided into much smaller strips (often the width of a scythe stroke).

The waste provided summer pasture for various animals of the manor: pigs, geese, cattle, and sheep. The animals of the whole manor normally grazed together under the watchful eyes of some young children or other attendants who could keep them from wandering too far afield, and bring them back to the village at night. The waste also was the source of wood for fuel and for building purposes, and helped to supplement the food supply with such things as nuts, berries, honey, and rabbits....

The fourth segment of the manor was the village itself, usually located in the center of the arable near a source of drinking water, and perhaps along a road or path or footpath leading to the outside world. The cottages of medieval peasants were extremely humble, usually consisting of a single room, with earthen floor and thatched roof. Around each cottage normally lay a small garden in which various vegetables and sometimes fruit trees were planted. In the village streets chickens, ducks, and dogs picked up a precarious living.

1. The author states that "on many manors meadow land was even more valuable than the arable" (lines 75–76) because:
   - **A.** the meadow produced the leaves and straw that fed the manor's various animals through the winter months.
   - **B.** when necessary, the meadow could be used to grow supplementary crops.
   - **C.** the strength of the manor's draught animals depended upon the meadow's production of winter fodder.
   - **D.** profit could be made selling hay to manors with insufficient winter fodder for their draught animals.

2. According to the passage, the fact that the peasants' individual strips of land were unfenced subdivisions of larger fields required each peasant to:
   - **F.** follow a fixed planting schedule so as to be able to harvest crops at the same time as the other peasants.
   - **G.** harvest crops independently of his neighbors.
   - **H.** limit the size of strips to what could be plowed in a single day.
   - **J.** maintain small garden plots in order to provide his family with enough food.

3. According to the second paragraph (lines 4–31), the fallow part of the arable had to be plowed a total of how many times in any given calendar year?
   - **A.** one
   - **B.** two
   - **C.** four
   - **D.** six

4. The passage suggests that the practice of peasants owning strips "scattered through the three fields in different parts" (lines 37–38) was instituted in order to:
   - **F.** divide resources fairly evenly.
   - **G.** preserve the wealth of elite landowners.
   - **H.** protect the three fields from overuse.
   - **J.** force neighbors to work only their own lands.

5. On the basis of the information in the passage, it may be inferred that people in medieval times did not think of sowing hay because:
   - **A.** hay sowing had not been done in the past.
   - **B.** the need for more hay was not great enough to warrant the extra work.
   - **C.** northern Europeans did not yet have the necessary farming techniques for successful hay cultivation.
   - **D.** the tight schedule of cultivating the arable meant that the peasants had no time to cultivate extra crops.

6. As it is used in line 53, the word "garnered" means:

F. planted
G. watered
H. gathered
J. plowed

7. According to the passage, if one of the arable's three great fields were left fallow one year, it would be:

A. left fallow for two more years in succession.
B. planted the next year with winter grain only.
C. planted the next year with spring grain only.
D. planted with either winter or spring grain the next year.

8. Which of the following conclusions is suggested by the fourth paragraph (lines 41–58)?

I. An individual was free to cultivate his own land in any way he wished.
II. The manor was run according to tradition.
III. Successful farming required cooperative methods.

F. I and II only
G. I and III only
H. II and III only
J. I, II, and III

9. According to the passage, a manor's value might be judged according to the number of its plows because:

A. the more plows a manor had, the less land had to be left fallow.
B. plows, while not in themselves valuable, symbolized great wealth.
C. manors with sufficient plows could continue plowing throughout the year.
D. the number of plows a manor owned determined how much land could be cultivated.

10. According to the passage, summer pasture for a manor's geese would be provided:

F. next to cottages, within the village.
G. on the fallow field of the arable.
H. on the communal ground of the waste.
J. on the whole of the meadow.

The Lay of the Land

Well, how'd you do? Did you remember to refer to the passage? You probably found that you had to do a more thorough check for some questions than for others.

This passage, like most nonfiction passages on the ACT, is organized in a fairly logical way around the main idea, which you might have expressed as "the structure and common practices of the medieval manor." Here's one possible road map you might have come up with:

- Paragraph 1 (just a single sentence, really): Intro to the topic of medieval manors (divided, as cited in the first line of next paragraph, into arable, meadow, waste, and village)
- Paragraphs 2, 3, and 4: Discussion of the arable and the practices associated with it
- Paragraph 5: Discussion of the meadow
- Paragraph 6: Discussion of the waste
- Paragraph 7: Discussion of the village

What about Roman Numerals?

A few ACT questions—like question 8 in this passage—are Roman numeral questions. You're given three or four statements, each labeled with a Roman numeral. The idea is to treat each one as a true-false statement. Decide which statements are true, and then select the choice that includes only those statements. Often you can save yourself some time on these questions. For instance, in question 8: Once you decide that Statement I is false, you can eliminate choices F, G, and J, all of which include Statement I. Thus, you can get your answer, choice H, without even looking at Statements II and III.

It should be obvious why, in your prereading step, you really need to get some sense of the layout of the passage like this. Many questions don't contain specific line references to help you locate information, and if you don't have a road map of the passage in your head or on paper, you might get lost.

Following is a key to the 10 questions attached to this passage.

Key to Passage I

(Nonfiction—Social Studies)

	Answer	Refer to	Type	Comments
1.	C	Lines 59–77	Detail	The entire paragraph supports this claim.
2.	F	Lines 46–52	Detail	"Uniform cropping was imperative . . ."
3.	B	Lines 19–21	Detail	Don't confuse fallow with planted fields.
4.	F	Lines 36–40	Inference	Every peasant got some fertile and some infertile land—inferably, to be fair to each.
5.	A	Lines 54–58, 62–64	Inference	No line reference so you had to have a sense of the structure to find this.
6.	H	Lines 52–54	Detail	Use context. The crop is ripe, and so must be ready to be gathered.
7.	B	Lines 14–15	Detail	No line reference; otherwise no problem.
8.	H	Lines 41–58	Inference	I: lines 42–44 says the opposite II: lines 41–46 III: lines 49–54
9.	D	Lines 26–28	Detail	No line reference; number of plows = amount of land.
10.	H	Lines 78–80	Detail	Whole paragraph devoted to describing waste.

Chapter Seven: **Science Workout 1: Look for Patterns**

- **The Kaplan Five-Step Method for ACT Science**
- **Reading Tables and Graphs**
- **The Real Thing: Practice Passage**

The Science subject test causes a lot of unnecessary anxiety among ACT takers. Many people get so overwhelmed by the terminology and technicality of the passages that they just give up. What they fail to realize is that Science is a little like the reverse of Math. In Math, you'll remember, we said that many of the questions are difficult problems based on elementary principles. In Science, on the other hand, many of the questions are elementary problems based on difficult material. So it's important not to panic if you don't understand the passage in Science. You can often get many of the questions right on a passage, even if you find it virtually incomprehensible!

Question Breakdown

The ACT Science test covers biology, chemistry, earth/space sciences, and physics. It includes:

- 15 Data Representation Questions
- 18 Experiment Questions
- 7 Conflicting Viewpoints Questions

Many ACT takers also tend to rely too heavily on what they've learned in school when approaching the Science subject test. But as we've said, "remembering" is not the mindset the ACT will reward. You couldn't possibly know the answers to ACT Science questions in advance: You have to pull them out of the passages. All the information you need to answer the questions is right on the page.

Worrying about science knowledge can be a problem no matter how good or bad your science background is. Students who have done poorly in science tend to panic because they think they don't know enough. Students who have done well in science might know too much. Some questions include wrong choices that are scientifically correct but don't relate to the passages. Choosing such answers will not earn you points on the ACT. So try not to rely primarily on your knowledge of science. Instead, use your ability to refer to the passages.

Emergency Plan

Here's how to use this chapter if you don't have much time. Learn the Kaplan Method for ACT Science Reasoning on the next page. Try the sample passage that follows. Then read the section called Reading Tables and Graphs.

ACT Science requires many of the same skills that ACT Reading does. The strategies discussed in Reading Workout I will therefore also work well for many Science passages. The most important difference between Reading and Science is that the "details" you have to find in the Science passages almost all relate to numbers or scientific processes, and they are often contained in graphs and tables rather than in paragraph form.

- **Reading graphs, tables, and research summaries.** Many questions involve only accurately retrieving data from a single graph or table. Others involve combining knowledge from two different graphs or tables. Still others involve understanding experimental methods well enough to evaluate information contained in summaries of experiments.
- **Looking for patterns in the numbers that appear.** Do these numbers get bigger or smaller? Where are the highest numbers? the lowest? At what point do the numbers change? A little calculation is sometimes required, but not much. In Science, you won't be computing with numbers so much as thinking about what they mean.

You Don't Need to Know Science

Knowing science is great, and it certainly can help your work in the Science subject test. But you don't need to know a truckload of scientific facts to answer ACT Science questions. The questions are answerable from the information in the passage.

In Science, as in Reading, it's crucial to consider the questions and at least try to answer them before looking at the answer choices. Refer to the passage to find the answer, and try to match it with one of the choices. Use the process of elimination as a fallback strategy for hard questions—but don't make it your main approach.

THE KAPLAN FIVE-STEP METHOD FOR ACT SCIENCE

The same Kaplan Method for Reading is also useful in Science. The steps, you'll remember, are:

1. Preread the passage
2. Consider the question stem
3. Refer to the passage (before looking at the choices)
4. Answer the question in your own words
5. Match your answer with one of the choices

But in Science, you have seven shorter passages to do instead of the four longer ones in Reading. Each passage should average five minutes. We recommend using just about one minute or so to preread the passage, and then a total of about four minutes to consider the questions and refer to the passage (that's about 40 seconds per question). Notice that this is less time prereading than in the Reading test.

Step 1: Preread the Passage

It's especially important in Science not to get bogged down in the details (we'll see that this is also critical in the Natural Sciences passage in Reading). Some of the material covered is extremely technical, and you'll just get frustrated trying to understand it completely. So it's crucial that you skim, to get a general idea of what's going on and—just as important—to get a sense of where certain types of data can be found.

Almost all Science passages have the same general structure. They begin with an introduction. Always read the introduction first to orient yourself. Some passages relate to material you may have already studied in high school. If you're familiar with the concepts, you may not need to do more than skim the introduction. If not, you'll want to read the introduction more carefully. But remember, don't focus on details.

After reviewing the introduction, quickly scan the rest of the passage. How is the information presented? Graphs? Diagrams? Are there experiments? What seems to be important? Size? Shape? Temperature? Speed? Chemical composition? Don't worry about details and don't try to remember it all. Plan to refer to the passage just as you would in Reading.

Example

> Scientists researching the relationship between birds and dinosaurs have chosen to carefully examine three fossils dating from the Jurassic period: an *archaeopteryx* (the oldest known bird) at the British Museum in London, a *compsognathus* (a dinosaur) at the Field Museum in Chicago, and a *teleosaurus* (a crocodile) at the National Museum in Beijing. All three creatures were about the same size as a turkey.

Remember to read actively. Ask yourself: Why would the scientists choose these three creatures? Since the scientists are studying birds and dinosaurs, the first two choices seem natural. But why should they include a crocodile? Maybe the National Museum in Beijing had a special deal on crocodile bones? More likely it's because crocodiles are somewhat like dinosaurs, but not extinct.

As you preread the passage, you also want to make sure you know what any tables and graphs in the passage are meant to represent. Feel free to take notes, mark up the test booklet, or circle important information. Get a sense of what kind of data is contained in each graph and table, but don't read the data carefully yet! You may want to take note of general trends in the data, but don't waste time taking in information that may not be relevant to the questions. Remember, your goal is to answer questions, *not* to learn and remember everything that goes on in the passage.

Scientific Terms

Scientific terms can be intimidating. But don't worry if you've never heard of things like *archaeopteryx* or *teleosaurus* before. If you need to know the meaning of a special scientific term, the test will normally define it. If the test doesn't tell you what a word means, you can usually figure it out from the context (or else you won't need to know it).

Step 2: Consider the Question Stem

Most of your time in Science will be spent considering questions and referring to the passage to find the answers. Here's where you should do most of your really careful reading. It's essential that you understand exactly what the question is asking. Then, go back to the passage and get a sense of what the answer should be before looking at the choices.

There are three basic kinds of Science questions:

- **Data Analysis Questions.** For these questions, you'll almost certainly be going back to the graphs and tables in the passage to analyze their data. Look for patterns in the data (you'll get some practice reading graphs and tables later in this Workout). And try to get a sense of what the answer should be before looking at the choices.

- **Experiment Questions.** Make sure you understand the purpose of the experiments. What are these scientists trying to prove? Try to identify the control group, if any, in each experiment, and the factor that is being varied from one trial to the next. (Experiments will be covered more fully in Science Workout 2.)
- **Principle Questions.** These questions ask you to apply a scientific principle, or to identify ways of defending or attacking a principle. This includes making predictions based on a given theory, or showing how a hypothesis might be strengthened or weakened by particular findings. (These questions will be especially important for the Conflicting Viewpoints passage, discussed in Science Workout 3.)

As we mentioned, one possible pitfall in answering the questions is relying too heavily on your own knowledge of science. In answering questions, use your knowledge of scientific *methods* and *procedures*. But don't rely heavily on any knowledge of specific *facts*. For example, the following question might have appeared with the passage excerpted above:

Example

1. The dinosaur studied by the scientists, *compsognathus*, was:

   A. definitely a reptile.
   B. definitely a bird.
   C. about the size of a turkey.
   D. larger than *archaeopteryx* or *teleosaurus*.

If you know that dinosaurs are usually classified as reptiles, choice A would be very tempting. But it's wrong. The passage doesn't say that. In fact, if we had seen the rest of this passage, we would have learned that the researchers were questioning whether dinosaurs should be classified as reptiles or birds. What the passage *does* say is that all three of the creatures tested are turkey sized, making the correct choice C.

Step 3: Refer to the Passage

As in Reading, you have to be diligent about referring to the passage. Your prereading of the passage should have given you an idea of where particular kinds of data can be found. Sometimes the questions themselves will direct you to the right place.

Be careful not to mix up units when taking information from graphs, tables, and summaries. Don't confuse *decreases* and *increases*: Many questions will hinge on whether you can correctly identify the factors that decrease and the ones that increase. The difference between a correct and an incorrect answer will often be a "decrease" where an "increase" should be. Read the questions carefully!

Step 4: Answer the Question in Your Own Words

The answers to the Science Questions are there in the passage. As we mentioned in Step 2 above, don't rely too much on your own knowledge of science. Instead think of paraphrasing the information in the passage.

Step 5: Match Your Answer with One of the Choices

Once you've paraphrased the information and matched it to an answer choice, double-check the question to make sure that you've actually answered the question asked. Many of the questions in Science are reversal questions. Always look for words like *not* and *except* in the questions.

READING TABLES AND GRAPHS

Most of the information in ACT Science passages is presented in tables or graphs, usually accompanied by explanatory material. Knowing how to read data from tables and graphs is critical to success on the Science subject test! In order to read most graphs and tables, you have to do four things:

- Determine what is being represented
- Determine what the axes (or columns and rows) represent
- Take note of units of measurement
- Look for trends in the data

Let's say you saw the following graph in a Science passage.

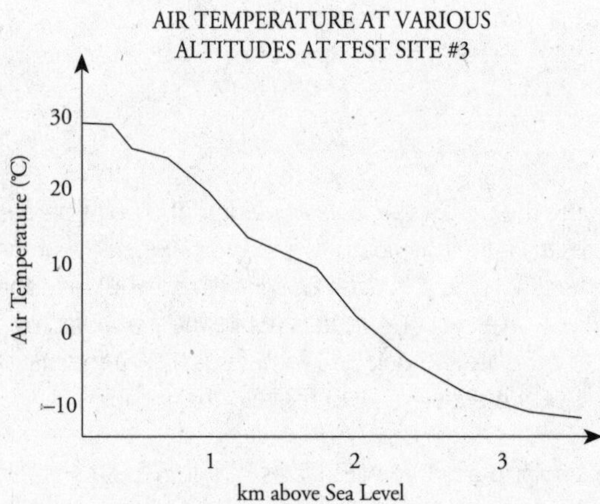

- **Determine what is being represented.** Most graphs and tables have titles that tell you what they represent. For some, though, you may have to get that information from the introduction. Here, the graph is representing how cold or hot the air is at various altitudes above a certain Test Site #3.

- **Determine what the axes represent.** These, too, are usually labeled. In the graph above, the *x*-axis represents distance above sea level in kilometers, while the *y*-axis represents the air temperature in degrees Celsius.
- **Take note of units of measurement.** Note that distance here is measured in *kilometers*, not miles or feet. Temperature is measured in degrees *Celsius*, not Fahrenheit.
- **Look for trends in the data.** The "pattern" of the data in this graph is pretty clear. As you rise in altitude, the temperature drops–the higher the altitude, the lower the temperature. (As we'll see later, this kind of trend is called an *inverse variation.*)

Don't Rush

Many students race through the section and do not read the questions carefully. If you just slow down and make sure of what you are being asked, you will find that these problems are not so bad after all.

The sloping line on the graph represents the various temperatures measured at the various altitudes. To find what the measured temperature was at, say, 2 km above sea level, find the 2 km point on the *x*-axis and trace your finger directly up from it until it hits the line. It does so at about the level of 3° C. In other words, at an altitude of 2 km above sea level at Test Site #3, the air temperature was about 3° C.

Be careful with units of measurement! Most passages use the metric system, but a few may use traditional or British units of measure. You won't be expected to remember oddball unit conversions like 8 furlongs = 1 mile or 2.54 cm = 1 in, and passages that use special units of measure such as microns or parsecs will define these units if necessary. But don't assume that all the units in the graphs match the units in the questions. For instance, try the following question.

Example

2. At what altitude did the meteorologists measure an air temperature of 10° C?

F. 1.4 m
G. 140 m
H. 1400 m
J. 14 km

Many test takers solving the problem above would find the point on the line at the level of 10° C on the *y*-axis, trace their fingers down to the *x*-axis, see that the altitude would be about halfway between 1 and 2 (a little closer to 1, maybe), and then quickly choose F. But F is wrong, since F gives you 1.4 *meters*, while the graph figures are given in *kilometers*. Remember to translate the data! A kilometer is 1,000 meters, so 1.4 kilometers would be 1.4 times 1,000 meters = 1,400 meters. That's choice H.

You should follow a similar procedure with tables of information. For instance, in the introduction to the passage in which the following table might have appeared, you would have learned that scientists were trying to determine the effects of two pollutants (Pb and Hg, lead and mercury) on the trout population of a particular river.

Table 1

Location	Water temperature (°C)	Presence of Pb (parts per million)	Presence of Hg (parts per million)	Population Density of Speckled Trout (# per 100 m^3)
1	15.4	0	3	7.9
2	16.1	0	1	3.5
3	16.3	1	67	0
4	15.8	54	3	5.7
5	16.0	2	4	9.5

- **Determine what is being represented.** There's no informative title for this table, but the introduction would have told you what the table represents.
- **Determine what the columns and rows represent.** In tables, you get columns and rows instead of *x*- and *y*-axes. But the principle is the same. Here, each row represents the data from a different numbered location on the river. Each column represents different data: water temperature, presence of the first pollutant, presence of the second pollutant, population of one kind of trout.
- **Take note of units of measurement.** Temperature is measured in degrees Celsius. The two pollutants are measured in parts per million (or ppm). The trout populations are measured in average number per 100 cubic meters of river.
- **Look for trends in the data.** Glancing at the table, it looks like locations where the Hg concentration is high (as in Location 3), the trout population is virtually nonexistent. This would seem to indicate that trout find a high Hg concentration incompatible. But notice the location where the other pollutant is abundant—in Location 4. Here, the trout population seems to be more in line with other locations. That would seem to indicate that this other pollutant—Pb—is NOT quite so detrimental to trout populations (though we'd have to do more studies if it turned out that all of the trout in that location had three eyes).

How Tables and Graphs Relate

To really understand tables and graphs, it helps to see how the same information can be represented in both. For instance, look at the next table and graph.

Concentration of *E. coli* in Cooling Pool B	
DISTANCE FROM EFFLUENT PIPE 3	1000s OF *E. COLI* PER CENTILITRE
zero m	.4
5 m	5.6
10 m	27.6
15 m	14.0
20 m	7.5

Concentration of *E. coli* in Cooling Pool B

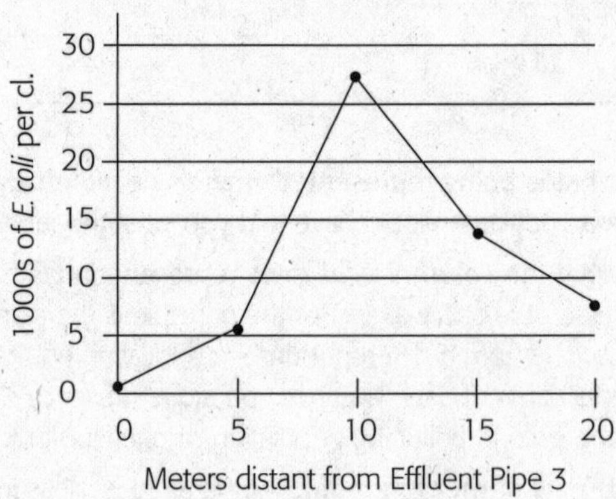

The table and graph above represent the exact same data. And here's yet another way of depicting the same data, in a bar chart.

Concentration of *E. coli* in Cooling Pool B

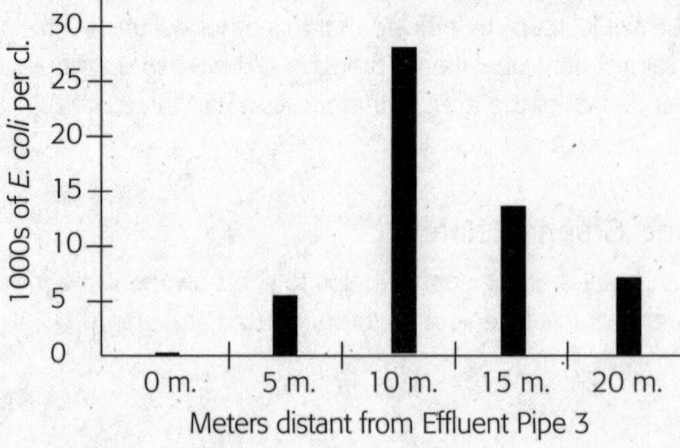

Remember that data can be represented in many different ways. But however it appears in the passage, whether it be in tables, graphs, or charts, you'll have to read and translate it to answer the questions.

Look for Patterns and Trends

When you first examine a graph or table, don't focus on exact numbers. Look for *patterns* in the numbers. But don't assume that there is *always* a pattern or trend: Finding that there isn't a pattern is just as important as finding that there is one. When looking for patterns and trends, you should keep three things in mind.

1. Extremes

Extremes—or maximums and minimums—are merely the highest and lowest points that things reach. In tables, the minimums and maximums will be represented by relatively high and low numbers. In graphs, they will be represented by highs and lows on the *x*- and *y*-axes. In bar charts, they will be represented by the tallest and shortest bars.

Look back at Table 1. What location on the river has the maximum concentration of Hg? Of Pb? A glance at the numbers tells you that Location 3—with 67 ppm—represents the maximum for Hg, while Location 4—with 54 ppm—represents the maximum for Pb.

How can taking note of maximums and minimums help you spot patterns in the data? Look again at Table 1. Notice that the maximum concentration of Hg, 67 ppm, just happens to coincide with the *minimum* for trout population—0 per 100 m^3. That's a good indication that there's some cause and effect going on here. Somehow, a maximum of Hg concentration correlates with a minimum of trout population. The obvious (though not airtight) conclusion is that a high concentration of Hg is detrimental to trout populations. And this kind of finding is much more evident when you look at maximums and minimums.

2. Critical Points

Critical points—or points of change—are values at which something dramatic happens. For example, at atmospheric pressure water freezes at 0° C and boils at about 100° C. If you examined water at various temperatures below the lower of these two critical points, it would be solid. If you examined water at various temperatures between the two points, it would be liquid. If you examined water above the higher critical point, it would be a gas.

When you scan the numbers in a chart or points on a graph, look for places where values bunch together or where suddenly something special happens. At atmospheric pressure 0° C is a critical point for water—as is 100° C—since something special happens: The substance changes form.

To find out how critical points can help you evaluate data, turn the page and take another look at the graph representing the concentration of *E. coli* (a common type of bacterium) in Cooling Pool B.

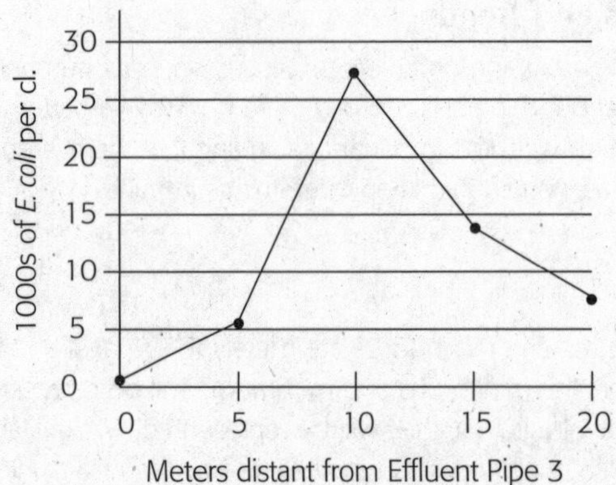

Notice how the concentration is low very near Effluent Pipe 3. From there, it rises until about 10 meters away from the pipe, then it falls again, tapering off as you get farther from the pipe. There's a critical point, then, right around 10 meters from Effluent Pipe 3. Somehow, that vicinity is most conducive to the growth of *E. coli*. As you move closer to or farther away from that point, the concentration falls off. So, in looking to explain the data, you'd want to focus on that location—10 meters from the pipe. What is it about that location that's so special? What makes it the hot new place for *E. coli* to see and be seen?

3. Variation

Variation is a bit more complex than extremes or critical points. Variation refers to the way two different things change *in relation to each other*. Direct variation means that two things vary in the same way: When one gets bigger, the other does too; when one gets smaller, so does the other. Inverse variation means that two things vary in *opposite* ways: When one gets bigger, the other gets smaller, and vice versa. We saw an example of inverse variation in the air temperature graph, where altitude and air temperature varied inversely—as altitude *in*creased, air temperature *de*creased.

Here's a more familiar example for nonscientists: As you walk home from school at a constant rate, time varies directly with the distance from school and indirectly with the distance from home. As time passes (as the amount of time increases) you move farther away from school (the distance from school increases). Both increase in the same direction. That's direct variation.

But as the amount of time *in*creases, the distance to your house *de*creases. The two change in opposite ways. That's inverse variation.

Many of the graphs on the ACT are intended to display variation. As we've just seen, graphs with *x-y* coordinates (horizontal and vertical axes) are used for this purpose. On such a graph, direct variation will be displayed by lines moving upward to the right. Inverse variations will plot out to lines moving downward to the right.

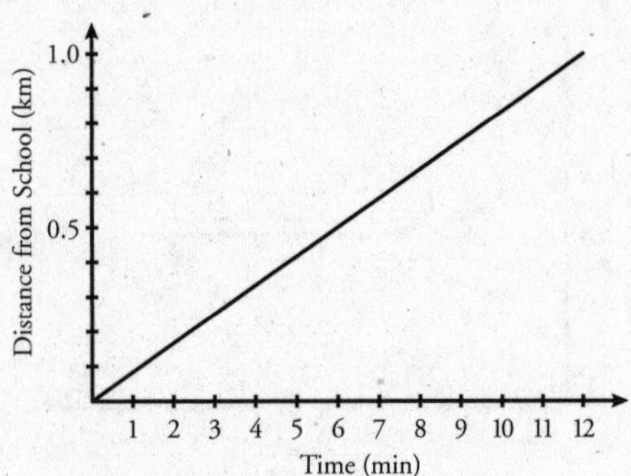

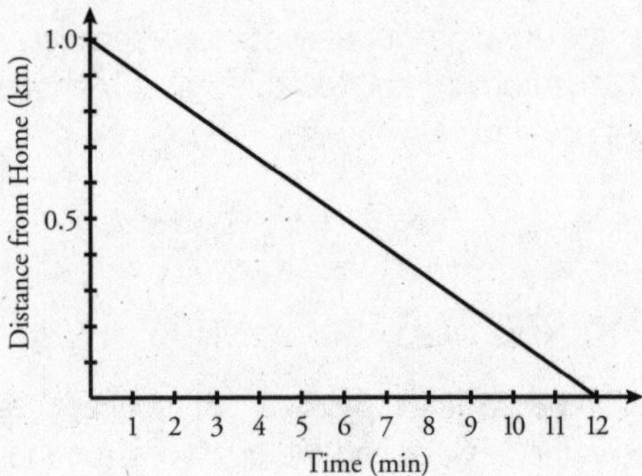

In the two graphs above, both variations make straight lines. This is because the speed at which you walked was constant. Sometimes, direct or inverse variations can be more complicated because the rates are not constant. Such variation could be called "nonlinear," because when plotted on a graph, it produces wavy, zigzag, broken, or curved lines. For example, if you started out from school running, then gradually slowed down as you got tired, then stopped for a while about halfway home to smell some roses before finally continuing home at a steady pace, the variation would not be linear. Distance from school would increase more slowly as time progressed, and for a while the distance wouldn't increase *at all*. Distance to home would decrease more slowly as you slowed down, and would also stop decreasing during the time you stopped to smell the roses.

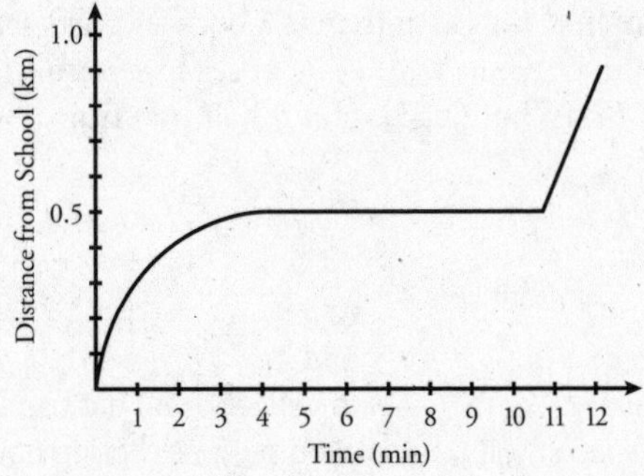

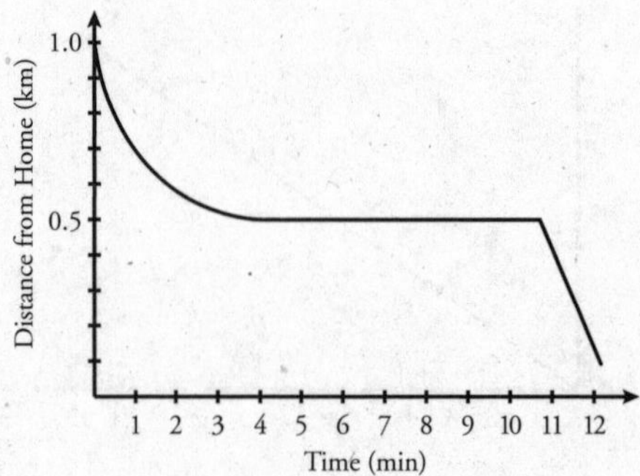

Graphs of this kind often look strange, but they can represent very ordinary activities. If you know how to walk home from school, you can probably understand the kinds of relationships and number patterns the ACT uses.

THE REAL THING: PRACTICE PASSAGE

Let's take a look at a full-fledged Science passage that requires these skills. Give yourself about seven minutes to do the passage and the questions (on the actual test, you'll want to move a bit faster).

Passage I

Although the effective acceleration due to gravity at the earth's surface is often treated as a constant ($g = 9.80$ m/sec^2) its actual value varies from place to place because of several factors.

First, a body on the surface of any rotating spheroid experiences an effective force perpendicular to the rotational axis and proportional to the speed of rotation. This centrifugal force, which counteracts gravity, varies with latitude, increasing from zero at the poles to a maximum at the equator. In addition, because the earth "bulges" at the equator, a body at equatorial sea level is farther from the center of the earth than is a body at polar sea level. Figure 1 shows the variation of mean values of g at sea level resulting from both effects; the contribution from "bulging" is about half that from rotation.

Figure 1

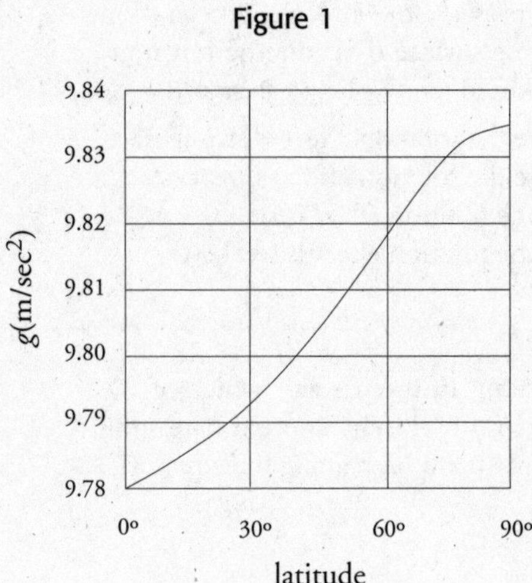

Measurements of *g* also vary depending on local rock density and altitude. Table 1 shows the effect of altitude on *g* at various points above sea level.

Table 1

Change in Altitude (km)	*g* (m/sec^2)
1	–0.0031
5	–0.0154
10	–0.0309
25	–0.0772
30	–0.1543

Example

3. If the earth's density were uniform, at approximately what latitude would calculations using an estimated value at sea level of $g = 9.80$ m/sec^2 produce the least error?

A. 0°
B. 20°
C. 40°
D. 80°

4. According to the passage, the effective acceleration due to gravity at the surface of a rotating but non-"bulging" sphere would tend to be greatest at the:

   F. equator, where the rotation effect is strongest.
   G. equator, where the rotation effect is weakest.
   H. poles, where the rotation effect is strongest.
   J. poles, where the rotation effect is weakest.

5. Given the information in the passage, which of the following figures most closely approximates the value of *g* at a point 10 km high along the equator?

   A. 9.75 m/sec^2
   B. 9.80 m/sec^2
   C. 9.81 m/sec^2
   D. 9.87 m/sec^2

6. Given the information presented in the passage, an increase in the speed of the earth's rotation would most likely cause which of the following results at sea level?

   I. An increase in *g* only along the equator
   II. A decrease in *g* at all nonpolar points
   III. No change in *g* at the poles
   IV. An increase in *g* at the poles

   F. II only
   G. I and III only
   H. II and III only
   J. II and IV only

7. Suppose that the earth stopped rotating but still "bulged." Based on information from the passage, the value of *g* at sea level at the equator would be:

   A. exactly 9.80 m/sec^2.
   B. greater than 9.78 m/sec^2.
   C. exactly 9.78 m/sec^2.
   D. less than 9.78 m/sec^2.

8. According to the information in Figure 1, the value of g:

   F. changes by a greater average amount per degree latitude between 30° and 60° than it does near the equator or poles.
   G. changes by a greater average amount per degree latitude near the equator or poles than it does between 30° and 60°.
   H. increases by an average of 5.8 m/sec^2 per degree latitude from the equator to the poles.
   J. decreases by an average of 3.1×10^{-3} m/sec^2 per degree latitude from the equator to the poles.

Answers and Explanations

This was actually a relatively simple, straightforward Science passage, but the terminology may have been intimidating nonetheless. The introduction tells you that the issue here is gravity, and how its pull (in other words, the acceleration due to gravity) changes because of several factors. Those factors—and the changes they cause—are represented in Figure 1 (which deals with the factor of latitude, which has an effect because of global "bulge" and the rotation effect) and Table 2 (which deals with the factor of altitude).

Analyzing Figure 1 as described above, you should have seen that the graph is supposed to show how g (the acceleration due to gravity) is affected by latitude (i.e., north-south location on the globe). The higher the latitude (the greater the distance from the equator), the greater the value of g. Thus, there's a direct variation between the two, though the variation isn't constant. As the curves at the beginning and ending of the line in Figure 1 tell you, the increase in g is "slower" near the equator and near the poles.

Confused?

Remember, you score points by answering the questions right, not by understanding the passages completely. You can get points on a Science passage, even if you don't understand it!

Notice how you could have answered **Question 3** just by understanding Figure 1. Question 3 asks, assuming the earth's density were uniform, "at what latitude would calculations using an estimated value at sea level of $g = 9.80$ m/sec^2 produce the least error?" First, figure out what that question is asking. You remember this question; we mentioned it in ACT Basics. It's simply asking you: Where would you get an actual value of g closest to 9.80 m/sec^2? Find 9.80 on the y-axis of the graph, follow across until you intersect with the curved line, and see where you are on the x-axis. That turns out to be about a third of the way from 30° to 60° latitude. In other words, choice C, 40°, is the answer.

Similarly, **Question 4** can be knocked off pretty easily. Where is the "effective acceleration due to gravity"(g, in other words) greatest (on a rotating but nonbulging sphere)? To answer this question you need to understand Figure 1. Although Figure 1 includes the effects of both rotation and bulging, it's clear that both factors cause the effective acceleration due to gravity to increase as the latitude increases from 0° to 90°. So the effective acceleration would be the greatest at 90° latitude—the poles. But that only narrows the choices down to H and J. To decide between them, we have to infer further whether the rotation effect is weakest or greatest at the poles. The second paragraph of the introduction gives you the answer: The effect of rotation ("centrifugal force") is zero at the poles. You can't get weaker than zero, so the answer is choice J.

Answers

3. C, 4. J, 5. A, 6. H, 7. B, 8. F

We'll get to **Question 5** below.

To answer **Question 6**, you again need only understand the introduction and Figure 1. This is a Principle Question, asking you to apply the principles about rotational effects on *g* to a hypothetical situation in which rotation *in*creased. Well, as you learned in the introduction, the effects of the earth's rotation tend to lessen the effects of gravity, so increasing the speed of rotation would lessen the effects of gravity even more—i.e., a lesser value for *g* except at the poles, where the effect of rotation is zero. So *g* would *de*crease everywhere but at the poles. Statements II and III are true, while Statements I and IV are false. Choice H is correct.

Question 7 requires more applications of principles, and is yet another question that can be answered by simply reading Figure 1. It asks you to suppose that rotation effects (one of the two factors affected by latitude) ceased, but that the earth still bulged at the equator. What would be the value of *g*? Well, again, rotation tends to "counteract" gravity, so it would have a depressing effect on *g*. Without rotation, then, *g* would be less depressed—it would go up, in other words. That means (reading from Figure 1 again) that *g* at 0° latitude (the equator) would, in the absence of rotation, go up from its current value of 9.78. That's why B is correct.

Question 8 (not to get monotonous) is still another that can be answered just by a proper reading of Figure 1. It asks you to describe what the graph tells you about the value of *g*. As we saw, the value rises slowly as you head away from 0° latitude (the equator), rises more rapidly in the middle latitudes, and slows down again near 90° latitude (the poles). That's best described by choice F. (Choice G gets it backwards—remember to read the choices carefully!) Choices H and J would involve you in some extensive calculations, at the end of which you'd realize that they were not true. But there's no reason to get that far. If you find yourself doing extensive calculation, you should know that you're on the wrong track. ACT Science will involve simple calculation only.

Notice how you could have answered five of the six questions with just a rudimentary grasp of the introduction and an understanding of how to "read" Figure 1.

The other question, **Question 5**, requires that you read both Figure 1 and Table 1 properly. It asks for the value of *g* at the equator (that information comes from Figure 1), but at an altitude of 10 km above sea level (that information comes from Table 1). Figure 1 tells you that the value of *g* at the equator at sea level would be 9.78 m/sec^2. But at 10 km above sea level, according to Table 1, *g* would be slightly lower—0.0309 m/sec^2 lower, to be precise. So, 9.78 minus 0.0309 would be about 9.75 m/sec^2. That's choice A.

Look for Patterns

The passage and questions above should convince you of one thing: To do well on Science, you have to be able to read graphs and tables, paying special attention to trends and patterns in the data. Sometimes, that's all you need to do to get most of the points on a passage.

Chapter Eight: **English Workout 2: Make It Make Sense**

- **Grammar Rules Tested by Sense Questions**
- **Nonstandard-Format English Questions**

In English Workout 1, we saw that the ACT expects you to use your words efficiently, and that, in fact, the shortest answer is correct remarkably often. But, obviously, the shortest answer is often wrong. What could make it wrong? It may not mean what it says.

Take this example: "Abraham Lincoln's father was a model of hard-working self-sufficiency. He was born in a log cabin he built with his own hands." Well, that's a cute trick, being born in a cabin you built yourself. Presumably the writer means that Abe was born in a cabin that his father built. But the literal meaning of the example is that the father somehow managed to be born in a cabin that he himself had built.

It's possible, of course, to analyze this example in terms of the rules of apostrophe use and pronoun reference. But that's not practical for the ACT, even for a student who has good grammar skills. There isn't time to carefully analyze every question, consider all the rules involved, and decide on an answer. You have to do 70 English questions in only 40 minutes—that's almost two questions per minute.

But there *is* plenty of time to approach examples like this one in a more pragmatic way. Ask yourself, *Does this stuff make sense*?

For the ACT, it's important to care. You need to adjust your mindset. After deciding whether or not the selection in a question is concise and relevant (Step 1 in the Three-Step Method), the next step is to make sure that the sentence *says* exactly what it's supposed to *mean*. If it doesn't, your job is to make it so. In other words, make it make sense.

We at Kaplan have a name for questions that test errors of meaning—Sense Questions. Once you get the hang of them, these questions can actually be fun. They're often funny once you see them. The following passage gives examples of the most common kinds of Sense Questions you'll find on the ACT.

Think

What you read always has two possible meanings: an intended meaning, and a literal meaning. The intended meaning is what the writer was trying to say. The literal meaning is what the author actually did say. The ACT demands that the intended and literal meanings of every passage be exactly the same.

Example

Passage I

Most people—even those who've never read Daniel Defoe's *Robinson Crusoe*—are familiar with the strange story of the sailor shipwrecked on a far-flung Pacific island. Relatively few of them, however, know that Crusoe's story. It was [1] actually based on the real-life adventures of a Scottish seaman, Alexander Selkirk. Selkirk came to the Pacific as a member of a 1703 privateering expedition led by a captain named William Dampier. During the voyage, Selkirk became dissatisfied with conditions aboard ship. After a bitter quarrel with his captain, he put Selkirk ashore [2] on tiny Mas a Tierra, one of the islands of Juan Fernandez, off the coast of Chile. Stranded, Selkirk lived there alone—in much the same manner as [3] Defoe's Crusoe—until 1709, when he was finally rescued by another English privateer. Upon his return to England, Selkirk found himself a celebrity, his [4] strange tale had already become the talk of pubs and coffeehouses throughout the British Isles. The story even reached the ears of Richard Steele, who featured it in his periodical, *The Tatler*. Eventually, he became [5] the subject of a

1. A. NO CHANGE
   B. story: was
   C. story, was
   D. story was

2. F. NO CHANGE
   G. Quarreling with his captain, the boat was put ashore
   H. Having quarreled with his captain, Selkirk was put ashore
   J. Having quarreled with his captain, they put Selkirk ashore

3. A. NO CHANGE
   B. same manner that
   C. identical manner that
   D. identical way as

4. F. NO CHANGE
   G. celebrity, but his
   H. celebrity. His
   J. celebrity his

5. A. NO CHANGE
   B. Selkirk became
   C. his became
   D. he becomes

bestselling book, *A Cruizing Voyage Round the World*, by Woodes Rogers. And while [6] there is some evidence that Defoe, a journalist, may actually have interviewed Selkirk personally, most literary historians believe that it was the reprinting of the Rogers book in 1718 that served as the real stimulus for Defoe's novel.

In *Crusoe*, which has been published [7] in 1719, Defoe took substantial liberties with the Selkirk story. For example, while Selkirk's presence on the island was of course known for many people [8] (certainly everyone in the crew that stranded him there), no one in the novel is aware of Crusoe's survival of the wreck and presence on the island. Moreover, while Selkirk's exile lasted just six years, Crusoe's goes on for a much more dramatic, though less credible, twenty-eight (over four times as long) [9]. But Defoe's most blatant embellishment of the tale is the invention of the character of Friday, for whom there was no counterpart whatsoever in the real-life story.

Because of [10] its basis in fact, Robinson Crusoe is often regarded as the first major novel in English

6. **F.** NO CHANGE
G. But since
H. And therefore
J. OMIT the underlined portion and start the sentence with "There."

7. **A.** NO CHANGE
B. was published
C. had been published
D. will have been published

8. **F.** NO CHANGE
G. widely known among people
H. known about many people
J. known to many people

9. **A.** NO CHANGE
B. (much longer)
C. (a much longer time, of course)
D. OMIT the underlined portion

10. **F.** NO CHANGE
G. Despite
H. Resulting from
J. As a consequence of

literature. Still popular today, contemporary audiences enjoyed the book as well. [11] In fact, two sequels, in which Crusoe returns to the island after his rescue, were eventually published. Though [12] to little acclaim. Meanwhile, Selkirk himself never gave a hoot about returning [13] to the island that had made him famous. Legend has it that he never gave up his eccentric living habits, spending his last years in a cave teaching alley cats to dance in his spare time. One wonders if even Defoe himself could have invented a more fitting end to the bizarre story of his shipwrecked sailor.

11. **A.** NO CHANGE
B. Still read today, Defoe's contemporaries also enjoyed it.
C. Viewed by many even then as a classic, the book is still popular to this day.
D. Much read in its day, modern audiences still find the book compelling.

12. **F.** NO CHANGE
G. published, though
H. published although
J. published; although

13. **A.** NO CHANGE
B. evinced himself as desirous of returning
C. could whip up a head of steam to return
D. expressed any desire to return

Items 14–15 ask about the passage as a whole.

14. Considering the tone and subject matter of the preceding paragraphs, is the last sentence an appropriate way to end the essay?
F. Yes, because it is necessary to shed some doubt on Defoe's creativity.
G. Yes, because the essay is about the relationship between the real Selkirk and Defoe's fictionalized version of him.
H. No, because there is nothing "bizarre" about Selkirk's story as it is related in the essay.
J. No, because the focus of the essay is more on Selkirk himself than on Defoe's fictionalized version of him.

15. This essay would be most appropriate as part of a:
A. scholarly study of eighteenth-century maritime history.
B. study of the geography of the islands off of Chile.
C. history of privateering in the Pacific.
D. popular history of English literature.

Most of the time, we may not notice when writers fail to say what they mean because we've taught ourselves to read for intended meaning only. We try to figure out what the author was *trying* to say, and we don't care much if an author isn't exactly clear.

You may have found these Sense Questions harder than the Economy Questions in English Workout 1. The shortest answers here aren't right nearly as often. But, all other things being equal, the shortest answer is still your best bet. It's correct about half of the time—seven out of fifteen questions: numbers 1, 3, 7, 8, 9, 10, and 13.

On some of the questions in Passage I above, you may not have gotten past Step 1 in the Three-Step Method. Question 9, for example, presented material that was clearly redundant. We certainly know that 28 years is longer than 6 (and if we're really up on our math we can even figure out that 28 is "more than four times" 6), so including any parenthetical aside like the ones given would be unnecessary. Remember, when in doubt, take it out. As we saw in English Workout 1, questions that include an "OMIT" option, and those in which some of the answers are much longer than others, are usually testing writing economy.

In the rest of the questions in this passage, the answers differ in other ways. They may join or fragment sentences, rearrange things, or add words that affect the meaning of the sentences. When the answers are all about the same length, as in most of the questions here, the question is more likely to test sense. Consider the shortest answer first, but don't be as quick to select it and move on. Think about the effect each choice has on the *meaning* of the sentence and pick longer answers if the shortest one doesn't make sense.

NOTE: Students tend to reject informal writing as "incorrect." But ACT passages are written at various levels of formality. Some are as stiff as textbooks. Others are as casual as a talk with friends. Pay attention to the tone of the words. Are they serious? Are they laid back? Stay with the author's tone. Don't always stay formal.

Answers

1. D, 2. H, 3. A, 4. H, 5. B, 6. F, 7. B, 8. J, 9. D, 10. G, 11. C, 12. G, 13. D, 14. G, 15. D

GRAMMAR RULES TESTED BY SENSE QUESTIONS

The ACT test makers include questions like those in Passage I to test many different rules of writing mechanics. Though it's not *necessary* to think about rules to answer the questions, familiarity with the rules can give you an alternative approach. The more ways to think about a question you have, the more likely you are to find the right answer.

We'll discuss some of these examples in groups based on what they're designed to test. That way we can briefly discuss the rules, but also show you how the basic strategic approach of "make it make sense" can get you the answers without a lot of technical analysis. Let's start with **Question 1**.

Completeness

...Relatively few of them, however, know that Crusoe's <u>story. It was</u> [1] actually based on the real-life adventures of a Scottish seaman, Alexander Selkirk.

1. A. NO CHANGE
   B. story: was
   C. story, was
   D. story was

If the underlined section for Question 1 were left as it is, the second sentence of the passage would be incomplete. It wouldn't make sense. "Relatively few people know that Crusoe's story" what? To make it make sense, you've got to continue the sentence so that it can tell us what it is that few people know about Crusoe's story. The three alternatives all do that, but B introduces a nonsensical colon, while C adds a comma when there's no pause in the sentence. D, however, continues the sentence—adding nothing unnecessary, but making it complete.

Question 1 is testing something we call completeness—the requirement that every sentence should consist of an entire thought. Don't just blindly judge the completeness of a sentence by whether or not it contains a subject and a verb. The alleged sentence—"Relatively few of them, however, know that Crusoe's story"—actually does contain a subject and a verb, but it's still not complete. It leaves a thought hanging. Don't leave thoughts hanging on the ACT. The test makers don't like it one bit.

Question 12 tests the same concept:

...In fact, two sequels, in which Crusoe returns to the island after his rescue, were eventually <u>published. Though to</u> [12] little acclaim.

12. F. NO CHANGE
    G. published, though
    H. published although
    J. published; although

Here, the fragment should be more obvious, since the clause that's trying to pass itself off as a sentence—"Though to little acclaim"—contains neither a subject nor a verb. That's the technical reason it's wrong, and if you recognized this, great. But on a more intuitive level, it just doesn't make sense to say, as a complete thought: "Though to little acclaim."

Clearly, that fragment has to be connected to the sentence before it, so F and J are wrong, since both would leave the fragment isolated. H goes too far in the other direction, omitting any punctuation at all between the fragment and the main body of the sentence, and that's no good. But the correct choice, G, does just what we need it to

do: It connects the fragment logically to the main sentence, but it provides a comma to represent the pause between the two.

Sentence Structure

Technically, of course, Questions 1 and 12 test sentence structure, which is the broad topic of which completeness is one part. The "rules" of good sentence structure require that every sentence contain a complete thought. A "sentence" without a complete thought is called a *fragment*. A "sentence" with *too many* complete thoughts (usually connected by commas) is called a *run-on*. That's what we find in **Question 4**:

...Upon his return to England, Selkirk found himself a <u>celebrity, his</u> (4) strange tale had already become the talk of pubs and coffeehouses throughout the British Isles.

4. F. NO CHANGE
   G. celebrity, but his
   H. celebrity. His
   J. celebrity his

Here we have two complete thoughts: (1) Selkirk found himself a celebrity upon his return, and (2) his tale was bandied about the pubs and coffeehouses. You can't just run these two complete thoughts together with a comma, as the underlined portion does. And you certainly can't just run them together *without* a comma or anything else, as choice J does. You can relate the two thoughts with a comma and a linking word (*and*, for instance), but choice G's inclusion of the word *but* makes no sense. It implies a contrast, while the two complete thoughts are actually very similar. Thus, you should create two sentences, one for each thought. That's what correct choice H does.

Make sure all of the sentences in a passage contain at least one, but not more than one, complete thought. Fragments and run-ons appear frequently on the English section of the ACT. Both are sense problems that need to be corrected.

Modifiers

Question 2 tests modifier problems:

...<u>After a bitter quarrel with his captain, he put Selkirk ashore</u> (2) on tiny Mas a Tierra, one of the islands of Juan Fernandez...

2. F. NO CHANGE
   G. Quarreling with his captain, the boat was put ashore
   H. Having quarreled with his captain, Selkirk was put ashore
   J. Having quarreled with his captain, they put Selkirk ashore

In a well-written sentence, it must be clear exactly what words or phrases in the sentence are modifying (or referring to) what other words or phrases in the sentence. In the underlined portion here, the clause "after a bitter quarrel with his captain" should modify the pronoun that follows it—he. But it doesn't. The *he* who put Selkirk ashore must be the captain, but it can't be the captain who had "a bitter quarrel with his captain." That doesn't make sense (unless the captain quarrels with himself). So put the thing modified next to the thing modifying it. The person who quarreled with his captain was Selkirk—not the boat and not "they," whoever they are—so H is correct.

If you recognized the problem with Question 2 as a "misplaced modifier," that's great. Fantastic, even. But you didn't have to know the technicalities to get the right answer here. You just had to make the sentence make sense.

Question 11 tests a similar problem:

...Still popular today, contemporary audiences enjoyed the book as well. 11

11. A. NO CHANGE
B. Still read today, Defoe's contemporaries also enjoyed it.
C. Viewed by many even then as a classic, the book is still popular to this day.
D. Much read in its day, modern audiences still find the book compelling.

The way the sentence is written, it basically means that contemporary audiences are "still popular today." That doesn't make sense. The *intended* meaning is that the *book* is still popular today, as it was then. Choice C fixes the sense problem by putting its modifier—"viewed by many even then as a classic"—next to the thing it modifies—"the book." Notice that the other choices all misplace their modifiers in the same way, making them modify "Defoe's contemporaries" (in B) and "modern audiences" (in D).

As a rule of thumb, you should always make sure that modifiers are as close as possible to the things they modify.

Idiom (Proper Word Form and Choice)

Question 3 tests a rather hazy linguistic concept known as *idiom*. The word "idiomatic" refers to language that, well, uses words in a peculiar way. Many words have special rules. If you're a native speaker of the language, you probably picked up many of these rules by ear before your eighth birthday; if you're not a native speaker, you had to learn them one by one.

...Stranded, Selkirk lived there alone—in much the <u>same manner as</u> [3] Defoe's Crusoe—until 1709, when he was finally rescued by another...

3. A. NO CHANGE
   B. same manner that
   C. identical manner that
   D. identical way as

The sentence as written actually makes perfect sense. Selkirk lived in "much the same manner as" Defoe's Crusoe. The phrase *much the same* calls for *as* to complete the comparison between Selkirk's and Crusoe's ways of life. Note how B and C would create completeness problems–in much the same (or identical) manner as Defoe's Crusoe what? Choice D, meanwhile, is just plain unidiomatic. In English, we just don't say "in much the identical way as," because the word identical is an absolute. You can't be more or partially identical; you either are or aren't identical to something else. But even if you didn't analyze D this carefully, it should have just sounded wrong to your ear. (In English Workout 3 we'll show you how "trusting your ear" can be a great way to get correct answers on the English subject test.)

Question 8 tests another idiom problem:

...For example, while Selkirk's presence on the island was of course <u>known for many people</u> [8] (certainly everyone in the crew that stranded him there), no one in the novel is aware of Crusoe's survival of the wreck and presence on the island.

8. F. NO CHANGE
   G. widely known among people
   H. known about many people
   J. known to many people

The underlined portion as written is unidiomatic. Selkirk's presence wasn't known *for* many people–it was known *by*, or known to, many people. When you're "known *for*" something, that means you have a reputation for doing such and such. That makes no sense in this context. But J *does* make sense, since it points out that Selkirk's presence on the island was known *to* many people–that is, it was something that many people knew about. G is unidiomatic; we just wouldn't say "among people" here, since it's not specific enough. That sounds as if we're talking about people as a species. H would have been acceptable if it had read "known about *by* many people," but without the *by* the correction just wouldn't make sense.

Idiom is a tough topic if you're not a native speaker. You have to think very carefully about the meaning of every word. But if you *are* a native speaker, use your many years of hearing English as a guide. Choose the correction that makes sense and doesn't sound weird.

Pronouns

Sometimes, the test will throw you a sentence in which the meaning of a pronoun is unclear. You won't be sure to whom or what the pronoun is referring. That's the kind of problem you were given in **Question 5**:

...The story even reached the ears of Richard Steele, who featured it in his periodical, *The Tatler*. Eventually, he became (5) the subject of a best-selling book...

5. **A.** NO CHANGE
B. Selkirk became
C. his became
D. he becomes

The *intended* meaning of the pronoun *he* here is "Selkirk." But what's the closest male name to the pronoun? Richard Steele, the publisher of *The Tatler*. That creates an unclear situation. Make it clear! Choice B takes care of the problem by naming Selkirk explicitly. C would create a sense problem—his *what* became the subject of a book? Meanwhile, D shifts the verb tense into the present, which makes no sense since this book was written over 250 years ago!

Mistakes of sense often involve pronouns. Make a habit of checking every underlined pronoun as you go along. What does the pronoun stand for? Can you tell? If not, there's an error. Does it make sense? If not, there's an error. Make sure it's perfectly clear to what or to whom all pronouns refer.

Logic

Remember when we talked about structural clues back in Reading Workout 1? (C'mon, it wasn't *that* long ago!) Structural clues are words that signal where an author is going in a piece of writing. They show how all of the pieces logically fit together. If the author uses the structural clue *on the other hand*, that means a contrast is coming up; if he or she uses the clue *moreover*, that means that a continuation is coming up—an addition that is more or less in the same vein as what came before.

Many ACT English questions mix up the logic of a piece of writing by giving you the wrong structural clue or other logic word. That's what happened in **Question 10**:

. . . Because of (10) its basis in fact, *Robinson Crusoe* is often regarded as the first major novel in English literature.

10. **F.** NO CHANGE
G. Despite
H. Resulting from
J. As a consequence of

As written, this sentence means that *Crusoe* was regarded as the first major novel because it was based on fact. But that makes no sense. If it was based on fact, that would work against its being regarded as a novel. There's a contrast between basis in "fact" (which implies nonfiction) and "first major novel" (which implies fiction). To show that contrast logically, you need a contrast word like *despite.* That's why G is correct here..

Question 6 also tests logic:

. . . the subject of a best-selling book, *A Cruizing Voyage Round the World,* by Woodes Rogers. <u>And while</u> [6] there is some evidence that Defoe, a journalist, may actually have interviewed Selkirk personally, most literary historians believe that it was the reprinting of the Rogers book in 1718 that served as the real stimulus for Defoe's novel.

6. **F.** NO CHANGE
   G. but since
   H. and therefore
   J. OMIT the underlined portion and start the sentence with "There."

The structural clue should convey a sense of continuation from the preceding sentence (since we're still talking about the book *A Cruizing Voyage*), but also a sense of contrast with the latter part of the sentence of which it's a part (since there is a contrast there between one possible stimulus and another). *And while* does the trick (or both tricks, actually). *And* provides the continuation; *while* provides the needed contrast.

G and H, however, introduce structural clues (*since, therefore*) that imply a cause-and-effect relationship between the two impulses—Defoe's interview and the appearance of *A Cruizing Voyage*—which makes no sense in context. Meanwhile, omitting the portion would create a run-on sentence with two complete thoughts—about Defoe's interview and about the opinion of "most literary historians"—without subordinating one to the other or connecting them with a linking word. Remember, don't pick "OMIT" simply because it's there!

Verb Usage

Verbs have an annoying habit of changing form depending on who's doing the action and when that person is doing it. Example: "I *hate* verbs; he hates verbs; and we both have hated verbs ever since we were kids." You have to be very careful to make sure verbs match their subject and the tense of the surrounding context.

...In *Crusoe*, which <u>has been published</u> (7) in 1719, Defoe took substantial liberties with the Selkirk story.

7. A. NO CHANGE
   B. was published
   C. had been published
   D. will have been published

The publication of *Robinson Crusoe* is something that took place in 1719—the past, in other words. So the underlined portion, which puts the verb in the present perfect tense, is flawed. Choices C and D, meanwhile, would put the verb into bizarre tenses normally used to convey a complex time relationship. C makes it seem as if publication of the book happened before Defoe took his liberties with the story. But that's nonsensical. The liberties were taken in the writing of the book. D, meanwhile, does strange things with the time sequence. The book was published in the past; Defoe also took his substantial liberties in the same past. So just use the simple past tense, choice B.

Tone

As we said earlier, the passages in the English subject test vary in tone. Some are formal; others are informal. Usually, you'll know which is which without having to think about it. If a passage contains slang, a few exclamation points, and a joke or two, the tone is informal; if it sounds like something a Latin instructor would say, it's probably formal.

Good style requires that the tone of a piece of writing be at the same level throughout. Sometimes the underlined portion might not fit the tone of the rest of the passage. If so, it's up to you to correct it. Look at **Question 13:**

Watch Out

Don't pick an answer just because it sounds "fancy." The word "desirous" in Question 13 might be tempting—but don't give in to the temptation. Pick commonsense, everyday words that express the meaning the author intends. Don't worry if it sounds plain.

...Meanwhile, Selkirk himself never <u>gave a hoot about returning</u> (13) to the island that had made him famous.

13. A. NO CHANGE
    B. evinced himself as desirous of returning
    C. could whip up a head of steam to return
    D. expressed any desire to return

Selkirk "never gave a hoot" about going back? No way! Slang doesn't belong in this passage. This isn't the most formally written passage in the world, but it's certainly no place for a phrase like *gave a hoot* or (just as bad) *whip up a head of steam* (that's choice C). B, meanwhile, goes too far in the opposite direction. "Evinced himself as desirous of returning" sounds like something no human being would say. But the rest of the passage sounds human. It makes no sense to shift tonal gears in the middle of a passage. Keep the tone consistent. Choose D.

NONSTANDARD-FORMAT ENGLISH QUESTIONS

The Nonstandard-Format questions ask about the passage as a whole. Keep in mind the main point of the passage—the "gist"—as well as the overall tone and style. For an entire passage to "make sense," it has to be consistent throughout, both in content and in tone and style.

Judging the Passage

Question 14 asks you to judge the passage. Was the last sentence an appropriate ending or not?

14. Considering the tone and subject matter of the preceding paragraphs, is the last sentence an appropriate way to end the essay?

- **F.** Yes, because it is necessary to shed some doubt on Defoe's creativity.
- **G.** Yes, because the essay is about the relationship between the real Selkirk and Defoe's fictionalized version of him.
- **H.** No, because there is nothing "bizarre" about Selkirk's story as it is related in the essay.
- **J.** No, because the focus of the essay is more on Selkirk himself than on Defoe's fictionalized version of him.

Think of the passage as a whole. It has been comparing Selkirk's real life with the one that Defoe made up for the character of Robinson Crusoe. Therefore, ending in this way, with an ironic reference to Defoe as writing a more fitting end to Selkirk's life, is perfectly appropriate. The answer to the question, then, should be yes (eliminating choices H and J). F says yes, but gives a nonsensical reason for saying yes. Why is it necessary to shed doubt on Defoe's creativity? Does the author hold a grudge against Defoe? Not that we can tell. So G is the best answer here.

Reading-Type Questions

If you thought **Question 15** looked like a Reading question hiding in the English part of the exam, you were right. As mentioned in ACT Basics, one reason that you should keep thinking about what the passage means—rather than focusing on picky rules of grammar or punctuation—is that the ACT often asks Reading-Type Questions.

15. This essay would be most appropriate as part of a:

A. scholarly study of eighteenth-century maritime history.
B. study of the geography of the islands off of Chile.
C. history of privateering in the Pacific.
D. popular history of English literature.

What was this passage principally about? How Defoe's *Robinson Crusoe* was loosely based on the life of a real shipwrecked sailor, Alexander Selkirk. Would that kind of thing belong in a study of geography (choice B)? No. The focus is on the fictionalization of a historical life, not on the physical features of the islands off Chile. The passage isn't principally about privateering or maritime history either, so C and A are wrong as well. This passage is about the relationship between a true story and a famous fictionalized story. And its tone isn't overly scholarly either. So it probably belongs in a popular history of English literature (choice D).

Guessing Hint

In Question 16, two answer choices list Sentence 3 first and two choices list Sentence 1 last. If the same sentence is listed as first or last in two answers, it's likely to belong at the beginning or ending of the passage. If a question had the following answers, what would be the best blind guess?

A. 1, 2, 3, 4, 5
B. 2, 5, 4, 3, 1
C. 3, 1, 2, 5, 4
D. 3, 4, 2, 5, 1

D is the best blind guess. Sentence 3 is likely to be first, and Sentence 1 is likely to be last, since they appear in these positions most. Note: Questions like this one, in which blind guessing would narrow the choices down to just one, are rare on the ACT. But you can often narrow the choices to two.

Structure and Purpose

There will also be questions that test your grasp of overall structure and purpose in a piece of prose. The test makers scramble the order of the sentences in a paragraph (or of the paragraphs in a passage). The question then asks you to decide on the best order for the scrambled parts. Take a look at **Question 16:**

[1] Only recently has new evidence led many scientists to question the accepted division between birds and dinosaurs. [2] Traditionally, they have been placed in entirely separate classes within the subphylum *Vertebrata*. [3] Birds and dinosaurs don't have many obvious similarities. [4] Birds formed the class *Aves*, while dinosaurs constituted two orders, *Saurischia* and *Ornithischia*, within the class *Reptilia*.

16. To best fulfill the author's purpose, the order of the sentences in the paragraph above should be:

F. 1, 2, 3, 4
G. 2, 3, 4, 1
H. 3, 2, 4, 1
J. 3, 2, 1, 4

Here again, the goal is to make it make sense. All of the sentences in this paragraph relate to the differences between birds and dinosaurs. Sentence 3 best introduces this idea. Notice that two of the answer choices begin with Sentence 3—H and J. The other two can be eliminated.

Look again at the logic of the sentences. Since Sentence 4 elaborates on the distinction introduced in Sentence 2, Sentence 4 should immediately follow Sentence 2. Only H has them in that order, so H looks like the answer.

Just to check, you'll want to read the entire paragraph in the order suggested by H. And if you do, you'll notice that the paragraph makes perfect sense, with Sentence 3 introducing the topic, Sentences 2 and 4 showing how that topic has been traditionally viewed, and Sentence 1 coming in naturally to show how that traditional view is no longer valid.

For questions like this, it's usually a good idea to start by trying to figure out the first (and sometimes the last) sentence, because first and last sentences usually have the most obvious functions in an ACT-style paragraph.

Chapter Nine: **Math Workout 2: Shake It Up!**

- **Ten Textbook Algebra and Coordinate Geometry Questions**
- **Four Ways to Shake It Up**
- **Typical Story Problems**
- **What to Do Next**

The main idea of Math Workout 1 was: Don't jump in headfirst and start crunching numbers until you've given a problem some thought. Make sure you know what you're doing—*and* that what you're doing won't take too long.

As we saw in Math Workout 1, sometimes you'll know how to proceed as soon as you understand the question. A good number of ACT algebra and coordinate geometry questions are straightforward textbook questions you may already be prepared for.

TEN TEXTBOOK ALGEBRA AND COORDINATE GEOMETRY QUESTIONS

When you take the ACT, you can be sure you'll see some of the following questions with only slight variations. You'll find answers and explanations for these questions in the 100 Key Math Concepts for the ACT section.

1. Evaluate an algebraic expression. *(See 100 Key Math Concepts for the ACT, #52)*

   Example: If $x = -2$, then $x^2 + 5x - 6 = ?$

2. Multiply binomials. *(See 100 Key Math Concepts for the ACT, #56)*

   Example: $(x + 3)(x + 4) = ?$

3. Factor a polynomial. *(See 100 Key Math Concepts for the ACT, #61)*

   Example: What is the complete factorization of $x^2 - 5x + 6$?

4. Simplify an algebraic fraction. *(See 100 Key Math Concepts for the ACT, #62)*

   Example: For all $x \neq \pm 3$, $\dfrac{x^2 - x - 12}{x^2 - 9} = ?$

5. Solve a linear equation. *(See 100 Key Math Concepts for the ACT, #63)*

   Example: If $5x - 12 = -2x + 9$, then $x = ?$

6. Solve a quadratic equation. *(See 100 Key Math Concepts for the ACT, #66)*

   Example: If $x^2 + 12 = 7x$, what are the two possible values of x ?

7. Solve a system of equations. *(See 100 Key Math Concepts for the ACT, #67)*

   Example: If $4x + 3y = 8$, and $x + y = 3$, what is the value of x ?

8. Solve an inequality. *(See 100 Key Math Concepts for the ACT, #69)*

   Example: What are all the values of x for which $-5x + 7 < -3$?

9. Find the distance between two points in the (x, y) coordinate plane. *(See 100 Key Math Concepts for the ACT, #71)*

   Example: What is the distance between the points with (x, y) coordinates $(-2, 2)$ and $(1, -2)$?

10. Find the slope of a line from its equation. *(See 100 Key Math Concepts for the ACT, #73)*

    Example: What is the slope of the line with the equation $2x + 3y = 4$?

These questions are all so straightforward and traditional, they could have come out of a high school algebra textbook. Do these questions the way you were taught. In case you'd like to review them, you'll find all the standard approaches succinctly summarized in 100 Key Math Concepts for the ACT. We're not so concerned in these Workouts with problems you may already know how to solve. Here we're going to focus on several situations where the quick and reliable solution method is not so obvious, where often the best method is one your algebra teacher never told you about.

FOUR WAYS TO SHAKE IT UP

It's bound to happen at some point on Test Day. You look at a math problem and you don't see what to do. Don't freak out. Think about the problem for a few seconds before you give up. When you don't see the quick and reliable approach right away, shake the problem up a little. Try one of these "shake-it-up" techniques:

1. Restate
2. Remove the disguise
3. Pick numbers
4. Backsolve

1. Restate the Problem

Often, the way to get over that stymied feeling is to change your perspective. Have you ever watched people playing Scrabble®? In their search to form high-scoring words with the letters on their seven tiles, they continually move the tiles around in their racks. Sometimes a good word becomes apparent only after rearranging the tiles. One might not see the seven-letter word in this arrangement:

R E B A G L A

But reverse the tiles and a word almost reveals itself:

A L G A B E R

The tiles can spell "ALGEBRA."

The same gimmick works on the ACT, too. When you get stuck, try looking at the problem from a different angle. Try rearranging the numbers, or changing fractions to decimals, or factoring, or multiplying out, or redrawing the diagram, or anything that might give you the fresh perspective you need to uncover a good solution method.

Here's a question you might not know what to do with at first glance:

Example

1. **Which of the following is equivalent to $7^{77} - 7^{76}$?**

   A. 7
   B. 7^{77-76}
   C. $7^{77 \div 76}$
   D. $7(77 - 76)$
   E. $7^{76}(6)$

Here's a hint: *Think of an easier problem testing the same principles*. The important thing to look for is the basic relationships involved—here, we have exponents and subtraction. That subtraction sign causes trouble, because none of the ordinary rules of exponents (see 100 Key Math Concepts for the ACT, #47–48) seem to apply when there is subtraction of "unlike" terms.

Another hint: How would you work with $x^2 - x$? Most test takers could come up with another expression for $x^2 - x$: they'd factor to $x(x - 1)$. Or if the problem asked for $x^{77} - x^{76}$, they'd factor to $x^{76}(x - 1)$. The rule is no different for 7 than for x. Factoring out the 7^{76} gives you: $7^{76}(7 - 1)$, which is $7^{76}(6)$, or choice E.

Sometimes an ACT algebra question will include an expression that isn't of much use in its given form. The breakthrough in such a case may be to restate the expression by either simplifying it or factoring it.

Example

2. If $\frac{x}{2} - \frac{x}{6}$ is an integer, which of the following statements must be true?

   F. x is positive.
   G. x is odd.
   H. x is even.
   J. x is a multiple of 3.
   K. x is a multiple of 6.

Reexpress: $\frac{x}{2} - \frac{x}{6} = \frac{3x}{6} - \frac{x}{6} = \frac{2x}{6} = \frac{x}{3}$

This form of the expression tells us a lot more. If $\frac{x}{3}$ is an integer, then x is equal to 3 times an integer:

$\frac{x}{3}$ = an integer

$x = 3 \times$ (an integer)

In other words, x is a multiple of 3, choice J.

2. Remove the Disguise

Sometimes it's hard to see the quick and reliable method immediately because the true nature of the problem is hidden behind a disguise. Look at this example:

Example

3. What are the (x, y) coordinates of the point of intersection of the line representing the equation $5x + 2y = 4$ and the line representing the equation $x - 2y = 8$?

   A. (2, 3)
   B. (–2, 3)
   C. (2, –3)
   D. (–3, 2)
   E. (3, –2)

Coordinate Geometry

Although this question turned out not to be a real coordinate geometry problem, the test makers do have a soft spot in their hearts for coordinate geometry. Typically 8 or more of the 60 math questions involve coordinate geometry. It's hard to get a top score without getting at least some of these geometry questions right. Use 100 Key Math Concepts for the ACT #71–77 to review the relevant rules and formulas.

This may look like a coordinate geometry question, but do you really have to graph the lines to find the point of intersection? Remember, the ACT is looking for creative thinkers, not mindless calculators! Think about it for a moment—what's the special significance of the point of intersection, the one point that the two lines have in common? That's the one point whose coordinates will satisfy *both* equations.

So what we realize now is that this is not a coordinate geometry question at all, but a "system-of-equations" question. All it's really asking you to do is solve the pair of equations for x and y. The question has nothing to do with slopes, intercepts, axes, or quadrants. It's a pure algebra question in disguise.

Now that we know we're looking at a system of equations, the method of solution presents itself more clearly. The first equation has a + $2y$, and the second equation has a − $2y$. If we just "add" the equations, the y terms cancel:

$$\begin{array}{r} 5x + 2y = 4 \\ x - 2y = 8 \\ \hline 6x \quad\quad = 12 \end{array}$$

If $6x = 12$, then $x = 2$. Plug that back into either of the original equations and you'll find that $y = -3$. The point of intersection is (2, −3), and the answer is C.

Example

4. A geometer uses the following formula to estimate the area A of the shaded portion of a circle as shown in the figure below when only the height h and the length of the chord c are known:

$$A = \frac{2ch}{3} + \frac{h^3}{2c}$$

What is the geometer's estimate of the area, in square inches, of the shaded region if the height is 2 inches and the length of the chord is 6 inches?

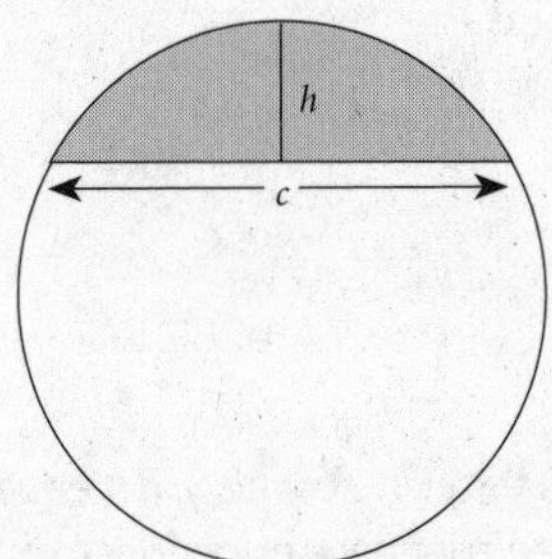

F. 6

G. $6\frac{2}{3}$

H. $7\frac{1}{2}$

J. $8\frac{2}{3}$

K. 12

At first glance, this looks like a horrendously esoteric geometry question. Who ever heard of such a formula? But when you think about the question a bit, you realize that you don't really have to understand the formula. You certainly don't have to remember it—it's right there in the question.

In fact, this is not really a geometry question at all. It's just an "evaluate the algebraic expression" question in disguise. All you have to do is plug the given values $h = 2$ and $c = 6$ into the formula:

$$A = \frac{2ch}{3} + \frac{h^3}{2c}$$
$$= \frac{2(6)(2)}{3} + \frac{(2)^3}{2(6)}$$
$$= 8 + \frac{2}{3} = 8\frac{2}{3}$$

Choice J is correct.

The people who wrote this question wanted you to freak out at first sight and give up. Don't give up on a question too quickly just because it looks like it's testing something you never saw before. In many such cases it's really a familiar problem in disguise.

3. Pick Numbers

Sometimes you can get stuck on an algebra problem because it's too general or abstract. A good way to get a handle on such a problem is to make it more explicit by temporarily substituting numbers for the variables.

Example

5. If a is an odd integer and b is an even integer, which of the following must be odd?

   A. $2a + b$
   B. $a + 2b$
   C. ab
   D. a^2b
   E. ab^2

Rather than try to think this one through abstractly, it's easier to pick numbers for a and b. There are rules that predict the evenness or oddness of sums, differences, and products, but there's no need to memorize those rules. When it comes to adding, subtracting, and multiplying evens and odds, what happens with one pair of numbers generally happens with all similar pairs.

Just say, for the time being, that $a = 1$ and $b = 2$. Plug those values into the answer choices, and there's a good chance only one choice will be odd:

A. $2a + b = 2(1) + 2 = 4$
B. $a + 2b = 1 + 2(2) = 5$
C. $ab = (1)(2) = 2$
D. $a^2b = (1)^2(2) = 2$
E. $ab^2 = (1)(2)^2 = 4$

Choice B was the only odd one for $a = 1$ and $b = 2$, so it *must* be the one that's odd no matter *what* odd number a actually stands for and even number b actually stands for.

4. Backsolve

With some ACT Math problems, it may actually be easier to try out each answer choice until you find the one that works, rather than attempt to solve the problem and then look among the choices for the answer. Since this approach involves working backwards from the answer choices to the question stem, it's called "backsolving." Here's a good example:

Example

6. All 200 tickets were sold for a particular concert. Some tickets cost \$10 apiece, and the others cost \$5 apiece. If total ticket sales were \$1,750, how many of the more expensive tickets were sold?

F. 20
G. 75
H. 100
J. 150
K. 175

There are ways to solve this problem by setting up an equation or two, but if you're not comfortable with the algebraic approach to this one, why not just try out each answer choice?

Start with choice H. If 100 tickets went for \$10, then the other 100 went for \$5. 100 at \$10 is \$1,000, and 100 tickets at \$5 is \$500, for a total of \$1,500—too small. There must have been more than 100 \$10 tickets.

Try choice J next. If 150 tickets went for \$10, then the other 50 went for \$5. So 150 tickets at \$10 is \$1,500, and 50 tickets at \$5 is \$250, for a total of \$1,750—that's it! The answer is J.

Backsolving your way to the answer may not be a method you'd show your algebra teacher with pride—but your algebra teacher won't be watching on Test Day. Remember, all that matters is right answers—it doesn't matter how you get them.

Backsolving

Answer choices are generally listed in numerical order. If the first number you try doesn't work, the process of plugging in that first number might tell you whether you'll need a smaller or a larger number. So when backsolving, start with the middle choice (C or H) to be safe.

TYPICAL STORY PROBLEMS

We find that about one-third of the questions on the Math test are Story Problems. Though some Story Problems present unique situations that must be analyzed on the spot, others are just variations on familiar themes.

Percent Problems

In Percent Problems, you're usually given two numbers and asked to find a third. The key is to identify what you have and what you're looking for. In other words identify the Part, the Percent, and the Whole.

Put the numbers and the unknown into the general form:

Part = Percent × Whole

Usually the Part is associated with the word *is,* and the Whole is associated with the word *of.*

Example

7. In a group of 250 students, 40 are seniors. What percentage of the group is seniors?

   A. 1.6%
   B. 6.25%
   C. 10%
   D. 16%
   E. 40%

The Percent is what we're looking for ("What percentage . . ."); the Whole is 250 (". . . of the group . . ."); and the Part is 40 (". . . are seniors"). Plug these into the general formula:

$$\text{Part} = \text{Percent} \times \text{Whole}$$
$$40 = 250x$$
$$x = \frac{40}{250} = .16 = 16\%$$

The answer is D.

Percent Change Trap

When a quantity is increased or decreased by a percent *more than once*, you cannot simply add and subtract the percents to get the answer. In this kind of percent problem:

- The first percent change is a percent of the starting amount, but
- The second percent change is a percent of the new amount.

Many ACT Percent Problems concern percent change. To increase a number by a certain percent, calculate that percent of the original number and add it on. To decrease a number by a certain percent, calculate that percent of the original number and then subtract. For example, to answer the question, "What number is 30% greater than 80?" first find 30% of 80—that's 24—and add that on to 80: 80 + 24 = 104.

The ACT has ways of complicating percent change problems. Especially tricky are problems with multiple changes, such as a percent increase followed by another percent increase, or a percent increase followed by a percent decrease.

Example

8. If a positive number is increased by 70 percent, and then the result is decreased by 50 percent, which of the following accurately describes the net change?

   F. a 20 percent decrease
   G. a 15 percent decrease
   H. a 12 percent increase
   J. a 20 percent increase
   K. a 120 percent increase

To get a handle on this one, pick a number. Suppose the original number is 100. After a 70 percent increase it rises to 170. That number, 170, is decreased by 50 percent, which means it's reduced by half to 85. The net change from 100 to 85 is a 15 percent decrease—choice G.

Average Problems

Instead of giving you a list of values to plug into the average formula, ACT Average Problems often put a slight spin on the question. They tell you the average of a group of terms and ask you to find the value of the missing term. Here's a classic example:

Pick 100 on Percent Problems

Picking numbers is a good strategy when the answer choices are all percents. And 99 percent of the time the best number to pick—the easiest to work with—will be 100.

Example

9. To earn a B for the semester, Linda needs an average of at least 80 on the five tests. Her average for the first four test scores is 79. What is the minimum score she must get on the fifth test to earn a B for the semester?

A. 80
B. 81
C. 82
D. 83
E. 84

The key to almost every Average Problem is to use the sum. Sums can be combined much more readily than averages. An average of 80 on five tests is more usefully thought of as a combined score of 400. To get a B for the semester, Linda's five test scores have to add up to 400 or more. The first four scores add up to $4 \times 79 = 316$. She needs another 84 to get that 316 up to 400. The answer is E.

Weighted Average Problems

Another spin ACT test makers put on Average Problems is to give you an average for part of a group and an average for the rest of the group and then ask for the combined average.

Example

10. In a class of 10 boys and 15 girls, the boys' average score on the final exam was 80 and the girls' average score was 90. What was the average score for the whole class?

F. 83
G. 84
H. 85
J. 86
K. 87

Don't just average 80 and 90 to get 85. That would work only if the class had exactly the same number of girls as boys. In this case, there are more girls, so they carry more "weight" in the overall class average. In other words, the class average should be somewhat closer to 90 (the girls' average) than to 80 (the boys' average).

As usual with averages, the key is to use the sum. The average score for the whole class is the total of the 25 individual scores divided by 25. We don't have 25 scores to add up, but we can use the boys' average and the girls' average to get two subtotals.

Probability Trap

The probability of what *will* happen is not affected by what already *has* happened. Whenever you flip a coin, the probability is $\frac{1}{2}$ that it will be heads. Even if you flip the coin and get heads ten times in a row, the probability is still $\frac{1}{2}$ on the eleventh flip. Of course, the odds against eleven heads in a row are huge, but once the first ten flips are history they're no longer relevant.

If 10 boys average 80, then their 10 scores add up to 10×80, or 800. If 15 girls average 90, then their 15 scores add up to 15×90, or 1,350. Add the boys' total to the girls' total: $800 + 1,350 = 2,150$. That's the class total, which can be divided by 25 to get the class average: $\frac{2,150}{25} = 86$. The answer is J.

Probability Problems

Probabilities are part-to-whole ratios. The whole is the total number of possible outcomes. The part is the number of "favorable" outcomes. For example, if a drawer contains two black ties and five other ties, and you want a black tie, the total number of possible outcomes is 7 (the total number of ties) and the number of "favorable" outcomes is 2 (the number of black ties). The probability of choosing a black tie at random is $\frac{2}{7}$.

WHAT TO DO NEXT

Because more than half the Math questions on the ACT involve algebra, it's a good idea to solidify your understanding of the basics before Test Day. Focus on #52–70 in 100 Key Math Concepts for the ACT. Keep things in perspective. Geometry questions are important, too, but algebra questions are more important.

Chapter Ten: **Reading Workout 2: Look It Up!**

- **Using the Kaplan Reading Method**
- **Important Question Types**
- **Find and Paraphrase...And Other Tips**

In Reading Workout 1, we discussed general strategies for approaching ACT Reading. Now let's look more closely at the types of questions you'll encounter. There are really three main types of Reading questions on the test: Specific Detail Questions and Inference Questions (which make up the bulk), as well as Big Picture Questions (of which there are usually just a few).

USING THE KAPLAN READING METHOD

Don't forget to use the Kaplan Five-Step Method for ACT Reading which we discussed in Reading Workout 1. Here's a reminder of how it works:

Step 1: Preread the Passage

In other words, quickly work through the passage before trying to answer the questions. Read actively, and assemble a mental "road map" or overall idea of how the passage is organized.

Step 2: Consider the Question Stem

Before plunging into the answer choices, take a moment to think about the question. Spend time thinking about the answer to the question before you look at the choices.

Step 3: Refer to the Passage

You don't need to refer to the whole passage. Just refer to the passage by finding the place where the answer to a question can be found. Sometimes a line reference will be included in the question; otherwise, rely on your road map of the passage.

Step 4: Answer the Question in Your Own Words

Do this before looking at the answer choices.

Step 5: Match Your Answer with One of the Choices

With an answer in mind, it'll be easier to spot the best choice.

IMPORTANT QUESTION TYPES

Try the following typical ACT nonfiction passage, this one from the Humanities. Afterward, we'll discuss selected questions from this set as examples of Specific Detail, Inference, and Big Picture Questions.

Passage II

Tragedy was the invention of the Greeks. In their Golden Age, the fifth century before Christ, they produced the world's greatest dramatists, new forms of tragedy and comedy that have been models ever since, and a theatre that every age goes back to for rediscovery of some basic principle....

Since it derived from primitive religious rites, with masks and ceremonial costumes, and made use of music, dance, and poetry, the Greek drama was at the opposite pole from the modern realistic stage. In fact, probably no other theatre in history has made fuller use of the intensities of art. The masks, made of painted linen, wood, and plaster, brought down from primitive days the atmosphere of gods, heroes, and demons. Our nineteenth- and twentieth-century grandfathers thought masks must have been very artificial. Today, however, we appreciate their exciting intensity and can see that in a large theatre they were indispensable. If they allowed no fleeting change of expression during a single episode, they could give for each episode in turn more intense expression than any human face could. When Oedipus comes back with bleeding eyes, the new mask could be more terrible than any facial makeup the audience could endure, yet in its sculpted intensity more beautiful than a real face.

Most essential of all intensities, and hardest for us to understand, was the chorus. Yet many playwrights today are trying to find some equivalent to do for a modern play what the chorus did for the Greeks. During the episodes played by the actors, the chorus would only provide a background of group response, enlarging and reverberating the emotions of the actors, sometimes protesting and opposing but in general serving as ideal spectators to stir and lead the reactions of the audience. But between episodes, with the actors out of the way, the chorus took over. We have only the words, not the music or dance, and some translations of the odes are in such formal, old-fashioned language that it is hard to guess that they were accompanied by vigorous, sometimes even wild dances and symbolic actions that filled an orchestra which in some cities was sixty to ninety feet in diameter. Sometimes the chorus expressed simple horror or lament. Sometimes it chanted and acted out, in unison and in precise formations of rows and lines, the acts of violence the characters were enacting offstage. When Phaedra rushes offstage in Hippolytus to hang herself from the rafters, the members of the chorus, all fifteen of them, perform in mime and chant the act of tying the rope and swinging from the rafters. Sometimes the chorus tells or reenacts an incident of history or legend that throws light on the situation in the play.

Sometimes the chorus puts into specific action what is a general intention in the mind of the main character. When Oedipus resolves to hunt out the guilty person and cleanse the city, he is speaking metaphorically, but the chorus invokes the gods of vengeance and dances a wild pursuit.

On the printed page, the choral odes seem static and formal, lyric and philosophical, emotional letdowns that punctuate the series of episodes, like intermissions between two acts of a play. The reader who skips the odes can get the main points of the play. A few are worth reading as independent poems, notably the famous one in Antigone beginning, "Many are the wonders of the world, but none is

more wonderful than man." Some modern acting versions omit the chorus or reduce it to a few background figures. Yet to the Greeks the odes were certainly more than mere poetic interludes: the wild Dionysian words and movements evoked primitive levels of the subconscious and at the same time served to transform primitive violence into charm and beauty and to add philosophical reflections on the meaning of human destiny.

For production today, we can only improvise some partial equivalent. In Athens the entire population was familiar with choral performances. Every year each of the tribes entered a dithyramb in a contest, rehearsing five hundred men and boys for weeks. Some modern composers have tried to write dramatic music for choruses: the most notable examples are the French composer Darius Milhaud, in the primitive rhythms, shouts, and chants of his operatic version of the *Oresteia*; George Gershwin, in the Negro funeral scenes of *Porgy and Bess*; and Kurt Weill, in the African choruses for *Lost in the Stars*, the musical dramatization of Alan Paton's novel, *Cry, the Beloved Country*. For revivals of Greek tragedies we have not dared use much music beyond a few phrases half shouted, half sung, and drumbeats and suggestive melodies in the background.

Reading Tip

Ordinary reading is too slow to find things and too fast to analyze text. Good test takers scan quickly to find what they need and then analyze intensely.

1. Combined with the passage's additional information, the fact that some Greek orchestras were sixty to ninety feet across suggests that:
   - **A.** few spectators were able to see the stage.
   - **B.** no one performer could dominate a performance.
   - **C.** choruses and masks helped overcome the distance between actors and audience.
   - **D.** Greek tragedies lacked the emotional force of modern theatrical productions.

2. Which of the following claims expresses the writer's opinion and not a fact?
   - **F.** The Greek odes contained Dionysian words and movements.
   - **G.** Greek theater has made greater use of the intensities of art than has any other theater in history.
   - **H.** Many modern playwrights are trying to find an equivalent to the Greek chorus.
   - **J.** The chorus was an essential part of Greek tragedy.

3. The description of the chorus' enactment of Phaedra's offstage suicide (lines 48–52) shows that, in contrast to modern theater, ancient Greek theater was:
   - **A.** more violent.
   - **B.** more concerned with satisfying an audience.
   - **C.** more apt to be historically accurate.
   - **D.** less concerned with a realistic portrayal of events.

4. It can be inferred that one consequence of the Greeks' use of masks was that:
   - **F.** the actors often had to change masks between episodes.
   - **G.** the characters in the play could not convey emotion.
   - **H.** the actors wearing masks played nonspeaking roles.
   - **J.** good acting ability was not important to the Greeks.

5. Which of the following is supported by the information in the second paragraph (lines 7–26)?
   - **A.** Masks in Greek drama combined artistic beauty with emotional intensity.
   - **B.** The use of masks in Greek drama was better appreciated in the nineteenth century than it is now.
   - **C.** Masks in Greek drama were used to portray gods but never human beings.
   - **D.** Contemporary scholars seriously doubt the importance of masks to Greek theater.

6. The author indicates in lines 57–58 that Oedipus's resolution "to hunt out the guilty person and cleanse the city" was:
   - **F.** at odds with what he actually does later in the performance.
   - **G.** misinterpreted by the chorus.
   - **H.** dramatized by the actions of the chorus.
   - **J.** angrily condemned by the chorus.

7. According to the passage, when actors were present on stage, the chorus would:
   - **A.** look on as silently as spectators.
   - **B.** inevitably agree with the actors' actions.
   - **C.** communicate to the audience solely through mime.
   - **D.** react to the performance as an audience might.

8. The main point of the fifth paragraph (lines 61–77) is that choral odes:
   - **F.** should not be performed by modern choruses.
   - **G.** have a meaning and beauty that are lost in modern adaptations.
   - **H.** can be safely ignored by a modern-day reader.
   - **J.** are only worthwhile in *Antigone.*

9. The passage suggests that modern revivals of Greek tragedies "have not dared use much music" (line 92) because:

A. modern instruments would appear out of place.
B. to do so would require a greater understanding of how choral odes were performed.
C. music would distract the audience from listening to the words of choral odes.
D. such music is considered far too primitive for modern audiences.

10. *Porgy and Bess* and *Lost in the Stars* are modern plays that:

F. are revivals of Greek tragedies.
G. use music to evoke the subconscious.
H. perform primitive Greek music.
J. have made use of musical choruses.

A quick preread of the passage should have given you a sense of its general organization:

- First paragraph: introduces the topic of Greek tragedy
- Second paragraph: discusses use of masks (artificial but intense)
- Third paragraph: discusses use of chorus (also artificial but intense)
- Fourth paragraph: expands discussion to choral odes
- Fifth paragraph: concludes with discussion of how Greek tragedy is performed today, and how it has influenced some modern art

That's really all the road map you need going into the questions. Aside from that, you should take away the author's main point: Greek tragedy included many artificial devices, but these devices allowed it to rise to a high level of intensity.

Now let's take a look at selected questions, which fall into three categories.

Specific Detail Questions

Questions 6 and 7 above are typical Detail Questions. Some Detail Questions give you a line reference to help you out; others don't, forcing you either to start tearing your hair out (if you're an unprepared test taker) or else to seek out the answer based on your sense of how the passage is laid out (one of the two key reasons to preread the passage).

Question 6 provides a line reference (lines 57–58), but to answer the question confidently, you should have also read a few lines *before* and a few lines *after* the cited lines. There you would have read: "Sometimes the chorus puts into action what is a general intention in the mind of the main character. When Oedipus resolves . . ." Clearly, the Oedipus example is meant to illustrate the point about the chorus acting out a character's intentions. So H is correct—they are "dramatizing" (or acting out) Oedipus's resolution. (By the way, G might have been tempting, but there's no evidence that the chorus is "misinterpreting," just that they're "putting a general intention into specific action.")

Look It Up

The answers are in the passage. Focus your attention on locating them. Your mindset should be: "Find the answer," not "Remember the answer."

Question 7 is a Detail Question *without* a line reference. Such questions are common on the ACT, and they require that you have a good sense of the structure of the passage as a whole, so that you can locate the place where the question is answered. This question's mention of the chorus should have sent you to paragraph 3, but that's a long paragraph, so you probably had to skim it to find the answer in line 36, where the author claims that the chorus serves to "lead the reactions of the audience"—captured by correct choice D.

Inference Questions

With Inference Questions, your job is to combine ideas logically to make an inference—something that's not stated explicitly in the passage but that is definitely said implicitly. Often, you'll see a word like *suggest, infer, inference,* or *imply* in the question stem to tip you off.

To succeed on Inference Questions, you have to "read between the lines." Common sense is your best tool here. You use various bits of information in the passage as evidence for your own logical conclusion.

Like Detail Questions, Inference Questions sometimes do and sometimes don't contain line references. **Question 9** does, referring you to line 92, but you really have to keep the context of the entire paragraph in mind when you make your inference. Why would modern revivals not have "dared" to use much music? Well, the paragraph opens by saying that modern productions "can only improvise some partial equivalent" to the choral odes. Inferably, since we can only improvise the odes, we don't understand very much about them. That's why the use of music would be considered daring, and why choice B is correct.

Question 4 provides no line reference, but the mention of masks should have sent you to the second paragraph of the passage. Lines 19–20 explain that masks "allowed no fleeting change of expression during a single episode." Treat that as your first piece of evidence. Your second comes in lines 20–22: "they [the masks] could give for each episode in turn more intense expression than any human face could." Put those two pieces of evidence together—masks can't change expression *during* a single episode, but they can give expression for each episode in *turn*.

Put Two and Two Together

Making inferences often requires that you combine bits of information from different parts of the passage. Common sense will then lead you to an appropriate inference—one that's not too extreme.

Clearly, the actors must have changed masks between episodes, so that they could express the different emotions that different episodes required. Choice F is correct.

One warning: Keep your inferences as "close" to the passage as possible. Don't make wild inferential leaps. An inference should follow naturally and inevitably from the evidence provided in the passage.

Big Picture Questions

About one-third of the ACT Reading questions are Detail Questions and most of the rest are Inference Questions. But there are also a few questions that test your understanding of the theme, purpose, and organization of the passage as a whole. Big Picture Questions tend to look for:

- Main point or purpose of a passage or part of a passage
- Author's attitude or tone
- Logic underlying the author's argument
- How ideas in different parts of the passage relate to each other
- Difference between fact and opinion

Missing the Big Picture?

If you're still stumped after reading the passage, try doing the Detail and Inference Questions first. They can help you fill in the Big Picture.

One way to see the Big Picture is to read actively. As you read, ask yourself, "What's this all about? What's the point of this? Why is the author saying this?"

Question 8 asks for the main idea of a particular paragraph—namely, the fourth, which our general outline indicates is the paragraph about choral odes. Skimming that paragraph, you find reference to how the odes seem to us modern people—"static and formal" (line 61–62), "like intermissions between two acts of a play" (lines 63–64). Later, the author states, by way of contrast (note the use of the clue word *yet*): "Yet to the Greeks the odes were certainly more than mere poetic interludes." Clearly, the author wants to contrast our modern static view of the odes with the Greeks' view of them as something more. That idea is best captured by choice G.

Question 2, meanwhile, is another common type of Big Picture Question—one that requires you to distinguish between expressions of fact and opinion in the passage. A simple test for fact (versus opinion) is this: Can it be proven objectively? If yes, it's a fact.

Fact or Opinion?

A good way to distinguish fact from opinion is to picture yourself as a fact checker for a newspaper. Is the point in question something you could verify in a book or with an expert? If not, it's probably not a fact.

The content of Greek odes (choice F) is a matter of fact; you can go to a Greek ode and find out whether it does or doesn't contain Dionysian words. Similarly, the efforts of modern playwrights to find an equivalent to the Greek chorus (choice H), and the central importance of the chorus to Greek tragedy (choice J) can be factually verified.

But the "intensities of art" are a subjective matter. What one person thinks is intense might strike another as boring. So G is the expression of opinion the question is looking for.

FIND AND PARAPHRASE . . . AND OTHER TIPS

The examples above show that your real task in Reading is not what you might expect. Your main job is to *find* the answers. Perhaps a better name for the Reading subtest would be "find and paraphrase." But students tend to think that their task in Reading is to "comprehend and remember." That's the wrong mindset.

Don't Be Afraid to Skip

Skip

Remember, answer the easy questions for each passage first. Skip the tough ones and come back to them later. Sometimes the thinking you do on an easy question will help you work out a hard one. When students can't finish on time, it's usually because they stubbornly refuse to skip.

Now that you've done a couple of full-length passages and questions, you've probably encountered at least a few questions that you found unanswerable. What do you do if you can't find the answer in the passage, or if you can find it but don't understand, or if you do understand but can't see an answer choice that makes sense? Skip the question. Skipping is probably more important in Reading than in any other ACT subject test. Many students find it useful to skip as many as half of the questions on the first pass through a set of Reading questions. That's fine.

When you come back to a Reading question the second time, it usually makes sense to use the process of elimination. The first time around, you tried to find the *right* answer but you couldn't. So, now try to identify the three *wrong* answers. Eliminating three choices is slower than finding one right choice, so don't make it your main strategy for Reading. But it is a good way to try a second attack on a question.

Another thing to consider when attacking a question for a second time is that the right answer may have been hidden. Maybe it's written in an unexpected way, with different vocabulary. Or maybe there is another good way that you haven't thought of to answer the question. But remember that it's still important to avoid getting bogged down when you come back to a question. Be willing to admit that there are some problems you just can't answer. Guess if you have to.

Here's a key to the Greek tragedy passage, so that you can check the answers to the questions not discussed above.

Key to Passage II
(Nonfiction—Humanities)

	Answer	Refer To	Type	Comments
1.	C	Lines 17–19, 29–44	Inference	Q-stem emphasizes distance between audience and stage; masks and choruses help to "enlarge" the action, so that it can be understood from a distance.
2.	G	Throughout	Big Picture	Discussed above.
3.	D	Lines 48–52	Inference	Combine info from lines 7–10, 48–52, 72–77.
4.	F	Lines 19–22	Inference	Discussed above.
5.	A	Lines 7–26	Inference	Combine info from lines 10–12, 22–27.
6.	H	Lines 57–60	Detail	Discussed above.
7.	D	Lines 31–36	Detail	Discussed above.
8.	G	Lines 61–77	Big Picture	Discussed above.
9.	B	Lines 91–94	Inference	Discussed above.
10.	J	Lines 83–91	Detail	"Some modern composers have tried to write dramatic music for choruses."

Chapter Eleven: **Science Workout 2: Always Know Your Direction**

- **How Scientists Think**
- **How Experiments Work**
- **Handling Experiment Questions**
- **The Real Thing: Practice Passage**

In Science Workout 1 you learned that to succeed on the ACT Science subtest, you've got to be able to spot trends and patterns in the data of graphs and tables. But that's not all you need to do well. You've also got to learn how to think like a scientist. You don't have to know very much science (though it certainly helps), but you should at least be familiar with how scientists go about getting and testing knowledge.

HOW SCIENTISTS THINK

Scientists use two very different kinds of logic, which (to keep things nontechnical) we'll call:

- General-to-Specific Thinking
- Specific-to-General Thinking

General-to-Specific

In some cases, scientists have already discovered a law of nature and wish to apply their knowledge to a specific case. For example, a scientist may wish to know how fast a pebble (call it Pebble A) will be falling when it hits the ground three seconds after being dropped. There is a law of physics from which it can be determined that: On Earth, falling objects accelerate at a rate of about 9.8 m/sec^2. The scientist could use this known general principle to calculate the specific information she needs: After three seconds, the object would be falling at a rate of about 3 sec × 9.8 m/sec^2, or roughly 30 m/sec. You could think of this kind of logic as *general-to-specific*. The scientist uses a *general* principle (the acceleration of any object falling on Earth) to find a *specific* fact (the speed of Pebble A).

Specific-to-General

But scientists use a different kind of thinking in order to discover a new law of nature. In this case, they examine many specific facts and then draw a general conclusion about what they've seen. For example, a scientist might watch hundreds of different kinds of frogs live and die, and might notice that all of them developed from tadpoles. She might then announce a conclusion: All frogs develop from tadpoles. You could think of this kind of logic as *specific-to-general*. The scientist looks at many *specific* frogs to find a *general* rule about all frogs.

This conclusion is called a "hypothesis," not a fact or a truth, because the scientist has not checked every single frog in the universe. She knows that there theoretically *could* be a frog somewhere that grows from pond scum or from a Dalmatian puppy. But until she finds such a frog, it is reasonable to think that her hypothesis is correct. Many hypotheses, in fact, are so well documented that they become the equivalent of laws of nature.

In your science classes in school, you mostly learn about general-to-specific thinking. Your teachers explain general rules of science to you and then expect you to apply these rules to answer questions and solve problems. Some ACT Science questions are like that as well. But a majority are not. Most ACT Science questions test specific-to-general thinking. The questions test your ability to see the kinds of patterns in specific data that, as a scientist, you would use to formulate your own general hypotheses. We did something like this in Science Workout 1, when we theorized—based on the trends we found in a table of data—that the pollutant Hg was in some way detrimental to trout populations.

HOW EXPERIMENTS WORK

Many ACT passages describe experiments and expect you to understand how they're designed. Experiments help scientists do specific-to-general thinking in a reliable and efficient way. Consider the tadpole researcher above. In a real-world situation, what would probably happen is that she would notice some of the frogs develop from tadpoles and wonder if maybe they all did. Then she'd know what to look for and could check all the frogs systematically. This process contains the two basic steps of any experiment:

- Forming a hypothesis (guessing that all frogs come from tadpoles)
- Testing a hypothesis (checking the frogs to see if this guess was right)

Experiments

The experimental method requires that the researcher focus on one factor that varies while other factors remain constant (a control group). Doing this helps to validate the results of the experiment, making sure that the factor investigated really is significant.

Scientists are often interested in cause-and-effect relationships. Having formed her hypothesis about tadpoles, a scientist might wonder what *causes* a tadpole to become a frog. To test causal relationships, a special kind of experiment is needed. She must test one possible cause at a time in order to isolate which one actually produces the effect in question. For example, the scientist might inject tadpoles with several different kinds of hormones. Some of these tadpoles might die. Others might turn into frogs normally. But a few—those injected with Hormone X, say—might remain tadpoles for an indefinite time. One reasonable explanation is that Hormone X in some way inhibited whatever causes normal frog development. In other words, the scientist would hypothesize a causal relationship between Hormone X and frog development.

Watch Your Tadpoles' Diets

The relationship between Hormone X and frog development, however, would not be demonstrated very well if the scientist also fed different diets to different tadpoles, kept some in warmer water, or allowed some to have more room to swim than others—or if she didn't also watch tadpoles who were injected with no hormones at all but who otherwise were kept under the same conditions as the treated tadpoles. Why? Because if the "eternal tadpoles" had diets that differed from that of the others, the scientist wouldn't know whether it was Hormone X or the special diet that kept the eternal tadpoles from becoming frogs. Moreover, if their water was warmer than that of the others, maybe it was the warmth that somehow kept the tadpoles from developing. And if she didn't watch untreated tadpoles (a control group), she couldn't be sure whether under the same conditions a normal, untreated tadpole would also remain undeveloped.

Thus, a scientist creating a well-designed experiment will:

- Ensure that there's a single variable (like Hormone X) that varies from test to test or group to group
- Ensure that all other factors (diet, temperature, space, etcetera) remain the same
- Ensure that there is a control group (tadpoles who don't get any Hormone X at all) for comparison purposes

Find What Varies

One of the advantages to knowing how experiments work is that you can tell what a researcher is trying to find out about by seeing what she allows to vary. That's what is being researched—in this case, Hormone X. Data about things other than hormones and tadpole-to-frog development would be outside the design of the experiment. Information about other factors might be interesting, but could not be part of a scientific proof.

For example, if some of the injected tadpoles that did grow into frogs later actually turned into princes, the data from experiments about the hormone they were given would not prove what causes frogs to become princes, though the data *could* be used to design another experiment intended to explore what could make a frog become a prince.

Therefore, whenever you see an experiment in Science, you should ask yourself:

1. **What's the factor that's being varied?** That is what is being tested.
2. **What's the control group?** It's the group that has nothing special done to it.
3. **What do the results show?** What differences exist between the results for the control group and those for the other group(s)? Or between the results for one treated group and those for another, differently treated group?

The Varying Factor

Many ACT Science questions ask you to determine the purpose of an experiment or to design one yourself. To figure out the purpose of an experiment, look to see what factor was allowed to change: That's what's being tested. To design an experiment yourself, keep everything constant except the factor you must investigate.

HANDLING EXPERIMENT QUESTIONS

On the next page is a full-fledged Science passage organized around two experiments. Use the Kaplan Method, but this time, ask yourself the three questions above. Take about 5 or 6 minutes to do the passage and its questions.

Passage II

A *mutualistic* relationship between two species increases the chances of growth or survival for both of them. Several species of fungi called *mycorrhizae* form mutualistic relationships with the roots of plants. The benefits to each species are shown in the figure below.

Figure 1

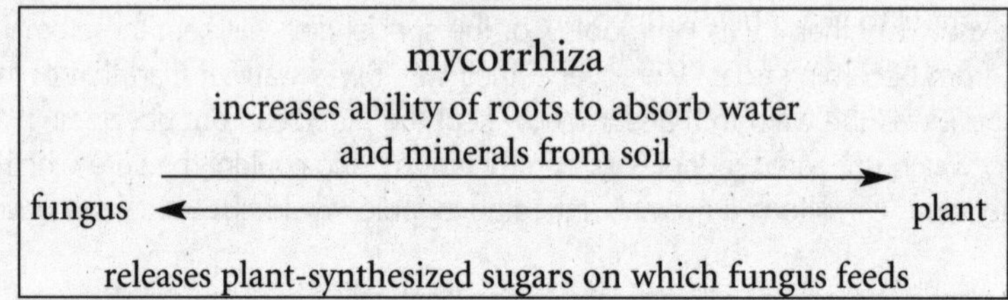

Some of the plant species that require or benefit from the presence of mycorrhizal fungi are noted below.

Cannot survive without mycorrhizae	Grow better with mycorrhizae
All conifers Some deciduous trees (e.g., birch, beech) Orchids	Citrus trees Ericaceae (heath, rhododendrons, azaleas) Grapes Soybeans

Agronomists investigated the effects of mycorrhizae on plant growth and survival in the following studies.

Study 1

Three 4-acre plots were prepared with soil from a pine forest. The soil for Plot A was mixed with substantial quantities of cultured mycorrhizal fungi. The soil for Plot B contained only naturally occurring mycorrhizal fungi. The soil for Plot C was sterilized in order to kill any mycorrhizal fungi. Additionally, Plot C was lined with concrete. After planting, Plot C was covered with a fabric that filtered out microorganisms while permitting air and light to penetrate. 250 pine seedlings were planted in each of the three plots. All plots received the same amount of water. The 6-month survival rates were recorded in the following table.

Table1

	Number of seedlings alive after 6 months	Utilization of available K (average)	Utilization of available P (average)
Plot A	107	18%	62%
Plot B	34	10%	13%
Plot C	0	N/A	N/A

N/A = not applicable

Study 2

The roots of surviving seedlings from Plots A and B were analyzed to determine how efficiently they absorbed potassium (K) and phosphorus (P) from the soil. The results were added to Table 1.

1. The most likely purpose of the concrete liner was:
   - **A.** to block the seedlings from sending out taproots to water below the plot.
   - **B.** to prevent mycorrhizal fungi in the surrounding soil from colonizing the plot.
   - **C.** to absorb potassium and phosphorus from the soil for later analysis.
   - **D.** to provide a firm foundation for mycorrhizal fungi in the plot.

2. Mycorrhizae are highly susceptible to acid rain. Given the information from the passage, acid rain is probably most harmful to:
   - **F.** wheat fields.
   - **G.** birch forests.
   - **H.** orange groves.
   - **J.** grape vines.

3. In a third study, pine seedlings were planted in soil from a different location. The soil was prepared as in Study 1. This time, the survival rates for seedlings planted in Plot A and Plot B were almost identical to each other. Which of the following theories would NOT help to explain these results?
   - **A.** Sterilization killed all the naturally occurring mycorrhizal fungi in the new soil.
   - **B.** The new soil was so mineral-deficient that it could not sustain life.
   - **C.** The new soil was naturally more fertile for pine seedlings than that used in Study 1.
   - **D.** Large quantities of mycorrhizal fungi occurred naturally in the new soil.

4. According to the passage, in which of the following ways do plants benefit from mycorrhizal associations?

   I. More efficient sugar production
   II. Enhanced ability to survive drought
   III. Increased mineral absorption

   - **F.** I only
   - **G.** III only
   - **H.** II and III only
   - **J.** I, II, and III

5. Which of the following generalizations is supported by the results of Study 2?
   - **A.** Mycorrhizal fungi are essential for the survival of pine seedlings.
   - **B.** Growth rates for pine seedlings may be improved by adding mycorrhizal fungi to the soil.
   - **C.** Mycorrhizal fungi contain minerals that are not normally found in pine forest soil.
   - **D.** Pine seedlings cannot absorb all the potassium that is present in the soil.

Answers and Explanations

Notice how many diagrams and tables were used here. That's common in experiment passages, where information is given to you in a wide variety of forms. Typically, though, the experiments themselves are clearly labeled, as Study 1 and Study 2 were here.

Answers

1. B, 2. G, 3. A, 4. H, 5. D

A quick preread of the introduction would have revealed the topic of the experiments here—the "mutualistic relationship" between some fungi and some plant roots, the fungi called mycorrhizae ("myco" for short). The first diagram just shows you who gets what out of this relationship. The benefit accruing to the plant (the arrow pointing to the word *plant*) is an increased ability to absorb water and minerals. The benefit accruing to the *fungus* (the other arrow) is the plant-synthesized sugars on which the fungus feeds. That's the mutual benefit that the myco association creates.

Notice, by the way, that reading this first diagram alone is enough to answer **Question 4**. The question is asking: What do the plants get out of the association? And we just answered that—increased ability to absorb water and minerals. Statement III is obviously correct, but so is Statement II, since increased water absorption would indeed enhance the plant's ability to survive drought (a drought is a shortage of water, after all). Statement I, though, is a distortion. We know that the *fungi* benefit from sugars produced by the plants, but we don't have any evidence that the association actually causes plants to produce sugar more efficiently. So I is out; II and III are in, making H the answer.

Can't Live without Those Fungi

Let's get back to the passage. We've just learned who gets what out of the myco association. Now we get a table that shows what *kinds* of plants enter into such associations. Some (those in the first column) are so dependent on myco associations that they can't live without them. Others (those in the second column) merely grow better with them; presumably they could live without them.

Watch for Reversals

Watch out for reversal questions that ask for the one choice that isn't true. Question 3 is a classic example. The wrong choices are things that could explain the results; the correct answer is the one that can't. Always double-check the question stem to make sure you're answering the right question!

Here again, there's a question we can answer based solely on information in this one table. **Question 2** tells us that mycos are highly susceptible to acid rain, and then asks what kind of plant communities would be most harmed by acid rain. Well, if acid rain hurts mycos, then the plants that are most dependent on myco fungi (that is, the ones listed in the first column) would be the most harmed by acid rain. Of the four choices, only birch forests—choice G—correspond to something in column 1 of the table. Birch trees can't even *survive* without myco fungi, so anything that hurts myco fungi would inferably hurt birch forests. (Grapevines and orange groves—which are citrus trees—would also be hurt by acid rain, but not as much, since they *can* survive without myco fungi; meanwhile, we're told nothing about wheat in the passage.)

Well, we've answered two of the five questions already and we haven't even gotten to the first experiment. That brings up an important point—namely, that even in passages that center around experiments, there are plenty of Data Analysis Questions. Don't expect there to be passages that have only Data Analysis Questions, other passages that have only Experiment Questions, and others that have only Principle Questions. Most passages will have a mixture of all three.

Study 1

Now look at the first experiment. Three plots, each with differently treated soil, are planted with pine seedlings. Plot A gets soil with cultivated myco fungi; Plot B gets untreated soil with only naturally occurring myco fungi; and Plot C gets no myco fungi at all, since the soil has been sterilized and isolated (via the concrete lining and the fabric covering). Now ask yourself the three important experiment questions.

1. **What's the factor being varied?** The factor being varied is the amount of myco fungi in the soil. Plot A gets lots; Plot B gets just the normal amount; Plot C gets none at all. It's clear, then, that the scientists are testing the effects of myco fungi on the growth of pine seedlings.
2. **What's the control group?** The plants in Plot B, since they get untreated soil. To learn the effects of the fungi, the scientists will then compare the results from fungi-rich Plot A with the control, and the results from fungi-poor Plot C with the same control.
3. **What do the results show?** The results are listed in the first column of the table. And they are decisive: No seedlings at all survived in Plot C; 34 did in Plot B; and 107 did in Plot A. The minimums and maximums coincide. Minimum fungi = minimum number of surviving seedlings; maximum fungi = maximum number of surviving seedlings. Clearly there's a cause-and-effect relationship here. Myco fungi probably help pine seedlings survive.

Questions 1 and 3 can be answered solely on the basis of Study 1. **Question 1** is merely a procedural question: Why the concrete liner in Plot C? Well, in the analysis of the experiment above, we saw that the factor being varied was the amount of myco fungi. Plot C was designed to have none at all. Thus, one can safely assume that the concrete liner was probably there to prevent any stray myco fungi from entering the sterilized soil—choice B.

Question 3 actually sets up an extra experiment based on Study 1. The soils were prepared in the exact same way, except that the soil came from a different location. The results? The number of surviving seedlings from Plots A and B were almost identical. What can that mean? Well, Plot A was supposed to be the fungi-rich plot, whereas Plot B (the control) was supposed to be the fungi-normal plot. But here they have the same results. However, notice that we're *not* told what those results are; it could be that no seedlings survived in any plots this time around.

The question—a reversal question—is phrased so that the three wrong choices are things that *could* explain the results; the correct choice will be the one that *can't*. Choices B, C, and D all *can* explain the results, since they all show how similar results could have been obtained from Plots A and B. If the new soil just couldn't support life—fungi or no fungi—well, Plots A and B would have gotten similar results; namely, no seedlings survive. On the other end of the spectrum, choices C and D show how the two plots might have gotten similar *high* survival rates. If there were lots of myco fungi naturally in this soil (that's choice D), then there wouldn't be all that much difference between the soils in Plots A and B. And if the soil were naturally extremely fertile for the pine seedlings (that's choice C), there must have been lots of fungi naturally present in the soil because pine tress (conifers) don't grow without fungi. So all three of these answers would help to explain similar results in Plots A and B.

Choice A, however, wouldn't help, since it talks about the sterilized soil that's in Plot C. The soil in Plot C won't affect the results in Plots A and B, so choice A is the answer here—the factor that *doesn't* help to explain the results.

Study 2

This study takes the surviving seedlings from Plots A and B in Study 1 and just tests how much potassium (K) and phosphorus (P) the roots have used. The results are listed in the second and third columns of the table. (Notice the "N/A"—not applicable—for Plot C in these columns, since there were no surviving seedlings to test in Plot C!) The data show much better utilization of both substances in the Plot A seedlings, the seedlings that grew in a fungi-rich soil. This data would tend to support a theory that the myco fungi aid in the utilization of K and P, and that this in turn aids survival in pine seedlings.

Some Points Are Quicker Than Others

Many questions on experiment passages will be answerable based solely on the data contained in a single graph or table. You can get these points with relative ease, even if you don't have time for, or don't fully understand, the experiments.

The only question that hinges on Study 2 is **Question 5**. It asks what generalization would be supported by the specific results of Study 2. Notice that Study 2 involved only measuring K and P. It did not involve survival rates (that was Study 1), so Choice A can't be right. And *neither* study measured growth rates, so B is out. The minerals K and P were in the control group's soil, which was natural, untreated pine forest soil, so choice C is clearly unsupported.

But the *data* did show that not all of the potassium (K) could be absorbed by pine seedlings. Only 18 percent was absorbed in Plot A, while only 10 percent was absorbed in Plot B. That's a long way from 100 percent, so choice D seems a safe generalization to make.

THE REAL THING: PRACTICE PASSAGE

Now that we've taken you step by step through a Science passage based on an experiment, it's time to try one on your own. Give yourself about 6 minutes for the next passage and questions. This time the explanations at the end will be very short:

Passage III

The following flowchart shows the steps used by a chemist in testing sample solutions for positive ions of silver (Ag), lead (Pb), and mercury (Hg).

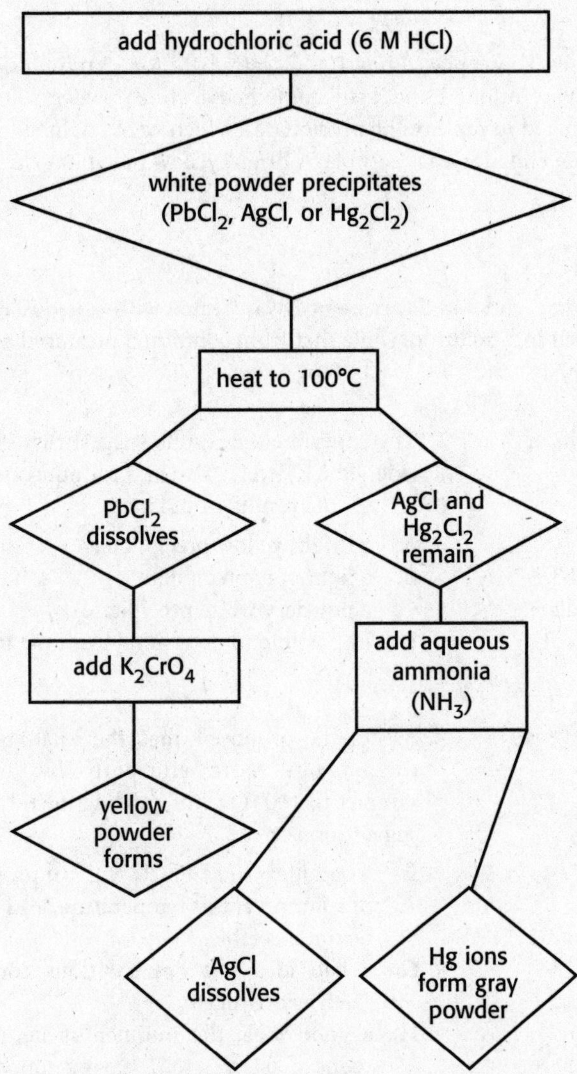

The following experiments were performed by the chemist:

Experiment 1

Hydrochloric acid (6 M HCl) was added to samples of four unknown solutions labeled 1, 2, 3, and 4. A white powder precipitated out of solutions 1, 2, and 3; no precipitate formed in solution 4.

Experiment 2

Each of the sample solutions from Experiment 1 was placed in a 100°C water bath for 15 minutes. The precipitate in solution 1 redissolved completely; solutions 2 and 3 still contained a white powder; solution 4 was unchanged. Solutions 2 and 3 were centrifuged to remove the precipitates, which were retained for further testing. Potassium chromate (K_2CrO_4) was then added to each sample. A bright yellow precipitate formed in solutions 1 and 2; none formed in solutions 3 or 4.

Experiment 3

The white powder centrifuged from solutions 2 and 3 in Experiment 2 was treated with aqueous ammonia (NH_3). The precipitate from solution 2 returned into solution, while that from solution 3 produced a gray powder.

6. Which conclusion is best supported by the results of Experiment 1 alone?

F. Silver ions are present only in solution 3.
G. No ions are present in solution 4.
H. Lead ions are present in solutions 1, 2, and 3.
J. No positive ions of silver, mercury, or lead are present in solution 4.

7. Based on the experimental results, which ions did solution 2 contain?

A. Lead ions only
B. Lead and silver ions only
C. Silver and mercury ions only
D. Silver ions only

8. The yellow precipitate that formed in Experiment 2 was most likely:

F. AgCl
G. Hg_2Cl_2
H. $PbCrO_4$
J. Ag_2CrO_4

9. The experimental results suggest that if lead chloride ($PbCl_2$) were treated with aqueous ammonia (NH_3), the results would be:

A. a bright yellow precipitate.
B. a light gray precipitate.
C. a powdery white precipitate.
D. impossible to determine from the information given.

10. A student proposed that the analysis could be carried out more efficiently by heating the samples to 100° C before adding the 6 M HCl. This suggestion is:

F. a bad idea; since $PbCl_2$ will not precipitate out of solution at this temperature, lead ions would be undetectable.
G. a bad idea; the hot solutions could not be safely centrifuged.
H. a good idea; the number of steps would be reduced from 3 to 2, saving much time and effort.
J. a good idea; the chloride-forming reaction would proceed faster, eliminating the necessity for a 15-minute water bath.

Answers and Explanations

This experiment passage was somewhat different from the preceding one. In the mycorrhiza experiment, the scientists were thinking in specific-to-general terms (observing the growth of *specific* pine seedlings to come to a conclusion about the general effect of myco fungi on pine seedlings). In this series of experiments, the general principle is known—silver, lead, and mercury will precipitate or dissolve when certain things are done to them—and the scientists are using this principle to test certain substances in order to identify them. In fact, this is more like a procedure than an experiment, since there's no control group. But the same kind of experimental thinking—using the results of varying procedures to make reasonable inferences about what's happening—will get you your answers.

Answers

6. J, 7. B, 8. H, 9. D, 10. F

This passage also introduces the idea of a flowchart. Basically, the flowchart indicates an order of procedures. You follow the flowchart from top to bottom. The things in squares indicate what's done to a specimen; the things in diamonds indicate possible results.

Flowcharts

Flowcharts are just what their name implies—charts depicting the "flow" of procedures. Follow a flowchart, either across or down, to find out what procedures come first, which come next, etcetera. Where flowcharts branch into two or more different arms, these represent alternative results.

Let's say you have an unknown substance. Following the flowchart, the first thing you do is add hydrochloric acid. If a white powder precipitates, that means there are positive ions of silver, lead, and/or mercury. (If nothing precipitates, the experiment is over; the substance is not of interest here.)

But, assuming you do get a white powder, how do you identify exactly which kind of white powder you have? You do the next procedure—heat it to 100°C. When you do this, any lead ions will dissolve, but any silver or mercury ions will remain as a powder. So, the flowchart has to divide here.

If part of your specimen dissolved when heated, that doesn't necessarily mean you have lead ions. To test for that, you add K_2CrO_4. If a yellow powder forms, then you know you've got lead; if not, you've got something else.

But what about the other branch? That tells you what has to be done if you *do* have some powder remaining after heating. And what you do is add NH_3. If the powder dissolves, you've got silver ions. If it forms a gray powder, on the other hand, what you've got are mercury (Hg) ions.

The three experiments here are actually three parts of a single experiment or procedure, each one using the results of the former in the way outlined in the flowchart. The questions ask for results at various points in the procedure, so let's look at them briefly now.

Key to Passage III

	Answer	Refer To	Comments
6.	J	Experiment 1 only	If any Ag, Pb, or Hg ions were present, they would have precipitated out as powder. Note that G is too extreme (could be ions of a fourth type not within scope of the experiment). Not enough testing in Exp. 1 to determine F or H.
7.	B	All 3 experiments	Heating left powder, so has to have Ag or Hg or both, so cut A. Addition of K_2CrO_4 left yellow precipitate, so must contain Pb (cut C and D).
8.	H	Experiment 2	Must be lead-based, because Ag and Hg precipitates were already removed (cut F, G, and J).
9.	D	Flowchart	No evidence for what would happen—two different branches of the flowchart.
10.	F	Flowchart	If the solutions were heated first, and then the HCl was added, the $PbCl_2$ would never form, and the chemist would not know whether lead ions were present.

As you've seen, not all experiments on the ACT Science subject test are specific-to-general experiments; some are general-to-specific procedures. But the same kind of strict thinking—manipulating factors to narrow down possibilities—can get you points, no matter what direction you're thinking in.

Chapter Twelve: **English Workout 3: Trust Your Ear**

- **Listen to the Choices**
- **Nineteen Classic Grammar Errors**

In the first two English workouts, we discussed English questions that hinged mostly on common sense. But there are also some English questions—we call them Technicality Questions—that may seem harder because they test for the technical rules of grammar, requiring you to correct errors that don't necessarily harm the economy or sense of the sentence. But don't worry. You don't have to be a grammar whiz to get these questions right. Luckily, you can often detect these errors because they "sound funny." Most of the time on the ACT, it's safe to trust your ear.

LISTEN TO THE CHOICES

Which of the following "sounds right" and which "sounds funny"?

- Bob doesn't know the value of the house he lives in.
- Bob don't know the value of the house he lives in.

Think

Technicality Questions test the rules of grammar. With questions of this type, the answers tend to all be about the same length, and there's no strong bias toward shorter answers. So trust your ears, not your eyes, on these questions.

The first sounds a lot better, right? For many of these questions, all you need to do is "listen" carefully in this way. You may not know the formal rules of grammar, punctuation, and diction, but you communicate in English every day. You wouldn't be communicating unless you had a decent feel for the rules.

You may have caught an apparent error in both of the examples above—ending a sentence with a preposition such as "in." This is undesirable in extremely formal writing. But ACT passages aren't usually that formal. The ACT test writers expect you to have a feel for the level of formality in writing. If the passage is informal, pick informal answers. If the passage is slightly formal (as most ACT passages are), pick slightly formal answers. If the passage is extremely formal, pick extremely formal answers. For example, if the passage starts off "You'll just love Bermuda—great beaches, good living . . . ." it won't end like this: "and an infinitely fascinating array of flora and fauna which may conceivably

Use "Standard" English

Some students are offended that the ACT expects them to talk like somebody else. That feeling is justified, but it won't help improve your score. Don't stubbornly pick an answer that "sounds" right to you but which you know wouldn't sound right to a "standard" English speaker. Your goal should be to get the best score you can, not to prove a point about regional or ethnic biases.

exceed, in range and scope, that of any alternative . . . ." It's too formal. Pick something like this: "You'll just love Bermuda—great beaches, good living, and lots of awesome plants and animals."

Although ACT passages differ in level of formality, they all are designed to test "standard" English—the kind used by people in most of America. Test takers who speak regional or ethnic dialects may therefore find it more difficult to follow their ears on some ACT questions. In much of the South, for instance, it's common to use the word "in" with the word "rate," like this: "Mortality declined *in* a rate of almost 2 percent per year." Most speakers of English, however, use the word "at" with "rate," like this: "Mortality declined *at* a rate of . . . ." Fortunately, ACT questions testing issues like this are rare. And even if you do speak a "nonstandard" dialect, you probably know what standard English sounds like. The dialect used on most television and radio programs would be considered "standard."

In the following short passage, "listen" carefully to each answer choice.

Example

Passage II

Halloween was first celebrated <u>among various</u>[1] Celtic tribes in Ireland in the fifth century B.C. It traditionally took place on the official last day of summer—October <u>31, and</u>[2] was named "All-Hallows' Eve." It was believed that all persons who had died during the previous year returned on this day to select persons or animals to inhabit for the next twelve months, until they could <u>pass peaceful</u>[3] into the afterlife.

On All-Hallows' Eve, the Celts <u>were dressing</u>[4] up as demons and monsters to frighten the spirits away, and tried to

1. A. NO CHANGE
   B. among varied
   C. between the various
   D. between various

2. F. NO CHANGE
   G. 31—and
   H. 31. And
   J. 31; and

3. A. NO CHANGE
   B. pass peacefully
   C. passed peacefully
   D. be passing peaceful

4. F. NO CHANGE
   G. were dressed
   H. dressed
   J. are dressed

make their homes as coldest as possible to prevent any
5
stray ghosts from crossing their thresholds. Late at night, the townspeople typically gathered outside the village, where a druidic priest would light a huge bonfire to frighten away ghosts and to honor the sun god for the past summer's harvest. Any villager whom was suspected of
6
being possessed would be captured, after which they
7
might be sacrificed in the bonfire as a warning to other spirits seeking to possess the living. When the Romans invaded the British Isles, they adopted Celtic—not Saxon—Halloween rituals, but outlawed human sacrifice in A.D. 61. Instead, they used effigies for their sacrifices. In time, as belief in spirit possession waned, Halloween
8
rituals lost their serious aspect and had been instead
9
performed for amusement.

Irish immigrants, fleeing from the potato famine in the 1840s, brought there Halloween customs to the
10
United States.

5. A. NO CHANGE
   B. colder
   C. coldest
   D. as cold

6. F. NO CHANGE
   G. whom were
   H. who was
   J. who were

7. A. NO CHANGE
   B. it
   C. he or she
   D. those

8. F. NO CHANGE
   G. belief for
   H. believing about
   J. belief of

9. A. NO CHANGE
   B. having been
   C. have been
   D. were

10. F. NO CHANGE
    G. brought they're
    H. brought their
    J. their brought-in

In New England, Halloween became a night of costumes and practical jokes. Some favorite pranks <u>included unhinging</u> [11] front gates and overturning outhouses. The Irish also introduced the custom of carving jack-o'-lanterns. The ancient Celts probably began the tradition by hollowing out a large turnip, carving it with a demon's face, and lighting it from inside with a candle. Since there were <u>far less</u> [12] turnips in New England than in Ireland, the Irish immigrants were forced to settle for pumpkins.

Gradually, Halloween celebrations spread to other regions of the United States. Halloween has been a popular holiday ever since, <u>although these days it's</u> [13] principal celebrants are children <u>rather than</u> [14] adults.

11. **A.** NO CHANGE
    B. include unhinging
    C. had included unhinged
    D. includes unhinged

12. **F.** NO CHANGE
    G. lots less
    H. not as much
    J. far fewer

13. **A.** NO CHANGE
    B. although these days its
    C. while now it's
    D. while not it is

14. **F.** NO CHANGE
    G. rather then
    H. rather
    J. else then

Key to Passage II

Answer	Problem	Explanation
1. A	*among/between* distinction	See Error 18 below
2. G	commas and dashes mixed	See Error 3 below
3. B	use of adjectives and adverbs	See Error 7 below
4. H	unnecessary *-ing* ending	See Error 16 below
5. D	comparative/superlative	See Error 17 below
6. H	*who/whom* confusion	See Error 11 below
7. C	pronoun usage error	See Error 1 below
8. F	preposition error	See Error 10 below
9. D	tense problem with *to be*	See Error 15 below
10. H	*they're/there/their* mixup	See Error 13 below
11. A	verb tense problem	See Error 14 below
12. J	*less/fewer* confusion	See Error 19 below
13. B	*it's/its* confusion	See Error 12 below
14. F	*then/than* confusion	See Error 17 below

Chances are, you were able to rely almost exclusively on your ear to correct many of the above errors. But there are a few English questions on every ACT that test errors your ear probably won't or can't catch. For these, you'll have to think about the rules more formally. But fortunately, only a small number of rules are typically involved, and we'll discuss them all in this workout. Even more fortunately, most of the technicalities tested on the ACT boil down to one general principle: *Make it all match.*

NINETEEN CLASSIC GRAMMAR ERRORS

The rest of this workout is designed to help you build your own "flag list" of common errors on the ACT that your ear might not catch. Consider each classic error. If it seems like common sense to you (or, better, if the error just sounds like bad English to you, while the correction sounds like good English), you probably don't have to add it to your flag list. On the other hand, if it doesn't seem obvious, add it to your list.

As we'll see, making things match works in two ways. Some rules force you to match one part of the sentence with another part. Other rules force you to match the right word or word form with the intended meaning.

Error 1: *They* and *It* (Singulars and Plurals)

The most tested "matching" rule on the ACT is this: Singular nouns must match with singular verbs and pronouns, and plural nouns must match with plural verbs and pronouns. The most common error in this area involves the use of the word *they*. It's plural, but in everyday speech, we often use it as a singular.

Sentence: "If a student won't study, they won't do well."

Problem: A *student* (singular) and *they* (plural) don't match.

Correction: "If students won't study, they won't do well," or "If a student won't study, he or she won't do well."

Error 2: *And* (Compound Subjects)

Another common matching error concerns "compound subjects" (lists).

Sentence: "The fool gave the wrong tickets to Bob and I."

Problem: *I* is a subject; it can't be the object of the preposition *to*.

Correction: "The fool gave the wrong tickets to Bob and me."

HINT: Try dropping the rest of the list (Bob and). "The fool gave the wrong tickets to I" should sound funny to you.

Error 3: Commas or Dashes (Parenthetical Phrases)

One rule of punctuation is tested far more often than any other on the ACT. Parenthetical phrases must begin and end with the same punctuation mark. Such phrases can be recognized because without them the sentence would still be complete. For instance: "Bob, on his way to the store, saw a large lizard in the street." If you dropped the phrase "on his way to the store," the sentence would still be complete. Thus, this phrase is parenthetical. It could be marked off with commas, parentheses, or dashes. But the same mark is needed at both ends of the phrase.

Sentence: "Bob—on his way to the store, saw a lizard."

Problem: The parenthetical phrase starts with a dash but finishes with a comma.

Correction: "Bob, on his way to the store, saw a lizard."

Error 4: Commas (Run-Ons and Comma Splices)

The ACT test makers expect you to understand what makes a sentence and what doesn't. You can't combine two sentences into one with a comma (though you can with a semicolon or conjunction).

Sentence: "Ed's a slacker, Sara isn't."

Problem: Two sentences are spliced together with a comma.

Correction: "Ed's a slacker, but Sara isn't." or "Ed's a slacker; Sara isn't." or "Ed, unlike Sara, is a slacker."

Usually, only one thing should happen in each sentence. There should be one "major event." There are only a few ways to put more than one event in a sentence. One way is to connect the sentences with a conjunction (a word like *and* or *but*), as in the first correction. Or, as in the second, a semicolon can stand for such a word. The other way is to "subordinate" one event to the other in a clause, as in the third correction.

Error 5: Fragment

This rule goes hand in hand with the one above. A sentence must have at least one "major event." A "fragment" is writing that could be a subordinate part of a sentence, but not a whole sentence itself.

Sentence: "Emily listened to music. While she studied."
Problem: "She studied" would be a sentence, but *while* makes this a fragment.
Correction: "Emily listened to music while she studied."

Error 6: Any Punctuation Mark

The ACT doesn't test tricky rules of punctuation. But it does expect you to know what the punctuation marks mean and to match their use to their meanings. Here are some common punctuation marks and their meanings:

Period (.): means "full stop" or "end of sentence."
Question mark (?): serves the same purpose, but for questions.
Exclamation mark (!): can be used instead of a period, but is generally inappropriate for all but very informal writing because it indicates extreme emotion.
Comma (,): means "little stop." In many cases a comma is optional. But never use a comma where a stop would be confusing, as in: "I want to go, to the, store."
Semicolon (;): used to separate two complete, but closely related thoughts.
Colon (:): works like an "=" sign, connecting two equivalent things. Colons are usually used to begin a list.
Dash (–): can be used for any kind of pause, usually a long one or one indicating a significant shift in thought.

Error 7: *-ly* Endings (Adverbs and Adjectives)

The ACT expects you to understand the difference between adverbs (the *-ly* words) and adjectives. The two are similar because they're both "modifiers." They modify, or refer to, or describe, another word or phrase in the sentence. The trick is that nouns and pronouns must be modified by adjectives, while other words, especially verbs and adjectives themselves, must be modified by adverbs.

Sentence: "Anna is an extreme gifted child, and she speaks beautiful too."

Problem: *Extreme* and *beautiful* are adjectives, but they're supposed to modify an adjective (*gifted*) and a verb (*speaks*) here, so they should be adverbs.

Correction: "Anna is an extremely gifted child, and she speaks beautifully too."

Error 8: *Good* or *Well*

In everyday speech, we often confuse the words *good* and *well*. But *good* is an adjective (it modifies a noun or pronoun); *well* is an adverb (it can modify verbs and adjectives).

Sentence: "Joe did good on the ACT."

Problem: *Good* is an adjective, but here it's modifying a verb (*did*), so use an adverb.

Correction: "Joe did well on the ACT."

One exception: *Well* can also be used as an adjective, when it means "healthy." So: "Joe was well again by the morning of the ACT" is correct, even though *well* is modifying the noun *Joe*.

Error 9: *Lie, Lay, Laid, Lain*

The words *lay* and *lie* are easy to confuse because they look alike and have similar meanings. The key difference in meaning is point of view. If the speaker is doing something without a direct object, he is "lying." If the speaker is doing it to something else, he is "laying." So, for example, "I will go lie down" (not *lay down*), but "I will lay this pencil on the desk" (not *lie* it).

It gets worse. The past tense of *lay* is *laid*. That's not too hard. The confusing word is *lie*. The past tense of *lie* is *lay*; when used for special tenses (with the words *had*, *have*, or *been*, for example), the form is *lain*. Thus, you'd say "I lay down" (meaning you, yourself, took a rest at some time in the past), or "I have lain down for a nap every afternoon for years now." But you'd say, "I laid that pencil on the desk yesterday, just as I have laid it on the desk every day for years now."

Don't confuse *lie* with the word *lie* that relates to dishonesty. The past tense of *lie* (meaning to tell an untruth) is *lied*.

Sentence: "I lied. I said that I had lain down, but I hadn't. In fact, I had just laid the pencil down. After I lied, though, I lay down to repent for having lied."

Problem: None. All uses of *lie*, *lied*, *lay*, *laid*, and *lain* above are correct.

Try not to get bogged down with *lie* and *lay*. If you don't get it, don't sweat it. It will account for one point if it appears at all.

Error 10: *In, Of, To, For* (Idiomatic Preposition Use)

Whenever you see a preposition, double check to make sure it makes sense and that it "matches" the other words. Many words require particular prepositions.

Sentences: "She tried to instill on me a respect to the law." "I want to protect you in all dangers."

Problem: The prepositions don't match the verbs.

Corrections: "She tried to instill in me a respect for the law." "I want to protect you from all dangers."

Error 11: *Who* or *Whom*

Many students fear the words *who* and *whom* more than any other grammatical conundrum. Fear no more. There's an easy way to remember when to use them: They work the same way *he* and *him* work. Turn the sentence into a question as we've done in the example below. If the answer to the question is *he*, the form should be *who*. If the answer is *him*, the form should be *whom*. Notice that the *m*'s go together.

Sentence: "Always remember who you're speaking to."

Problem: Who is wrong. Ask: Speaking to who? Speaking to him, not to he. So, it should be whom.

Correction: "Always remember whom you're speaking to."

Some students try to avoid the who/whom problem by using the word *which* instead. Nope. It's not nice to call people "whiches." Never use the word *which* for a person.

Error 12: *Its* or *It's* (Apostrophe Use)

Probably the trickiest rule on the ACT is the proper use of apostrophes. Apostrophes are used primarily for two purposes: possessives and contractions. When you make a *noun* (not a pronoun) possessive by adding an "s," you use an apostrophe. Examples: *Bob's, the water's, a noodle's*. You NEVER use an apostrophe to make a pronoun possessive—pronouns have special possessive forms. You'd never write "her's." When you run two words together to form a single word, you use an apostrophe to join them. For example: *You'd, he's, they're*.

Apostrophes also have a few unusual uses, but luckily they're almost never tested on the ACT. So, master the basics and you're in good shape. The most common apostrophe issue on the ACT is usage of the words *its* and *it's*. A good way to remember which is which is that *its* and *it's* follow the same rule as do *his* and *he's*. Both *its* and *his* are possessive pronouns: so they have *no* apostrophes. Both *it's* and *he's* are contractions—so they *do* have apostrophes.

Sentence: "The company claims its illegal to use it's name that way."

Problem: *It's* is a contraction of *it is*; *its* is the possessive form of *it*.

Correction: "The company claims it's illegal to use its name that way."

Error 13: *There*, *Their*, or *They're* and *Are* or *Our* (Proper Word Usage)

Some students confuse the words *there*, *their*, and *they're*. A good way to remember which is *they're* is to remember that contractions use apostrophes—so *they're* is the contraction for *they are*. You can tell which is *there* because it's spelled like *here*, and the words *here* and *there* match. (*Their* means "of or belonging to them"; you'll just have to remember that one the old-fashioned way.)

Students also frequently confuse the words *are* (a verb) and *our* (a possessive). You can remember that *our* is spelled like *your*, another, less confusing possessive.

Error 14: *Sang*, *Sung*, *Brang*, *Brung*, etcetera (Verb Forms)

When the answers differ because of different forms of the same or similar verbs (for example, *live*, *lives*, *lived*), ask yourself *who* did it and *when* did they do it? We would say "I now live" but "he now lives." In these sentences, the *who* is different—and so the verb changes. Similarly, we would say "I now live" but "I lived in the past." In these sentences, the *when* is different—so the verb changes.

Most verbs are "regular" in this way, with only the endings "s" and "d" to worry about. You use the "s" when the point of view is "he," "she," or "it" and the time is now (present tense). You use the "d" for times in the past. For times in the future, or several steps backward in time, there are no special endings. You use the words *will*, *will have*, *have*, and *had* for these time sequences. "I *will* live. I *will* have lived for twenty-five years by the time the next century begins. I *had* lived in Nebraska, but we moved. I *have* lived in Indiana since then."

But a few verbs are irregular. They have special forms. For example, we say "sang" rather than "singed" and "have sung" rather than "have singed" or "have sang." Each of these verbs must be learned separately.

One irregular verb commonly tested on the ACT is *bring*.

Sentence: "I've brung my umbrella to work."
Problem: *Brang* and *brung* aren't used in standard English.
Correction: "I've brought my umbrella to work."

Error 15: *Be* and *Was* (Forms of the Verb *to Be*)

The ACT tests the use of proper verb forms, especially of the verb *to be*. You must use the following forms. Memorize them if you have to:

Present Tense: I *am*, we *are*, you *are*, they *are*, he *is*, she *is*, it *is*
Past Tense: I *was*, we *were*, you *were*, they *were*, he/she/it *was*
Future Tense: I/we/you/they/he/she/it *will be*
Perfect Tense: I/we/you *have been*, he/she/it *has been*
Past Perfect: I/we/you/he/she/it *had been*
Future Perfect: I/we/you/he/she/it *will have been*

Notice that different forms of the *verb* (*am, are, is, were, was, will be, have been, had been, will have been*) are used depending on point of view (called "case" in grammar) and whether the action is now, in the past, or in the future (called "tense" in grammar). In many dialects, the words *be* and *was* are used instead of the special forms given. For example, many speakers might say "They *be* going home," or "They *was* going home." But the ACT would require you to write "They *are* (or *were*) going home."

Error 16: *-ing* Endings (Unidiomatic Verb Use)

Don't use *-ing* endings where they aren't needed. They are used to indicate repeated or continuous action and shouldn't be used for a single action that occurs once.

Sentence: "When I left for the store, I was forgetting my list."

Problem: The *-ing* ending isn't necessary.

Correction: "When I left for the store, I forgot my list."

Error 17: *-er* and *-est, More,* and *Most* (Comparatives and Superlatives)

Whenever you see the endings *-er* or *-est*, or the words *more* or *most*, double-check to make sure they're used logically. Words with *-er* or with *more* should be used to compare only two things. If there are more than two things involved, use *-est* or *most*.

Sentence: "Bob is the fastest of the two runners."

Problem: The comparison is between just two things, so *-est* is inappropriate.

Correction: "Bob is the faster of the two runners."

Don't use the words *more* or *most* if you can use the endings instead. Say "I think vanilla is tastier than chocolate," not "I think vanilla is more tasty than chocolate." Never use both *more* or *most and* an ending. Don't say "Of the five flavors of frozen yogurt I've eaten, strawberry delight is the most tastiest." Just say it's "the tastiest."

A note on "than" and "then": "Than" is used in comparisons such as "Bob is faster than Jim." "Then" refers to time, as in "Bob ran and then stopped."

Error 18: *Between* or *Among*

Make sure that you use the word *between* only when there are two things involved. When there are more than two things, or an unknown number of things, use *among*.

Sentence: "I will walk among the two halves of the class." "I will walk between the many students in class."

Problem: Use *between* for two things; *among* for more than two.

Correction: "I will walk between the two halves of the class." "I will walk among the many students in class."

Error 19: *Less* or *Fewer*

Make sure that you use the word *less* only for uncountable things. When things can be counted, they are *fewer*.

Sentence: "I have fewer water than I thought, so I can fill less buckets."

Problem: You can count buckets; you can't count water.

Correction: "I have less water than I thought, so I can fill fewer buckets."

HINT: People are always countable, so use *fewer* when writing about them.

For a more thorough account of the grammar points you should know for the ACT, refer to the English Review for the ACT section at the back of this book.

Chapter Thirteen: **Math Workout 3: Figuring It Out**

- **Ten Textbook Geometry Questions**
- **Tackling More Complex Geometry Questions**

Every ACT Math subject test has about 14 geometry questions and exactly 4 trigonometry questions. Depending on what kind of score you're aiming for, you might be able to blow off those few trigonometry questions. But you probably don't want to blow off that many geometry questions.

Fortunately, a good number of the geometry questions are straightforward. Nothing is distorted or disguised. With these questions, you know what to do—if you know your geometry—the instant you understand them.

TEN TEXTBOOK GEOMETRY QUESTIONS

Here's a set of ten such questions. When you take the ACT you will see quite a few questions just like these—possibly reworded and certainly with different numbers and figures. Use these questions to find out how well you remember your geometry.

Example

1. In the figure below, line t crosses parallel lines m and n. What is the degree measure of $\angle x$?

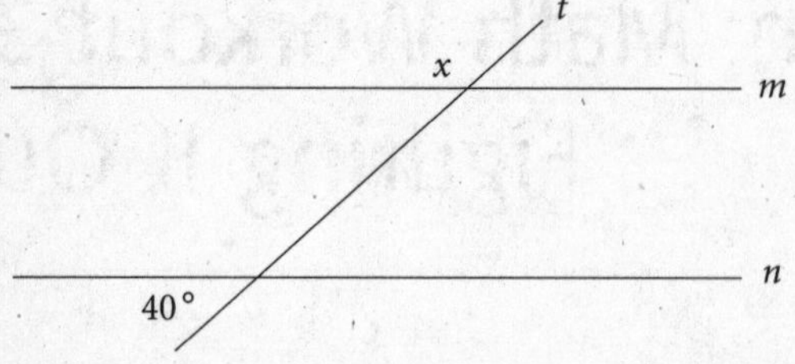

A. 40
B. 50
C. 60
D. 130
E. 140

2. In the figure below, ΔABC is isosceles with $AB = BC$. What is the degree measure of $\angle x$?

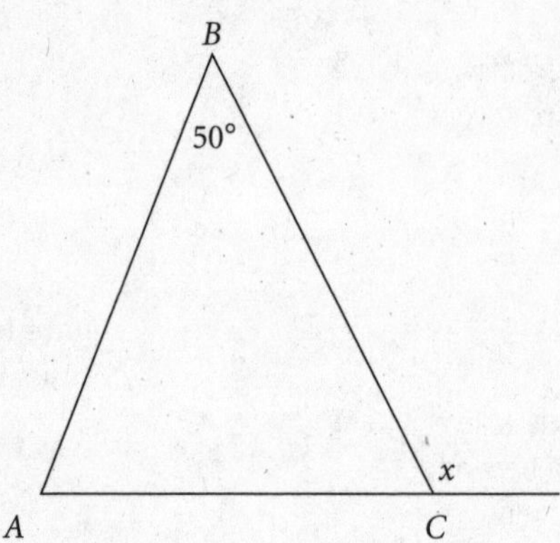

F. 50
G. 65
H. 100
J. 115
K. 130

3. In the figure below, $\angle B$ is a right angle and the lengths of $\overline{AB}$, $\overline{BC}$, and $\overline{CD}$ are given in units. What is the area of ΔACD, in square units?

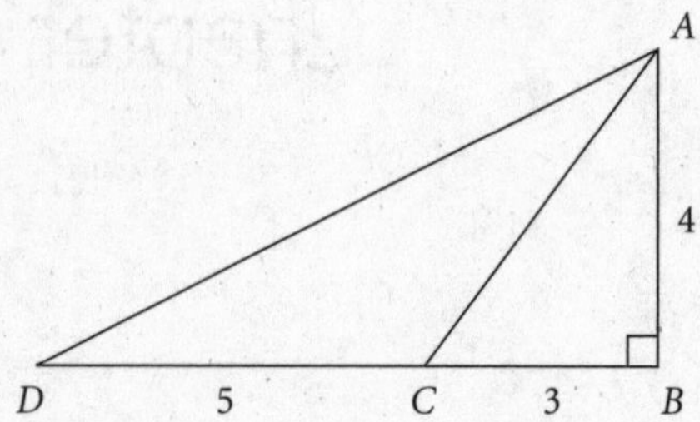

A. 10
B. 12
C. 16
D. 20
E. 32

4. In the figure below, ΔABC is similar to ΔDEF. $\angle A$ corresponds to $\angle D$, $\angle B$ corresponds to $\angle E$, and $\angle C$ corresponds to $\angle F$. If the given lengths are of the same unit of measure, what is the value of x?

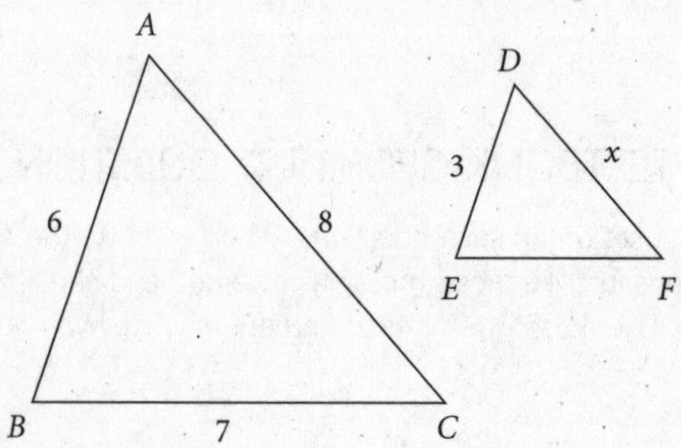

F. 3
G. 3.5
H. 4
J. 5
K. 6

5. In ΔABC below, $\angle B$ is a right angle. If $\overline{AB}$ is 1 unit long and $\overline{BC}$ is 2 units long, how many units long is $\overline{AC}$?

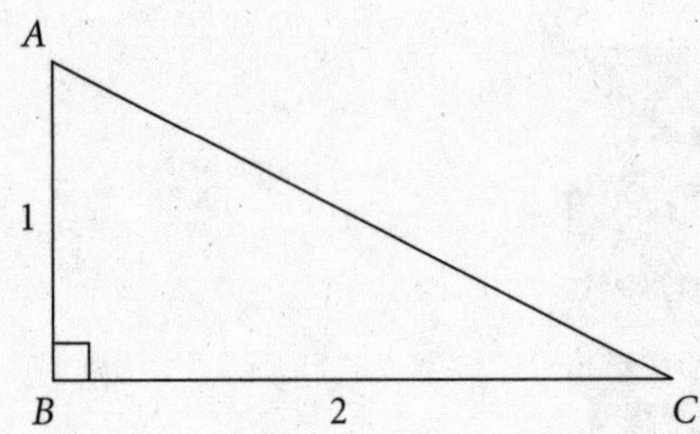

A. $\sqrt{2}$
B. $\sqrt{3}$
C. 2
D. $\sqrt{5}$
E. 3

6. In the figure below, $\overline{AC}$ is perpendicular to $\overline{BD}$, the measure of $\angle D$ is 30° and the measure of $\angle B$ is 45°. If $\overline{AD}$ is 6 units long, how many units long is $\overline{AB}$?

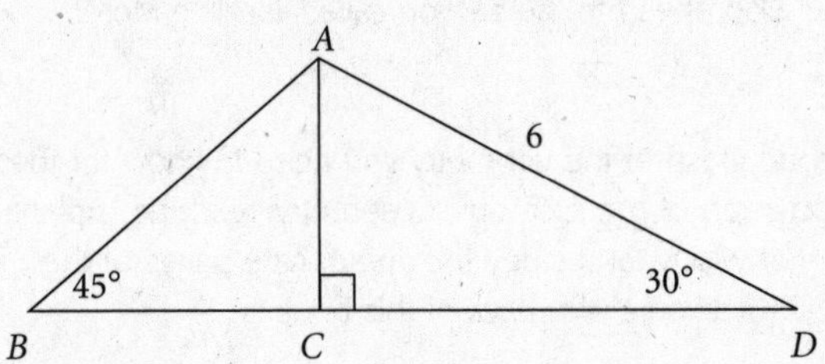

F. 3
G. $3\sqrt{2}$
H. $2\sqrt{6}$
J. $3\sqrt{3}$
K. 6

7. In the figure below, $\overline{BE}$ is perpendicular to $\overline{AD}$, and the lengths of $\overline{AB}$, $\overline{BC}$, $\overline{CD}$, and $\overline{BE}$ are given in inches. What is the area, in square inches, of trapezoid $ABCD$?

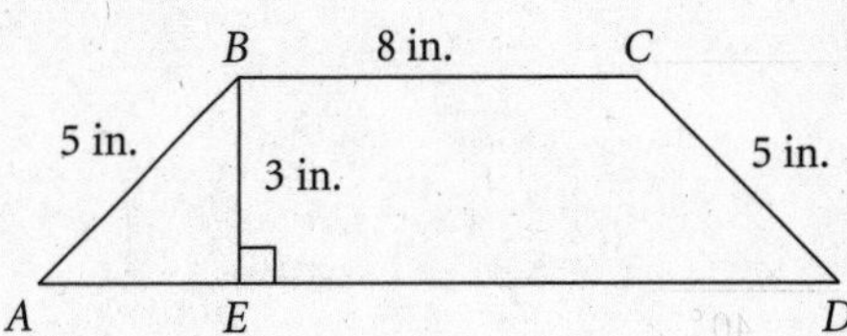

A. 24
B. 30
C. 32
D. 34
E. 36

8. What is the area, in square inches, of a circle with a diameter of 8 inches?

F. 4π
G. 8π
H. 16π
J. 32π
K. 64π

9. In the circle centered at O in the figure below, the measure of $\angle AOB$ is 40°. If $\overline{OA}$ is 9 units long, how many units long is minor arc AB?

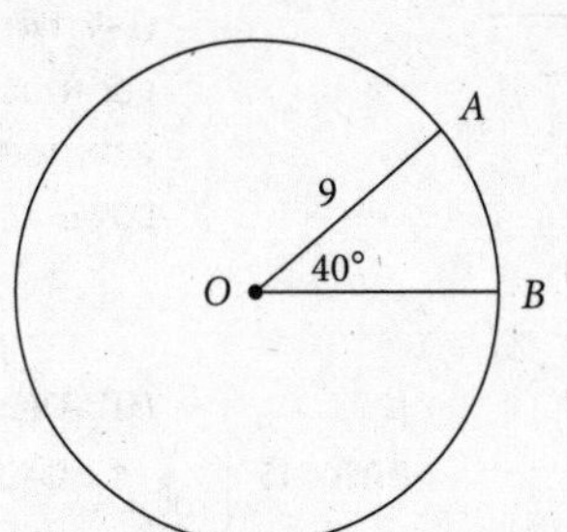

A. π
B. 2π
C. 9
D. 9π
E. 40

10. In the figure below, *ABCD* is a square and $\overline{AB}$ is a diameter of the circle centered at *O*. If $\overline{AD}$ is 10 units long, what is the area, in square units, of the shaded region?

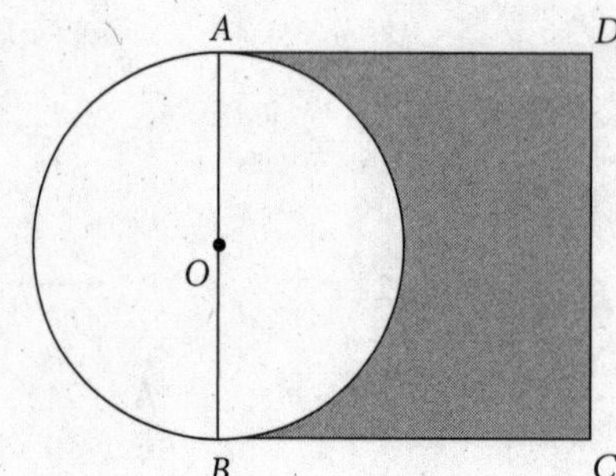

F. $100 - 50\pi$
G. $100 - 25\pi$
H. $100 - \frac{25\pi}{2}$
J. $100 - 10\pi$
K. $100 - 5\pi$

Scoring

10 correct: You have a solid grounding in geometry. Straightforward textbook geometry questions are no problem for you. Skip ahead to the section called Tackling More Complex Geometry Questions.

8–9 correct: You have a pretty good grasp of the geometry you need to know for the ACT. Before moving on to the discussion of more complex geometry, read the explanations below of the questions you got wrong, and study the appropriate pages of the 100 Key Math Concepts for the ACT section at the back of this book.

0–7 correct: You have gaps in your knowledge of geometry. Before you can hope to get much out of our discussion of more complex geometry, you had better solidify your geometry foundations. Look at the explanations below and study the corresponding pages of the 100 Key Math Concepts for the ACT section at the back of this book.

Answers and Explanations

Answers

1. E, 2. J, 3. A, 4. H, 5. D
6. G, 7. E, 8. H, 9. B, 10. H

1. When a transversal crosses parallel lines, the four acute angles formed are all equal, the four obtuse angles formed are all equal, and any angles that are not equal are supplementary. The angle marked *x* is obtuse, so it's supplementary to the given 40° angle. 180 – 40 = 140. The answer is E. (*100 Key Math Concepts for the ACT, #79*)

2. The three angles of any triangle add up to 180°. Furthermore, the two angles opposite the equal sides of an isosceles triangle are equal. The given angle measures 50°, so the other two angles split the remaining 130°. Since those other two angles

are equal, they each measure 65°. The angle marked x is adjacent and supplementary to a 65° angle, so $x = 180 - 65 = 115$. The answer is J. (*100 Key Math Concepts for the ACT, #80*)

3. The formula for the area of a triangle is $A = \frac{1}{2}bh$. To apply this formula, you need the base and the height. Here you can use $\overline{CD}$ for the base and $\overline{AB}$ for the height. So: Area $= \frac{1}{2}(CD)(AB) = \frac{1}{2}(5)(4) = 10$. The answer is A. (*100 Key Math Concepts for the ACT, #83*)

4. In similar triangles, corresponding sides are proportional. $\overline{DE}$ corresponds to $\overline{AB}$, and $\overline{DF}$ corresponds to $\overline{AC}$, so we can set up this proportion:

   $\frac{AB}{DE} = \frac{AC}{DF}$

   $\frac{6}{3} = \frac{8}{x}$

   $6x = 3 \times 8$

   $6x = 24$

   $x = 4$

   The answer is H. (*100 Key Math Concepts for the ACT, #82*)

5. The Pythagorean theorem says: $(\text{leg}_1)^2 + (\text{leg}_2)^2 = (\text{hypotenuse})^2$. Here the legs have lengths of 1 and 2, so plug them into the formula:

   $(1)^2 + (2)^2 = (\text{hypotenuse})^2$

   $1 + 4 = x^2$

   $x^2 = 5$

   $x = \sqrt{5}$

   The answer is D. (*100 Key Math Concepts for the ACT, #84*)

6. The indicated angles tell you that ΔABC is a 45°-45°-90° triangle and that ΔACD is a 30°-60°-90° triangle. $\overline{AD}$ is the hypotenuse and $\overline{AC}$ is the shorter leg of the 30°-60°-90° triangle, so $AC = \frac{1}{2}(AD) = 3$. $\overline{AC}$ is also the shorter leg of the 45°-45°-90°, and $\overline{AB}$, the side we're looking for, is the hypotenuse. Therefore, $AB = (AC)\sqrt{2} = 3\sqrt{2}$. The answer is G. (*100 Key Math Concepts for the ACT, #85*)

7. The formula for the area of a trapezoid is $A = \left(\frac{b_1 + b_2}{2}\right)h$, where b_1 and b_2 are the lengths of the parallel sides. You could think of it as the height times the average of the bases. You're given the height (3 inches), one base (8 inches), and enough

information to figure out the other base. Notice that ΔABE is a 3-4-5 triangle, so $AE = 4$ inches. And if you were to drop an altitude down from point C, you'd get another 3-4-5 triangle on the right:

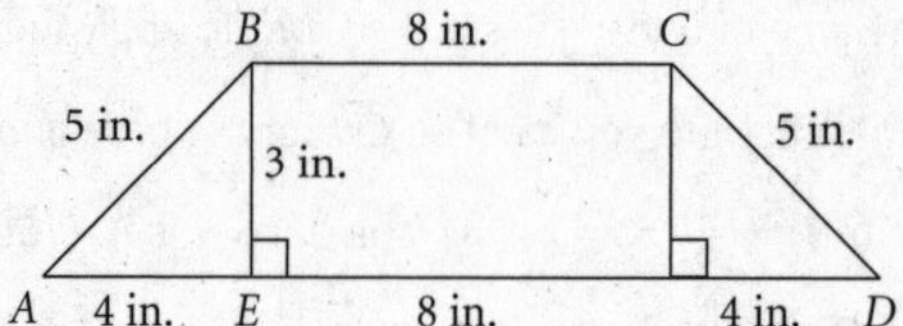

Now you can see that the bottom base is 16 inches. Plug these numbers into the formula:

$$A = \left(\frac{b_1 + b_2}{2}\right)h$$

$$= \left(\frac{8 + 16}{2}\right) \times 3$$

$$= 12 \times 3 = 36$$

The answer is E. (*100 Key Math Concepts for the ACT, #87*)

8. The formula for the area of a circle is $A = \pi r^2$, where r is the radius. If the diameter is 8 inches, then the radius is 4 inches, which we plug into the formula:

$$A = \pi r^2$$

$$= \pi(4)^2$$

$$= 16\pi$$

The answer is H. (*100 Key Math Concepts for the ACT, #91*)

9. The central angle of minor arc AB is 40°,which is $\frac{1}{9}$ of the whole circle's 360°. The length of minor arc AB, therefore, is $\frac{1}{9}$ of the whole circle's circumference.

$$C = 2\pi r = 2\pi(9) = 18\pi$$

$$\frac{1}{9}C = \frac{1}{9}(18\pi) = 2\pi$$

The answer is B. (*100 Key Math Concepts for the ACT, #90*)

10. The shaded region is equal to the area of the square minus the area of the semicircle. The area of the square is $10 \times 10 = 100$. The radius of the circle is half of 10, or 5, so the area of the whole circle is $\pi(5)^2 = 25\pi$, and the area of the semicircle is $\frac{25\pi}{2}$. The square minus the semicircle, then, is:

$100 - \frac{25\pi}{2}$. The answer is H. (*100 Key Math Concepts for the ACT, #87, #91*)

TACKLING MORE COMPLEX GEOMETRY QUESTIONS

ACT geometry questions are not all straightforward. The test writers have ways of further complicating them. It's not always obvious at first what the question is getting at. Sometimes you really have to think about the figure and the given information before that light bulb goes on in your head. Often the inspiration that brings illumination is finding the hidden information.

Example

1. In the figure below, ΔABC is a right triangle and $\overline{AC}$ is perpendicular to $\overline{BD}$. If $\overline{AB}$ is 6 units long, and $\overline{AC}$ is 10 units long, how many units long is $\overline{AD}$?

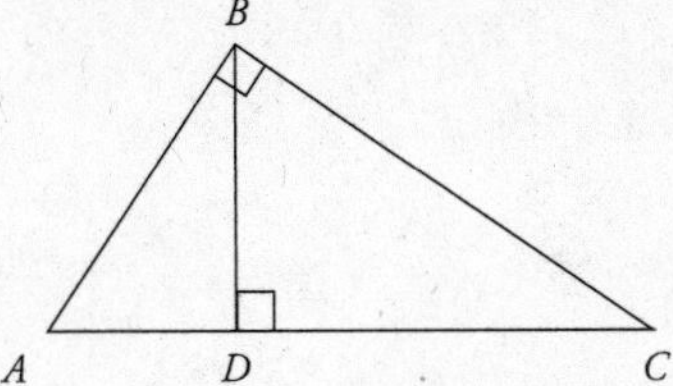

A. 3
B. $2\sqrt{3}$
C. 3.6
D. 4
E. $3\sqrt{2}$

At first this looks like a Pythagorean theorem question. In fact, the two given sides of ΔABC identify it as the 6-8-10 version of the 3-4-5 special right triangle. (*100 Key Math Concepts for the ACT, #85*) So we know that $BC = 8$. So what? How's that going to help us find *AD*?

The inspiration here is to realize that this is a "similar triangles" problem. We don't see the word *similar* anywhere in the question stem, but the stem and the figure combined actually tell us that all three triangles in the figure—ΔABC, ΔADB, and ΔBDC—are similar. We know the triangles are similar because they all have the same three angles. Here are the three triangles separated and oriented to show the correspondences:

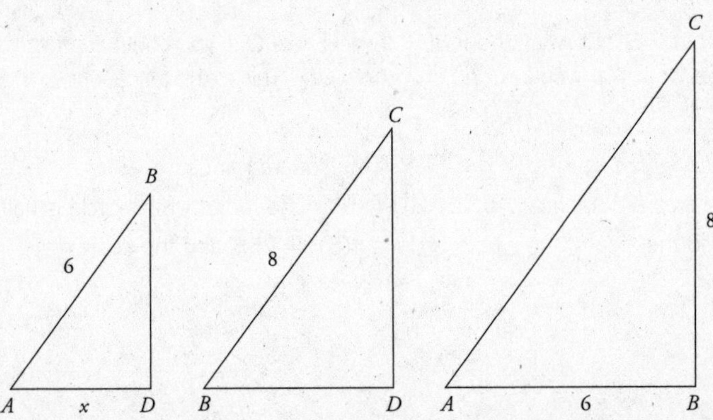

In this orientation it's easy to see the proportion setup that will solve the problem:

$$\frac{10}{6} = \frac{6}{x}$$
$$10x = 36$$
$$x = 3.6$$

The answer is C.

Example

2. In the figure below, the area of the circle centered at O is 25π, and $\overline{AC}$ is perpendicular to $\overline{OB}$. If $\overline{AC}$ is 8 units long, how many units long is $\overline{BD}$?

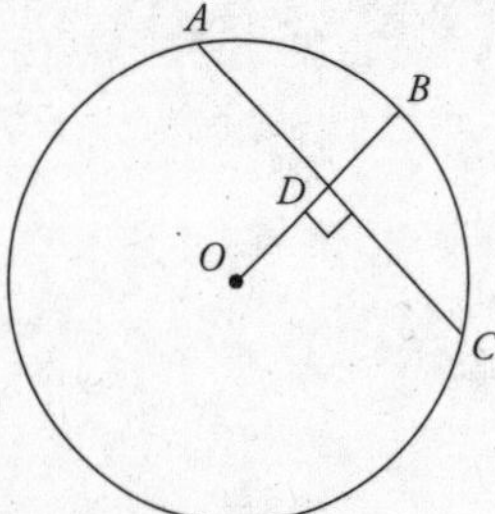

F. 2
G. 2.5
H. 3
J. 3.125
K. 4

This is a tough one. It's not easy to see how to get $\overline{BD}$ from the given information. You can use the area—25π—to figure out the radius, and then you'd know the length of $\overline{OB}$:

$$\text{Area} = \pi r^2$$
$$25\pi = \pi r^2$$
$$25 = r^2$$
$$r = 5$$

So you know $\overline{OB} = 5$, but what about $\overline{BD}$? If you knew $\overline{OD}$, you could subtract that from $\overline{OB}$ to get what you want. But do you know $\overline{OD}$? This is the place where most people get stuck.

The inspiration that will lead to a solution is that you can take advantage of the right angle at *D*. Look what happens when you take a pencil and physically add $\overline{OA}$ and $\overline{OC}$ to the figure:

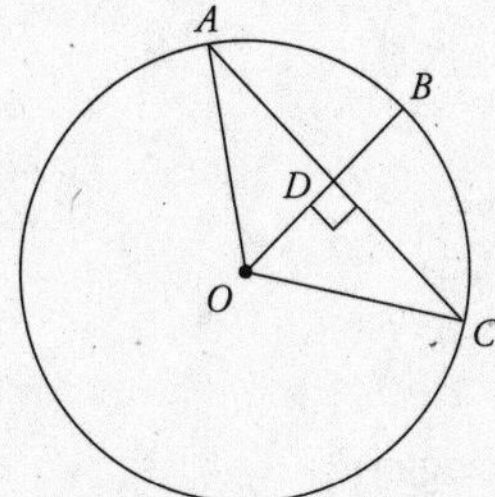

ΔOAD and ΔOCD are right triangles. And when we write in the lengths, we discover some special right triangles:

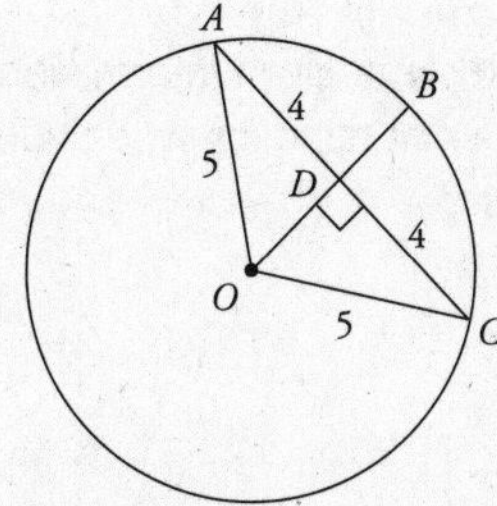

Now it's apparent that $OD = 3$. Since $OB = 5$, BD is $5 - 3 = 2$. The answer is F.

Figureless Problems

Some ACT geometry problems present an extra challenge because they don't provide a figure. You have to "figure it out" for yourself. Try this one:

Example

3. If one side of a right triangle is 3 units long, and a second side is 4 units long, which of the following could be the length, in units, of the third side?

A. 1
B. 2
C. $\sqrt{7}$
D. $3\sqrt{2}$
E. $3\sqrt{3}$

The key to solving most figureless problems is to sketch a diagram, but sometimes that's not so easy because the test makers deliberately give you less information than you might like. Question 3 is the perfect example. It gives you two sides of a right triangle and asks for the third. Sounds familiar. And the two sides it gives you—3 and 4—*really* sound familiar. It's a 3-4-5, right?

5
3
4

So the answer's 5 . . .

Whoops! There's no 5 among the answer choices! What's going on?!

Better check back. Notice that the question asks, "Which of the following *could* be the length . . ." That *could* is crucial. It suggests that there's more than one possibility. Our answer of 5 was too obvious. There's another one somewhere.

Can you think of another way of sketching the figure with the same given information? Who says that the 3 and 4 have to be the two legs? Look at what happens when you make one of them—the larger one, of course—the *hypotenuse*:

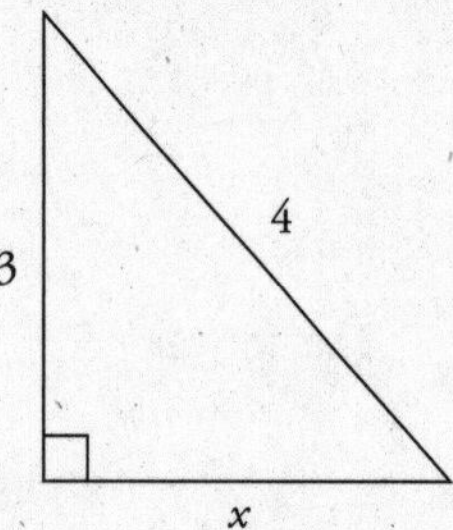

This is not a 3-4-5 triangle, because in a 3-4-5, the 3 and the 4 are the legs. This is no special right triangle; to figure out the length of the third side, resort to the Pythagorean theorem:

$$
\begin{aligned}
(\text{leg}_1)^2 + (\text{leg}_2)^2 &= (\text{hypotenuse})^2 \\
3^2 + x^2 &= 4^2 \\
9 + x^2 &= 16 \\
x^2 &= 7 \\
x &= \sqrt{7}
\end{aligned}
$$

The answer is C.

Many Steps and Many Concepts

Some of the toughest ACT geometry questions are ones that take many steps to solve and combine many different geometry concepts. The following is an example.

Example

4. In the figure below, $\overline{AB}$ is tangent to the circle at A. If the circumference of the circle is 12π units and $\overline{OB}$ is 12 units long, what is the area, in square units, of the shaded region?

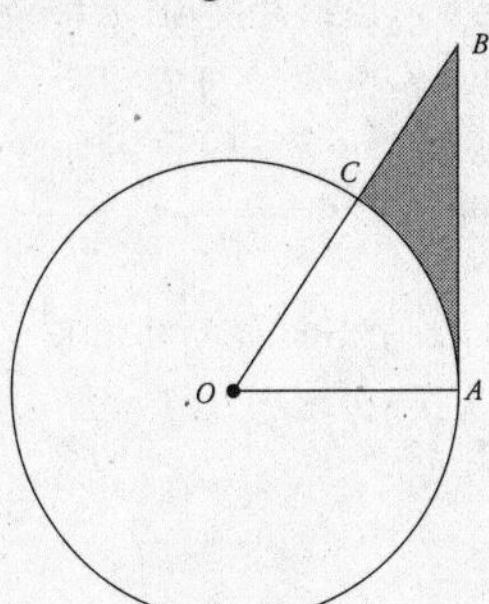

F. $18\sqrt{3} - 6\pi$
G. $24\sqrt{3} - 6\pi$
H. $18\sqrt{3} - 2\pi$
J. $12\pi - 12$
K. $243 - 2\pi$

This is about as hard as they come on the ACT. It is by no means clear how the given information—the circumference of the circle and the length of $\overline{OB}$—will lead you to the area of the shaded region.

So what do you do? Give up? No. *Don't* give up immediately unless you're really short on time or you know for sure you can't do the problem.

So then should you just plow ahead blindly and figure out every length, angle, and area you can and see where that leads you? *Well, not exactly*. It would be better to be more systematic.

The key to success with a circuitous problem like this is to focus on your destination—what you're looking for—and think about what you need to get there. Then go back to the given information and see what you can do to get you going in the right direction. Think about where you're headed before you take even one step; otherwise you may just have to backtrack.

Your destination in question 4 is "the area of the shaded region." That region is a shape that has no name, let alone an area formula. Like most shaded regions, this one is in fact the difference between two familiar shapes with names and area formulas. Think of the shaded region in question 4 as:

(the area of ΔAOB) – (the area of sector AOC)

So now, you know you need to figure out the area of the triangle and the area of the sector.

First, the triangle. You are explicitly given $\overline{OB} = 12$. You are also given that $\overline{AB}$ is tangent to the circle at A, which tells you that $\overline{OA}$ is a radius and that $\angle OAB$ is a right angle. So if you can figure out the radius of the circle, you'll have two sides of a right triangle, which will enable you to figure out the third side, and then figure out the area.

You can get the radius from the given circumference. Plug what you know into the formula and solve for r:

$$\text{Circumference} = 2\pi r$$
$$12\pi = 2\pi r$$
$$r = \frac{12\pi}{2\pi} = 6$$
$$OA = 6$$

Trigonometry

It's always obvious when you've come to the trigonometry questions, as they are among the most straightforward and predictable math questions on the ACT. "SOHCAHTOA" alone is usually enough to get you two right answers. If you can master 100 Key Math Concepts for the ACT, #96–100, you can get all four. But if you never "got" trigonometry, SKIP THE TRIG QUESTIONS. In other words, do the ones you understand; guess on the ones you don't.

Aha! So it turns out that ΔAOB is no ordinary right triangle. Since one leg—6—is exactly half the hypotenuse—12—you're looking at a 30°-60°-90° triangle. By applying the well-known side ratios ($1{:}\sqrt{3}{:}2$) for a 30°-60°-90° triangle (*100 Key Math Concepts for the ACT, #85*), you determine that $AB = 6\sqrt{3}$. Now plug the lengths of the legs in for the base and altitude in the formula for the area of a triangle, and you'll get:

$$\text{Area} = \frac{1}{2}bh$$
$$= \frac{1}{2}(6\sqrt{3})(6)$$
$$= 18\sqrt{3}$$

Already it looks like the answer is going to be F or H—they're the choices that begin with $18\sqrt{3}$. You could just guess F or H and move on, but if you've come this far, you might as well go all the way.

Next, you need to determine the area of the sector. Fortunately, while working on the triangle, you figured out the two things you need to get the area of the sector: the radius of the circle (6) and the measure of the central angle (60°). The radius tells you that the area of the whole circle (πr^2) is 36π. And the central angle tells you that the sector is $\frac{60}{360}$ or $\frac{1}{6}$ of the circle. One sixth of 36π is 6π. So the area of the shaded region is $18\sqrt{3} - 6\pi$, choice F.

Chapter Fourteen: **Reading Workout 3: Arts and Sciences**

- **The Prose Fiction Passage**
- **The Natural Sciences Passage**
- **Emergency Strategy for Test Day**

Now that you've learned the general approach to ACT Reading and the approach for each of the specific question-types, let's look more closely at the two passage types that give students the most trouble—the *Prose Fiction* passage and the *Natural Sciences* passage.

The passage breakdown for the ACT Reading test is as follows:

Prose Fiction—one passage per test.

Nonfiction—three passages per test, one each in:

- Social Studies
- Natural Sciences
- Humanities

Your approach will be essentially the same for all three nonfiction passages, since they're all well-organized essays. Your approach to the Prose Fiction passage, however, will be somewhat different.

What follows are two full ACT Reading passages—one Prose Fiction passage and one Natural Sciences passage (which, for convenience, we'll call just Science)—complete with questions. We'll talk about specific strategies for each, but, just as important, we'll talk about how you can bring together everything you've learned so far and combine this knowledge into a plan of attack for *all* Reading passages. At the end of the Workout, we'll also show you how to salvage a few extra points if you find yourself near the end of the test with not enough time to read the final passage.

THE PROSE FICTION PASSAGE

The Prose Fiction passage differs from the three nonfiction passages in that it is not a well-structured essay designed to communicate ideas in a logical, orderly way. It is, usually, a story in which characters fully equipped with their own motivations and emotions interact with each other in revealing ways. For that reason, the Prose Fiction passage won't break down into an orderly outline or road map, so don't even try to characterize the function of each paragraph. Pay attention instead to the *story*.

In the Prose Fiction passage, almost all of the questions relate to the characters. Your job is to find the answers to the following questions:

- **Who are these people?** What are they like? How are they related to each other?
- **What is their state of mind?** Are they angry? Sad? Reflective? Excited?
- **What's going on?** What's happening on the surface? What's happening beneath the surface?

What a Character!

In the Prose Fiction passage, you want to focus on the characters. Who are they? What are they like? The author won't usually tell you outright. You have to figure it out for yourself, judging from what they say and do.

Most of the passages focus on one person, or are written from the point of view of one of the characters. Figure out who this main character is and pay special attention to what he or she is like. Read between the lines to determine unspoken emotions and attitudes. Little hints—a momentary frown, a pointed or sarcastic comment—are sometimes all you have to go on, so *pay attention*. In fact, you'll probably want to spend more time prereading the Prose Fiction passage than you do any of the other three passages. It's important to get a good feel for the tone and style of the passage as a whole before going to the questions.

Fortunately, the questions that accompany these passages tend to go more quickly than those for the other passages, so you'll be able to make up some of that time you lose reading the passage.

Make It a Movie in Your Head

Try to make the passage into a movie! Imagine the scenes, the characters, the events. In the Prose Fiction passage, it should be easy to imagine the story unfolding like a movie. Pay careful attention not only to what the characters say but how they say it as well.

And don't forget to read actively, as always. Don't just read and then react. Once you have an idea of the personality of the characters, you should be able to anticipate how they will react to the events of the passage.

The Real Thing: Practice Passage

What follows is a typical ACT Prose Fiction passage, complete with questions. Before trying it, you might want to glance back at the techniques discussed in our first Reading Workout. Review the Kaplan Reading Method. Recall that you should probably plan to spend about three minutes prereading (a little more, actually, since this is the Prose Fiction passage). Then do whichever questions you can figure out quickly. Skip any hard or time-consuming problems and come back for them later.

When you work on the questions, constantly refer to the passage. Plan to spend much more time with your eyeballs pointed at the passage than at the questions. And don't forget to answer the questions in your own words (based on what you've preread and reread in the passage) before you look at the answers.

What's Past Is Past

Once you've finished reading a passage and its questions, put it out of your mind. There's no connection at all between passages, so don't carry your stress or doubt to the next one. Approach each passage as if it were the only one. Stay active and confident!

Passage III

I recall a mist starting in as I crossed the lawn that afternoon. I was making my way up to the summer house for the purpose of clearing away the remains of his lordship's taking tea there with some guest a little while earlier. I can recall spotting from some distance .... Miss Kenton's figure moving about inside the summerhouse. When I entered she had seated herself on one of the wicker chairs scattered around its interior, evidently engaged in some needlework. On closer inspection, I saw she was performing repairs to a cushion. I went about gathering up the various items of crockery from amidst the plants and the cane furniture, and as I did so, I believe we exchanged a few pleasantries, perhaps discussed one or two professional matters. For the truth was, it was extremely refreshing to be out in the summerhouse after many continuous days in the main building and neither of us was inclined to hurry with our tasks .... In fact, I was looking out over the lawn to where the mist was thickening down around the poplar trees planted along the cart-track, when I finally introduced the topic of the previous year's dismissals. Perhaps a little predictably, I did so by saying:

"I was just thinking earlier, Miss Kenton. It's rather funny to remember now, but you know, only this time a year ago, you were still insisting you were going to resign. It rather amused me to think of it." When I finally turned to look at her, she was gazing through the glass at the great expanse of fog outside.

"You probably have no idea, Mr. Stevens," she said eventually, "how seriously I really thought of leaving this house. I felt so strongly about what happened. Had I been anyone worthy of any respect at all, I dare say I would have left Darlington Hall long ago." She paused for a while, and I turned my gaze back out to the poplar trees down in the distance. Then she continued in a tired voice: "It was cowardice, Mr. Stevens. Simple cowardice. Where could I have gone? I have no family. Only my aunt. I love her dearly, but I can't live with her for a day without feeling my whole life is wasting away. I did tell myself, of course, I would soon find some situation.

"But I was so frightened, Mr. Stevens. Whenever I thought of leaving, I just saw myself going out there and finding nobody who knew or cared about me. There, that's all my high principles amount to. I feel so ashamed of myself. But I just couldn't leave, Mr. Stevens. I just couldn't bring myself to leave."

Miss Kenton paused again and seemed to be deep in thought. I thus thought it opportune to relate at this point, as precisely as possible, what had taken place earlier between myself and Lord Darlington. I proceeded to do so and concluded by saying:

"What's done can hardly be undone. But it is at least a great comfort to hear his lordship declare so unequivocally that it was all a terrible misunderstanding. I just thought you'd like to know, Miss Kenton, since I recall you were as distressed by the episode as I was."

"I'm sorry, Mr. Stevens," Miss Kenton said behind me in an entirely new voice, as though she had just been jolted from a dream, "I don't understand you." Then as I turned to her, she went on: "As I recall, you thought it was only right and proper that Ruth and Sarah be sent packing. You were positively cheerful about it."

"Now really, Miss Kenton, that is quite incorrect and unfair. The whole matter caused me great concern, great concern indeed. It is hardly the sort of thing I like to see happen in this house."

"Then why, Mr. Stevens, did you not tell me so at the time?"

I gave a laugh, but for a moment was rather at a loss for an answer. Before I could formulate one, Miss Kenton put down her sewing and said:

"Do you realize, Mr. Stevens, how much it would have meant to me if you had thought to share your feelings last year? You knew how upset I was when my girls were dismissed. Do you realize how much it would have helped me? Why, Mr. Stevens, why, why, why do you always have to pretend?"

I gave another laugh at the ridiculous turn the conversation had suddenly taken. "Really, Miss Kenton," I said, "I'm not sure I know what you mean. Pretend? Why, really . . . ."

"I suffered so much over Ruth and Sarah leaving us. And I suffered all the more because I believed I suffered alone."

1. Based on the details in the passage, it can be inferred that Mr. Stevens and Miss Kenton are Lord Darlington's:

A. guests.
B. relatives.
C. acquaintances.
D. employees.

2. The statement "Had I been anyone worthy of any respect at all, I dare say I would have left Darlington Hall long ago" (lines 36–38) can be interpreted to mean:

F. No one at Darlington Hall truly respects Miss Kenton.
G. Miss Kenton has little respect for Mr. Stevens.
H. Miss Kenton feels she betrayed her principles by staying.
J. Miss Kenton senses that Mr. Stevens feels superior to her.

3. According to the passage, the intent of Mr. Stevens's recollection of Miss Kenton's desire to resign (lines 26–30) is most likely to:

A. open up a discussion of an event that had upset Miss Kenton.
B. turn the conversation to the professional topic of furniture repair.
C. indulge in nostalgic reminiscences of happier days.
D. irritate Miss Kenton by mocking the seriousness of that desire.

4. Mr. Stevens gives "a laugh" (line 79) because he is suddenly:

F. amused.
G. insecure.
H. suspicious.
J. sarcastic.

5. The main point of Miss Kenton's references to her own family (lines 42–45) is that:

A. she would have nowhere to turn if she left her job.
B. children often reject those they should love.
C. she was afraid of discovering that she did not love her aunt.
D. life becomes very tedious when one visits relatives.

6. What is it that Mr. Stevens describes as "done" (line 60)?

F. Lord Darlington's earlier conversation with him
G. Miss Kenton's talk of leaving Darlington Hall
H. Ruth and Sarah's dismissal
J. Any talk of Miss Kenton's dismissal

7. As he is revealed in the passage, Mr. Stevens is:

A. bored with their conversation in the summer house.
B. increasingly hostile to Miss Kenton's depiction of his actions.
C. uncomfortable with expressing his deep affection for Miss Kenton.
D. unaware of how his past behavior had affected Miss Kenton.

8. Which of the following would be out of character for the narrator?

I. Pointing out to Miss Kenton why she was unfairly characterizing his actions
II. Spending time thinking about Miss Kenton's accusations
III. Ridiculing Miss Kenton for poorly repairing the cushion

F. I only
G. II only
H. I and II only
J. III only

9. Miss Kenton interacts with Mr. Stevens in a way that can best be described as:

A. sincere but formal.
B. indifferent but polite.
C. timid but angry.
D. patronizing but kindly.

10. At the end of the passage, Miss Kenton asks "Why, Mr. Stevens, why, why, why do you always have to pretend?" (lines 86–88) What specific action of Mr. Stevens does she have in mind?

F. His apparent cheerfulness at Ruth and Sarah's dismissal
G. His simulation of great affection for her
H. His phony concern for her own future employment
J. His empty expressions of sympathy for her own suffering

Answers and Explanations

It should be clear now why trying to build a mental road map of the Prose Fiction passage is not such a good idea. Unlike the paragraphs in the nonfiction passages, those in the Prose Fiction passage tend not to be organized around a single topic. They just move the story forward. Instead of building a road map, then, your prereading step should have been spent finding answers to the important questions about character and action.

- **Who are these people?** The first paragraphs are peppered with hints about who these people are. Lines 3–4 discuss Mr. Stevens "clearing away the remains of his lordship's taking tea." Lines 11–12 describes Miss Kenton "performing repairs to a cushion." Lines 28–29 discusses her previous plans for resigning. Clearly, Mr. Stevens and Miss Kenton are servants (we later learn—in lines 57–58—that their employer is Lord Darlington). Notice how, by answering this basic question, you've already answered Question 1.
- **What is their state of mind?** We read of "the previous year's dismissals" (line 23–24) and Miss Kenton's intentions to leave the house (lines 34–36) as a result of them. She "felt so strongly about what happened" (lines 35–36) but she was afraid to take the step of actually leaving in protest ("It was cowardice," she admits in line 41). It sounds like some other servants were dismissed unfairly last year, and that this upset Miss Kenton. Apparently, Mr. Stevens also found the incident distressing (lines 64–65), but Miss Kenton hadn't realized this at the time.
- **What's going on?** These are obviously very formal people, but there are strong emotions rumbling beneath the surface. It's clear that Miss Kenton is very upset because she didn't realize that Mr. Stevens disapproved of the dismissals, too ("Do you realize, Mr. Stevens, how much it would have meant to me if you had thought to share your feelings last year?"—lines 82–84. And later: "Why, Mr. Stevens, why, why, why do you always have to *pretend*?"—lines 86–88). We get the impression that Mr. Stevens is not a man who very readily shows his feelings and emotions—as Miss Kenton puts it, he always *pretends*.

Notice how many inference-type questions there are. This is typical of the Prose Fiction passage, where so much information is conveyed implicitly—"between the lines." In most cases, you have to read around the specific line references in order to find your answer. If you've done your preread properly, however, you should be able to knock off most of the questions quickly.

Key to Passage III

(Prose Fiction)

	Answer	Refer To	Type	Comments
1.	D	First 2 paragraphs	Inference	Discussed above.
2.	H	Lines 36–38, 50–51	Inference	"There, that's all my high principles amount to," she says.

3.	A	Lines 26–30, 55–58	Inference	Lines 55–58 show that Mr. Stevens has just been discussing this subject with Lord Darlington, and now wants to discuss it with Miss Kenton.
4.	G	Lines 79–80	Inference	He is "at a loss for an answer," and clearly not laughing out of amusement.
5.	A	Lines 42–45	Detail	"Where could I have gone? I have no family."
6.	H	Lines 60–65	Detail	Refers to "the previous year's dismissals," first mentioned in lines 23–24.
7.	D	Throughout	Big Picture	Mr. Stevens' nervous laughs hint that he had no idea how deeply Miss Kenton was affected.
8.	J	Throughout	Inference	I—He does this in lines 73–76. II—He wishes to respond to the accusations in lines 70–72. III—This kind of blatant harshness would be uncharacteristic of so discreet and proper a man.
9.	A	Throughout	Big Picture	Miss Kenton freely expresses her feelings to him throughout, so she is sincere. But she never loses her formal language and demeanor.
10.	F	Lines 82–86, 66–72	Inference	She wishes that he "had thought to share [his] feelings;" she was under the impression that he was "positively cheerful about [the dismissals]."

THE NATURAL SCIENCES PASSAGE

The Science passage in the Reading subject test is often similar in appearance to a passage on the Science subject test. Illustrations, graphs, and tables of information may be included. Usually, though, the emphasis in Reading is more on understanding ideas than on analyzing experiments and data.

Approaching the Science passage is really not any different from approaching the other nonfiction passages, since all are well-organized essays that lay out ideas in a straightforward, logical way. But you may be more likely to find unfamiliar vocabulary in Science passages. *Don't panic*. Any unfamiliar terms will usually be defined in the passage, or else will have definitions inferable from context.

Don't Get Lost!

In the Science passage, it's easy to lose yourself in complex details. Don't do it. It's *especially* important not to get bogged down in the Science passage! Many students try to understand and remember everything as they read. But that's not the right ACT mindset. In your preread of the passage, just get the "gist" and the outline; don't sweat the details. As always, use line references in the questions when possible. They will lead you back to the details that are important. You'd be surprised how many questions you can answer on a passage you don't really understand.

Weak in Science?

Don't freak out if you find yourself in a fog as you read the Science passage. Keep your head, and quickly get to the questions. Focus on the detail questions with line references. You can score points on the Science passage, even if you don't completely understand it.

The Real Thing: Practice Passage

The next passage is a typical ACT-style Science passage with questions. Try to attack it with the same Kaplan Method you use for other passages. Don't worry if you don't understand everything. Your only goal is to get a sense of the passage and its outline.

Passage IV

Atoms can be excited in many ways other than by absorbing a photon. The element phosphorous spontaneously combines with oxygen when exposed to air. There is a transfer of energy to the phosphorous electrons during this chemical reaction which excites them to sufficiently high energy states that they can subsequently emit light when dropping into a lower state. This is an example of what is termed chemiluminescence, the emission of light as a result of chemical reaction.

A related effect is bioluminescence, when light is produced by chemical reactions associated with biological activity. Bioluminescence occurs in a variety of life forms and is more common in marine organisms than in terrestrial or freshwater life. Examples include certain bacteria, jellyfish, clams, fungi, worms, ants, and fireflies. There is considerable diversity in how light is produced. Most processes involve the reaction of a protein with oxygen, catalyzed by an enzyme. The protein varies from one organism to another, but all are grouped under the generic name luciferin. The enzymes are known as luciferase. Both words stem from the Latin lucifer meaning light-bearing. The various chemical steps leading to bioluminescence are yet to be explained in detail, but in some higher organisms the process is known to be activated by the nervous system.

The firefly is best understood. Its light organ is located near the end of the abdomen. Within it luciferin is combined with other atomic groups in a series of processes in which oxygen is converted into carbon dioxide. The sequence culminates when the luciferin is split off from the rest, leaving it in an excited state. The excess energy is released as a photon. The peak in the emission spectrum lies between 550 and 600 nm depending on the type of luciferase. This flash produced by the simultaneous emission of many photons serves to attract mates, and females also use it to attract males of other species, which they devour.

Certain bacteria also produce light when stimulated by motion. This is why the breaking sea or a passing boat generate the greenish light seen in some bodies of water such as Phosphorescent Bay in Puerto Rico. Some fish have a symbiotic relationship with bacteria. The "flashlight fish" takes advantage of the light created by bacteria lodged beneath each eye. Certain other fish produce their own bioluminescence, which serves as identification. However, the biological advantage if any of bioluminescence in some other organisms such as fungi remains a mystery.

Triboluminescence is the emission of light when one hard object is sharply struck against another. This contact, when atom scrapes against atom, excites electrons and disrupts electrical bonds. Light is then created when the electrons

find their way to lower states. Triboluminescence is not to be confused with the glow of small particles that may be broken off by the impact. Such "sparks" are seen as a result of their high temperature. Light given off by hot objects is known as thermoluminescence, or incandescence.

Another form of thermoluminescence is the basis for dating ancient ceramic objects. Quartz and other constituents of clay are continually irradiated by naturally occurring radioactive elements (e.g., uranium and thorium) and by cosmic rays. This produces defects in the material where electrons may be trapped. Heating pottery to 500°C releases the trapped electrons, which can then migrate back to their original atoms, where on returning to an atomic orbit they then emit a photon. The intensity of thermoluminescence is therefore a measure of the duration of irradiation since the time when the pottery had been previously fired.

Excitation is also possible by other means. The passage of an electrical current (electroluminescence) is one. The impact of high energy particles is another. The *aurora borealis* and its southern counterpart the *aurora australis* arise when a stream of high energy particles from the sun enters the earth's upper atmosphere and literally shatters some of the molecules of the air. This leaves their atoms in excited states, and the light subsequently given off is characteristic of the atoms. Although the oxygen molecule, a major constituent of our atmosphere, has no emission in the visible, the oxygen atom can emit photons in either the red or green portions of the spectrum. Other atoms contribute to light at other wavelengths.

11. According to the information in the sixth paragraph (lines 65–78), the brighter the thermoluminescence of a heated piece of ancient pottery:

A. the younger the piece is.
B. the older the piece is.
C. the less irradiation has occurred within the piece's clay.
D. the fewer electrons have become trapped within the clay.

12. If an ancient ceramic bowl is heated to 500°C, light is emitted when certain electrons:

F. release radioactive elements found in the clay.
G. scrape against other electrons.
H. become superheated.
J. return to their former atoms.

13. Compared to bioluminescence, chemiluminescence is NOT produced by:

A. organic proteins that have been catalyzed.
B. a chemical reaction.
C. any reaction involving oxygen.
D. a change in energy states.

14. It can be inferred from the passage that the description of the firefly's production of light is a good example of the degree to which researchers understand:

F. why light attracts fireflies.
G. how a chemical process can trigger bioluminescence.
H. how female fireflies attack male fireflies.
J. how to measure the intensity of a firefly's bioluminescence.

15. In both chemiluminescence and bioluminescence, photons are emitted:

A. as excess energy.
B. only by certain marine organisms.
C. only when luciferase is present.
D. only when phosphorous is present.

16. Based on details in the passage, the word *excited* as used in line 1 means:

F. split off from a molecule.
G. agitated until glowing.
H. raised to a higher energy level.
J. heated to the point of disintegration.

17. In discussing the creation of the two kinds of aurora, the passage asserts that the oxygen molecule "has no emission in the visible [spectrum]" (line 90–91) but also states that "the oxygen atom can emit photons in either the red or the green portions of the spectrum" (lines 91–92). Is the passage logically consistent?

A. Yes, because visible light is emitted after the oxygen molecules have been broken apart into oxygen atoms.
B. Yes, because the passage presents factual information and therefore cannot be illogical.
C. No, because the oxygen molecule forms the largest part of the atmosphere and scientific theories must account for its invisible emissions.
D. No, because the writer has failed to adequately differentiate between the oxygen molecule's behavior and that of the oxygen atom.

18. Assume that two meteors have collided and shattered. Astronomers see both a burst of light and then a subsequent glow. Such a visual phenomenon could best be explained as the result of:

I. chemiluminescence
II. triboluminescence
III. thermoluminescence

F. II only
G. II and III only
H. I and III only
J. I, II, and III

19. Based on information presented in the passage, which of the following is a hypothesis, rather than a fact?

A. Fireflies use bioluminescence to attract mates.
B. Thermoluminescence and triboluminescence are two distinctly different kinds of light emission.
C. A firefly's type of luciferase determines the peak of its light emission's intensity.
D. All organisms that produce bioluminescence do so for some biological advantage.

20. According to the last paragraph (lines 79–94), both the *aurora borealis* and the *aurora australis*:

F. demonstrate the effects on atoms of high energy particles.
G. occur without the presence of oxygen.
H. emit light due to the presence of electrical currents.
J. are visible from the surface of the earth.

Answers and Explanations

Feeling a little numb? Unless you're a real science buff, you probably found this passage a lot less exciting than the atoms did. And you may have found yourself adrift in a sea of bewildering terms—*chemiluminescence, luciferin, aurora australis*.

We hope, though, that you didn't panic. You could still get points—and lots of them—from this passage even if all that you took away from your preread was a sense that the passage was mainly about things in nature glowing when their atoms are excited. That, and a sense of a road map, was really all you needed. Most of the questions were answerable by referring to the appropriate lines in the passage and paraphrasing what you read there.

Here's a possible road map for the passage:

- First paragraph: Introduction of idea of excited atoms releasing photons (i.e., luminescence). Discusses *chemiluminescence* (resulting from a chemical reaction).
- Second paragraph: Discusses *bioluminescence* (associated with biological activity—that is, with things that are alive).
- Third paragraph: Example of *bioluminescence*—fireflies.
- Fourth paragraph: More examples of *bioluminescence*—sea life.
- Fifth paragraph: Discusses *triboluminescence* (things hitting each other) and *thermoluminescence* (hot objects).
- Sixth paragraph: Example of *thermoluminescence*—refired ceramic objects.
- Seventh paragraph: Concludes with discussion of *electroluminescence* (associated with electrical currents).

Basically, the author is giving us a rundown on the various kinds of luminescence in nature. When the questions ask about one kind or another, you simply refer to the appropriate paragraph and lines.

Below is a key to the answers for this passage. Notice how you could have gotten an answer to number 12, for instance, *even if you were totally confused*. If you found "500°" in the passage (line 71), the sentence more or less spelled out the answer for you, requiring a minimum of paraphrasing.

Key to Passage IV

(Nonfiction—Natural Sciences)

	Answer	Refer To	Type	Comments
11.	B	Lines 65–78	Inference	More time since last firing to trap more electrons, creating brighter glow.
12.	J	Line 73	Detail	"migrate back to their original atoms"
13.	A	Paragraph 2	Detail	Be careful with the reversal word NOT in the question. Organic means "having to do with life."
14.	G	Lines 19–28, 29–41	Inference	Remember, passage is about luminescence, not fireflies.
15.	A	Lines 4–10, 38–40	Inference	B and C aren't chemi-; D isn't bio-. Only A is both.
16.	H	Line 2–10, 56–66	Detail	Lines 4–8 say it all.
17.	A	Lines 79–104	Big Picture	Note difference between oxygen molecule and oxygen atom.
18.	G	Lines 54–64	Inference	I—No, since no chemical reaction II—Yes, since impact reaction III—Yes, since "subsequent glow" (probably a heat reaction)
19.	D	Throughout	Big Picture	Any statement about "all organisms" is probably a hypothesis, since no one can verify what's true of every organism in existence.
20.	F	Lines 79–94	Detail	"a stream of high energy particles from the sun."

EMERGENCY STRATEGY FOR TEST DAY

If you're nearly out of time and you've still got an entire passage untouched, you need to shift to last-minute strategies. Don't try to preread the passage; you'll just run out of time before you answer any questions. Instead, scan the questions without reading the passage and look first for the ones that mention line numbers or specific paragraphs. You can often get quick points on these questions by referring back to the passage as the question stem directs, reading a few lines around the reference, and taking your best shot.

Of course, the most important thing is to make sure you have gridded in at least a random guess on every question. If some of your blind guesses are right (as some of them statistically *should* be), they'll boost your score just as much as well-reasoned, thought-out answers would!

Chapter Fifteen: **Science Workout 3: Keep Your Viewpoints Straight**

- **Prereading the Conflicting Viewpoints Passage**
- **The Real Thing: Practice Passage**
- **The Deep End: Facing Tough Science Passages**

On the Science test you'll find one "Conflicting Viewpoints" passage, in which two scientists propose different theories about a particular scientific phenomenon. Often, the two theories are just differing interpretations of the same data; other times, each scientist offers his own data to support his own opinion. In either case, it's essential that you know more or less what theory each scientist is proposing, and that you pay careful attention to how and where their theories differ.

In Science Workout 2, we talked about how scientists think, and you should bring all of that information to bear on the Conflicting Viewpoints passage. Since the scientists are disagreeing on interpretation, it's usually the case that they're engaging in specific-to-general thinking. They're each using specific data, sometimes the *same* specific data, but they're coming to very different general conclusions.

Your job is *not* to figure out which scientist is right and which is wrong. Instead, you'll be tested on whether you *understand* each scientist's position and the thinking behind it.

Points and Viewpoints

You may find yourself understanding one scientist's viewpoint but not the other's. Don't let that upset you. Many of the questions will involve just one scientist's theory, so you can still do well on those questions.

PREREADING THE CONFLICTING VIEWPOINTS PASSAGE

When tackling the Conflicting Viewpoints passage, you'll probably want to spend a little more time than usual on the prereading step of the Kaplan Reading Method. As we saw on other Science passages, your goal in prereading is to get a general idea of what's going on so that you can focus when you do the questions. But we find that it pays to spend a little extra time with the Conflicting Viewpoints passage in order to get a clearer idea of the opposing theories and the data behind them.

The passage will usually consist of a short introduction laying out the scientific issue in question, followed by the different viewpoints. Sometimes these viewpoints are presented under the headings Scientist 1 and Scientist 2, or Theory 1 and Theory 2, or Hypothesis 1 and Hypothesis 2.

A scientific viewpoint on the ACT will typically consist of two parts:

- A statement of the general theory
- A summary of the data behind the theory

Remember

The Kaplan Method:

1. Preread the passage
2. Consider the question stem
3. Refer to the passage (before looking at the choices)
4. Answer the question in your own words
5. Match your answer with one of the choices

Usually, the first line of each viewpoint expresses the general theory. Scientist 1's first sentence might be something like: *The universe will continue to expand indefinitely.* This is Scientist 1's viewpoint boiled down to a single statement. Scientist 2's first sentence might be: *The force of gravity will eventually force the universe to stop expanding and to begin contracting.* This is Scientist 2's viewpoint, and it clearly contradicts Scientist 1's opinion.

While it's important that you understand these basic statements of theory, it is just as important that you see how they oppose each other. In fact, you might want to circle the theory statement for each viewpoint, right there in the test booklet, to fix the two positions in your mind.

After each statement of theory will come the data that's behind it. As we said, sometimes the scientists are just drawing different interpretations from the same data. But usually, each will have different supporting data. There are two different kinds of data:

- Data that support the scientist's own theory
- Data that weaken the opposing scientist's theory

Keep Your Theories Straight

In the heat of the moment, it's easy to confuse the two opposing theories. Always double check to make sure you haven't assigned the ideas of Scientist 1 to Scientist 2, and vice versa.

It's normally a good idea to identify the major points of data for each theory. You might underline a phrase or sentence that crystallizes each, or even take note of whether it primarily supports the scientist's own theory or shoots holes in the opposing theory.

Once you understand each scientist's theory and the data behind it, you'll be ready to move on to the questions. Remember that some of the questions will refer to only one of the viewpoints. Whatever you do, *don't mix up the two viewpoints*! A question asking about the data supporting Theory 2 may have wrong answers that perfectly describe the data for Theory 1. If you're careless, you can easily fall for one of these wrong answers.

THE REAL THING: PRACTICE PASSAGE

What follows is a full-fledged, ACT-style Conflicting Viewpoints passage. Give yourself six minutes or so to do the passage and all seven questions.

Passage V

Tektites are natural, glassy objects that range in size from the diameter of a grain of sand to that of a human fist. They are found in only a few well-defined areas, called strewn fields. Two theories about the origin of tektites are presented below.

Scientist 1

Tektites almost certainly are extraterrestrial, probably lunar, in origin. Their forms show the characteristics of air-friction melting. In one study, flanged, "flying saucer" shapes similar to those of australites (a common tektite form) were produced by ablating lenses of tektite glass in a heated airstream that simulated atmospheric entry.

Atmospheric forces also make terrestrial origin extremely improbable. Aerodynamic studies have shown that because of atmospheric density, tektite-like material ejected from the earth's surface would never attain a velocity much higher than that of the surrounding air, and therefore would not be shaped by atmospheric friction. Most likely, tektites were formed either from meteorites or from lunar material ejected in volcanic eruptions.

Analysis of specimen #14425 from the *Apollo 12* lunar mission shows that the sample strongly resembles some of the tektites from the Australasian strewn field. Also, tektites contain only a small fraction of the water that is locked into the structure of terrestrial volcanic glass. And tektites never contain unmelted crystalline material; the otherwise similar terrestrial glass produced by some meteorite impacts always does.

Don't Give Up

Many students are intimidated by Science problems and they often skip them. Take your time and figure out what you can, even if you're not sure how it may lead to the correct answer. You'll be surprised at how far you get.

Scientist 2

Nonlocal origin is extremely unlikely, given the narrow distribution of tektite strewn fields. Even if a tightly focused jet of lunar matter were to strike the earth, whatever was deflected by the atmosphere would remain in a solar orbit. The next time its orbit coincided with that of the earth, some of the matter would be captured by earth's gravity and fall over a wide area.

There are striking similarities not only between the composition of the earth's crust and that of most tektites but between the proportions of various gases found in the earth's atmosphere and in the vesicles of certain tektites.

Tektites were probably formed by meteorite impacts. The shock wave produced by a major collision could temporarily displace the atmosphere above. Terrestrial material might then splatter to suborbital heights and undergo air-friction melting upon reentry. And tektite fields in the Ivory Coast and Ghana can be correlated with known impact craters.

1. The discovery that many tektites contain unmelted, crystalline material would:

   A. tend to weaken Scientist 1's argument.
   B. tend to weaken Scientist 2's argument.
   C. be incompatible with both scientists' views.
   D. be irrelevant to the controversy.

2. Which of the following is a reason given by Scientist 2 for believing that tektites originate on the earth?

   F. The density of the earth's atmosphere would prevent any similar lunar or extraterrestrial material from reaching the earth's surface.
   G. Tektites have a composition totally unlike that of any material ever brought back from the Moon.
   H. Extraterrestrial material could not have been as widely dispersed as tektites are.
   J. Material ejected from the Moon or beyond would eventually have been much more widely distributed on Earth.

3. Scientist 1 could best answer the point that some tektites have vesicles filled with gases in the same proportion as the earth's atmosphere by:

   A. countering that not all tektites have such gas-filled vesicles.
   B. demonstrating that molten material would be likely to trap some gases while falling through the terrestrial atmosphere.
   C. suggesting that those gases might occur in the same proportions in the Moon's atmosphere.
   D. showing that similar vesicles, filled with these gases in the same proportions, are also found in some terrestrial volcanic glass.

4. How did Scientist 2 answer the argument that tektitelike material ejected from the earth could not reach a high enough velocity relative to the atmosphere to undergo air-friction melting?

   F. By asserting that a shock wave might cause a momentary change in atmosphere density, permitting subsequent aerodynamic heating
   G. By pointing out that periodic meteorite impacts have caused gradual changes in atmospheric density over the eons
   H. By attacking the validity of the aerodynamic studies cited by Scientist 1
   J. By referring to the correlation between tektite fields and known impact craters in the Ivory Coast and Ghana

5. The point of subjecting lenses of tektite glass to a heated airstream was to:

   A. determine their water content.
   B. see if gases became trapped in their vesicles.
   C. reproduce the effects of atmospheric entry.
   D. simulate the mechanism of meteorite formation.

6. Researchers could best counter the objections of Scientist 2 to Scientist 1's argument by:

   F. discovering some phenomenon that would quickly remove tektite-sized objects from orbit.
   G. proving that most common tektite shapes can be produced by aerodynamic heating.
   H. confirming that active volcanoes once existed on the moon.
   J. mapping the locations of all known tektite fields and impact craters.

7. Which of the following characteristics of tektites is LEAST consistent with the theory that tektites are of extraterrestrial origin?

   A. Low water content
   B. "Flying saucer" shapes
   C. Narrow distribution
   D. Absence of unmelted material

Answers and Explanations

Your preread of the introduction should have revealed the issue at hand—namely, tektites, which are small glassy objects found in certain areas known as strewn fields. The conflict is about the *origin* of these objects: In other words, where did they come from?

Answers

1. A, 2. J, 3. B, 4. F, 5. C, 6. F, 7. C

Scientist 1's theory is expressed in his first sentence: "Tektites almost certainly are extraterrestrial, probably lunar, in origin." Put that into a form you can understand: In other words, Scientist 1 believes that tektites come from space, probably the moon. Scientist 2, on the other hand, has an opposing theory, also expressed in her first sentence: "Nonlocal origin is extremely unlikely." In other words, it's unlikely that tektites came from a nonlocal source; instead, they probably came from a *local* source, i.e., right here on Earth. The conflict is clear. One says that tektites come from space; the other says they come from Earth. You might have even labeled the two positions: "space origin" and "Earth origin."

But how do these scientists support their theories? Scientist 1 presents three points of data:

1. Tektite shapes show characteristics of "air-friction melting" (supporting the theory of space origin).
2. "Atmospheric forces" wouldn't be great enough to shape tektitelike material ejected from Earth's surface (weakening the theory of Earth origin).
3. Tektites resemble moon rocks gathered by *Apollo 12* but not Earth rocks (strengthening the theory of space origin).

Scientist 2 also presents three points of data:

1. Any matter coming from space would "fall over a wide area" instead of being concentrated in strewn fields (weakening the theory of space origin).
2. There are "striking similarities" between tektites and the composition of the earth's crust (strengthening the theory of Earth origin).
3. "Meteorite impacts" could create shock waves, explaining how terrestrial material could undergo air-friction melting (strengthening the theory of Earth origin by counteracting Scientist 1's first point).

Obviously, you wouldn't want to write out the supporting data for each theory the way we've done above. But it probably would be a good idea to underline the key phrases in the data descriptions ("air-friction melting," "*Apollo 12*," etcetera) and number them. What's important is that you have an idea of what data supports which theory. The questions, once you get to them, will then force you to focus.

Question 1 asks how it would affect the scientists' arguments if it were discovered that many tektites contain unmelted crystalline material. Well, Scientist 1 says that tektites never contain unmelted crystalline material, and that the terrestrial glass produced by some meteorite impacts *always* does. Therefore, by showing a resemblance between tektites and Earth materials, this discovery would weaken Scientist 1's argument for extraterrestrial origin. Choice A is correct.

For **Question 2**, you had to identify which answer choice was used by Scientist 2 to support the argument that tektites are terrestrial in origin. You should have been immediately drawn to choice J, which expresses what we've identified above as Scientist 2's first data point. Notice how choice F is a piece of evidence that Scientist 1 cites. (Remember not to confuse the viewpoints!) As for G, Scientist 2 says that tektites *do* resemble earth materials, but never says that they *don't* resemble lunar materials. And choice H gets it backwards; Scientist 2 says that extraterrestrial material *would* be widely dispersed, and that the tektites are *not* widely dispersed, rather than vice versa.

For **Question 3**, you need to find the best way for Scientist 1 to counter the point that some tektites have vesicles filled with gases in the same proportion as the earth's atmosphere. First, make sure you understand the meaning of that point. The idea that these gases must have been trapped in the vesicles (little holes) while the rock was actually being formed is being used by Scientist 2 to suggest that tektites are of terrestrial origin. Scientist 1 *could* say that not all tektites have such gas-filled vesicles—Choice A—but that's not a great argument. If any reasonable number of them *do*, Scientist 1 would have to come up with an alternative explanation (Scientist 2 never claimed that *all* tektites contained these vesicles). But if, as B suggests, Scientist 1 could demonstrate that molten material would be likely to trap some terrestrial gases while falling through earth's atmosphere, this would explain how tektites might have come from beyond the earth and still contain vesicles filled with Earthlike gases. Choice C is easy to eliminate if you know that the moon's atmosphere is extremely thin and totally different in composition from the Earth's atmosphere, so it doesn't make much sense to suggest that those gases might occur in the same proportions as in the moon's atmosphere. Finally, since it's Scientist 2 who claims that tektites are terrestrial in origin, choice D, showing that similar gas-filled vesicles occur in some terrestrial volcanic glass, wouldn't help Scientist 1 at all.

In **Question 4**, you're asked how Scientist 2 answered the argument that tektitelike material ejected from the earth could not reach a high enough velocity to undergo air-friction melting. Well, that was Scientist 2's third data point. The shock wave produced by a major meteorite collision could momentarily displace the atmosphere right above the impact site (meaning the air moved out of the way for a brief time). So, when the splattered material reentered the atmosphere, it would undergo air-friction melting. That's basically what choice F says, so F is correct.

In **Question 5**, the concept of subjecting lenses of tektite glass to a heated airstream was mentioned toward the beginning of Scientist 1's argument. The point was to simulate the entry of extraterrestrial tektite material through Earth's atmosphere, and that's closest to choice C.

Know Your Evidence

As you can see, many questions on the Conflicting Viewpoints passage involve evidence: what evidence was presented, what evidence would hurt or help one scientist's views, what evidence was used for what purpose. It's important that you take note of the evidence (data) each scientist uses.

Question 6 shows again why it pays to keep each scientist's viewpoint straight. You can't counter the objections of Scientist 2 to Scientist 1's argument unless you know what Scientist 2 was objecting to. Scientist 2's first data point is the only one designed to shoot holes in the opposing viewpoint. There, Scientist 2 takes issue with the idea that lunar material could strike the earth without being dispersed over a far wider area than the known strewn fields. But if, as correct choice F says, researchers found some force capable of removing tektite-sized objects from orbit *quickly*, it would demolish the objection that Scientist 2 raises in her first paragraph. The tektite material would strike the earth or be pulled away quickly, instead of remaining in a solar orbit long enough to be captured by the earth's gravity and subsequently be distributed over a wide area of the earth.

Question 7 wasn't too tough if you read the question stem carefully. You want to find the tektite characteristic that is LEAST consistent with the theory that tektites came from the moon or beyond. This is Scientist 1's theory, so you want to pick the answer choice that doesn't go with his argument. Scientist 1's evidence *does* include tektites' low water content, "flying saucer" shapes, and absence of unmelted material. The only answer choice that she didn't mention was the narrow distribution of the strewn fields. And with good reason. That's part of Scientist 2's argument *against* an extraterrestrial origin. So the correct answer is choice C.

THE DEEP END: FACING TOUGH SCIENCE PASSAGES

Now we're going to do something very cruel. We're going to to throw you a Science passage of such technical difficulty that you will want to go screaming for the exit before you finish reading it.

We're doing this for a reason. Sometimes on the ACT Science test, you'll find yourself encountering a bear of a passage—one that seems entirely incomprehensible. The secret to success with these passages is: *Don't panic*. As we'll show you, you can get points on even the most difficult Science passage in the entire history of the ACT—as long as you keep your cool and approach it in a savvy, practical way. Here's the passage.

Passage VI

Neutrinos (n) are subatomic particles that travel at approximately the speed of light. They can penetrate most matter, because they are electrically neutral and effectively massless.

Generally accepted theory holds that the nuclear reactions that power the Sun create vast quantities of neutrinos as byproducts. Three proposed stages (PPI, PPII, and PPIII) of the most important solar reaction are shown in Figure 1, along with their neutrino-producing subpaths. Equations for the subpaths are shown in Table 1, as are the predicted neutrino energies and fluxes.

Figure 1

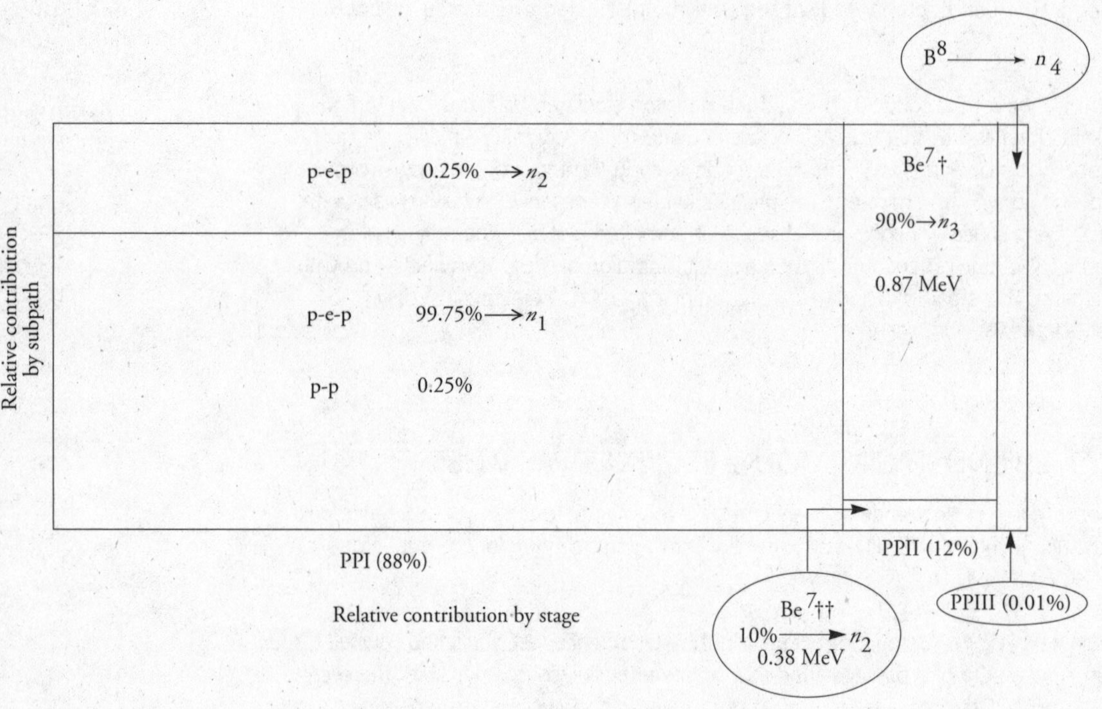

Table 1

Subpath name	Subpath equation	Neutrino energy (MeV)	Expected flux on Earth (10^{10}cm^{-2}sec^{-1})
p-p	${}_1H^1 + {}_1H^1 \longrightarrow {}_1H^2 + \beta^+ + n$	0.42	6.06781
p-e-p	${}_1H^1 + \beta^- + {}_1H^1 \longrightarrow {}_1H^2 + n$	1.44	0.01524
Be^7†	${}_4Be^7 + \beta^- \longrightarrow {}_3Li^7 + n$	0.87	0.43924
Be^7††	${}_4Be^7 + \beta^- \longrightarrow {}_3Li^7 + n$	0.38	0.04880
B^8	${}_5B^8 \longrightarrow {}_4Be^8 + \beta^+ + n$	14.05*	0.00054

†Be^7 subpath 1
††Be^7 subpath 2

*Maximum

8. According to the information presented in the passage, which of the following stages or subpaths should contribute the smallest portion of the total solar neutrino flux on Earth?

F. p-p
G. PPI
H. PPII
J. PPIII

9. Of the neutrinos that are produced in the subpaths described in the passage, which type can have the greatest energy?

A. n_1
B. n_2
C. n_3
D. n_4

10. Based on the information presented in the passage, the percentage of solar neutrinos produced by Be7 subpath 2 is approximately:

F. 1.2%
G. 10%
H. 12%
J. 90%

11. Solar neutrinos are detected through a reaction with $_{37}Cl$ for which the minimum neutrino energy is approximately 0.8 MeV. Of the neutrinos discussed in the passage, this method would detect:

A. all of the neutrinos produced in PPI and PPII.
B. some of the neutrinos produced in PPI, PPII, and PPIII.
C. only neutrinos produced in Be^7 subpath 1 of PPII.
D. only neutrinos produced in PPIII.

12. The symbol β represents a beta particle, a particle emitted during nuclear decay. Beta particles may be positively or negatively charged. During which of the following subpaths are beta particles emitted?

I. p-p
II. p-e-p
III. B^8

F. II only
G. I and III only
H. II and III only
J. I, II, and III

Answers and Explanations

Confused? If you aren't, you should stick close to your phone, because the Nobel Prize committee will probably be calling sometime soon! On the other hand, if you *are* confused, don't sweat it. As we said in ACT Basics, some ACT questions are so hard that even your *teachers* would have a hard time getting them correct.

Answers
8. J, 9. D, 10. F, 11. B, 12. G

The good news is that you don't have to understand a passage to get a few questions right. Here's how you might have approached the passage above.

Getting Points Even if You Don't Get the Point

Your preread of the introduction should have told you that the passage is about neutrinos coming from the sun. But that may be all you were able to get from this gibberish. You may have been in a total fog looking at Figure 1 and Table 1. But if you didn't panic, you might have noticed a few things: First, that whatever Figure 1 illustrates, there are some really big parts and some really small parts. If you look at the *x*-axis of the chart, you'll see that, whatever PPI, PPII, and PPIII are, the first is 88%, the second only 12%, and the third only .01%.

Is that tiny, vague insight enough to get a point? Yes! Look at **Question 8**. It asks which stage or subpath contributes the *smallest* portion of flux. Well, look for a small portion. PPIII's figure of 0.01% is a very small number, whatever it's supposed to be referring to, so PPIII would be a good guess here. And indeed, choice J is correct for Question 8.

What about Table 1? This is a little easier to understand, especially if you ignore the column about subpath equations. But "neutrino energy" sounds like something we can comprehend. Apparently, each subpath produces a different level of neutrino energy. Some have high energy (like B^8, with 14.06) and some have low energy (like B^7++, with only 0.38). Energy is mentioned in **Question 9**. Which type of neutrinos can have the greatest energy? Well, if B^8 were a choice, we'd pick that. But the choices are *n*'s, not B's. Well, try to find B^8 somewhere in the other chart—Figure 1. There we find it somehow associated with n_4 neutrinos. So take a gamble; choose n_4—which is choice D—for this question. If you did that, you'd still have gotten another point, still without really understanding much more than before.

You're hot; keep it going. **Question 10** refers to Be^7 subpath 2. You may have noticed in the note under Table 1 that the Be^7 with two little dagger marks signifies subpath 2. So far, so good. Notice that the choices are all percentages. Where are percentages mentioned? In Figure 1. So find Be^7 with two dagger marks in Figure 1. You find it in the area of PPII, which is 12 percent of the *x*-axis in that chart. But notice that Be^7 with two dagger marks represents only *part* of that part of the figure—10 percent, to be exact. So, 10 percent of 12 percent would be 1.2%. That's choice F. It's also the correct answer.

Things get a little harder with **Question 11**, but you still might have gotten the answer if you used common sense. Here we get some mumbo jumbo about $_{37}$Cl, but the part of the question that should have caught your eye was the bit about a minimum neutrino energy of 0.8 MeV. Neutrino energy was represented in the third column of Table 1. According to that table, only three subpaths have an energy greater than 0.8—p-e-p (with 1.44), Be^7 with one dagger mark (with 0.87), and B^8 (the champion, with 14.06). Unfortunately, the answer choices aren't expressed in those terms; they're expressed in terms of PPI, II, and III, so we're going to have to translate from table to figure again, just as we did with Question 9.

Take p-e-p first. That's part (but not all) of the PPI portion of Figure 1. Be^7 with one dagger mark, similarly, is part (but not all) of the PPII portion. And B8 is all of the PPIII portion. So there are at least parts of PPI, PPII, and PPIII implicated here. That should have led you to Choice B, which would have gotten you yet another point. Notice that choice A is inaccurate because it talks about *all* of something in PPI and PPII, and doesn't mention PPIII at all. Choices C and D, meanwhile, seem too limited, since they only mention one of the PP areas (whatever they are). So B was definitely the closest answer choice.

Finally, **Question 12** talks about beta particles. Well, that little beta symbol appears only in the subpath column of Table 1. There we find beta symbols in the equations for *all* of the subpaths in the table. That may have led you to believe that all three Roman numerals should be included, and no one would have blamed you for choosing choice J (I, II, and III). You would have been wrong, but you can't win them all when you're winging questions you don't really understand.

Of course, if you noticed that the question was asking for beta particles *emitted*, and if you knew that in the subpath equations everything *before* the arrow is what you start with while everything *after* the arrow is what you finish with, you might have been able to make a better guess. You would have realized that those equations with a beta symbol *before* the arrow were ones in which a beta particle was *absorbed*, while those with a beta symbol *after* the arrow were ones in which a beta particle was *emitted*. In that case, then, you would have seen that the equations for p-p and B^8 do have beta particles emitted, while the equation for p-e-p does not. That might have led you to choice G—I and III only—which is the correct answer.

Six questions, six points—and all without understanding the passage in any deep or thorough way. Of course, if you understand the mysteries of neutrino flux and p-e-p subpaths, congratulations. You're probably enough of a science whiz to ace the subject test anyway. But if you're like most ACT test takers, you won't understand everything the passages talk about. Sometimes you'll even find yourself totally lost.

The moral of the story, of course, is don't give up on a passage just because you don't understand it. You may not be able to get *every* point associated with the passage, but you may be able to get at least one or two (or three or four). Remember: The test is designed in such a way that you can *figure out* many of the questions, even if you don't know the subject area.

Let's conclude now with another quick point about getting quick points. If you're nearly out of time and you've still got a whole Science passage left, you need to shift to last-minute strategies. As in Reading, don't try to preread the passage, or you'll just run out of time before you answer any questions. Instead, scan the questions without reading the passage and look first for the ones that require only reading data off of a graph or table. You can often get a couple of quick points just by knowing how to find data quickly.

Again, the most important thing is to make sure you have gridded in at least a random guess on every question.

Chapter Sixteen: **Writing Workout: Write What Counts**

- **Just the Facts**
- **The Kaplan Four-Step Method for the ACT Essay**
- **Know the Score: Sample Essays**
- **Preparing for the Essay**
- **Practice Essay**

A growing number of colleges want an assessment of your written communication skills. If you consider yourself a good writer and are accustomed to scoring well on essays, there may be a temptation to skip this chapter. Don't. Top scores are not given out easily, and writing a scored first draft in under a half hour is unlike most of your past writing experiences.

Let's start with the facts.

JUST THE FACTS

Writing has always been an essential skill for college success. An optional Writing test will be available when you take the ACT. Some colleges require it; others do not. Before registering for the ACT, find out if the schools to which you're applying want applicants to take the Writing test.

The ACT English test already measures knowledge of effective writing skills, including grammar, punctuation, organization, and style. The Writing test complements that evaluation of technical skill with an example of your simple, direct writing.

How the ACT Essay Is Scored

Your essay will be graded on a holistic scale of 1–6 (6 being the best). Graders will be looking for an overall sense of your essay, not assigning separate scores for specific elements like grammar or organization. Two readers read and score each essay; then those scores are added together to arrive at your Writing subscore (from 2–12). If there's a difference of more than a point between the two readers' scores, your essay will be read by a third reader.

Statistically speaking, there will be few essays that score 6. If each grader gives your essay a 4 or 5, that will place you at the upper range of those taking the exam.

What Skills Are Tested?

The readers realize you're writing under time pressure and expect you to make some mistakes. The content of your essay is not relevant; readers are not checking your facts. Nor will they judge you on your opinions. What they want is to see how well you can communicate a relevant, coherent point of view.

The test makers identify the following as the skills tested in the Writing test:

- Stating a clear perspective on an issue
- Providing supporting evidence and logical reasoning
- Maintaining focus and organizing ideas logically
- Writing clearly

The first of these involves answering the question in the prompt. The second means offering relevant support for your opinion—building an argument. The third means being organized: avoiding digressions and tying all your ideas together sensibly. The fourth is the only one addressing your "writing" directly, and it's limited to clarity. The Writing test is not principally a test of your grammar and punctuation (which are tested in the English test)—colleges want a chance to see your reasoning and communication skills.

The skill they didn't mention is speed. The skills they list would be relevant if you were writing an essay over the course of several weeks. On the ACT, you have to do all this in 30 minutes. This *cannot* be done using the process you learned for essay writing in the past. There is no opportunity to choose a topic and do research; there is no time to write and rewrite.

Do You Need to Prepare for the Essay?

So, the ACT essay is not like other writing experiences. It's a first draft that will be graded. Not only must it be complete and well organized, but it must also be easy for a grader to see that it is complete and well organized (and the grader may spend as little as a minute reading your essay). That's a lot to do in 30 minutes, so preparation and practice are a good idea.

By the way, practicing the ACT essay also reinforces what you've learned for the English test and strengthens your Reading test skills: in Reading, you take an argument apart; in Writing, you put together an argument.

THE KAPLAN FOUR-STEP METHOD FOR THE ACT ESSAY

Step 1: Pause to Know the Prompt

Step 2: Plan

Step 3: Produce

Step 4: Proofread

If you plan your essay and adhere to your plan when you write, the result will be solidly organized. Between now and Test Day, you can't drastically change your overall writing skills—and you probably don't need to. If your plan is good, all you need to do in the writing and proofreading steps is draw on your strengths and avoid your weaknesses. Get to know what those are as you practice.

Write What Counts: To maximize your score, use the Kaplan Method to help you focus on writing what the scorers will look for—*and nothing else*.

Step:	A high-scoring essay:	A low-scoring essay:
Prompt	clearly develops a position on the prompt	does not clearly state a position
Plan	supports with concrete, detailed examples	is general or repetitious
Produce	maintains clear focus and organization	digresses or has weak organization
Proofread	shows competent use of language	contains errors that reduce clarity

Kaplan has found this approach useful in its many years of experience with hundreds of sample essay statements on a wide range of tests. Let's look at what the test makers tell you about how the essays are scored.

To score Level 4, you must:

- Answer the question
- Support ideas with examples
- Show logical thought and organization
- Avoid major or frequent errors that make your writing unclear

Tip

Note that you can't earn a 5 or 6 if you haven't met the basic requirements for a 4, so think of the requirements as building blocks and be sure you have the foundation in place.

Organization and clarity are key to an above-average essay. If the reader can't follow your train of thought—if ideas aren't clearly organized or if grammatical errors, misspellings, and incorrect word choices make your writing unclear—you can't do well.

To score Level 5, all you have to add to a 4 is:

- Address the topic in depth

That is, offer more examples and details. The test makers' graders love specific examples, and the more concrete your examples are the more they clarify your thinking and keep you focused.

To score Level 6, all you have to add to a 5 is:

- Make transitions smoother and show variety in syntax and vocabulary.

Use words from the prompt to tie paragraphs together, rather than relying exclusively on connectors like "however" and "therefore." Vary your sentence structure, sometimes using simple sentences and other times using compound and complex ones. Adding a few college-level vocabulary words will also boost your score.

Now let's apply the Kaplan Method to a practice prompt:

Step 1: Pause to Know the Prompt

Spend less than a minute on this.

Know the General Directions: Before Test Day, you should be familiar with the general directions, which will look like this:

> In many high schools, the administration has provided guidelines for the publication of student newspapers. These guidelines often determine which topics can and cannot be discussed in the newspaper and prohibit what the administration deems inappropriate language. Many administrators and teachers feel that these restrictions enable them to provide a safe learning environment for students. Others feel that any restriction on the student newspaper is a violation of freedom of speech. In your opinion, should high schools place restrictions on student newspapers?
>
> In your essay, take a position on this question. You may write about either one of the two points of view given, or you may present a different point of view on this question. Use specific reasons and examples to support your position.

The final paragraph is always the same. Notice that there are two distinct parts to the assignment (we've highlighted them for you): (1) state a position and (2) provide support for your position.

Stay on Target

The assignment is not to write something vaguely inspired by the information given—that's where many good, creative writers go wrong.

Many scores are lower than they could be simply because these standard directions are ignored: the writer does not present a point of view or does not provide support for it.

Answer the Question: There is no right or wrong answer. Just decide what you will choose as your position, and then back it up with reasoning and examples. Highlight key words in the prompt and use them in your paragraphs to show how your ideas relate to the prompt. You can also add depth by defining or providing background about these words. Terms that might be explored in this statement include: *topic, inappropriate language, safe,* and *free speech.*

Step 2: Plan

Take 5 minutes or less to build a Plan before you write. Focus on what kinds of reasoning and examples you can use to support your position. If you find you have more examples for a position different from the one you thought you would take, change your position.

Subject Matter: Avoid highly emotional examples that will tend to reduce your clarity and organization. Avoid potentially offensive examples or extreme positions that are hard to defend.

A 6 essay can have a single well-developed example; two or more can make strong essays, but won't guarantee a 5 or 6. However, an abundance of undeveloped examples makes weak, low-scoring essays.

Literary or historical examples won't necessarily do better than personal experience. Choose examples that you can write about with confidence; don't try to impress the readers with your content—it doesn't count. If you do choose personal experiences, choose self-improvement, positive acts, or creative work. Remember that colleges may use these essays as additional personal statements.

Controlled Brainstorming: In your high school classes, many of you learned to "brain-storm"—perhaps using a "clustering" approach to organize your ideas. These are excellent strategies if you have the luxury of days or weeks to write your essay. They lead to unbalanced, disorganized essays if you have to write in 30 minutes.

The Kaplan Method is designed to produce balanced and integrated essays in the 30 minutes allotted. Controlled brainstorming means staying very focused on coming up with workable examples and arguments as quickly as possible, and then moving on. You aren't looking for the perfect argument or example—just ones that you can write about with clarity and detail.

Information Banks: Don't wait until Test Day to think of examples you can use to support your ideas. Regardless of what question is raised in the prompt, you will draw your support from the things you know best and are most comfortable writing about—things that you know a fair amount of concrete detail about.

Refresh your memory about your favorite or most memorable books, school subjects, historical events, personal experiences, activities—anything. By doing so, you strengthen mental connections to those ideas and details—that will make it easier to connect to the right examples on Test Day.

Structure Your Essay: Plan a clear introduction, a distinct middle section, and a strong conclusion. Choose your best examples, decide in what order you'll handle them, and plan your paragraphs.

With that in mind, we suggest:

- Use an effective *hook* to bring the reader in.
- Use regular *transitions* to provide the glue that holds your ideas together.
- End with a *bang* to make your essay memorable.

Reminder

You don't have to respond to the points of view offered in the prompt—you can if you wish, and they can be good sources of ideas and details for your essay. But you can also take an entirely different approach to the issue and never mention them.

Be Creative

One high-scoring essay on "whether secrecy is good" used as an example a squirrel hiding nuts for the winter.

A "hook" means avoiding an essay that opens (as thousands of other essays will): "In my opinion, ..., because...." Try a more general statement that introduces one or more of the "keywords" you will use from the prompt.

A "bang" means a closing that ties the three paragraphs together. Good choices can be a clear, succinct statement of your thesis in the essay or a vivid example that's right on point.

Let's look at a plan for our prompt. The answer we've chosen is that:

> I agree that restrictions on student newspapers violate freedom of speech and I also believe restrictions impede student learning.

This position clearly responds to the assignment, and adding some reasoning *not* taken directly from the prompt immediately tells the reader "I have ideas of my own."

Next, working with our proposed response, comb your memory or your imagination for supporting reasons and examples to use. We'll use:

> Point: student newspapers should mimic real life newspapers
> Point: not being in the school paper doesn't mean it's not discussed
> Point: students can avoid "harming" others as well as adults
> Point: censorship is anti-democratic

Fill in the details mentally. Jot down any notes you need to ensure that you use the details you've developed, but don't take the time to write full sentences. When you have enough ideas for a few supporting paragraphs, decide what your introduction and conclusion will be and the order in which you'll discuss each supporting idea.

Save the Best for Last

Save your best example for last and stress its relative importance.

Here's our sample plan:

> Para 1: I agree with "free speech." Student newspapers should prepare for real life.
> Para 2: Press is treated specially in real life
> Para 3: Potential harm not a good argument
> Para 4: Censorship vs. democracy
> Para 5: Better to have discussion out in the open
> Para 6: Restate thesis

If you take our advice and use examples that are very familiar to you, you won't have to write much in your plan in order to remember the point being made. Learn how brief you can make your notes and still not lose sight of what you mean to say.

A good plan:

- Responds to the prompt
- Has an introduction
- Has strong examples, usually one per paragraph
- Has a strong conclusion

In addition to writing practice essays, practice just making Plans on your own whenever you have a few spare minutes, using ideas for changes in high school curriculum, events, lifestyle, and activities such as: longer vs. shorter class sessions; students should/should not be allowed off campus during the school day; study halls should/should not be eliminated; vocational options vs. all college prep. The more you do this, the easier it will become.

Timing

You'll have at least 22 minutes for this step. If you want to make Test Day seem easy, practice writing in only 20 minutes.

Step 3: Produce

Appearances Count: In purely physical terms, your essay will make a better impression if you fill a significant portion of the space provided, and if it is clearly divided into three to five reasonably equal paragraphs (except that the final paragraph can be short). Use one paragraph for your introduction, one for each example or line of reasoning, and one for your conclusion so your essay will be easy for readers to follow.

Write neatly: graders can't help but feel negative about your essay if it's hard to decipher—and negative feelings affect holistic scoring. If your handwriting is a problem, print.

Stick With the Plan: Given the short time you have for the essay, it's vital to the clarity of your writing that you use the ideas and organization you established in your plan. Resist any urge to introduce new ideas—no matter how good you think they are—or to digress from the central focus or organization of each paragraph.

Write Carefully: Write mentally before you write on paper. If your essays are littered with misspellings and grammatical mistakes, you may get a low score simply because the reader cannot follow what you are trying to say.

Use Topic Sentences: Each paragraph should be organized around a topic sentence that you should finish in your mind before you start to write:

- *I believe...*
- *One example...*
- *Another example...*
- *Another example...*
- *Therefore we can conclude...*

Reminder

This isn't the place for creative flights of fancy. Make your writing direct, persuasive, and grammatical.

You don't have to write it this way in the essay, but completing these sentences in your mind ensures that you focus on what idea organizes each paragraph.

Choose Words Carefully: Use some college-level vocabulary, but only words you know are correct. If you are trying to impress the reader, you may *obfuscate* more than *elucidate* what you are *articulating*.

Vary your sentence structure. A couple of common weaknesses to keep in mind:

- avoid using "I" excessively
- avoid slang

Use Transitions: Think about the relationship between ideas as you write, and spell them out clearly. This makes it easy for the readers to follow your reasoning, and they'll appreciate it. Use key words from the prompt as well as the kinds of words you've learned about in Reading that indicate contrast, opinion, relative importance, and support.

Essay Length: While many poor essays can be quite long, there will be few 6 essays under about 300 words, so take this into consideration as you practice. The length of an essay is no assurance of its quality. However, it's hard to develop an argument in depth—something the graders look for—in one or two short paragraphs. Don't ramble, digress, or write off topic just to make your essay longer. Practice writing organized essays with developed examples, and you'll find yourself writing more naturally. Aim for 350–450 words.

Don't Sweat the Small Stuff: Do not obsess over every little thing. If you cannot remember how to spell a word, do your best and just keep going. Even the top scoring essays can have minor errors. The essay readers understand that you are writing first drafts and have no time for research or revision.

Step 4: Proofread

Always leave yourself two or three minutes to review your work—the time spent will definitely pay off. Very few of us can avoid the occasional confused sentence or omitted word when writing under pressure. Quickly review your essay to be sure your ideas are on the page, not just in your head.

Don't hesitate to make corrections on your essay—these are timed first drafts, not term papers. But keep it clear: use a single line through deletions and an asterisk to mark where text should be inserted.

Keep Track of Time

In addition to checking the quality of your writing, saving time to proofread also helps ensure that you will complete your essay on Test Day. An incomplete essay will undermine your confidence.

You don't have time to look for every minor error or to revise substantially. Learn the types of mistakes you tend to make and look for them. Some of the most common mistakes in students' essays are those found in the English test questions.

Common Errors

- omitted words
- sentence fragments
- subject-verb agreement or verb tense errors
- misplaced modifiers
- pronoun agreement errors
- misused words—especially homonyms like "their" for "there" or "they're"
- spelling errors

Common Style Problems

- choppy sentences (combine some)
- too many long, complex sentences (break some up)
- too many stuffy-sounding words (replace some with simple words)
- too many simple words (add a few college-level words)

KNOW THE SCORE: SAMPLE ESSAYS

The best way to be sure you've learned what the readers will look for is to try scoring some essays yourself.

Let's look at a sample essay based on the prompt and plan we've been looking at.

Here's the prompt:

> In many high schools, the administration has provided guidelines for the publication of student newspapers. These guidelines often determine which topics can and cannot be discussed in the newspaper and prohibit what the administration deems inappropriate language. Many administrators and teachers feel that these restrictions enable them to provide a safe learning environment for students. Others feel that any restriction on the student newspaper is a violation of freedom of speech. In your opinion, should high schools place restrictions on student newspapers?
>
> In your essay, take a position on this question. You may write about either one of the two points of view given, or you may present a different point of view on this question. Use specific reasons and examples to support your position.

You Make the Call

Don't cheat yourself by reading our explanation without first deciding what holistic grade you would give the sample essay.

Sample Essay 1

> In many high schools, the administration has provided guidelines for the publication of student newspapers. These guidelines often determine which topics can and cannot be discussed in the newspaper, and prohibit what the administration deems inappropriate language. Many administrators and teachers feel that these restrictions enable them to provide a safe, appropriate learning environment for students. Others feel that any restriction on the student newspaper is a violation of freedom of speech. In my opinion, students should be free to write on any topic.
>
> Firstly, restrictions will not stop certain topics being talked about. Students will always discuss topics that they are interested in. Second, students are more aware of what is or is not appropriate than the administration might think. A newspaper is there to tell news and students will therefore write about the news.
>
> Finally and most importantly, a right such as freedom of speech should not be checked at the school door. Students not being able to cognizant and value rights such as these if they are not taught their importance in school. So high schools should not place restrictions on student newspapers.

Score: _____/6

It should have been fairly easy to see that this isn't a strong essay. The author does state a clear opinion, but half of the essay is a direct copy of the prompt—something the graders will notice and, if anything, be annoyed by. The time and space spent just quoting the prompt was completely wasted—it earned the writer zero points.

The rest of the essay is organized and uses transition words ("firstly" and "finally"). The author states her thesis, follows with three supporting reasons, and then a conclusion. However, none of this is discussed fully enough—no concrete detail or examples are given. In the second paragraph, for instance, the author should have added an example demonstrating that students are aware of what is appropriate or an example of topics that students will discuss.

Using the Prompt

This doesn't mean you shouldn't quote from the prompt. On the contrary, you should use as much language from the prompt as possible, but always tie language from the prompt to your own ideas.

The language is understandable but there are significant errors affecting clarity. For instance, the second sentence of paragraph 3 is a fragment—there is no verb. Some vocabulary words are clearly plugged in without a clear understanding of their meaning: In paragraph 3 "not being able to cognizant" is incorrect; perhaps the student meant, "not being able to understand".

This essay looks like the writer couldn't think of "good" ideas, waited too long, and had to write in a hurry.

Keep Planning Simple

Never spend more than 5 minutes planning, no matter how much you wish you could think of "better" ideas. The content doesn't count; fullness of communication does.

Let's try another, better essay. Read quickly and select a score before reading our evaluation.

Sample Essay 2

Many high schools place restrictions on appropriate topics and language for student newspapers. Many people disagree with these restrictions. While arguments can be made for either side, I believe that newspapers, as part of the school, should be placed under guidelines of the school.

First, a high school necessarily has stricter rules than normal society. These rules are not in place to punish students. They protect them and providing a suitable learning environment. In this way, when students leave high school they will have grown from children to adults, ready to succeed in the larger world. For example, the strict time schedule, with exactly three or four minutes given between classes, prepares students for strict schedules in the broader world.

Second, students interested in journalism should have instruction in how to write and publish newspaper articles. A student newspaper, which for obvious reasons has limited scope, is a perfect laboratory for students to experiment with journalistic writing. The administration and faculty dedicated to the newspaper can guide students in choosing appropriate topics, such as student elections. Then they can write articles on politics in the future. Imagine a student whose high school teacher taught the proper techniques for reporting on the race for student council president, joining a major news organization and reporting on the United States Presidential election.

Lastly, students may not realize the harm which their writing may cause. In my school, a student discovered a teacher's affair and "reported" on it in a story on the student's TV network, before the school could interfere. The teacher's career was destroyed and his marriage fell apart. Perhaps he deserved it, but student television should not have been the vehicle that ruined his life. The student reporter felt terribly in the end, as she had not thought through the consequences of her story. The same consequences could occur in a student newspaper that was restricted by no guidelines from the school.

Therefore, while many people argue that freedom of speech is a right too precious to give up, it is more important to provide guidelines for young people.

Score: _____/6

The graders will be scoring holistically, not checking off "points"—but to learn what makes a good essay, it may help to consider these questions, based on the test makers' scoring criteria:

Does the author answer the question?

Is the author's position clearly stated?

Does the body of the essay support and develop the position taken?

Are there at least three supporting paragraphs?

Is the relevance of each supporting paragraph clear?

Is the essay a reasonable length?

Is the essay organized, with a clear introduction, middle, and end?

Did the author use one paragraph for each new idea?

Is each sentence in a paragraph relevant to the point made in that paragraph?

Are transitions clear?

Is the essay easy to read? Is it engaging?

Are sentences varied?

Is vocabulary used effectively? Is college-level vocabulary used?

Don't just answer "yes" or "no"—locate specific text in the essay that answers the question.

OK, now do you want to revise the score you gave this essay?

Actually, this sample exceeds the basic requirements for a 4; it's a 5.

This essay addresses the assignment. The writer's position is clear and the personal example in the fourth paragraph provides good support. The organization is good and the author uses transition words. Each paragraph discusses a different aspect of the writer's argument. Let's look at why it doesn't rate a 6.

Some of the support isn't explained enough. The second paragraph, for example, doesn't show the connection between strict schedules and restrictions on newspaper reporting—the subject of the essay. The idea, in paragraph 3, of a student growing up to be a presidential reporter is interesting, but it doesn't particularly address the idea of restrictions. The final paragraph doesn't tie back to the main argument about newspapers; it only generally mentions "guidelines for young people."

The author's writing is good, but unexceptional. There are a few examples of complex sentences. For example, in paragraph 2, "A student newspaper, which for obvious reasons has limited scope, is a perfect laboratory for students to experiment with journalistic writing." The essay includes grammar mistakes, however—such as, in paragraph 2: "They protect them and providing a suitable learning environment." In paragraph 3, the sentence "Then they can write articles on politics in the future" includes the ambiguous *they*, which could refer to the administration and teachers or the students.

Reminder

Since Kaplan's Method will ensure solid organization, the difference between a 4 and a 5 comes down to how fully you develop your examples. The difference between a 5 and a 6 is the liveliness of your writing.

Let's look at another essay. Read it quickly and decide how you would score it.

Sample Essay 3

School administrations and teachers who support restrictions believe that these restrictions are needed to form an appropriate learning environment. But I agree with those who oppose such restrictions because they violate freedom of speech and these limits impede student progress and success after high school.

Despite the true need for rules in high schools, newspapers should be exempt. Students need discipline in the form of detention for misbehavior or demerits for poor study, but the student newspaper should not be a part of that system. Rather, it should mimic "real world" journalism.

Student editors, usually seniors aged seventeen or eighteen, are well aware of the overall environment in which they publish, and understand what is or is not appropriate. High school should give students practice at being cognizant of the larger arena in which they act. The few negative incidents that free press will admittedly cause will teach students that in life, one must take responsibility for one's actions.

Therefore, the argument for freedom of speech in student newspapers advances substantial educational goals for students, as well as our unalienable right of freedom of speech. This right, however, is paramount. The American public school is an extension of the American government and community, and censorship is inconsistent with American democracy. Again, students need to be prepared for the world they will live in; depriving them of rights that are promoted in the greater community prepares students poorly for life after high school.

Finally, censoring information in the student newspaper will not remove the subject from student discussion. Rather, it will remove a balanced, informative viewpoint, and often make the "inappropriate" action more desirable and "cool." Placing restrictions on student newspapers would be a serious mistake that would hinder students from learning what it is to participate in a free society.

Score: ____/6

Did you recognize this as an essay based on the plan we did earlier?

Para 1: I agree with "free speech." Student newspapers should prepare for real life.
Para 2: Press is treated specially in real life
Para 3: Potential harm not a good argument
Para 4: Censorship vs. democracy
Para 5: Not discussing in press doesn't mean not discussing in school

This essay is pretty good—it would earn a 4. The position is clearly stated, and some supporting reasoning is given. There is some good vocabulary here (for example paragraph 1, last sentence "impede," paragraph 3, third sentence "cognizant," paragraph 4, second sentence "paramount," and fourth sentence "inconsistent").

However, the reasoning is too general and the writing is too ordinary to earn the top score. Let's see how it could be improved.

Turning a 4 into a 6

The essay plunges right into the two points of view offered in the prompt. It could be improved by introducing the issue with a general statement, like:

There seems to be considerable debate nationwide over the role and proper control of student newspapers.

In the last sentence of the first paragraph, the writer introduces some additional reasoning *not* included in the prompt. That's excellent, but it would be better to make it clear where the position from the prompt ends and the author's position begins, perhaps like this:

But I agree with those who oppose such restrictions because they violate freedom of speech. I would further argue that these limits impede student progress and success after high school.

The second paragraph is relevant and organized—it covers one of the two positions offered in the prompt. But it would be better if the writer tied this argument more clearly to something specific in the prompt, perhaps with an opening sentence using language from the prompt, like:

Some people claim that high school students need strict guidelines in order to prepare for life after school.

Moreover, at the end of the paragraph the reference to mimicking "real world" journalism would be improved by telling the reader what "real world" journalism is:

Rather, it should mimic "real world" journalism, which strives to provide valid, balanced reporting on events important to the public, or in this case the student body.

The third paragraph addresses the view in the prompt that students can cause harm by printing inappropriate articles. But, again, it should be made clearer what part of the prompt this paragraph is responding to, with a first sentence like:

> Others believe that students may cause unintended harm with newspaper articles written on controversial subjects. I think that is laughable.

Paragraph four is pretty good, as is. It states clearly what the author considers the most important argument. The fifth paragraph raises good arguments, but leaves them undeveloped. It would be best to provide an example of what type of story would help promote "balanced, informative" discussion to counteract "inappropriate…cool" actions, like:

> For instance, a reporter for my high school paper researched and wrote an in-depth story on the increasing drug problem among students. The administration quickly intervened and stopped the story, declaring that drugs were an inappropriate topic for student discussion. This story, however, would have focused discussion on a crucial issue for students, so that they can make the right choice when offered drugs or when they see friends using drugs. Unfortunately, this is a situation most students will face, and they need to be prepared. Suppressing the story made drugs seem even more rebellious and mysterious and most importantly did not give students facts with which they could prepare.

This makes it clear why the writer saved this argument for the last—an important, detailed example.

Finally, since this writer offers a fair number of supporting ideas, it would also be a good idea to add some transitions that establish the relative importance of those ideas. For example, in the third paragraph:

> <u>First of all,</u> student editors, usually seniors aged seventeen or eighteen, are well aware of the overall environment in which they publish, and understand what is or is not appropriate. <u>But even more importantly,</u> high school should give students practice at being cognizant of the larger arena in which they act.

Here's how this essay would look with the improvements we've suggested.

> <u>There seems to be considerable debate nationwide over the role and proper control of student newspapers.</u> School administrations and teachers who support restrictions believe that these restrictions are needed to form an appropriate learning environment. But I agree with those who oppose such restrictions because they violate freedom of speech<u>. I would further argue that</u> these limits impede student progress and success after high school.
>
> <u>Some people claim that high school students need strict guidelines in order to prepare for life after school.</u> Despite the true need for

rules in high schools, newspapers should be exempt. Students need discipline in the form of detention for misbehavior or demerits for poor study, but the student newspaper should not be a part of that system. Rather, it should mimic "real world" journalism, which strives to provide valid, balanced reporting on events important to the public, or in this case the student body.

Others believe that students may cause unintended harm with newspaper articles written on controversial subjects. I think that is laughable. First of all, student editors, usually seniors aged seventeen or eighteen, are well aware of the overall environment in which they publish, and understand what is or is not appropriate. But even more importantly, high school should give students practice at being cognizant of the larger arena in which they act. The few negative incidents that free press will admittedly cause will teach students that in life, one must take responsibility for one's actions.

Therefore, the argument for freedom of speech in student newspapers advances substantial educational goals for students, as well as our unalienable right of freedom of speech. This right, however, is paramount. The American public school is an extension of the American government and community, and censorship is inconsistent with American democracy. Again, students need to be prepared for the world they will live in; depriving them of rights that are promoted in the greater community prepares students poorly for life after high school.

Finally, censoring information in the student newspaper will not remove the subject from student discussion. Rather, it will remove a balanced, informative viewpoint, and often make the "inappropriate" action more desirable and "cool." For instance, a reporter for my high school paper researched and wrote an in-depth story on the increasing drug problem among students. The administration quickly intervened and stopped the story, declaring that drugs were an inappropriate topic for student discussion. This story, however, would have focused discussion on a crucial issue for students, so that they can make the right choice when offered drugs or when they see friends using drugs. Unfortunately, this is a situation most students will face, and they need to be prepared. Suppressing the story made drugs seem even more rebellious and mysterious and most importantly did not give students facts with which they could prepare.

Placing restrictions on student newspapers would be a serious mistake that would hinder students from learning what it is to participate in a free society.

Reminder

There are no right or wrong opinions. You can earn a 6 with an essay for or against the issue raised in the prompt

This is now a 6 essay. It addresses the task both fully and concretely. It addresses both sides of the argument, refutes two opposing arguments, and then moves to the bulk of the author's own reasoning. The first paragraph introduces all the lines of reasoning that will be used, demonstrating to the reader that the writer knew right from the start where this essay was headed. The development of ideas is clear and logical and the paragraphs reflect this organization.

The author shows a high level of skill with language. The transitions between paragraphs are clear and guide the reader through the reasoning. The sentence structure varies throughout the passage, and is at times complex.

So what did we do to our 4 to make it a 6?

- We added examples and detail.
- We varied sentence structure and added more college-level vocabulary ("strives," "laughable," "intervened," and "suppressing").
- While length alone doesn't make a 6, we've added significantly to our original essay. Those extra words provide more room for detail and the "superior language" the test maker is looking for in a 6 essay.
- The conclusion, rather than being lost in the fifth paragraph, is now a strong, independent statement that concisely sums up the writer's point of view.

Remember that your graders will be reading *holistically.* They will not be grading you by assigning points to particular aspects of your writing. However, as you practice essay writing, you can build an otherwise humdrum essay into a 6 by working on specific elements, with the net effect of giving your essay that 6 glow.

PREPARING FOR THE ESSAY

Information Banks

Don't wait until Test Day to think about what subjects you can draw on for your examples to create animated and engaging essays. Examples can be drawn from anywhere: your life experience, a story you saw on the news, literature, history, or other subjects. So prepare yourself by refreshing your memory about your favorite subjects—collect examples that can be used for a variety of topics.

Don't hesitate to use your examples broadly. If the topic is about school, that doesn't mean you have to use school-based examples. It's better to write about things that you are comfortable with and know a lot about—but be sure to make it clear how they are relevant to the topic.

Outside Reading

The outside reading you do for Reading will also help develop your writing skills for the essay. Adopt persuasive language that you find in articles you read. After reading them, flex your own persuasive capacities by asking yourself:

- What is the author's point?
- How is it supported?
- What kinds of people would disagree, and why?

Establish and Adhere to a Practice Schedule

Don't try to cut corners. Learn the Kaplan Method and practice writing at least one essay a week; last minute cramming will not be effective. If you intend to maximize your score, you must establish and adhere to a practice schedule. And practice at the same time of day that you will be writing on Test Day.

Be hard on yourself. Always time yourself to internalize the necessary pacing. Don't allow yourself any extra minutes to complete an essay. Never start to write until you have a complete plan, and then adhere to your plan. Always reserve two minutes to look over the essay and make needed additions or corrections.

Self-Evaluation

After each practice essay, score yourself based on the guidelines provided. As part of your self-evaluation, determine which types of example are most useful to you and what types of error you make most often. Then analyze how well you followed the Kaplan Method in constructing your essay, and what you might focus on to improve. Do you have a tendency to rush your plan, or do you find that you haven't left two minutes to proofread? Practice to make your pacing reliable.

Get a Second Opinion

Ask someone else to read and critique your practice essays. If you know someone else who's taking the ACT, you might agree to assist each other in this way. Knowing whether another person can follow your reasoning is the single most important learning aid you can have for the essay.

If You're Not a "Writer"

Writing essays may not be your favorite pastime, but you can still succeed on the ACT essay. If your writing is weak, focus on building a well-supported argument; if you have that, weaknesses and errors in writing will be less important.

Emergency Plan

It's difficult to create a good essay in the last few minutes, so it's best not to let an emergency happen. If you're down to the wire, allow yourself a few minutes to plan and then write, based on that plan, no matter how much you wish you could think of other ideas. Remember that the essay tests your ability to convey those ideas—not the quality of the ideas.

If English Is Your Second Language

The ACT essay can be a special challenge for the international student or ESL student here in the United States. On the ACT, you will be taking a position on the prompt, something that sometimes, but not always, happens on the TOEFL® (Test of English as a Foreign Language). However, plan your essay using all the tools in this chapter and write according to your plan. Make a special point of spending time proofreading your practice essays when you finish them, and edit anything that makes your writing unclear. There's a strong connection between your English reading skills and your writing skills, so keep reading as well (and don't forget to look for material for your Information Banks as well).

PRACTICE ESSAY

Try out the Kaplan Method on the following essay prompt. After you're finished, read over your essay and if possible, have someone else read it as well. You can compare it to the model essay that follows the lined pages. Good luck!

> Many city councils have introduced proposals that would give them the power to ban certain books from the children's and young adult sections of local public libraries. Some citizens support such proposals because they hope to limit young people's exposure to inappropriate materials. However, other people believe that these measures are equivalent to censorship. In your opinion, should the government have the right to restrict the materials available to young people in libraries?
>
> In your essay, take a position on this question. You may write about either one of the two points of view given, or you may present a different point of view on this question. Use specific reasons and examples to support your position.

Model Essay

Here's one possible way to approach this essay prompt. Remember that the opinion you express is less important than the way you present it. Notice how this response includes a logically arranged argument with specific examples.

In some districts, city councils and other governing bodies have suggested that they be given the power to ban certain teen and children's books from public libraries. While some citizens believe that it would be beneficial for an outside party to screen the books that are available to young people, others are upset at what they see as censorship of the library's offerings.

Leaving the question of censorship aside, I believe that decisions about which books are appropriate for young people should be left to the young people themselves and their parents, not to city councils or librarians. Young people's reading levels and maturity levels can vary dramatically even within the same age group, and parents are the best judges of what kinds of books are suitable for their children. The proposal to have the city council make these decisions also fails to take into account the huge variations in parents' own preferences for their children; the idea of inappropriateness is a very subjective one. While some parents may agree with the city council's decisions, others may feel that the city council bans too many books, or even too few. In the end, parents must be responsible for knowing what books their children are reading and making their own decisions about those books' appropriateness within the context of their own values.

Additionally, whether certain books are appropriate or not, it's unrealistic to think that removing "objectionable" material from public libraries will keep young people from ever encountering that kind of material. Between television, the Internet, and interactions with friends and classmates, young people encounter all sorts of situations that may not necessarily be age appropriate. It's understandable that adults are concerned, but trying to keep potentially objectionable books away from young readers doesn't ensure that they won't encounter the language or situations used in those books elsewhere. To my mind, the best solution is for adults to encourage young people to analyze these situations thoughtfully, ask questions, and form their own opinions, rather than trying to shield them from the realities of the world.

Finally, although certain books contain elements that some people may find offensive or upsetting, those elements don't necessarily outweigh the literary merits of the books in question. One example of this is *Huckleberry Finn*, which all of the students at my school read as a requirement in English classes. It is widely recognized as a classic of American literature, even though it also includes portrayals of African-American characters that many people find offensive. The historical context that is necessary to understand *The Diary of Anne Frank* may be upsetting to younger readers, but the diary is still a significant historical document. Many books with controversial content are still worth reading, and a policy that screens out books based on their potential to offend may exclude important works of literature from libraries.

In conclusion, I believe that the power to make determinations about a book's appropriateness should lie not with a city council or a librarian, but with young readers and their parents. The role of a library is to make information available, not to make or enforce judgments about what its patrons should or should not be reading.

Chapter Seventeen: **Strategic Summaries**

- **English Test**
- **Math Test**
- **Reading Test**
- **Science Test**
- **Writing Test**

ENGLISH TEST

The English subject test:

- Is 45 minutes long.
- Includes five passages, representing a range of writing styles and levels of formality.
- Consists of 75 questions, divided among the five passages. They test many points of grammar, punctuation, writing mechanics, usage, and rhetorical skills, by proposing ways of expressing information underlined at various points in the passages. We divide the questions strategically into three groups:
  1. Economy Questions
  2. Sense Questions
  3. Technicality Questions

There are also a few Nonstandard-Format Questions that require different strategies, as outlined in Special Strategies below.

The questions do *not* get harder as you proceed through the section.

Emergency Plan

If you have two weeks or fewer to prep for the ACT, read this chapter. It reviews the key facts and strategies for the English, Math, Reading, Science, and Writing tests.

Test Prep and Admissions

Mindset

- When in doubt, take it out. Make sure that everything is written as concisely as possible. If you think something doesn't belong in a sentence, it probably doesn't, so choose an answer that leaves it out.
- Make it make sense. Grammar allows language to communicate meaning clearly. Most grammatically faulty sentences on the ACT don't say what the author obviously intended to say. If a sentence has more than one possible meaning, figure out what the author intended to say, and fix the sentence so it conveys that meaning properly.
- Trust your ear. Mistakes in grammar often sound bad to your ear. Trust that instinct. Don't choose the answer that "sounds fancy," choose the one that "sounds right." But keep in mind that there are some errors your ear won't catch. For these errors, use your flag list.

The Kaplan Method

For each question, ask yourself three things. Note that you may actually have your answer before getting to all three questions:

1. **Ask: Does this stuff belong here?** Is it redundant? Is it relevant? Is this a long way to say a short idea? If so, choose an answer that gets rid of the stuff that doesn't belong.
2. **Ask: Does this stuff make sense?** The ACT test makers want short, simple, easy-to-understand prose. They expect everything to fit together logically. Choose the answer that turns nonsense into sense.
3. **Ask: Does this stuff sound like English?** If not, choose the answer that does. Recognize items on your "flag list" from English Workout 3 and let them help out when your ear isn't sure. These classic errors appear again and again on ACT English subject tests.

Special Strategies

A few questions will require you to rearrange the words in a sentence, the sentences in a paragraph, or even the paragraphs in a passage. Others may ask questions about the meaning of all or part of the passage, or about its structure. Your approach to these Nonstandard-Format Questions should be:

1. **Determine your task.** What are you being asked to do?
2. **Consider the passage as a whole.** Most passages will have a well-defined theme, laid out in a logical way. Choose the answer that expresses this theme, or the arrangement of elements that best continues the logical "flow" of the passage.
3. **Prephrase your answer.** As in Reading, you should have an idea of what the answer is before looking at the choices.

Test Prep and Admissions

Timing

We recommend that you *not* skip around in the English subject test. Although you can certainly use the usual Two-Pass Approach, you might prefer to go straight from beginning to end, answering all of the questions as you go. Unlike in other sections, in English you'll usually have at least a sense of what the right answer should be rather quickly. Remember, even the correct answer will start to sound wrong if you think about it too much!

Set your watch to 12:00 at the beginning of the subject test. Although you should go faster if you can, here's roughly where you should be at the following checkpoints.

12:09 . . . . . One passage finished and answers gridded in
12:18 . . . . . Two passages finished and answers gridded in
12:27 . . . . . Three passages finished and answers gridded in
12:36 . . . . . Four passages finished and answers gridded in
12:45 . . . . . Five passages finished and answers for the entire section gridded in

Note that you should do at least some work on all 75 English questions, and make sure you have at least one guess gridded in for every question when time is called.

When You're Running Out of Time

If you have no time left even to read the last few questions, choose the shortest answer for each one. Remember that "OMIT," when it appears, counts as the shortest answer.

Scoring

Your performance on the English subject test will be averaged into your ACT Composite Score, weighted equally with your scores on the other three major subject tests. You will also receive:

- English subject score—from 1 to 36—for the entire English subject test
- Usage/Mechanics subscore—from 1 to 18—based on your performance on the questions testing grammar, usage, punctuation, and sentence structure
- Rhetorical Skills subscore—from 1 to 18—based on your performance on the questions testing strategy, organization, and style
- Writing subscore—from 2 to 12—based on the optional Writing test
- Combined English-Writing score—from 1 to 36—if you take the optional Writing test

MATH TEST

The Math subject test:

- Is 60 minutes long.
- Consists of 60 questions, which test your grasp of prealgebra, algebra, coordinate geometry, plane geometry, and trigonometry. We break down the questions into the following strategic categories:
  1. Diagram Questions
  2. Story Questions
  3. Concept Questions

The questions tend to test more advanced math concepts as you proceed through the section.

Mindset

- The end justifies the means. That means getting as many correct answers as quickly as possible. If that means doing straightforward questions in a straightforward way, that's fine. But many questions can be solved faster by unorthodox methods.
- Take time to save time. It sounds paradoxical, but to go your fastest on the Math test you've got to slow down. Never dive in headlong, wildly crunching numbers or manipulating equations without first giving the problem some thought.
- When in doubt, shake it up. ACT Math questions are not always what they seem at first glance. Sometimes all you need is a new perspective to break through the disguise.

The Kaplan Method

1. **Understand.** First focus on the question stem and make sure you understand the problem. Sometimes you'll want to read the stem twice, or rephrase it in a way you can better understand. Think to yourself: "What kind of problem is this? What am I looking for? What am I given?" When you begin, don't pay too much attention to the answer choices, though you may want to glance to see what form they're in.
2. **Analyze.** Think for a moment and decide on a plan of attack. Don't start crunching numbers right away. "What's a quick and reliable way to find the correct answer?" Look for patterns and shortcuts, using common sense and your knowledge of the test. You want to find the creative solutions that will get you more right answers in less time. Try to solve the problem without focusing on the answer choices.
3. **Select.** Once you get an answer—or once you get stuck—check the answer choices. If you got an answer and it's listed as one of the choices, chances are it's right—fill in the appropriate bubble and move on. But if you didn't get an answer, narrow down the choices as best you can by a process of elimination, and then guess.

Special Strategies

We offer several recommendations for what to do when you get stuck. If after a few moments of thought you find you still can't come up with a reasonable way of doing the problem, try one of these techniques:

1. **Backsolve.** We recommend that you normally attempt to solve a problem before looking at the answer choices. But when you're stuck, take advantage of the multiple-choice format. In some of the questions, you can just try out each answer choice until you find the one that works.
2. **Pick numbers.** Some problems are hard because they're general or abstract. Bring these down to earth by temporarily replacing variables with specific numbers.
3. **Guesstimate.** Sometimes you'll understand what a problem is asking for, but you just won't know what algorithm, formula, or theorem to apply. If you can figure out some ballpark estimate for the correct answer, you'll probably be able to eliminate at least one or two answer choices.
4. **Eyeball.** Even though the directions warn you that diagrams are "not necessarily" drawn to scale, eyeballing is a surprisingly effective guessing strategy. When you don't fully fathom the geometry of a situation, but you do have a diagram to work with, see how many answer choices you can eliminate just by sizing things up with your eyes.

Timing

Remember the Two-Pass Approach. Spend about 45 minutes on your first pass through the Math subject test: Do the easier questions, guess on the questions you know you'll never get, and mark the tough ones that you'll want to come back to. Spend the last 15 minutes picking up those questions that you skipped on the first pass.

We recommend that you grid your answers at the end of every page or two. In the last five minutes or so, start gridding your answers one by one. And make sure that you have an answer (even if it's a blind guess) gridded for every question by the time the test is over.

Don't worry if you have to guess on a lot of the Math questions. You can miss a lot of questions on the subject test and still get a great score. Remember that the average ACT test taker gets less than half the Math questions right!

When You're Running Out of Time

If at some point you realize you have more questions left than you have time for, be willing to skip around, looking for questions you understand right away. Pick your spots. Concentrate on the questions you have the best chance of correctly answering. Just be sure to grid an answer—even if it's just a wild guess—for every question.

Scoring

Your performance on the Math subject test will be averaged into your ACT Composite Score, equally weighted with your scores on the other three major subject tests. You will also receive:

- Math subject score—from 1 to 36—for the entire Math subject test
- Prealgebra/Elementary Algebra subscore—from 1 to 18
- Intermediate Algebra/Coordinate Geometry subscore—from 1 to 18
- Plane Geometry/Trigonometry subscore—from 1 to 18

READING TEST

The Reading subject test:

- Is 35 minutes long.
- Includes four passages:
    - Three Nonfiction passages (one each in Social Studies, Natural Sciences, and Humanities, though there is no significant difference among them except subject matter)
    - One Prose Fiction passage (an excerpt from a short story or novel)
- Consists of 40 questions, 10 on each passage. They include:
    1. Specific Detail Questions
    2. Inference Questions
    3. Big Picture Questions

The questions do NOT get harder as you go through the section.

Mindset

- Know where you're going. Try to read passages actively, anticipating where the author is going by paying attention to structural clues and common sense. Pay attention to the structure of each passage and don't get bogged down in the details.
- Look it up. Find the answers, don't remember them. Think of the passages as reference books, not textbooks. Refer.

The Kaplan Method

1. **Preread the passage.** Try to understand the "gist" of the passage. Get a sense of the overall structure of the passage. Create a mental road map (except on the Prose Fiction passage) to make referring back easier.
2. **Consider the question stem.** Understand the question first, without looking at the array of answer choices. Remember that many wrong choices are designed to mislead test takers who just jump past the question stem and start comparing choices to each other.

3. **Refer to the passage before looking at the choices.** Always refer to the passage before answering the question. If the question includes a line reference, use it. Only then look at the choices. Make sure your answer matches the passage in meaning, and that it doesn't just use the same words as the passage.
4. **Answer the question in your own words** before looking at the choices.
5. **Match your answer with one of the choices.** Having an answer in mind will keep you from getting bogged down.

Special Strategies

Prose Fiction Passage

When you preread the passage, pay attention to the characters, especially the main character. Read between the lines to determine unspoken emotions and attitudes. Ask yourself:

- Who are these people? What are they like? How are they related to each other?
- What is their state of mind? Are they angry, sad, reflective, excited?
- What's going on? What's happening on the surface? What's happening beneath the surface?

Nonfiction Passages

Don't be thrown by unfamiliar vocabulary. If you find a difficult term, odds are the definition will be given to you in context (or else it simply might not matter what the word means). Remember, you can still get lots of questions right, even if you don't fully understand the passage. The answers to all of the questions can be found.

Timing

You might want to take a few seconds at the beginning of the subject test to page through the passages, gauging the difficulty of each one. At first glance you may wish to skip an entire passage if it seems very difficult.

We recommend that you treat each passage and its questions as a block. Take two passes through each block before moving on to the next (skip around if you like, but watch your answer grid if you do!). Get the easy questions on the first pass through and save the tougher ones for the second pass. Just make sure to keep track of time.

Set your watch to 12:00 at the beginning of the subject test. Although you should go faster if you can, here's roughly where you should be at the following checkpoints.

12:09 . . . . . One passage finished and answers gridded in
12:18 . . . . . Two passages finished and answers gridded in
12:27 . . . . . Three passages finished and answers gridded in
12:35 . . . . . Four passages finished and answers for entire section gridded in

Don't spend time agonizing over specific questions. Avoid thinking long and hard about the answer choices. Once you've spent a minute or so on a question, make your best guess and keep moving on.

Don't panic if you can't finish all four passages. Make sure you do a good job on at least three passages—and remember to grid answers (even if they're blind guesses) for all questions by the end. Even if you try all four passages, you probably won't really work on all forty questions. For many questions, you'll just have to guess. Just make sure you guess on the tough ones and actually work on the easy ones!

When You're Running Out of Time

If you have less than 5 minutes left for the last passage, do the following:

1. Skip the prereading step.
2. Look for questions with specific line references and do them.
3. Refer to the cited location in the passage and answer the question as best you can, based on what you see there.
4. Make sure you have gridded in an answer for every question before time is called.

Scoring

Your performance on the Reading subject test will be averaged into your ACT Composite Score, weighted equally with your scores on the other three major subject tests. You will also receive:

- Reading subject score—from 1 to 36—for the entire Reading subject test
- Social Science/Sciences subscore—from 1 to 18—based on your performance on the nonfiction passages drawn from Social Studies and Natural Sciences
- Arts/Literature subscore—from 1 to 18—based on your performance on the nonfiction passage (drawn from the Humanities) and on the Prose Fiction passage

SCIENCE TEST

The Science subject test:

- Is 35 minutes long.
- Includes 7 passages, or sets of scientific information, involving graphs, tables, and research summaries. Typically, one of the passages involves two conflicting viewpoints on a single scientific issue.
- Consists of 40 questions, divided among the 7 passages. We divide the questions strategically into three categories:
  1. Data Analysis Questions
  2. Experiment Questions
  3. Principle Questions

The questions do not get harder as you proceed through the section.

Mindset

- Look for patterns. Usually, the exact data contained in Science passages are not as important as are changes in the data. Look for extremes (maximums and minimums), critical points (points of change), and variation (direct and inverse).
- Know your direction. There are two kinds of scientific reasoning—general-to-specific and specific-to-general. Always be aware of when scientists are inferring a specific case from a general rule, and when they are using specific data to form a (general) hypothesis.
- Refer, don't remember. Don't even think of trying to remember data. It's always there, right on the page, for you to refer to when needed.

The Kaplan Method

1. **Preread the passage.** Look for the overall topic. What is being researched? Look for the purpose of each experiment. How do the experiments differ? Don't get bogged down in details and don't worry about understanding everything.
2. **Consider the question stem.** Make sure you understand exactly what the question is asking. Get a sense of what the answer should be without looking at the choices, many of which are designed to mislead you if you're indecisive.
3. **Refer to the passage before looking at the choices.** Always refer back to the passage before looking at the choices and selecting one. Make sure you read charts and graphs accurately, and that you do not confuse different kinds of units.
4. **Answer the question in your own words.** Don't rely too much on your knowledge of science. Paraphrase the information in the passage.
5. **Match your answer with one of the choices.** Having an answer in mind will help you to avoid falling for a wrong answer.

Special Strategies

Reading Tables and Graphs

When reading tables and graphs, you should:

- Determine what is being represented
- Determine what the axes (or columns and rows) represent
- Take note of units of measurement
- Look for trends in the data

Experiments

Remember how experiments work. There is typically (though not always) a control group plus an experimental group or groups. In a well-designed experiment, the only difference between the groups will be a variation in the factor that's being tested. Ask yourself:

- What's the factor that's being varied?
- What's the control group, if any?
- What do the results show? What differences exist between the results for one group and those for another?

Conflicting Viewpoints Passage

Spend a little more time than usual on the prereading step of this passage. Focus on the two points of view. What are the scientists arguing about? What do they agree on, if anything? What do they differ on? Identify the following for each scientist:

- Basic theory statement (usually the first sentence of each scientist's presentation)
- Major pieces of data behind the theory (keeping in mind whether each supports the scientist's own theory or weakens the opposing scientist's theory)

Timing

Some Science passages are a lot harder than others, and they're not arranged in order of difficulty, so you might want to take a few seconds at the beginning of the subject test to page through the passages, gauging the difficulty of each one. You may wish to skip an entire passage if it seems very difficult (but remember that a very difficult passage may have very easy questions).

As in Reading, treat each passage and its questions as a block, taking two passes through each block before moving on to the next. Get the easy questions on the first pass through and save the tougher ones for the second pass. Some questions will probably be impossible for you to answer; take an intuitive guess on these.

Set your watch to 12:00 at the beginning of the subject test. Although you should go faster if you can, here's where you should be at the following checkpoints:

12:05 . . . . . One passage finished and answers gridded in
12:10 . . . . . Two passages finished and answers gridded in
12:15 . . . . . Three passages finished and answers gridded in
12:20 . . . . . Four passages finished and answers gridded in
12:25 . . . . . Five passages finished and answers gridded in
12:30 . . . . . Six passages finished and answers gridded in
12:35 . . . . . Seven passages finished and answers for the entire section gridded in

Don't spend time agonizing over specific questions. Avoid thinking long and hard about the answer choices. If you've spent a minute or so on a question and don't seem to be making any headway, make your best guess and move on.

Don't panic if you can't finish all seven passages, but try to do a good job on at least five of them. And make sure you remember to grid answers (even if they're blind guesses) for all questions by the end.

When You're Running Out of Time

If you have fewer than three minutes left for the last passage, do the following:

1. Skip the prereading step.
2. Look for questions that refer to specific experiments or to specific graphs or tables.
3. Refer to the cited location in the passage and answer the question as best you can, based on what you see there.
4. Make sure you have gridded in an answer for every question before time is called.

Scoring

Your performance on the Science subject test will be averaged into your ACT Composite Score, weighted equally with your scores on the other three major subject tests. You will also receive:

- Science subject score—from 1 to 36—for the entire Science subject test

Unlike the other three subject scores, the Science score is not divided into subscores.

WRITING TEST

The Writing test:

- Is optional (check with the schools to which you are applying and with your guidance counselor about whether you should take the test).
- Is 30 minutes long.
- Includes just one prompt about which you must write an essay. The essay must
  1. State a point of view on the issue.
  2. Support the point of view with concrete, detailed examples.
  3. Provide a clear and coherent argument.

Mindset

Don't wait until Test Day to think of examples you can use to support your ideas. Regardless of what question is raised in the prompt, you will draw your support from the things you know best and are most comfortable writing about—things that you know a fair amount of concrete detail about.

Refresh your memory about your favorite or most memorable books, school subjects, historical events, current events, personal experiences, activities—anything. By doing so, you strengthen mental connections to those ideas and details—that will make it easier to connect to the right examples on Test Day.

The Kaplan Method

1. **Pause to Know the Prompt.** Read about the issue and take a position on it. There is no right or wrong answer, but make sure you address the issue. In other words, answer the question.
2. **Plan.** Take 5 minutes or less to plan the essay before you write. Focus on what kinds of reasoning and examples you can use to support your position. If you find you have more examples for a position different from the one you thought you would take, change your position.
3. **Produce.** Write your draft, sticking closely to your plan. The essay should have three to five well-developed paragraphs with topic sentences and supporting details. Include an introductory paragraph stating your position and a concluding paragraph. Aim for 350 to 450 words, and write neatly.
4. **Proofread.** Always leave yourself two minutes to review your work—the time spent will definitely pay off. Very few of us can avoid the occasional confused sentence or omitted word when writing under pressure. Quickly review your essay to be sure your ideas are on the page, not just in your head.

Special Strategies

To write a complete, coherent essay in 30 minutes, you must be very focused. Spend five minutes up front on your plan, listing the topic of each paragraph. Then stick to the plan as you write the essay. Don't change the plan in midstream if another idea suddenly comes to you; it might derail the essay. Keep your focus on the issue and don't digress.

Make the structure of your essay very easy to for the reader to see. Have an introductory paragraph, two or three middle paragraphs, each focused on one example or bit of evidence, and a concluding paragraph.

Write neatly: graders can't help but feel negative about your essay if it's hard to decipher—and negative feelings affect holistic scoring. If your handwriting is a problem, print.

Timing

With only 30 minutes, efficient use of time is critical. Divide your time as follows:

5 minutes—Read the prompt and plan the essay.

20–22 minutes—Draft the essay, sticking to the plan.

3–5 minutes—Proofread and correct any errors.

When You're Running Out of Time

Try not to. Running out of time doesn't just mean guessing the last few questions as it does on the other tests; it means your essay won't be as complete and coherent as it should be. If you do start running out of time, forget the proofreading stage. If absolutely necessary, leave out one of your example paragraphs and go on to the concluding paragraph.

Scoring

Your essay will be graded on a holistic scale of 1–6 (6 being the best). Graders will be looking for an overall sense of your essay, not assigning separate scores for specific elements like grammar or organization. Two readers read and score each essay; then those scores are added together to arrive at your Writing subscore (from 2–12), which is reported as part of your English score. If there's a difference of more than a point between the two readers' scores, your essay will be read by a third reader. A combined English-Writing score also will be recorded. Two-thirds of this score is based on your English score and one-third is based on your writing subscore. The Combined English-Writing score does not count towards your Composite Score.

Statistically speaking, there will be few essays that score 6. If each grader gives your essay a 4 or 5, that will place you at the upper range of those taking the exam.

Chapter Eighteen: **Last-Minute Tips**

- **Three Days before the Test**
- **Two Days before the Test**
- **The Day before the Test**
- **The Morning of the Test**
- **During the Test**
- **After the Test**

Is it starting to feel like your whole life is a buildup to the ACT? You've known about it for years, you've worried about it for months, and now you've spent at least a few hours in solid preparation for it. As the test gets closer, you may find your anxiety is on the rise. But you really shouldn't worry. After the preparation you've received from this book, you're in good shape for Test Day.

To calm any pretest jitters you may have (and assuming you've left yourself at least some breathing time before your ACT), let's go over a few last-minute strategies for the couple of days before and after the test.

Emergency Plan

If you have two weeks or fewer to prep for the ACT, read this chapter. It tells you how to use your time wisely before, during, and after the test.

THREE DAYS BEFORE THE TEST

- If you haven't already done so, take one of the the full-length practice tests in this book under timed conditions or take one of the practice tests on the CD-ROM, if you've bought the version of this book with the CD-ROM. If you have already worked through all the tests in the book and on the CD, try an actual published ACT (your guidance counselor might have one).
- Try to use all of the techniques and tips you've learned in this book. Take control. Approach the test strategically and creatively.

WARNING: Don't take a full practice ACT unless you have at least 48 hours left before the test! Doing so will probably exhaust you, hurting your scoring potential on the actual test! You wouldn't run a marathon the day before the real thing, would you?

TWO DAYS BEFORE THE TEST

- Go over the results of your practice test. Don't worry too much about your score or whether you got a specific question right or wrong. Remember the practice test doesn't count. But do examine your performance on specific questions with an eye to how you might get through each one faster and with greater accuracy on the actual test to come.
- After reviewing your test, look over the Strategic Summaries. If you feel a little shaky about any of the areas mentioned, quickly read the relevant workouts.
- This is the day to do your last studying—review a couple of the more difficult principles we've covered, do a few more practice problems, and call it quits. It doesn't pay to make yourself crazy right before the test. Besides, you've prepared. You'll do well.

Get in the Zone

Being easily distracted diminishes your ability to pick up on every subtle and not-so-subtle component of the text. Everything from traffic outside to a proctor's noisy watch can distract on Test Day. You can train to get into the test "zone" by practicing with a radio on, or in a busy coffee shop.

THE DAY BEFORE THE TEST

- Don't study.
- Get together an "ACT survival kit" containing the following items:
  - Watch
  - At least three sharpened No. 2 pencils
  - Pencil sharpener
  - Two erasers
  - Photo ID card (if you're not taking the test at your high school, make sure your ID is official)
  - Calculator
  - Your admission ticket
  - Snack—there's a break, and you'll probably get hungry
  - Your lucky rabbit's foot
- Know exactly where you're going and how you're getting there. It's probably a good idea to visit your test center sometime before Test Day, so that you know what expect on the big day.
- Relax! Read a good book, take a bubble bath, watch TV. Exercise can be a good idea early in the afternoon. Working out makes it easier to sleep when you're nervous, and it also makes many people feel better. Of course, don't work so hard that you can't get up the next day!
- Get a good night's sleep. Go to bed early and allow for some extra time to get ready in the morning.

THE MORNING OF THE TEST

- Eat breakfast. Make it something substantial, but not anything too heavy or greasy. Don't drink a lot of coffee if you're not used to it; bathroom breaks cut into your time, and too much caffeine—or any other kind of drug—is a bad idea.
- Dress in layers so that you can adjust to the temperature of the test room.
- Read something. Warm up your brain with a newspaper or a magazine. Don't let the ACT be the first thing you read that day.
- Be sure to get there early. Allow yourself extra time for traffic, mass-transit delays, and any other possible problems.
- If you can, go to the test with a friend (even if he or she isn't taking the test). It's nice to have somebody supporting you right up to the last minute.

DURING THE TEST

- Don't get rattled. If you find your confidence slipping, remind yourself how well you've prepared. You've followed the Three Commandments of ACT Success. You know the test; you know the strategies; you know the material tested. You're in great shape, as long as you relax!
- Even if something goes really wrong, don't panic. If the test booklet is defective—two pages are stuck together or the ink has run—try to stay calm. Raise your hand, and tell the proctor you need a new book. If you accidentally misgrid your answer page or put the answers in the wrong section, again don't panic. Raise your hand, and tell the proctor. He or she might be able to arrange for you to regrid your test after it's over, when it won't cost you any time.

AFTER THE TEST

Once the test is over, put it out of your mind. If you don't plan to take the ACT again, shelve this book and start thinking about more interesting things.

You might walk out of the ACT thinking that you blew it. This is a normal reaction. Lots of people—even the highest scorers—feel that way. You tend to remember the questions that stumped you, not the many that you knew. If you're really concerned, call us for advice. Also call us if you had any problems with your test experience—a proctor who called time early, a testing room whose temperature hovered just below freezing. We'll do everything we can to make sure that your rights as a test taker are preserved!

But remember, unless you've ignored our recommendation about *not* listing any schools to receive your scores automatically, you've got nothing to worry about (provided that there is still time to get the scores there before the deadline). If you really did blow the test, you can take it again and no admissions officer will be the wiser.

Odds are, though, you didn't really blow it. Most people only remember their disasters on the test; they don't remember the numerous small victories that kept piling up the points.

ACT Practice Test One
Answer Sheet

English Test	10. F G H J	20. F G H J	30. F G H J	40. F G H J	50. F G H J	60. F G H J	70. F G H J
1. A B C D	11. A B C D	21. A B C D	31. A B C D	41. A B C D	51. A B C D	61. A B C D	71. A B C D
2. F G H J	12. F G H J	22. F G H J	32. F G H J	42. F G H J	52. F G H J	62. F G H J	72. F G H J
3. A B C D	13. A B C D	23. A B C D	33. A B C D	43. A B C D	53. A B C D	63. A B C D	73. A B C D
4. F G H J	14. F G H J	24. F G H J	34. F G H J	44. F G H J	54. F G H J	64. F G H J	74. F G H J
5. A B C D	15. A B C D	25. A B C D	35. A B C D	45. A B C D	55. A B C D	65. A B C D	75. A B C D
6. F G H J	16. F G H J	26. F G H J	36. F G H J	46. F G H J	56. F G H J	66. F G H J	
7. A B C D	17. A B C D	27. A B C D	37. A B C D	47. A B C D	57. A B C D	67. A B C D	
8. F G H J	18. F G H J	28. F G H J	38. F G H J	48. F G H J	58. F G H J	68. F G H J	
9. A B C D	19. A B C D	29. A B C D	39. A B C D	49. A B C D	59. A B C D	69. A B C D	

Math Test	9. A B C D E	18. F G H J K	27. A B C D E	36. F G H J K	45. A B C D E	54. F G H J K
1. A B C D E	10. F G H J K	19. A B C D E	28. F G H J K	37. A B C D E	46. F G H J K	55. A B C D E
2. F G H J K	11. A B C D E	20. F G H J K	29. A B C D E	38. F G H J K	47. A B C D E	56. F G H J K
3. A B C D E	12. F G H J K	21. A B C D E	30. F G H J K	39. A B C D E	48. F G H J K	57. A B C D E
4. F G H J K	13. A B C D E	22. F G H J K	31. A B C D E	40. F G H J K	49. A B C D E	58. F G H J K
5. A B C D E	14. F G H J K	23. A B C D E	32. F G H J K	41. A B C D E	50. F G H J K	59. A B C D E
6. F G H J K	15. A B C D E	24. F G H J K	33. A B C D E	42. F G H J K	51. A B C D E	60. F G H J K
7. A B C D E	16. F G H J K	25. A B C D E	34. F G H J K	43. A B C D E	52. F G H J K	
8. F G H J K	17. A B C D E	26. F G H J K	35. A B C D E	44. F G H J K	53. A B C D E	

Reading Test	6. F G H J	12. F G H J	18. F G H J	24. F G H J	30. F G H J	36 F G H J
1. A B C D	7. A B C D	13. A B C D	19. A B C D	25. A B C D	31. A B C D	37. A B C D
2. F G H J	8. F G H J	14. F G H J	20. F G H J	26. F G H J	32. F G H J	38. F G H J
3. A B C D	9. A B C D	15. A B C D	21. A B C D	27. A B C D	33. A B C D	39 A B C D
4. F G H J	10. F G H J	16. F G H J	22. F G H J	28. F G H J	34. F G H J	40. F G H J
5. A B C D	11. A B C D	17. A B C D	23. A B C D	29. A B C D	35. A B C D	

Science Test	6. F G H J	12. F G H J	18. F G H J	24. F G H J	30. F G H J	36. F G H J
1. A B C D	7. A B C D	13. A B C D	19. A B C D	25. A B C D	31. A B C D	37. A B C D
2. F G H J	8. F G H J	14. F G H J	20. F G H J	26. F G H J	32. F G H J	38. F G H J
3. A B C D	9. A B C D	15. A B C D	21. A B C D	27. A B C D	33. A B C D	39 A B C D
4. F G H J	10. F G H J	16. F G H J	22. F G H J	28. F G H J	34. F G H J	40. F G H J
5. A B C D	11. A B C D	17. A B C D	23. A B C D	29. A B C D	35. A B C D	

Practice Test One

HOW TO TAKE THESE PRACTICE TESTS

Practice Tests One and Two are Kaplan-created tests, similar to the actual ACT test booklet. Before taking a practice test, find a quiet room where you can work uninterrupted for three hours. Make sure you have a comfortable desk, your calculator, and several No. 2 pencils. Use the answer sheet to record your answers. Once you start a practice test, don't stop until you've finished. Remember: You can review any questions within a section, but you may not jump from one section to another.

You'll find the answers and explanations to the test questions immediately following each test.

ENGLISH TEST

45 Minutes—75 Questions

Directions: In the following five passages, certain words and phrases have been underlined and numbered. You will find alternatives for each underlined portion in the right-hand column. Select the one that best expresses the idea, that makes the statement acceptable in standard written English, or that is phrased most consistently with the style and tone of the entire passage. If you feel that the original version is best, select "NO CHANGE." You will also find questions asking about a section of the passage or about the entire passage. For these questions, decide which choice gives the most appropriate response to the given question. For each question in the test, select the best choice, and fill in the corresponding space on the answer sheet. You may wish to read each passage through before you begin to answer the questions associated with it. Most answers cannot be determined without reading several sentences around the phrases in question. Make sure to read far enough ahead each time you choose an alternative.

Passage I

Since primitive times, societies have created, and told [1] legends. Even before the development of written language, cultures would orally pass down these popular stories.

[2] These stories served the dual purpose of entertaining audiences and of transmitting values and beliefs from generation to generation. Indeed [3] today we have many more permanent ways of handing down our beliefs to future generations, we continue to create and tell legends. In our technological society, a new form of

1. **A.** NO CHANGE
   B. created then subsequently told
   C. created and told
   D. created, and told original

2. Suppose that the author wants to insert a sentence here to describe the different kinds of oral stories told by these societies. Which of the following sentences would best serve that purpose?
   F. These myths and tales varied in substance, from the humorous to the heroic.
   G. These myths and tales were often recited by paid storytellers.
   H. Unfortunately, no recording of the original myths and tales exists.
   J. Sometimes it took several evenings for the full story to be recited.

3. **A.** NO CHANGE
   B. However,
   C. Indeed,
   D. Although

GO ON TO THE NEXT PAGE

folk tale has emerged: <u>the</u> urban legend. 4

[2]

Urban legends are stories we all have heard; they are supposed to have really happened, but are never <u>verifiable however.</u> 5 It seems that the people involved can never be found. Researchers of the urban legend call the elusive participant in such supposed "real-life" events a FOAF—a Friend of a Friend.

[3]

Urban legends have some characteristic features. They are often humorous in nature with a surprise <u>ending and a conclusion.</u> 6 One such legend is the tale of the hunter who was returning home from an unsuccessful hunting trip. On his way home, he accidentally hit and killed a deer on a deserted highway. Even though he knew it was illegal, he decided to keep the deer, and he <u>loads it in</u> 7 the back of his station wagon.

As the hunter continued driving, the deer, <u>he was</u> 8 only temporarily knocked unconscious by the car, woke up and began thrashing around. The hunter panicked, stopped the car, ran to the ditch, and watched the enraged deer destroy his car.

4. F. NO CHANGE
   G. it is called the
   H. it being the
   J. known as the

5. A. NO CHANGE
   B. verifiable, however.
   C. verifiable, furthermore.
   D. verifiable.

6. F. NO CHANGE
   G. ending.
   H. ending, which is a conclusion.
   J. ending or conclusion.

7. A. NO CHANGE
   B. loaded it in
   C. is loading it in
   D. had loaded it in

8. F. NO CHANGE
   G. which being
   H. that is
   J. which was

GO ON TO THE NEXT PAGE

[4]

One legend involves alligators in the sewer systems of major metropolitan areas. According to the story, before alligators were a protected species, people [9] vacationing in Florida purchased baby alligators to take home as souvenirs. Between 1930 and 1940, nearly a million alligators in Florida were killed for the value of their skin, used to make expensive leather products such as boots and wallets. [10] After the novelty of having a pet alligator wore off, many people flushed their baby souvenirs down toilets. Legend has it that the baby alligators found a perfect growing and breeding environment in city sewer systems, where they thrive to this day on the ample supply of rats.

[5]

In addition to urban legends that are told from friend to friend, a growing number of urban legends are passed along through the Internet and e-mail. One of the more popular stories are about [11] a woman who was unwittingly charged $100 for a cookie recipe she requested at an upscale restaurant. To get her money's

9. **A.** NO CHANGE
   B. species; people
   C. species. People
   D. species people

10. **F.** NO CHANGE
    G. Because their skin is used to make expensive leather products such as boots and wallets, nearly a million alligators in Florida were killed between 1930 and 1940.
    H. Killed between 1930 and 1940, the skin of nearly a million alligators from Florida was used to make expensive leather products such as boots and wallets.
    J. OMIT the underlined portion.

11. **A.** NO CHANGE
    B. would be about
    C. is about
    D. is dealing with

GO ON TO THE NEXT PAGE

worth, this <u>woman supposed</u> 12 copied the recipe for the delicious cookies and forwarded it via e-mail to everyone she knew.

12. F. NO CHANGE
G. woman supposedly
H. women supposedly
J. women supposed to

[6]

Although today's technology enhances our ability to tell and retell urban legends, the Internet can also serve as a monitor of urban legends. <u>Dedicated to commonly told urban legends, research is done by many websites.</u> 13 According to those websites, most legends, including the ones told here, have no basis in reality.

13. A. NO CHANGE
B. Many websites are dedicated to researching the validity of commonly told urban legends.
C. Researching the validity of commonly told urban legends, many websites are dedicated.
D. OMIT the underlined portion.

Items 14–15 ask about the passage as a whole.

14. The author wants to insert the following sentence:

Other urban legends seem to be designed to instill fear.

What would be the most logical placement for this sentence?

F. After the last sentence of paragraph 2
G. After the second sentence of paragraph 3
H. Before the first sentence of paragraph 4
J. After the last sentence of paragraph 4

15. Suppose that the author had been assigned to write an essay comparing the purposes and topics of myths and legends in primitive societies and in our modern society. Would this essay fulfill that assignment?

A. Yes, because the essay describes myths and legends from primitive societies and modern society.
B. Yes, because the essay provides explanations of possible purposes and topics for myths and legends from primitive societies and modern society.
C. No, because the essay does not provide enough information about the topics of the myths and legends in primitive societies to make a valid comparison.
D. No, because the essay doesn't provide any information on the myths and legends of primitive societies.

GO ON TO THE NEXT PAGE

Passage II

What does it mean to be successful? Do one [16] measure success by money? If I told you about a man: working [17] as a teacher, a land surveyor, and a factory worker (never holding any of these jobs for more than a few years), would that man sound like a success to you? If I told you that he spent two solitary years living alone [18] in a small cabin that he built for himself, and that he spent those years looking at plants and writing in a diary—would you think of him as a celebrity or an important figure? What if I told you that he rarely ventured [19] far from the town where he was born, that he was thrown in jail for refusing to pay his taxes, and that he died at the age of forty-five? Do any of these facts seem to point to a man whose life should be studied and emulated?

You may already know about this man. You may even have read some of his writings. His name was: Henry David Thoreau, and he [20] was, in addition to the jobs listed above, a poet, an essayist, a naturalist, and a social critic. Although the facts listed about him may

16. **F.** NO CHANGE
G. Does we
H. Does one
J. Did you

17. **A.** NO CHANGE
B. man who worked
C. man and worked
D. man, which working

18. **F.** NO CHANGE
G. two years living alone
H. two solitary years all by himself
J. a couple of lonely years living in solitude

19. **A.** NO CHANGE
B. he ventured rarely
C. he has rare ventures
D. this person was to venture rarely

20. **F.** NO CHANGE
G. was Henry David Thoreau and he
H. was: Henry David Thoreau, who
J. was Henry David Thoreau, and he

GO ON TO THE NEXT PAGE

not seem to add up to much, he <u>was, in fact a</u> (21) tremendously influential person. Along with writers such as Ralph Waldo Emerson, Mark Twain, and Walt Whitman, Thoreau helped to create the first literature and philosophy that most people identify as <u>unique</u> (22) "American."

In 1845, Thoreau built a <u>cabin. Near</u> (23) Walden Pond and remained there for more than two years, living alone, fending for himself, and observing the nature around him. He kept scrupulous notes in his diary, notes that he later distilled into his most famous work titled *Walden*. <u>*Walden* is read by many literature students today.</u> (24)

[1] To protest slavery, Thoreau refused to pay his taxes in 1846. [2] Thoreau was a firm believer in the abolition of slavery, and he objected to the practice's extension into the new territories of the West. [3] For this act of rebellion, he was thrown in the Concord jail. [25]

21. **A.** NO CHANGE
B. was, in fact, a
C. was in fact a
D. was in fact, a

22. **F.** NO CHANGE
G. uniquely
H. uniqueness
J. the most unique

23. **A.** NO CHANGE
B. cabin. On
C. cabin, by
D. cabin near

24. **F.** NO CHANGE
G. This book is read by many literature students today.
H. Today, many literature students read *Walden*.
J. OMIT the underlined portion.

25. What is the most logical order of sentences in this paragraph?
A. NO CHANGE
B. 3, 2, 1
C. 2, 1, 3
D. 3, 1, 2

GO ON TO THE NEXT PAGE

Thoreau used his writing to spread his message of resistance and <u>activism; he published</u> [26] an essay entitled *Civil Disobedience* (also known as *Resistance to Civil Government*). In it, Thoreau laid out his argument for refusing to obey unjust laws.

26. **F.** NO CHANGE
    G. activism and he published
    H. activism; which is why he published
    J. activism to publish

Although Thoreau's life was very brief, <u>his</u> [27] works and his ideas continue to touch and influence people. Students all over the country—all over the world—continue to read his essays and hear his unique voice, urging them to lead lives of principle, individuality, and freedom. [28]

27. **A.** NO CHANGE
    B. he's
    C. their
    D. those

28. The purpose of this paragraph is to:
    F. explain why Thoreau was put in jail.
    G. prove a point about people's conception of success.
    H. suggest that Thoreau may be misunderstood.
    J. discuss Thoreau's importance in today's world.

To be able to live out the ideas that burn in <u>the heart of a person</u> [29]—surely that is the meaning of success.

29. **A.** NO CHANGE
    B. one's heart
    C. the heart and soul of a person
    D. through the heart of a person

Question 30 asks about the preceding passage as a whole.

30. By including questions throughout the entire first paragraph, the author allows the reader to:
    F. answer each question as the passage proceeds.
    G. think about the meaning of "success."
    H. assess the quality of Thoreau's work.
    J. form an opinion about greed in modern society.

GO ON TO THE NEXT PAGE

Passage III

[1]

More than half of the world's currently living plant 31 and animal species live in tropical rainforests. Four square miles of a Central American rainforest can be home to up to 1,500 different species of flowering plants, 700 species of trees, 400 species of birds, and 125 species of mammals. Of these mammals, the sloth is one of the most unusual.

31. **A.** NO CHANGE
B. currently existing plant
C. living plant
D. plant

[2]

Unlike most mammals, the sloth is usually upside down. A sloth does just about everything upside down, including sleeping, eating, mating, and giving birth. Its' unique 32 anatomy allows the sloth to spend most of the time hanging from one tree branch or another, high in the canopy of a rainforest tree. About the size of a large domestic cat, the 33 sloth hangs from its unusually long limbs and long hook-like claws. Specially designed for limbs, the sloth's muscles seem to cling to things. 34

32. **F.** NO CHANGE
G. It's unique
H. Its unique
J. Its uniquely

33. **A.** NO CHANGE
B. cat; the
C. cat. The
D. cat, but the

34. **F.** NO CHANGE
G. The sloth's muscles seem to cling to things for specially designed limbs.
H. The muscles in a sloth's limbs seem to be specially designed for clinging to things.
J. OMIT the underlined portion.

GO ON TO THE NEXT PAGE

[3]

In fact, a sloth's limbs are <u>so specific</u> (35) adapted to upside-down life that a sloth is essentially incapable of walking on the ground. <u>Instead, they</u> (36) must crawl or drag itself with its massive claws. This makes it easy to see why the sloth rarely leaves its home in the trees. <u>Because</u> (37) it can not move swiftly on the ground, the sloth is an excellent swimmer.

[4]

[38] A sloth can hang upside down and, without moving the rest of its <u>body turn</u> (39) its face 180 degrees so that it <u>was looking</u> (40) at the ground. A sloth can rotate its forelimbs in all directions, so it can easily reach the leaves that make up its diet. The sloth can also roll itself up into a ball in order to <u>protect and defend itself</u> (41) from

35. **A.** NO CHANGE
B. so specific and
C. so specified
D. so specifically

36. **F.** NO CHANGE
G. Instead, it
H. However, they
J. In addition, it

37. **A.** NO CHANGE
B. Despite
C. Similarly,
D. Though

38. The author wants to insert a sentence here to help connect paragraph 3 and paragraph 4. Which of the following sentences would best serve that purpose?
F. Of course, many other animals are also excellent swimmers.
G. Another unique characteristic of the sloth is its flexibility.
H. In addition to swimming, the sloth is an incredible climber.
J. Flexibility is a trait that helps the sloth survive.

39. **A.** NO CHANGE
B. body turns
C. body, it has the capability of turning
D. body, turn

40. **F.** NO CHANGE
G. had been looking
H. will have the ability to be looking
J. can look

41. **A.** NO CHANGE
B. protect, and defend itself
C. protects itself
D. protect itself

GO ON TO THE NEXT PAGE

predators. The howler monkey, another inhabitant of the rainforest, is not as flexible as the sloth. 42

[5]

The best defense a sloth has from predators such as jaguars and large snakes, though, is its camouflage. During the rainy season, a sloth's thick brown or gray fur is usually covered with a coat of blue-green algae. Which 43 helps it blend in with its forest surroundings. Another type of camouflage is the sloth's incredibly slow movement: it often moves less than 100 feet during a 24-hour period.

[6]

It is this slow movement that earned the sloth its name. *Sloth* is also a word for laziness or an aversion to work. But even though it sleeps an average of 15 hours a day, the sloth isn't necessarily lazy. It just moves, upside down, at its own slow pace through its world of rainforest trees. [44]

42. **F.** NO CHANGE
G. Another inhabitant of the rainforest, the howler monkey, is not as flexible as the sloth.
H. Not as flexible as the sloth is the howler monkey, another inhabitant of the rainforest.
J. OMIT the underlined portion.

43. **A.** NO CHANGE
B. algae, which
C. algae, being that it
D. algae

44. The author is considering deleting the last sentence of paragraph 6. This change would:
F. diminish the amount of information provided about the habits of the sloth.
G. make the ending of the passage more abrupt.
H. emphasize the slothful nature of the sloth.
J. make the tone of the essay more consistent.

GO ON TO THE NEXT PAGE

Question 45 asks about the preceding passage as a whole.

45. The author wants to insert the following description:

> An observer could easily be tricked into thinking that a sloth was just a pile of decaying leaves.

What would be the most appropriate placement for this sentence?

A. After the last sentence of paragraph 1
B. After the third sentence of paragraph 2
C. Before the last sentence of paragraph 5
D. Before the first sentence of paragraph 6

GO ON TO THE NEXT PAGE

Passage IV

During the summer of 1988, I watched Yellowstone National Park go up in flames. In June, <u>fires ignited by lightning</u> 46 had been allowed to burn unsuppressed because park officials expected that the usual summer rains would douse the flames. However, the rains never <u>will have come</u> 47. A plentiful fuel supply of fallen logs and pine needles was available, and winds of up to 100 mph whipped the spreading fires along and carried red-hot embers to other areas, creating new fires. By the time park officials succumbed to the pressure of public opinion and <u>decide</u> 48 to try to extinguish the <u>flames. It's</u> 49 too late. The situation remained out of control in spite of the efforts of 9,000 fire fighters who were using state-of-the-art equipment. By September, more than 720,000 acres of Yellowstone had been affected by fire. <u>Nature was only able to curb the destruction</u> 50; the smoke did not begin to clear until the first snow arrived on September 11.

46. **F.** NO CHANGE
G. fires having been ignited by lightning
H. fires, the kind ignited by lightning,
J. fires ignited and started by lightning

47. **A.** NO CHANGE
B. came
C. were coming
D. have come

48. **F.** NO CHANGE
G. are deciding
H. decided
J. OMIT the underlined portion.

49. **A.** NO CHANGE
B. flames, it's
C. flames, it was
D. flames; it was

50. **F.** NO CHANGE
G. Only curbing the destruction by able nature
H. Only nature was able to curb the destruction
J. Nature was able to curb only the destruction

GO ON TO THE NEXT PAGE

Test Prep and Admissions

<u>Being that I was</u> (51) an ecologist who has studied forests for 20 years, I knew that this was not nearly the tragedy it seemed to be. Large fires are, after all, necessary <u>in order that the continued health in the forest ecosystem be maintained</u> (52). Fires thin out overcrowded areas and allow the sun to reach species of plants stunted by shade. Ash fertilizes the soil, and fire smoke kills forest bacteria. In the case of the lodgepole pine, fire is essential to reproduction: the <u>pines' cone</u> (53) open only when exposed to temperatures greater than 112 degrees.

The fires in Yellowstone did result in some loss of wildlife, but overall, the region's animals proved to be fire-tolerant and fire-adaptive. <u>However,</u> (54) large animals such as bison were often seen <u>grazing, and</u> (55) bedding down in meadows near burning forests. Also, the fire posed little threat to the members of any endangered animal species in the park.

My confidence in the natural resilience of the forest has been borne out in the years since the fires

51. **A.** NO CHANGE
B. Being that I am
C. I'm
D. As

52. **F.** NO CHANGE
G. for the continued health of the forest ecosystem to be maintained.
H. in order to continue the maintenance of the health of the forest ecosystem.
J. for the continued health of the forest ecosystem.

53. **A.** NO CHANGE
B. pines cones'
C. pine's cones
D. pine's cone

54. **F.** NO CHANGE
G. Clearly,
H. In fact,
J. Instead,

55. **A.** NO CHANGE
B. grazing; and bedding
C. grazing: and bedding
D. grazing and bedding

GO ON TO THE NEXT PAGE

ravaged Yellowstone. <u>Judged from recent pictures of the park</u> [56] the forest was not destroyed; <u>it</u> [57] was rejuvenated.

56. **F.** NO CHANGE
G. Recent pictures of the park show that
H. Judging by the recent pictures of the park,
J. As judged according to pictures taken of the park recently,

57. **A.** NO CHANGE
B. they
C. the fires
D. I

Items 58–59 pose questions about the passage as a whole.

58. The writer is considering inserting the following true statement after the first sentence of the second paragraph:

> Many more acres of forest burned in Alaska in 1988 than in Yellowstone Park.

Would this addition be appropriate for the essay?

F. Yes, the statement would add important information about the effects of large-scale forest fires.
G. Yes, the statement would provide an informative contrast to the Yellowstone fire.
H. No, the statement would not provide any additional information about the effect of the 1988 fire in Yellowstone.
J. No, the statement would undermine the author's position as an authority on the subject of forest fires.

59. Suppose that the writer wishes to provide additional support for the claim that the fire posed little threat to the members of any endangered animal species in the park. Which of the following additions would be most effective?

A. A list of the endangered animals known to inhabit the park
B. A discussion of the particular vulnerability of endangered species of birds to forest fires
C. An explanation of the relative infrequency of such an extensive series of forest fires
D. A summary of reports of biologists who monitored the activity of endangered species in the park during the fire

GO ON TO THE NEXT PAGE

Passage V

[1]

White water rafting being [60] a favorite pastime of mine for several years. I have drifted down many challenging North American rivers, including the Snake, the Green, and the Salmon, and there are many other rivers in America as well. [61] I have spent some of my best moments in dangerous rapids, yet nothing has matched the thrill I experienced facing my first rapids, on the Deschutes River. [62]

[2]

My father and I spent the morning floating down a calm and peaceful stretch of the Deschutes in his wooden MacKenzie river boat. This trip it being [63] the wooden boat's first time down rapids, as well as mine. Rapids are rated according to a uniform scale of relative difficulty. [64]

[3]

Roaring, I was in the boat approaching Whitehorse Rapids. [65] I felt much like a novice skier peering down her first steep slope: I was scared, but even more excited.

60. **F.** NO CHANGE
G. have been
H. has been
J. was

61. **A.** NO CHANGE
B. Salmon, just three of many rivers existing in North America.
C. Salmon; many other rivers exist in North America.
D. Salmon.

62. **F.** NO CHANGE
G. rapids: on Deschutes River.
H. rapids; on the Deschutes River.
J. rapids on the Deschutes River.

63. **A.** NO CHANGE
B. it happened that it was
C. was
D. being

64. **F.** NO CHANGE
G. Rated according to a uniform scale, rapids are relatively difficult.
H. (Rapids are rated according to a uniform scale of relative difficulty.)
J. OMIT the underlined portion.

65. **A.** NO CHANGE
B. It roared, and the boat and I approached Whitehorse Rapids.
C. While the roaring boat was approaching Whitehorse Rapids, I could hear the water.
D. I could hear the water roar as we approached Whitehorse Rapids.

GO ON TO THE NEXT PAGE

The water churned and covering me (66) with a refreshing spray. My father, towards the stern, controlled the oars. The carefree expression he usually wore on the river had been replaced and instead he adopted (67) a look of intense concentration as he maneuvered around boulders dotting our path. To release tension, we began to holler like kids on a roller coaster, our voices echoing across (68) the water as we lurched violently about.

Suddenly we came to a jarring halt and we stopped (69); the left side of the bow was wedged on a large rock. A whirlpool whirled around us; if we capsized we would be sucked into the undertow. Instinctively, I threw all of my weight towards the right side of the tilting boat. Luckily, it was (70) just enough force to dislodge us, and we continued on down for about ten more minutes of spectacular rapids.

[5]

Later that day we went through Buckskin Mary Rapids and Boxcar Rapids. When we pulled up on the bank that evening, we saw that the boat had received its first scar: that scar was a (71) small hole on the upper bow

66. F. NO CHANGE
G. churned, and covering me
H. churning and covering me
J. churned, covering me

67. A. NO CHANGE
B. with
C. by another countenance altogether:
D. instead with some other expression;

68. F. NO CHANGE
G. throughout
H. around
J. from

69. A. NO CHANGE
B. which stopped us
C. and stopped
D. OMIT the underlined portion.

70. F. NO CHANGE
G. it's
H. it is
J. its

71. A. NO CHANGE
B. that was a
C. which was a
D. a

GO ON TO THE NEXT PAGE

from the boulder we had wrestled with. In the years to come, we went down many rapids and the boat receiving many [72] bruises, but Whitehorse is the most memorable rapids of all. [73]

72. F. NO CHANGE
G. received many
H. received much
J. receives many

73. Which of the following concluding sentences would most effectively emphasize the final point made in this paragraph while retaining the style and tone of the narrative as a whole?
A. The brutal calamities that it presented the unwary rafter were more than offset by its beguiling excitement.
B. Perhaps it is true that your first close encounter with white water is your most intense.
C. Or, if not the most memorable, then at least a very memorable one!
D. Call me crazy or weird if you want, but white water rafting is the sport for me.

Items 74–75 pose questions about the passage as a whole.

74. The writer has been assigned to write an essay that focuses on the techniques of white water rafting. Would this essay meet the requirements of that assignment?
F. No, because the essay's main focus is on a particular experience, not on techniques.
G. No, because the essay mostly deals with the relationship between father and daughter.
H. Yes, because specific rafting techniques are the essay's main focus.
J. Yes, because it presents a dramatic story of a day of white water rafting.

75. Suppose that the writer wants to add the following sentence to the essay:

It was such a peaceful summer day that it was hard to believe dangerous rapids awaited us downstream.

What would be the most logical placement of this sentence?
A. After the last sentence of paragraph 1
B. After the last sentence of paragraph 2
C. Before the first sentence of paragraph 4
D. After the last sentence of paragraph 4

IF YOU FINISH BEFORE TIME IS CALLED, YOU MAY CHECK YOUR WORK ON THIS SECTION ONLY. DO NOT TURN TO ANY OTHER SECTION IN THE TEST.

MATH TEST

60 Minutes—60 Questions

Directions: Solve each of the following problems, select the correct answer, and then fill in the corresponding space on your answer sheet.

Don't linger over problems that are too time-consuming. Do as many as you can, then come back to the others in the time you have remaining.

Calculator use is permitted, but some problems can best be solved without a calculator.

Note: Unless otherwise noted, all of the following should be assumed.

1. Illustrative figures are *not* necessarily drawn to scale.

2. All geometric figures lie in a plane.

3. The term *line* indicates a straight line.

4. The term *average* indicates arithmetic mean.

Do Your Figuring Here.

1. In a recent survey, 14 people found their mayor to be "very competent." This number is exactly 20% of the people surveyed. How many people were surveyed?

A. 28
B. 35
C. 56
D. 70
E. 84

2. A train traveled at a rate of 90 miles per hour for x hours and then at a rate of 60 miles per hour for y hours. Which expression represents the train's average rate in miles per hour for the entire distance traveled?

F. $\frac{540}{xy}$

G. $\frac{90}{x} \times \frac{60}{y}$

H. $\frac{90}{x} + \frac{60}{y}$

J. $\frac{90x + 60y}{x + y}$

K. $\frac{150}{x + y}$

GO ON TO THE NEXT PAGE

Do Your Figuring Here.

3. In a certain string ensemble, the ratio of men to women is 5:3. If there are a total of 24 people in the ensemble, how many women are there?

A. 12
B. 11
C. 10
D. 9
E. 8

4. If $x \neq 0$, and $x^2 - 3x = 6x$, then $x = ?$

F. −9
G. −3
H. $\sqrt{3}$
J. 3
K. 9

5. The two overlapping circles below form three regions, as shown:

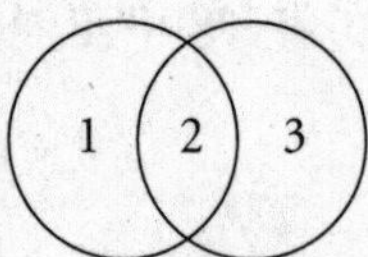

What is the maximum number of regions that can be formed by three overlapping circles?

A. 5
B. 6
C. 7
D. 8
E. 9

6. If $x^2 + 6x + 8 = 4 + 10x$, then x equals which of the following?

F. −2
G. −1
H. 0
J. 1
K. 2

GO ON TO THE NEXT PAGE

Do Your Figuring Here.

7. Nine less than the number c is the same as the number d, and d less than twice c is 20. Which two equations could be used to determine the value of c and d?

A. $d - 9 = c$
$d - 2c = 20$

B. $c - 9 = d$
$2c - d = 20$

C. $c - 9 = d$
$d - 2c = 20$

D. $9 - c = d$
$2c - d = 20$

E. $9 - c = d$
$2cd = 20$

8. An ice cream parlor offers 5 flavors of ice cream and 4 different toppings (sprinkles, hot fudge, whipped cream, and butterscotch). There is a special offer that includes one flavor of ice cream and one topping, served in a cup, sugar cone, or waffle cone. How many ways are there to order ice cream with the special offer?

F. 4
G. 5
H. 12
J. 23
K. 60

9. At a recent audition for a school play, 1 out of 3 students who auditioned were asked to come to a second audition. After the second audition, 75% of those asked to the second audition were offered parts. If 18 students were offered parts, how many students went to the first audition?

A. 18
B. 24
C. 48
D. 56
E. 72

GO ON TO THE NEXT PAGE

Do Your Figuring Here.

10. One number is 5 times another number and their sum is –60. What is the lesser of the two numbers?

F. –5
G. –10
H. –12
J. –48
K. –50

11. In the figure below, which is composed of equilateral triangles, what is the greatest number of parallelograms that can be found?

A. 6
B. 9
C. 12
D. 15
E. 18

12. The circle in the figure below is inscribed in a square with a perimeter of 16 inches. What is the area of the shaded region?

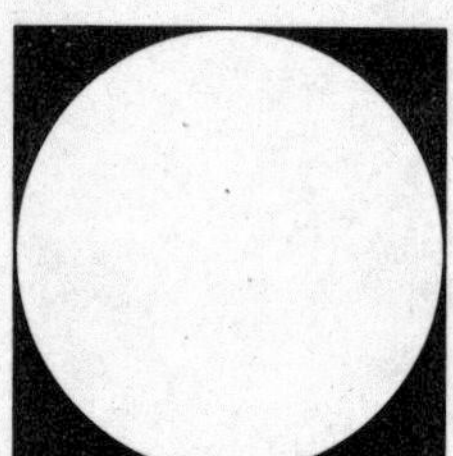

F. 4π
G. $16 - 2\pi$
H. $16 - 4\pi$
J. $8 - 2\pi$
K. $8 - 4\pi$

GO ON TO THE NEXT PAGE

Do Your Figuring Here.

13. How many positive integers less than 50 are multiples of 4 but <u>not</u> multiples of 6?

A. 4
B. 6
C. 8
D. 10
E. 12

14. What is the value of $f(3)$ where $f(x) = (8 - 3x)(x^2 - 2x - 15)$?

F. −30
G. −18
H. 12
J. 24
K. 30

15. A class contains five juniors and five seniors. If one member of the class is assigned at random to present a paper on a certain subject, and another member of the class is randomly assigned to assist him, what is the probability that both will be juniors?

A. $\frac{1}{10}$
B. $\frac{1}{5}$
C. $\frac{2}{9}$
D. $\frac{2}{5}$
E. $\frac{1}{2}$

16. In triangle XYZ below, $\overline{XS}$ and $\overline{SZ}$ are 3 and 12 units, respectively. If the area of triangle XYZ is 45 square units, how many units long is altitude $\overline{YS}$?

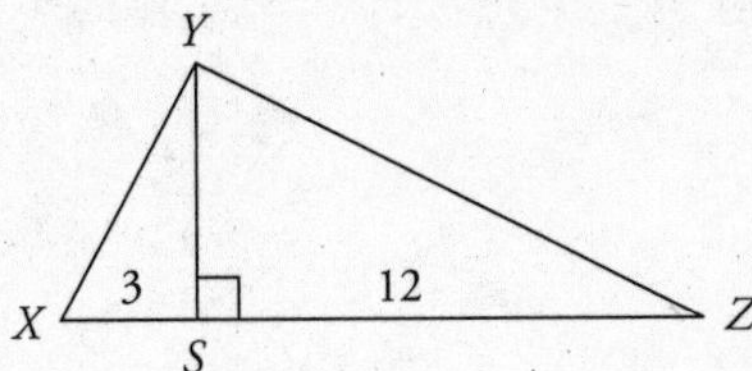

F. 3
G. 6
H. 9
J. 12
K. 15

GO ON TO THE NEXT PAGE

17. At which *y*-coordinate does the line described by the equation $6y - 3x = 18$ intersect the *y*-axis?

A. 18
B. 9
C. 6
D. 3
E. 2

Do Your Figuring Here.

18. If $x^2 - y^2 = 12$ and $x - y = 4$, what is the value of $x^2 + 2xy + y^2$?

F. 3
G. 8
H. 9
J. 12
K. 16

19. What is the area in square units of the figure below?

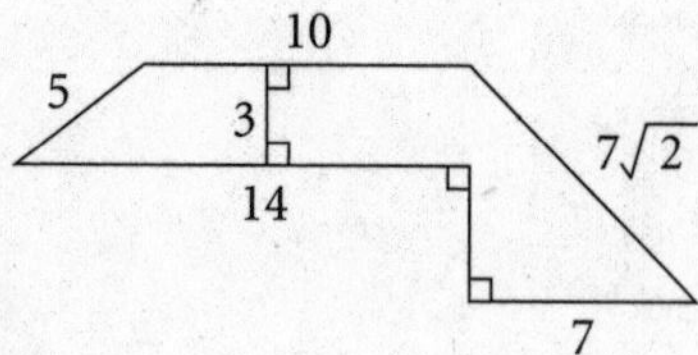

A. 147
B. 108.5
C. 91
D. 60.5
E. $39 + 7\sqrt{2}$

20. A carpenter is cutting wood to make a new bookcase with a board that is 12 feet long. If the carpenter cuts off 3 pieces, each of which is 17 inches long, how many inches long is the remaining fourth and final board? (A foot contains 12 inches.)

F. 36
G. 51
H. 93
J. 108
K. 144

GO ON TO THE NEXT PAGE

21. If $x^2 - 4x - 6 = 6$, what are the possible values for x?

A. 4, 12
B. −6, 2
C. −6, −2
D. 6, 2
E. 6, −2

Do Your Figuring Here.

22. If −3 is a solution for the equation $x^2 + kx - 15 = 0$, what is the value of k?

F. 5
G. 2
H. −2
J. −5
K. cannot be determined from the information given

23. If the lengths, in inches, of all three sides of a triangle are integers, and one side is 7 inches long, what is the smallest possible perimeter of the triangle, in inches?

A. 9
B. 10
C. 12
D. 15
E. 18

24. If $0° < \theta < 90°$ and $\sin\theta = \frac{\sqrt{11}}{2\sqrt{3}}$, then $\cos\theta = ?$

F. $\frac{1}{2\sqrt{3}}$
G. $\frac{1}{\sqrt{11}}$
H. $\frac{2}{\sqrt{3}}$
J. $\frac{2\sqrt{3}}{\sqrt{11}}$
K. $\frac{11}{2\sqrt{3}}$

GO ON TO THE NEXT PAGE

Do Your Figuring Here.

25. Which of the following expressions is equivalent to $\frac{\sqrt{3+x}}{\sqrt{3-x}}$ for all x such that $-3 < x < 3$?

A. $\frac{3-x}{3+x}$

B. $\frac{3+x}{3-x}$

C. $\frac{-3\sqrt{3+x}}{3-x}$

D. $\frac{\sqrt{9-x^2}}{3-x}$

E. $\frac{x^2-9}{3+x}$

26. In a certain cookie jar containing only macaroons and gingersnaps, the ratio of macaroons to gingersnaps is 2 to 5. Which of the following could be the total number of cookies in the cookie jar?

F. 24
G. 35
H. 39
J. 48
K. 52

27. What is the sum of $\frac{3}{16}$ and .175?

A. .3165
B. .3500
C. .3625
D. .3750
E. .3875

28. What is the maximum possible area, in square inches, of a rectangle with a perimeter of 20 inches?

F. 15
G. 20
H. 25
J. 30
K. 40

GO ON TO THE NEXT PAGE

Do Your Figuring Here.

29. $\dfrac{\dfrac{3}{2}+\dfrac{7}{4}}{\left(\dfrac{15}{8}-\dfrac{3}{4}\right)-\left(\dfrac{4+3}{-4+3}\right)}=?$

A. $\frac{3}{8}$
B. $\frac{2}{5}$
C. $\frac{9}{13}$
D. $\frac{5}{2}$
E. $\frac{8}{3}$

30. If $x - 15 = 7 - 5(x - 4)$, then $x = ?$

F. 0
G. 2
H. 4
J. 5
K. 7

31. The sketch below shows the dimensions of a flower garden. What is the area of this garden in square meters?

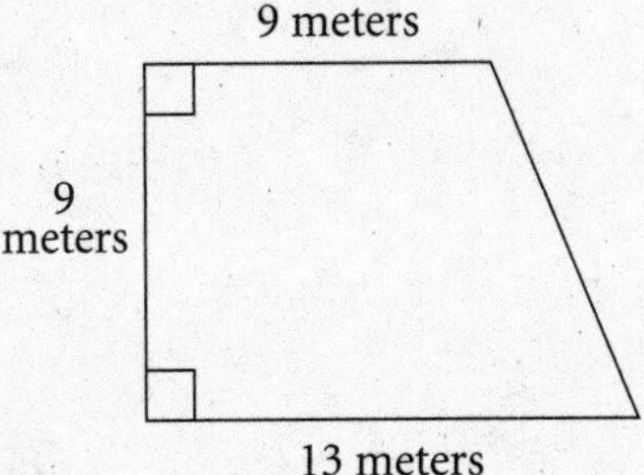

A. 31
B. 85
C. 99
D. 101
E. 117

32. What is the slope of the line described by the equation $6y - 3x = 18$?

F. -2

G. $-\frac{1}{2}$

H. $\frac{1}{2}$

J. 2

K. 3

33. Line m passes through the point (4, 3) in the standard (x, y) coordinate plane, and is perpendicular to the line described by the equation $y = -\frac{4}{5}x + 6$. Which of the following equations describes line m?

A. $y = \frac{5}{4}x + 2$

B. $y = -\frac{5}{4}x + 6$

C. $y = \frac{4}{5}x - 2$

D. $y = -\frac{4}{5}x + 2$

E. $y = \frac{5}{4}x - 2$

34. Line t in the standard (x, y) coordinate plane has a y-intercept of -3 and is parallel to the line having the equation $3x - 5y = 4$. Which of the following is an equation for line t?

F. $y = -\frac{3}{5}x + 3$

G. $y = -\frac{5}{3}x - 3$

H. $y = \frac{3}{5}x + 3$

J. $y = \frac{5}{3}x + 3$

K. $y = \frac{3}{5}x - 3$

Do Your Figuring Here.

GO ON TO THE NEXT PAGE

Do Your Figuring Here.

35. If $y = mx + b$, which of the following equations expresses x in terms of y, m, and b?

A. $x = \frac{y-b}{m}$

B. $x = \frac{b-y}{m}$

C. $x = \frac{y+b}{m}$

D. $x = \frac{y}{m} - b$

E. $x = \frac{y}{m} + b$

36. In the figure below, $\overline{AB} = 20$, $\overline{BC} = 15$, and $\angle ADB$ and $\angle ABC$ are right angles. What is the length of $\overline{AD}$?

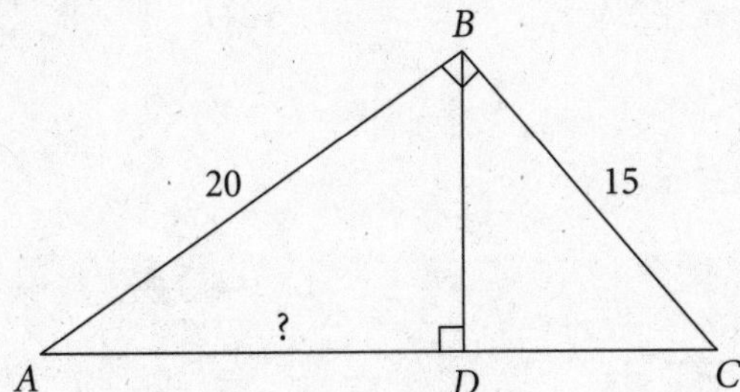

F. 9
G. 12
H. 15
J. 16
K. 25

GO ON TO THE NEXT PAGE

37. In the standard (x, y) coordinate plane shown in the figure below, points A and B lie on line m, and point C lies below it. The coordinates of points A, B, and C are (0, 5), (5, 5), and (3, 3), respectively. What is the shortest possible distance from point C to a point on line m?

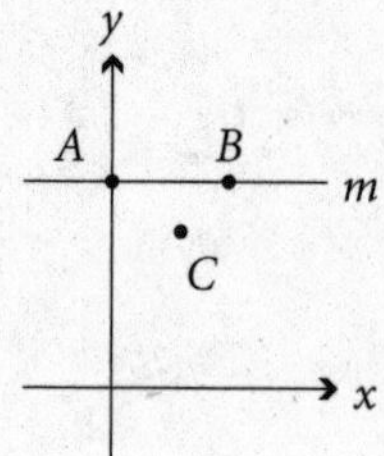

A. 2
B. $2\sqrt{2}$
C. 3
D. $\sqrt{13}$
E. 5

38. For all $x \neq 8$, $\frac{x^2 - 11x + 24}{8 - x} = ?$

F. $8 - x$
G. $3 - x$
H. $x - 3$
J. $x - 8$
K. $x - 11$

39. Points A and B lie in the standard (x, y) coordinate plane. The (x, y) coordinates of A are (2, 1) and the (x, y) coordinates of B are (–2, –2). What is the distance from A to B ?

A. $3\sqrt{2}$
B. $3\sqrt{3}$
C. 5
D. 6
E. 7

Do Your Figuring Here.

GO ON TO THE NEXT PAGE

Do Your Figuring Here.

40. In the figure below, $\overline{AB}$ and $\overline{CD}$ are both tangent to the circle as shown, and $ABCD$ is a rectangle with side lengths $2x$ and $5x$ as shown. What is the area of the shaded region?

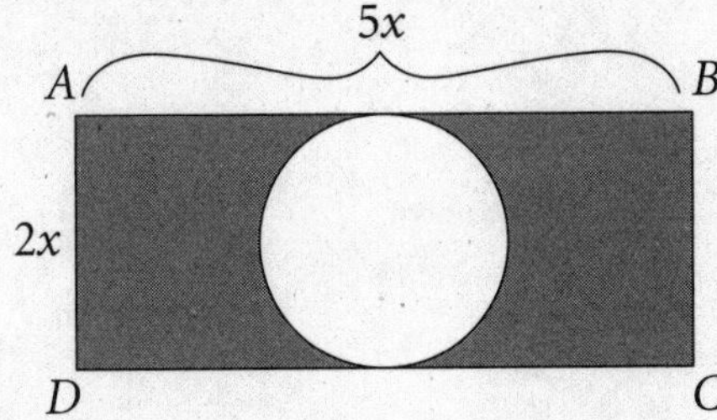

F. $10\pi x^2$
G. $10x^2 - \pi x^2$
H. $10x^2 - 2\pi x$
J. $9\pi x^2$
K. $6\pi x^2$

41. If $0° < \theta < 90°$ and $\cos \theta = \frac{5\sqrt{2}}{8}$, then $\tan \theta = ?$

A. $\frac{5}{\sqrt{7}}$

B. $\frac{\sqrt{7}}{5}$

C. $\frac{\sqrt{14}}{8}$

D. $\frac{8}{\sqrt{14}}$

E. $\frac{8}{5\sqrt{2}}$

42. Consider fractions of the form $\frac{7}{n}$, where n is an integer. How many integer values of n make this fraction greater than .5 and less than .8?

F. 3
G. 4
H. 5
J. 6
K. 7

GO ON TO THE NEXT PAGE

Do Your Figuring Here.

43. The circumference of circle X is 12π and the circumference of circle Y is 8π. What is the greatest possible distance between two points, one of which lies on the circumference of circle X and one of which lies on the circumference of circle Y?

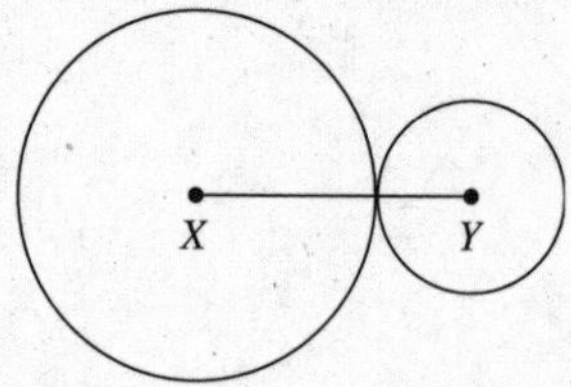

A. 6
B. 10
C. 20
D. 10π
E. 20π

44. $\sqrt{(x^2 + 4)^2} - (x + 2)(x - 2) = ?$

F. $2x^2$
G. $x^2 - 8$
H. $2(x - 2)$
J. 0
K. 8

45. If $s = -3$, then $s^3 + 2s^2 + 2s = ?$

A. −15
B. −10
C. −5
D. 5
E. 33

46. How many different numbers are solutions for the equation $2x + 6 = (x + 5)(x + 3)$?

F. 0
G. 1
H. 2
J. 3
K. Infinitely many

GO ON TO THE NEXT PAGE

47. In square $ABCD$ below, $\overline{AC} = 8$. What is the perimeter of $ABCD$?

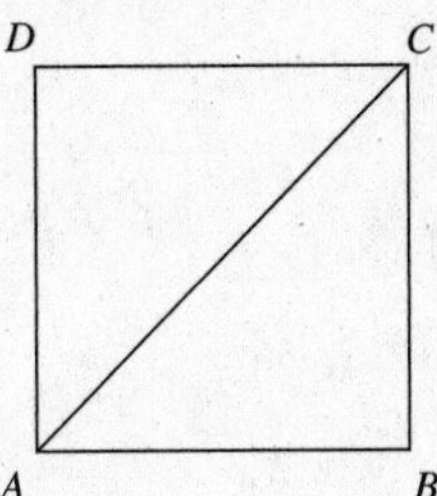

A. $4\sqrt{2}$
B. 8
C. $8\sqrt{2}$
D. 16
E. $16\sqrt{2}$

48. The front surface of a fence panel is shown below with the lengths labeled representing inches. The panel is symmetrical along its center vertical axis. What is the surface area of the front surface of the panel in square inches?

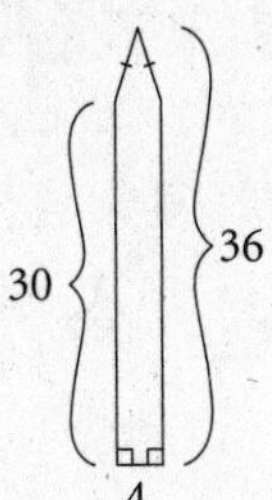

F. 144
G. 132
H. 120
J. 80
K. $64 + 6\sqrt{5}$

Do Your Figuring Here.

GO ON TO THE NEXT PAGE

49. In the figure below, O is the center of the circle, and C, D, and E are points on the circumference of the circle. If $\angle OCD$ measures 70° and $\angle OED$ measures 45°, what is the measure of $\angle CDE$?

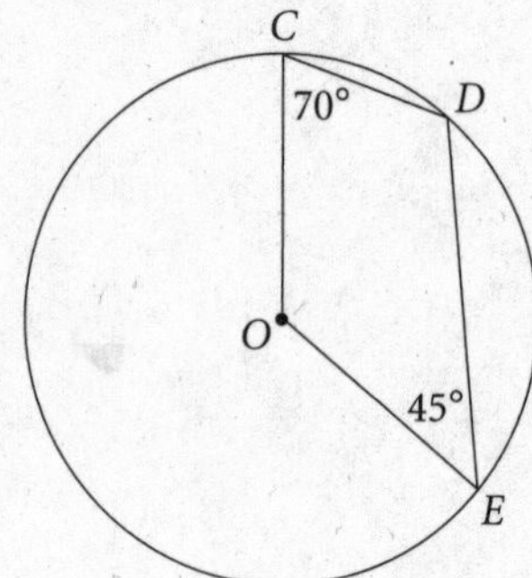

A. 25°
B. 45°
C. 70°
D. 90°
E. 115°

50. Which of the following systems of equations does NOT have a solution?

F. $x + 3y = 19$
$3x + y = 6$

G. $x + 3y = 19$
$x - 3y = 13$

H. $x - 3y = 19$
$3x - y = 7$

J. $x - 3y = 19$
$3x + y = 6$

K. $x + 3y = 6$
$3x + 9y = 7$

51. What is the 46th digit to the right of the decimal point in the decimal equivalent of $\frac{1}{7}$?

A. 1
B. 2
C. 4
D. 7
E. 8

Do Your Figuring Here.

GO ON TO THE NEXT PAGE

52. Which of the following inequalities is equivalent to $-2 - 4x \leq -6x$?

F. $x \geq -2$
G. $x \geq 1$
H. $x \geq 2$
J. $x \leq -1$
K. $x \leq 1$

Do Your Figuring Here.

53. If $x > 0$ and $y > 0$, $\frac{\sqrt{x}}{x} + \frac{\sqrt{y}}{y}$ is equivalent to which of the following?

A. $\frac{2}{xy}$
B. $\frac{\sqrt{x}+\sqrt{y}}{\sqrt{xy}}$
C. $\frac{x+y}{xy}$
D. $\frac{\sqrt{x}+\sqrt{y}}{\sqrt{x+y}}$
E. $\frac{x+y}{\sqrt{xy}}$

54. In the diagram below, $\overline{CD}$, $\overline{BE}$, and $\overline{AF}$ are all parallel and are intersected by two transversals as shown. What is the length of $\overline{EF}$?

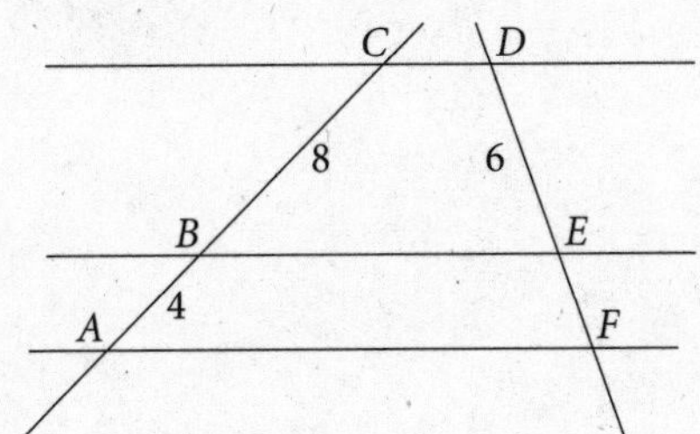

F. 2
G. 3
H. 4
J. 6
K. 9

55. What is the area, in square units, of the square whose vertices are located at the (x, y) coordinate points indicated in the figure below?

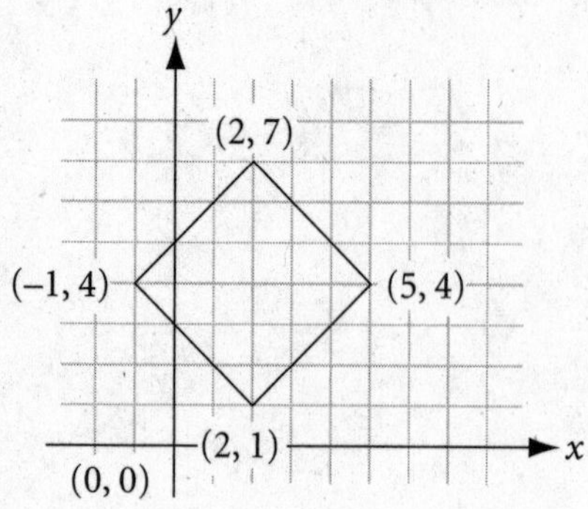

A. 9
B. 12
C. 16
D. 18
E. 24

56. Compared to the graph of $y = \cos \theta$, the graph of $y = 2 \cos \theta$ has:

F. twice the period and the same amplitude.
G. half the period and the same amplitude.
H. twice the period and half the amplitude.
J. half the amplitude and the same period.
K. twice the amplitude and the same period.

57. Brandy has a collection of comic books. If she adds 15 to the number of comic books in her collection and multiplies the sum by 3, the result will be 65 less than 4 times the number of comic books in her collection. How many comic books are in her collection?

A. 50
B. 85
C. 110
D. 145
E. 175

Do Your Figuring Here.

GO ON TO THE NEXT PAGE

Do Your Figuring Here.

58. One empty cylinder has three times the height and twice the diameter of another empty cylinder. How many fillings of the smaller cylinder would be equivalent to one filling of the larger cylinder?

(Note: The volume of a cylinder of radius r and height h is $\pi r^2 h$.)

F. 6
G. $6\sqrt{2}$
H. 12
J. 18
K. 24

59. What is the perimeter of a 30°-60°-90° triangle with a long leg of 12 inches?

A. $6\sqrt{3} + 12$
B. $4\sqrt{3} + 18$
C. $8\sqrt{3} + 18$
D. $12\sqrt{3} + 12$
E. $12\sqrt{3} + 18$

60. A baseball team scores an average of x points in its first n games and then scores y points in its next and final game of the season. Which of the following represents the team's average score for the entire season?

F. $x + \frac{y}{n}$
G. $x + \frac{y}{n+1}$
H. $\frac{x + ny}{n+1}$
J. $\frac{nx + y}{n+1}$
K. $\frac{n(x + y)}{n+1}$

IF YOU FINISH BEFORE TIME IS CALLED, YOU MAY CHECK YOUR WORK ON THIS SECTION ONLY. DO NOT TURN TO ANY OTHER SECTION IN THE TEST. **STOP**

Test Prep and Admissions

READING TEST

35 Minutes—40 Questions

Directions: This test contains four passages, each followed by several questions. After reading a passage, select the best answer to each question and fill in the corresponding oval on your answer sheet. You are allowed to refer to the passages while answering the questions.

Passage I

Emma Woodhouse, handsome, clever, and rich, with a comfortable home and happy disposition, seemed to unite some of the best blessings of existence. She had lived nearly twenty-one years in the world with very little to distress or vex her. She was the youngest of the two daughters of a most affectionate, indulgent father, and had, in consequence of her sister's marriage, been mistress of his house from a very early period. Her mother had died too long ago for her to have more than an indistinct remembrance of her caresses, and her place had been taken by an excellent governess who had fallen little short of a mother in affection.

Sixteen years had Miss Taylor been in Mr. Woodhouse's family, less as a governess than a friend, very fond of both daughters, but particularly of Emma. Between them it was more the intimacy of sisters. Even before Miss Taylor had ceased to hold the nominal office of governess, the mildness of her temper had hardly allowed her to impose any restraint. The shadow of authority being now long passed away, they had been living together as friend and friend very mutually attached, and Emma doing just what she liked, highly esteeming Miss Taylor's judgment, but directed chiefly by her own. The real evils, indeed, of Emma's situation were the power of having rather too much her own way, and a disposition to think a little too well of herself; these were the disadvantages which threatened alloy to her many enjoyments. The danger, however, was at present so unperceived, that they did not by any means rank as misfortunes with her.

Sorrow came—a gentle sorrow—but not at all in the shape of any disagreeable consciousness. Miss Taylor married. It was Miss Taylor's loss which first brought grief. It was on the wedding-day of this beloved friend that Emma first sat in mournful thought of any continuance. The wedding over, and the bride-people gone, she and her father were left to dine together, with no prospect of a third to cheer a long evening. Her father composed himself to sleep after dinner, as usual, and she had then only to sit and think of what she had lost.

The marriage had every promise of happiness for her friend. Mr. Weston was a man of unexceptionable character, easy fortune, suitable age, and pleasant manners. There was some satisfaction in considering with what self-denying, generous friendship she had always wished and promoted the match, but it was a black morning's work for her. The want of Miss Taylor would be felt every hour of every day. She recalled her past kindness—the kindness, the affection of sixteen years—how she had taught her and how she had played with her from five years old—how she had devoted all her powers to attach and amuse her in health—and how she had nursed her through the various illnesses of childhood. A large debt of gratitude was owing here, but the intercourse of the last seven years, the equal footing and perfect unreserve which had soon followed Isabella's marriage, on their being left to each other, was yet a dearer, tenderer recollection. She had been a friend and companion such as few possessed: intelligent, well-informed, useful, gentle, knowing all the ways of the family, interested in all its concerns, and peculiarly interested in her, in every

GO ON TO THE NEXT PAGE

pleasure, every scheme of hers—one to whom she could speak every thought as it arose, and who had such an affection for her as could never find fault.

How was she to bear the change? It was true that her friend was going only half a mile from them, but Emma was aware that great must be the difference between a Mrs. Weston, only half a mile from them, and a Miss Taylor in the house. With all her advantages, natural and domestic, she was now in great danger of suffering from intellectual solitude.

This passage is an adapted excerpt from Jane Austen's novel *Emma*. In this passage, Emma confronts a change in her previously happy life.

1. According to the passage, what are the greatest disadvantages facing Emma?

A. Her father is not a stimulating conversationalist, and she is bored.
B. She is lonely and afraid that Mrs. Weston will not have a happy marriage.
C. She is used to having her way too much, and she thinks too highly of herself.
D. She misses the companionship of her mother, her sister, and Miss Taylor.

2. The name of Emma's sister is:

F. Mrs. Weston.
G. Isabella.
H. Miss Taylor.
J. Mrs. Woodhouse.

3. As described in the passage, Emma's relationship with Miss Taylor can be characterized as:

A. similar to a mother-daughter relationship.
B. similar to the relationship of sisters or best friends.
C. weaker than Emma's relationship with her sister.
D. stronger than Miss Taylor's relationship with her new husband.

4. As used in line 29, *disposition* can most closely be defined as:

F. a tendency.
G. control.
H. placement.
J. transfer.

5. Which of the following are included in Emma's memories of her relationship with Miss Taylor?

I. Miss Taylor taking care of Emma during childhood illnesses
II. Miss Taylor's interest in all of the concerns of Emma's family
III. Miss Taylor teaching her mathematics
IV. Miss Taylor scolding her for being selfish

A. I, III, and IV only
B. I and III only
C. II, III, and IV only
D. I and II only

6. It is most reasonable to infer from Emma's realization that "great must be the difference between a Mrs. Weston, only half a mile from them, and a Miss Taylor in the house" (lines 77–79) that:

F. Miss Taylor will no longer be a part of Emma's life.
G. Emma is happy about the marriage because now she will have more freedom.
H. Emma regrets that her relationship with Miss Taylor will change.
J. Emma believes that her relationship with Miss Taylor will become stronger.

7. Based on the passage, Emma could best be described as:

A. sweet and naïve.
B. self-centered and naïve.
C. self-centered and headstrong.
D. unappreciative and bitter.

GO ON TO THE NEXT PAGE

Test Prep and Admissions

8. The passage suggests that the quality Emma values most in a friend is:
   F. charisma.
   G. devotion.
   H. honesty.
   J. intelligence.

9. How does Emma view Mr. Weston?
   A. She thinks that he is an excellent match, and it required considerable self-sacrifice not to pursue him herself.
   B. She considers him to be a respectable if somewhat average match for her friend.
   C. She sees him as an intruder who has carried away her best friend in "a black morning's work" (line 53).
   D. She believes he is an indulgent, easily swayed man, reminiscent of her father.

10. From the passage, it can be inferred that Emma is accustomed to:
   F. behaving according to the wishes of her affectionate father.
   G. taking the advice of Miss Taylor when faced with deciding upon a course of action.
   H. doing as she pleases without permission from her father or governess.
   J. abiding by strict rules governing her behavior.

GO ON TO THE NEXT PAGE

Passage II

Learning and its result, memory, are processes by which we retain acquired information, emotions, and impressions that can influence our behavior. At the psychological level, memory is not a single process. Sensory memory, the first of three main systems of memory, describes the momentary lingering of perceptual information as it is initially sensed and briefly recorded. When an image strikes the eyes it lingers in the visual system for an instant while the image is interpreted, and is quickly overwritten by new information. In the visual system this is called *iconic memory*, in the auditory system it is *echoic memory*, and in reference to touch it is *haptic memory*.

If sensory information is processed it can move into the second main system of memory, working memory. This was once known as short-term memory (and that term is still popularly used). But working memory is viewed as a more accurate term, since this system not only stores information for short periods of time, but also enables the use and manipulation of information processed there. However, only a limited number of items can be held in working memory (the average for most people is seven), and decay of the memory occurs rapidly, although it can be held longer if the information is mentally or vocally repeated. Unless we make a conscious effort to retain it, a working memory may disappear forever.

Long-term memory is the most comprehensive of the three, with apparently infinite capacity. Memories recorded in long-term memory are never lost, although at times there may be difficulty accessing them. There are three independent categories of long-term memory which interact extensively: *episodic* involves personal memories and details of daily life, and is closely identified with its time and place; *semantic* contains facts and general knowledge that are not tied to when or how they were learned; and *procedural* retains skills used to perform certain activities that eventually may not require conscious effort.

Although the main systems of memory are widely accepted, controversy continues about memory formation and retrieval. It was once believed that for a memory to enter long-term memory it must first be held in working memory. However, this idea has been challenged by an alternate theory suggesting that sensory memories can be directly entered into long-term memory through a pathway that runs parallel to, rather than in series with, working memory. Memories therefore can register simultaneously in both systems.

Likewise, all agree that the retrieval of long-term memories is facilitated by repetition, but there is no agreement about the accuracy of these memories. For many years the scientific community viewed human memory as similar to computer memory, with the mind recording each detail just as it was presented. However, there is a growing consensus that our memory is sometimes flawed. An inference or assumption made by an individual when a memory is created may later be recalled as fact, or the mind may fill in details that were originally missing. Moreover, when we try to recall a particular memory, an unrelated memory may alter it through a process called interference. There is even evidence that an entirely false memory can be incorporated as a memory indistinguishable from true memories. Although for most purposes these discrepancies are harmless, concerns regarding the accuracy of human memory challenge the reliability of eyewitness testimony.

11. The main purpose of the passage is to:

A. describe the main memory systems and why they are increasingly controversial.

B. describe the main memory systems and some views of memory formation and retrieval.

C. demonstrate that early ideas about memory formation and retrieval were incorrect.

D. demonstrate that theories about the main memory systems are incorrect.

GO ON TO THE NEXT PAGE

12. Based on information in the passage, which of the following would be recalled from semantic long-term memory?

    F. Ballet steps
    G. A childhood birthday
    H. Multiplication tables
    J. Riding a bicycle

13. It can be reasonably inferred from the passage that, if a man in a car accident is unable to remember details of his life and family, but does remember how to perform his job, his:

    A. episodic memories have been lost.
    B. episodic memories have become inaccessible.
    C. procedural memories have been lost.
    D. procedural memories have become inaccessible.

14. The fact that the scientific community once viewed human memory as similar to computer memory is mentioned in the last paragraph in order to:

    F. illustrate that memory is now viewed as complex rather than mechanical.
    G. explain that memory is now viewed as an exact record of events.
    H. illustrate that memory is always inaccurate.
    J. explain that memories are formed the same way computers encode data.

15. If a person reads, "The baseball hit the window," and, when asked to recall the sentence, remembers "The baseball broke the window," according to the passage this is probably an example of:

    A. interference altering a memory.
    B. a memory that became inaccessible.
    C. a reader's assumption altering a memory.
    D. a completely false memory being created.

16. According to the passage, all the following are examples of episodic memory EXCEPT:

    F. the meal you ate last night
    G. the name of an old classmate
    H. the year your class won a trophy
    J. the face of a stranger passed on the street

17. Based on information in the passage the term *short-term memory* was most likely replaced with *working memory* in order to:

    A. refute the idea that memories in this category degrade quickly.
    B. emphasize that memories in this category can be manipulated.
    C. show that memories in this category become long-term memories.
    D. demonstrate that echoic memories are held in the visual system.

18. As it is used in the passage, the word *iconic* (line 12) most nearly means relating to:

    F. something sacred.
    G. a symbolic representation.
    H. visual sensory memory.
    J. a picture that represents a computer command.

19. According to the passage, most of the scientific community now agrees that:

    A. there are really four main categories of memory, not three.
    B. memories held in long-term memory remain forever.
    C. memories must be held in working memory before long-term memory.
    D. repetition does not affect the duration of memory.

20. According to the passage, which of the following is a characteristic of working memory?

    F. A slight echo in the ear
    G. Quick replacement by new sensory information
    H. Rapid forgetting
    J. Infinite capacity

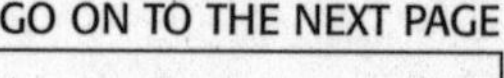

Passage III

There can be little doubt that women artists have been most prominent in photography and that they have made their greatest contribution in this field. One reason for this is not difficult to ascertain. As several historians of photography have pointed out, photography, being a new medium outside the traditional academic framework, was wide open to women and offered them opportunities that the older fields did not....

All these observations apply to the first woman to have achieved eminence in photography, and that is Julia Margaret Cameron.... Born in 1815 in Calcutta into an upper-middle-class family and married to Charles Hay Cameron, a distinguished jurist and member of the Supreme Court of India, Julia Cameron was well-known as a brilliant conversationalist and a woman of personality and intellect who was unconventional to the point of eccentricity. Although the mother of six children, she adopted several more and still found time to be active in social causes and literary activities. After the Camerons settled in England in 1848 at Freshwater Bay on the Isle of Wight, she became the center of an artistic and literary circle that included such notable figures as the poet Alfred Lord Tennyson and the painter George Frederick Watts. Pursuing numerous activities and taking care of her large family, Mrs. Cameron might have been remembered as still another rather remarkable and colorful Victorian lady had it not been for the fact that, in 1863, her daughter presented her with photographic equipment, thinking her mother might enjoy taking pictures of her family and friends. Although forty-eight years old, Mrs. Cameron took up this new hobby with enormous enthusiasm and dedication. She was a complete beginner, but within a very few years she developed into one of the greatest photographers of her period and a giant in the history of photography. She worked ceaselessly as long as daylight lasted and mastered the technical processes of photography, at that time far more cumbersome than today, turning her coal house into a darkroom and her chicken house into a studio. To her, photography was a "divine art," and in it she found her vocation. In 1864, she wrote triumphantly under one of her photographs, "My First Success," and from then until her death in Ceylon in 1874, she devoted herself wholly to this art.

Working in a large format (her portrait studies are usually about 11 inches by 14 inches) and requiring a long exposure (on the average five minutes), she produced a large body of work that stands up as one of the notable artistic achievements of the Victorian period. The English art critic Roger Fry believed that her portraits were likely to outlive the works of artists who were her contemporaries. Her friend Watts, then a very celebrated portrait painter, inscribed on one of her photographs, "I wish I could paint such a picture as this." ...Her work was widely exhibited, and she received gold, silver, and bronze medals in England, America, Germany, and Austria. No other female artist of the nineteenth century achieved such acclaim, and no other woman photographer has ever enjoyed such success.

Her work falls into two main categories on which her contemporaries and people today differ sharply. Victorian critics were particularly impressed by her allegorical pictures, many of them based on the poems of her friend and neighbor Tennyson.... Contemporary taste much prefers her portraits and finds her narrative scenes sentimental and sometimes in bad taste. Yet, not only Julia Cameron, but also the painters of that time loved to depict subjects such as *The Five Foolish Virgins* or *Pray God, Bring Father Safely Home.* Still, today her fame rests upon her portraits for, as she herself said, she was intent upon representing not only the outer likeness but also the inner greatness of the people she portrayed.

GO ON TO THE NEXT PAGE

Working with the utmost dedication, she produced photographs of such eminent Victorians as Tennyson, Browning, Carlyle, Trollope, Longfellow, Watts, Darwin, Ellen Terry, Sir John Herschel, who was a close friend of hers, and Mrs. Duckworth, the mother of Virginia Woolf.

21. Which of the following conclusions can be reasonably drawn from the passage's discussion of Julia Margaret Cameron?

A. She was a traditional homemaker until she discovered photography.
B. Her work holds a significant place in the history of photography.
C. She was unable to achieve in her lifetime the artistic recognition she deserved.
D. Her eccentricity has kept her from being taken seriously by modern critics of photography.

22. According to the passage, Cameron is most respected by modern critics for her:

F. portraits.
G. allegorical pictures.
H. use of a large format.
J. service in recording the faces of so many twentieth century figures.

23. The author uses which of the following methods to develop the second paragraph (lines 10–49)?

A. A series of anecdotes depicting Cameron's energy and unconventionality
B. A presentation of factual data demonstrating Cameron's importance in the history of photography
C. A description of the author's personal acquaintance with Cameron
D. A chronological account of Cameron's background and artistic growth

24. As it is used in the passage, *cumbersome* (line 42) most closely means:

F. difficult to manage.
G. expensive.
H. intense.
J. enjoyable.

25. When the author says that Cameron had found "her vocation" (lines 45–46), his main point is that photography:

A. offered Cameron an escape from the confines of conventional social life.
B. became the main interest of her life.
C. became her primary source of income.
D. provided her with a way to express her religious beliefs.

26. The main point of the third paragraph is that Cameron:

F. achieved great artistic success during her lifetime.
G. is the greatest photographer who ever lived.
H. was considered a more important artist during her lifetime than she is now.
J. revolutionized photographic methods in the Victorian era.

27. According to the passage, the art of photography offered women artists more opportunities than did other art forms because it:

A. did not require expensive materials.
B. allowed the artist to use family and friends for subject matter.
C. was non-traditional.
D. required little artistic skill.

GO ON TO THE NEXT PAGE

28. *The Five Foolish Virgins* and *Pray God, Bring Father Safely Home* are examples of:

F. portraits of celebrated Victorians.
G. allegorical subjects of the sort that were popular during the Victorian era.
H. photographs in which Cameron sought to show a subject's outer likeness and inner greatness.
J. photographs by Cameron that were scoffed at by her contemporaries.

29. According to the passage, which of the following opinions of Cameron's work was held by Victorian critics but is NOT held by modern critics?

A. Photographs should be based on poems.
B. Her portraits are too sentimental.
C. Narrative scenes are often in bad taste.
D. Her allegorical pictures are her best work.

30. The author's treatment of Cameron's development as a photographer can best be described as:

F. admiring.
G. condescending.
H. neutral.
J. defensive.

GO ON TO THE NEXT PAGE

Passage IV

The harbor seal, *Phoca vitulina*, lives amphibiously along the northern Atlantic and Pacific coasts. This extraordinary mammal, which does most of its fishing at night when visibility is low and in places where noise levels are high, has developed several unique adaptations that have sharpened its acoustic and visual acuity. The need for such adaptations has been compounded by the varying behavior of sound and light in each of the two habitats of the harbor seal—land and water.

While the seal is on land, its ear operates much like the human ear, with sound waves traveling through air and entering the inner ear through the auditory canal. The directions from which sounds originate are distinguishable because the sound waves arrive at each inner ear at different times. In water, however, where sound waves travel faster than they do in air, the ability of the brain to differentiate arrival times between each ear is severely reduced. Yet it is crucial for the seal to be able to pinpoint the exact origins of sound in order to locate both its offspring and its prey. Therefore, the seal has developed an extremely sensitive quadraphonic hearing system, composed of a specialized band of tissue that extends down from the ear to the inner ear. In water, sound is conducted to the seal's inner ear by this special band of tissue, making it possible for the seal to identify the exact origins of sounds.

The eye of the seal is also uniquely adapted to operate in both air and water. The human eye, adapted to function primarily in air, is equipped with a cornea, which aids in the refraction and focusing of light onto the retina. As a result, when a human eye is submerged in water, light rays are further refracted and the image is blurry. The seal's cornea, however, refracts light as water does. Therefore, in water, light rays are transmitted by the cornea without distortion, and are clearly focused on the retina. In air, however, the cornea is astigmatic, resulting in a distortion of incoming light rays. The seal compensates for this by having a stenopaic pupil, which constricts into a vertical slit. Since the astigmatism is most pronounced in the horizontal plane of the eye, the vertical pupil serves to minimize its effect on the seal's vision.

Since the harbor seal hunts for food under conditions of low visibility, some scientists believe it has echolocation systems akin to those of bats, porpoises, and dolphins. This kind of natural radar involves the emission of high frequency sound pulses that reflect off obstacles such as predators, prey, or natural barriers. The reflections are received as sensory signals by the brain, which processes them into an image. The animal, blinded by unfavorable lighting conditions, is thus able to perceive its surroundings. Such echolocation by harbor seals is suggested by the fact that they emit "clicks," high frequency sounds produced in short, fast bursts that occur mostly at night, when visibility is low.

Finally, there is speculation that the seal's whiskers, or vibrissae, which are unusually well developed and highly sensitive to vibrations, act as additional sensory receptors. Scientists speculate that the vibrissae may sense wave disturbances produced by nearby moving fish, allowing the seal to home in on and capture prey.

31. The harbor seal's eye compensates for the distortion of light rays on land by means of its:

A. vibrissae
B. cornea
C. stenopaic pupil
D. echolocation

32. The passage implies that a harbor seal's vision is:

F. inferior to a human's vision in the water, but superior to it on land.
G. superior to a human's vision in the water, but inferior to it on land.
H. inferior to a human's vision both in the water and on land.
J. equivalent to a human's vision both in the water and on land.

GO ON TO THE NEXT PAGE

33. According to the passage, scientists think vibrissae help harbor seals to catch prey by:

A. improving underwater vision.
B. sensing vibrations in the air.
C. camouflaging predator seals.
D. detecting underwater movement.

34. According to the passage, the speed of sound in water is:

F. faster than the speed of sound in air.
G. slower than the speed of sound in air.
H. the same as the speed of sound in air.
J. unable to be determined exactly.

35. According to the passage, which of the following have contributed to the harbor seal's need to adapt its visual and acoustic senses?

I. Night hunting
II. The need to operate in two habitats
III. A noisy environment

A. I and II only
B. II and III only
C. I and III only
D. I, II, and III

36. Which of the following claims expresses the writer's opinion and not a fact?

F. The human eye is adapted to function primarily in air.
G. When the seal is on land, its ear operates like a human ear.
H. The "clicks" emitted by the harbor seal mean it uses echolocation.
J. The need for adaptation is increased if an animal lives in two habitats.

37. The passage suggests that the harbor seal lives in:

A. cold ocean waters with accessible coasts.
B. all areas with abundant fish populations.
C. most island and coastal regions.
D. warm coastlines with exceptionally clear waters.

38. According to the passage, a special band of tissue extending from the ear to the inner ear enables the harbor seal to:

F. make its distinctive "clicking" sounds.
G. find prey by echolocation.
H. breathe underwater.
J. determine where a sound originated.

39. The author compares harbor seal sensory organs to human sensory organs primarily in order to:

A. point out similarities among mammals.
B. explain how the seal's sensory organs function.
C. prove that seals are more adaptively successful than humans.
D. prove that humans are better adapted to their environment than seals.

40. According to the passage, one way in which seals differ from humans is:

F. that sound waves enter the inner ear through the auditory canal.
G. the degree of refraction of light by their corneas.
H. they focus light rays on the retina.
J. they have adapted to live in a certain environment.

IF YOU FINISH BEFORE TIME IS CALLED, YOU MAY CHECK YOUR WORK ON THIS SECTION ONLY. DO NOT TURN TO ANY OTHER SECTION IN THE TEST.

SCIENCE TEST

35 Minutes—40 Questions

Directions: Each of the following seven passages is followed by several questions. After reading each passage, decide on the best answer to each question and fill in the corresponding oval on your answer sheet. You are allowed to refer to the passages while answering the questions. Calculator use is not allowed on this test.

Passage I

The table below contains some physical properties of common optical materials. The refractive index of a material is a measure of the amount by which light is bent upon entering the material. The transmittance range is the range of wavelengths over which the material is transparent.

Table 1

Physical Properties of Optical Materials				
Material	Refractive index for light of 0.589 μm	Transmittance range (μm)	Useful range for prisms (μm)	Chemical resistance
Lithium fluoride	1.39	0.12–6	2.7–5.5	Poor
Calcium fluoride	1.43	0.12–12	5–9.4	Good
Sodium chloride	1.54	0.3–17	8–16	Poor
Quartz	1.54	0.20–3.3	0.20–2.7	Excellent
Potassium bromide	1.56	0.3–29	15–28	Poor
Flint glass*	1.66	0.35–2.2	0.35–2	Excellent
Cesium iodide	1.79	0.3–70	15–55	Poor

*Flint glass is lead oxide doped quartz

1. According to the table, which material(s) will transmit light at 25 μm?
   - **A.** Potassium bromide only
   - **B.** Potassium bromide and cesium iodide
   - **C.** Lithium fluoride and cesium iodide
   - **D.** Lithium fluoride and flint glass

2. A scientist hypothesizes that any material with poor chemical resistance would have a transmittance range wider than 10 μm. The properties of which of the following materials contradicts this hypothesis?
   - **F.** Lithium fluoride
   - **G.** Flint glass
   - **H.** Cesium iodide
   - **J.** Quartz

3. When light travels from one medium to another, total internal reflection can occur if the first medium has a higher refractive index than the second. Total internal reflection could occur if light were travelling from:
   - **A.** lithium fluoride to flint glass.
   - **B.** potassium bromide to cesium iodide.
   - **C.** quartz to potassium bromide.
   - **D.** flint glass to calcium fluoride.

GO ON TO THE NEXT PAGE

4. Based on the information in the table, how is the transmittance range related to the useful prism range?
   - F. The transmittance range is always narrower than the useful prism range.
   - G. The transmittance range is narrower than or equal to the useful prism range.
   - H. The transmittance range increases as the useful prism range decreases.
   - J. The transmittance range is wider than and includes within it the useful prism range.

5. The addition of lead oxide to pure quartz has the effect of:
   - A. decreasing the transmittance range and the refractive index.
   - B. decreasing the transmittance range and increasing the refractive index.
   - C. increasing the transmittance range and the useful prism range.
   - D. increasing the transmittance range and decreasing the useful prism range.

GO ON TO THE NEXT PAGE

Passage II

Osmosis is the diffusion of a solvent (often water) across a semipermeable membrane from the side of the membrane with a lower concentration of dissolved material to the side with a higher concentration of dissolved material. The result of osmosis is an equilibrium—an even distribution—on both sides of the membrane. In order to prevent osmosis, external pressure must be applied to the side with the higher concentration of dissolved material. *Osmotic pressure* is the external pressure required to prevent osmosis. The apparatus shown below was used to measure osmotic pressure in the following experiments.

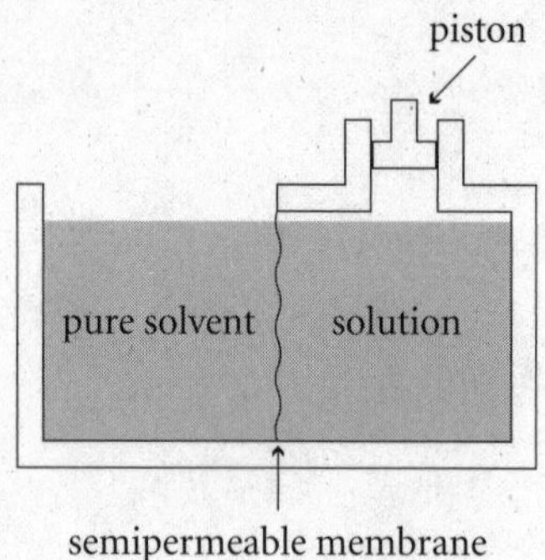

Experiment 1

Aqueous (water-based) solutions containing different concentrations of sucrose were placed in the closed side of the apparatus. The open side was filled with water. The sucrose solutions also contained a blue dye that binds to the sucrose. The osmotic pressure created by the piston was measured for each solution at various temperatures. The results are given in Table 1.

Table 1

Concentration of sucrose solution (mol/L)	Temperature (K)	Osmotic pressure (atm)
1.00	298.0	24.47
0.50	298.0	12.23
0.10	298.0	2.45
0.05	298.0	1.22
1.00	348.0	28.57
0.50	348.0	14.29
0.10	348.0	2.86
0.05	348.0	1.43

Experiment 2

Sucrose solutions of 4 different organic solvents were investigated in the same manner as in Experiment 1 with all trials at 298 K. The results are shown in Table 2.

Table 2

Solvent	Concentration of sucrose solution (mol/L)	Osmotic pressure (atm)
Ethanol	0.50	12.23
Ethanol	0.10	2.45
Acetone	0.50	12.23
Acetone	0.10	2.45
Diethyl ether	0.50	12.23
Diethyl ether	0.10	2.45
Methanol	0.50	12.23
Methanol	0.10	2.45

6. According to the experimental results, osmotic pressure is dependent upon the:

F. solvent and temperature only.
G. solvent and concentration only.
H. temperature and concentration only.
J. solvent, temperature, and concentration.

7. According to Experiment 2, if methanol was used as a solvent, what pressure must be applied to a 0.5 mol/L solution of sucrose at 298 K to prevent osmosis?

A. 24.46 atm
B. 12.23 atm
C. 2.45 atm
D. 1.23 atm

8. A 0.10 mol/L aqueous sucrose solution is separated from an equal volume of pure water by a semipermeable membrane. If the solution is at a pressure of 1 atm and a temperature of 298 K, the sucrose solution:

F. will diffuse across the semipermeable membrane from the sucrose solution side to the pure water side.
G. will diffuse across the semipermeable membrane from the pure water side to the sucrose solution side.
H. will not diffuse across the semipermeable membrane.
J. will diffuse across the semipermeable membrane, but the direction of diffusion cannot be determined.

9. In Experiment 1, the scientists investigated the effect of:

A. solvent and concentration on osmotic pressure.
B. volume and temperature on osmotic pressure.
C. concentration and temperature on osmotic pressure.
D. temperature on atmospheric pressure.

10. Which of the following conclusions can be drawn from the experimental results?

I. Osmotic pressure is independent of the solvent used.
II. Osmotic pressure is only dependent upon the temperature of the system.
III. Osmosis occurs only when the osmotic pressure is exceeded.

F. I only
G. III only
H. I and II only
J. I and III only

11. What was the most likely purpose of the dye placed in the sucrose solutions in Experiments 1 and 2?

A. The dye showed when osmosis was completed.
B. The dye showed the presence of ions in the solutions.
C. The dye was used to make the experiment more colorful.
D. The dye was used to make the onset of osmosis visible.

GO ON TO THE NEXT PAGE

Passage III

A chemist investigating the influence of molecular weight and structure on the boiling point (transition from liquid to gaseous state) of different compounds recorded the data in the tables below. Two types of compounds were investigated: organic carbon compounds (shown in Table 1) and inorganic compounds (shown in Table 2).

Table 1

Straight-Chain Hydrocarbons		
Molecular formula	**Molar weight* (g/mol)**	**Boiling point (°C)**
CH_4	16	–162
C_2H_6	30	–88
C_3H_8	44	–42
C_4H_{10}	58	0
C_5H_{12}	72	36
C_8H_{18}	114	126
$C_{20}H_{42}$	282	345

*Molar weight is the weight of one mole, or an *Avogadro's Number* of molecules ($\approx 6 \times 10^{23}$), in grams.

Table 2

Other Substances (Polar and Non-Polar)		
Molecular formula	**Molar weight (g/mol)**	**Boiling point (°C)**
N_2*	28	–196
SiH_4*	32	–112
GeH_4*	77	–90
Br_2*	160	59
CO**	28	–192
PH_3**	34	–85
AsH_3**	78	–55
ICl**	162	97

* *Non-Polar*: molecule's charge is evenly distributed

***Polar*: molecule's negative and positive charges are partially separated

12. Which of the following straight-chain hydrocarbons would NOT be a gas at room temperature?

F. C_2H_6
G. C_3H_8
H. C_4H_{10}
J. C_5H_{12}

13. Which of the following conclusions is supported by the observed results?

I. Boiling point varies directly with molecular weight.
II. Boiling point varies inversely with molecular weight.
III. Boiling point is affected by molecular structure.

A. I only
B. II only
C. I and III only
D. II and III only

14. Based on the data in Table 1, the boiling point of the straight-chain hydrocarbon C_6H_{14} (molecular weight 86 g/mol) is most likely:

F. 30° C.
G. 70° C.
H. 130° C.
J. impossible to predict.

15. Based on the data in Table 2, as molecular weight increases, the difference between the boiling points of polar and non-polar substances of similar molecular weight:

A. increases.
B. decreases.
C. remains constant.
D. varies randomly.

GO ON TO THE NEXT PAGE

16. A polar substance with a boiling point of 0° C is likely to have a molar weight closest to which of the following:

F. 58
G. 80
H. 108
J. 132

17. Which of the following places the compound types in ascending order according to the rate at which the boiling point increases with increasing molar weight?

A. straight-chain hydrocarbons, non-polar inorganic compounds, polar inorganic compounds
B. straight-chain hydrocarbons, polar inorganic compounds, non-polar inorganic compounds
C. non-polar inorganic compounds, straight-chain hydrocarbons, polar inorganic compounds
D. non-polar inorganic compounds, polar inorganic compounds, straight-chain hydrocarbons

Passage IV

A series of experiments was performed to study the environmental factors affecting the size and number of leaves on the *Cyas* plant.

Experiment 1

Five groups of 25 *Cyas* seedlings, all from 2–3 cm tall, were allowed to grow for 3 months, each group at a different humidity level. All of the groups were kept at 75° F and received 9 hours of sunlight a day. The average leaf lengths, widths, and densities are given in Table 1.

Table 1

%Humidity	Average length (cm)	Average width (cm)	Average density* (leaves/cm)
15	5.6	1.6	0.13
35	7.1	1.8	0.25
55	9.8	2.0	0.56
75	14.6	2.6	0.61
95	7.5	1.7	0.52

*Number of leaves per 1 cm of plant stalk

Experiment 2

Five new groups of 25 seedlings, all from 2–3 cm tall, were allowed to grow for 3 months, each group receiving different amounts of sunlight at a constant humidity of 55%. All other conditions were the same as in Experiment 1. The results are listed in Table 2.

Table 2

Sunlight (hrs/day)	Average length (cm)	Average width (cm)	Average density* (leaves/cm)
0	5.3	1.5	0.32
3	12.4	2.4	0.59
6	11.2	2.0	0.56
9	8.4	1.8	0.26
12	7.7	1.7	0.19

*Number of leaves per 1 cm of plant stalk

GO ON TO THE NEXT PAGE

Experiment 3

Five new groups of 25 seedlings, all from 2–3 cm tall, were allowed to grow at a constant humidity of 55% for 3 months at different daytime and nighttime temperatures. All other conditions were the same as in Experiment 1. The results are shown in Table 3.

Table 3

Day/Night temperature (° F)	Average length (cm)	Average width (cm)	Average density* (leaves/cm)
85/85	6.8	1.5	0.28
85/65	12.3	2.1	0.53
65/85	8.1	1.7	0.33
75/75	7.1	1.9	0.45
65/65	8.3	1.7	0.39

*Number of leaves per 1 cm of plant stalk

18. Which of the following conclusions can be made based on the results of Experiment 2 alone?

F. The seedlings do not require long daily periods of sunlight to grow.
G. The average leaf density is independent of the humidity the seedlings receive.
H. The seedlings need more water at night than during the day.
J. The average length of the leaves increases as the amount of sunlight increases.

19. Seedlings grown at a 40% humidity level under the same conditions as in Experiment 1 would have average leaf widths closest to:

A. 1.6 cm.
B. 1.9 cm.
C. 2.2 cm.
D. 2.5 cm.

20. According to the experimental results, under which set of conditions would a *Cyas* seedling be most likely to produce the largest leaves?

F. 95% humidity and 3 hours of sunlight
G. 75% humidity and 3 hours of sunlight
H. 95% humidity and 6 hours of sunlight
J. 75% humidity and 6 hours of sunlight

21. Which variable remained constant throughout all of the experiments?

A. The number of seedling groups
B. The percent of humidity
C. The daytime temperature
D. The nighttime temperature

22. It was assumed in the design of the 3 experiments that all of the *Cyas* seedlings were:

F. more than 5 cm tall.
G. equally capable of germinating.
H. equally capable of producing flowers.
J. equally capable of further growth.

23. As a continuation of the 3 experiments listed, it would be most appropriate to next investigate:

A. how many leaves over 6.0 cm long there are on each plant.
B. which animals consume *Cyas* seedlings.
C. how the mineral content of the soil affects the leaf size and density.
D. what time of year the seedlings have the darkest coloring.

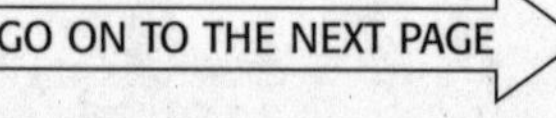

Passage V

The resistance (R) of a conductor is the extent to which it opposes the flow of electricity. Resistance depends not only on the conductor's resistivity (ρ), but also on the conductor's length (L) and cross-sectional area (A). The resistivity of a conductor is a physical property of the material that varies with temperature.

A research team designing a new appliance was researching the best type of wire to use in a particular circuit. The most important consideration was the wire's resistance. The team studied the resistance of wires made from four metals—gold (Au), aluminum (Al), tungsten (W), and iron (Fe). Two lengths and two gauges (diameters) of each type of wire were tested at 20° C. The results are recorded in the following table.

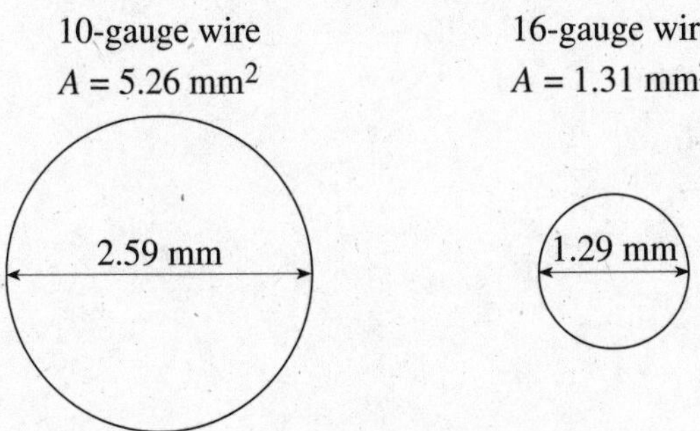

Note: area of circle = πr^2

Table 1

Material	Resistivity (μΩ ⊇ cm)	Length (cm)	Cross-sectional area (mm²)	Resistance (μΩ)
Au	2.44	1.0	5.26	46.4
Au	2.44	1.0	1.31	186.0
Au	2.44	2.0	5.26	92.8
Au	2.44	2.0	1.31	372.0
Al	2.83	1.0	5.26	53.8
Al	2.83	1.0	1.31	216.0
Al	2.83	2.0	5.26	107.6
Al	2.83	2.0	1.31	432.0
W	5.51	1.0	5.26	105.0
W	5.51	1.0	1.31	421.0
W	5.51	2.0	5.26	210.0
W	5.51	2.0	1.31	842.0
Fe	10.00	1.0	5.26	190.0
Fe	10.00	1.0	1.31	764.0
Fe	10.00	2.0	5.26	380.0
Fe	10.00	2.0	1.31	1,528.0

24. Of the wires tested, resistance increases for any given material as which parameter is decreased?

F. Length
G. Cross-sectional area
H. Resistivity
J. Gauge

25. Given the data in the table, which of the following best expresses resistance in terms of resistivity (ρ), cross-sectional area (A), and length (L)?

A. $\frac{\rho A}{L}$

B. $\frac{\rho L}{A}$

C. ρAL

D. $\frac{AL}{\rho}$

GO ON TO THE NEXT PAGE

26. Which of the following wires would have the highest resistance?

F. A 1-cm aluminum wire with a cross-sectional area of 3.31 mm^2
G. A 2-cm aluminum wire with a cross-sectional area of 3.31 mm^2
H. A 1-cm tungsten wire with a cross-sectional area of 0.33 mm^2
J. A 2-cm tungsten wire with a cross-sectional area of 0.33 mm^2

27. According to the information given, which of the following statements is (are) correct?

I. 10-gauge wire has a larger diameter than 16-gauge wire.
II. Gold has a higher resistivity than tungsten.
III. Aluminum conducts electricity better than iron.

A. I only
B. II only
C. III only
D. I and III only

28. Which of the following graphs best represents the relationship between the resistivity of a tungsten wire and its length?

F.

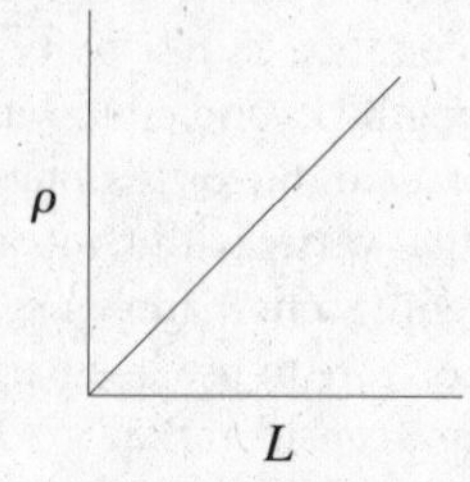

ρ

L

G.

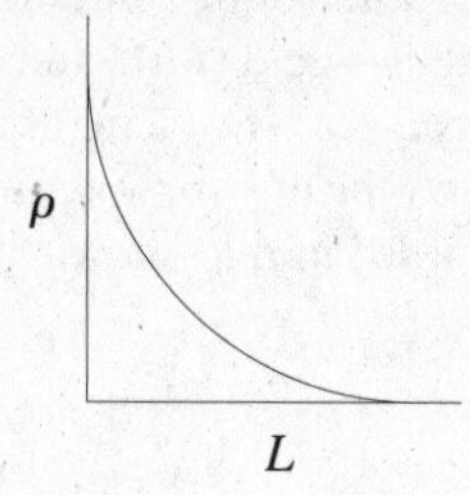

ρ

L

H.

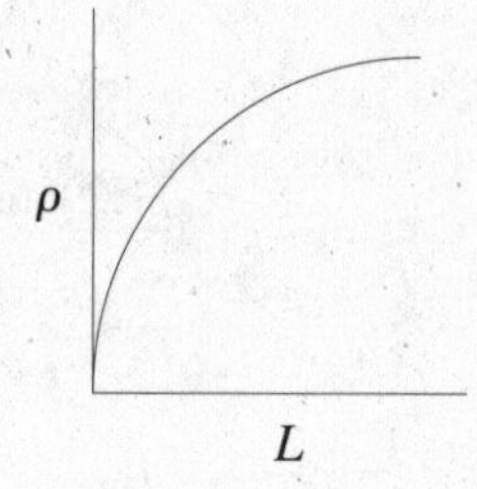

ρ

L

J.

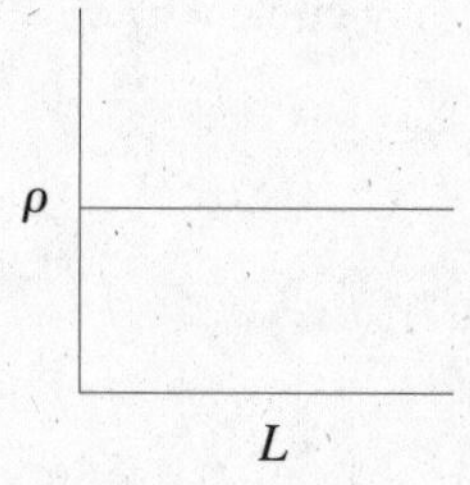

ρ

L

GO ON TO THE NEXT PAGE

Passage VI

How does evolution occur? Two views are presented below.

Scientist 1

Evolution occurs by natural selection. Random mutations are continually occurring in a species as it propagates. A number of these mutations result in traits that help the species adapt to environmental changes. Because these mutant traits are advantageous, the members of the species who possess them tend to survive and pass on their genes more often than those who do not have these traits. Therefore, the percentage of the population with an advantageous trait increases over time. Long necks evolved in giraffes by natural selection. The ancestors of giraffes had necks of various sizes, however their average neck length was much shorter than the average neck length of modern-day giraffes. Since the food supply was limited, the individuals with necks on the long range of the spectrum had access to more food (the leaves of trees) and therefore were more likely to survive and pass on their traits than individuals with shorter necks. Therefore, the proportion of the individuals with long necks is slightly greater in each subsequent generation.

Scientist 2

Evolution occurs by the inheritance of acquired characteristics. Characteristics that are acquired by an individual member of a species during its lifetime are passed on to its offspring. Therefore, each generation's traits are partially accounted for by all the changes that occurred in the individuals of the previous generation. This includes changes that occurred as a result of accidents, changes in the environment, overuse of muscles, etc. The evolution of long necks of giraffes is an example. Ancestors of giraffes had short necks and consequently had to stretch their necks to reach the leaves of trees that were their main source of food. This repeated stretching of their necks caused them to elongate slightly. This trait was passed on, so that the individuals of the next generation had slightly longer necks. Each subsequent generation also stretched their necks to feed; therefore, each generation had slightly longer necks than the previous generation.

29. Both scientists agree that:

- **A.** the environment affects evolution.
- **B.** the individuals of a generation have identical traits.
- **C.** acquired characteristics are inherited.
- **D.** random mutations occur.

30. How would the two hypotheses be affected if it were found that all of the offspring of an individual with a missing leg due to an accident were born with a missing leg?

- **F.** It would support Scientist 1's hypothesis, because it is an example of random mutations occurring within a species.
- **G.** It would refute Scientist 1's hypothesis, because it is an example of random mutations occurring within a species.
- **H.** It would support Scientist 2's hypothesis, because it is an example of an acquired characteristic being passed on to the next generation.
- **J.** It would support Scientist 2's hypothesis, because it is an example of random mutations occurring within a species.

GO ON TO THE NEXT PAGE

31. Which of the following characteristics can be inherited according to Scientist 2?

I. Fur color
II. Bodily scars resulting from a fight with another animal
III. Poor vision

A. I only
B. II only
C. I and III only
D. I, II, and III

32. Scientist 1 believes that the evolution of the long neck of the giraffe:

F. is an advantageous trait which resulted from overuse of neck muscles over many generations.
G. is an advantageous trait that resulted from a random mutation.
H. is an advantageous trait that resulted from a mutation that occurred in response to a change in the environment.
J. is a disadvantageous trait that resulted from a random mutation.

33. The fundamental point of disagreement between the two scientists is whether:

A. giraffes' ancestors had short necks.
B. evolved traits come from random mutations or from the previous generation.
C. the environment affects the evolution of a species.
D. the extinction of a species could be the result of random mutations.

Passage VII

Bovine spongiform encephalopathy (BSE) is caused by an unconventional pseudovirus that eventually kills infected cattle. BSE is diagnosed post mortem from the diseased cavities that appear in brain tissue, and is associated with the use in cattle feed of ground-up meat from scrapie-infected sheep. A series of experiments was performed to determine the mode of transmission of BSE. The results are given in the table below.

Experiment 1

Sixty healthy cows were divided into two equal groups. Group A's feed included meat from scrapie-free sheep; and Group B's feed included meat from scrapie-infected sheep. Eighteen months later, the two groups were slaughtered and their brains examined for BSE cavities.

Experiment 2

Researchers injected ground-up sheep brains directly into the brains of two groups of thirty healthy cows. The cows in Group C received brains from scrapie-free sheep. The cows in Group D received brains from scrapie-infected sheep. Eighteen months later, both groups were slaughtered and their brains examined for diseased cavities.

Table 1

Group	Mode of transmission	Scrapie present	Number of cows infected with BSE*
A	feed	no	1
B	feed	yes	12
C	injection	no	0
D	injection	yes	3

*As determined visually by presence/absence of spongiform encephalopathy

GO ON TO THE NEXT PAGE

34. Which of the following hypotheses was investigated in Experiment 1?

F. The injection of scrapie-infected sheep brains into cows' brains causes BSE.
G. The ingestion of wild grasses causes BSE.
H. The ingestion of scrapie-infected sheep meat causes scrapie.
J. The ingestion of scrapie-infected sheep meat causes BSE.

35. What is the purpose of Experiment 2?

A. To determine whether BSE can be transmitted by injection
B. To determine whether BSE can be transmitted by ingestion
C. To determine whether ingestion or injection is the primary mode of BSE transmission
D. To determine the healthiest diet for cows

36. Which of the following assumptions is made by the researchers in Experiments 1 and 2?

F. Cows do not suffer from scrapie.
G. A year and a half is a sufficient amount of time for BSE to develop in a cow.
H. Cows and sheep suffer from the same diseases.
J. Cows that eat scrapie-free sheep meat will not develop BSE.

37. A researcher wishes to determine whether BSE can be transmitted through scrapie-infected goats. Which of the following experiments would best test this?

A. Repeating Experiment 1, using a mixture of sheep and goat meat in Group C's feed
B. Repeating Experiments 1 and 2, replacing sheep with healthy goats
C. Repeating Experiments 1 and 2, replacing healthy sheep with healthy goats and scrapie-infected sheep with scrapie-infected goats
D. Repeating Experiment 2, replacing healthy cows with healthy goats

38. What is the control group in Experiment 1?

F. Group A
G. Group B
H. Group C
J. Group D

39. Which of the following conclusions is (are) supported by the experiments?

I. Cows that are exposed to scrapie-infected sheep are more likely to develop BSE than cows that are not.
II. BSE is only transmitted by eating scrapie-infected sheep meat.
III. A cow that eats scrapie-infected sheep meat is more likely to develop BSE than a cow that is injected with scrapie-infected sheep brains.

A. II only
B. III only
C. I and III only
D. II and III only

40. Which of the following statements is consistent with the results of Experiment 1?

F. All cows that are fed scrapie-infected sheep meat develop BSE.
G. All cows that are injected with scrapie-infected sheep brains develop BSE.
H. Some cows that are fed scrapie-infected sheep meat develop BSE.
J. Some cows that are injected with scrapie-infected sheep brains develop BSE.

IF YOU FINISH BEFORE TIME IS CALLED, YOU MAY CHECK YOUR WORK ON THIS SECTION ONLY. DO NOT TURN TO ANY OTHER SECTION IN THE TEST.

WRITING TEST

30 Minutes—1 Question

Directions: This section will test your writing ability. You will have thirty (30) minutes to compose an essay in English. Prior to planning your essay, pay close attention to the essay prompt so that you understand exactly what you are supposed to do. Your essay's grade will be based on how well it expresses an opinion on the question in the prompt, as well as its logical construction, supporting evidence, and clarity of expression based on the standards of written English.

You may use the unlined space on the next page to plan your essay. Anything written in this space will not be scored by the graders. Your essay must be written on the lined pages. While you may not need all the space to finish, you should not skip lines. Corrections and additions may be written neatly in between lines but not in the margins. Be sure to write clearly. Illegible work will not receive credit.

If you finish in under thirty minutes, you may review your essay. When time is called, lay your pencil down immediately.

DO NOT CONTINUE UNTIL TOLD TO DO SO.

GO ON TO THE NEXT PAGE

While some high schools offer art and music courses to their students, these courses are not always mandatory. Some teachers, students, and parents think that schools should emphasize traditional academic subjects like math and science, as those skills will help the students more in the future when they join the workforce. Others feel that requiring all high school students to take classes in music or the visual arts would teach equally valuable skills that the students may not learn otherwise, and would also help them do better in traditional academic subject areas. In your opinion, should art or music classes be mandatory for all high school students?

In your essay, take a position on this question. You may write about either one of the two points of view given, or you may present a different point of view on this question. Use specific reasons and examples to support your position.

Use this space to *plan* your essay. Your work here will not be graded. Write your essay on the lined pages that follow.

GO ON TO THE NEXT PAGE

KAPLAN
Test Prep and Admissions

KAPLAN
Test Prep and Admissions

KAPLAN
Test Prep and Admissions

Practice Test One: **Answer Key**

ENGLISH TEST			MATH TEST		READING TEST		SCIENCE TEST	
1. C	26. F	51. D	1. D	31. C	1. C	21. B	1. B	21. A
2. F	27. A	52. J	2. J	32. H	2. G	22. F	2. F	22. J
3. D	28. J	53. C	3. D	33. E	3. B	23. D	3. D	23. C
4. F	29. B	54. H	4. K	34. K	4. F	24. F	4. J	24. G
5. D	30. G	55. D	5. C	35. A	5. D	25. B	5. B	25. B
6. G	31. D	56. G	6. K	36. J	6. H	26. F	6. H	26. J
7. B	32. H	57. A	7. B	37. A	7. C	27. C	7. B	27. D
8. J	33. A	58. H	8. K	38. G	8. G	28. G	8. G	28. J
9. A	34. H	59. D	9. E	39. C	9. B	29. D	9. C	29. A
10. J	35. D	60. H	10. K	40. G	10. H	30. F	10. F	30. H
11. C	36. G	61. D	11. D	41. B	11. B	31. C	11. D	31. E
12. G	37. D	62. J	12. H	42. H	12. H	32. G	12. J	32. G
13. B	38. G	63. C	13. C	43. C	13. B	33. D	13. C	33. B
14. H	39. D	64. J	14. H	44. K	14. F	34. F	14. G	34. J
15. C	40. J	65. D	15. C	45. A	15. C	35. D	15. A	35. A
16. H	41. D	66. J	16. G	46. G	16. J	36. H	16. H	36. G
17. B	42. J	67. B	17. D	47. E	17. B	37. A	17. D	37. C
18. G	43. B	68. F	18. H	48. G	18. H	38. J	18. F	38. F
19. A	44. G	69. D	19. D	49. E	19. B	39. B	19. B	39. B
20. J	45. C	70. F	20. H	50. K	20. H	40. G	20. G	40. H
21. B	46. F	71. D	21. E	51. E				
22. G	47. B	72. G	22. H	52. K				
23. D	48. H	73. B	23. D	53. B				
24. J	49. C	74. F	24. F	54. G				
25. C	50. H	75. B	25. D	55. D				
			26. G	56. K				
			27. C	57. C				
			28. H	58. H				
			29. B	59. D				
			30. K	60. J				

Answers and Explanations

ENGLISH TEST

Passage I

1. (C)

(C) is the most correct and concise answer choice. (A) uses an unnecessary comma. (B) is unnecessarily wordy. (D) is redundant—if the societies created the legends, there is no need to describe the legends as original.

2. (F)

The question stem gives an important clue to the best answer: the purpose of the inserted sentence is "to describe the different kinds" of stories. (F) is the only choice that does this. (G) explains how the stories were told. (H) explains why more is not known about the stories. (J) describes the length of some stories.

3. (D)

Answer choices (A), (B), and (C) create run-on sentences. (D) describes a relationship that makes sense between our "many more permanent ways of handing down our beliefs" and the fact that "we continue to create and tell legends." It also creates a complete sentence.

4. (F)

(H) and (J) are ungrammatical after a colon. Answer choices (G), (H), and (J) are unnecessarily wordy.

5. (D)

In addition to other problems, answer choices (A), (B), and (C) are redundant or unnecessarily wordy. Because the contrasting word *but* is already used, *however* is repetitive and should be eliminated.

6. (G)

Answer choices (F), (H), and (J) are all redundant. The word *conclusion* is unnecessary because it expresses the same thing as the word *ending*, which has already been used.

7. (B)

(B) is the only choice that stays consistent with the verb tense established by *knew* and *decided*.

8. (J)

(F) creates a run-on sentence and also makes it seem that the hunter, not the deer, "was only temporarily knocked unconscious by the car." (G) and (H) use incorrect verb tenses.

9. (A)

(B) is incorrect because the words preceding the semicolon could not be a complete sentence on their own. (C) would create a sentence fragment. (D) would create a run-on sentence.

10. (J)

Regardless of the sequence of the words, the information provided in choices (F), (G), and (H) is irrelevant to the passage's topic of urban legends.

11. (C)

The subject of the sentence is *One*, so the verb must be singular. (B) and (D) use incorrect verb tenses.

12. (G)

(F) creates a sentence that does not make sense. (H) and (J) use the plural *women* instead of the singular *woman*.

13. (B)

(B) most clearly expresses the idea that several websites research "the validity of commonly told urban legends." Because this information is relevant to the topic of urban legends, "OMIT the underlined portion" is not the best answer.

14. (H)

Paragraph 3 describes an urban legend that is "humorous in nature." Paragraph 4 describes a rather frightening legend: alligators living underneath the city in the sewer system. The sentence "Other urban legends seem to be designed to instill fear" is an appropriate topic sentence for paragraph 4, and it also serves as a needed transition between paragraph 3 and paragraph 4.

15. (C)

Although the third and fourth sentences of paragraph 1 provide some general information about the purpose and topics of the myths and legends of primitive societies, no specifics are given. This makes (C) the best answer.

Passage II

16. (H)

The choices here would be *do you* or *does one*. The latter appears as an answer choice.

17. (B)

(A) incorrectly uses a colon. (C) and (D) are grammatically incorrect.

18. (G)

Solitary and *alone* are redundant in the same sentence. (H) and (J) also have redundancy.

19. (A)

The underlined portion is clearest the way it is written.

20. (J)

The colon is incorrect, so eliminate (F) and (H). Because it is a compound sentence, a comma is needed before *and*.

21. (B)

In fact is nonessential—it should be set off by commas.

22. (G)

American (an adjective) is the word being modified. Therefore, the adverb form of *unique* is needed.

23. (D)

Near Walden Pond ... is a long sentence fragment. The best way to fix the error is to simply combine the sentences.

24. (J)

This paragraph and the ones that immediately follow outline Thoreau's life. His influence on the people of today is not discussed until the end of the essay. Therefore, the underlined sentence does not belong.

25. (C)

Sentence 3 comes immediately after sentence 1. (C) is the only choice that lists it this way.

26. (F)

There is one independent clause on each side of the semicolon, so the sentence is punctuated correctly. (G) needs a comma before *and*. (H) is incorrect because the second half of the sentence is not an independent clause. (J) does not make sense.

27. (A)

A possessive pronoun is needed because the works belong to Thoreau. Eliminate (B) and (D). (C) relates to more than one person, so it is incorrect as well.

28. (J)

This paragraph is all about what Thoreau means to us today.

29. (B)

(A), (C), and (D) are excessively wordy.

30. (G)

The use of questions forces the reader to think about the answers. (F) is too literal, and (J) is too broad for the topic of the essay. (H) is incorrect because the author establishes the quality of Thoreau's work.

Passage III

31. (D)

Because the word *live* is used later in the sentence, (A), (B), and (C) contain redundant information.

32. (H)

In this sentence, the *its* must be possessive because the *unique anatomy* belongs to the sloth. The word describing *anatomy* must be an adjective, not an adverb.

33. (A)

The comma is correctly used in (A) to separate the nonessential descriptive phrase *about the size of a large domestic cat* from the rest of the sentence.

34. (H)

The information about the sloth's limbs is relevant to the topic, so it should not be omitted. (H) makes the most sense in the context of the passage.

35. (D)

Adapted needs to be modified by an adverb, so (D) is the best answer choice.

36. (G)

Instead describes the right relationship between the two sentences. The pronouns must be consistent, and since *its* is already used in the sentence, (G) is the best answer choice.

37. (D)

(D) is the only choice that correctly describes the relationship between the sloth's inability to "move swiftly on the ground" and its ability to swim.

38. (G)

(G) connects the sloth's unique characteristics discussed in paragraph 3 with the description of its flexibility in paragraph 4.

39. (D)

(D) correctly uses the second comma necessary to separate the phrase *without moving the rest of its body* from the rest of the sentence. (C) can be eliminated because it is unnecessarily wordy.

40. (J)

(J) is the only choice that contains a consistent verb tense.

41. (D)

(A) and (B) contain redundant information. (C) uses an incorrect form of the verb.

42. (J)

This information about the howler monkey is irrelevant to the topic of the passage.

43. (B)

(A) creates a sentence fragment. (C) is unnecessarily wordy and awkward. (D) creates a run-on sentence.

44. (G)

The last sentence serves as a conclusion for the entire passage, and removing it would make the ending more abrupt.

45. (C)

The description of the sloth's "camouflage" is in paragraph 5.

Passage IV

46. (F)

The underlined portion is best left as is. The other answer choices make the sentence unnecessarily wordy.

47. (B)

The verb tense must agree with the tense that has been established up to this point. The passage is in past tense, so the past tense choice (B) is correct.

48. (H)

Like the previous question, the simple past tense is correct.

49. (C)

(A) creates a sentence fragment and uses an incorrect verb tense. (B) also uses the wrong verb tense. (D) incorrectly uses a semicolon, as the words preceding the semicolon do not constitute an independent clause.

50. (H)

In the context of the rest of the passage, only (H) makes sense. The fire fighters' attempts to extinguish the flames failed; only nature could stop the fire with the first snowfall.

51. (D)

(A) and (B) are unnecessarily wordy and awkward. (C) creates a run-on sentence.

52. (J)

All of the other answer choices are unnecessarily wordy and/or repetitive.

53. (C)

From the word *open*, you can determine that the best answer will contain *cones*. This makes (C) the only possible answer, as the apostrophe is incorrectly used in (B).

54. (H)

This is the only answer choice that makes sense in the context of the passage. The sighting of the large animals near burning forests is used as evidence that the animals of the region were "fire-tolerant and fire-adaptive."

55. (D)

The comma in (A) is unnecessary because the sentence has a list of only two examples, not three. The semicolon in (B) is incorrectly used because *and bedding down* does not begin an independent clause. The colon in (C) is incorrectly used because it is not being used to introduce or emphasize information.

56. (G)

The problem with *judging from the recent pictures of the park* is that the phrase is modifying *forest*, and a forest obviously can't judge anything. The phrase would have been okay if the sentence read "judging from the recent pictures of the park, I think that the forest was not destroyed." In this case the phrase modifies *I*, the author, who is capable of judging. Choice (G) takes care of the problem by rewriting the sentence so that the modifying phrase is gone.

57. (A)

The pronoun refers to *forest*.

58. (H)

The introduction of information about fires in Alaska is unwarranted, so (F) and (G) can be eliminated. (J) is incorrect because the additional information would actually uphold the author's position as an authority.

59. (D)

The reports mentioned in (D) would substantiate the author's claims much more so than any of the other answer choices.

Passage V

60. (H)

(F) creates a sentence fragment, and (G) incorrectly uses a plural verb with a singular subject. The context of the paragraph makes (H) a better choice than (J).

61. (D)

The final part of the sentence, "...and there are many other rivers in America as well," is completely irrelevant to the rest of the sentence and the paragraph, in which the author discusses white water rafting and the rivers she's rafted.

62. (J)

The phrase *on the Deschutes River* is essential information and, therefore, should not be set off by a comma. (G) and (H) incorrectly use the colon and semicolon, respectively.

63. (C)

(A) and (D) create sentence fragments, and (B) is extremely awkward.

64. (J)

This sentence is irrelevant to the topic of the passage.

65. (D)

This sentence makes it sound as though the author were roaring, not the rapids; *roaring* is a misplaced modifier. (B) doesn't fix the problem because the reader has no idea what *it* refers to. (C) has *the boat* roaring. (D) is the clearest choice.

66. (J)

The word *cover* must either be in past tense, or the structure of the sentence must change. (J) does the latter.

67. (B)

(B) is the simplest, most concise way of expressing the idea. Replacing *and instead he adopted* with *with* makes the sentence much less awkward.

68. (F)

(G) and (J) make it sound as though the author were in the water. (F) expresses the idea better than (H).

69. (D)

The phrase *and we stopped* is redundant because *we came to a jarring halt* says the same thing much more expressively. Omit the underlined portion.

70. (F)

It was is fine here because the author is telling her story in the past tense. (G) and (H) are the present tense, and (J) incorrectly introduces the possessive form.

71. (D)

The other answer choices are unnecessarily wordy; the simplest choice is the best.

72. (G)

The participle *receiving* has to be changed into a verb in the past tense, *received*, in order to be consistent with *went*. (G) is correct as opposed to (H) because the number of bruises something has can be counted, which necessitates *many bruises*, not *much bruises*.

73. (B)

(A) wouldn't work as a concluding sentence because its style and tone are off; nowhere in the passage does the writer use language such as *brutal calamities* and *beguiling excitement*. Also, the writer and her father were not "unwary rafters." (C) contradicts the writer's main theme that nothing was as memorable as her first ride through the rapids. The tone in (D), "call me crazy or weird...," is much different from the writer's. (B) is the choice that closely matches the author's style and tone while restating the main theme of the passage.

74. (F)

This essay relates a personal experience of the writer: her first time rafting down the rapids. There is very little mention of the techniques of white water rafting, so the essay would not meet the requirements of the assignment. (G) is wrong because the essay does not focus on the relationship between father and daughter, but on their first rafting experience together.

75. (B)

The sentence is a preface of things to come, so it must appear towards the beginning of the essay. That eliminates (C) and (D). The second paragraph is about the peaceful setting, so (B) is the most sensible answer.

MATH TEST

1. (D)

You know that 14 people are 20% of the total, and you need to find 100% of the total. You could set up an equation, or you could multiply 14 by 5, since 100% is 5 times as much as 20%. The number of people surveyed is 14×5, or 70.

2. (J)

One safe way to answer this question is by picking numbers. For instance, if you let $x = 2$ and $y = 3$, the train would have traveled $90 \times 2 + 60 \times 3 = 360$ miles in 5 hours, or $\frac{360}{5} = 72$ miles per hour. If you then plug $x = 2$ and $y = 3$ into the answer choices looking for 72, it's clear that the correct answer is (J). No other answer choice equals 72 when $x = 2$ and $y = 3$.

3. (D)

If the ratio of men to women is 5:3, then the ratio of women to the total is 3:8. Since you know the total number of string players is 24, you can set up the equation $\frac{3}{8} = \frac{x}{24}$ to find that $x = 9$. Also, without setting up the proportion, you could note that the total number of players is 3 times the ratio total, so the number of women will be 3 times the part of the ratio that represents women.

4. (K)

In a pinch you could backsolve on this question, but this one is fairly easy to solve algebraically, like so:

$$x^2 - 3x = 6x$$

$$x^2 = 9x$$

Now you can divide both sides by x because $x \neq 0$:

$$\frac{x^2}{x} = \frac{9x}{x}$$

$$x = 9$$

5. (C)

With visual perception problems such as this one, the key is to play around with possibilities as you try to draw a solution. Eventually, you should be able to come up with a picture like this:

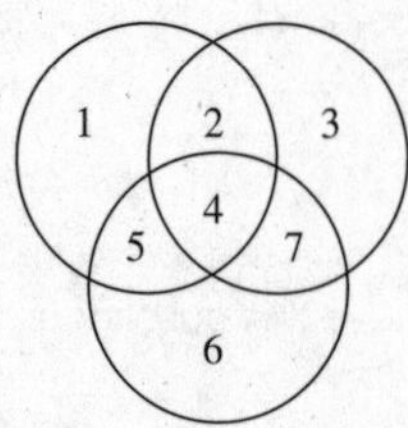

6. (K)

This problem could be solved algebraically, but look at the answer choices. They are all simple numbers, making this a great opportunity for backsolving. Begin with choice (H). Plugging in 0, you get:

$(0)^2 + 6(0) + 8 = 4 + 10(0)$

$8 = 4$

Since 8 does not equal 4, you know this isn't the correct answer. But it is difficult to know which answer to try next. Should you aim higher or lower? If you're unsure of which direction to go, just try whatever looks easiest. Choice (J), 1, looks like a good candidate:

$(1)^2 + 6(1) + 8 = 4 + 10(1)$

$1 + 6 + 8 = 4 + 10$

$15 = 14$

So (J) doesn't work either, but it looks like the numbers are getting closer, so you're going in the right direction. Try out choice (K) just to be sure.

$(2)^2 + 6(2) + 8 = 4 + 10(2)$

$4 + 12 + 8 = 4 + 20$

$24 = 24$

Choice (K) is the correct answer.

7. (B)

Translate piece by piece:

"Nine less than c" indicates subtraction: $c - 9$.

"Nine less than c is the same as the number d": $c - 9 = d$. There's one equation.

"d less than" also indicates subtraction: $-d$.

"d less than twice c is 20": $2c - d = 20$. There's the second equation.

Choice (B) matches what we found.

8. (K)

To determine the total number of possible arrangements on a question like this one, simply determine the number of possibilities for each component, and then multiply them together. There are 3 ways of serving the ice cream, 5 flavors, and 4 toppings. Therefore there are $3 \times 5 \times 4 = 60$ ways to order ice cream, and choice (K) is correct.

9. (E)

Backsolving is a great technique to use for this problem. Start with (C). The director asked one out of 3 students to come to the second audition and $\frac{1}{3}$ of 48 is 16, so 16 students were invited to a second audition. Then 75% of 16, which is $\frac{3}{4}(16) = 12$ students were offered parts. The question states that 18 students were offered parts, so you already know that (C) is too small. You can also eliminate (A) and (B). Since the director invited $\frac{1}{3}$ of the students to a second audition, the number of students at the first audition must be divisible by 3. (You can't have a fraction of a student.) That eliminates (D), which leaves only (E).

10. (K)

Begin by translating the English into math: $x + 5x = -60$, $6x = -60$, so $x = -10$, and the two numbers are -10 and -50. Thus the lesser number is -50.

By the way, this is where most people mess up. They forget that the "lesser" of two negative numbers is the negative number with the larger absolute value (since *less* means *to the left of* on the number line):

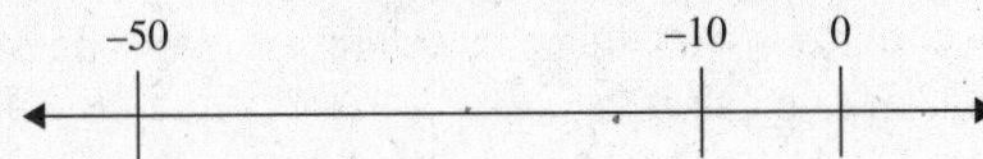

11. (D)

You're looking for the total number of parallelograms that can be found among the triangles, and parallelograms could be formed two ways from these triangles, either from two adjacent triangles, or from four adjacent triangles, like so:

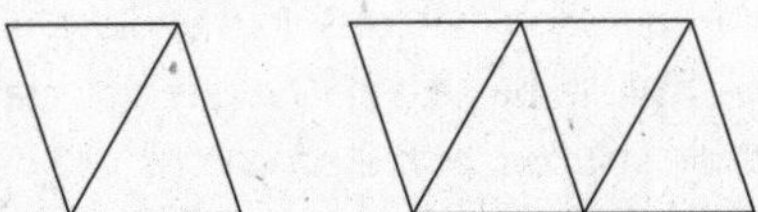

Begin by looking for the smaller parallelograms. If you look for parallelograms leaning in the same direction as the one we drew, you'll find three. But there are two other possible orientations for the smaller parallelogram; it could be flipped horizontally, or it could be rotated 90 degrees so that one triangle sits atop the other in the form of a diamond; both of these orientations also have three parallelograms, for a total of nine smaller parallelograms.

Now look for larger parallelograms. Perhaps the easiest way to count these is to look along the sides of the larger composite triangle. You should be able to spot two of the larger parallelograms along each side, one originating at each vertex, for a total of six larger parallelograms. Thus there are a total of $9 + 6 = 15$ parallelograms in all.

12. (H)

The square has a perimeter of 16 inches, so each side of the square is 4 inches, and the area of the square is, therefore, 16 square inches. If the side of the square is 4 inches, then the diameter of the circle is also 4 inches. The radius of the circle is then 2 inches. The area of the circle is 4π square inches. The area of the shaded region is then $16 - 4\pi$ square inches.

13. (C)

The safest strategy is simply to list out the possibilities. It's also helpful to realize that multiples of both 4 and 6 are multiples of 12 (the least common multiple between the two), so skip over all multiples of 12:

4, 8, ~~12~~, 16, 20, ~~24~~, 28, 32, ~~36~~, 40, 44, ~~48~~

So there are 8 in all.

14. (H)

Don't be intimidated by the expression $f(x)$. In this case, that just means that you should plug in the number that appears in the parentheses for the x in the expression they have given you. So, if $f(x) = (8 - 3x)(x^2 - 2x - 15)$, $f(3) = [8 - 3(3)][(3)^2 - 2(3) - 15]$. Once you get to this point, just remember PEMDAS. $[8 - 3(3)][(3)^2 - 2(3) - 15] = (8 - 9)(9 - 6 - 15) = (-1)(-12) = 12$, choice (H).

15. (C)

A class contains five juniors and five seniors. If one member of the class is assigned at random to present a paper on a certain subject, and another member of the class is randomly assigned to assist him, then:

The probability that the first student picked will be a junior $= \frac{\text{\# of Juniors}}{\text{Total \# of Students}} = \frac{5}{10} = \frac{1}{2}$

The probability that the second student picked will be a junior, given that the first student picked was a junior $= \frac{\text{\# of Juniors Remaining}}{\text{Total \# of Students Remaining}}$

So the probability that both students will be juniors $= \frac{1}{2} \times \frac{4}{9} = \frac{2}{9}$

16. (G)

Since the formula to find the area of a triangle is $\frac{1}{2}$ (*base*)(*height*), you can plug in the base and area to find the height. You know that the area of this triangle is 45 units and that the base is 3 + 12 = 15. Let x be the length of altitude $\overline{YS}$. Plug these into the area formula to get $45 = \frac{15x}{2}$. Solve for x to get $x = 6$.

17. (D)

The y-coordinate is the point on which the x value is zero, so plug $x = 0$ into the equation:

$6y - 3(0) = 18$

$6y = 18$

$y = 3$

18. (H)

This question involves common quadratics, so the key is to write these quadratic expressions in their other forms. For instance $x^2 - y^2 = 12$, so $(x + y)(x - y) = 12$. Since $x - y = 4$, $(x + y)(4) = 12$, so $x + y = 3$. Finally, $x^2 + 2xy + y^2 = (x + y)^2 = (3)^2 = 9$.

19. (D)

This shape must be divided into 3 simple shapes. By drawing downward two perpendicular line segments from the endpoints of the side which is 10 units long, you are left with a 3 × 10 rectangle, a triangle with a base of 4 and a height of 3, and a triangle with a base of 7 and a hypotenuse of $7\sqrt{2}$. The rectangle has an area of 3 × 10 = 30 square units. The smaller triangle has an area of $\frac{4 \times 3}{2} = 6$ square units. The larger triangle is a 45°-45°-90° triangle, so the height must be 7. Therefore, it has an area of $\frac{7 \times 7}{2} = 24.5$ square units. The entire shape has an area of 6 + 30 + 24.5 = 60.5 square units.

20. (H)

Although backsolving is certainly possible with this problem, it's probably quicker to solve with arithmetic. The board is 12 feet long, which means it is 12 × 12 = 144 inches. The carpenter cuts off 3 × 17 = 51 inches. That leaves 144 – 51 = 93 inches.

21. (E)

To answer this question, begin by setting the right side of the equation to equal zero:

$x^2 - 4x - 6 = 6$

$x^2 - 4x - 12 = 0$

Now use reverse-FOIL to factor the left side of the equation:

$(x - 6)(x + 2) = 0$

Thus either $x - 6 = 0$ or $x + 2 = 0$, so $x = 6$ or -2.

22. (H)

Here's another question that tests your understanding of FOIL, but you have to be careful. The question states that –3 is a possible solution for the equation $x^2 + kx - 15 = 0$, so in its factored form, one set of parentheses with a factor inside must be $(x + 3)$. Since the last term in the equation in its expanded form is –15, that means that the entire factored equation must read $(x + 3)(x - 5) = 0$, which in its expanded form is $x^2 - 2x - 15 = 0$. Thus $k = -2$.

23. (D)

To solve this problem you need to understand the triangle inequality theorem, which states: The sum of the lengths of any two sides of a triangle is always greater then the length of the third side. Therefore, the other sides of this triangle must add up to more than 7. You know from the problem that every side must be an integer. That means that the sides must add up to at least 8 inches (4 inches and 4 inches, or 7 inches and 1 inch, for example). The smallest possible perimeter is 7 + 8 = 15.

24. (F)

It's time to use SOHCAHTOA, and drawing a triangle might help as well. If the sine of θ (opposite side over hypotenuse) is $\frac{\sqrt{11}}{2\sqrt{3}}$, then one of the legs of the right triangle is $\sqrt{11}$ and the hypotenuse is $2\sqrt{3}$. Now apply the Pythagorean theorem to come up with the other (adjacent) leg: $(\sqrt{11})^2 + (n)^2 = (2\sqrt{3})^2$, so $11 + n^2 = 12$, which means that $n^2 = 1$, and $n = 1$. Thus cosine (adjacent side over hypotenuse) θ is $\frac{1}{2\sqrt{3}}$.

25. (D)

Take a quick look at the answer choices before simplifying an expression like this one. Notice that none of these choices contain a radical sign in their denominators. So when you simplify the expression, try to eliminate that radical sign. Your calculations should look something like this:

$$\frac{\sqrt{3+x}}{\sqrt{3-x}} \times \frac{\sqrt{3-x}}{\sqrt{3-x}} = \frac{\sqrt{(3+x)(3-x)}}{\sqrt{(3-x)^2}} =$$

$$\frac{\sqrt{9-3x+3x-x^2}}{3-x} = \frac{\sqrt{9-x^2}}{3-x}.$$

So choice (D) is correct.

26. (G)

If the ratio of the parts is 2:5, then the ratio total is 2 + 5 = 7. Thus the actual total number of cookies must be a multiple of 7. The only answer choice that's a multiple of 7 is (G), 35.

27. (C)

This question is a great opportunity to use your calculator. Notice that all your answer choices are decimals. In order to solve, convert $\frac{3}{16}$ into a decimal and add that to .175. $\frac{3}{16}$ = .1875, so the sum equals .1875 + .175 = .3625.

So choice (C) is correct.

28. (H)

Remember that if you are given a perimeter for a rectangle, the rectangle with the greatest area for that perimeter will be a square. So we are looking for the area of a square with a perimeter of 20. The perimeter of a square equals $4s$, where s is the length of one side of the square. If $4s = 20$, then $s = 5$. The area of the square equals $s^2 = 5^2 = 25$, choice (H).

29. (B)

Be careful on this one. You can't start plugging numbers into your calculator without paying attention to the order of operations. This one is best solved on your own.

$$\frac{\frac{3}{2}+\frac{7}{4}}{\left(\frac{15}{8}-\frac{3}{4}\right)-\left(\frac{4+3}{-4+3}\right)} = \frac{\frac{3}{2}+\frac{7}{4}}{\left(\frac{9}{8}\right)-\left(\frac{7}{-1}\right)} = \frac{\frac{13}{4}}{\frac{9}{8}+\frac{7}{1}}$$

$$= \frac{\frac{13}{4}}{\frac{65}{8}} = \frac{13}{4} \times \frac{8}{65} = \frac{2}{5}$$

30. (K)

You could solve this algebraically for x as follows:

$x - 15 = 7 - 5(x - 4)$

$x - 15 = 7 - 5x + 20$

$x - 15 = -5x + 27$

$6x = 42$

$x = 7$

Remember also that if you are ever stuck, you can try to backsolve with the answer choices. Here if you try them all out, only 7 works:

$7 - 15 = 7 - 5(7 - 4)$

$-8 = 7 - 5(3)$

$-8 = 7 - 15$

$-8 = -8$

31. (C)

Break strange figures like this one up into shapes that are more familiar and easier to handle. In this case, the quadrilateral can be split into a square and a right triangle. The square is 9×9, so the area of that part of the figure is 81 square meters. The right triangle has a height of 9 and a base of 4, so the area of the triangle would be $\frac{1}{2}bh = \frac{1}{2}(4 \times 9) = \frac{1}{2}(36) = 18$ square meters. So the total area of the figure is $(81 + 18)$ square meters $= 99$ square meters, choice (C).

32. (H)

The easiest way to solve this question is to put it in the form $y = mx + b$, in which case m equals the slope. In other words, you want to isolate y:

$$6y - 3x = 18$$

$$6y = 3x + 18$$

$$y = \frac{3x + 18}{6}$$

$$y = \frac{1}{2}x + 3$$

So the slope equals $\frac{1}{2}$.

33. (E)

To answer this question you have to know that perpendicular lines on the standard (x, y) coordinate plane have slopes that are negative reciprocals of each other. In other words, the line described by the equation $y = -\frac{4}{5}x + 6$ has a slope of $-\frac{4}{5}$, so a line perpendicular to it has a slope of $\frac{5}{4}$. Looking at the answer choices, you can immediately eliminate (B), (C), and (D). Now just plug the coordinates you're given, (4, 3), into one of the remaining equations. Let's try choice (A):

$$3 = \frac{5}{4}(4) + 2$$

$$3 = 5 + 2$$

This does not compute, so the answer must be (E). (Try it out if you're not convinced.)

34. (K)

Since the problem gives you the y-intercept, it is easy to look at the answer choices and rule out (F), (H), and (J). Put the equation from the question in slope-intercept form to find its slope:

$$3x - 5y = 4$$

$$-5y = -3x + 4$$

$$y = \frac{-3x + 4}{-5}$$

$$y = \frac{3}{5}x - \frac{4}{5}$$

Since line t is parallel, it has the same slope. This matches (K).

35. (A)

To solve for x in the equation $y = mx + b$, isolate x on one side of the equation. Begin by subtracting b from both sides. You will be left with $y - b = mx$. Then divide both sides by m, and you will be left with $x = \frac{y - b}{m}$, choice (A).

36. (J)

In this figure there are many right triangles, and many similar triangles. If you know to be on the lookout for 3-4-5 triangles, it should be easy to spot that triangle ABC has sides of 15-20-25, so $\overline{AC}$ is 25. Now turn your attention to triangle ABD. Since it's a right triangle that shares $\angle BAC$ with triangle ABC, it too must be a 3-4-5 triangle. So if the hypotenuse is 20, the shorter leg ($\overline{BD}$) must have a length of 12, and the longer leg ($\overline{AD}$) must have a length of 16.

37. (A)

The shortest distance to line *m* will be a line perpendicular to *m*. So, the distance will be the difference between the *y*-coordinates of point *C* and the nearest point on line *m*. Since every point on *m* has a *y*-coordinate of 5, and point *C* has a *y*-coordinate of 3, the difference is 2.

38. (G)

Perhaps the easiest approach here is to pick numbers. Pick a simple number such as $x = 2$. Thus

$$\frac{x^2 - 11x + 24}{8 - x} = \frac{(2)^2 - 11(2) + 24}{6} = \frac{4 - 22 + 24}{6}$$

$= \frac{6}{6} = 1$. So 1 is your target number. When you plug $x = 2$ into the answer choices, the only choice that gives you 1 is (G).

39. (C)

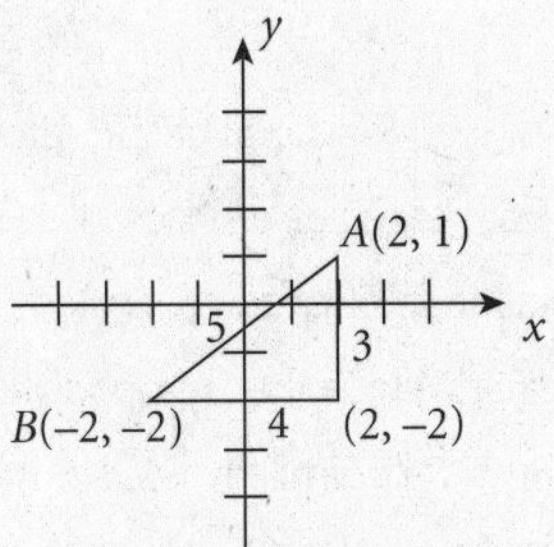

It may help you to draw a picture. Draw a right triangle into the coordinate plane as we've done above. Note that the distance between the two points represents the hypotenuse of the triangle. The legs of the triangle have lengths of 3 and 4, so the distance between the two points must be 5, choice (C).

40. (G)

To find the area of the shaded region, you must subtract the area of the circle from the area of the rectangle. Since the sides of the rectangle are $2x$ and $5x$, it has an area of $2x \times 5x = 10x^2$. By examining the diagram, you can see that the circle has a diameter of $2x$, so it has a radius of x. Its area is, therefore, πx^2. The shaded region, therefore, has an area of $10x^2 - \pi x^2$.

41. (B)

Since you are not given a diagram for this problem, it's best to draw a quick sketch of a right triangle to help keep the sides separate in your mind. Mark one of the acute angles θ. Since $\cos \theta = \frac{5\sqrt{2}}{8}$, mark the adjacent side $5\sqrt{2}$ and the hypotenuse as 8. (Remember SOHCAH-TOA.) Use the Pythagorean theorem to find that the side opposite θ is $\sqrt{14}$. The problem asks you to find $\tan \theta$. Tangent $= \frac{\text{opposite}}{\text{adjacent}}$, so $\tan \theta = \frac{\sqrt{14}}{5\sqrt{2}}$, which can be simplified to $\frac{\sqrt{7}}{5}$.

42. (H)

This question is one where your calculator can come in handy. Divide 7 by integer values for *n*, and look for values between .5 and .8. Begin by looking for the integer values of *n* where $\frac{7}{n}$ is greater than .5. If $n = 14$, then $\frac{7}{n} = .5$, so *n* must be less than 14. Work through values of *n* until you get to the point where $\frac{7}{n} \geq .8$. When $n = 9$, $\frac{7}{n} = .778$, but when $n = 8$, $\frac{7}{n} = .875$. So the integer values that work for *n* in this case are $n = 9, 10, 11, 12$, and 13. Five integer values work, so choice (H) is correct.

43. (C)

The points are as far apart as possible when separated by a diameter of *X* and a diameter of *Y*.

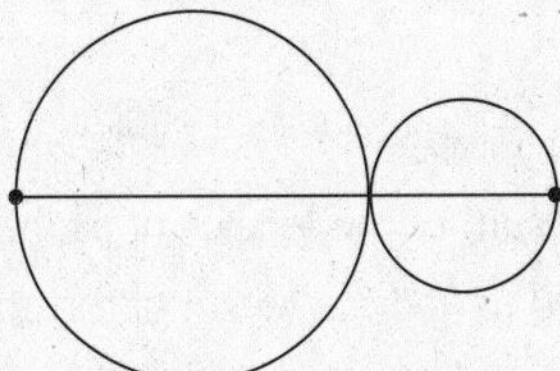

The circumference of a circle is $\pi \times$ (diameter), so the diameter of circle X is 12 and the diameter of circle Y is 8. The greatest possible distance between points then is $12 + 8 = 20$.

44. (K)

Begin by getting rid of the square root sign. If $y \geq 0$, then $\sqrt{y^2} = y$, so $\sqrt{(x^2 + 4)^2} = x^2 + 4$. $(x + 2)(x - 2) = x^2 - 4$, so you now have $(x^2 + 4) - (x^2 - 4) = ?$ Get rid of the parentheses and you have $x^2 + 4 - x^2 + 4 = x^2 - x^2 + 4 + 4 = 8$.

45. (A)

Here you need to substitute -3 for s and solve. That gives you the expression $(-3)^3 + 2(-3)^2 + 2(-3)$, which equals $-27 + 18 - 6$, or -15. If you missed this problem, you probably made a mistake with the signs of the numbers.

46. (G)

Be careful on this one. Begin by simplifying the equation by FOILing one side:

$$2x + 6 = (x + 5)(x + 3)$$

$$2x + 6 = x^2 + 8x + 15$$

Then get the right side of the equation to equal zero: $x^2 + 6x + 9 = 0$.

The left side of this equation is the perfect square $(x + 3)^2$, so $(x + 3)^2 = 0$, which has only one solution, $x = -3$. Choice (G) is correct.

47. (E)

This is a great eyeballing question. The perimeter is greater than $\overline{AC}$, so you can get rid of choices (A) and (B). It appears to be quite a bit greater than $\overline{AC}$, more than twice as great, so choices (C) and (D) are out as well. That only leaves choice (E).

If you wanted to solve this the conventional way, since the perimeter is the sum of the lengths of all the sides of the square, you need to find the length of the square's sides. Let the length of each of the square's sides be x. $\overline{AC}$ divides the square into two right triangles, so we can apply the Pythagorean theorem: $\overline{AB}^2 + \overline{BC}^2 = \overline{AC}^2$. Since $\overline{AB}$ and $\overline{BC}$ are sides of the square they have the same length. We can write that as $x^2 + x^2 = \overline{AC}^2$. $\overline{AC} = 8$, so $2x^2 = 8^2$; $2x^2 = 64$; $x^2 = 32$; $x = \sqrt{32} = \sqrt{16 \times 2} = 4\sqrt{2}$. So each side of the square is $4\sqrt{2}$, and the perimeter of the square is $4 \times 4\sqrt{2} = 16\sqrt{2}$.

48. (G)

To find the area of this complex shape, you could divide it into 2 simple shapes by drawing a line 30 inches up, parallel to the horizontal base. This leaves you with a 4×30 rectangle and a triangle with height of 6 and a base of 4. The rectangle has an area of $4 \times 30 = 120$ square inches, and the triangle has an area of $\frac{4 \times 6}{2} = 12$ square inches. That makes a total of $120 + 12 = 132$ square inches.

49. (E)

Drawing $\overline{OD}$ divides quadrilateral $OCDE$ into two triangles, OCD and ODE. Both triangles are isosceles because $\overline{OC}$, $\overline{OD}$, and $\overline{OE}$ are all radii of circle O. Angles ODC and OCD have equal measures, since they're opposite equal sides, so $\angle ODC$ measures 70°. Similarly, $\angle ODE$ measures 45°. Together, angles ODC and ODE make up $\angle CDE$, so its measure is $70° + 45° = 115°$.

50. (K)

Remember that lines intersect at the point that is a solution to both equations. So, equations with no common solution don't intersect—they have the same slope and are parallel. To solve this problem, search through the answer choices to find the pair of equations representing lines with the same slope. If you write the equations in (K) in slope-intercept form, you'll get $y = -\frac{1}{3}x + 2$, $y = -\frac{1}{3}x + \frac{7}{9}$, so the slope is clearly the same for both equations.

51. (E)

To solve a repeating decimal question, begin by determining the pattern of the decimal on your calculator. $\frac{1}{7}$ = 0.142857142857 . . ., so you know that this fraction repeats every 6 decimal places. Since we are looking for the 46th decimal place, we need to determine where in the 6-term pattern we would be at the 46th place. Divide 46 by 6, and look for the remainder. The remainder in this case is 4, so we are looking for the fourth term in the sequence, which is 8, choice (E).

52. (K)

Remember that you treat an inequality exactly like an equality, except that you need to flip the sign when you multiply or divide by a negative number. In this problem, you start with the inequality $-2 - 4x \leq -6x$. Add $4x$ to both sides to get $-2 \leq -2x$. Divide by -2 and flip the sign to get $1 \geq x$, which matches (K).

53. (B)

For this problem, it would probably be easiest to pick numbers. Since you will be taking the square root of the numbers, it's easiest to pick perfect squares, like 4 and 9. $\frac{\sqrt{4}}{4} + \frac{\sqrt{9}}{9} = \frac{2}{4} + \frac{3}{9} = \frac{1}{2} + \frac{1}{3} = \frac{5}{6}$. When you plug 4 and 9 into the answer choices, only (B) gives you $\frac{5}{6}$.

54. (G)

When transversals intersect parallel lines, corresponding line segments on the transversals are proportional. In other words, $\frac{\overline{DE}}{\overline{CB}} = \frac{\overline{EF}}{\overline{BA}}$. Thus $\frac{6}{8} = \frac{\overline{EF}}{4}$, so $\overline{EF} = 3$.

55. (D)

Divide the square into two right triangles by drawing the diagonal from (2, 7) to (2, 1). Remember that the area of each triangle is half its base times its height. Treat the diagonal as the base of a triangle. Its length is the distance from (2, 7) to (2, 1). Since the x-coordinates are the same, that distance is simply the difference between the y-coordinates, 7 – 1, or 6. The diagonal bisects the square, so the height of the triangle is half the distance from (–1, 4) to (5, 4). We already know that a diagonal of this square is 6, so half the distance is 3. Therefore, the base and height of either triangle are 6 and 3, so the area of each triangle is $\frac{6 \times 3}{2}$ or 9 square units. The square is made up of two such triangles and so has twice the area, or 18 square units.

56. (K)

Compared to the graph of $y = \cos \theta$, the graph of $y = 2 \cos \theta$ would have twice the amplitude and the same period, choice (K). Here you are doubling y, which represents the vertical coordinates, but the θ coordinates stay the same. The amplitude of a trigonometric equation refers to how high or low the curve moves from the horizontal axis. The period refers to the distance required to complete a single wave along the horizontal axis.

57. (C)

To solve this problem with algebra, you need to translate each phrase into mathematics. Translated, the problem is $3(x + 15) = 4x - 65$. Solve for x to get 110. Alternatively, you could backsolve.

58. (H)

The volume of a cylinder is $\pi r^2 h$, so pick numbers to make this question more concrete and plug them into this volume formula. Let's say the smaller cylinder has a height of 1 and a radius of 1 (diameter of 2), for a volume of $\pi(1)^2 \times 1 = \pi$. The larger cylinder would then have a height of 3 and a radius of 2 (diameter of 4), for a volume of $\pi(2)^2 \times 3 = 12\pi$. Thus it would take 12 fillings of the smaller cylinder to fill the larger cylinder.

59. (D)

Draw a picture of the triangle, and carefully apply your knowledge of the ratio of the lengths of the sides of a 30°-60°-90° triangle ($x : x\sqrt{3} : 2x$). So if the longer leg has a length of 12, the shorter leg has a length of $\frac{12}{\sqrt{3}} = \frac{12\sqrt{3}}{\sqrt{3} \times \sqrt{3}} = \frac{12\sqrt{3}}{3} = 4\sqrt{3}$. Thus the hypotenuse is twice this, or $8\sqrt{3}$. So the perimeter is the sum of the three sides, or $4\sqrt{3} + 12 + 8\sqrt{3} = 12\sqrt{3} + 12$.

60. (J)

Remember the average formula on this one. The average formula states, Average $= \frac{\text{Sum of the terms}}{\text{Number of terms}}$. So to find the total average, find the total sum and divide it by the total number of terms. If a team averages x points in n games, then it scored nx points in n games. In the final game of the season, it scored y points. So the total sum of points for the season is $nx + y$, and the total number of games is $n + 1$. So the team's average score for the entire season is $\frac{nx + y}{n + 1}$, choice (J).

READING TEST

Passage I

1. (C)
The answer can be found in lines 26–31: "The real evils, indeed, of Emma's situation were the power of having rather too much her own way, and a disposition to think a little too well of herself; these were the disadvantages which threatened alloy to her many enjoyments."

2. (G)
Isabella's name is given in line 64.

3. (B)
The answer can be found in lines 17–18: "Between them it was more the intimacy of sisters."

4. (F)
As it is used in the sentence, *disposition* means "tendency" or "inclination." It would not make sense for Emma to have (G) control, (H) placement, or (J) transfer "to think a little too well of herself" (lines 28–29).

5. (D)
The answer can be found in lines 55–61: "She recalled her past kindness—the kindness, the affection of sixteen years—how she had taught her and...how she had devoted all her powers to attach and amuse her in health—and how she had nursed her through the various illnesses of childhood."

6. (H)
Miss Taylor will continue to be a part of Emma's life, but they will not be as close because Miss Taylor no longer lives with Emma and because Miss Taylor will be primarily concerned with her husband's, not Emma's, well-being.

7. (C)
Emma is self-centered, as evidenced by her description of her relationship with Miss Taylor. Among Miss Taylor's admirable qualities, Emma includes the fact that Miss Taylor was "interested in her, in every pleasure, every scheme of hers—one to whom she could speak every thought as it arose, and who had such an affection for her as could never find fault" (lines 70–74). Emma is also clearly headstrong. She is described as "having rather too much her own way" (lines 27–28).

8. (G)

Emma's description of her friendship with Miss Taylor suggests that Emma most highly values devotion in her friends.

9. (B)

The description of Mr. Weston is in lines 47–50: "The marriage had every promise of happiness for her friend. Mr. Weston was a man of unexceptionable character, easy fortune, suitable age, and pleasant manners." None of the other choices match this description.

10. (H)

The answer to the question is in lines 24–26: "Emma doing just what she liked, highly esteeming Miss Taylor's judgment, but directed chiefly by her own."

Passage II

11. (B)

The passage presents the three main systems of memory and states that these systems are widely accepted—so eliminate (A)—but gives alternate theories about the way long-term memories are formed and possible flaws in the process. Although the passage mentions two early ideas about memory that were too simplistic (C) and (D), this is not the main focus of the passage.

12. (H)

Described in paragraph three, semantic memory holds facts and general knowledge, like the multiplication tables (H). Ballet steps (F) and riding a bicycle (J) would be in procedural memory, a childhood memory (G) would be in episodic.

13. (B)

All the information you need is in paragraph three. Memories of one's personal life would be held in episodic memory, therefore the man's episodic memory was affected. Eliminate (C) and (D). Long-term memories are "never lost," but they may become inaccessible, therefore the author would most likely agree that the man's episodic memories had become inaccessible to him.

14. (F)

While memory was once viewed as relatively simple and automatic with memories being held exactly as they were originally received, it is now believed that many factors alter the way memories are formed and retrieved. (G) and (J) contradict this. (H) is too extreme.

15. (C)

In the last paragraph the author states that assumptions and inferences can affect memory. A person might assume that if the ball hits a window the window will break. Interference (A) is when one, unrelated memory alters another. The memory described in the question is not inaccessible (B), but wrong. And most of the memory was still correct, not false (D).

16. (J)

This detail question requires very careful reading. Refresh your memory by looking at *episodic* in paragraph three. It's in long-term memory, and involves personal events closely identified with a time and place. (F), (G), and (H) fit that idea closely. If you're unsure, look at the description of working (short-term) memory in paragraph two. You'll see that it includes those things briefly remembered and then lost forever—like the face of a stranger passed on the street.

17. (B)

Paragraph two describes this change in terminology. The term *short-term memory* did not accurately describe all the functions of this category of memory. *Working memory* is more accurate since, although these memories degrade quickly—eliminating (A)—these memories can also be used and manipulated as described in the second paragraph. (C) and (D) confuse information in other paragraphs.

18. (H)

Don't panic. All you have to do is look at the line where this term is defined for you. The term doesn't relate to any of the usual meanings of the word *icon*.

19. (B)

The second sentence in paragraph three states, "Memories recorded in long-term memory are never lost...." Although absolute statements are often too extreme to be correct in Reading, when the passage explicitly supports an absolute statement don't be afraid to choose it. You might choose

(A) if you mistook "short-term" and "working" memory for two separate categories. (C) is contradicted in paragraph four, and (D) is contradicted at the end of paragraph two and again at the start of paragraph five.

20. (H)

Paragraph two states that working memories decay rapidly, which means that they are quickly forgotten. (F) and (G) relate to sensory memory. (J) is characteristic of long-term memory.

Passage III

21. (B)

In lines 10–11 Julia Margaret Cameron is described as "the first woman to have achieved eminence in photography." The other answer choices contradict information supplied in the passage.

22. (F)

The answer to this question can be found in lines 72–73: "Contemporary taste much prefers her portraits..." and in line 78: "today her fame rests upon her portraits...".

23. (D)

The dates used in the passage tell you that this is a chronological account; the author begins with Cameron's birth in 1815, tells of her marriage and then her move to England in 1848, points out that she received her first photographic equipment in 1863, describes one of her photographs from 1864, and then concludes the paragraph with her death in 1874.

24. (F)

The dictionary definition of *cumbersome* is "difficult to handle because of weight or bulk." (F) most closely fits this definition, and it is the only answer choice that makes sense within the context of the sentence.

25. (B)

(A) contradicts information from the passage, which suggests that Cameron led anything but a conventional life. Neither the money that Cameron earned as a photographer nor her religious beliefs are discussed in the passage, making (C) and (D) incorrect answers.

26. (F)

Lines 53–55 say, "She produced a large body of work that stands up as one of the notable artistic achievements of the Victorian period." To say that she is "the greatest photographer who ever lived" goes beyond anything stated or implied in the passage. The third paragraph does not compare her importance as an artist during her lifetime to her importance today. The passage also does not state that she "revolutionized" any photographic methods.

27. (C)

The answer to this question can be found in lines 6–9: "photography, being a new medium outside the traditional academic framework, was wide open to women and offered them opportunities that the older fields did not...".

28. (G)

These titles refer to allegorical pictures, as described in lines 69–72: "Victorian critics were particularly impressed by her allegorical pictures, many of them based on the poems of her friend and neighbor Tennyson..."

29. (D)

The answer to this question can be found in lines 72–74: "Contemporary taste much prefers her portraits and finds her narrative scenes sentimental and sometimes in bad taste."

30. (F)

The author says that Cameron "achieved eminence" (line 11) in her field, that she "devoted herself wholly to this art" (line 49), and that "no other woman photographer has ever enjoyed such success" (lines 65–66). Only (F) fits these descriptions.

Passage IV

31. (C)

For details about the eye, look at paragraph three. Only the cornea and stenopaic pupil are relevant, eliminating (A) and (D). But the cornea (B) is helpful underwater, not on land.

32. (G)

The eye is covered in paragraph three. The seal's cornea improves vision in the water (note the comparison to human underwater vision), but distorts light moving through the air. Another adaptation was then needed to "minimize" distortion, but that doesn't mean distortion is completely eliminated, so the seal's vision in the air is distorted, (G).

33. (D)

The vibrissae are discussed only in the last paragraph. They sense wave disturbances made by nearby moving fish, so (D) is correct.

34. (F)

This is stated in the second paragraph, where the seal's hearing is discussed.

35. (D)

This appears in the first paragraph, which introduces the influences on the seal's adaptations. They include that the seal "does most of its fishing at night," that "noise levels are high," and that these factors are compounded by the seal's "two habitats."

36. (H)

Locating each of these claims in the passage, we find that (H) is "suggested" and the subject of speculation, rather than stated as fact. All of the others are given in support of claims.

37. (A)

We find in the first paragraph that they live along the northern Atlantic and Pacific coasts. Since they live in both the land and water, the coastlines must be accessible. We can infer that the waters are cold rather than warm, eliminating (D). (B) and (C) are too broad.

38. (J)

This feature is mentioned at the end of paragraph two. It shouldn't be confused with echolocation, which is discussed in paragraph four, but not connected with any particular sensory organ.

39. (B)

The entire passage is about how the seal's sensory organs have adapted to life on land and in the water, making (B) the best choice. Generally, we are told about differences, not similarities, between the two, eliminating (A). The relative success of human and seal adaptation to their environments isn't discussed, (C) and (D).

40. (G)

In paragraph three, we see that human corneas refract light badly in water, and the seal's corneas perform well.

SCIENCE TEST

Passage I

1. (B)

To answer this question, you have to examine the third column of the table, transmittance range. For a material to transmit light at a wavelength of 25 μm, its transmittance range—the range of wavelengths over which the material is transparent—must include 25 μm. Only potassium bromide (0.3–29 μm) and cesium iodide (0.3–70 μm) have transmittance ranges that include 25 μm, so (B) is correct.

2. (F)

The material that contradicts this hypothesis is going to have poor chemical resistance, but a transmittance range less than 10 μm. Lithium fluoride (F) fits the bill: its chemical resistance is poor, and its transmittance range is less than 6 μm wide. (G) and (J) are wrong because both flint glass and quartz have excellent chemical resistance. (H) is out because cesium iodide has a transmittance range nearly 70 μm wide.

3. (D)

The correct answer is a pair of materials in which the refractive index of the first material is greater than that of the second. In (A), (B), and (C), the refractive index of the first material is less than that of the second. In (D), however, flint glass has a refractive index of 1.66 while calcium fluoride's refractive index is only 1.43. That makes (D) the correct answer.

4. (J)

The easiest way to answer this question is to use the first couple of materials and test each hypothesis on them. (F) and (G) are incorrect because the transmittance range of lithium fluoride is wider than its useful prism range. Comparing the data on lithium fluoride and calcium fluoride rules out (H) because transmittance range does NOT increase as useful prism range decreases. In fact, looking down the rest of the table, you see that transmittance range seems to decrease as useful prism range decreases. (J) is the only one left, and the data on lithium fluoride and calcium fluoride as well as all the other materials confirms that the transmittance range is always wider than, and includes within it, the useful prism range.

5. (B)

According to the footnote to the table, quartz infused with lead oxide is flint glass. A comparison of the properties of pure quartz and flint glass shows that the transmittance range of flint glass is narrower than that of quartz but that its refractive index is greater. This supports (B).

Passage II

6. (H)

Use the results of both experiments to answer this question. The answer choices all involve temperature, concentration, and solvent in different combinations. To determine whether osmotic pressure is dependent upon a variable, look for a pair of trials in which all conditions except for that variable are identical. In doing so, you see that temperature and concentration affect osmotic pressure, but solvent does not.

7. (B)

Find methanol at 0.5 mol/L, which is in Table 2. The text above the table states that all the trials were conducted under the same temperature (298 K). Therefore, simply look across the row that you identified. The osmotic pressure is 12.23, (B).

8. (G)

To figure out whether or not the sucrose solution will diffuse across the membrane under the conditions described in the question, go back to the definition of osmotic pressure given in the introduction. Once the external pressure reaches the osmotic pressure, osmosis will not occur. In order for osmosis to occur, the external pressure must be less than the osmotic pressure of the solution. The solution in this question is a 0.1 mol/L aqueous sucrose solution at 298 K; those conditions correspond to an osmotic pressure of 2.45 atm. Since the external pressure is 1 atm, which is less than the osmotic pressure, osmosis will occur. From the definition of osmosis in the passage, it is clear that the solution will diffuse from the side of the membrane with a lower concentration of dissolved material, in this case pure water, to the side with a higher concentration, in this case sucrose solution. (G) is correct.

9. (C)

To determine what the scientists investigated in Experiment 1, look at what they varied and what they measured. In Experiment 1, the scientists varied the concentration and the temperature of sucrose solutions, and they measured the osmotic pressure. Therefore, they were investigating the effect of concentration and temperature on osmotic pressure (C). Watch out for (A): it states what was investigated in Experiment 2, not Experiment 1.

10. (F)

The results in Table 2 indicate that osmotic pressure doesn't depend on the solvent, as discussed in the explanation to Question 1. So Statement I is a valid conclusion, and (G) can be eliminated. Statement II is false. The results in Table 1 indicate that osmotic pressure is dependent on concentration as well as temperature. So (H) can be ruled out. Now consider Statement III. It is not a valid conclusion because osmotic pressure is the pressure required to prevent osmosis, so osmosis occurs only if the external pressure is less than the osmotic pressure.

11. (D)

To answer questions that ask about the design of an experiment, look at what the scientists are trying to measure. You're told that osmotic pressure is the pressure required to prevent osmosis. In order to measure the osmotic pressure of a solution, scientists need to be able to tell when osmosis begins. If you have two clear solutions with sucrose dissolved in one of them, how can you tell when there's any movement of solvent between the two of them? If the sucrose is dyed, the blue solution will become paler when osmosis starts, i.e., when solvent moves across the membrane to create an equilibrium. Therefore, (D) is correct.

Passage III

12. (J)

Even if you do not know how many °C are equivalent to room temperature, you can eliminate all of the incorrect answer choices. Choices (F), (G), and (H) all reach a boiling point at low temperatures and, therefore, would all be gases at room temperature. (J), at 36° C, is the only logical choice.

13. (C)

To answer this question, you have to look for trends in each table and draw conclusions. This can be done by looking at the values in each category and seeing how they vary with respect to each other. If you look at Tables 1 and 2, you can see that there is a direct variation between boiling point and molecular weight: as one increases, the other increases. Therefore, Statement I is correct, Statement II is false, and you can eliminate (B) and (D). Now consider Statement III. To investigate the relationship between molecular structure and boiling point, you have to keep the third variable—molecular weight—constant. Look at the data for two compounds with different molecular structures but the same molecular weight: N_2 and CO; their boiling points differ. Therefore, Statement III is correct, and (C) is the correct response.

14. (G)

In order to answer this question, you need to establish where C_6H_{14} would fit in Table 1. It is clear from Table 1 that the boiling point increases as the molecular weight increases, so the boiling point of C_6H_{14} will be between the boiling points of molecules with greater and lesser molecular weights. The molecular weight of C_6H_{14} is 86 g/mol, so it will lie between those hydrocarbons with molecular weights of 72 g/mol and 114 g/mol. Therefore, its boiling point will be between 36° C and 126° C. (G), with a value of 70° C, is the only choice that lies between these two boiling points.

15. (A)

N_2, a non-polar molecule, and CO, a polar molecule, have identical molecular weights and their boiling points differ by only 4° C. SiH_4 (non-polar) and PH_3 (polar) have nearly identical molecular weights as well, but the difference between their boiling points is 27° C—much greater than the difference between the boiling points of N_2 and CO, which have lower molecular weights than SiH_4 and PH_3. The difference between the boiling points of polar and non-polar substances of similar molecular weight increases as molecular weight increases, so (A) is correct.

16. (H)

If you refer to Table 2, you'll see that for polar substances, as the molar weight goes from 78 to 162, the boiling point goes from –55° C to 97° C. You know the molar weight

has to be somewhere between 78 and 162, so (F) is clearly out, and (G), 80, is too close to 78 to be the answer. You would expect the molar weight to be closer to 78 than 162, since 0 is closer to −55 than 97. Therefore (J), 132, is out, and (H) is the answer.

17. (D)

To figure this out, it is best to examine how much the boiling point rises when dealing with similar molar weight gains. For instance, you can roughly compare rates by looking at what happens to straight-chain hydrocarbons when the molar weight goes from 30 to 72 (boiling point change of 124° C), to what happens to non-polar inorganic compounds when the molar weight goes from 32 to 77 (boiling point change of 22° C), to what happens to polar inorganic compounds when the molar weight goes from 34 to 78 (boiling point change of 30° C). From these figures it is clear that the rate at which the boiling point increases with increasing molar weight is the least for non-polar inorganic compounds, and greatest for straight-chain hydrocarbons, so (D) is correct.

Passage IV

18. (F)

The question refers to Experiment 2 only, so the correct answer will involve sunlight. Table 2 shows that the average length of the leaves increased from 5.3 cm to 12.4 cm as the amount of sunlight increased from 0 to 3 hours per day. But as the amount of sunlight increased further, leaf size decreased. Therefore, (J) is incorrect. Neither humidity (G) nor water (H) is relevant to Experiment 2.

19. (B)

Table 1 gives leaf widths at 35% and 55% humidity as 1.8 cm and 2.0 cm, respectively. The leaf width at 40% humidity would most likely be between those two figures. (B) is the only choice within that range.

20. (G)

All the answer choices involve humidity and sunlight, which were investigated in Experiments 1 and 2, respectively. In Table 1, leaf length and width were greatest at 75% humidity. In Table 2, they were greatest at 3 hours per day of sunlight. Combining those two conditions, as in (G), would probably produce the largest leaves.

21. (A)

This question relates to the method of the study. Each experiment begins with a statement that 5 groups of seedlings were used. Therefore, (A) is correct. The other answer choices list variables that were manipulated.

22. (J)

(J) is an assumption that underlies the design of all three experiments. If the seedlings were not equally capable of further growth, then changes in leaf size and density could not be reliably attributed to researcher-controlled changes in humidity, sunlight, and temperature. (F) is wrong because all the seedlings were 2–3 cm tall. The seedlings' abilities to germinate (G) or to produce flowers (H) were not mentioned in the passage.

23. (C)

Each of the three experiments investigated a different factor. To produce the most useful new data, researchers would probably vary a fourth condition. Soil mineral content would be an appropriate factor to examine. None of the other choices relate directly to the purpose of the experiments as expressed in paragraph 1 of the passage.

Passage V

24. (G)

According to the table, decreasing the cross-sectional area of a given wire always increases resistance, so (G) is correct. (H) is wrong because resistivity, displayed in the second column, is constant for each material and thus cannot be responsible for variations in resistance for any given material. Gauge varies inversely with cross-sectional area, so (J) is incorrect.

25. (B)

Because resistance varies inversely with cross-sectional area A, as discussed in the previous explanation, the correct answer to this question must place A in the denominator. The only choice that does so is (B).

26. (J)

Compare the choices two at a time. The wires in (F) and (G) are made of the same material and have the same cross-sectional area; only their length is different. Doubling the length doubles the resistance, so (G) would have a higher resistance than (F). By similar reasoning, (J) would have a higher resistance than (H). The only difference between (G) and (J) is the material. Even though the research team didn't test wire with a 0.33 mm^2 cross-sectional area, it's safe to assume that the tungsten wire would have a higher resistance than the aluminum one.

27. (D)

The larger circle represents 10-gauge wire; its diameter is 2.59 mm. The smaller circle has a diameter of only 1.29 mm, but it represents 16-gauge wire, so Statement I is true, and you can eliminate choices (B) and (C) without even checking Statements II or III. To check Statement III, the table shows that the resistance of an iron (Fe) wire is much higher than that of an aluminum (Al) wire with the same length and cross-sectional area. The first sentence of paragraph 1 defined the resistance of a conductor as "the extent to which it opposes the flow of electricity." Since iron has a higher resistance than aluminum, iron must not conduct electricity as well. Therefore, Statement III is true, and (D) is correct.

28. (J)

The data indicate that the resistivity of a material doesn't change when wire length changes. Therefore, the graph of resistivity versus length for tungsten (or any other) wire is a horizontal line.

Passage VI

29. (A)

To answer this question, you have to refer to the examples presented by the scientists to find a point of agreement. Both use the example of giraffes to show how scarcity of food and the need to reach higher and higher branches led to the evolution of long necks; thus they both agree that environment affects evolution.

30. (H)

This Principle question requires that you figure out how new evidence affects the two hypotheses. To answer it, all you have to consider are the hypotheses of the two scientists. Scientist 2 believes that characteristics acquired by an individual over a lifetime are passed on to its offspring, a theory that would be supported by this finding.

31. (E)

This question requires some reasoning. Scientist 2 states that all of the changes that occur in an individual's life can be passed on to offspring. Since he believes that any characteristic can undergo change, he must also believe that any characteristic can be inherited.

32. (G)

You don't need any information other than the hypotheses of Scientist 1 to answer this question. He believes that random mutations continually occur within a species as it propagates, and that advantageous mutations, such as long necks on giraffes, help the species adapt to environmental changes, and thus become more prevalent within the species, which is what (G) states.

33. (B)

Here you don't need any information other than the hypotheses of the two scientists. The crux of their disagreement is over how evolution occurs—whether through random mutations or through the inheritance of acquired characteristics.

Passage VII

34. (J)

In Experiment 1, the researchers vary what is fed to the cows by giving them meat from scrapie-free sheep and from scrapie-infected sheep. The cows are later examined for signs of BSE. One common type of wrong answer choice for Experiment questions are choices, such as choice (G) for this question, that include factors that are outside the parameters of the experiment.

35. (A)

In Experiment 2, the researchers vary what is injected into cows' brains. Any answer choice that discusses ingestion as a focus of this experiment is wrong. This eliminates (B), (C), and (D). Often, wrong answer choices for Experiment questions, such as choice (B) for this question, will include the appropriate information from the wrong experiment.

36. (G)

By examining the method used in a given experiment, one can determine the assumptions the researchers made in carrying out the experiment and the sources of error. Often error enters the experiment because of the assumptions researchers make. In Experiments 1 and 2, the researchers examined the brains of cows a year and a half after the cows were fed scrapie-infected sheep meat or were injected with scrapie-infected sheep brains. If a year and a half is not a sufficient amount of time for BSE to develop, some of the cows that were counted as not infected might have developed BSE if they had been given more time.

37. (C)

To answer this question, you need to determine how to test whether BSE can be transmitted via scrapie-infected goats. To test this one would compare the effects of feeding cows scrapie-free goat meat with the effects of feeding cows scrapie-infected goat meat and compare the effects of injecting cows with scrapie-free goat brains with the effects of injecting them with scrapie-infected goat brains.

38. (F)

Remember that control groups are used as standards of comparison. The control group used in Experiment 1 is the group that is fed scrapie-free sheep meat. If the same proportion of Group A developed BSE as that of Group B, then the researchers would not have any evidence to support the hypothesis that the ingestion of scrapie-infected sheep meat causes BSE.

39. (B)

Since the proportion of the group of cows that ate scrapie-infected sheep meat and developed BSE was greater than the proportion of the group that were injected with scrapie-infected sheep brains and developed BSE, one can conclude that a cow that eats scrapie-infected sheep meat is more likely to develop BSE than a cow that is injected with scrapie-infected sheep brains. Mere exposure to scrapie-infected sheep, as opposed to ingestion thereof, is never studied in either experiment, so conclusion I can be eliminated.

40. (H)

To answer this question, consider only the results of Experiment 1. In Experiment 1, the researcher varies what is fed to the cows. The number of cows that developed BSE after eating scrapie-infected sheep meat was much greater than the number of cows that developed BSE after eating scrapie-free sheep meat. This is evidence that the ingestion of scrapie-infected sheep meat causes the development of BSE.

WRITING TEST

Model Essay

Below is an example of what a high-scoring essay might look like. Notice the author states her position clearly in the introductory paragraph and supports that position with evidence in the following paragraphs. This essay also uses transitions, some advanced vocabulary, and an effective "hook" to draw in the reader.

When people think about what students should learn in high school, they often focus on "the three Rs": reading, writing, and arithmetic. It's true that in an increasingly competitive global economy, those skills are more important than ever. However, in our society's rush to make sure students are keeping up through required standardized testing and increased computer education, are we forgetting another important aspect of education? Are we forgetting to teach our students how to think creatively and express themselves artistically? I think that requiring all high school students to take music or visual arts classes would benefit our country's students in several ways.

Learning about art and music actually helps students do better in other subjects. People often forget that studying art or music isn't just about putting paint to canvas or lips to trumpet. There is a lot of background information that students learn as well. When students study music they also have to learn a lot of history: who was the composer, where was he or she from, what was happening politically and socially during the time the music was composed, and how does the work compare historically to music by other composers. The same holds true for the visual arts; students can learn a lot from art history, not just about the artist but also about different cultures and time periods. Studies have shown that students who take music classes do better at math, maybe because these classes emphasize dividing up measures of music and counting out times.

With so much focus on standardized test scores and grade point averages, schools today emphasize individual academic performance and overlook the teaching of teamwork skills. Through playing in my high school's band, I have learned that even though it is important for me to practice so that I can play my best (and maybe move up a chair), what really matters is how we sound as a group. My bandmates and I push each other to succeed, and we get together outside of school to practice for big games and competitions. Band is also where I have made most of my friends. Participation in the arts is a great way for students to build social skills and create school spirit. It teaches students to help one another so that going to school isn't just about getting good grades for one's own benefit.

Learning about art or music is also helpful to students because it teaches them how to think creatively. When you take a photograph or paint a portrait you have to look at things in a new way, and you must try to synthesize your perception into a medium that other people can relate to. Between all the pressure to do well academically and all the social pressure teenagers face to fit in, being a teenager can be really stressful. Art and music can allow students to express their feelings in a positive, constructive way. Such classes can give students who aren't good at traditional academic subjects like math or science a chance to shine.

In conclusion, I think requiring all high school students to take music or visual arts classes would help students not only academically but socially and emotionally as well. Studying the arts actually helps students succeed in traditional subject areas, builds their confidence and social skills, and gives them the opportunity to learn to think creatively, all skills that will help them once they reach the workforce.

You can evaluate your essay and the model essay based on the following criteria, covered in chapter 16.

- Does the author answer the question?
- Is the author's position clearly stated?
- Does the body of the essay support and develop the position taken?
- Are there at least three supporting paragraphs?
- Is the relevance of each supporting paragraph clear?
- Is the essay a reasonable length?
- Is the essay organized, with a clear introduction, middle, and end?
- Did the author use one paragraph for each new idea?
- Is each sentence in a paragraph relevant to the point made in that paragraph?
- Are transitions clear?
- Is the essay easy to read? Is it engaging?
- Are sentences varied?
- Is vocabulary used effectively? Is college-level vocabulary used?

ACT Practice Test Two Answer Sheet

English Test	10. F G H J	20. F G H J	30. F G H J	40. F G H J	50. F G H J	60. F G H J	70. F G H J
1. A B C D	11. A B C D	21. A B C D	31. A B C D	41. A B C D	51. A B C D	61. A B C D	71. A B C D
2. F G H J	12. F G H J	22. F G H J	32. F G H J	42. F G H J	52. F G H J	62. F G H J	72. F G H J
3. A B C D	13. A B C D	23. A B C D	33. A B C D	43. A B C D	53. A B C D	63. A B C D	73. A B C D
4. F G H J	14. F G H J	24. F G H J	34. F G H J	44. F G H J	54. F G H J	64. F G H J	74. F G H J
5. A B C D	15. A B C D	25. A B C D	35. A B C D	45. A B C D	55. A B C D	65. A B C D	75. A B C D
6. F G H J	16. F G H J	26. F G H J	36. F G H J	46. F G H J	56. F G H J	66. F G H J	
7. A B C D	17. A B C D	27. A B C D	37. A B C D	47. A B C D	57. A B C D	67. A B C D	
8. F G H J	18. F G H J	28. F G H J	38. F G H J	48. F G H J	58. F G H J	68. F G H J	
9. A B C D	19. A B C D	29. A B C D	39. A B C D	49. A B C D	59. A B C D	69. A B C D	

Math Test	9. A B C D E	18. F G H J K	27. A B C D E	36. F G H J K	45. A B C D E	54. F G H J K
1. A B C D E	10. F G H J K	19. A B C D E	28. F G H J K	37. A B C D E	46. F G H J K	55. A B C D E
2. F G H J K	11. A B C D E	20. F G H J K	29. A B C D E	38. F G H J K	47. A B C D E	56. F G H J K
3. A B C D E	12. F G H J K	21. A B C D E	30. F G H J K	39. A B C D E	48. F G H J K	57. A B C D E
4. F G H J K	13. A B C D E	22. F G H J K	31. A B C D E	40. F G H J K	49. A B C D E	58. F G H J K
5. A B C D E	14. F G H J K	23. A B C D E	32. F G H J K	41. A B C D E	50. F G H J K	59. A B C D E
6. F G H J K	15. A B C D E	24. F G H J K	33. A B C D E	42. F G H J K	51. A B C D E	60. F G H J K
7. A B C D E	16. F G H J K	25. A B C D E	34. F G H J K	43. A B C D E	52. F G H J K	
8. F G H J K	17. A B C D E	26. F G H J K	35. A B C D E	44. F G H J K	53. A B C D E	

Reading Test	6. F G H J	12. F G H J	18. F G H J	24. F G H J	30. F G H J	36 F G H J
1. A B C D	7. A B C D	13. A B C D	19. A B C D	25. A B C D	31. A B C D	37. A B C D
2. F G H J	8. F G H J	14. F G H J	20. F G H J	26. F G H J	32. F G H J	38. F G H J
3. A B C D	9. A B C D	15. A B C D	21. A B C D	27. A B C D	33. A B C D	39 A B C D
4. F G H J	10. F G H J	16. F G H J	22. F G H J	28. F G H J	34. F G H J	40. F G H J
5. A B C D	11. A B C D	17. A B C D	23. A B C D	29. A B C D	35. A B C D	

Science Test	6. F G H J	12. F G H J	18. F G H J	24. F G H J	30. F G H J	36. F G H J
1. A B C D	7. A B C D	13. A B C D	19. A B C D	25. A B C D	31. A B C D	37. A B C D
2. F G H J	8. F G H J	14. F G H J	20. F G H J	26. F G H J	32. F G H J	38. F G H J
3. A B C D	9. A B C D	15. A B C D	21. A B C D	27. A B C D	33. A B C D	39 A B C D
4. F G H J	10. F G H J	16. F G H J	22. F G H J	28. F G H J	34. F G H J	40. F G H J
5. A B C D	11. A B C D	17. A B C D	23. A B C D	29. A B C D	35. A B C D	

Practice Test Two

ENGLISH TEST

45 Minutes—75 Questions

Directions: In the following five passages, certain words and phrases have been underlined and numbered. You will find alternatives for each underlined portion in the right-hand column. Select the one that best expresses the idea, that makes the statement acceptable in standard written English, or that is phrased most consistently with the style and tone of the entire passage. If you feel that the original version is best, select "NO CHANGE." You will also find questions asking about a section of the passage or about the entire passage. For these questions, decide which choice gives the most appropriate response to the given question. For each question in the test, select the best choice, and fill in the corresponding space on the answer sheet. You may wish to read each passage through before you begin to answer the questions associated with it. Most answers cannot be determined without reading several sentences around the phrases in question. Make sure to read far enough ahead each time you choose an alternative

Passage I

[1]

By the time Duke Ellington published his autobiography, *Music is My Mistress* in 1973 he had (1) traveled to dozens of countries and every continent. "I pay rent in New York City," he answered when asked of his residence.

[2]

In the 1920s though, Ellington pays (2) more than rent in New York; he paid his dues on the bandstand. Having moved to Harlem from Washington, DC in 1923, Ellington established: his own (3) band and achieved critical recognition with a polished sound and appearance. The first New York review of the Ellingtonians in 1923 commented, "The boys look neat in dress suits and labor hard but not in vain at their music." As Ellington made a name for himself as a leader arranger and pianist, (4) his Harlem Renaissance compositions and recordings

1. **A.** NO CHANGE
   B. 1973. He had
   C. 1973, it had
   D. 1973, he had

2. **F.** NO CHANGE
   G. paid
   H. has to pay
   J. pay

3. **A.** NO CHANGE
   B. established the following: his own
   C. established his own
   D. took the time and effort to establish his own

4. **F.** NO CHANGE
   G. leader arranger, and pianist,
   H. leader, arranger, and pianist
   J. leader, arranger, and pianist,

GO ON TO THE NEXT PAGE

Test Prep and Admissions

highlighted two enduring characteristics of the man. First, Ellington lived for jazz. Second, Harlem sustained it, (5) physically and spiritually.

[3]

Ellington himself admitted he was not a very good pianist. As a teenager (6) in Washington. He missed more piano lessons then he took (7) with his teacher, Mrs. Clinkscales, and spent more time going to dances than practicing the piano. Mrs. Clinkscales was really the name of his piano teacher! (8) In the clubs, therefore, (9) Ellington and his friends eventually caught word of New York and the opportunities that awaited and were there for (10) young musicians. Ellington wrote, "Harlem, to our minds, did indeed have the world's most glamorous atmosphere. We had to go there." He left Washington with drummer Sonny Greer. (11) Before they could even unpack in Harlem, though, they found themselves penniless. Not until Ellington was lucky enough to find fifteen dollars on the street could he return to Washington and recollect himself.

5. **A.** NO CHANGE
B. him,
C. them,
D. itself,

6. **F.** NO CHANGE
G. good pianist as a teenager
H. good pianist, a teenager
J. good pianist, as a teenager

7. **A.** NO CHANGE
B. lessons then he had taken
C. lessons; he took
D. lessons than he took

8. **F.** NO CHANGE
G. That was really the name of his piano teacher: Mrs. Clinkscales!
H. Mrs. Clinkscales was really the name of his piano teacher.
J. OMIT the underlined portion.

9. **A.** NO CHANGE
B. however
C. despite
D. then

10. **F.** NO CHANGE
G. awaiting and being there for
H. that awaited
J. which were there for

11. **A.** NO CHANGE
B. With drummer Sonny Greer, it was Washington that he left.
C. Leaving Washington, he, Ellington, left with drummer Sonny Greer.
D. OMIT the underlined portion.

GO ON TO THE NEXT PAGE

[4]

Ellington eventually did return to Harlem, and he achieved great success as the bandleader at the Cotton Club from 1927 to 1932. Located in the heart of Harlem at 142nd Street and Lenox Avenue, he played at the Cotton Club, which was frequented [12] by top entertainers and rich patrons. Harlem's nightlife, "cut out of a very luxurious, royal-blue bolt of velvet," was an inspirational backdrop, and Ellington composed, arranged, and recorded prolifically to the rave of excited critical acclaim. "Black and Tan Fantasy," "Hot and Bothered," and "Rockin' in Rhythm" were Ellington's early hits during this period. [13] They exhibited his unique ability to compose music that animated both dancers in search of a good time and improvising musicians in search of good music. Before long, the once fumbling pianist from Washington, DC became the undisputed leader of hot jazz in decadent Harlem. [14]

12. F. NO CHANGE
G. he played at the Cotton Club, a club that was frequented
H. the Cotton Club, which was frequented
J. the Cotton Club was frequented

13. The purpose of including the names of Ellington's songs is to:
A. provide some details about Ellington's early music.
B. contradict an earlier point that Ellington did not create his own music.
C. illustrate the complexity of Ellington's music.
D. discuss the atmosphere at the Cotton Club.

14. The purpose of paragraph 4, as it relates to the previous paragraphs, is primarily to:
F. demonstrate how accomplished Ellington had become.
G. suggest that Ellington did not like living in New York.
H. remind us how difficult it is to be a musician.
J. make us skeptical of Ellington's abilities.

GO ON TO THE NEXT PAGE

Question 15 asks about the preceding passage as a whole.

15. The writer wishes to insert the following detail into the essay:

> The combination of fun and seriousness in his music led to critical acclaim and wide mass appeal.

The sentence would most logically be inserted into paragraph:

A. 1, after the last sentence.
B. 3, before the first sentence.
C. 4, after the first sentence.
D. 4, before the last sentence.

Passage II

The paragraphs in this passage may not be in the most logical order. Each paragraph is numbered in brackets, and question 29 will ask you to choose the appropriate order.

[1]

Some animals change its [16] coloring with the seasons. The ptarmigan sheds its brown plumage in winter, replacing [17] it with white feathers. The stoat, a member of the weasel family is known [18] as the *ermine* in winter because its brown fur changes to white. The chameleon is perhaps the most versatile of all animals which change [19] their protective coloration. The chameleon changes its color in just a few minutes to whatever surface it happens to be sitting on.

16. **F.** NO CHANGE
G. their
H. it's
J. there

17. **A.** NO CHANGE
B. winter and replacing
C. winter: replacing
D. winter replacing

18. **F.** NO CHANGE
G. weasel family known
H. weasel family, which is known
J. weasel family, is known

19. **A.** NO CHANGE
B. who changes
C. that change
D. that changed

GO ON TO THE NEXT PAGE

[2]

While animals like the chameleon use their coloring [20] as a way of hiding from predators, the skunk uses its distinctive white stripe as a way of standing out from its surroundings. Far from placing it in danger; the skunk's [21] visibility actually protects it. By distinguishing itself from other animals. The [22] skunk warns its predators to avoid its infamous stink. Think about it: the question is would your appetite be whetted by the skunk's odor? [23]

[3]

Researchers have been investigating [24] how animal species have come to use coloring as a means of protecting themselves. One study has shown that certain animals have glands that release special hormones, resulting in the change of skin or fur color. Therefore, [25] not all the animals that camouflage themselves have these glands. The topic remains and endures as [26] one of the many mysteries of the natural world.

20. F. NO CHANGE
G. their use coloring
H. use coloring their
J. coloring their use

21. A. NO CHANGE
B. danger, the skunk's
C. danger; the skunks'
D. danger, it is the skunk's

22. F. NO CHANGE
G. animals, therefore, the
H. animals because
J. animals, the

23. A. NO CHANGE
B. would your appetite be whetted by the skunk's odor?
C. the question is as follows, would your appetite be whetted by the skunk's odor?
D. the question is would your appetite be whetted by the odor of the skunk?

24. F. NO CHANGE
G. investigated
H. were investigating
J. investigate

25. A. NO CHANGE
B. Nevertheless,
C. However,
D. Finally,

26. F. NO CHANGE
G. remaining and enduring as
H remains and endures
J. remains

GO ON TO THE NEXT PAGE

[4]

Animals have a variety of ways of protecting themselves from enemies. Some animals adapt in shape and color to their environment. The tree frog, for example, blends perfectly into its surroundings. When it sits motionless, <u>a background of leaves completely hides the tree frog.</u> 27

<u>This camouflage enables the tree frog to hide from other animals that would be interested in eating the tree frog.</u> 28

27. A. NO CHANGE
    B. the tree frog is completely hidden in a background of leaves.
    C. completely hidden is the tree frog in a background of leaves.
    D. a background of leaves and the tree frog are completely hidden.

28. F. NO CHANGE
    G. This camouflage enables the tree frog to hide from predators.
    H. This camouflage enables the tree frog to hide from other animals interested in eating the tree frog.
    J. OMIT the underlined portion.

Items 29–30 ask about the passage as a whole.

29. What would be the most logical order of paragraphs for this essay?

- **A.** 3, 1, 4, 2
- **B.** 1, 2, 4, 3
- **C.** 4, 1, 2, 3
- **D.** 2, 1, 3, 4

30. Suppose the author had been asked to write an essay on how animals use their colorings to protect themselves in the wild. Would this essay meet the requirement?

- **F.** Yes, because the author covers several aspects of how animals use their colorings to protect themselves.
- **G.** Yes, because the author thoroughly investigates how one animal protects itself with its colorings.
- **H.** No, because the author does not consider animals that exist in the wild.
- **J.** No, because the author does not include information from research studies.

GO ON TO THE NEXT PAGE

Passage III

The word *chocolate* is used to describe a variety of foods made 31 from the beans of the cacao tree. The first people known to have made chocolate were the Aztecs, a people who used 32 cacao seeds to make a bitter but tasty drink. However, it was not until Hernan Cortez's exploration of Mexico in 1519. That 33 Europeans first learned of chocolate.

Cortez came to the New World in search of gold, but his interest was also fired by the Aztecs' strange drink. When Cortez returned to Spain, his ship's cargo included and held 34 three chests of cacao beans. It was from these beans that Europe experienced its first taste of what seemed to be 35 a very unusual beverage. The drink soon became popular among those people wealthy enough to afford it. Over the next century cafes specializing 36 in chocolate drinks began to appear throughout Europe. [37]

31. **A.** NO CHANGE
B. foods, which are made
C. foods and made
D. foods and are

32. **F.** NO CHANGE
G. Aztecs, and they used
H. Aztecs a people that use
J. Aztecs, who used

33. **A.** NO CHANGE
B. 1519 that
C. 1519, that
D. 1519:

34. **F.** NO CHANGE
G. included, held
H. included
J. including and holding

35. **A.** NO CHANGE
B. seems to be
C. seemingly is
D. to seemed be

36. **F.** NO CHANGE
G. Over the next century cafes specialize
H. Over the next century, cafes specializing
J. Over the next century, there were cafes specializing

37. The author is considering the addition of another sentence here that briefly describes one of the first European cafes to serve a chocolate drink. This addition would:

A. weaken the author's argument.
B. provide some interesting details.
C. contradict the topic of the paragraph.
D. highlight the author's opinion of chocolate.

Test Prep and Admissions

GO ON TO THE NEXT PAGE

Of course, chocolate is very popular today. People all over the world enjoy <u>chocolate bars chocolate sprinkles and even chocolate soda.</u> 38

38. F. NO CHANGE
    G. chocolate, bars, chocolate, sprinkles, and even chocolate soda.
    H. chocolate bars chocolate sprinkles—even chocolate soda.
    J. chocolate bars, chocolate sprinkles, and even chocolate soda.

<u>In fact,</u> 39 Asia has cultivated the delicacy of chocolate-covered ants! People enjoy this food as a snack at the movies or sporting events. The chocolate ant phenomenon has yet to take over America, <u>but enjoy their chocolate Americans do</u> 40 nonetheless.

39. A. NO CHANGE
    B. Unfortunately,
    C. In spite of this,
    D. The truth is,

40. F. NO CHANGE
    G. but Americans enjoy their chocolate
    H. but enjoy their chocolate is what Americans do
    J. but Americans do enjoy their chocolate

Many chocolate lovers around the world were ecstatic to hear that chocolate may actually be good for you. Researchers <u>say: chocolate contains</u> 41 a chemical that could prevent cancer and heart disease. New research measures the amount of catechins, the chemical thought to be behind the benefits, in different types of chocolate.

41. A. NO CHANGE
    B. have said the following: chocolate contains
    C. say that chocolate contains
    D. say: chocolate contained

<u>The substance is also found in tea.</u> 42 The studies show that chocolate is very high in catechins. The research is likely to be welcomed <u>by those</u> 43 with a sweet tooth, although dentists <u>may less be pleased.</u> 44

42. F. NO CHANGE
    G. Another place where the substance is found is tea.
    H. Also, tea contains the substance.
    J. OMIT the underlined portion.

43. A. NO CHANGE
    B. with them
    C. by us
    D. to those

44. F. NO CHANGE
    G. pleased less they will be.
    H. may be pleased less.
    J. may be less pleased.

GO ON TO THE NEXT PAGE

Question 45 asks about the preceding passage as a whole.

45. Suppose the author had been given the assignment of writing about culinary trends in history. Would this essay satisfy the requirement?

A. Yes, because the essay discusses many culinary trends in history.
B. Yes, because the essay shows how chocolate has been used over time.
C. No, because the essay focuses too much on chocolate in present times.
D. No, because the essay only covers chocolate.

Passage IV

[1]

Scientists, in programs <u>administers by</u> (46) the United States Army, are experimenting to develop the military uniform of the future. As imagined, it <u>would be light as silk, bulletproof, and able to</u> (47) rapidly change at the molecular level to adapt to biological or chemical threats. In response to a detected anthrax threat, for example, it would become an impermeable shield. The pant leg of a <u>soldier who's</u> (48) leg had been broken <u>would have been</u> (49) able to morph into a <u>splint, or, even form</u> (50) an artificial muscle. Nanosensors would transmit vital signs back to a medical team, or monitor the breath for increased nitric oxide, a sign of stress.

46. F. NO CHANGE
G. administering by
H. administered by
J. administers with

47. A. NO CHANGE
B. would: be light as silk, bulletproof, and able to
C. would be light as silk bulletproof and able to
D. light as silk, bulletproof, and was able to

48. F. NO CHANGE
G. soldier whose
H. soldier, who's
J. soldier that's

49. A. NO CHANGE
B. would be
C. will have been
D. is

50. F. NO CHANGE
G. splint or even form
H. splint, or even, form
J. splint or, even, form

GO ON TO THE NEXT PAGE

[2]

The especially promising Invisible Soldier program aims to make the long-held dream of human invisibility a reality by using technology. To create (51) a covering capable of concealing a soldier and making him invisible (52) from most wavelengths of visible light. [53] [54]

[3]

A solution proposed in the early stages near the beginning of (55) the program's development would construct a suit or cape from fabric linked to sensors that can detect the coloring and pattern of the background. The sensors would then send varying intensities of electrical current to the appropriate areas of the fabric, they (56) would be impregnated with chemicals sensitive to electricity. The coveralls would change colors continually as the soldier moved.

51. A. NO CHANGE
B. technology to create
C. technology, which were creating
D. technology; create

52. F. NO CHANGE
G. making a soldier invisible and concealing him
H. concealing a soldier making that soldier invisible
J. concealing a soldier

53. The writer's description of the U.S. Army's Invisible Soldier program seems to indicate that the army's opinion of the program is:
A. skeptical
B. curious
C. enthusiastic
D. detailed

54. What is the purpose of this paragraph, as it relate to the rest of the essay?
F. To highlight one of the successes of the scientists' programs
G. To predict the future of U.S. military uniforms
H. To outline what will follow in the essay
J. To introduce a specific example of the uniform of the future

55. A. NO CHANGE
B. beginning and the early stages of
C. early stages of
D. OMIT the underlined portion.

56. F. NO CHANGE
G. that
H. it
J. which

GO ON TO THE NEXT PAGE

[4]

The problem with this solution from a military standpoint, you know, is [57] power: the fact that the suit [58] would require a continuous flow of electricity means that a soldier would have to carry a large number of batteries, which would hardly contribute to ease of movement and camouflage.

[5]

[1] But army researchers have developed a new kind of color-changing pixel, known as the intererometric modulator or i-mod, that may successfully address this problem. [2] The researchers hope that a flexible suit made of i-mod pixels could completely blend into any background. [3] In addition to matching a background, the pixels could also be set to show other colors, for example, a camouflage mode that would render a soldier effectively invisible in the forest and a flash mode that would enhance a soldier's visibility in a rescue situation. [4] Changing the distance between the mirrors changes the color of the light that they reflect. [5] Each i-mod pixel is made up of a pair of tiny mirrors. [59]

57. **A.** NO CHANGE
B. is, like,
C. however, is
D. therefore, is

58. **F.** NO CHANGE
G. power; the fact that the suit
H. power the fact that the suit
J. power the fact that, the suit

59. Which of the following sequences will make paragraph 5 most logical?
A. 2, 4, 5, 3, 1
B. 2, 3, 1, 5, 4
C. 1, 4, 5, 2, 3
D. 1, 5, 4, 2, 3

Question 60 asks about the preceding passage as a whole.

60. The writer wishes to insert the following material into the passage:

"When H.G. Wells wrote *The Invisible Man*, there was no interest in camouflaging soldiers; the British army was garbed in bright red uniforms. Since that time, governments have learned the value of making soldiers difficult to see, first by using camouflage fabrics, and today by envisioning something even more effective that would change color to match the terrain."

The new material would most logically be placed in paragraph:
F. 2
G. 3
H. 4
J. 5

GO ON TO THE NEXT PAGE

Passage V

It lasted fewer than 10 years, but when it was over, the United States had been radically and forever changed. The population had exploded on the west coast of the country, fortunes had been made and those same fortunes were lost 61, and a new state had entered the union—a state that would become a state of mind for all Americans: California 62.

The United States acquiring 63 the territory that would later become California during the Mexican War (1846–1848). One of the many settlers who traveled to the new territory was John Sutter who was a shopkeeper 64 from Switzerland who had left behind his wife, his children, and his debts, in search of a new life. Hired he did 65 a carpenter named James Marshall to build a sawmill for him on the American River in the foothills of the Sierra Nevada mountains.

On January 24, 1848, while inspecting the mill's runoff into the river 66, Marshall saw two shiny objects below the surface of the water. He took the nuggets to Sutter, who was annoyed by the discovery; Sutter didn't

61. **A.** NO CHANGE
B. fortunes had been made and lost,
C. fortunes, which had been made, were then lost,
D. made and lost were fortunes,

62. **F.** NO CHANGE
G. Americans, and that place was called California.
H. Americans, California.
J. Americans. California.

63. **A.** NO CHANGE
B. had acquired
C. is acquiring
D. acquired

64. **F.** NO CHANGE
G. John Sutter, a shopkeeper
H. John Sutter; a shopkeeper
J. John Sutter, who was a shopkeeper

65. **A.** NO CHANGE
B. He hired
C. Hiring
D. He did hire

66. **F.** NO CHANGE
G. (he was inspecting the mill's runoff into the river)
H. inspecting the mill's runoff into the river all the while,
J. OMIT the underlined portion.

GO ON TO THE NEXT PAGE

want <u>them</u> mill workers distracted by gold fever.
67

67. A. NO CHANGE
B. this
C. his
D. there

<u>Keeping the discovery</u> quiet for a while, but then he
68
couldn't resist bragging about it. Word got out, and workers began quitting their jobs and heading into the hills to look for the source of the gold that had washed down the river.

68. F. NO CHANGE
G. The discovery he was keeping
H. He kept the discovery
J. Keeps he the discovery

[69] Thousands of people poured into California in search of fortune and glory. <u>This is similar to recent stock market increases.</u>
70
During the two years after Marshall's discovery, more than 90,000 people made their way to California, looking for gold. In fact, so many people moved west in just <u>singularly one</u> of those years,
71
1849, that all the prospectors, regardless of when they arrived, became known as Forty-niners. By 1850, so many people had moved to the California territory that the United States Congress was forced to declare it a new state. In 1854, the population had increased by

69. Which of the following would provide the best transition here, guiding the reader from the topic of the previous paragraph to the new topic of this paragraph?
A. Sutter and Marshall did not make a profit.
B. The Gold Rush had officially begun.
C. Can you image how a small discovery led to such a large state?
D. Most of the "gold" turned out to be a hoax.

70. F. NO CHANGE
G. The rush for gold was similar to recent stock market increases.
H. This was similar to recent stock market increases.
J. OMIT the underlined portion.

71. A. NO CHANGE
B. one
C. one and only one
D. singular

GO ON TO THE NEXT PAGE

another 300,000 people. In fact, [72] one out of every 90 people then living in the United States was living in California.

Even after all of the gold had been taken from the ground, California remained a magical place in the American imagination. The 31st state had become a place that [73] lives could change, fortunes could be made, and dreams could come true. For many people, and California [74] is still such a place.

Question 75 asks about the preceding passage as a whole.

72. F. NO CHANGE
G. In spite of this,
H. Believe it or not,
J. Therefore,

73. A. NO CHANGE
B. where
C. through which
D. in

74. F. NO CHANGE
G. Forty-niners, California
H. people and California
J. people, California

75. Suppose the writer had been assigned to write a brief essay detailing the life of a Forty-niner during the California Gold Rush. Would this essay successfully fulfill the assignment?
A. Yes, because the essay tells about the lives of John Sutter and James Marshall.
B. No, because the essay covers a historical rather than biographical perspective of the Gold Rush.
C. Yes, because one can imagine the life of a Forty-niner from the details provided in the essay.
D. No, because the essay does not discuss Forty-niners.

IF YOU FINISH BEFORE TIME IS CALLED, YOU MAY CHECK YOUR WORK ON THIS SECTION ONLY. DO NOT TURN TO ANY OTHER SECTION IN THE TEST. STOP

MATH TEST

60 Minutes—60 Questions

Directions: Solve each of the following problems, select the correct answer, and then fill in the corresponding space on your answer sheet.

Don't linger over problems that are too time-consuming. Do as many as you can, then come back to the others in the time you have remaining.

Calculator use is permitted, but some problems can best be solved without a calculator.

Note: Unless otherwise noted, all of the following should be assumed.

1. Illustrative figures are *not* necessarily drawn to scale.

2. All geometric figures lie in a plane.

3. The term *line* indicates a straight line.

4. The term *average* indicates arithmetic mean.

Do Your Figuring Here.

1. The regular price for a certain bicycle is $125.00. If that price is reduced by 20%, what is the new price?

A. $100.00
B. $105.00
C. $112.50
D. $120.00
E. $122.50

2. If $x = -5$, then $2x^2 - 6x + 5 = ?$

F. −15
G. 15
H. 25
J. 85
K. 135

3. How many distinct prime factors does the number 36 have?

A. 2
B. 3
C. 4
D. 5
E. 6

4. In the figure below, what is the value of x ?

Do Your Figuring Here.

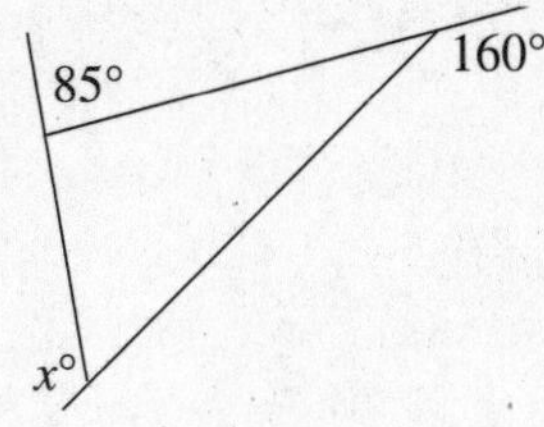

F. 105°
G. 115°
H. 135°
J. 245°
K. 255°

5. What is the average of $\frac{1}{20}$ and $\frac{1}{30}$?

A. $\frac{1}{25}$
B. $\frac{1}{24}$
C. $\frac{2}{25}$
D. $\frac{1}{12}$
E. $\frac{1}{6}$

6. The toll for driving a segment of a certain freeway is \$1.50 plus 25 cents for each mile traveled. Joy paid a \$25.00 toll for driving a segment of the freeway. How many miles did she travel?

F. 10
G. 75
H. 94
J. 96
K. 100

7. For all x, $3x^2 \cdot 5x^3 = ?$

A. $8x^5$
B. $8x^6$
C. $15x^5$
D. $15x^6$
E. $15x^8$

GO ON TO THE NEXT PAGE

Do Your Figuring Here.

8. How many units apart are the points $P(-1, -2)$ and $Q(2, 2)$ in the standard (x, y) coordinate plane?

F. 2
G. 3
H. 4
J. 5
K. 6

9. In a group of 25 students, 16 are female. What percentage of the group is female?

A. 16%
B. 40%
C. 60%
D. 64%
E. 75%

10. For how many integer values of x will $\frac{7}{x}$ be greater than $\frac{1}{4}$ and less than $\frac{1}{3}$?

F. 6
G. 7
H. 12
J. 28
K. infinitely many

11. Which of the following is a polynomial factor of $6x^2 - 13x + 6$?

A. $2x + 3$
B. $3x - 2$
C. $3x + 2$
D. $6x - 2$
E. $6x + 2$

12. What is the value of a if $\frac{1}{a} + \frac{2}{a} + \frac{3}{a} + \frac{4}{a} = 5$?

F. $\frac{1}{2}$
G. 2
H. 4
J. $12\frac{1}{2}$
K. 50

GO ON TO THE NEXT PAGE

Do Your Figuring Here.

13. In the figure below, $\overline{AD}$, $\overline{BE}$, and $\overline{CF}$ all intersect at point G. If the measure of $\angle AGB$ is 40° and the measure of $\angle CGE$ is 105°, what is the measure of $\angle AGF$?

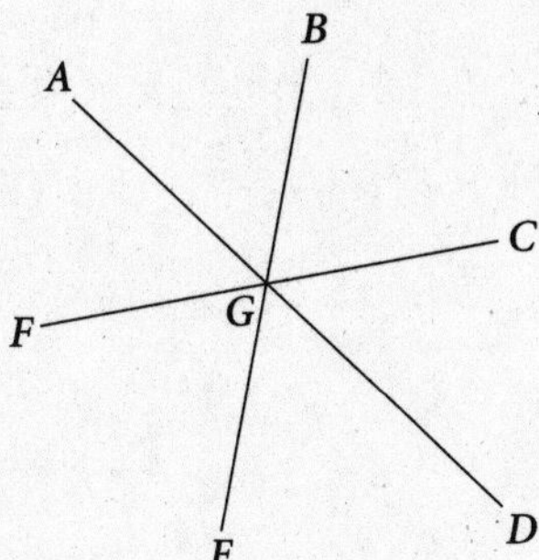

A. 35°
B. 45°
C. 55°
D. 65°
E. 75°

14. Which of the following is the solution statement for the inequality $-3 < 4x - 5$?

F. $x > -2$
G. $x > \frac{1}{2}$
H. $x < -2$
J. $x < \frac{1}{2}$
K. $x < 2$

15. In the figure below, $\overline{BD}$ bisects $\angle ABC$. The measure of $\angle ABC$ is 100° and the measure of $\angle BAD$ is 60°. What is the measure of $\angle BDC$?

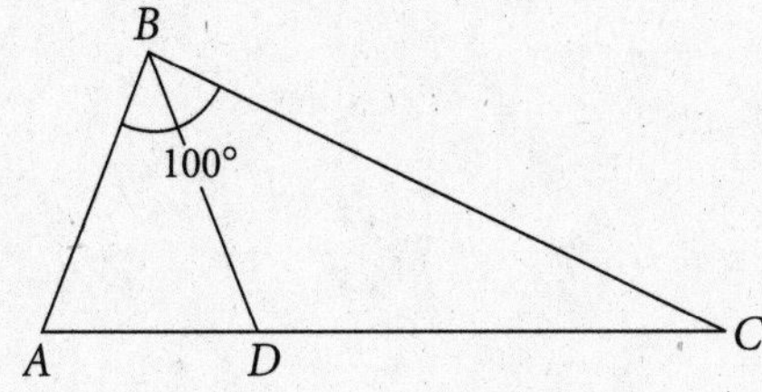

A. 80°
B. 90°
C. 100°
D. 110°
E. 120°

GO ON TO THE NEXT PAGE

Do Your Figuring Here.

16. If $x + 2y - 3 = xy$, where x and y are positive, then which of the following equations expresses y in terms of x ?

F. $y = \dfrac{3-x}{2-x}$

G. $y = \dfrac{3-x}{x-2}$

H. $y = \dfrac{x-3}{2-x}$

J. $y = \dfrac{x-2}{x-3}$

K. $y = \dfrac{6-x}{x-2}$

17. In a group of 50 students, 28 speak English and 37 speak Spanish. If everyone in the group speaks at least one of the two languages, how many speak both English and Spanish?

A. 11
B. 12
C. 13
D. 14
E. 15

18. A car travels 288 miles in 6 hours. At that rate, how many miles will it travel in 8 hours?

F. 216
G. 360
H. 368
J. 376
K. 384

19. When $\frac{4}{11}$ is written as a decimal, what is the 100th digit after the decimal point?

A. 3
B. 4
C. 5
D. 6
E. 7

Do Your Figuring Here.

20. What is the solution for x in the system of equations below?

$$3x + 4y = 31$$
$$3x - 4y = -1$$

F. 4
G. 5
H. 6
J. 9
K. 10

21. In the standard (x, y) coordinate plane, points P and Q have coordinates $(2, 3)$ and $(12, -15)$, respectively. What are the coordinates of the midpoint of $\overline{PQ}$?

A. $(6, -12)$
B. $(6, -9)$
C. $(6, -6)$
D. $(7, -9)$
E. $(7, -6)$

22. In the figure below, $\angle B$ is a right angle, and the measure of $\angle C$ is θ. What is the value of $\cos\theta$?

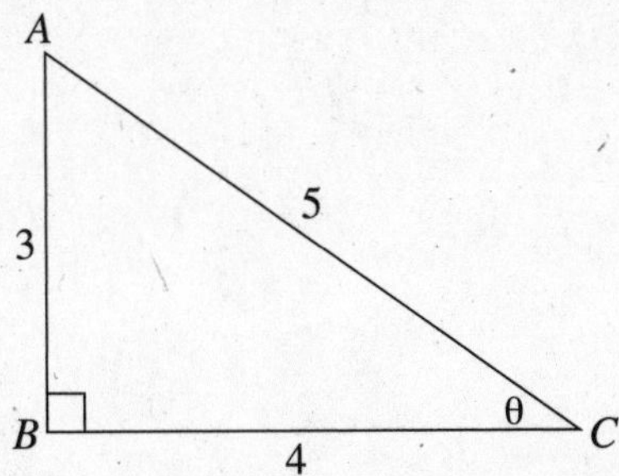

F. $\frac{3}{4}$
G. $\frac{3}{5}$
H. $\frac{4}{5}$
J. $\frac{5}{4}$
K. $\frac{4}{3}$

GO ON TO THE NEXT PAGE

23. In the figure below, the circle centered at P is tangent to the circle centered at Q. Point Q is on the circumference of circle P. If the circumference of circle P is 6 inches, what is the circumference, in inches, of circle Q ?

Do Your Figuring Here.

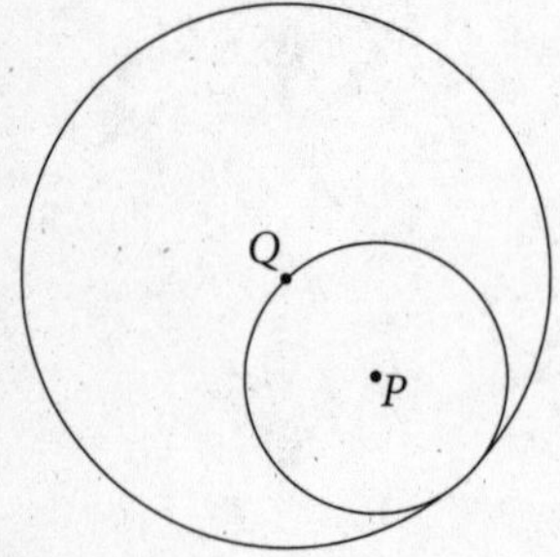

A. 12
B. 24
C. 36
D. 12π
E. 36π

24. If $f(x) = x^3 - x^2 - x$, what is the value of $f(-3)$?

F. –39
G. –33
H. –21
J. –15
K. 0

25. If the lengths, in inches, of all three sides of a triangle are integers, and one side is 7 inches long, what is the least possible perimeter of the triangle, in inches?

A. 9
B. 10
C. 15
D. 21
E. 24

26. What is the complete factorization of $2x + 3x^2 + x^3$?

F. $x(x^2 + 2)$
G. $x(x - 2)(x + 3)$
H. $x(x - 1)(x + 2)$
J. $x(x + 1)(x + 2)$
K. $x(x + 2)(x + 3)$

GO ON TO THE NEXT PAGE

27. If $xyz \neq 0$, which of the following is equivalent to $\frac{x^2y^3z^4}{(xyz^2)^2}$?

A. $\frac{1}{y}$

B. $\frac{1}{z}$

C. y

D. $\frac{x}{yz}$

E. xyz

Do Your Figuring Here.

28. As a decimal, what is the sum of $\frac{2}{3}$ and $\frac{1}{12}$?

F. 0.2
G. 0.5
H. 0.75
J. 0.833
K. 0.875

29. The formula for converting a Fahrenheit temperature reading to Celsius is $C = \frac{5}{9}(F - 32)$, where C is the reading in degrees Celsius and F is the reading in degrees Fahrenheit. Which of the following is the Fahrenheit equivalent to a reading of 95° Celsius?

A. 35° F
B. 53° F
C. 63° F
D. 203° F
E. 207° F

30. A jar contains 4 green marbles, 5 red marbles, and 11 white marbles. If one marble is chosen at random, what is the probability that it will be green?

F. $\frac{1}{3}$

G. $\frac{1}{4}$

H. $\frac{1}{5}$

J. $\frac{1}{16}$

K. $\frac{5}{15}$

GO ON TO THE NEXT PAGE

31. What is the average of the expressions $2x + 5$, $5x - 6$, and $-4x + 2$?

A. $x + \frac{1}{3}$

B. $x + 1$

C. $3x + \frac{1}{3}$

D. $3x + 3$

E. $3x + 3\frac{1}{3}$

32. The line that passes through the points (1, 1) and (2, 16) in the standard (*x*, *y*) coordinate plane is parallel to the line that passes through the points (–10, –5) and (*a*, 25). What is the value of *a* ?

F. –8
G. 3
H. 5
J. 15
K. 20

33. In the figure below, $\overline{QS}$ and $\overline{PT}$ are parallel, and the lengths of QR and PQ, in units, are as marked. If the perimeter of ΔQRS is 11 units, how many units long is the perimeter of ΔPRT ?

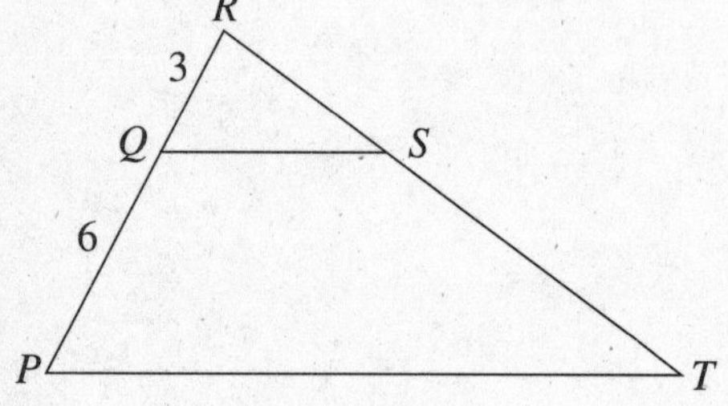

A. 22
B. 33
C. 66
D. 88
E. 99

Do Your Figuring Here.

GO ON TO THE NEXT PAGE

Do Your Figuring Here.

34. The figure shown below belongs in which of the following classifications?

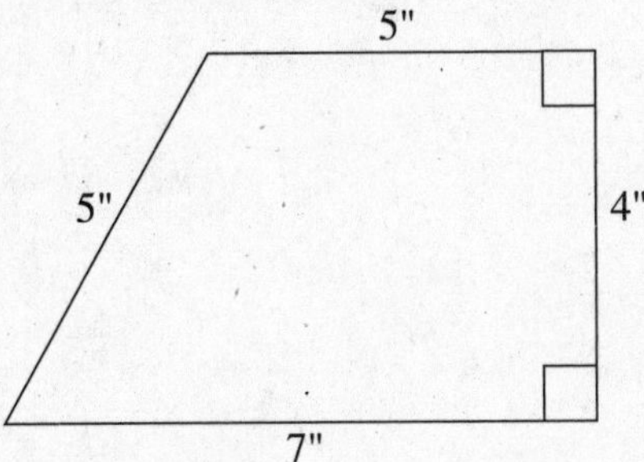

I. Polygon
II. Quadrilateral
III. Rectangle
IV. Trapezoid

F. I only
G. II only
H. IV only
J. I, II, and III only
K. I, II, and IV only

35. If one solution to the equation $2x^2 + (a - 4)x - 2a = 0$ is $x = -3$, what is the value of a ?

A. 0
B. 2
C. 4
D. 6
E. 12

36. A menu offers 4 choices for the first course, 5 choices for the second course, and 3 choices for dessert. How many different meals, consisting of a first course, a second course, and a dessert, can one choose from this menu?

F. 12
G. 24
H. 30
J. 36
K. 60

GO ON TO THE NEXT PAGE

Do Your Figuring Here.

37. If an integer is divisible by 6 and by 9, then the integer must be divisible by which of the following?

I. 12
II. 18
III. 36

A. I only
B. II only
C. I and II only
D. I, II, and III
E. None

38. For all $x \neq 0$, $\frac{x^2 + x^2 + x^2}{x^2} = ?$

F. 3
G. $3x$
H. x^2
J. x^3
K. x^4

39. Joan has q quarters, d dimes, n nickels, and no other coins in her pocket. Which of the following represents the total number of coins in Joan's pocket?

A. $q + d + n$
B. $5q + 2d + n$
C. $.25q + .10d + .05n$
D. $(25 + 10 + 5)(q + d + n)$
E. $25q + 10d + 5n$

40. Which graph below represents the solutions for x of the inequality $5x - 2(1 - x) \geq 4(x + 1)$?

F. –4 –3 –2 –1 0 1 2 3 4

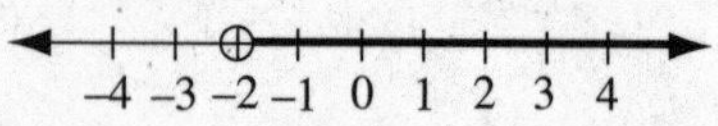

G. –4 –3 –2 –1 0 1 2 3 4

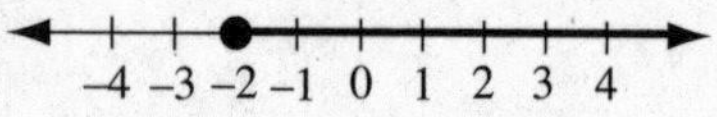

H. –4 –3 –2 –1 0 1 2 3 4

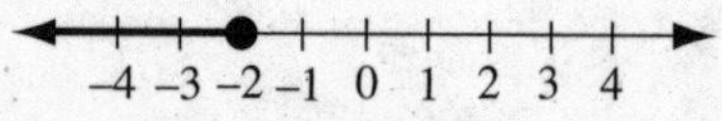

J. –4 –3 –2 –1 0 1 2 3 4

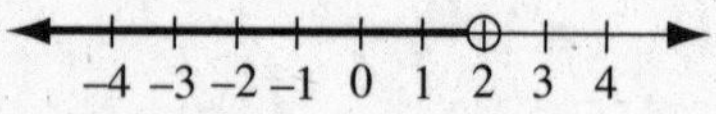

K. –4 –3 –2 –1 0 1 2 3 4

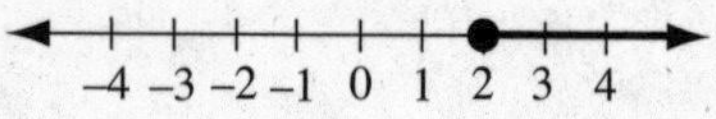

GO ON TO THE NEXT PAGE

Do Your Figuring Here.

41. In the standard (x, y) coordinate plane, line m is perpendicular to the line containing the points (5, 6) and (6, 10). What is the slope of line m ?

A. –4

B. $-\frac{1}{4}$

C. $\frac{1}{4}$

D. 4

E. 8

42. In the right triangle below, $\sin \theta = ?$

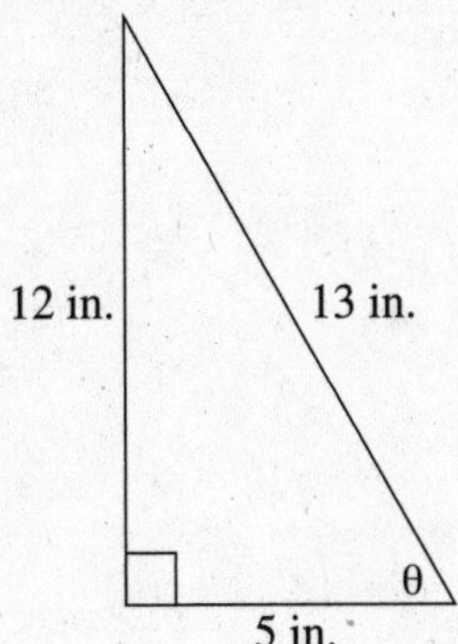

F. $\frac{5}{13}$

G. $\frac{5}{12}$

H. $\frac{12}{13}$

J. $\frac{13}{12}$

K. $\frac{13}{5}$

43. If $9^{2x-1} = 3^{3x+3}$, then $x = ?$

A. –4

B. $-\frac{7}{4}$

C. $-\frac{10}{7}$

D. 2

E. 5

GO ON TO THE NEXT PAGE

44. From 1970 through 1980, the population of City *Q* increased by 20%. From 1980 through 1990, the population increased by 30%. What was the combined percent increase for the period 1970–1990?

F. 25%
G. 26%
H. 36%
J. 50%
K. 56%

45. Martin's average score after 4 tests is 89. What score on the 5th test would bring Martin's average up to exactly 90?

A. 90
B. 91
C. 92
D. 93
E. 94

46. Which of the following is an equation for the circle in the standard (*x*, *y*) coordinate plane that has its center at (–1, –1) and passes through the point (7, 5)?

F. $(x-1)^2+(y-1)^2=10$
G. $(x+1)^2+(y+1)^2=10$
H. $(x-1)^2+(y-1)^2=12$
J. $(x-1)^2+(y-1)^2=100$
K. $(x+1)^2+(y+1)^2=100$

47. Which of the following is an equation for the graph in the standard (*x*, *y*) coordinate plane below?

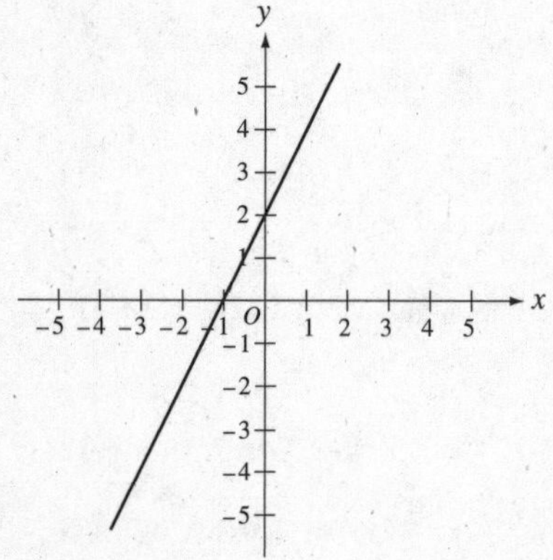

A. $y=-2x+1$
B. $y=x+1$
C. $y=x+2$
D. $y=2x+1$
E. $y=2x+2$

Do Your Figuring Here.

GO ON TO THE NEXT PAGE

Do Your Figuring Here.

48. What is $\frac{1}{4}$% of 16 ?

F. 0.004
G. 0.04
H. 0.4
J. 4
K. 64

49. For all s, $(s + 4)(s - 4) + (2s + 2)(s - 2) = ?$

A. $s^2 - 2s - 20$
B. $3s^2 - 12$
C. $3s^2 - 2s - 20$
D. $3s^2 + 2s - 20$
E. $5s^2 - 2s - 20$

50. Which of the following is an equation of the parabola graphed in the (x, y) coordinate plane below?

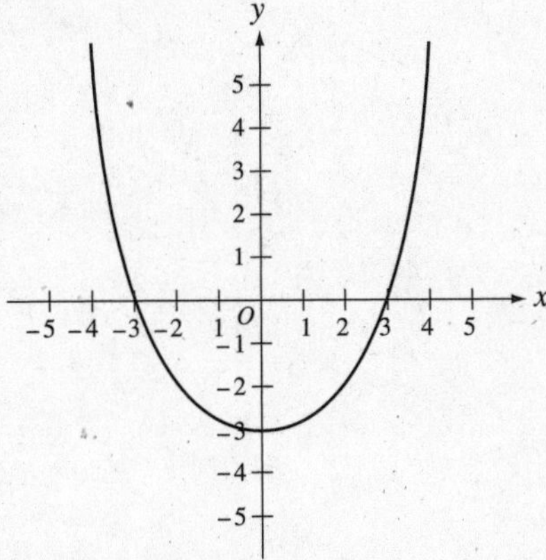

F. $y = \frac{x^2}{3} - 3$

G. $y = \frac{x^2 - 3}{3}$

H. $y = \frac{x^2}{3} + 3$

J. $y = \frac{x^2 + 3}{3}$

K. $y = 3x^2 - 3$

GO ON TO THE NEXT PAGE

51. In the figure below, $\sin a = \frac{4}{5}$. What is $\cos b$?

Do Your Figuring Here.

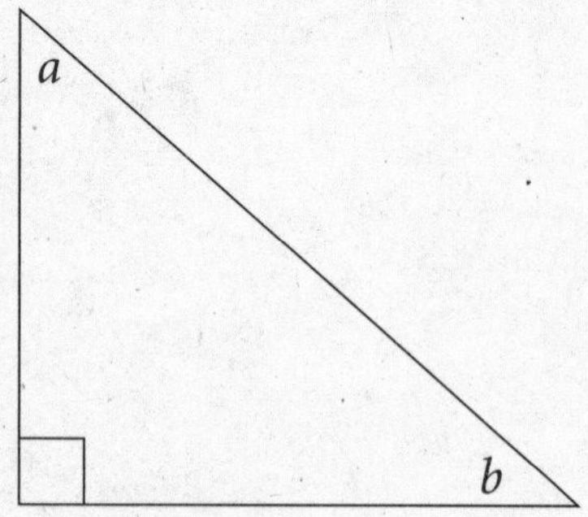

A. $\frac{3}{4}$

B. $\frac{3}{5}$

C. $\frac{4}{5}$

D. $\frac{5}{4}$

E. $\frac{4}{3}$

52. For all $x \neq 0$, $\frac{x^2 + x^2 + x^2}{x} = ?$

F. $3x$
G. x^3
H. x^5
J. x^7
K. $2x^2 + x$

53. One can determine a student's score S on a certain test by dividing the number of wrong answers (w) by 4 and subtracting the result from the number of right answers (r). This relation is expressed by which of the following formulas?

A. $S = \frac{r - w}{4}$

B. $S = r - \frac{w}{4}$

C. $S = \frac{r}{4} - w$

D. $S = 4r - w$

E. $S = r - 4w$

GO ON TO THE NEXT PAGE

54. What is the volume, in cubic inches, of the cylinder shown in the figure below?

Do Your Figuring Here.

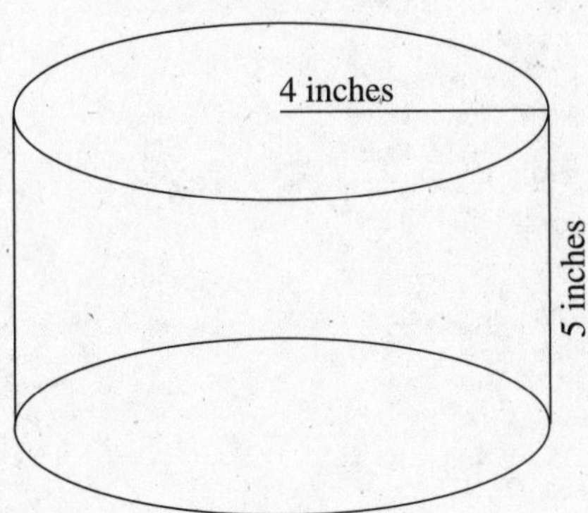

F. 20π
G. 40π
H. 60π
J. 80π
K. 100π

55. In the figure below, $\overline{AB}$ is perpendicular to $\overline{BC}$. The lengths of $\overline{AB}$ and $\overline{BC}$, in inches, are given in terms of x. Which of the following represents the area of ΔABC, in square inches, for all $x > 1$?

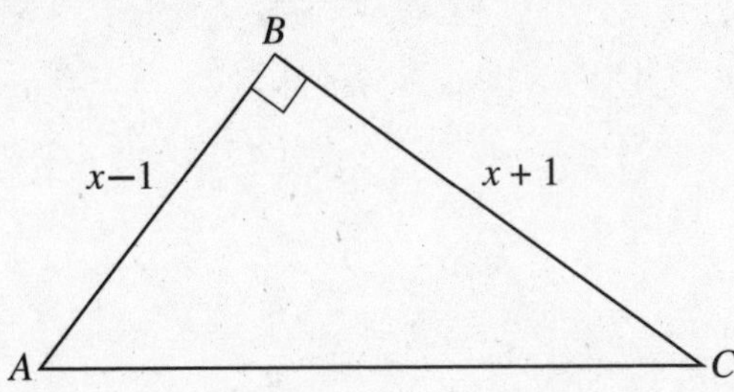

A. x
B. $2x$
C. x^2
D. $x^2 - 1$
E. $\frac{x^2 - 1}{2}$

GO ON TO THE NEXT PAGE

Do Your Figuring Here.

56. In 1990, the population of Town A was 9,400 and the population of Town B was 7,600. Since then, each year, the population of Town A has decreased by 100, and the population of Town B has increased by 100. Assuming that in each case the rate continues, in what year will the two populations be equal?

F. 1998
G. 1999
H. 2000
J. 2008
K. 2009

57. In a certain club, the average age of the male members is 35 and the average age of the female members is 25. If 20% of the members are male, what is the average age of all the club members?

A. 26
B. 27
C. 28
D. 29
E. 30

58. To determine the height h of a tree, Roger stands b feet from the base of the tree and measures the angle of elevation to be θ, as shown in the figure below. Which of the following relates h and b ?

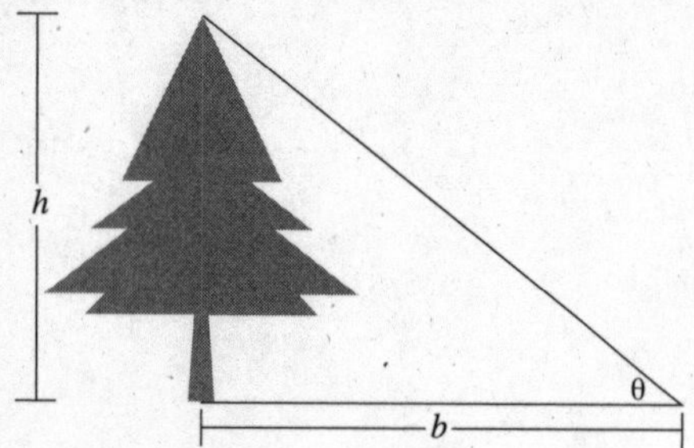

F. $\sin \theta = \frac{h}{b}$

G. $\sin \theta = \frac{b}{h}$

H. $\sin \theta = \frac{b}{\sqrt{b^2 + h^2}}$

J. $\sin \theta = \frac{h}{\sqrt{b^2 + h^2}}$

K. $\sin \theta = \frac{\sqrt{b^2 + h^2}}{b}$

GO ON TO THE NEXT PAGE

Do Your Figuring Here.

59. The formula for the lateral surface area S of a right circular cone is $S = \pi r\sqrt{r^2 + h^2}$, where r is the radius of the base and h is the altitude. What is the lateral surface area, in square feet, of a right circular cone with base radius 3 feet and altitude 4 feet?

A. $3\pi\sqrt{5}$
B. $3\pi\sqrt{7}$
C. 15π
D. 21π
E. $\frac{75\pi}{2}$

60. In the figure below, line t crosses parallel lines m and n. Which of the following statements must be true?

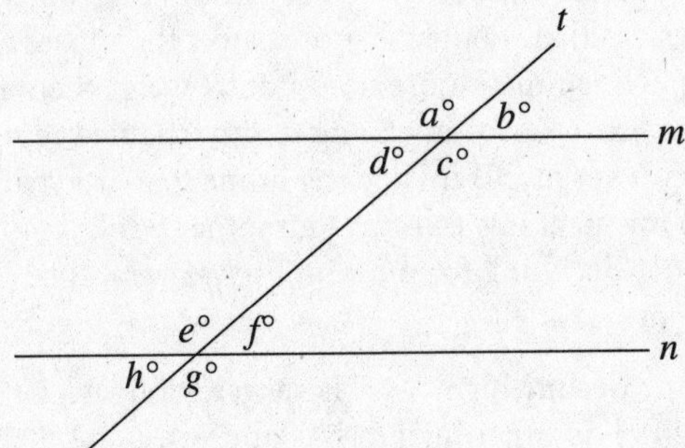

F. $a = b$
G. $a = d$
H. $b = e$
J. $c = g$
K. $d = g$

IF YOU FINISH BEFORE TIME IS CALLED, YOU MAY CHECK YOUR WORK ON THIS SECTION ONLY. DO NOT TURN TO ANY OTHER SECTION IN THE TEST.

STOP

READING TEST

35 Minutes—40 Questions

Directions: This test contains four passages, each followed by several questions. After reading a passage, select the best answer to each question and fill in the corresponding oval on your answer sheet. You are allowed to refer to the passages while answering the questions.

Passage I

I can remember, when I was a very little girl indeed, I used to say to my doll when we were alone together, "Now, Dolly, I am not clever, you know very well, and you must be patient with me, like a dear!"

...My dear old doll! I was such a shy little thing that I seldom dared to open my lips, and never dared to open my heart, to anybody else. It almost makes me cry to think what a relief it used to be to me when I came home from school of a day to run upstairs to my room and say, "Oh, you dear faithful Dolly, I knew you would be expecting me!" and then to sit down on the floor, leaning on the elbow of her great chair, and tell her all I had noticed since we parted....

I was brought up, from my earliest remembrance—like some of the princesses in the fairy stories, only I was not charming—by my godmother. At least, I only knew her as such. She was a good, good woman! She went to church three times every Sunday, and to morning prayers on Wednesdays and Fridays, and to lectures whenever there were lectures; and never missed. She was handsome; and if she had ever smiled, would have been (I used to think) like an angel—but she never smiled. She was always grave and strict. She was so very good herself, I thought, that the badness of other people made her frown all her life.... It made me very sorry to consider how good she was and how unworthy of her I was, and I used ardently to hope that I might have a better heart; and I talked it over very often with the dear old doll, but I never loved my godmother as I ought to have loved her and as I felt I must have loved her if I had been a better girl....

I had never heard my mama spoken of.... I had never been shown my mama's grave. I had never been told where it was....

Although there were seven girls at the neighboring school where I was a day boarder, and although they called me little Esther Summerson, I knew none of them at home. All of them were older than I, to be sure (I was the youngest there by a good deal), but there seemed to be some other separation between us besides that, and besides their being far more clever than I was and knowing much more than I did. One of them in the first week of my going to the school (I remember it very well) invited me home to a little party, to my great joy. But my godmother wrote a stiff letter declining for me, and I never went. I never went out at all.

It was my birthday. There were holidays at school on other birthdays—none on mine. There were rejoicings at home on other birthdays, as I knew from what I heard the girls relate to one another—there were none on mine. My birthday was the most melancholy day at home in the whole year....

Dinner was over, and my godmother and I were sitting at the table before the fire. The clock ticked, the fire clicked; not another sound had been heard in the room or in the house for I don't know how long. I happened to look timidly up from my stitching, across the table at my godmother, and I saw in her face, looking gloomily at me, "It would have been far better, little Esther, that you had had no birthday, that you had never been born!"

GO ON TO THE NEXT PAGE

I broke out crying and sobbing, and I said, "Oh, dear godmother, tell me, pray do tell me, did Mama die on my birthday?"

"No," she returned. "Ask me no more, child!"

...I put up my trembling little hand to clasp hers or to beg her pardon with what earnestness I might, but withdrew it as she looked at me, and laid it on my fluttering heart. She...said slowly in a cold, low voice—I see her knitted brow and pointed finger—"The time will come—and soon enough—when you will understand this better and will feel it too.... I have forgiven her"—but her face did not relent—"the wrong she did to me, and I say no more of it, though it was greater than you will ever know.... Forget your mother and leave all other people to forget her.... Now, go!"

...I went up to my room, and crept to bed, and laid my doll's cheek against mine wet with tears, and holding that solitary friend upon my bosom, cried myself to sleep. Imperfect as my understanding of my sorrow was, I knew that I had brought no joy at any time to anybody's heart and that I was to no one upon earth what Dolly was to me.

Dear, dear, to think how much time we passed alone together afterwards, and how often I repeated to the doll the story of my birthday and confided to her that I would try as hard as ever I could to repair the fault I had been born with.... I hope it is not self-indulgent to shed these tears as I think of it.

Adapted excerpt from *Bleak House*, by Charles Dickens. In this passage, Esther recounts some of her childhood experiences.

1. According to the passage, Esther only remembers:

A. being brought up by her parents for a short time.
B. being brought up by her mother for a short time.
C. being brought up by her godmother for a short time.
D. being brought up by her godmother.

2. It is most likely that Esther thought of her doll as:

F. only an amusing plaything.
G. her only friend and confidante.
H. a princess in a fairy tale.
J. a beautiful toy that was too fragile to touch.

3. As it is used in the passage, *stiff* (line 50) most closely means:

A. difficult to bend.
B. rigidly formal.
C. unchanging.
D. not moving easily or freely.

4. Which of the following most likely contributed to Esther's belief that she had been born with a fault (line 97)?

I. She had never heard anyone talk about her mother.
II. Her birthday was never celebrated.
III. Her godmother told her that she should never have been born.

F. I and III only
G. I and II only
H. I only
J. I, II, and III

5. Esther's godmother's words, actions, and facial expression as described in paragraph 10 (lines 74–85) suggest that she:

A. had a change of heart about celebrating Esther's birthday.
B. did not know what had happened to Esther's mother.
C. continued to resent Esther's mother.
D. had truly forgiven Esther's mother.

GO ON TO THE NEXT PAGE

6. According to the passage, Esther's childhood could be most accurately characterized as:

F. an adventure.
G. a time of loneliness and confusion.
H. a period of dedication to education and self-improvement.
J. a period of attempting to become more like her godmother.

7. From Esther's statement, "I was to no one upon earth what Dolly was to me" (lines 91–92), it is reasonable to infer that Esther:

A. believed that her godmother loved her.
B. believed that she would be able to become friends with the girls at school.
C. believed that no one loved her.
D. believed that her mother was alive.

8. In the passage, it is implied that all of the following contributed to separating Esther from the other girls at her school EXCEPT:

F. the other girls were older than Esther.
G. Esther's godmother did not allow Esther to socialize with the other girls outside of school.
H. Esther believed that the other girls were much smarter.
J. Esther was self-indulgent.

9. According to the passage, one reason that Esther thinks of her godmother as a "good, good woman" (line 20) is:

A. that when she smiles, she looks like an angel.
B. that she forgave Esther's mother.
C. that she frequently attends church services.
D. that she gave Esther a doll.

10. In the passage, Esther describes herself as a child as:

F. self-indulgent and not very clever.
G. shy and not very clever.
H. shy and faithful.
J. self-indulgent and faithful.

GO ON TO THE NEXT PAGE

Passage II

Marcos Nunes is not likely to forget his first holiday in Brazil's Pantanal wilderness. One afternoon last October he was coaxing his horse through a lonely tuft of woods when he suddenly found himself staring down a fully grown spotted jaguar. He held his breath while the painted cat and her cub paraded silkily through the grove, not 10 meters away.... "Thank you," he wrote later in a hotel visitor's log, "for the wonderful fright!"

As Nunes and other ecotourists are discovering, these big, beautiful animals, once at the brink of extinction, are now staging a comeback. Exactly how dramatic a comeback is difficult to say because jaguars—*Panthera onca*, the largest feline in the New World—are solitary, secretive, nocturnal predators. Each cat needs to prowl at least 35 square kilometers by itself. Brazil's Pantanal, vast wetlands that spill over a 140,000-square-kilometer swath of South America the size of Germany, gives them plenty of room to roam. Nevertheless, scientists who have been tagging jaguars with radio transmitters for two decades have in recent years been reporting a big increase in sightings. Hotels, campgrounds, and bed-and-breakfasts have sprung up to accommodate the half-million tourists a year (twice the number of five years ago) bent on sampling the Pantanal's wildlife, of which the great cats must be the most magnificent example.

Most sightings come from local cattle herders—but their jaguar stories have a very different ring. One day last September, ranch hand Abel Monteiro was tending cattle near the Rio Vermelho, in the southern Pantanal, when, he says, a snarling jaguar leaped from the scrub and killed his two bloodhounds. Monteiro barely had time to grab his .38 revolver and kill the angry cat. Leonelson Ramos da Silva says last May he and a group of field hands had to throw flaming sticks all night to keep a prowling jaguar from invading their forest camp.... The Brazilian interior, famous for its generous spirit and cowboy *bonhomie*, is now the scene of a political cat fight between the scientists, environmentalists, and ecotourists who want to protect the jaguars and the embattled ranchers who want to protect themselves and their livelihood.

The ranchers, to be sure, have enough headaches coping with the harsh, sodden landscape without jaguars attacking their herds and threatening their livelihoods. Hard data on cattle losses due to jaguars in the Pantanal are nonexistent, but there are stories. In 1995, Joo Julio Dittmar bought a 6,200-hectare strip of ideal breeding ground, only to lose 152 of his 600 calves to jaguars, he claims. Ranchers chafe at laws that forbid them to kill the jaguars. "This is a question of democracy," says Dittmar. "We ranchers ought to be allowed to control our own environment."

Man and jaguar have been sparring for territory ever since 18th-century settlers, traders, and herdsmen began to move into this sparsely populated serto, or back lands. By the 1960s, the Pantanal was a vast, soggy canvas, white with gleaming herds of Nelore cattle. Game hunters were bagging 15,000 jaguars a year in the nearby Amazon Basin (no figures exist on the Pantanal) as the worldwide trade in pelts reached $30 million a year. As the jaguars grew scarce, their chief food staple, the capybaras—a meter-long rodent, the world's largest—overran farmers' fields and spread trichomoniasis, a livestock disease that renders cows sterile.

Then in 1967, Brazil outlawed jaguar hunting, and a world ban on selling pelts followed in 1973. Weather patterns also shifted radically—due most likely to global warming—and drove annual floods to near-Biblical proportions. The waters are only now retreating from some inundated pasturelands. As the Pantanal herds shrank from 6 million to about 3.5 million head, the jaguars advanced. Along the way they developed a taste for the bovine intruders.

The ranchers' fear of the big cats is partly cultural. The ancient Inca and Maya believed that jaguars possessed supernatural powers. In Brazil, the most treacherous enemy is said to be *o amigo da onca*, a friend to the jaguar....

Some people believe there may be a way for ranchers and jaguars to coexist. Sports hunters on "green safaris" might shoot jaguars with immobilizing drugs, allowing scientists to fit the cats with

GO ON TO THE NEXT PAGE

radio collars. Fees would help sustain jaguar research and compensate ranchers for livestock losses. (Many environmentalists, though, fear fraudulent claims.) Scientists are setting up workshops to teach ranchers how to protect their herds with modern husbandry, pasture management, and such gadgets as blinking lights and electric fences.

Like many rural folk, however, the wetland ranchers tend to bristle at bureaucrats and foreigners telling them what to do. When the scholars go home and the greens log off, the *pantaneiros* will still be there—left on their own to deal with the jaguars as they see fit.

11. As it is used in the passage, *canvas* (line 63) most closely means:

A. a survey of public opinion.
B. a background.
C. a coarse cotton fabric.
D. a painting.

12. According to the passage, one result of the decline of the jaguar population during the 1960s was:

F. the increase in the population of the settlers.
G. an increase in Brazil's ecotourist business.
H. an increase in the price of a jaguar pelt.
J. an increase in the population of their most common source of food, the capybaras.

13. According to the passage, it is difficult to determine the extent of the jaguar's comeback because:

A. the area they inhabit is so large.
B. the stories that the local ranchers tell about jaguars contradict the conclusions reached by scientists.
C. jaguars are solitary, nocturnal animals that can have a territory of 35 square kilometers.
D. scientists have only used radio transmitters to track the movements of the jaguar population.

14. The information about ecotourism in the first and second paragraphs of the passage (lines 1–28) suggests that:

F. the jaguars are seen as a threat to the safety of tourists.
G. the jaguars are important to the success of Brazil's growing ecotourism industry.
H. the growth of the ecotourism industry is threatening the habitat of the jaguars.
J. it is common for ecotourists to spot one or more jaguars.

15. According to the passage, which of the following is NOT a method for protecting cattle herds that scientists are teaching ranchers?

A. "Green safaris"
B. Pasture management
C. The use of blinking lights and electric fences
D. Modern husbandry

16. It is most likely that the author of the passage included the jaguar stories of three ranchers (lines 29–40, 52–58) in order to:

F. express more sympathy toward the ranchers than toward the environmentalists and scientists.
G. illustrate the dangers and economic losses that the jaguars currently pose to ranchers.
H. show the violent nature of the ranchers.
J. provide a complete picture of the Pantanal landscape.

GO ON TO THE NEXT PAGE

17. From information in the passage, it is most reasonable to infer that the cattle herds "shrank from 6 million to about 3.5 million head" (lines 79–80) because:

    A. the jaguars had killed so many cattle.
    B. environmentalists and scientists worked to convert pastureland into refuges for the jaguars.
    C. many cows had become sterile from trichomoniasis and annual floods submerged much of the pastureland used by ranchers.
    D. the cattle could not tolerate the increase in the average temperature caused by global warming.

18. The main conclusion reached about the future of the relationship between the people and the jaguars in the Pantanal is that:

    F. the increase in ecotourism will ensure the continued growth in the jaguar population.
    G. the ranchers themselves will ultimately determine how they will cope with the jaguars.
    H. the jaguar population will continue to fluctuate with the number of tourists coming into Pantanal.
    J. the scientists' new ranching methods will make it easy for the ranchers and jaguars to coexist.

19. According to the passage, which of the following groups want to protect the jaguar?

    I. Ecotourists
    II. Environmentalists
    III. Scientists

    A. I and II only
    B. I and III only
    C. II and III only
    D. I, II, and III

20. According to the passage, there is no accurate data available on:

    F. the number of cattle killed by jaguars.
    G. the number of ranchers attacked by jaguars.
    H. the growth rate of ecotourism in Brazil.
    J. the percentage of the Pantanal wetlands inhabited by jaguars.

GO ON TO THE NEXT PAGE

Passage III

Greek instruments can be classified into two general categories—string and pipe, or lyre and aulos. Our knowledge of them comes from representations on monuments, vases, statues, and friezes and from the testimony of Greek authors. The lyre was the national instrument and included a wide variety of types. In its most antique form, the chelys, it is traced back to the age of fable and allegedly owed its invention to Hermes. Easy to carry, this small lyre became the favorite instrument of the home, amateurs, and women, a popular accompaniment for drinking songs and love songs as well as more noble kinds of poetry.... Professional Homeric singers used a kithara, a larger, more powerful instrument, which probably came from Egypt. The kithara had a flat wooden sound box and an upper horizontal bar supported by two curving arms. Within this frame were stretched strings of equal length, at first but three or four in number. Fastened to the performer by means of a sling, the kithara was played with both hands. We are not sure in just what manner the instrument was used to accompany the epics. It may have been employed for a pitch-fixing prelude and for interludes, or it may have paralleled or decorated the vocal melody in more or less free fashion.

...Two types of tuning were used: the dynamic, or pitch method, naming the degrees "according to function"; and the thetic, or tablature, naming them "according to position" on the instrument.

As early as the eighth century B.C., lyres of five strings appeared. Terpander (fl. c. 675 B.C.), one of the first innovators, is said to have increased the number of strings to seven. He is also supposed to have completed the octave and created the Mixolydian scale. Aristoxenos claimed that the poetess Sappho, in the seventh century B.C., in addition to introducing a mode in which Dorian and Lydian characteristics were blended, initiated use of the plectrum or pick. At the time of Sophocles (495–406 B.C.), the lyre had eleven strings.

Another harplike instrument was the magadis, whose tone was described as trumpetlike. Of foreign importation, it had twenty strings, which, by means of frets, played octaves. As some of the strings were tuned in quartertones, it was an instrument associated with the enharmonic mode. Smaller versions, the pectis and the barbitos, were also tuned in quartertones. Greek men and boys had a style of singing in octaves that was called magadizing, after the octave-playing instruments.

The kithara was identified with Apollo and the Apollonian cult, representing the intellectual and idealistic side of Greek art. The aulos or reed pipe was the instrument of Dionysians, who represented the unbridled, sensual and passionate aspect of Greek culture.

Although translated as "flute," the aulos is more like our oboe. Usually found in double form, the pipes set at an angle, the aulos was imputed to have a far more exciting effect than that produced by the subdued lyre. About 600 B.C., the aulos was chosen as the official instrument of the Delphian and Pythian festivals. It was also used in performances of the Dionysian dithyramb as well as a supplement of the chorus in classic Greek tragedy and comedy.

There was a complete family of auloi covering the same range as human voices. One authority names three species of simple pipes and five varieties of double pipes. (The double pipe was the professional instrument.) An early specimen was supposed to have been tuned to the chromatic tetrachord D, C sharp, B flat, A—a fact that points to Oriental origin. Elegiac songs called aulodia were composed in this mode to be accompanied by an aulos. Although the first wooden pipes had only three or four finger holes, the number later

GO ON TO THE NEXT PAGE

increased so that the Dorian, Phrygian and Lydian modes might be performed on a single pair. Pictures of auletes show them with a bandage or phorbeia over their faces; this might have been necessary to hold the two pipes in place, to modulate the tone or, perhaps, to aid in storing air in the cheeks for the purpose of sustained performance.

21. The passage suggests that the aulos was considered "the official instrument of the Dionysians" (lines 56–59) because:

A. it expressed the excitement and passion of that aspect of Greek culture.
B. it was chosen as the official instrument of the Delphian and Pythian festivals.
C. it represented the intellectual and idealistic side of Greek art.
D. it was invented around the time that the Dionysian cult originated.

22. The statement that the chelys can be "traced back to the age of fable" (line 8) implies that the chelys:

F. was invented by storytellers.
G. was used to accompany the epics.
H. probably existed in legend only.
J. was a particularly ancient instrument.

23. The main purpose of the passage is to describe the:

A. use of the lyre in different musical settings.
B. connection between the ancient Greek arts of music and drama.
C. references to music in ancient Greek literature.
D. origin and development of various Greek instruments.

24. According to the passage, the kithara was:

F. most likely of Greek origin.
G. played with one hand.
H. used by professional musicians.
J. less powerful than a chelys.

25. Which of the following is NOT cited as a change that occurred to the lyre between the eighth and fifth centuries B.C.?

A. Musicians began to use a plectrum.
B. Lyres featured increasing numbers of strings.
C. Musicians began to use different scales and modes.
D. Lyres were used to accompany dramatic productions.

26. It can be inferred from the passage that the chromatic tetrachord D, C sharp, B flat, A (lines 75–76) was:

F. not appropriate for elegaic songs.
G. only used by professional musicians.
H. impossible on the first wooden pipes.
J. present in ancient Oriental music.

27. According to the passage, the most ancient form of the lyre was called a:

A. magadis.
B. kithara.
C. chelys.
D. barbitos.

28. According to the passage, one of Sappho's contributions to ancient Greek music was that she:

F. completed the octave and created the Mixolydian scale.
G. introduced a mode blending Dorian and Lydian characteristics.
H. incorporated poetry into recitals of lyre music.
J. helped increase the number of strings on the lyre.

GO ON TO THE NEXT PAGE

29. According to the passage, which of the following is/are characteristic of the aulos?

I. It was used in performances of the Dionysian dithyramb.
II. It sounded more exciting than the lyre.
III. It resembles the modern-day flute more than it does the oboe.

A. I only
B. I and II only
C. II and III only
D. I, II, and III

30. Which of the following does the passage suggest is true about our knowledge of ancient Greek instruments?

F. Our knowledge is dependent on secondary sources.
G. Little is known about how instruments were tuned.
H. Very few pictures of ancient Greek instruments have survived.
J. More is known about string instruments than about pipe instruments.

GO ON TO THE NEXT PAGE

Passage IV

Astronomers noted more than 150 years ago that sunspots wax and wane in number in an 11-year cycle. Ever since, people have speculated that the solar cycle might exert some influence on the Earth's weather. In this century, for example, scientists have linked the solar cycle to droughts in the American Midwest. Until recently, however, none of these correlations has held up under close scrutiny.

One problem is that sunspots themselves are so poorly understood. Observations have revealed that the swirly smudges represent areas of intense magnetic activity where the sun's radiative energy has been blocked and that they are considerably cooler than bright regions of the sun. Scientists have not been able, however, to determine just how sunspots are created or what effect they have on the solar constant (a misnomer that refers to the sun's total radiance at any instant).

The latter question, at least, now seems to have been resolved by data from the *Solar Maximum Mission* satellite, which has monitored the solar constant since 1980, the peak of the last solar cycle. As the number of sunspots decreased through 1986, the satellite recorded a gradual dimming of the sun. Over the past year, as sunspots have proliferated, the sun has brightened. The data suggest that the sun is 0.1 percent more luminous at the peak of the solar cycle, when the number of sunspots is greatest, than at its nadir, according to Richard C. Willson of the Jet Propulsion Laboratory and Hugh S. Hudson of the University of California at San Diego.

The data show that sunspots do not themselves make the sun shine brighter. Quite the contrary. When a sunspot appears, it initially causes the sun to dim slightly, but then after a period of weeks or months islands of brilliance called faculas usually emerge near the sunspot and more than compensate for its dimming effect. Willson says faculas may represent regions where energy that initially was blocked beneath a sunspot has finally breached the surface.

Does the subtle fluctuation in the solar constant manifest itself in the Earth's weather? Some recent reports offer statistical evidence that it does, albeit rather indirectly. The link seems to be mediated by a phenomenon known as the quasi-biennial oscillation (QBO), a 180-degree shift in the direction of stratospheric winds above the Tropics that occurs about every two years.

Karin Labitzke of the Free University of Berlin and Harry van Loon of the National Center for Atmospheric Research in Boulder, Colorado, were the first to uncover the QBO link. They gathered temperature and air-pressure readings from various latitudes and altitudes over the past three solar cycles. They found no correlation between the solar cycle and their data until they sorted the data into two categories: those gathered during the QBO's west phase (when the stratospheric winds blow west) and those gathered during its east phase. A remarkable correlation appeared: temperatures and pressures coincident with the QBO's west phase rose and fell in accordance with the solar cycle.

Building on this finding, Brian A. Tinsley of the National Science Foundation discovered a statistical correlation between the solar cycle and the position of storms in the North Atlantic. The latitude of storms during the west phase of the QBO, Tinsley found, varied with the solar cycle: storms occurring toward the peak of a solar cycle traveled at latitudes about six degrees nearer the Equator than storms during the cycle's nadir.

Labitzke, van Loon, and Tinsley acknowledge that their findings are still rather mysterious. Why does the solar cycle seem to exert more of an influence during the west phase of the QBO than it does during the east phase? How does the 0.1 percent variance in solar radiation trigger the much larger changes—up to six degrees Celsius in polar regions—observed by Labitzke and van Loon? Van Loon says simply, "We can't explain it."

GO ON TO THE NEXT PAGE

John A. Eddy of the National Center for Atmospheric Research, nonetheless, thinks these QBO findings as well as the *Solar Maximum Mission* data "look like breakthroughs" in the search for a link between the solar cycle and weather. With further research, for example, into how the oceans damp the effects of solar flux, these findings may lead to models that have some predictive value. The next few years may be particularly rich in solar flux.

31. According to the passage, the main source of information about the effect of sunspots on the solar constant is provided by:

A. studies of droughts in the Midwest.
B. data from the *Solar Maximum Mission* satellite.
C. temperature and air pressure readings taken in Colorado.
D. discussions between various eminent astronomers.

32. As it is used in the passage, the term *solar constant* refers to:

F. magnetic activity.
G. the sun's total radiance.
H. the sun's surface temperature.
J. wind direction.

33. The main purpose of this passage is to:

A. explain why scientists have failed to find any direct correlation between sunspots and the Earth's weather.
B. describe a possible correlation between the solar cycle and the Earth's weather.
C. describe the solar cycle and its relation to the solar constant.
D. prove conclusively that sunspots dramatically influence the Earth's weather.

34. As it is used in line 27, the word *proliferated* means:

F. grown in size.
G. brightened.
H. decreased in number.
J. increased in number.

35. Which of the following explains why the sun appears brighter during periods of sunspot activity?

A. Energy that has been blocked is finally released.
B. The sun shines brighter when sunspots first appear.
C. Magnetic activity increases the sun's temperature.
D. Air pressure in the Earth's atmosphere falls.

36. The shift in the direction of stratospheric winds that occurs every two years is known as:

F. a facula.
G. the solar flux.
H. North Atlantic storms.
J. the quasi-biennial oscillation.

37. Which of the following best summarizes the main point of the last paragraph?

A. Scientists will soon be in a position to accurately predict the Earth's weather.
B. Many findings of the *Solar Maximum Mission* cannot yet be explained.
C. The relationship between the solar cycle and the Earth's weather may become clear with further research.
D. Scientists disagree as to whether studying sunspots will ever have any practical value.

GO ON TO THE NEXT PAGE

38. According to the passage, changes in the solar cycle may influence the Earth's weather in which of the following ways?

I. Changing the direction of stratospheric winds
II. Altering temperature and pressure levels
III. Influencing the latitude of storms

F. I only
G. I and II only
H. II and III only
J. I, II, and III

39. From the information in the first paragraph, it may be inferred that scientists now consider a correlation between the solar cycle and droughts in the American Midwest to be:

A. probable.
B. unlikely.
C. confusing.
D. useful.

40. According to the passage, which of the following statements best describes the current understanding of the relationship between sunspot activity and solar luminosity?

F. At the peak of sunspot activity, the solar constant decreases in magnitude.
G. At the peak of sunspot activity, the solar constant increases in magnitude.
H. At the low point of sunspot activity, the sun is 0.1 percent brighter than it is at the peak of such activity.
J. Scientists have yet to demonstrate a relationship between the two phenomena.

IF YOU FINISH BEFORE TIME IS CALLED, YOU MAY CHECK YOUR WORK ON THIS SECTION ONLY. DO NOT TURN TO ANY OTHER SECTION IN THE TEST. STOP

SCIENCE TEST

35 Minutes—40 Questions

Directions: Each of the following seven passages is followed by several questions. After reading each passage, decide on the best answer to each question and fill in the corresponding oval on your answer sheet. You are allowed to refer to the passages while answering the questions. Calculator use is not allowed on this test.

Passage I

Acid-base indicators are used to determine changes in pH. The pH is a quantitative measure of the hydrogen ion concentration of a solution. For any solution, the pH ranges from 0 to 14. An acid-base indicator is a weak acid or base that is sensitive to the hydrogen ion concentration and changes color at a known pH. At any other pH, the acid-base indicator is clear.

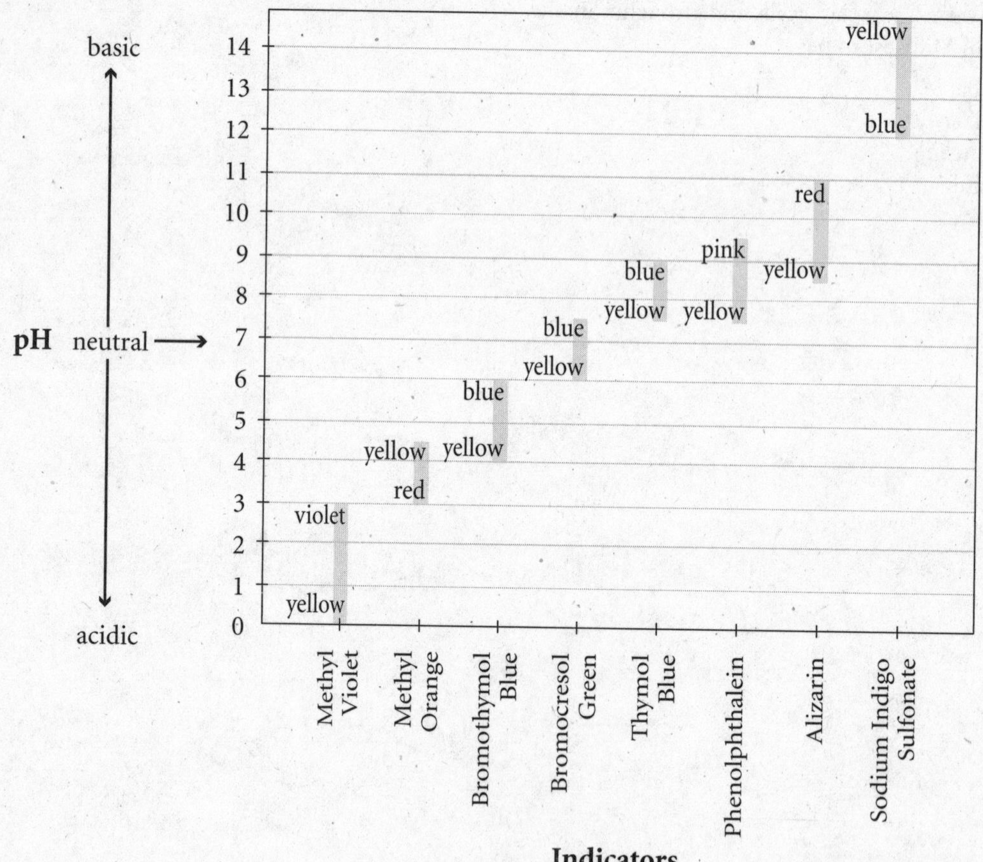

1. Which indicators undergo a color change in the region from pH 8 to pH 12?

A. Bromocresol green, bromothymol blue, and thymol blue
B. Thymol blue, phenolphthalein, and alizarin
C. Phenolphthalein, alizarin, and sodium indigo sulfonate
D. Phenolphthalein and bromothymol blue

2. Which of the following indicators undergoes a red-to-yellow or yellow-to-red color change?

I. Alizarin
II. Thymol blue
III. Methyl orange

F. I only
G. II only
H. I and III only
J. I, II, and III

3. A chemist is running an experiment in a solution that becomes basic upon completion. According to the diagram, the reaction is complete when:

A. the addition of bromocresol green results in a blue color.
B. any indicator turns violet.
C. a white solid appears.
D. the addition of bromothymol blue results in a blue color.

4. Which of the following hypotheses is consistent with the information in the passage and the diagram?

F. Color changes for any given acid-base indicator occur in a solution with a pH less than 7.
G. Color changes for any given acid-base indicator occur in a solution with a pH greater than 7.
H. Color changes for acid-base indicators always occur within the same pH range.
J. Color changes for acid-base indicators vary within the pH range.

5. Compared to bromothymol blue, phenolphthalein undergoes a color change at:

A. a higher pH.
B. a lower pH.
C. the same pH.
D. Cannot be determined from the data provided.

GO ON TO THE NEXT PAGE

Passage II

The Brazilian tree frog (*Hyla faber*) exchanges gases through both its skin and lungs. The exchange rate depends on the temperature of the frog's environment. A series of experiments was performed to investigate this dependence.

Experiment 1

Fifty frogs were placed in a controlled atmosphere that, with the exception of temperature, was designed to simulate their native habitat. The temperature was varied from 5° C to 25° C, and equilibrium was attained before each successive temperature change. The amount of oxygen absorbed by the frogs' lungs and skin per hour was measured, and the results for all the frogs were averaged. The results are shown in Table 1.

Table 1

	Moles O_2 absorbed/hr	
Temperature (°C)	**Skin**	**Lungs**
5	15.4	8.3
10	22.7	35.1
15	43.6	64.9
20	42.1	73.5
25	40.4	78.7

Experiment 2

The same frogs were placed under the same conditions as in Experiment 1. For this experiment, the amount of carbon dioxide eliminated through the skin and lungs was measured. The results are averaged and given in Table 2.

Table 2

	Moles CO_2 released/hr	
Temperature (°C)	**Skin**	**Lungs**
5	18.9	2.1
10	43.8	12.7
15	79.2	21.3
20	91.6	21.9
25	96.5	21.4

6. The results of Experiment 1 suggest that the total amount of O_2 absorbed per hour is:
   F. correlated to the temperature.
   G. independent of the temperature.
   H. an indication of how healthy a Brazilian tree frog is.
   J. always less than the total amount of CO_2 eliminated per hour.

7. According to Experiment 2, the total amount of CO_2 eliminated per hour at 17° C is closest to:
   A. 21 mol/hr
   B. 85 mol/hr
   C. 106 mol/hr
   D. 115 mol/hr

8. Ectotherms are animals whose bodily functions are affected by the temperature of their environment. Which of the following results supports the conclusion that *Hyla fabers* is an ectotherm?
   F. The oxygen absorbed at 25° C
   G. The carbon dioxide released by the lungs
   H. The oxygen absorbed over the entire temperature range
   J. The results do not support this conclusion.

9. According to the results of Experiment 2, which of the following plots best represents the amount of carbon dioxide eliminated through the skin and lungs as a function of temperature?

   A.
   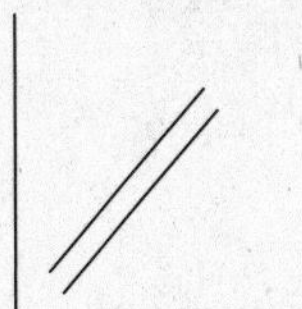

   B.
   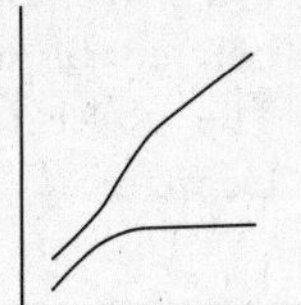

   C.
   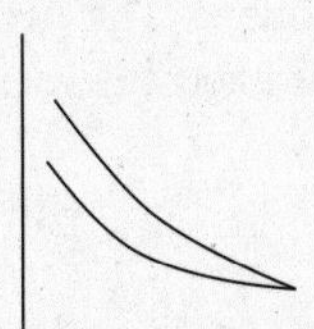

   D.
   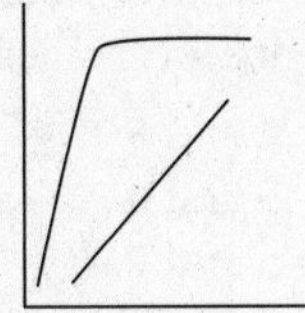

10. On the basis of the experimental results, one could conclude that as temperature increases:
    F. O_2 absorbed by the lungs increases and CO_2 released by the skin decreases.
    G. O_2 absorbed by the lungs increases and CO_2 released by the skin increases.
    H. O_2 absorbed by the lungs decreases and CO_2 released by the lungs increases.
    J. O_2 absorbed by the lungs decreases and CO_2 released by the lungs decreases.

11. According to the results of these experiments, as the temperature rises above 15° C, which of the following phenomena can be observed?
    A. The Brazilian tree frog's ability to absorb oxygen through the skin decreases, as does its ability to release carbon dioxide through the lungs.
    B. The Brazilian tree frog's ability to absorb oxygen through the skin decreases, while its ability to release carbon dioxide through the lungs remains about the same.
    C. The Brazilian tree frog's ability to absorb oxygen through the skin remains about the same, as does its ability to release carbon dioxide through the lungs.
    D. The Brazilian tree frog's ability to absorb oxygen through the skin increases, while its ability to release carbon dioxide through the lungs remains about the same.

GO ON TO THE NEXT PAGE

Passage III

A scientist wants to use a certain organic reagent to develop a means of extracting valuable elements from radioactive nuclear power plant effluent. Using the organic reagent, she measured extraction curves for six different elements: tungsten (W), molybdenum (Mo), ytterbium (Yb), erbium (Er), thulium (Tm), and europium (Eu).

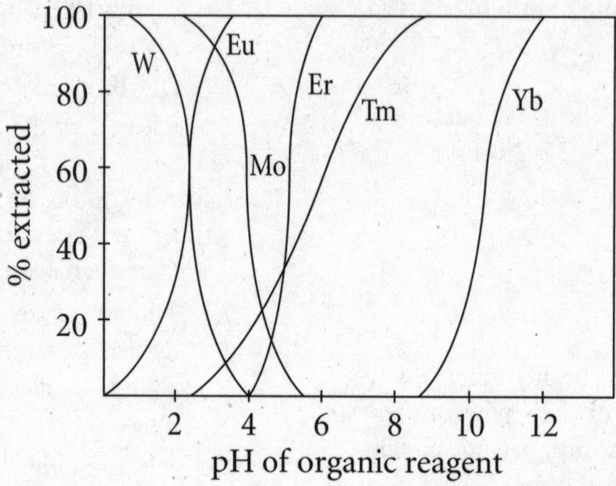

12. At which pH level is the organic reagent most effective in extracting molybdenum?
    - F. 3
    - G. 4
    - H. 5
    - J. 6

13. The engineers who run a power plant that ejects waste with high levels of erbium and tungsten isotopes would like to extract as much of both elements as possible. Assuming a single-step extraction, this could be accomplished by using the organic reagent at a pH of:
    - A. less than 1.5 or greater than 5.5
    - B. 4
    - C. 4.6
    - D. It is impossible to extract large amounts of both elements using the reagent at any pH.

14. Based on the data given, which of the following conclusions can be drawn about the effect of pH on the percentage extracted?
    - F. The percentage of an element extracted increases as pH increases.
    - G. The percentage of an element extracted decreases as pH increases.
    - H. The percentage of an element extracted is independent of pH.
    - J. The effect of pH is different for different elements.

15. The researcher was able to extract 45% of the thulium from the plant's effluent. The pH level of the organic reagent was most likely between:
    - A. 4 and 5
    - B. 5 and 6
    - C. 6 and 7
    - D. 7 and 8

GO ON TO THE NEXT PAGE

16. If erbium is among the elements being extracted by the organic reagent at a certain pH, which of the following cannot be among the other elements being extracted?

F. Europium
G. Thulium
H. Molybdenum
J. Ytterbium

17. If at a certain pH the organic reagent extracts the same percentages of europium and molybdenum, which of the following statements are also true?

I. More than 90% of each of these elements is being extracted.
II. Of the six elements being studied, the organic reagent at this pH is extracting only these two.
III. The pH of the organic reagent is between 3 and 4.

A. I and II
B. I and III
C. II and III
D. I, II, and III

Passage IV

While the focus (point of origin) of most earthquakes lies less than 20 km below the Earth's surface, certain unusual seismographic readings indicate that some activity originates at considerably greater depths. Below, two scientists discuss the possible causes of deep-focus earthquakes.

Scientist 1

Surface earthquakes occur when rock in the Earth's crust fractures to relieve stress. However, below 50 km, rock is under too much pressure to fracture normally. Deep-focus earthquakes are caused by the pressure of fluids trapped in the Earth's tectonic plates. As a plate is forced down into the mantle by convection, increases in temperature and pressure cause changes in the crystalline structure of minerals such as serpentine. In adopting a denser configuration, the crystals dehydrate, releasing water. Other sources of fluid include water trapped in pockets of deep-sea trenches and carried down with the plates. Laboratory work has shown that fluids trapped in rock pores can cause rock to fail at lower shear stresses. In fact, at the Rocky Mountain Arsenal, the injection of fluid wastes into the ground accidentally induced a series of shallow-focus earthquakes.

Scientist 2

Deep-focus earthquakes cannot result from normal fractures because rock becomes ductile at the temperatures and pressures that exist at depths greater than 50 km. Furthermore, mantle rock below 300 km is probably totally dehydrated because of the extreme pressure. Therefore, trapped fluids could not cause quakes below that depth. A better explanation is that deep-focus quakes result from the slippage that occurs when rock in a descending tectonic plate undergoes a phase change in its crystalline structure along a thin plane parallel to a stress. Just such a phase change and resultant slippage can be produced in the laboratory by compressing a slab of calcium magnesium silicate. The pattern of deep-quake activity supports this theory. In most seismic zones, the recorded incidence of deep-focus earthquakes corresponds to the depths at which phase changes are predicted to occur in mantle rock. For example, little or no phase change is thought to occur at 400 km, and indeed, earthquake activity at this level is negligible. Between 400 and 680 km, activity once again increases. Although seismologists initially believed that earthquakes could be generated at depths as low as 1,080 or 1,200 km, no foci have been confirmed below 700 km. No phase changes are predicted for mantle rock below 680 km.

GO ON TO THE NEXT PAGE

18. Scientists 1 and 2 agree on which point?

F. Deep-earthquake activity does not occur below 400 km.
G. Fluid allows tectonic plates to slip past one another.
H. Water can penetrate mantle rock.
J. Rock below 50 km will not fracture normally.

19. Which of the following is evidence that would support Scientists 1's hypothesis?

A. The discovery that water can be extracted from mantle-like rock at temperatures and pressures similar to those found below 300 km
B. Seismographic indications that earthquakes occur 300 km below the surface of the Earth
C. The discovery that phase changes occur in the mantle rock at depths of 1,080 km
D. An earthquake underneath Los Angeles that was shown to have been caused by water trapped in sewer lines

20. Both scientists assume that:

F. deep-focus earthquakes are more common than surface earthquakes.
G. trapped fluids cause surface earthquakes.
H. the Earth's crust is composed of mobile tectonic plates.
J. deep-focus earthquakes cannot be felt on the Earth's crust without special recording devices.

21. To best refute Scientist 2's hypothesis, Scientist 1 might:

A. find evidence of other sources of underground water.
B. record a deep-focus earthquake below 680 km.
C. find a substance that doesn't undergo phase changes even at depths equivalent to 680 km.
D. show that rock becomes ductile at depths of less than 50 km.

22. According to Scientist 1, the earthquake at Rocky Mountain Arsenal occurred because:

F. serpentine or other minerals dehydrated and released water.
G. fluid wastes injected into the ground compressed a thin slab of calcium magnesium silicate.
H. fluid wastes injected into the ground flooded pockets of a deep-sea trench.
J. fluid wastes injected into the ground lowered the shear stress failure point of the rock.

23. Scientist 2's hypothesis would be strengthened by evidence showing that:

A. water evaporates at high temperatures and pressures.
B. deep-focus earthquakes can occur at 680 km.
C. stress has the same effect on mantle rock that it has on calcium magnesium silicate.
D. water pockets exist at depths below 300 km.

GO ON TO THE NEXT PAGE

Passage V

Astronomers want to know the effects of atmospheric conditions on the impact of an asteroid-to-Earth collision. The most common hypothesis is that the presence of moisture in the Earth's atmosphere significantly reduces the hazardous effects of such a collision. One researcher has decided to create a laboratory model of the Earth. The researcher has the ability to control the amount of moisture surrounding the model. The researcher has also created models of asteroids at various sizes. The researcher will use a collision indicator (see table below) based on the Torino Scale to measure the results of two experiments.

Collision Indicator	
0 to 0.9	A collision capable of little destruction
1 to 3.9	A collision capable of localized destruction
4 to 6.9	A collision capable of regional destruction
7 to 10	A collision capable of global catastrophe

Experiment 1

The researcher simulated collisions on the Earth model with asteroid models equivalent to mass ranging from 1,000 kg to 1,000,000 kg. The controlled moisture level of the model Earth's atmosphere was 86%. The effects of the collisions were recorded and rated according to the collision indicator.

Experiment 2

The researcher simulated collisions on the Earth model with asteroid models equivalent to the same mass as in Experiment 1. The controlled moisture level of the model Earth's atmosphere in this experiment was 12%. The effects of the collisions were recorded and rated according to the collision indicator. The results of both experiments are shown in the graph.

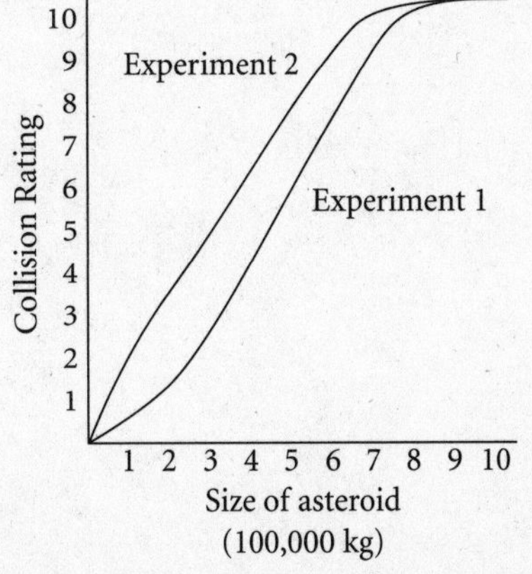

GO ON TO THE NEXT PAGE

24. How was the experimental design of Experiment 1 different from that of Experiment 2?

F. The impacts of more asteroids were measured.
G. The impacts of larger asteroids were measured.
H. There was more moisture in the atmosphere.
J. There was a different collision indicator.

25. If the atmospheric moisture in Experiment 2 was increased to 50%, the collision rating for an asteroid with a mass of 400,000 kg would most likely be between:

A. 2 and 3.
B. 4.5 and 5.5.
C. 6 and 7.
D. 9 and 10.

26. Based on the experimental results, one can generalize that an increase of moisture in the atmosphere would:

F. decrease the impact of an asteroid-to-Earth collision, regardless of the size of the asteroid.
G. decrease the impact of an asteroid-to-Earth collision with asteroids under 700,000 kg.
H. increase the impact of an asteroid-to-Earth collision, regardless of the size of the asteroid.
J. increase the impact of an asteroid-to-Earth collision with asteroids under 700,000 kg.

27. In a simulated asteroid-to-Earth collision, a 400,000 kg asteroid received a collision rating of 4. The amount of moisture in the atmosphere was most likely closest to:

A. 0%
B. 12%
C. 86%
D. 100%

28. According to the researcher's model, a 100,000 kg asteroid colliding in an atmosphere with a moisture level of 12% would be likely to have the same impact as an asteroid colliding in an atmosphere with a moisture level of 86% with a size closest to which of the following?

F. 50,000 kg
G. 120,000 kg
H. 270,000 kg
J. 490,000 kg

29. To be minimally capable of regional destruction, an asteroid entering an atmosphere with a moisture level of 86% would have to be roughly what percent larger than an asteroid capable of the same level of destruction entering an atmosphere with a moisture level of 12%?

A. 20%
B. 70%
C. 150%
D. 220%

GO ON TO THE NEXT PAGE

Passage VI

The electrical conductivity of a material determines how it will react to various temperature conditions in a consumer product. Product researchers need to know how a material will react in order to determine its safety for consumer use. The electrical conductivity of two different samples of a platinum dithiolate compound was measured from 10 K to 275 K. The results and general conductivity versus temperature plots for conductors and semiconductors are shown below.

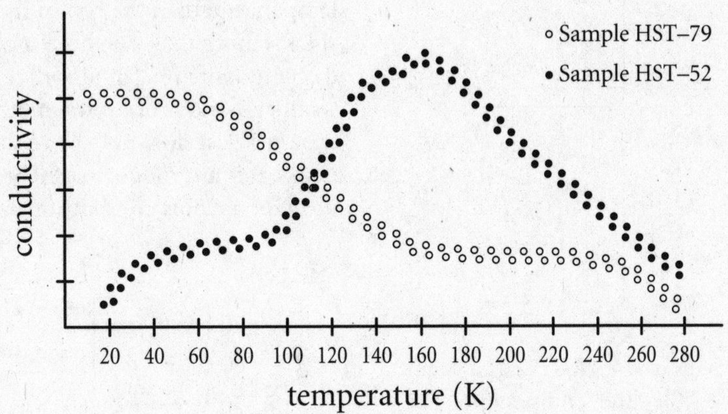

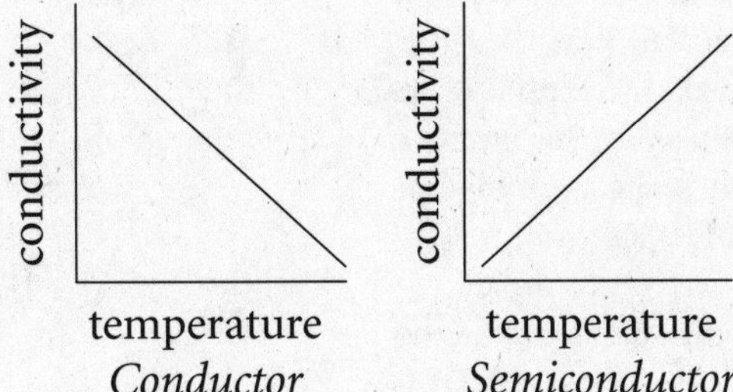

30. For Sample HST-52, which of the following describes its behavior when the temperature is dropped from 200 K to 100 K?

- **F.** The sample remains a semiconductor.
- **G.** The sample remains a conductor.
- **H.** The sample undergoes a conductor to semiconductor transition.
- **J.** The sample undergoes a semiconductor to conductor transition.

31. In a material exhibiting conductor-like behavior, the conductivity:

- **A.** increases as the temperature increases.
- **B.** decreases as the temperature increases.
- **C.** decreases as the temperature decreases.
- **D.** remains the same at all temperatures.

32. A newly developed material has a semiconductor to conductor transition at about 10 K as the temperature increases. Its conductivity versus temperature plot would resemble which of the following?

F.

G.

H.

J.

33. An industrial firm wishes to use HST-52 as a semiconductor in an assembly line component. The experimental results indicate that:

A. HST-52 is not a semiconductor; a new material will have to be chosen.
B. HST-52 is suitable for the planned application.
C. HST-52 is too brittle to be used in this manner.
D. HST-52 will be usable only if the assembly line is maintained at less than 150 K.

34. The temperature at which a compound's conductivity-versus-temperature plot declines most quickly is known as its "optimal conductor" temperature. Which of the following could be the optimal conductor temperature for Sample HST-52?

F. 20 K
G. 80K
H. 160 K
J. 180 K

35. Over which of the following temperatures would Sample HST-79 be best suited for use as a conductor?

A. Between 20 and 60 K
B. Between 80 and 120 K
C. Between 140 and 180 K
D. Between 190 and 220 K

Passage VII

Siamese cats have a genotype for dark fur, but the enzymes that produce the dark coloring function best at temperatures below the cat's normal body temperature. A Siamese cat usually has darker fur on its ears, nose, paws, and tail, because these parts have a lower temperature than the rest of its body. If a Siamese cat spends more than one hour a day for six consecutive days outdoors (an "outdoor" cat) during very cold weather, darker fur grows in other places on its body. If a Siamese cat does not spend this amount of time outdoors, it is an "indoor" cat. The amount of dark fur on its body remains constant throughout the year.

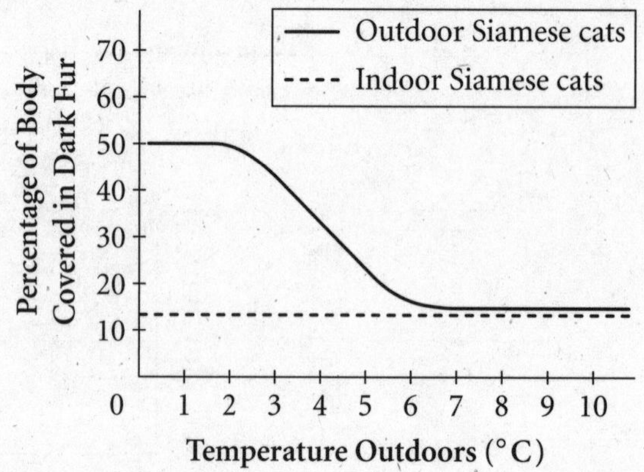

36. A particular Siamese cat goes outdoors a total of 3 hours per week during the coldest part of the year. One could predict that the percentage of its body covered by dark fur would be closest to:

F. 0%
G. 10%
H. 40%
J. 60%

37. According to the graph, what is the most likely temperature outside if outdoor Siamese cats have 45% of their bodies covered in dark fur?

A. 0° C
B. 3° C
C. 6° C
D. 9° C

GO ON TO THE NEXT PAGE

38. If a Siamese cat that lived indoors was lost and later found with dark fur over 30% of its body, which of the following could be inferred about the period during which it was missing:

I. It was living in an area where temperatures fell below 5° C.
II. It spent more time outdoors than indoors.
III. It was missing for at least 6 days.

F. I and II only
G. I and III only
H. II and III only
J. I, II, and III

39. If a Siamese cat has dark fur over 10% of its body, which of the following must be true about the cat?

A. It lives indoors.
B. It lives in an area where the temperature outdoors is usually 7° C or higher.
C. It either lives indoors or it lives in an area where the temperature outdoors is usually 7° C or higher.
D. None of the above

40. If a researcher wants to find out how fur color is affected by the amount of time a Siamese cat spends outside in cold weather, which experiment would be the most helpful?

F. The "indoor" cats in the original experiment should be used as the control group and their fur color should be compared to a group of Siamese cats spending six hours or more a day outside in cold weather for six consecutive days.
G. A new group of Siamese cats should be formed and kept outside two or more hours a day at varying temperatures. Their fur color at different outdoor temperatures should be compared to the "outdoor" cats already charted.
H. Siamese cats should be split into two groups, one group spending only one hour per day outside for six consecutive days in cold weather, and the other group spending at least two hours a day outside for six consecutive days in the same weather.
J. No new experiment is needed. The data already gathered shows that the more time a Siamese cat spends outside in cold weather, the darker its fur will be.

IF YOU FINISH BEFORE TIME IS CALLED, YOU MAY CHECK YOUR WORK ON THIS SECTION ONLY. DO NOT TURN TO ANY OTHER SECTION IN THE TEST.

WRITING TEST

30 Minutes—1 Question

Directions: This section will test your writing ability. You will have thirty (30) minutes to compose an essay in English. Prior to planning your essay, pay close attention to the essay prompt so that you understand exactly what you are supposed to do. Your essay's grade will be based on how well it expresses an opinion on the question in the prompt, as well as its logical construction, supporting evidence, and clarity of expression based on the standards of written English.

You may use the unlined space on the next page to plan your essay. Anything written in this space will not be scored by the graders. Your essay must be written on the lined pages. While you may not need all the space to finish, you should not skip lines. Corrections and additions may be written neatly in between lines but not in the margins. Be sure to write clearly. Illegible work will not receive credit.

If you finish in under thirty minutes, you may review your essay. When time is called, lay your pencil down immediately.

DO NOT CONTINUE UNTIL TOLD TO DO SO.

School athletics has become increasingly competitive in recent years, as professional athletes are drafted at younger ages and the money and fame that professional athletes enjoy has risen to astronomical levels. Some students and school administrators believe that all student athletes should be required to maintain a minimum grade point average or be barred from playing, to ensure that they still get a good education. Others believe this requirement would be unfair because athletics and academics are unrelated, and because such a rule would make it too difficult for coaches to do their jobs. In your opinion, should student athletes be required to maintain a minimum grade point average?

In your essay, take a position on this question. You may write about either one of the two points of view given, or you may present a different point of view on this question. Use specific reasons and examples to support your position.

Use this space to *plan* your essay. Your work here will not be graded. Write your essay on the lined pages that follow.

GO ON TO THE NEXT PAGE

KAPLAN
Test Prep and Admissions

Practice Test Two: **Answer Key**

ENGLISH TEST		
1. D	26. J	51. B
2. G	27. B	52. J
3. C	28. G	53. C
4. J	29. C	54. J
5. B	30. F	55. C
6. G	31. A	56. J
7. D	32. J	57. C
8. J	33. B	58. F
9. B	34. H	59. D
10. H	35. A	60. F
11. A	36. H	61. B
12. J	37. B	62. F
13. A	38. J	63. D
14. F	39. A	64. G
15. D	40. G	65. B
16. G	41. C	66. F
17. A	42. J	67. C
18. J	43. A	68. H
19. C	44. J	69. B
20. F	45. D	70. J
21. B	46. H	71. B
22. J	47. A	72. F
23. B	48. G	73. B
24. F	49. B	74. J
25. C	50. G	75. B

MATH TEST	
1. A	31. A
2. J	32. F
3. A	33. B
4. G	34. K
5. B	35. D
6. H	36. K
7. C	37. B
8. J	38. F
9. D	39. A
10. F	40. K
11. B	41. B
12. G	42. H
13. D	43. E
14. G	44. K
15. D	45. E
16. F	46. K
17. E	47. E
18. K	48. G
19. D	49. C
20. G	50. F
21. E	51. C
22. H	52. F
23. A	53. B
24. G	54. J
25. C	55. E
26. J	56. G
27. C	57. B
28. H	58. J
29. D	59. C
30. H	60. J

READING TEST	
1. D	21. A
2. G	22. J
3. B	23. D
4. G	24. H
5. C	25. D
6. G	26. J
7. C	27. C
8. J	28. G
9. C	29. B
10. G	30. F
11. B	31. B
12. J	32. G
13. C	33. B
14. G	34. J
15. A	35. A
16. G	36. J
17. C	37. C
18. G	38. H
19. D	39. A
20. F	40. G

SCIENCE TEST	
1. B	21. B
2. H	22. J
3. A	23. C
4. J	24. H
5. A	25. B
6. F	26. G
7. C	27. C
8. H	28. H
9. B	29. B
10. G	30. H
11. B	31. B
12. F	32. H
13. D	33. D
14. J	34. J
15. B	35. B
16. J	36. G
17. B	37. B
18. J	38. G
19. A	39. C
20. H	40. H

Answers and Explanations

ENGLISH TEST

Passage I

1. (D)

A comma is needed to set off the introductory phrase, so (A) cannot be correct. (B) creates a sentence fragment, and the pronoun *it* in (C) does not match the subject of the sentence—Duke Ellington.

2. (G)

The whole passage is in past tense, and there is no reason why this verb should not be in past tense as well. Also, the part of the sentence on the other side of the semicolon gives you a big clue by using *paid*.

3. (C)

The colon is used incorrectly in the original sentence, and (B) does not solve the problem. (D) is unnecessarily wordy.

4. (J)

Commas are needed between items in a series, so eliminate (F) and (G). A comma is also needed to set off the introductory phrase, so eliminate (H).

5. (B)

In order to figure out the appropriate pronoun, identify the noun to which the pronoun refers. The only possible corresponding noun is *Ellington*; therefore, (B) is the correct answer.

6. (G)

As a teenager in Washington is not a complete sentence. (H) does not make sense, and (J) is incorrect because the comma is unnecessary.

7. (D)

The word *then* should be *than*—(D) is the choice that makes this correction.

8. (J)

Even though the piano teacher's name is mentioned in the preceding sentence, more information about her name is unnecessary.

9. (B)

There is a contrast between Ellington's not being a good pianist and his hearing about the opportunities for musicians in New York. The best contrast is established by (B).

10. (H)

Awaited and *were there for* mean the same thing, so one part of the underlined portion should be deleted—that eliminates (F) and (G). (J) incorrectly uses *which* instead of *that*, so it too can be eliminated.

11. (A)

The sentence is logical in the flow of the paragraph, so eliminate (D). (A) is the simplest and most correct way to phrase the sentence.

12. (J)

The subject of the sentence is the Cotton Club, so answer choices with the pronoun *he*—(F) and (G)—should be eliminated. (H) creates a sentence fragment.

13. (A)

This list of songs simply provides some detail. The songs do not contradict anything, so eliminate (B). The names of the songs themselves do not illustrate complexity; therefore, (C) is incorrect. This part of the paragraph is no longer about the Cotton Club, so eliminate (D).

14. (F)

The last paragraph of the essay lists the accomplishments of Ellington. (F) is the only answer choice that makes sense.

15. (D)

Paragraph 4 is the only paragraph that covers elements of Ellington's music. The logical place for the insertion is before the last sentence of the essay.

Passage II

16. (G)

The subject is *animals*, so a plural pronoun is needed. (F) is a singular pronoun, (H) is a contraction, and (J) uses "there" instead of "their."

17. (A)

The comma is needed to set off the second clause from the first.

18. (J)

The phrase *a member of the weasel family* is a nonessential clause and should be set off by commas. Eliminate (G) and (H) because they create sentence fragments.

19. (C)

Which should be *that*—rule out (A) and (B). The whole passage is in present tense, so eliminate (D) because it is in past tense.

20. (F)

Choose the most logical order of the words. (F) is the choice that makes the most sense.

21. (B)

Far from placing it in danger is an introductory phrase and should be set off by a comma. Eliminate (A) and (C). (D) is unnecessarily wordy and doesn't make sense with the rest of the sentence.

22. (J)

By distinguishing itself from other animals is a sentence fragment. These words make sense as an introductory phrase and should therefore be set off by a comma. (J) is the choice that accomplishes this.

23. (B)

(B) is the simplest and most correct way to phrase the question.

24. (F)

The investigating has occurred in the past, and it is still occurring. The tense of the answer choice should reflect this. (G) and (H) only refer to the past, and (J) refers only to the present.

25. (C)

The previous sentence speaks of special glands, but this sentence says that some animals do not have these glands. This is a contrast, and *however* sets it up best.

26. (J)

Remains and *endures as* are the same thing, so the correct choice will eliminate one of them. (J) does just that.

27. (B)

The pronoun *it* refers to the tree frog, not a background of leaves. (B) fixes the error.

28. (G)

The information is useful in the paragraph, so eliminate (J). (G) is a simple and logical way of rephrasing all of the excess words.

29. (C)

Paragraph 4 begins with an introduction, and Paragraph 3 ends with a conclusion. (C) is the only choice that reflects this.

30. (F)

The author covers a range of topics in the area and uses several animals as examples. All of the other answer choices are incorrect because they contradict things that the author does in the essay.

Passage III

31. (A)

The other answer choices are unnecessarily wordy.

32. (J)

The other answer choices are unnecessarily wordy.

33. (B)

The sentences on both sides of the period are fragments. The best way to fix this mistake is to simply combine the sentences.

34. (H)

Included and *held* relay the same information. (H) deletes one of the unnecessary words.

35. (A)

The drink was unusual to the people who never experienced it before. In other words, the verb form should be past tense. Eliminate (B) and (C). (D) does not make sense, so eliminate it.

36. (H)

Over the next century is an introductory phrase and should be set off by a comma. (H) and (J) add the comma, but (J) also adds unnecessary words.

37. (B)

This description would provide some "color" to the essay. It would not weaken or contradict anything, so eliminate (A) and (C). It would not say anything about the author's opinion of chocolate either, so eliminate (D).

38. (J)

Commas are needed between items in a series. (G) is incorrect because there are too many commas.

39. (A)

The sentence provides an example of the uses of chocolate worldwide. (B) and (C) set up an unwarranted contrast. (D) is not a good transition between the two sentences.

40. (G)

The word *do* is unnecessary in the sentence, especially with the presence of *nonetheless*. (G) is the most concise statement of the information.

41. (C)

The colon is not used properly here, so eliminate (A), (B), and (D).

42. (J)

Tea has nothing to do with the topic, so the sentence should be eliminated.

43. (A)

The research will be welcomed "by" people, not "to" or "with" them. Therefore, eliminate (B) and (D). *Us with a sweet tooth* does not make sense, so (A) is the correct answer.

44. (J)

(F) and (G) do not make any sense at all. Between (H) and (J), the latter is the better sounding choice.

45. (D)

This essay is about only chocolate, and it does not cover any other culinary trends in history. Therefore, it would not meet the requirement.

Passage IV

46. (H)

Here, the verb is being used as part of a modifying phrase. Choice (H) is idiomatically correct.

47. (A)

Commas are needed in a series, so eliminate (C). A colon is not appropriate; eliminate (B). (D) incorrectly switches to the past tense.

48. (G)

The form needed is the possessive of *who* so (G) is correct.

49. (B)

This sentence is part of a list of proposed *uniform of the future* developments. The other sentences in that list use the verbs *would be*, *would become*, and *would transmit*. So the correct form is (B).

50. (G)

No commas are needed in a list of only two items.

51. (B)

Be wary of sentences that begin with *to*; they are often fragments like the one here. (B) is the best way to combine the two parts of the sentence.

52. (J)

Two words in the underlined portion of the sentence telling what the proposed covering does to a soldier have closely related meanings: "concealing" means *keeping from being observed* or *hiding*, and "invisible" means *hidden* or *impossible to see*. Because these words convey

the same idea, this is a simple redundancy that can be fixed by eliminating one of the two words. Therefore, we can eliminate choices (F), (G), and (H), and select (J) as the answer.

53. (C)

To determine the U.S. Army's opinion of the Invisible Soldier program, look at the words used to introduce and describe it: the army has dreamed of such a program and invested in it. So the army attitude is positive; we can eliminate the negative word *skeptical* in (A) and the neutral words *curious* and *detailed* in (B) and (D), leaving *enthusiastic*, (C).

54. (J)

In context, this paragraph offers a specific example of the more general issues raised in paragraph 1.

55. (C)

Having *beginning* and *early stages* is redundant. (C) is the most concise way to rephrase this.

56. (J)

As written, this is a run-on sentence, so eliminate (F). To correct it, the new clause should be made subordinate by replacing the pronoun with a relative pronoun, so eliminate (H). The correct form, since it follows a comma, is *which* rather than *that*, so eliminate (G).

57. (C)

The passage has a formal, technical tone. It would, therefore, be inappropriate for the author to use the highly informal expressions *you know, is* or *is, like*; eliminate (A) and (B). The choice *however, is* is appropriate since this paragraph contrasts with the preceding one. (D) would be appropriate if this paragraph drew a conclusion based on the prior paragraph, but it doesn't.

58. (F)

A colon is correct punctuation here because the material that follows it is an explanation of what precedes it.

59. (D)

Only sentence 2 and sentence 1 are choices for a first sentence. To put the sentences in logical order, first look for a good transition from paragraph 4, which discusses a problem. Sentence 1 explicitly refers to addressing the problem, so it's the better choice. Eliminate (A) and (B). The second sentence should follow logically from sentence 1's description of the new color-changing pixel, and our choices are sentences 4 and 5. Sentence 4 in (C) refers to mirrors, which we haven't encountered before in the passage, rather than pixels, so we can eliminate this choice. That leaves us with (D), sentence 5, which refers to the pixels introduced in the first sentence.

60. (F)

To answer this question, we need an idea of the purpose of each paragraph. Paragraph 1 introduces the *uniform of the future*, paragraph 2 the *Invisible Soldier* program, paragraph 3 the program's early-stage solution, paragraph 4 a problem with that solution, and paragraph 5 a new advance that may solve that problem. The new sentences to be inserted do not discuss a problem with such a program. We can therefore eliminate choices (G), (H), and (J). The material properly belongs in paragraph 2, choice (G), because it introduces camouflage generally.

Passage V

61. (B)

(A) and (C) are too wordy, and (D) does not continue the verb tense established in the series.

62. (F)

The colon is used here to dramatically introduce California. The commas in (G) and (H) do not do this well, and the separate sentence in (J) does not work either.

63. (D)

This paragraph is in the past tense, so the introductory sentence should be in the past tense as well.

64. (G)

This is a long nonessential clause that should be set off by a comma. (J) is incorrect because it unnecessarily adds more words.

65. (B)

The word order is incorrect in (A). (C) creates a sentence fragment, and *did* in (D) is unnecessary.

66. (F)

The information is pertinent to the topic, and (F) is the clearest statement.

67. (C)

The only choice that works here is (C). *Their* would have also worked, but it does not appear as one of the answer choices.

68. (H)

(F) is a sentence fragment. (G) and (J) are very awkward.

69. (B)

The last sentence of the previous paragraph talks about how workers began to quit their jobs to join the Gold Rush. The first sentence of this paragraph magnifies this point. (B) is the only logical transition.

70. (J)

This information is not pertinent to the Gold Rush back in 1849.

71. (B)

Singularly and *one* are redundant. (C) is too wordy, and (D) is incorrect within the context of the sentence.

72. (F)

This sentence is a more specific detail that illustrates the preceding sentence. (F) is the best transition between the two sentences.

73. (B)

(A) makes it sound as though lives are changing the place rather than the other way around. (C) does not make sense, and (D) is grammatically incorrect.

74. (J)

(H) and (F) do not make sense because of the word *and*. (G) is incorrect because the sentence is talking about people today, not the Forty-niners.

75. (B)

Though the Forty-niners are mentioned, the focus of the essay is on the history of the California Gold Rush. Therefore, the essay would not meet the requirements of the assignment.

MATH TEST

1. (A)—Percent Increase and Decrease

100 Key Math Concepts for the ACT, #33. To reduce a number by 20%, you could take 20% of the original number and subtract the result, or you could just take 80% of the original number:

$$\begin{aligned}\text{New price} &= 80\% \text{ of original price}\\ &= (.80)(\$125)\\ &= \$100\end{aligned}$$

2. (J)—Evaluating an Algebraic Expression

100 Key Math Concepts for the ACT, #52. Plug in $x = -5$ and see what you get:

$$\begin{aligned}2x^2 - 6x + 5 &= 2(-5)^2 - 6(-5) + 5\\ &= 2 \times 25 - (-30) + 5\\ &= 50 + 30 + 5\\ &= 85\end{aligned}$$

3. (A)—Prime Factorization

100 Key Math Concepts for the ACT, #11. The prime factorization of 36 is $2 \times 2 \times 3 \times 3$. That factorization includes 2 distinct prime factors, 2 and 3.

4. (G)—Exterior Angles of a Triangle

100 Key Math Concepts for the ACT, #81. The exterior angles of a triangle (or any polygon, for that matter) add up to 360°:

$$\begin{aligned}x + 85 + 160 &= 360\\ x &= 115\end{aligned}$$

5. (B)—Average Formula, Adding/Subtracting Fractions

100 Key Math Concepts for the ACT, #41, #22. Don't jump to hasty conclusions—don't just average the denominators. Do it right—add the fractions and divide by 2:

$$\text{Average of 2 numbers} = \frac{\text{Sum}}{2}$$

$$\frac{\frac{1}{20}+\frac{1}{30}}{2} = \frac{\frac{3}{60}+\frac{2}{60}}{2} = \frac{\frac{5}{60}}{2} = \frac{\frac{1}{12}}{2} = \frac{1}{12} \times \frac{1}{2} = \frac{1}{24}$$

6. (H)—Rate

100 Key Math Concepts for the ACT, #39. Everyone pays \$1.50, and the rest of the toll is based on the number of miles traveled. Subtract \$1.50 from Joy's toll to see how much is based on distance traveled: \$25.00 – \$1.50 = \$23.50. Then divide that amount by 25 cents per mile:

$$\frac{\$23.50}{\$0.25 \text{ per mile}} = 94 \text{ miles}$$

7. (C)—Multiplying and Dividing Powers, Multiplying Monomials

100 Key Math Concepts for the ACT, #47, #55. Multiply the coefficients and add the exponents:

$$3x^2 \times 5x^3 = 3 \times 5 \times x^{2+3} = 15x^5$$

8. (J)—Finding the Distance Between Two Points

100 Key Math Concepts for the ACT, #71. You could use the distance formula, but it's easier here to think about a right triangle. One leg is the difference between the x's, which is 3, and the other leg is the difference between the y's, which is 4, so you're looking at a 3-4-5 triangle, and the hypotenuse, which is the distance from P to Q, is 5.

9. (D)—Percent Formula

100 Key Math Concepts for the ACT, #32. Percent times Whole equals Part:

$$(\text{Percent}) \times 25 = 16$$

$$\text{Percent} = \frac{16}{25} = 0.64 = 64\%$$

10. (F)—Comparing Fractions

100 Key Math Concepts for the ACT, #28. For $\frac{7}{x}$ to be greater than $\frac{1}{4}$, the denominator x has to be less than 4 times the numerator, or 28. And for $\frac{7}{x}$ to be less than $\frac{1}{3}$, the denominator x has to be greater than 3 times the numerator, or 21. Thus x could be any of the integers 22 through 27, of which there are 6.

11. (B)—Factoring Other Polynomials–FOIL in Reverse

100 Key Math Concepts for the ACT, #61. To factor $6x^2 - 13x + 6$, you need a pair of binomials whose "first" terms will give you a product of $6x^2$ and whose "last" terms will give you a product of 6. And since the middle term of the result is negative, the two last terms must both be negative. You know that one of the factors is among the answer choices, so you can use them in your trial-and-error effort to factor. You know you're looking for a factor with a minus sign in it, so the answer's either B or D.

Try B first: Its first term is $3x$, so the other factor's first term would have to be $2x$ (to get that $6x^2$ in the product). B's last term is –2, so the other factor's last term would have to be –3. Check to see if $(3x - 2)(2x - 3)$ works:

$$(3x - 2)(2x - 3)$$
$$= (3x \cdot 2x) + [3x(-3)] + [(-2)(2x)] + [(-2)(-3)]$$
$$= 6x^2 - 9x - 4x + 6$$
$$= 6x^2 - 13x + 6$$

It works. There's no need to check D.

12. (G)—Adding/Subtracting Fractions

100 Key Math Concepts for the ACT, #22. The four fractions on the left side of the equation are all ready to be added, because they already have a common denominator: a.

$$\frac{1}{a} + \frac{2}{a} + \frac{3}{a} + \frac{4}{a} = 5$$
$$\frac{1+2+3+4}{a} = 5$$
$$\frac{10}{a} = 5$$
$$10 = 5a$$
$$a = 2$$

13. (D)—Intersecting Lines

100 Key Math Concepts for the ACT, #78. $\angle CGE$ and $\angle BGF$ are vertical angles, so they're equal, and $\angle BGF$ measures 105°. If you subtract $\angle AGB$ from $\angle BGF$, you're left with $\angle AGF$, the angle you're looking for. So, $\angle AGF$ measures 105° – 40°, or 65°.

14. (G)—Solving an Inequality

100 Key Math Concepts for the ACT, #69. You solve an inequality much the way you solve an equation: Do the same things to both sides until you've isolated what you're solving for. (Just remember to flip the sign if you ever multiply or divide both sides by a negative number.) Here you want to isolate x:

$$-3 < 4x - 5$$
$$2 < 4x$$
$$\frac{2}{4} < x$$
$$x > \frac{1}{2}$$

15. (D)—Interior Angles of a Triangle, Exterior Angles of a Triangle

100 Key Math Concepts for the ACT, #80, #81. Because $\overline{BD}$ bisects $\angle ABC$, the measure of $\angle ABD$ is 50°. Now you know 2 of the 3 angles of ΔABD, so the third angle measures 180° – 60° – 50° = 70°.

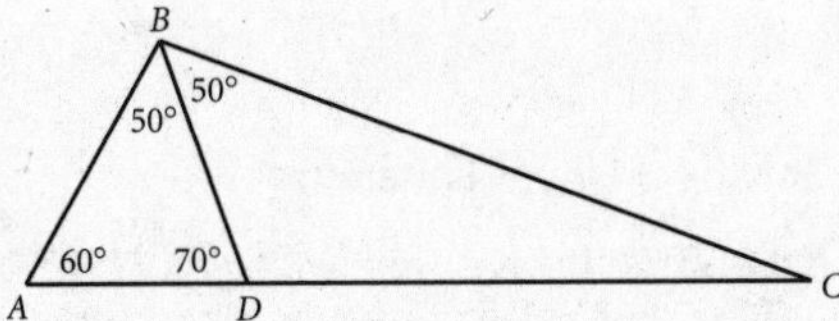

$\angle BDC$, the angle you're looking for, is supplementary to the 70° angle, so $\angle BDC$ measures 180° – 70° = 110°.

16. (F)—Solving "In Terms Of", Factoring out a Common Divisor

100 Key Math Concepts for the ACT, #64, #58. To express y in terms of x, isolate y:

$$x + 2y - 3 = xy$$
$$2y - xy = -x + 3$$
$$y(2 - x) = 3 - x$$
$$y = \frac{3 - x}{2 - x}$$

17. (E)—Parts and Whole

If you add the number of English-speakers and the number of Spanish-speakers, you get 28 + 37 = 65. But there are only 50 students, so 65 – 50 = 15 of them are being counted twice—because those 15 speak both languages.

18. (K)—Rate

100 Key Math Concepts for the ACT, #39. Set up a proportion:

$$\frac{288 \text{ miles}}{6 \text{ hours}} = \frac{x \text{ miles}}{8 \text{ hours}}$$
$$6x = 288 \cdot 8$$
$$6x = 2{,}304$$
$$x = 384$$

19. (D)—Repeating Decimals

100 Key Math Concepts for the ACT, #30. To convert a fraction to a decimal, you divide the denominator into the numerator. Clearly you don't have time to take the division out to 100 places after the decimal point. There must be a pattern you can take advantage of. Start dividing and continue just until you see what the pattern is:

$$11\overline{)4.000000\ldots}$$

The 1st, 3rd, 5th, etc. digits are 3; and the 2nd, 4th, etc. digits are 6. In other words, every odd-numbered digit is a 3 and every even-numbered digit is a 6. The 100th digit is an even-numbered digit, so it's a 6.

20. (G)—Solving a System of Equations

100 Key Math Concepts for the ACT, #67. Since it's x you're looking for, eliminate y. Fortunately, the equations are all ready for you—just add them and the $+4y$ cancels with the $-4y$:

$$3x + 4y = 31$$
$$3x - 4y = -1$$
$$6x = 30$$
$$x = 5$$

21. (E)—Finding the Distance Between Two Points

100 Key Math Concepts for the ACT, #71. The coordinates of the midpoint are the averages of the coordinates of the endpoints. The average of the x's is $\frac{2 + 12}{2} = 7$, and the average of the y's is $\frac{3 + (-15)}{2} = -6$, so the coordinates of the midpoint are (7, –6).

22. (H)—Sine, Cosine, and Tangent of Acute Angles

100 Key Math Concepts for the ACT, #96. Cosine is "adjacent over hypotenuse." Here the leg adjacent to θ is 4 and the hypotenuse is 5, so $\cos\theta = \frac{4}{5}$.

23. (A)—Circumference of a Circle

100 Key Math Concepts for the ACT, #89. The radius of circle *Q* is twice the radius of circle *P*. You could use the circumference of circle *P* to find the radius of circle *P*, then double that radius to get the radius of circle *Q*, and finally use that radius to calculate the circumference of circle *Q*. It's much easier and faster, however, if you realize that "double the radius means double the circumference." If the circumference of circle *P* is 6, then the circumference of circle *Q* is twice that, or 12.

24. (G)—Evaluating an Algebraic Expression

100 Key Math Concepts for the ACT, #52. This looks like a functions question, but in fact it's just a "plug-in-the-number-and-see-what-you-get" question.

$$\begin{aligned} f(x) &= x^3 - x^2 - x \\ f(-3) &= (-3)^3 - (-3)^2 - (-3) \\ &= -27 - 9 + 3 \\ &= -33 \end{aligned}$$

25. (C)—Integer/Noninteger, Miscellaneous Triangles

100 Key Math Concepts for the ACT, #3. If the two unknown side lengths are integers, and the sum of the two lengths has to be greater than 7, then the least amount the two unknown sides could add up to would be 8, which would make the perimeter 7 + 8 = 15.

26. (J)—Factoring Other Polynomials—FOIL in Reverse, Factoring out a Common Divisor

100 Key Math Concepts for the ACT, #61. First factor out an *x* from each term, then factor what's left:

$$\begin{aligned} 2x + 3x^2 + x^3 &= x(2 + 3x + x^2) \\ &= x(x^2 + 3x + 2) \\ &= x(x + 1)(x + 2) \end{aligned}$$

27. (C)—Simplifying an Algebraic Fraction, Multiplying and Dividing Powers, Raising Powers to Powers

100 Key Math Concepts for the ACT, #62, #47, #48. Get rid of the parentheses in the denominator, and then cancel factors the numerator and denominator have in common:

$$\frac{x^2y^3z^4}{(xyz^2)^2} = \frac{x^2y^3z^4}{x^2y^2z^4} = \frac{x^2}{x^2} \cdot \frac{y^3}{y^2} \cdot \frac{z^4}{z^4} = y$$

28. (H)—Adding/Subtracting Fractions, Converting Fractions to Decimals

100 Key Math Concepts for the ACT, #22, #29. Normally you would have a choice: Either convert the fractions to decimals first and then add, or add the fractions first and then convert the sum to a decimal. In this case, however, both fractions would convert to endlessly repeating decimals, which might be a bit unwieldy when adding. In this case it seems to make sense to add first, then convert:

$$\frac{2}{3} + \frac{1}{12} = \frac{8}{12} + \frac{1}{12} = \frac{9}{12} = \frac{3}{4} = 0.75$$

29. (D)—Solving a Linear Equation

100 Key Math Concepts for the ACT, #63. This looks like a physics question, but in fact it's just a "plug-in-the-number-and-see-what-you-get" question. Be sure you plug 95 in for *C* (not *F*):

$$\begin{aligned} C &= \frac{5}{9}(F - 32) \\ 95 &= \frac{5}{9}(F - 32) \\ \frac{9}{5} \times 95 &= F - 32 \\ F - 32 &= 171 \\ F &= 171 + 32 = 203 \end{aligned}$$

30. (H)—Probability

100 Key Math Concepts for the ACT, #46. Probability equals the number of favorable outcomes divided by the total number of possible outcomes. In this problem, a "favorable outcome" is choosing a green marble—that's 4. The "total number of possible outcomes" is the total number of marbles, or 20:

$$\text{Probability} = \frac{\text{Favorable Outcomes}}{\text{Total Number of Possible Outcomes}}$$
$$= \frac{4}{20}$$
$$= \frac{1}{5}$$

31. (A)—Adding and Subtracting Polynomials, Average Formula

100 Key Math Concepts for the ACT, #54, #41. To find the average of three numbers—even if they're algebraic expressions—add them and divide by 3:

$$\text{Average} = \frac{\text{Sum of terms}}{\text{Number of terms}}$$
$$= \frac{(2x + 5) + (5x - 6) + (-4x + 2)}{3}$$
$$= \frac{3x + 1}{3}$$
$$= x + \frac{1}{3}$$

32. (F)—Using Two Points to Find the Slope

100 Key Math Concepts for the ACT, #72. Parallel lines have the same slope. Use the first pair of points to figure out the slope:

$$\text{Slope} = \frac{y_2 - y_1}{x_2 - x_1} = \frac{16 - 1}{2 - 1} = 15$$

Then use the slope to figure out the missing coordinate in the second pair of points:

$$\text{Slope} = \frac{y^2 - y^1}{x^2 - x^1}$$
$$15 = \frac{(25 - (-5))}{a - (-10)}$$
$$15 = \frac{30}{a + 10}$$
$$15a + 150 = 30$$
$$15a = -120$$
$$a = -8$$

33. (B)—Similar Triangles

100 Key Math Concepts for the ACT, #82. When parallel lines make a big triangle and a little triangle as they do here, the triangles are similar (because they have the same angle measurements). Side $\overline{PR}$ is three times the length of $\overline{QR}$, so each side of the big triangle is three times the length of the corresponding side of the smaller triangle, and therefore the ratio of the perimeters is also 3:1. So the perimeter of ΔPRT is 3 times 11, or 33.

34. (K)—Special Quadrilaterals

100 Key Math Concepts for the ACT, #86. It is a polygon because it's composed of straight line segments. It is a quadrilateral because it has four sides. It is not a rectangle because opposite sides are not equal. It is a trapezoid because it has one pair of parallel sides.

35. (D)—Evaluating an Algebraic Expression, Solving a Linear Equation

100 Key Math Concepts for the ACT, #52, #63.

Plug in $x = -3$ and solve for a:

$$2x^2 + (a - 4)x - 2a = 0$$
$$2(-3)^2 + (a - 4)(-3) - 2a = 0$$
$$18 - 3a + 12 - 2a = 0$$
$$30 - 5a = 0$$
$$-5a = -30$$
$$a = 6$$

36. (K)—Counting the Possibilities

100 Key Math Concepts for the ACT, #45. The total number of combinations of a first course, second course, and dessert is equal to the product of the 3 numbers:

$$\text{Total possibilities} = 4 \times 5 \times 3 = 60$$

37. (B)—Prime Factorization, Least Common Multiple

100 Key Math Concepts for the ACT, #11, #14. An integer that's divisible by 6 has at least one 2 and one 3 in its prime factorization. An integer that's divisible by 9 has at least two 3's in its prime factorization. Therefore, an integer that's divisible by both 6 and 9 has at least one 2 and two 3's in its prime factorization. That means it's divisible by 2, 3, $2 \times 3 = 6$, $3 \times 3 = 9$, and $2 \times 3 \times 3 = 18$. It's not necessarily divisible by 12 or 36, each of which includes two 2's in its prime factorization.

You could also do this one by **picking numbers**. Think of a common multiple of 6 and 9 and use it to eliminate some options. $6 \times 9 = 54$ is an obvious common multiple—and it's not divisible by 12 or 36, but it is divisible by 18. The *least* common multiple of 6 and 9 is 18, which is also divisible by 18. It looks like every common multiple of 6 and 9 is also a multiple of 18.

38. (F)—Simplifying an Algebraic Fraction

100 Key Math Concepts for the ACT, #62.

$$\frac{x^2 + x^2 + x^2}{x^2} = \frac{3x^2}{x^2} = 3$$

39. (A)—Translating from English into Algebra

100 Key Math Concepts for the ACT, #65. Read carefully. This question's a lot easier than you might think. It's asking for the total number of coins, not the total value. q quarters, d dimes, and n nickels add up to a total of $q + d + n$ coins.

40. (K)—Solving an Inequality and Graphing Inequalities

100 Key Math Concepts for the ACT, #69, #70. You solve an inequality much the way you solve an equation: Do the same things to both sides until you've isolated what you're solving for. (Just remember to flip the sign if you ever multiply or divide both sides by a negative number.)

$$5x - 2(1 - x) \geq 4(x + 1)$$
$$5x - 2 + 2x \geq 4x + 4$$
$$5x + 2x - 4x \geq 4 + 2$$
$$3x \geq 6$$
$$x \geq 2$$

The "greater-than-or-equal-to" symbol is graphed as a solid circle.

41. (B)—Using Two Points to Find the Slope

100 Key Math Concepts for the ACT, #72. First find the slope of the line that contains the given points:

$$\text{Slope} = \frac{y_2 - y_1}{x_2 - x_1} = \frac{10 - 6}{6 - 5} = 4$$

Line m is perpendicular to the above line, so the slope of m is the negative reciprocal of 4, or $-\frac{1}{4}$.

42. (H)—Sine, Cosine, and Tangent of Acute Angles

100 Key Math Concepts for the ACT, #96. Sine is "opposite over hypotenuse." Here the leg opposite θ is 12 and the hypotenuse is 13, so:

$$\sin \theta = \frac{12}{13}.$$

43. (E)—Raising Powers to Powers, Solving a Linear Equation

100 Key Math Concepts for the ACT, #48, #63. Express the left side of the equation so that both sides have the same base:

$$9^{2x-1} = 3^{3x+3}$$
$$(3^2)^{2x-1} = 3^{3x+3}$$
$$3^{4x-2} = 3^{3x+3}$$

Now that the bases are the same, just set the exponents equal:

$$4x - 2 = 3x + 3$$
$$4x - 3x = 3 + 2$$
$$x = 5$$

44. (K)—Combined Percent Increase and Decrease

100 Key Math Concepts for the ACT, #35. Be careful with combined percent increase. You cannot just add the two percents, because they're generally percents of different wholes. In this instance, the 20% increase is based on the 1970 population, but the 30% increase is based on the larger 1980 population. If you just added 20% and 30% to get 50%, you fell into the test maker's trap.

The best way to do a problem like this one is to pick a number for the original whole and just see what happens. As usual, the best number to pick is 100. (That may be a small number for the population of a city, but verisimilitude is not important—all that matters is the math.)

If the 1970 population was 100, then a 20% increase would put the 1980 population at 120. Now, to figure the 30% increase, multiply 120 by 130%:

New # = (Original #) + (30% of Original #)

New # = 130% of Original #

$$x = 1.3(120)$$
$$= 156$$

Since the population went from 100 to 156, that's a 56% increase.

45. (E)—Finding the Missing Number

100 Key Math Concepts for the ACT, #44. The best way to deal with changing averages is go by way of the sums. Use the old average to figure out the total of the first 4 scores:

Sum of first 4 scores = $4 \times 89 = 356$

And use the new average to figure out the total he needs after the 5th score:

Sum of 5 scores = $5 \times 90 = 450$

To get his sum up from 356 to 450, Martin needs to score $450 - 356 = 94$.

46. (K)—Equation for a Circle

100 Key Math Concepts for the ACT, #75. If you find the distance from the center to the given point on the circle, you'll have the radius. The difference between the *x*'s is 8, and the difference between the *y*'s is 6. If 8 and 6 are the lengths of the legs of a right triangle, then the hypotenuse is 10. The radius, then, is 10. Now you can plug the radius and the coordinates of the center point into the general form of the equation of a circle:

$$(x - h)^2 + (y - k)^2 = r^2$$
$$(x + 1)^2 + (y + 1)^2 = 10^2$$
$$(x + 1)^2 + (y + 1)^2 = 100$$

47. (E)—Using Two Points to Find the Slope, Using an Equation to Find the Slope and the Intercept

100 Key Math Concepts for the ACT, #72, #73, #74. Use the points where the line crosses the axes—(–1, 0) and (0, 2)—to find the slope:

$$\text{Slope} = \frac{y_2 - y_1}{x_2 - x_1} = \frac{2 - 0}{0-(-1)} = 2$$

The *y*-intercept is 2. Now plug $m = 2$ and $b = 2$ into the slope-intercept equation form:

$$y = mx + b$$
$$y = 2x + 2$$

48. (G)—Percent Formula

100 Key Math Concepts for the ACT, #32. Be careful. The question is not asking, "What is $\frac{1}{4}$ of 16?" It's asking, "What is $\frac{1}{4}$ *percent* of 16?" One-fourth of 1 percent is 0.25%, or 0.0025:

$$\frac{1}{4}\% \text{ of } 16 = 0.0025 \times 16 = 0.04$$

49. (C)—Multiplying Binomials—FOIL

100 Key Math Concepts for the ACT, #56. Use FOIL to get rid of the parentheses, and then combine like terms:

$$(s + 4)(s - 4) + (2s + 2)(s - 2)$$
$$= (s^2 - 16) + (2s^2 - 2s - 4)$$
$$= s^2 + 2s^2 - 2s - 16 - 4$$
$$= 3s^2 - 2s - 20$$

50. (F)—Equation for a Parabola and Evaluating an Algebraic Expression

100 Key Math Concepts for the ACT, #76, #52. The easiest way to find the equation of a given parabola is to take a point or two from the graph and plug the coordinates into the answer choices, eliminating the choices that don't work. Start with a point with coordinates that are easy to work with. Here you could start with (3, 0). Plug $x = 3$ and $y = 0$ into each answer choice and you'll find that only F works.

51. (C)—Sine, Cosine, and Tangent of Acute Angles

100 Key Math Concepts for the ACT, #96. Since $\sin a = \frac{4}{5}$, you could think of this as a 3-4-5 triangle:

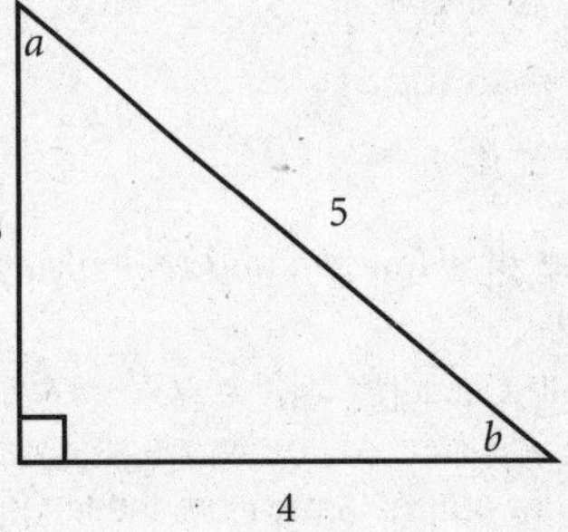

Cosine is "adjacent over hypotenuse." Here the leg adjacent to *b* is 4, and the hypotenuse is 5, so $\cos b = \frac{4}{5}$. (Notice that the sine of one acute angle in a right triangle is equal to the cosine of the other acute angle.)

52. (F)—Adding and Subtracting Monomials, Simplifying an Algebraic Fraction

100 Key Math Concepts for the ACT, #53, #62. Add the like terms in the numerator and then divide by the denominator:

$$\frac{x^2 + x^2 + x^2}{x} = \frac{3x^2}{x} = 3x$$

If you weren't careful, you might have confused this with problem 38 and missed the change in the denominator.

53. (B)—Translating from English into Algebra

100 Key Math Concepts for the ACT, #65. When you divide w by 4, you get $\frac{w}{4}$. When you subtract that result from r, you get $r - \frac{w}{4}$.

54. (J)—Volume of Other Solids

100 Key Math Concepts for the ACT, #95. The formula for the volume of a cylinder is $V = \pi r^2h$, where r is the radius of the circular base and h is the height. Here $r = 4$ and $a = 5$, so:

$$\begin{aligned} \text{Volume} &= \pi r^2h \\ &= \pi(4)^2(5) \\ &= \pi(16)(5) \\ &= 80\pi \end{aligned}$$

55. (E)—Area of a Triangle and Multiplying Binomials—FOIL

100 Key Math Concepts for the ACT, #83, #56. With a right triangle you can use the two legs as the base and the height to figure out the area. Here the leg lengths are expressed algebraically. Just plug the two expressions in for b and h in the triangle area formula:

$$\text{Area} = \frac{1}{2}(x - 1)(x + 1) = \frac{1}{2}(x^2 - 1) = \frac{x^2 - 1}{2}$$

56. (G)—Rate

100 Key Math Concepts for the ACT, #39. The difference between the populations in 1990 was 9,400 – 7,600 = 1,800. Each year, as the larger population goes down by 100 and the smaller population goes up by 100, the difference decreases by 200. Thus it will take 1,800 ÷ 200 = 9 years to erase the difference.

57. (B)—Miscellaneous Averages: Weighted Average

The overall average is not simply the average of the two average ages. Because there are a lot more women than men, women carry more weight, and the overall average will be closer to 25 than 35. Pick particular numbers for the females and males, say 4 females and 1 male. The ages of the 4 females total 4 times 25, or 100, and the age of the 1 male totals 35. The average, then, is (100 + 35) divided by 5, or 27.

58. (J)—Sine, Cosine, and Tangent of Acute Angles and Pythagorean Theorem

100 Key Math Concepts for the ACT, #96, #84. The height h of the tree is the leg opposite θ. The distance b from the base of the tree is the leg adjacent to θ. "Opposite over adjacent" is tangent, but all the answer choices are in terms of the sine. Sine is "opposite over hypotenuse," so you're going to have to figure out the hypotenuse. Use the Pythagorean theorem:

$$\begin{aligned} (\text{hypotenuse})^2 &= (\text{leg}_1)^2 + (\text{leg}_2)^2 \\ (\text{hypotenuse})^2 &= b^2 + h^2 \\ \text{hypotenuse} &= \sqrt{b^2 + h^2} \end{aligned}$$

Now, to get the sine, put the opposite h over the hypotenuse $\sqrt{b^2 + h^2}$: $\sin\theta = \frac{h}{\sqrt{b^2 + h^2}}$

59. (C)—Evaluating an Algebraic Expression

100 Key Math Concepts for the ACT #52. This looks like a solid geometry question, but in fact it's just a "plug-in-the-numbers" question.

$$S = \pi r\sqrt{r^2 = h^2} = \pi(3)\sqrt{3^2 + 4^2} = 3\pi\sqrt{9 + 16}$$
$$3\pi\sqrt{25} = 3\pi \times 5 = 15\pi$$

60. (J)—Parallel Lines and Transversals

100 Key Math Concepts for the ACT #79. When a transversal crosses parallel lines, all the resulting acute angles are equal and all the resulting obtuse angles are equal. You can generally tell at sight which angles are equal. In this problem's figure, $a = c = e = g$, and $b = d = f = h$. Only J is true: c and g are both obtuse. In all the other choices you'll find an obtuse and an acute.

READING TEST

Passage I

1. (D)

Lines 16–19 provide the answer: "I was brought up, from my earliest remembrance…by my godmother."

2. (G)

From the description of Dolly in the first two paragraphs, it is clear that Esther viewed her doll as her only friend. "I was such a shy little thing that I seldom dared to open my lips, and never dared to open my heart, to anybody else" (lines 6–8). This idea is repeated in lines 86–89: "I went up to my room, and crept to bed, and laid my doll's cheek against mine wet with tears, and holding that solitary friend upon my bosom, cried myself to sleep."

3. (B)

In this case, *stiff* is used to describe the tone of the letter that Esther's godmother wrote to decline the invitation to another student's birthday party. (B), "rigidly formal," is the most appropriate definition in this context.

4. (G)

Esther only *imagines* that her godmother tells her she should never have been born. "I saw in her face, looking gloomily at me, 'It would have been far better, little Esther, that you had no birthday, that you had never been born!'" (lines 66–69).

5. (C)

Although Esther's godmother says that she has forgiven Esther's mother, her facial expression directly contradicts this. "I see her knitted brow and pointed finger…her face did not relent…" (lines 78–82).

6. (G)

Esther is clearly lonely, as evidenced by her description of Dolly as her only friend and her explanation that there is a separation dividing her from the other girls at school. The birthday scene with her godmother also shows that Esther is quite confused about her own family past.

7. (C)

Her confrontation with her godmother gives Esther further reason to believe that no one loves her. The phrase before the cited line also points to (C) as the best answer: "I knew that I had brought no joy at any time to anybody's heart" (lines 90–91).

8. (J)

Answers (F), (G), and (H) are all mentioned in paragraph 5 (lines 39–52). At the end of the passage, Esther says, "I hope it is not self-indulgent to shed these tears as I think of it" (lines 98–99).

9. (C)

Esther's evidence that her godmother is a "good, good woman" is explained in lines 20–23: "She went to church three times every Sunday, and to morning prayers on Wednesdays and Fridays, and to lectures whenever there were lectures; and never missed."

10. (G)

In the first paragraph, Esther says, "Now, Dolly, I am not clever…" (line 3). In the second paragraph, Esther describes herself as "such a shy little thing" (line 6).

Passage II

11. (B)

In the phrase "the Pantanal was a vast, soggy canvas, white with gleaming herds of Nelore cattle" (lines 62–64), *canvas* is used to mean "a background." None of the other choices makes sense.

12. (J)

The answer to this question can be found in lines 68–70: "As the jaguars grew scarce, their chief food staple, the capybaras—a meter-long rodent, the world's largest—overran farmers' fields…."

13. (C)

The answer to this question can be found in lines 12–17: "Exactly how dramatic a comeback is difficult to say because jaguars—*Panthera onca*, the largest feline in the New World—are solitary, secretive, nocturnal predators. Each cat needs to prowl at least 35 square kilometers by itself."

14. (G)

The last sentence of the second paragraph provides the answer. "Hotels, campgrounds, and bed-and-breakfasts have sprung up to accommodate the half-million tourists a year…bent on sampling the Pantanal's wildlife, of which the great cats must be the most magnificent example" (lines 23–28). Tourists want to see the jaguars, and not having the jaguars might negatively affect the booming ecotourist business.

15. (A)

The "green safari" example is mentioned as a way for "scientists to fit the cats with radio collars" (lines 89–92). The other three examples provided are listed in lines 95–99 as methods the scientists are teaching the ranchers.

16. (G)

In lines 50–53, the author says, "Hard data on cattle losses due to jaguars in the Pantanal are nonexistent…." One reason for providing anecdotal information, then, is to tell the story of the hardships faced by the ranchers due to the jaguars. The author does not suggest that he empathizes with the ranchers more than the jaguars—in fact, he refers to the jaguars as "magnificent." The only example that shows rancher violence is Abel Monteiro shooting an attacking jaguar who had killed his two dogs (lines 34–36), an act of self-defense. The landscape of the Pantanal is not the focus of these two paragraphs, so (J) can be eliminated.

17. (C)

The passage explains that because of the decrease in the jaguar population, the capybara population increased. These rodents "spread trichomoniasis, a livestock disease that renders cows sterile" (lines 71–72). Lines 75–79 describe the effect of weather patterns and floods on the ranchers' land. "Weather patterns also shifted radically—due most likely to global warming—and drove annual floods to near-Biblical proportions. The waters are only now retreating from some inundated pasturelands."

18. (G)

The last sentence of the paragraph reads, "When the scholars go home and the greens log off, the *pantaneiros* will still be there—left on their own to deal with the jaguars as they see fit" (lines 102–105).

19. (D)

Evidence is given throughout the passage that all three groups support protecting the jaguars. It is most concisely stated in lines 42–45: "a political cat fight between the scientists, environmentalists, and ecotourists who want to protect the jaguars and the embattled ranchers…."

20. (F)

The answer to this question can be found in lines 50–53: "Hard data on cattle losses due to jaguars in the Pantanal are nonexistent, but there are stories."

Passage III

21. (A)

This Inference Question asks you why the aulos was considered "the instrument of the Dionysians." In the fifth paragraph, you find out that the Dionysians "represented the unbridled, sensual and passionate aspect of Greek culture" (lines 57–59). The passage also says that the aulos had a "far more exciting effect" (line 63) than the lyre. The suggestion here is clearly that the aulos must have been able to express the unbridled passion and excitement of the Dionysians, making (A) the best answer. (B) is out because the fact that the aulos was chosen as the official instrument of the Delphian and Pythian festivals doesn't explain why it was the instrument of the Dionysians. (C) contradicts the passage: the kithara, not the aulos, represented the intellectual, idealistic side of Greek art. Finally, the author never says when the Dionysian cult originated, so (D) is also out.

22. (J)

All the author means by saying that the chelys can be "traced back to the age of fable" is that it is an ancient instrument. The chelys was an actual, not an imaginary, instrument, so (H) is wrong. (G) is out because the kithara was used to accompany the epics, not the chelys.

23. (D)

(D) is the only answer choice to this Big Picture Question that adequately covers the entire passage. (A) focuses only on the lyre. The connection between Greek music and drama (B) is mentioned only in passing, as are the references to music in ancient Greek literature (C). The passage is really all about the "origin and development of various Greek instruments" (D).

24. (H)

The first thing the author says about the kithara is that it was used by professional Homeric singers. The kithara, according to the author, probably came from Egypt, so (F) is wrong. (G) and (J) contradict information in the paragraph to the effect that the kithara was more powerful than the chelys and was played with both hands.

25. (D)

Skim through the third paragraph to find the changes that occurred to the lyre between the eighth and fifth centuries B.C. Musicians began to use a plectrum in the seventh century B.C. (A), lyres featured an increasing number of strings (B) during this period, and musicians also began to use different scales and modes (C). That leaves (D). Nothing in the paragraph indicates that lyres were used to accompany dramatic productions.

26. (J)

The final paragraph says that "an early specimen" of the aulos was tuned to the chromatic tetrachord, "a fact that points to Oriental origin" (lines 74–77). From this you can infer that the chromatic tetrachord must have been used in ancient Oriental music (J). (F) is contradicted by the author's assertion that elegiac songs were composed in the mode of the chromatic tetrachord. There is no evidence to support either (G) or (H).

27. (C)

In the fourth sentence of the first paragraph (lines 7–9), the author indicates that the chelys is the most antique form of the lyre.

28. (G)

Sappho did two things that we know about from lines 39–41. She introduced a mode in which Dorian and Lydian characteristics were blended, and she initiated the use of the plectrum.

29. (B)

All of the details you need to answer this question are in the sixth paragraph (lines 60–69). The first sentence states that the aulos is more like our oboe than our flute, so Roman numeral III is false. This means (C) and (D) can be eliminated. The second sentence of the paragraph confirms that the aulos sounded more exciting than the lyre (Roman numeral II). Since (B) is the only remaining answer choice that includes II, you know it has to be the best answer.

30. (F)

Greek instruments are discussed as a whole at the very beginning of the passage. The author says that our knowledge of Greek instruments comes from "representations on monuments, vases, statues, and friezes and from the testimony of Greek authors" (lines 3–5). These are all "secondary sources" of information about the instruments, so (F) is the best answer. (G) is wrong because quite a bit is known about the tuning of the instruments, as represented in the second paragraph. (H) is contradicted by the same sentence that supports (F). Finally, there is no evidence to suggest that more is known about one type of instrument than the other (J).

Passage IV

31. (B)

Lines 15–18 state that "Scientists have not been able, however, to determine just how sunspots are created or what effect they have on the solar constant...." This is followed by the statement that the question might be answered with "data from the *Solar Maximum Mission* satellite, which has monitored the solar constant since 1980" (lines 21–23).

32. (G)

The definition of *solar constant* is given in lines 18–19: "a misnomer that refers to the sun's total radiance at any instant."

33. (B)

The second sentence of the passage says, "People have speculated that the solar cycle might exert some influence on the earth's weather" (lines 3–5). The concluding paragraph suggests that the findings discussed in the passage point to "a link between the solar cycle and weather" (lines 89–90).

34. (J)

From the sentence alone, it may be difficult to determine the answer. But the preceding sentence clarifies that *proliferated* means "increased in number." Lines 24–25 read, "As the number of sunspots decreased through 1986...."

35. (A)

The answer to this question can be found in lines 36–43: "When a sunspot appears, it initially causes the sun to dim slightly, but then after a period of weeks or months islands of brilliance called faculas usually emerge near the sunspot and more than compensate for its dimming effect. Wilson says faculas may represent regions where energy that initially was blocked beneath a sunspot has finally breached the surface."

36. (J)

The answer to this question is found in lines 48–51: "the quasi-biennial oscillation (QBO), a 180-degree shift in the direction of stratospheric winds above the Tropics that occurs about every two years."

37. (C)

The last paragraph quotes a scientist as believing that there will be "breakthroughs" in our understanding of the relationship between the solar cycle and the weather.

38. (H)

As described in the passage, the QBO changes directions every two years independently of the solar cycle. Lines 64–66 state that: "temperatures and pressures coincident with the QBO's west phase rose and fell in accordance with the solar cycle." Lines 70–72 state that: "The latitude of storms during the west phase of the QBO...varied with the solar cycle..."

39. (A)

Lines 7–9 read: "Until recently, however, none of these correlations has held up under close scrutiny." This suggests that recently they have begun to hold up under scrutiny.

40. (G)

The answer to this question can be found in lines 28–30: "The data suggest that the sun is 0.1 percent more luminous at the peak of the solar cycle, when the number of sunspots is greatest...."

SCIENCE TEST

Passage I

1. (B)

Look at the *y*-axis of the graph between the region of pH 8 and pH 12 and then scan across at that level. The indicators that undergo color change at this pH range are thymol blue, phenolphthalein, and alizarin. These indicators correspond to (B).

2. (H)

Looking carefully at the graph, you can see that methyl orange changes from red to yellow between pH 3 and pH 5, and alizarin changes from yellow to red between pH 9 and pH 11. Thymol blue undergoes a yellow to blue color change, so it is not correct.

3. (A)

In order to determine when the reaction is complete and the solution is basic, the chemist should select an indicator that turns color when the pH has risen into the region of basicity (above 7). When bromocresol green inches above the pH of 7, it turns blue, so (A) is correct.

4. (J)

This question requires you to make a broad conclusion about acid-base indicators. (F) and (G) are incorrect because there are plenty of indicators that change colors above or below pH 7. (H) is incorrect because different indicators change colors at different pH levels, which explains why (J) is correct.

5. (A)

Compare the two indicators on the graph and you'll find that phenolphthalein undergoes a color change at a higher pH than bromothymol blue.

Passage II

6. (F)

The quickest way to answer the question is to eliminate the wrong answer choices. A look at Table 1 rules out (G) because the total amount of oxygen absorbed is clearly affected by temperature. (H) is wrong because frog health is never an issue. The very mention of CO_2 makes (J) incorrect—Experiment 1 was only concerned with oxygen.

7. (C)

There is no data for 17° C, so an estimate is necessary. The total (skin plus lungs) amount of carbon dioxide released per hour was about 100 mol/hr at 15° C and about 110 mol/hr at 20° C. The only choice that falls between these is (C).

8. (H)

To show that *Hyla faber* is an ectotherm, one must find evidence demonstrating that changes in temperature cause changes in gas exchange. Table 1 demonstrates that as temperature increases, *Hyla faber*'s oxygen absorption increases, so (H) is correct. (F) is not good evidence because data for only one temperature does not give an idea of how temperature changes affect gas exchange. (G) is incorrect because the amount of carbon dioxide eliminated by the lungs is the same for 15° C, 20° C, and 25° C, which makes it look as though changes in temperature have little effect on gas exchange in the frog.

9. (B)

The amount of carbon dioxide eliminated by the skin increases over the range of temperatures; the increase levels off at the highest temperature. Carbon dioxide release by the lungs increases a bit over the lower temperatures and then levels off almost completely. The curve for skin release has to be much higher on the graph than the curve for lung release because the skin eliminated more carbon dioxide at each temperature than did the lungs. (B) is the only graph that fits these patterns.

10. (G)

When the answer choices all look similar like in this problem, find the differences between them and rule out the ones that cannot be correct. You can eliminate (H) and (J) right away because the results show that as temperature increases, O_2 absorbed by the lungs increases. (F) is not correct either—as temperature increases, CO_2 released by the skin increases, which is stated by (G).

11. (B)

Here again you want to be careful and refer to the answer choices as you review the tables to observe what happens as the temperature rises above 15° C. Since each of the answer choices refers to the tree frog's ability to absorb oxygen through the skin, start there. From Table 1 you can see that the skin's oxygen absorption rate goes down, so (C) and (D) are out. Now you need to refer to Table 2 to see what happens to the rate at which carbon dioxide is released from the lungs. It appears to remain about the same, so the correct answer is (B).

Passage III

12. (F)

A good way to approach this question would be to draw a vertical line on the graph from 100% extraction of molybdenum (Mo) to the *x*-axis. This line lands closest to the pH of 3. Therefore, (F) is correct.

13. (D)

To answer this question, you need to look at the extraction curves for both erbium and tungsten and observe how they change with pH. For tungsten, the percentage extracted decreases from 100% to 0% as the pH increases from 1 to 2. The percentage of erbium extracted increases from 0% to 100% as the pH increases from 4 to 6. There is no overlap between the two ranges. "A single-step extraction" could not remove both at the same time.

14. (J)

In the graph, there are two types of slopes: one in which the percentage of an element extracted increases as the pH increases, and one in which the percentage of an element extracted decreases with increasing pH. Since there are two types of slopes, (J) is the correct response. (F) or (G) would be correct if the question pertained to a specific element, but the question asks you to consider the graph as a whole. If the percentage of an element extracted was independent of pH, you would expect to see the same percentage extracted at every pH. In other words, the graph for each element would be a horizontal line. This is not the case, so (H) is incorrect.

15. (B)

Draw a line on the graph from 45% to the line for thulium (Tm). Then draw a vertical line from that point to the *x*-axis. You should land on the *x*-axis between 5 and 6.

16. (J)

To answer this question, refer to the extraction curve for erbium. Erbium begins to be extracted when the pH level of the organic reagent is 4 or greater, and by a pH of 6 all of it is being extracted. Ytterbium (J) does not begin to be extracted until pH reaches approximately 9.

17. (B)

Refer to extraction curves for europium and molybdenum, the first of which goes up while the second goes down. Where these curves cross is where the percentages being extracted are the same. According to the vertical scale, this point appears to be higher than 90%, so statement I is correct and (C) can be eliminated. Statement II, however, is not correct. If you drop a vertical line down from where these curves meet, you'll see that thulium and tungsten are also being extracted at this pH. By eliminating answer choices that contain II, (A) and (D), you can see that (B) has to be the correct answer even without examining statement III.

Passage IV

18. (J)

Scientist 1 states that "below 50 km, rock is under too much pressure to fracture normally." Scientist 2 gives the fact that "rock becomes ductile at the temperatures and pressures that exist at depths greater than 50 km" as the reason that "deep-focus earthquakes cannot result from normal fractures."

19. (A)

Scientist 1's theory is invalid unless water can be shown to exist in mantle rock at the level of deep-focus earthquakes. If researchers could subject mantle-like rock to those temperatures and pressures, and then extract water from it (A), their experimental results would support the hypothesis of Scientist 1.

20. (H)

Both scientists believe that the Earth's crust (surface layer) is composed of mobile tectonic plates. In describing the plates as being "forced down into the mantle," Scientist 1 implies that they are normally in the crust and Scientist 2 makes reference to "a descending tectonic plate." The introductory paragraph says that "most" earthquakes originate less than 20 km below the Earth's surface, so (F) is wrong. Neither scientist assumes that surface quakes are caused by trapped fluids (G); both state that such quakes are caused by normal fractures in the Earth's crust. Neither scientist discusses how deep-focus earthquakes are detected, so (J) is not an assumption made by either scientist.

21. (B)

Scientist 2 believes that deep-focus quakes are the result of slippage caused by phase changes. Scientist 2 would, therefore, not expect deep quakes to occur below 680 km where, according to the last sentence of the passage, "no phase changes are predicted." Recording a quake with an origin below that depth would send Scientist 2 back to the drawing board, or at least in search of deeper phase changes.

22. (J)

The final sentence of Scientist 1's paragraph mentions that when fluids were injected into the ground at the Rocky Mountain Arsenal, the unintended result was "a series of shallow-focus earthquakes." The opening words *in fact* signal that this final sentence is meant to illustrate the previous sentence, which refers to experiments in which trapped fluids caused rock to fail at lower than normal shear stresses. The implication is that the quakes at the arsenal occurred because the fluid wastes lowered the shear stress failure point of the rock, (J). Dehydration (F) and the slab of calcium magnesium silicate (G) belong in Scientist 2's paragraph. (H) confuses the Rocky Mountain Arsenal incident with the deep-sea trenches that are mentioned in the previous two sentences.

23. (C)

Scientist 2 claims that the slippage involved in deep-focus quakes results from phase changes. To support this contention, she cites laboratory work that produced similar phase changes and slippage in a slab of calcium magnesium silicate. But neither scientist says that mantle rock is composed of calcium magnesium silicate. If the slippery slab is to serve as evidence for Scientist 2's theory, it must at least be similar to mantle rock, so (C) is correct. (A) might help refute Scientist 1's viewpoint, but would not strengthen Scientist 2's theory. (B) and (D) would tend to weaken Scientist 2's theory.

Passage V

24. (H)

The one variable that changes is the amount of moisture. (G) cannot be correct because Experiment 2 says that the researcher used models equivalent to the same mass as in Experiment 1. There is no evidence for (F) or (J).

25. (B)

The moisture in Experiment 1 is 86%, and the moisture in Experiment 2 is 12%. If the moisture was changed to 50%, the collision rating would fall between the lines of the two experiments on the graphs. At 400,000 kg, the collision rating would be between 4.5 and 5.5.

26. (G)

The collision ratings for Experiment 1, with a high percentage of moisture in the atmosphere, were mostly lower than those in Experiment 2. Therefore, an increase in moisture would decrease the impact of a collision. Eliminate (H) and (J). However, for asteroids over 700,000 kg, the lines on the graph meet—the presence of moisture loses its effect. (G) is correct.

27. (C)

Feel free to draw on the graph (you can write on your test booklet during the ACT). Draw a line from 4 on the *x*-axis straight up. Draw a line from the 4 on the *y*-axis straight across. Those two lines meet on the line for Experiment 1. The moisture level for Experiment 1 was 86%, so (C) is correct.

28. (H)

Again it might help to draw on the graph to answer this question. Draw a vertical line up from 1 (100,000 kg) on the horizontal scale to see where it hits the curve representing Experiment 2. Then draw a horizontal line from this curve to the curve representing Experiment 1 and draw from that point down to the horizontal scale once again. You'll see that the size is closest to (H), 270,000 kg.

29. (B)

To be minimally capable of regional destruction, an asteroid must have a collision rating of 4, so draw a horizontal line over from 4 on the vertical scale. If you do so you'll see that size of an asteroid capable of such destruction goes from roughly 250,000 kg at a 12% moisture level to about 400,000 kg at an 86% moisture level. 400,000 is roughly 70% larger than 250,000, so (B) is the correct answer.

Passage VI

30. (H)

Following HST-52 from right to left across the first figure (because the temperature is decreasing), conductivity increases and temperature decreases —just like the conductivity of a conductor—until 160 K, at which point HST-52's conductivity starts to decrease with decreasing temperature, like a semiconductor. With decreasing temperature, the sample undergoes a conductor to semiconductor transition (H).

31. (B)

The plot for conductor-like behavior indicates that as the temperature increases, its conductivity decreases. (A) and (C) describe the behavior of semiconductors, not conductors. (D) is incorrect: if the conductivity of conductors were the same at all temperatures, the plot of conductivity vs. temperature for conductors would be a horizontal line.

32. (H)

A material that has a semiconductor to conductor transition at 10 K will show a brief increase and then, starting at 10 K, a steady decrease as the temperature increases. (H) is the plot that shows this brief increase at low temperatures and then the decrease as the temperature rises.

33. (D)

The figure shows that HST-52 displays semiconductor behavior only up to about 150 K. Therefore, HST-52 will be usable as a semiconductor only at temperatures below about 150 K (D). (A) is wrong because HST-52 is a semiconductor at certain temperatures, and (B) is wrong because HST-52 is not a semiconductor at all temperatures. The brittleness of HST-52 is never discussed in the passage, so (C) should be eliminated from the outset.

34. (J)

You are looking for the temperature at which the downward slope for Sample HST-52 is the steepest. This is somewhat difficult to determine, but this much is clear: the slope does not begin to go down until the temperature rises above 160 K. Thus the only answer that could make sense is (J), 180 K.

35. (B)

Again you are looking for where the downward slope is the steepest, only here you're looking for a range of temperatures. The plot for Sample HST-72 is fairly flat until the temperature rises above 60 K, then it declines at a fairly good pace until about 160 K, at which point it becomes fairly flat again until about 230 K. The only answer choice that covers the range of fairly steep decline is (B), between 80 and 120 K.

Passage VII

36. (G)

The key to this question is determining whether the cat in question is an outdoor or indoor cat. This cat goes outdoors a total of three hours per week, whereas an outdoor cat would spend at least six hours outdoors per week. Therefore, this cat is an indoor cat, and the percentage of dark fur on its body would remain just above 10%.

37. (B)

You can draw a line from 45% dark fur across to the solid line representing outdoor cats. If you draw a line from that intersection straight down to the *x*-axis, you will hit 3° C.

38. (G)

If the cat grew dark fur over 30% of its body, it must have been an "outdoor" cat as defined in the passage, and, according to the table, been exposed to temperature below 5° C (Statement I). To be an outdoor cat, a cat does not have to spend more time outdoors than indoors (Statement II) but it has to spend time outdoors for 6 consecutive days (Statement III).

39. (C)

If a Siamese cat does not have dark fur over more than 10% of its body, then it must *either* be an indoor cat *or* live in an area where it is not regularly exposed to temperatures below 7° C.

40. (H)

Choice (F) is wrong because the "indoor" cats will not help us, since they don't go outside. (G) is not a good choice because the "outdoor" cats of the original experiment cannot be used as a control group: The time they spent outside was not monitored—we only know that they spent more than one hour outside a day. (J) is incorrect because the data already gathered only showed that outdoor cats turn darker in cold weather than indoor cats and doesn't provide any data about how varying the amount of time outdoors affects fur color. The correct answer is (H): a completely new experiment would have to be set up.

WRITING TEST

Model Essay

Below is an example of what a high-scoring essay might look like. Notice the author states her position clearly in the introductory paragraph and supports that position with evidence in the following paragraphs.. This essay also uses transitions, some advanced vocabulary, and an effective "hook" to draw in the reader.

While some people believe academics and athletics are not related, I think it is important to hold student athletes responsible for earning a minimum grade point average. We live in a sports-obsessed world, where professional athletes receive multi-million dollar contracts and where highly paid athletes are becoming younger and younger. For example, LeBron James, still in high school, obtained a lucrative endorsement deal with Nike and was a highly sought-after NBA draft pick. Sadly, when teams are recruiting young athletes, the last thing they often look at is grades. It is also unfortunate that, feeling the pressure from alumni and fans to have successful teams, schools are often willing to overlook poor grades in their high-performing athletes. With so much money and fame at stake, and with so many institutions turning a blind eye, is it any wonder that many young athletes will sacrifice anything to get ahead, even their academic performance? Requiring student athletes to maintain a minimum grade point average is important for several reasons.

As an educational institution, a school's number-one priority should be the education of its students. The school does its student athletes a disservice when it doesn't push them to do their best at academics and learn as much as they can. It is unfair to hold other students, who may not be lucky enough to have the same natural athletic abilities, to a higher academic standard than athletes, and devalues any effort they make to get good grades by showing them in effect that what really matters in life is how good you are at sports. Also, since sports place so many demands on students' time and energy, what incentive do athletes have to take the extra time to keep up with schoolwork if they aren't required to do so?

When a school does not require student athletes to achieve a specified grade point average, it sets them up for failure later in life. The hard truth is that there are not enough jobs in professional sports for every student athlete. If students don't get drafted to play sports once they finish school, or if they do get chosen and then get injured and can no longer play the sport as well or at all, they only will have their grades and grade point average to show for their time in school. If their grades aren't good, they will have difficulty finding a job and starting a new career.

I am not trying to say that high-school sports are bad, or that they don't offer benefits to students involved in them. Not only do those students get in shape, but they also get to be on a team and feel like a part of something important. I think, however, that when schools treat academics as secondary they are taking the focus off all the positive things students get by participating in sports. When students think their athletic performance is their best chance for a post-high school career, they no longer think about accomplishments like learning discipline and improving self-esteem. They only focus on winning at all costs. Schools encourage this by making athletic performance more important than academics. If students know that they have a high enough grade point average to succeed if their sport doesn't become their career, maybe sports can go back to being fun again.

Participating in sports is a great thing for students to do. It builds self-confidence, fosters school spirit, and teaches determination. However, high schoolers should be students first. Requiring student athletes to maintain a certain grade point average would ensure that students get the education they need whether or not they go on to play professional sports. Schools' number-one priority should be making sure that all of their students, whether they are athletes or not, have the education required to succeed in life.

You can evaluate your essay and the model essay based on the following criteria, covered in chapter 16.

- Does the author answer the question?
- Is the author's position clearly stated?
- Does the body of the essay support and develop the position taken?
- Are there at least three supporting paragraphs?
- Is the relevance of each supporting paragraph clear?
- Is the essay a reasonable length?
- Is the essay organized, with a clear introduction, middle, and end?
- Did the author use one paragraph for each new idea?
- Is each sentence in a paragraph relevant to the point made in that paragraph?
- Are transitions clear?
- Is the essay easy to read? Is it engaging?
- Are sentences varied?
- Is vocabulary used effectively? Is college-level vocabulary used?

Compute Your Score

1 **Figure out your score in each section.** Refer to the answer keys to figure out the number right in each test section. Enter the results below:

Raw Scores		TEST 1	TEST 2		TEST 1	TEST 2
	English:			Reading:		
	Math:			Science:		

2 **Find your practice test scores.** Find your raw score on each section in the table below. The score in the far left column indicates your estimated scaled score if this were an actual ACT.

SCALED SCORE	RAW SCORES			
	Test 1 English	Test 2 Mathematics	Test 3 Reading	Test 4 Science
36	75	60	40	40
35	74	60	40	40
34	73	59	39	39
33	72	58	39	39
32	71	57	38	38
31	70	55–56	37	37
30	69	53–54	36	36
29	68	50–52	35	35
28	67	48–49	34	34
27	65–66	45–47	33	33
26	63–64	43–44	32	32
25	61–62	40–42	31	30–31
24	58–60	38–39	30	28–29
23	56–57	35–37	29	26–27
22	53–55	33–34	28	24–25
21	49–52	31–32	27	21–23
20	46–48	28–30	25–26	19–20
19	44–45	26–27	23–24	17–18
18	41–43	23–25	21–22	16
17	39–40	20–22	19–20	15
16	36–38	17–19	17–18	14
15	34–35	15–16	15–16	13
14	30–33	13–14	13–14	12
13	28–29	11–12	12–13	11
12	25–27	9–10	10–11	10
11	23–24	8	9	9
10	20–22	7	8	8
9	17–19	6	7	7
8	14–16	5	6	6
7	12–13	4	5	5
6	9–11	3	4	4
5	7–8	2	3	3
4	4–6	1	2	2
3	3	1	1	1
2	2	0	0	0
1	1	0	0	0

Test Prep and Admissions

Scaled Scores

	TEST 1	TEST 2
English:		
Math:		
Reading:		
Science:		

3 **Find your estimated composite score.** To calculate your estimated composite score, simply add together your scaled scores on each subsection and divide by four.

	TEST 1	TEST 2
Composite Score:		

English Review for the ACT

PUNCTUATION REVIEW

Commas

1. Use Commas to Separate Items in a Series

If more than two items are listed in a series, they should be separated by commas. The final comma—the one that precedes the word "and"—may be omitted. An omitted final comma would not be considered an error on the ACT.

> Example: My recipe for buttermilk biscuits includes flour, baking soda, salt, shortening, and buttermilk.

> ALSO RIGHT: My recipe for buttermilk biscuits includes flour, baking soda, salt, shortening and buttermilk.

Be watchful for commas placed **before** the first element of a series or **after** the last element.

> WRONG: My recipe for chocolate cake includes, flour, baking soda, sugar, eggs, milk and chocolate.

> WRONG: Flour, baking soda, sugar, eggs, milk and chocolate, are the ingredients in my chocolate cake.

2. Use Commas to Separate Two or More Adjectives before a Noun

Example: I can't believe you sat through that long, dull movie three times in a row.

> It is incorrect to place a comma after the last adjective in a series.

> WRONG: The manatee is a blubbery, bewhiskered, creature.

3. Use Commas to Set Off Parenthetical Clauses and Phrases

If a phrase or clause is not necessary to the main idea expressed by a sentence, it should be set off by commas.

> Example: Phillip, who never had any formal chef's training, bakes excellent cheesecake.

The main idea here is that Phillip bakes an excellent cheesecake. The intervening clause merely serves to further identify Phillip; it should therefore be enclosed in commas.

4. Use Commas after Introductory Phrases

> Example: Having watered his petunias every day during the drought, Harold was disappointed when his garden was destroyed by aphids.

> Example: After the banquet, Harold and Melissa went dancing.

5. Use Commas to Separate Independent Clauses

Use a comma before a conjunction (*and, but, nor, yet,* etcetera) that connects two independent clauses.

> Example: Marta is good at basketball, but she's better at soccer.

Semicolons

Like commas, semicolons can be used to separate independent clauses. As we saw above, two related independent clauses that are connected by a conjunction such as *and, but, nor,* or *yet* should be punctuated by a comma. If the words *and, but, nor,* or *yet* aren't used, the clauses should be separated by a semicolon.

Example: Whooping cranes are an endangered species; there are only fifty of them alive today.

Example: Whooping cranes are an endangered species, and they are unlikely to survive if we continue to pollute their habitat.

Semicolons may also be used between independent clauses connected by words like *therefore, nevertheless*, and *moreover.* For more on this topic, see the section on "Sentence Structure" in this chapter.

Colons

In Standard Written English, the colon is used only as a means of signaling that what follows is a list, definition, explanation, or restatement of what has gone before. A word or phrase such as *like the following, as follows, namely*, or *this* is often used along with the colon to make it clear that a list, summary, or explanation is coming up.

Example: This is what I found in her refrigerator: a moldy lime and a jar of peanut butter.

Example: Your instructions are as follows: Read the passage carefully, answer the questions, and turn over your answer sheet.

The Dash

The dash has two uses. One is to indicate an abrupt break in thought.

Example: The alligator, unlike the crocodile, will usually not attack humans—unless, that is, she feels that her young are in danger.

The dash can also be used to set off a parenthetical expression from the rest of the sentence.

Example: At 32° Fahrenheit—which is zero on the Celsius scale—water will freeze.

The Apostrophe

The apostrophe has two distinct functions. It is used with contracted verb forms to indicate that one or more letters have been eliminated:

Example: The **boy's** an expert at chess. (The boy is an expert at chess.)

Example: The **boy's** left for the day. (The boy has left for the day.)

The apostrophe is also used to indicate the possessive form of a noun.

Example: The **boy's** face was covered with mosquito bites after a day in the swamp.

GRAMMAR REVIEW

Subject-Verb Agreement

The form of a verb must match, or agree with, its subject in two ways: person and number.

1. Agreement of Person

When we talk about person, we're talking about whether the subject and verb of a sentence show that the author is making a statement about himself (first person), about the person he is speaking to (second person), or about some other person, place, or thing (third person).

- First Person Subjects: I, we.

  Example: I am going to Paris. We are going to Rome.
- Second Person Subject: you.

  Example: Are you sure you weren't imagining that flying saucer?
- Third Person Subjects: he, she, they, it, and names of people, places and things.

  Example: He is driving me crazy.

2. Agreement of Number

When we talk about number, we're talking about whether the subject and verb show that one thing is being discussed (singular) or that more than one thing is being discussed (plural). Subjects and verbs must agree in number. Subjects and verbs that don't agree in number appear very frequently on the ACT.

WRONG: The **children catches** the school bus every morning.

RIGHT: The **children catch** the school bus every morning.

Be especially careful of subject-verb agreement when the subject and verb are separated by a long string of words.

WRONG: **Wild animals** in jungles all over the world is endangered.

RIGHT: **Wild animals** in jungles all over the world **are** endangered.

Pronouns

A pronoun is a word that is used in place of a noun. The antecedent of a pronoun is the word to which the pronoun refers.

Example: Mary (ANTECEDENT) was late for work because she (PRONOUN) forgot to set the alarm.

Occasionally, an antecedent will appear in a sentence after the pronoun.

Example: Because he (PRONOUN) sneezes so often, Arthur (ANTECEDENT) always thinks he (PRONOUN) might have the flu.

1. Pronouns and Agreement

In clear, grammatical writing, a pronoun must clearly refer to and agree with its antecedent.

Number agreement of pronouns is more frequently tested on the ACT than person agreement, although you may see a question that tests person agreement.

Number and Person

	Singular	Plural
First Person	I, me my, mine	we, us our, ours
Second Person	you your, yours	you your, yours
Third Person	he, him she, her it one his her, hers its one's	they, them their, theirs

Number Agreement

Pronouns must agree in number with their antecedents. A singular pronoun should stand in for a singular antecedent. A plural pronoun should stand in for a plural antecedent. Here's a typical ACT pronoun error.

WRONG: The bank turned Harry down when he applied for a loan because **their** credit department discovered that he didn't have a job.

What does the plural possessive *their* refer to? The singular noun *bank*. The singular possessive *its* is what we need here.

RIGHT: The bank turned Harry down for a loan because **its** credit department discovered that he didn't have a job.

Person Agreement

Pronouns must agree with their antecedents in person too. A first-person pronoun should stand in for a first-person antecedent, and so on. One more thing to remember about *which* pronoun to use with which antecedent: Never use the relative pronoun *which* to refer to a human being. Use *who* or *whom* or *that.*

WRONG: The woman **which** is standing at the piano is my sister.

RIGHT: The woman **who** is standing at the piano is my sister.

2. Pronouns and Case

A more subtle type of pronoun problem is one in which the pronoun is in the wrong case. Look at the following chart:

	Case	
	Subjective	Objective
First Person	I we	me us
Second Person	you	you
Third Person	he she it they one	him her it them one
Relative Pronouns	who that which	whom that which

When to Use Subjective Case Pronouns

- Use the subjective case for the subject of a sentence.

Example: **She** is falling asleep.

WRONG: Nancy, Claire, and **me** are going to the ballet.

RIGHT: Nancy, Claire, and **I** are going to the ballet.

- Use the subjective case after a linking verb like *to be*.

Example: It is **I**.

- Use the subjective case in comparisons between the subject of verbs that are not stated, but understood.

Example: Gary is taller than **they** (are).

When to Use Objective Case Pronouns

- Use the objective case for the object of a verb.

Example: I called **her**.

- Use the objective case for the object of a preposition.

Example: I laughed at **him**.

- Use the objective case after gerunds and infinitives.

Example: Asking **him** to go was a big mistake.

Example: To give **him** the scare of his life, we all jumped out of his closet.

- Use the objective case in comparisons between objects of verbs that are not stated but understood.

Example: She calls you more than (she calls) **me**.

3. Who and Whom

Another thing you'll need to know is when to use the relative pronoun *who* (subjective case) and when to use the relative pronoun *whom* (objective case: *whom* goes with *him* and *them*). The following method is very helpful when you're deciding which one to use.

Example: Sylvester, (*who* or *whom*?) is afraid of the dark, sleeps with a Donald Duck night-light on.

- Look only at the relative pronoun in its clause. Ignore the rest of the sentence.

(Who or whom?) is afraid of the dark.

- Turn the clause into a question. Ask yourself:

Who or whom is afraid of the dark?

- Answer the question with an ordinary personal pronoun.

He is.

- If you've answered the question with a subjective case pronoun (as you have here), you need the subjective case *who* in the relative clause.

Sylvester, **who** is afraid of the dark, sleeps with a Donald Duck night-light on.

If you answer the question with an objective case pronoun, you need the objective case *whom* in the relative clause.

Try answering the question with *he* or *him*. *Who* goes with *he* (subjective case) and *whom* goes with *him* (objective case).

Sentence Structure

A sentence is a group of words that can stand alone because it expresses a complete thought. To express a complete thought, it must contain a subject, about which something is said, and a verb, which says something about the subject.

Example: Dogs bark.

Example: The explorers slept in yak-hide tents.

Example: Looking out of the window, John saw a flying saucer.

Every sentence consists of at least one clause. Many sentences contain more than one clause (and phrases, too).

A **clause** is a group of words that contains a subject and a verb. "Dogs bark," "The explorers slept in a yak-hide tent," and "John saw a flying saucer" are all clauses.

A **phrase** is a group of words that does not have both a subject and a verb.

Looking out of the window is a phrase.

1. Sentence Fragments

On the ACT, some of those innocent-looking groups of words beginning with capital letters and ending with periods are only masquerading as sentences. In reality, they're sentence fragments.

A sentence fragment is a group of words that seems to be a sentence but which is *grammatically* incomplete because it lacks a subject or a verb, **or** which is *logically* incomplete because other elements necessary for it to express a complete thought are missing.

WRONG: Eggs and fresh vegetables on sale at the farmers' market.

This is not a complete sentence because there's no verb to say something about the subject, *eggs and fresh vegetables*.

WRONG: Because Richard likes hippopotamuses.

Even though this contains a subject (Richard) and a verb (likes), it's not a complete sentence because it doesn't express a complete thought. We don't know what's true "*because* Richard likes hippopotamuses."

WRONG: Martha dreams about dinosaurs although.

This isn't a complete sentence because it doesn't express a complete thought. What makes Martha's dreaming about dinosaurs in need of qualification or explanation?

2. Run-On Sentences

Just as unacceptable as an incomplete sentence is a "too-complete" sentence, a run-on sentence.

A run-on sentence is actually two complete sentences stuck together either with just a comma or with no punctuation at all.

WRONG: The children had been playing in the park, they were covered with mud.

WRONG: The children had been playing in the park they were covered with mud.

There are a number of ways to fix this kind of problem. They all involve a punctuation mark or a connecting word that can properly connect two clauses.

- Join the clauses with a semicolon.

RIGHT: The children had been playing in the park; they were covered with mud.

- Join the clauses with a coordinating conjunction and a comma.

RIGHT: The children had been playing in the park, and they were covered with mud.

(Coordinating Conjunctions: *and, but, for, nor, or, so, yet*)

- Join the clauses with a subordinating conjunction.

  RIGHT: Because the children had been playing in the park, they were covered with mud.

OR

RIGHT: The children were covered with mud because they had been playing in the park.

(Subordinating Conjunctions: *after, although, if, since, while*)

- And, of course, the two halves of a run-on sentence can be written as two separate, complete sentences.

RIGHT: The children had been playing in the park. They were covered with mud.

Verbs

On the ACT you'll find items that are wrong because a verb is in the wrong tense. To spot this kind of problem, you need to be familiar both with the way each tense is used and with the ways the tenses are used together. English has six tenses, and each has a simple form and a progressive form.

	Simple	Progressive
PRESENT	I work	I am working
PAST	I worked	I was working
FUTURE	I will work	I will be working
PRESENT PERFECT	I have worked	I have been working
PAST PERFECT	I had worked	I had been working
FUTURE PERFECT	I will have worked	I will have been working

1. Using the Present Tense

Use the present tense to describe a state or action occurring in the present time.

Example: I **am** a student.

Example: They **are studying** the Holy Roman Empire.

Use the present tense to describe habitual action.

Example: They **eat** at Joe's Diner every night.

Example: My father never **drinks** coffee.

Use the present tense to describe things that are always true.

Example: The earth **is** round.

Example: Grass **is** green.

2. Using the Past Tense

Use the simple past tense to describe an event or state that took place at a specific time in the past and is now over and done with.

Example: Norman **broke** his toe when he tripped over his son's tricycle.

3. Using the Future Tense

Use the future tense for actions expected in the future.

Example: I **will call** you on Wednesday.

We often express future actions with the expression *to be going to:*

Example: I **am going to move** to another apartment soon.

4. Using the Present Perfect Tense

Use the present perfect tense for actions and states that started in the past and continue up to and into the present time.

Example: I **have been living** here for the last two years.

Use the present perfect for actions and states that happened a number of times in the past and may happen again in the future.

Example: I **have heard** that song several times on the radio.

Use the present perfect for something that happened at an unspecified time in the past.

Example: Anna **has seen** that movie already.

5. Using the Past Perfect Tense

The past perfect tense is used to represent past actions or states that were completed before other past actions or states. The more recent past event is expressed in the simple past, and the earlier past event is expressed in the past perfect.

Example: When I turned my computer on this morning, I realized that I **had exited** the program yesterday without saving my work.

6. Using the Future Perfect Tense

Use the future perfect tense for a future state or event that will take place before another future event.

Example: By the end of the week, I **will have worked** four hours of overtime.

Adjectives and Adverbs

On the ACT, you may find an occasional item that's wrong because it uses an adjective where an adverb is called for, or vice versa.

An adjective modifies, or describes, a noun or pronoun.

Example: A woman in a **white** dress stood next to the **old** tree.

Example: The boat, **leaky** and **dirty**, hadn't been used in years.

An adverb modifies a verb, an adjective, or another adverb. Most, but not all, adverbs end in *-ly*. (Don't forget that some **adjectives**—*friendly, lovely*—also end in *-ly*.)

Example: The interviewer looked *approvingly* at the *neatly* dressed applicant.

STYLE REVIEW

Pronouns and Reference

When we talk about pronouns and their antecedents, we say pronouns refer to or refer back to their antecedents. We talked earlier about pronouns that didn't agree in person or number with their antecedents. But a different kind of pronoun reference problem exists when a pronoun either doesn't refer to any antecedent at all or doesn't refer clearly to one, and only one, antecedent.

Sometimes an incorrectly used pronoun has no antecedent.

POOR: Joe doesn't like what **they play** on this radio station.

Who are they? We can't tell, because there is no antecedent for *they*. On the ACT, this sort of usage is an error.

RIGHT: Joe doesn't like what **the disc jockeys play** on this radio station.

Don't use pronouns without antecedents when doing so makes a sentence unclear. Sometimes a pronoun seems to have an antecedent until you look closely and see that the word that appears to be the antecedent is not a noun, but an adjective, a possessive form, or a verb. The antecedent of a pronoun must be a noun.

WRONG: When you are painting, make sure you don't get **it** on the floor.

RIGHT: When you are painting, make sure you don't get **paint** on the floor.

Other examples of pronoun reference problems:

WRONG: I've always been interested in astronomy and finally have decided to become **one**.

RIGHT: I've always been interested in astronomy and finally have decided to become an **astronomer**.

Don't use pronouns with remote references. A pronoun that is too far away from what it refers to is said to have a remote antecedent.

WRONG: Jane quit smoking and, as a result, temporarily put on a lot of weight. **It** was very bad for her health.

RIGHT: Jane quit smoking because **it** was very bad for her health, and, as a result, she temporarily gained a lot of weight.

Don't use pronouns with faulty broad reference. A pronoun with broad reference is one that refers to a whole idea instead of to a single noun.

WRONG: He built a fence to stop people from looking into his backyard. **That's** not easy.

RIGHT: He built a fence to stop people from looking into his backyard. The fence was not easy **to build**.

Redundancy

This type of style error is frequently tested on the ACT. Words or phrases are redundant when they have basically the same meaning as something already stated in the sentence. Don't use two phrases when one is sufficient.

WRONG: The school was **established and founded** in 1906.

RIGHT: The school was **established** in 1906.

Relevance

Irrelevant asides, even when set off in parentheses, are to be avoided on the ACT. Everything in the sentence should serve to get across the point in question. Something unrelated to that point should be cut.

POOR: No one can say for sure just how successful the new law will be in the fight against crime (just as no one can be sure whether he or she will ever be a victim of a crime).

BETTER: No one can say for sure just how successful the new law will be in the fight against crime.

Verbosity

Sometimes having extra words in a sentence results in a style problem. Conciseness is something that is valued on the ACT.

WORDY: The supply of **musical instruments that are antique** is limited, so they become more valuable each year.

BETTER: The supply of **antique musical instruments** is limited, so they become more valuable each year.

WORDY: We **were in agreement with each other** that Max was an unsuspecting old fool.

BETTER: We **agreed** that Max was an unsuspecting old fool.

Commonly Misused Words

Among/Between

In most cases, you should use *between* for two items and *among* for more than two.

Example: The competition **between** Anne and Michael has grown more intense.

Example: He is always at his best **among** strangers.

But use common sense. Sometimes *among* is not appropriate.

Example: Plant the trees in the area **between** the road, the wall, and the fence.

Amount/Number

Amount should be used to refer to an uncountable quantity. *Number* should refer to a countable quantity.

Example: The **amount** of food he threw away would feed a substantial **number** of people.

As/Like

Like is a preposition; it takes a noun object. *As*, when functioning as a conjunction, introduces a subordinate clause. Remember, a clause is a part of a sentence containing a subject and verb.

Example: He sings **like** an angel.

Example: He sings **as** an angel sings.

As . . . As . . .

The idiom is *as . . . as . . .*, **not** *as . . . than . . .*

WRONG: That suit is **as** expensive **than** this one.

RIGHT: That suit is **as** expensive **as** this one.

Fewer/Less

Use *fewer* before a plural noun; use *less* before a singular one.

Example: There are **fewer** apples on this tree than there were last year.

Example: He makes **less** money than she does.

Neither . . . Nor . . .

The correlative conjunction is *neither . . . nor . . .*, **not** *neither . . . or . . .*

Example: He is *neither* strong *nor* flexible.

Avoid the redundancy caused by using *nor* following a negative.

WRONG: Alice's departure was **not** noticed by Debby **nor** Sue.

RIGHT: Alice's departure was **not** noticed by Debby **or** Sue.

Its/It's

Many people confuse *its* and *it's*. *Its* is possessive; *It's* is a contraction of *it is*:

Example: The cat licked **its** paws.

Example: **It's** raining cats and dogs.

Their/They're/There

Many people confuse *their*, *there*, and *they're*. *Their* is possessive; *they're* is a contraction of *they are*:

Example: The girls rode **their** bikes home.

Example: **They're** training for the big race.

There has two uses: It can indicate place and it can be used as an expletive—a word that doesn't do anything in a sentence except delay the subject.

Example: Put the book over **there**.

Example: **There** will be fifteen runners competing for the prize.

Math Glossary

ABSOLUTE VALUE—the magnitude of a number, irrespective of its sign. Written as a number inside vertical lines: $|3|=3$ and $|-3|=3$.

ACUTE ANGLE—an angle measuring less than 90°. *A triangle with three acute angles is called an acute triangle.*

ADJACENT ANGLES—two angles having a common side and a common vertex.

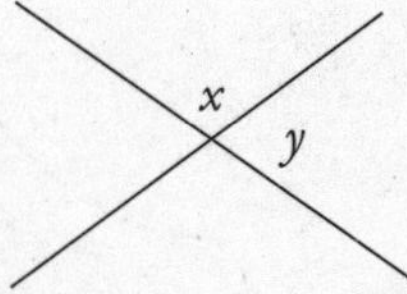

In the figure above, angles x and y are adjacent. (They are also supplementary.)

ALGEBRAIC EXPRESSION—one or more algebraic terms connected with plus and minus signs. *An algebraic expression is not an equation because it has no equal sign.*

ALTITUDE—a perpendicular segment whose length can be used in calculating the area of a triangle or other polygon.

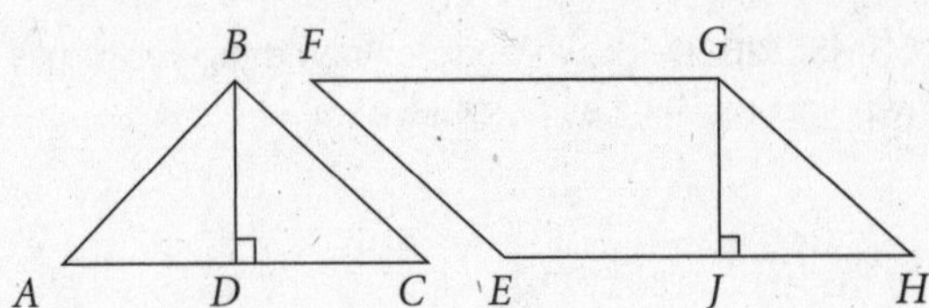

In the figure above, $\overline{BD}$ is an altitude of ΔABC, and $\overline{GJ}$ is an altitude of parallelogram EFGH.

ANGLE—two line segments coming together at a point called the vertex.

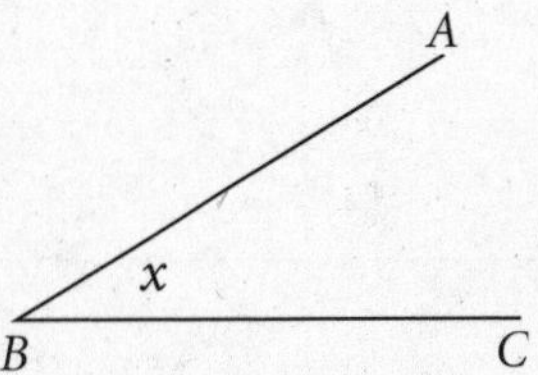

The angle above could be called $\angle ABC$, $\angle B$, or $\angle x$.

ARC—a portion of the circumference of a circle.

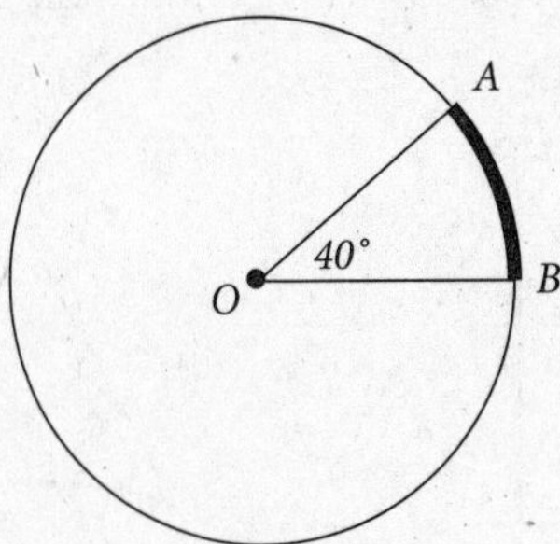

Because the central angle is $\frac{1}{9}$ of a full circle's 360°, the length of minor arc AB is $\frac{1}{9}$ the circumference.

AREA—a measure, in square units, of the size of a region in a plane. *Finding the area of a figure invariably involves multiplying two dimensions, such as length and width, or base and height.*

AVERAGE—the sum of a group of numbers divided by the number of numbers in the group. To find the average of 2, 7, and 15, divide the sum (2 + 7 + 15 = 24) by the number of numbers (3): 24 ÷ 3 = 8.

AVERAGE RATE—Average *A* per *B* = $\frac{\text{Total } A}{\text{Total } B}$. Average speed = $\frac{\text{Total distance}}{\text{Total time}}$. *To get the average speed, don't just average the speeds.*

AXES—the perpendicular "number lines" in the coordinate plane.

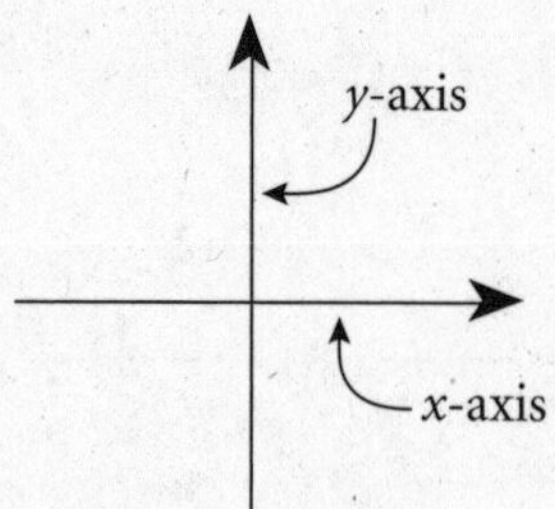

BASE—a side of a polygon that will be used with an altitude in calculating the area; a face of a solid, the area of which will be used with an altitude in calculating the volume.

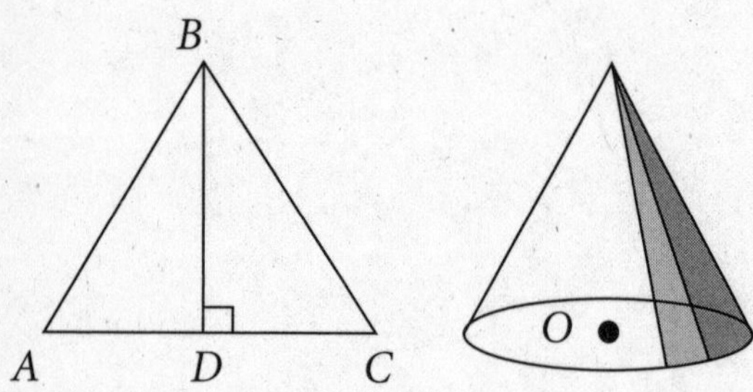

In the figure above, $\overline{AC}$ is the base of the triangle, and circle O is the base of the cone.

BINOMIAL—an algebraic expression with two terms. *The FOIL method of multiplying works only for a pair of binomials.*

BISECTOR—a line or line segment that divides an angle in half. *The bisector of a 90° angle divides it into two 45° angles.*

CENTRAL ANGLE—an angle formed by two radii of a circle.

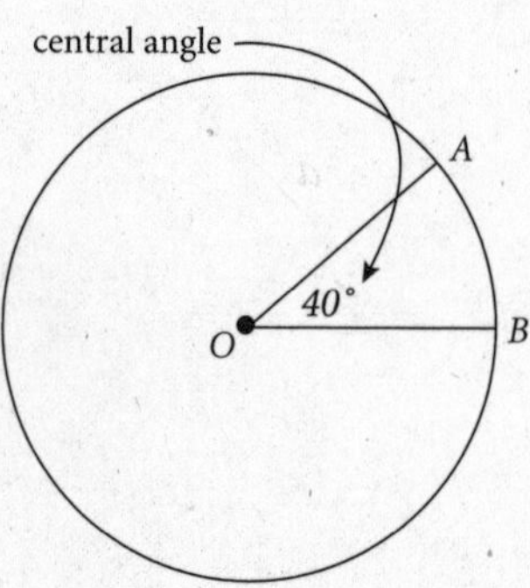

In the figure above, ∠*AOB* is a central angle.

CHORD—a line segment connecting two points on a circle.

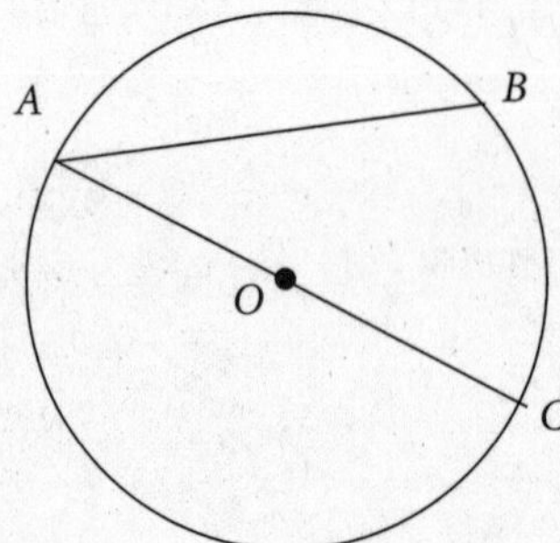

In the figure above, $\overline{AB}$ and $\overline{AC}$ are chords of circle O. Because it passes through the center, $\overline{AC}$ is also a diameter.

CIRCLE—the set of points in a plane at a particular distance from a central point. *A circle is not a polygon because it is not made up of straight sides.*

CIRCUMFERENCE—the distance around a circle. *The circumference of a circle is analogous to the perimeter of a polygon.*

CIRCUMSCRIBED—drawn outside another figure with as many points touching as possible.

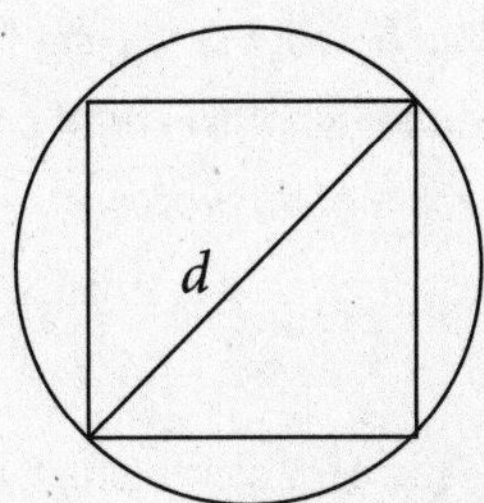

In the figure above, the circle is circumscribed about the square; d is both a diagonal of the square and a diameter of the circle.

COEFFICIENT—the numerical or "constant" part of an algebraic term. *In the monomial $-4x^2y$, the coefficient is –4. In the expression $ax^2 + bx + c$, a, b, and c are the coefficients.*

COMMON DENOMINATOR—a number that can be used as the denominator for two or more fractions so that they can be added or subtracted. *Before you can add the fractions $\frac{5}{6}$ and $\frac{5}{8}$, you first re-express them with a common denominator, such as 24:* $\frac{5}{6} = \frac{20}{24}$ and $\frac{5}{8} = \frac{15}{24}$.

COMMON FACTOR—a factor shared by two integers. *Any two integers will have at least 1 for a common factor.*

COMMON MULTIPLE—a multiple shared by two integers. *You can always get a common multiple for two integers by multiplying them, though that will not necessarily be the least common multiple.*

COMPLEMENTARY ANGLES—two angles whose measures add up to 90°. *A 30° angle and a 60° angle are complementary.*

CONE—a solid with a circle at one end and a single point at the other.

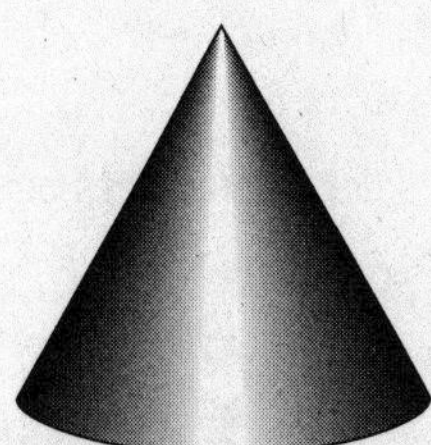

CONGRUENT—identical; of the same size and shape. *Congruent polygons have the same angles and side lengths.*

CONSECUTIVE—one after another, in order, without skipping any. *The numbers 6, 9, 12, 15, 18, and 21 are consecutive multiples of 3.*

COORDINATES—the pair of numbers, written inside parentheses, that specifies the location of a point in the coordinate plane. *The first number is the x-coordinate and the second number is the y-coordinate.*

COSECANT—the ratio of the hypotenuse to the opposite leg. *The cosecant of ∠A in the figure below is* $\frac{\text{hypotenuse}}{\text{opposite}} = \frac{13}{5}$.

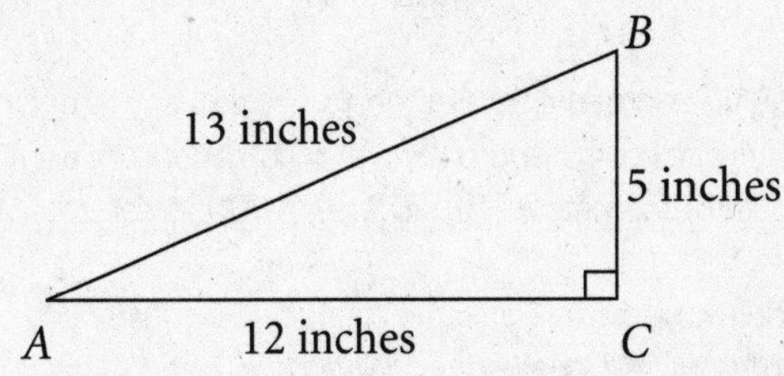

COSINE—the ratio of the adjacent leg to the hypotenuse. *The cosine of ∠A in the figure above is* $\frac{\text{adjacent}}{\text{hypotenuse}} = \frac{12}{13}$.

COTANGENT—the ratio of the adjacent leg to the opposite leg. *The cotangent of* $\angle A$ *in the figure above is* $\frac{\text{adjacent}}{\text{opposite}} = \frac{12}{5}$.

CUBE—a rectangular solid whose faces are all squares.

CUBE (of a number)—the third power. *The cube of a negative number is negative.*

CYLINDER—a solid with two circular ends connected by "straight" sides.

DECIMAL—a noninteger written with digits and a decimal point. *A decimal is equivalent to a common fraction whose denominator is 10, 100, or 1,000, etcetera.*

DEGREE—one 360th of a full rotation. *A right angle measures 90 degrees—often written 90°.*

DEGREE OF AN EQUATION—the greatest exponent in a single-variable equation. The equation $x^3 - 9x = 0$ *is a third-degree equation because the biggest exponent is 3.*

DENOMINATOR—the number below the fraction bar. *When you increase the denominator of a positive fraction, you decrease the value of the fraction:* $\frac{7}{11}$ *is less than* $\frac{7}{10}$.

DIAGONAL—a line segment connecting two nonadjacent vertices of a polygon. *A diagonal divides a rectangle into two right triangles.*

DIAMETER—(the length of) a line segment connecting two points on a circle and passing through the center. *A diameter is a chord of maximum length.*

DIFFERENCE—the result of subtraction. *The positive difference between 3 and 7 is 4.*

DIGIT—one of the numbers from 0 through 9. *In the 3-digit number 355, the hundreds' digit is 3, the tens' digit is 5, and the ones' digit is 5.*

DISTINCT—different, distinguishable. *The number 355 has 2 distinct digits: 3 and 5.*

EDGE—a line segment formed by the intersection of two faces.

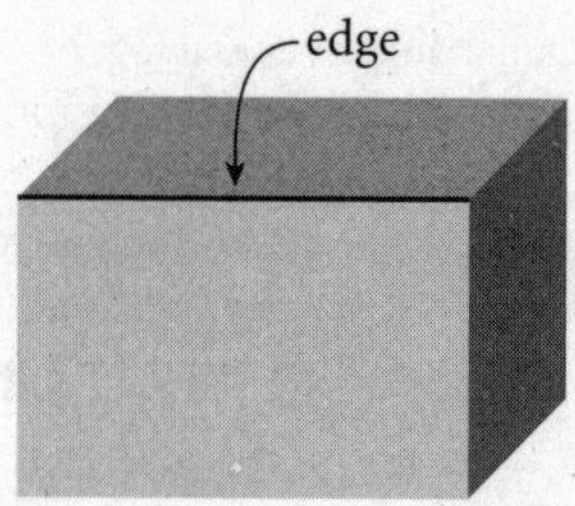

A rectangular solid has 12 edges.

ELLIPSE—a set of points in a plane for which the sum of the distances from two points (called *foci*) is constant.

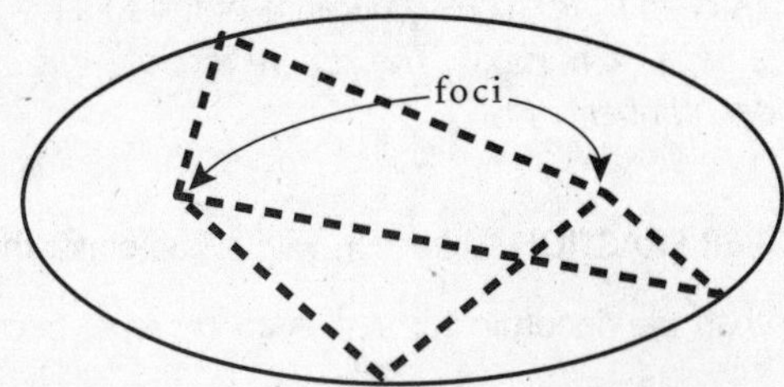

EQUATION—a statement of equality between two quantities. *It's an equation if it includes an equal sign.*

EQUATION OF A LINE—an equation that describes the relationship between the x- and y-coordinates of every point on the line in the coordinate plane. *The equation of the x-axis is $y = 0$, and the equation of the y-axis is $x = 0$.*

EQUILATERAL TRIANGLE—a triangle with three equal sides.

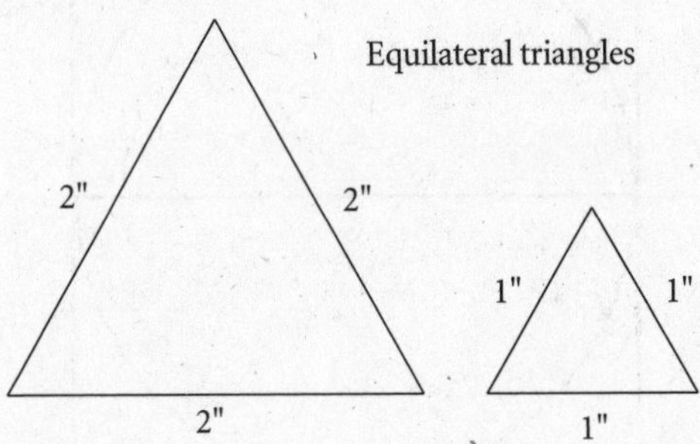

All equilateral triangles are similar—they all have three 60° angles.

EVEN NUMBER—a multiple of 2. *The set of even numbers includes not only 2, 4, 6, etcetera, but also 0, −2, −4, −6, etcetera.*

EXPONENT—the small, raised number written to the right of a variable or number, indicating the number of times that variable or number is to be used as a factor. *In the expression $-4x^3$, the exponent is 3, so $-4x^3 = -4 \cdot x \cdot x \cdot x$.*

EXTERIOR ANGLE—the angle created outside a polygon when one side is extended. *The exterior angles of any polygon add up to 360°.*

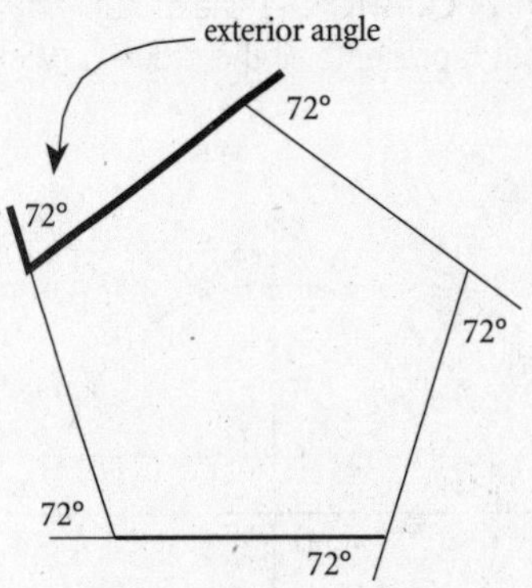

The exterior angles of a regular pentagon each measure 72°.

FACE—a polygon formed by edges of a solid.

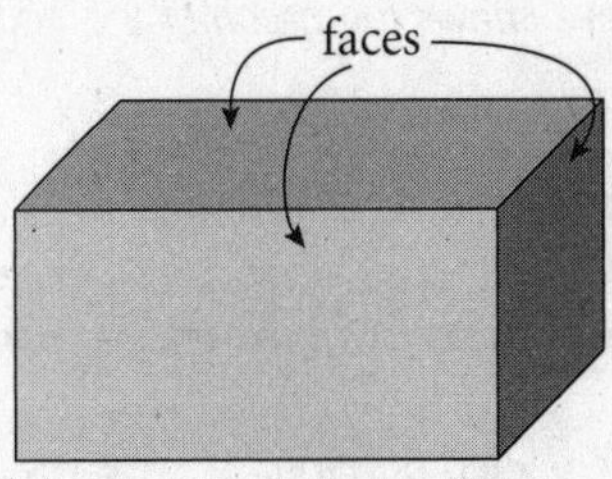

A rectangular solid has 6 faces.

FACTOR (of n)—a positive integer that divides into n with no remainder. *The complete list of factors of 18 is: 1, 2, 3, 6, 9, and 18.*

FACTORING (a polynomial)—re-expressing a polynomial as the product of simpler expressions. *The complete factorization of $2x^2 + 7x + 3$ is $(2x + 1)(x + 3)$.*

FRACTION—a number expressed as a ratio. *In everyday speech, the word fraction implies something less than 1, but to a mathematician, any number written in the form $\frac{A}{B}$ is a fraction.*

GRAPH OF AN EQUATION—a line or curve in the coordinate plane that represents all the ordered pair solutions of an equation.

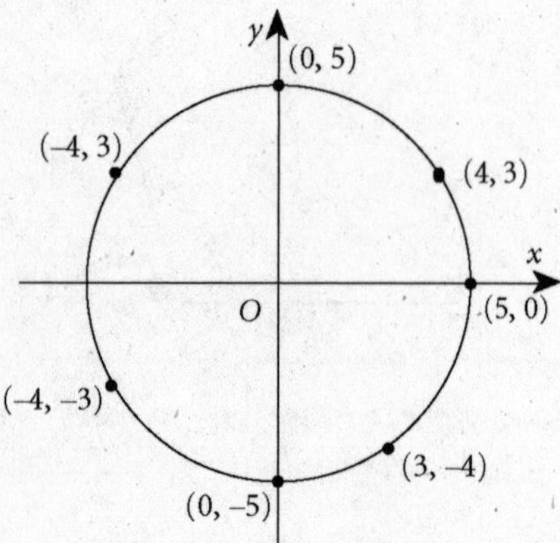

The figure above shows the graph of the equation $x^2 + y^2 = 25$.

GREATEST COMMON FACTOR—the greatest integer that is a factor of both numbers under consideration. *The greatest common factor (GCF) of relative primes is 1.*

HEXAGON—a six-sided polygon.

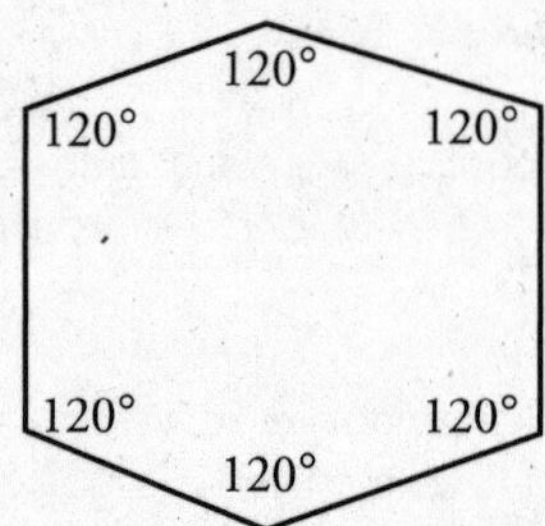

The six angles of a regular hexagon each measure 120°.

HYPOTENUSE—the side of a right triangle opposite the right angle.

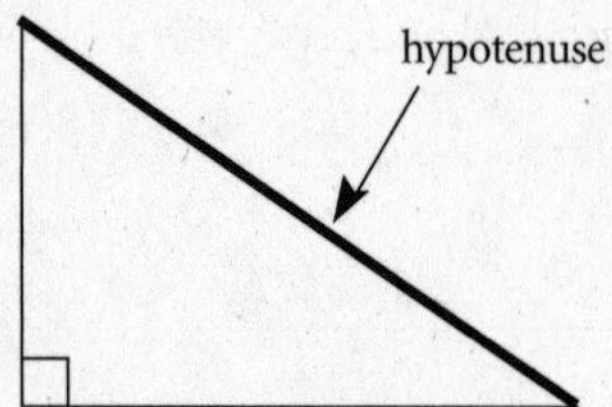

The hypotenuse is always the longest side.

IMAGINARY—not real, usually because of the square root of a negative number. *The square root of −4 is an imaginary number.*

IMPROPER FRACTION—a fraction with a numerator that's greater than the denominator. $\frac{35}{8}$ is an improper fraction and is therefore greater than 1.

INEQUALITY—a statement that compares the size of two quantities. *There are four inequality symbols: < ("less than"), ≤ "(less than or equal to"), > ("greater than"), and ≥ ("greater than or equal to").*

INSCRIBED—drawn inside another figure with as many points touching as possible.

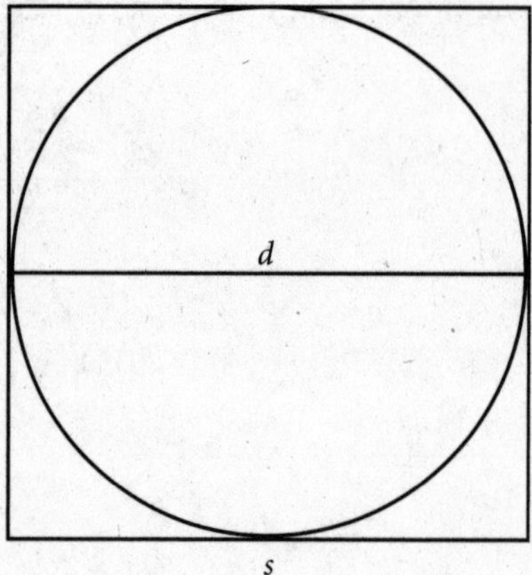

When a circle is inscribed within a square, the diameter d of the circle is the same as a length of a side s of the square.

INTEGER—a whole number; 325, 0, and −29 are integers.

INTERCEPT—the point where a given line crosses the *x*-axis or *y*-axis.

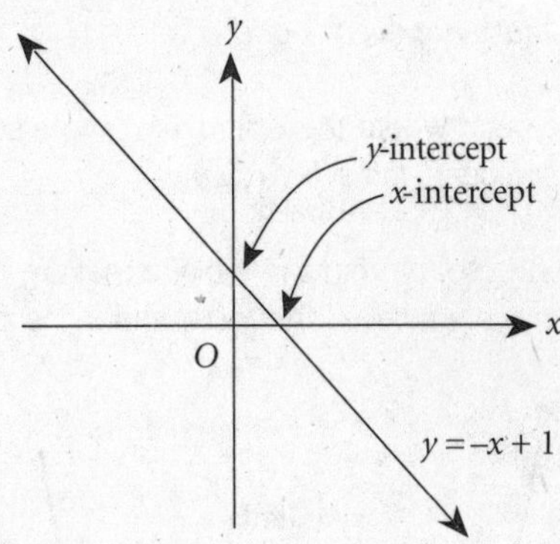

The y-intercept is the b in the slope-intercept form $y = mx + b$.

INTERIOR ANGLE—an angle inside a polygon formed by two adjacent sides. *Every polygon has the same number of interior angles as sides.*

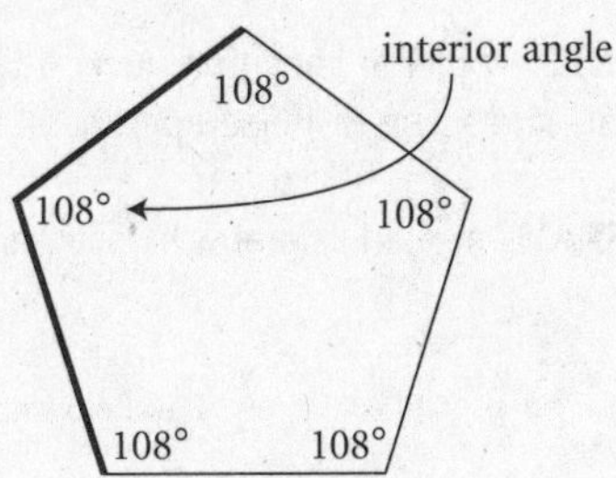

The interior angles of a regular pentagon each measure 108°.

IRRATIONAL—real, but not capable of being expressed as a ratio of integers. *$\sqrt{2}$, $\sqrt{3}$, and π are irrational numbers.*

ISOSCELES TRIANGLE—a triangle with two sides of equal length.

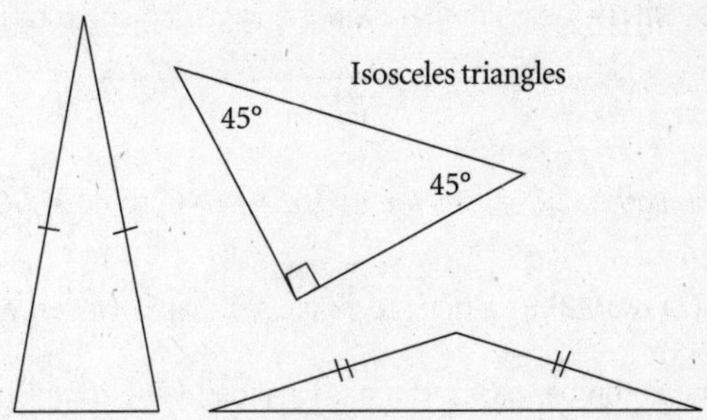

The angles opposite the equal sides of an isosceles triangle are also equal.

LEAST COMMON MULTIPLE—the smallest number that is a multiple of both given numbers. *The least common multiple of relative primes is their product.*

LEGS (of a right triangle)—the sides that make up the right angle.

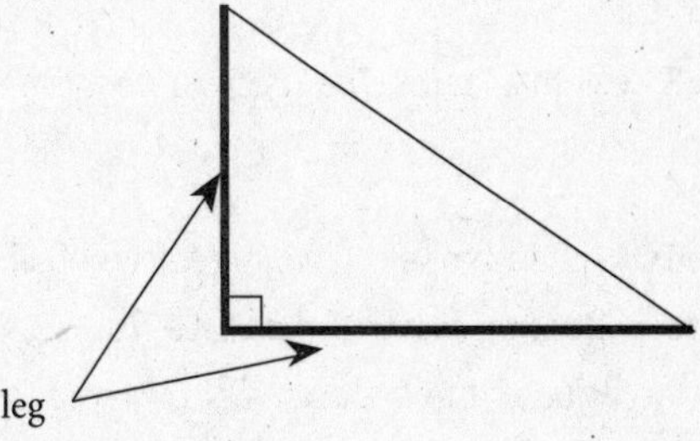

You can use the legs as the base and altitude to find the area of a right triangle.

LIKE TERMS—algebraic terms in which the elements other than the coefficients are alike. *$2ab$ and $3ab$ are like terms, and so they can be added: $2ab + 3ab = 5ab$.*

LINE—a straight row of points extending infinitely in both directions. *A line has only one dimension.*

LINE SEGMENT—a straight row of points connecting two endpoints. *Each side of a polygon is a line segment.*

LINEAR EQUATION—a single-variable equation with no exponent greater than 1. *A linear equation is also called a first-degree equation.*

MIDPOINT—the point that divides a line segment in half.

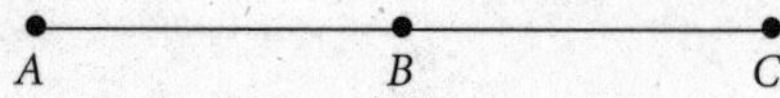

In the figure above, B is the midpoint of $\overline{AC}$, so $AB = BC$.

MIXED NUMBER—a noninteger greater than 1 written with a whole number part and a fractional part. *The mixed number $4\frac{2}{3}$ can also be expressed as the improper fraction $\frac{14}{3}$.*

MONOMIAL—an algebraic expression consisting of exactly one term.

MULTIPLE (of *n*)—a number that *n* will divide into with no remainder. *Some of the multiples of 18 are: 0, 18, and 90.*

NEGATIVE—less than zero. *The greatest negative integer is −1.*

NUMERATOR—the number above the fraction bar. *When you increase the numerator of a positive fraction, you increase the value of the fraction: $\frac{13}{17}$ is greater than $\frac{12}{17}$.*

OBTUSE ANGLE—an angle measuring more than 90° and less than 180°. *An obtuse triangle is one that has one obtuse angle.*

OCTAGON—an eight-sided polygon.

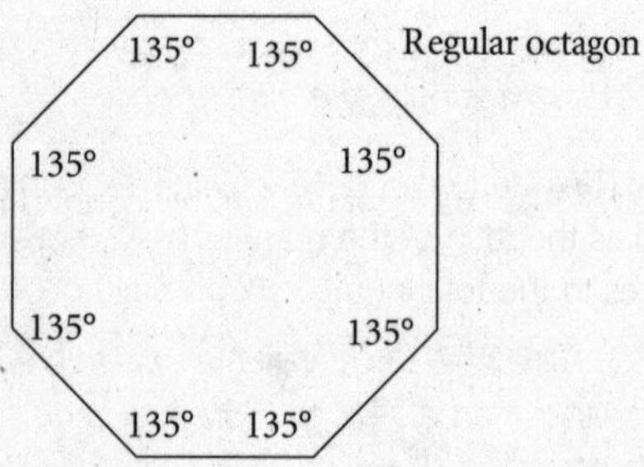

Each of the interior angles of a regular octagon measures 135°.

ODD NUMBER—an integer that is not a multiple of 2. *Any integer that's not even is odd.*

ORIGIN—the point where the *x*- and *y*-axes intersect. *The origin represents the point (0,0).*

PARABOLA—the set of points in a plane that are the same distance from a point called the *focus* and a line called the *directrix*.

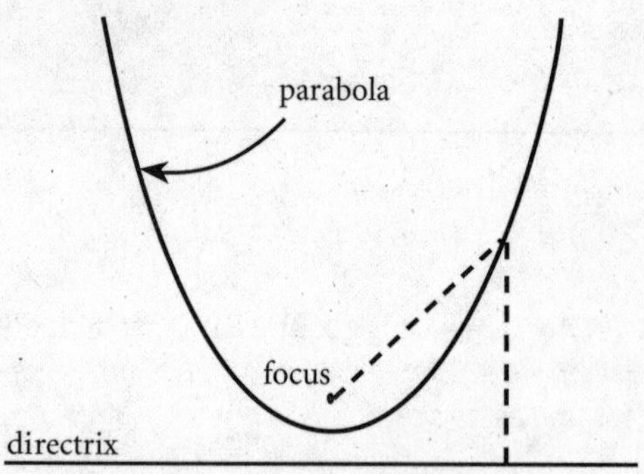

PARALLEL LINES—coplanar lines that never intersect. Parallel lines are the same distance apart at all points.

PARALLELOGRAM—a quadrilateral with two pairs of parallel sides.

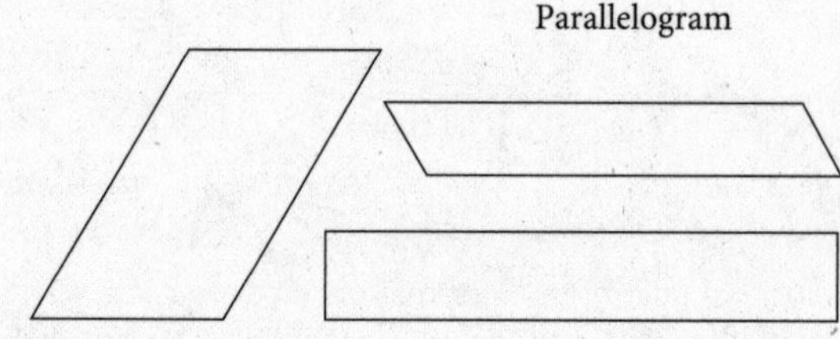

Opposite sides of a parallelogram are equal; opposite angles of a parallelogram are also equal.

PENTAGON—a five-sided polygon.

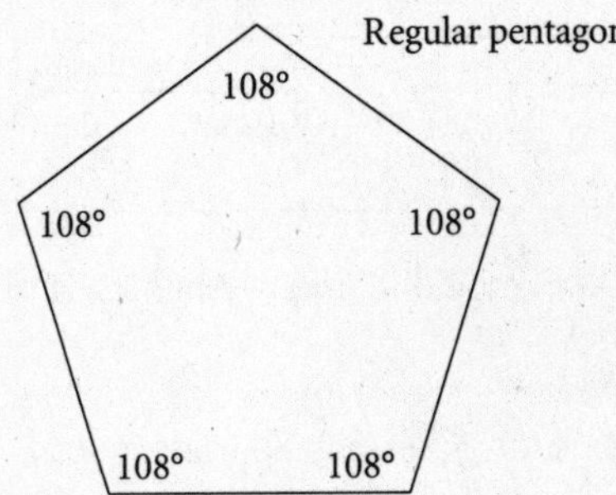

The interior angles of any pentagon add up to 540°. Each of the interior angles of a regular pentagon measures 108°.

PERCENT—one hundredth. 20% means 20 hundredths, or $\frac{20}{100} = \frac{1}{5}$.

PERCENT INCREASE/DECREASE—amount of increase or decrease expressed as a percent of the original amount. *A decrease from 100 to 83 is a 17% decrease.*

PERIMETER—the sum of the lengths of the sides of a polygon. *Two polygons with the same area do not necessarily have the same perimeter.*

PERPENDICULAR—intersecting at a right angle. *The altitude and base of a triangle are perpendicular.*

PI—an irrational number, approximately 3.14, which is equal to the ratio of the circumference of any circle to its diameter. The symbol for pi is π. *Pi appears in the formulas for the circumference and area of a circle, as well for the volumes of a sphere, a cylinder, and a cone.*

POINT—a precise position in space. *A point has no length, breadth, or thickness.*

POLYGON—a closed figure composed of any number of straight sides.

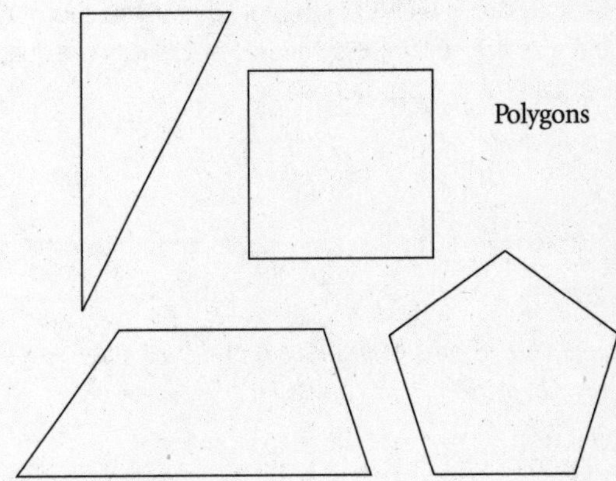

Triangles, squares, trapezoids, and pentagons are all polygons, but circles and ellipses are not.

POLYNOMIAL—an algebraic expression that is the sum of two or more terms. *Binomials and trinomials are just two types of polynomials.*

POSITIVE—greater than zero. *Zero is not a positive number.*

POWER—a product obtained by multiplying a quantity by itself one or more times. *The fifth power of 2 is 32.*

PRIME FACTORIZATION—an integer expressed as the product of prime numbers. *The prime factorization of 60 is $2 \times 2 \times 3 \times 5$.*

PRIME NUMBER—an integer greater than 1 that has no factors other than 1 and itself. The first 10 prime numbers are: 2, 3, 5, 7, 11, 13, 17, 19, 23, and 29. Notice that 2 is the only even prime number.

PROBABILITY—the likelihood of a particular event, expressed as the ratio of the number of "favorable" occurrences to the total number of possible occurrences. *Probability is a part-to-whole ratio and can therefore never be greater than 1.*

PRODUCT—the result of multiplication. *The product of 3 and 4 is 12.*

PROPORTION—an expression of the equality of ratios. *Corresponding sides of similar figures are proportional.*

PYTHAGOREAN THEOREM—the rule that states, "for any right triangle, the sum of the squares of the legs is equal to the square of the hypotenuse."

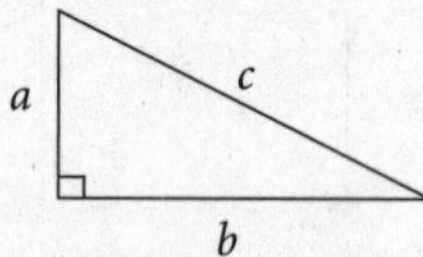

If you call the lengths of the legs a and b and the length of the hypotenuse c, you can write "$a^2 + b^2 = c^2$."

QUADRANT—one of the four regions into which the axes divide the coordinate plane.

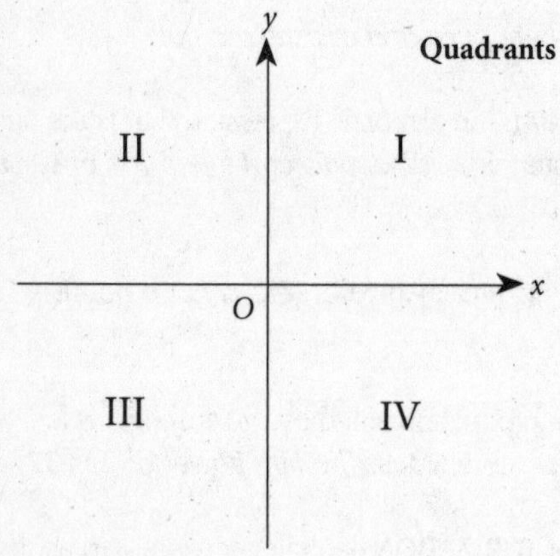

When you know the signs of the coordinates, you know which quadrant contains that point. For any point in Quadrant IV, for example, the x-coordinate is positive and the y-coordinate is negative.

QUADRATIC EQUATION—a second-degree equation. *Quadratic equations with one unknown often have two solutions.*

QUADRILATERAL—a four-sided polygon. *Squares, rectangles, parallelograms, and trapezoids are all quadrilaterals.*

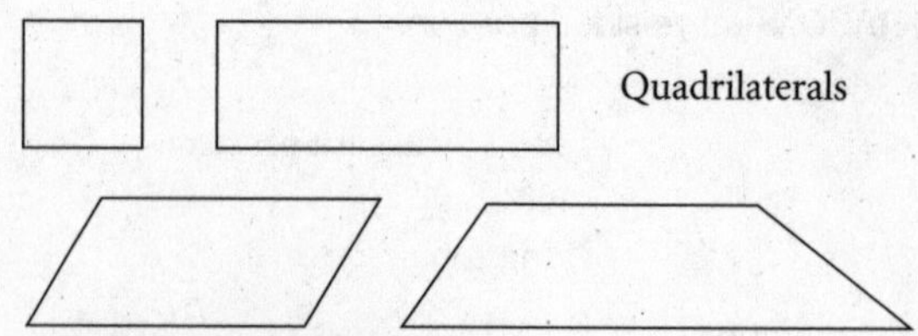

QUOTIENT—the result of division. When 12 is divided by 3, the quotient is 4.

RADIAN—a unit for expressing the measure of an angle.

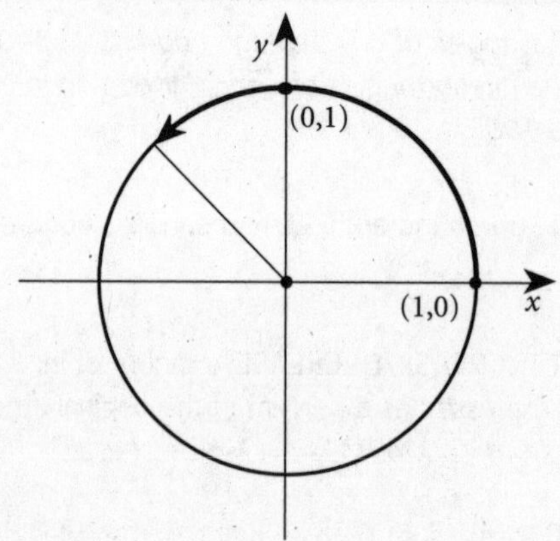

The angle shown in the figure above measures $\frac{3\pi}{4}$ radians, which is the same as 135°. It's no coincidence that $\frac{3\pi}{4}$ is also the length of the arc shown.

RADICAL—*the symbol $\sqrt{}$, which by itself represents the positive square root, and with a little number written in—as in $\sqrt[3]{32}$—represents a higher root. By convention, $\sqrt{}$ represents the positive square root only.*

RADIUS—(the length of) a line segment connecting the center and a point on a circle. *The radius is half the diameter.*

RATE—a ratio of quantities measured in different units. *The most familiar rates have units of time after the word per, such as: meters per second, pages per hour, inches per year.*

RATIO—a fraction that expresses the relative sizes of two quantities. *A ratio is generally expressed with the words "of" and "to": as in "the ratio of girls to boys."*

RATIONAL—capable of being expressed as a ratio of integers. *The repeating decimal .074074074074 . . . is a rational number because it can be written as* $\frac{2}{27}$.

REAL—having a place on the number line. *π is a real number because it has a location—somewhere just to the right of 3.14—on the number line.*

RECIPROCALS—a pair of numbers whose product is 1. *To get the reciprocal of a fraction, switch the numerator and denominator: the reciprocal of* $\frac{2}{7}$ is $\frac{7}{2}$.

RECTANGLE—a quadrilateral with four right angles. *All rectangles are parallelograms, but not all parallelograms are rectangles.*

RECTANGULAR SOLID—a solid whose faces are all rectangles.

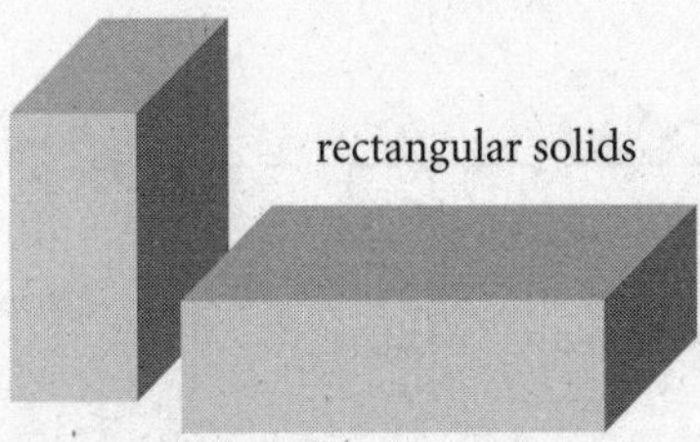

REDUCING A FRACTION—expressing a fraction in lowest terms by factoring out and canceling common factors. $\frac{6}{8}$ reduces to $\frac{3}{4}$.

REGULAR POLYGON—a polygon with all equal sides and all equal angles. *Equilateral triangles and squares are regular polygons.*

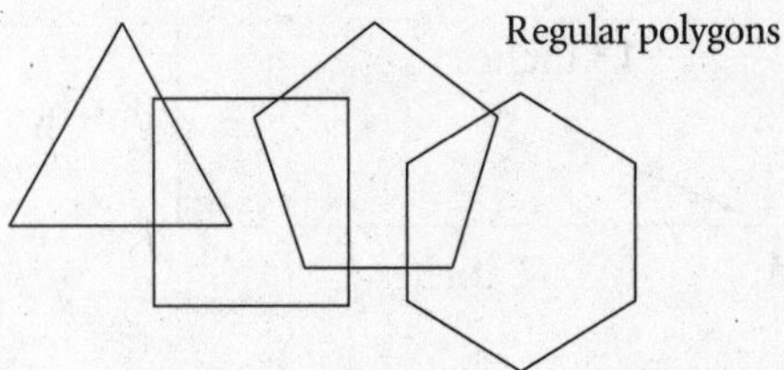

RELATIVE PRIMES—positive integers that have no factors in common. *Thirty-five and 54 are relative primes because their prime factorizations (35 = 5 × 7, and 54 = 2 × 3 × 3 × 3) have nothing in common.*

REPEATING DECIMAL—a decimal with a digit or cluster of digits that repeats indefinitely. *The fraction* $\frac{1}{7}$ *is equivalent to the repeating decimal .142857142857142857. . . , which can be written as* $.\overline{142857}$.

RHOMBUS—a quadrilateral with four equal sides.

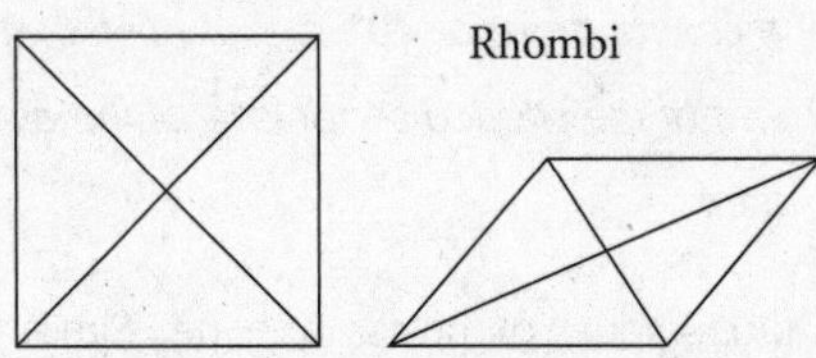

The diagonals of a rhombus are perpendicular.

RIGHT ANGLE—an angle measuring 90°. *A rectangle is a polygon with four right angles.*

RIGHT TRIANGLE—a triangle with a right angle. *Every right triangle has exactly two acute angles.*

ROOT—a number that multiplied by itself a certain number of times will yield the given quantity. The third root of 8 is 2.

SCALENE TRIANGLE—a triangle with sides of different lengths. *A 3-4-5 triangle is a scalene triangle.*

SECANT—the ratio of the hypotenuse to the adjacent leg. *The secant is the reciprocal of the cosine.*

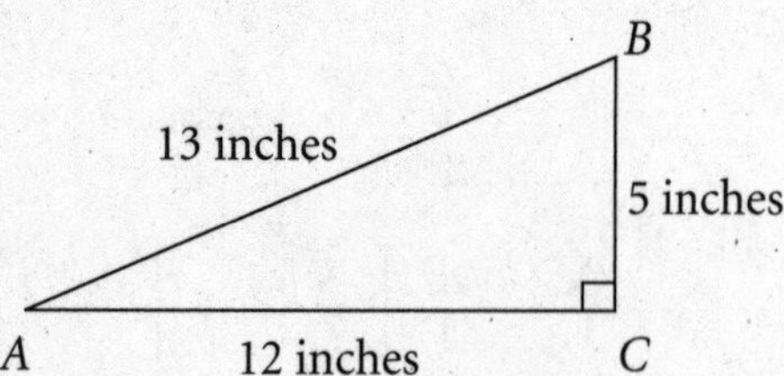

In the figure above, the secant of $\angle A$ *is* $\frac{13}{12}$.

SECTOR—a region bounded by two radii and an arc.

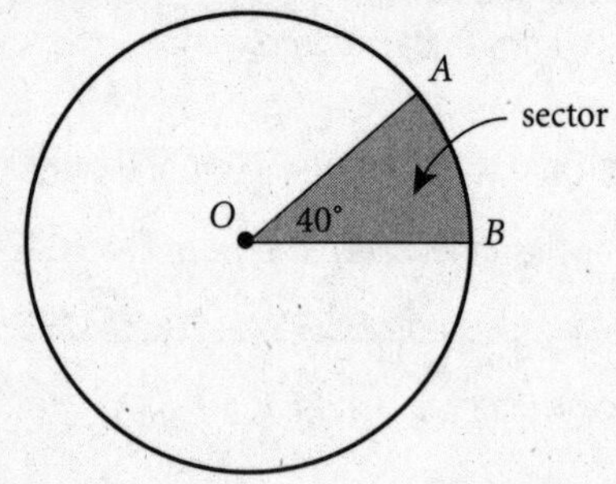

Because the central angle of 40° is $\frac{1}{9}$ *of the full circle's 360°, the area of the shaded sector is* $\frac{1}{9}$ *of the area of the whole circle.*

SIMILAR—proportional; of the same shape. Similar polygons have the same angles.

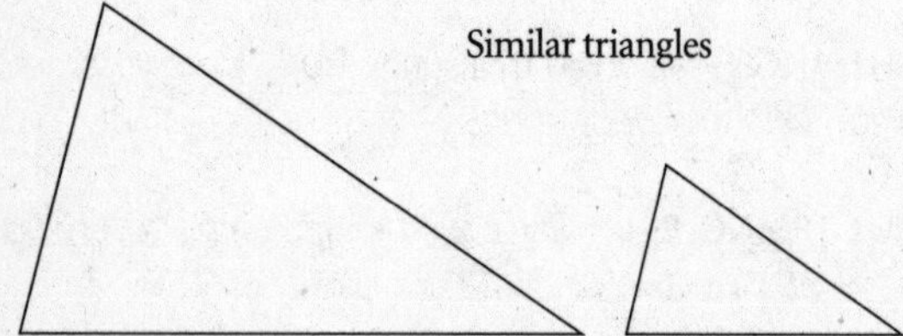

SINE—the ratio of the opposite leg to the hypotenuse.

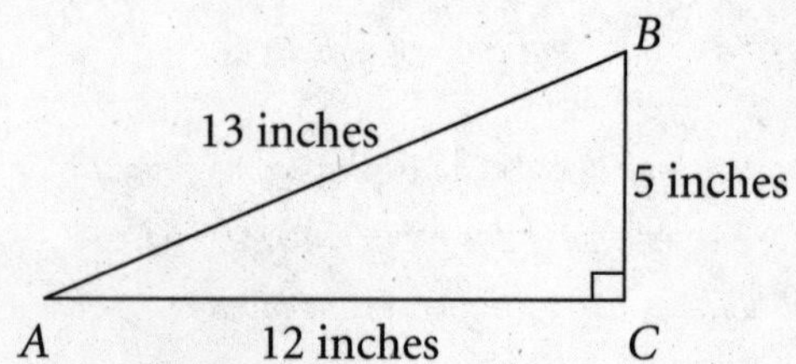

In the figure above, the sine of $\angle A$ *is* $\frac{5}{13}$.

SLOPE—a description of the "steepness" of a line in the coordinate plane, defined as $\frac{\text{Change in } y}{\text{Change in } x}$. *Lines that go "uphill" (left to right) have positive slopes, and lines that go "downhill" have negative slopes. A horizontal line—that is, a line parallel to the x-axis—is "flat" and has a slope of 0.*

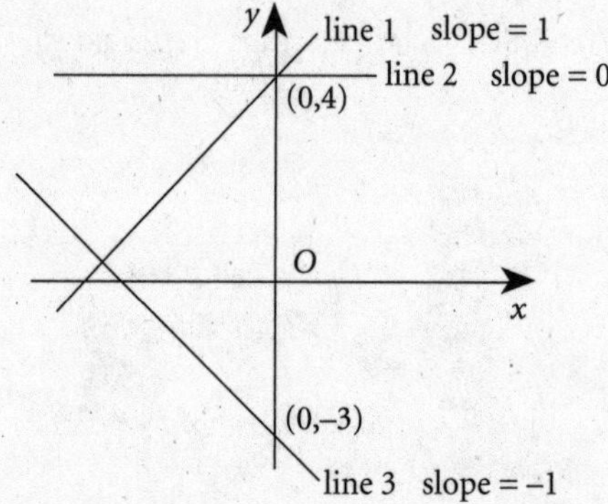

SLOPE-INTERCEPT FORM—an equation in the form $y = mx + b$. *In this form, m is the slope and b is the y-intercept. Line 1 in the figure above has a slope of 1 and a y-intercept of 4, so its equation is* $y = x + 4$. *Line 2's equation is* $y = 4$. *Line 3's equation is* $y = -x - 3$.

SOLID—a three-dimensional figure.

Cubes, cylinders, cones, and spheres are all solids.

SOLVING—isolating the given variable.

SPHERE—the set of all points in space a particular distance from a central point. *Visualize a sphere as a ball.*

SQUARE—a quadrilateral with four equal sides and four right angles. *A square can be thought of as a rectangular rhombus.*

SQUARE ROOT—a number that when squared yields the given quantity. *Positive numbers each have two square roots, but negative numbers have no real square roots.*

SUM—the result of addition. *The sum of 3 and 4 is 7.*

SUPPLEMENTARY ANGLES—two angles whose measures add up to 180°.

SURFACE AREA—the sum of the areas of the surfaces of a solid. *Surface area is measured in square units.*

SYSTEM OF EQUATIONS—two or more equations in which each variable represents the same quantity in one equation as in another.

TANGENT—the ratio of the opposite leg of a right triangle to the adjacent leg.

TANGENT (of a circle)—a line that intersects a circle at exactly one point. *Visualize a tangent as a line that just barely "touches" the circle.*

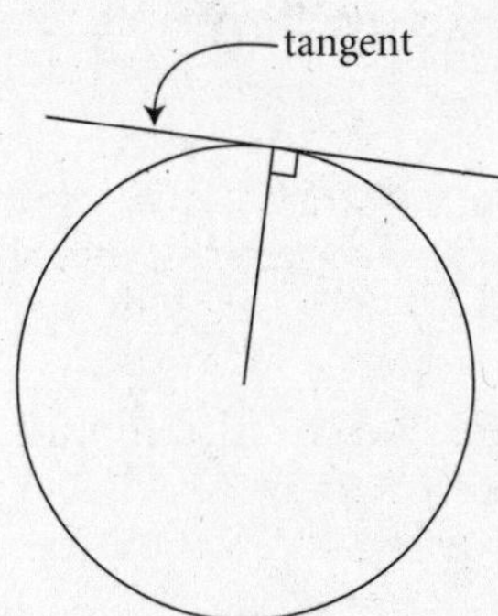

TERM—a part of an algebraic expression that either stands by itself or is connected to other terms with plus and minus signs. *A term has three parts: the coefficient, the variable(s), and the exponent(s).*

TRANSVERSAL—a line that intersects two parallel lines.

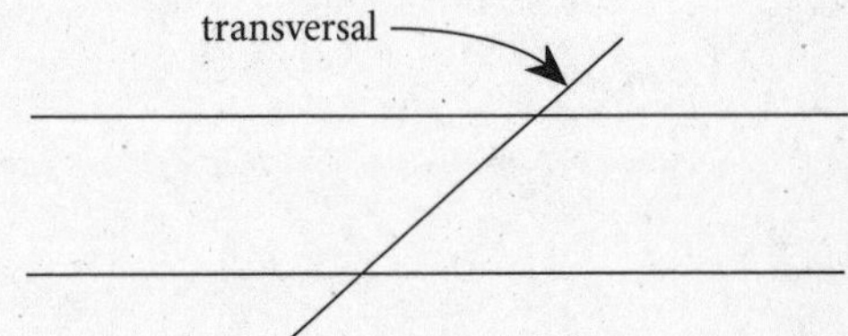

A transversal across parallel lines creates two sets of four equal angles.

TRAPEZOID—a quadrilateral with one pair of parallel sides.

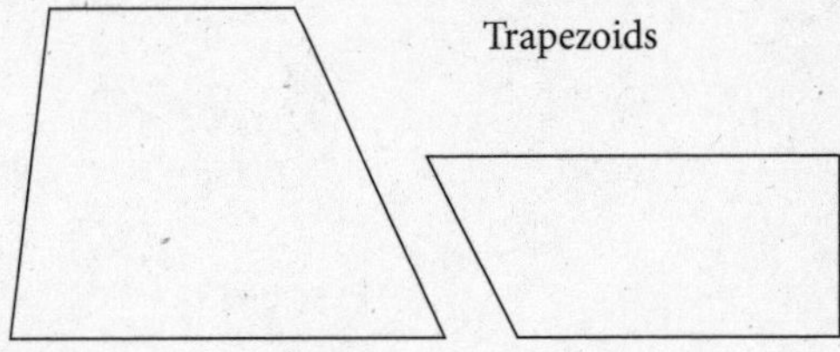

TRIANGLE—a three-sided polygon. *The three angles of a triangle add up to 180°.*

UNDEFINED—not covered by the rules. *Division by 0 is undefined.*

VARIABLE—a letter representing an unknown or unspecified quantity. *The letter most commonly used for a variable is x.*

VERTEX—a point of intersection, such as a corner of a rectangular solid or a polygon.

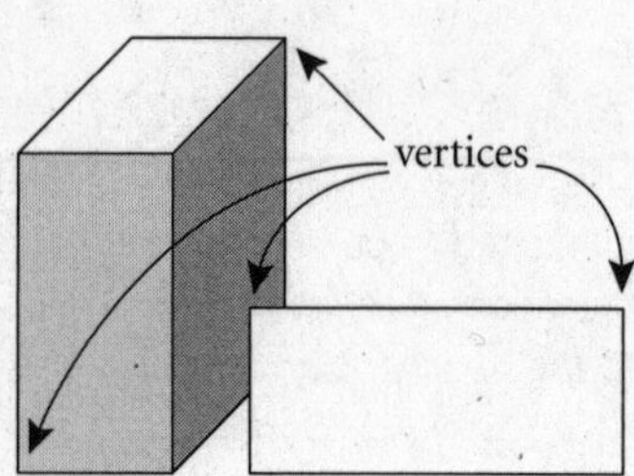

VERTICAL ANGLES—angles across the vertex of intersecting lines. *Vertical angles are equal.*

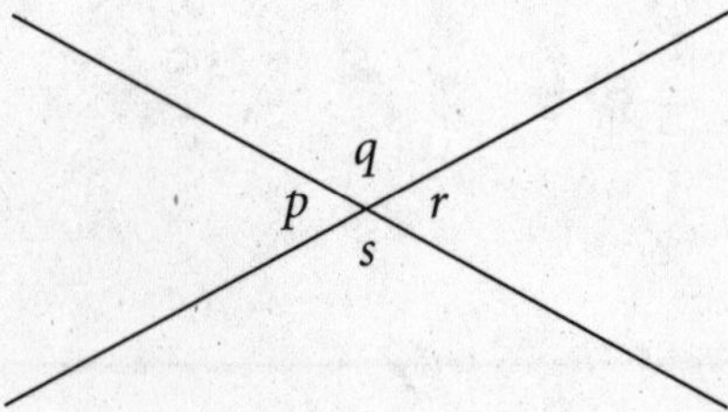

In the figure above, $\angle q$ and $\angle s$ are vertical angles, as are $\angle p$ and $\angle r$.

VOLUME—a measure of the amount of "space" contained within a solid. *Computing volume invariably involves multiplying three dimensions, such as length, width, and height.*

100 Key Math Concepts for the ACT

NUMBER PROPERTIES

1. **UNDEFINED**

   On the ACT, *undefined* almost always means **division by zero**. The expression $\frac{a}{bc}$ is undefined if either b or c equals 0.

2. **REAL/IMAGINARY**

   A real number is a number that has a **location on the number line**. On the ACT, imaginary numbers are numbers that involve the square root of a negative number. $\sqrt{-4}$ is an imaginary number.

3. **INTEGER/NONINTEGER**

   Integers are **whole numbers**; they include negative whole numbers and zero.

4. **RATIONAL/IRRATIONAL**

   A **rational number** is a number that can be expressed as a **ratio of two integers. Irrational numbers** are real numbers—they have locations on the number line—they just **can't be expressed precisely as a fraction or decimal**. For the purposes of the ACT, the most important **irrational numbers** are $\sqrt{2}$, $\sqrt{3}$, and π.

5. **ADDING/SUBTRACTING SIGNED NUMBERS**

   To **add a positive and a negative**, first ignore the signs and find the positive difference between the number parts. Then attach the sign of the original number to the larger number part. For example, to add 23 and −34, first we ignore the minus sign and find the positive difference between 23 and 34—that's 11. Then we attach the sign of the number with the larger number part—in this case it's the minus sign from the −34. So, $23 + (-34) = -11$.

   Make **subtraction** situations simpler by turning them into addition. For example, think of $-17 - (-21)$ as $-17 + (+21)$.

   To **add or subtract a string of positives and negatives**, first turn everything into addition. Then combine the positives and negatives so that the string is reduced to the sum of a single positive number and a single negative number.

6. **MULTIPLYING/DIVIDING SIGNED NUMBERS**

   To multiply and/or divide positives and negatives, treat the number parts as usual and **attach a negative sign if there were originally an odd number of negatives**. To multiply −2, −3, and −5, first multiply the number parts: $2 \times 3 \times 5 = 30$. Then go back and note that there were three—an odd number—negatives, so the product is negative: $(-2) \times (-3) \times (-5) = -30$.

7. PEMDAS

When performing multiple operations, remember **PEMDAS**, which means **Parentheses** first, then **Exponents**, then **Multiplication** and **Division** (left to right), then **Addition** and **Subtraction** (left to right).

In the expression $9 - 2 \times (5 - 3)^2 + 6 \div 3$, begin with the parentheses: $(5 - 3) = 2$. Then do the exponent: $2^2 = 4$. Now the expression is: $9 - 2 \times 4 + 6 \div 3$. Next do the multiplication and division to get $9 - 8 + 2$, which equals 3.

8. ABSOLUTE VALUE

Treat absolute value signs a lot like **parentheses**. Do what's inside them first and then take the absolute value of the result. Don't take the absolute value of each piece between the bars before calculating. In order to calculate $|(-12) + 5 - (-4)| - |5 + (-10)|$, first do what's inside the bars to get: $|-3| - |-5|$, which is $3 - 5$, or -2.

9. COUNTING CONSECUTIVE INTEGER S

To count consecutive integers, **subtract the smallest from the largest and add 1**. To count the integers from 13 through 31, subtract: $31 - 13 = 18$. Then add 1: $18 + 1 = 19$.

DIVISIBILITY

10. FACTOR/MULTIPLE

The **factors** of integer *n* are the positive integers that divide into *n* with no remainder. The **multiples** of *n* are the integers that *n* divides into with no remainder. 6 is a factor of 12, and 24 is a multiple of 12. 12 is both a factor and a multiple of itself.

11. PRIME FACTORIZATION

A **prime number** is a positive integer that has exactly two positive integer factors: 1 and the integer itself. The first eight prime numbers are 2, 3, 5, 7, 11, 13, 17, and 19.

To find the prime factorization of an integer, just keep breaking it up into factors until **all the factors are prime**. To find the prime factorization of 36, for example, you could begin by breaking it into 4×9:

$$36 = 4 \times 9 = 2 \times 2 \times 3 \times 3$$

12. RELATIVE PRIMES

To determine whether two integers are relative primes, break them both down to their prime factorizations. For example: $35 = 5 \times 7$, and $54 = 2 \times 3 \times 3 \times 3$. They have **no prime factors in common**, so 35 and 54 are relative primes.

13. COMMON MULTIPLE

You can always get a common multiple of two numbers by **multiplying** them, but, unless the two numbers are relative primes, the product will not be the least common multiple. For example, to find a common multiple for 12 and 15, you could just multiply: $12 \times 15 = 180$.

14. LEAST COMMON MULTIPLE (LCM)

To find the least common multiple, check out the **multiples of the larger number** until you find one that's **also a multiple of the smaller**. To find the LCM of 12 and 15, begin by taking the multiples of 15: 15 is not divisible by 12; 30's not; nor is 45. But the next multiple of 15, 60, is divisible by 12, so it's the LCM.

15. GREATEST COMMON FACTOR (GCF)

To find the greatest common factor, break down both numbers into their prime factorizations and take **all the prime factors they have in common**. $36 = 2 \times 2 \times 3 \times 3$, and $48 = 2 \times 2 \times 2 \times 2 \times 3$. What they have in common is two 2s and one 3, so the GCF is $= 2 \times 2 \times 3 = 12$.

16. EVEN/ODD

To predict whether a sum, difference, or product will be even or odd, just **take simple numbers like 1 and 2 and see what happens**. There are rules—"odd times even is even," for example—but there's no need to memorize them. What happens with one set of numbers generally happens with all similar sets.

17. MULTIPLES OF 2 AND 4

An integer is divisible by 2 if the **last digit is even**. An integer is divisible by 4 if the **last two digits form a multiple of 4**. The last digit of 562 is 2, which is even, so 562 is a multiple of 2. The last two digits make 62, which is not divisible by 4, so 562 is not a multiple of 4.

18. MULTIPLES OF 3 AND 9

An integer is divisible by 3 if the **sum of its digits is divisible by 3**. An integer is divisible by 9 if the **sum of its digits is divisible by 9**. The sum of the digits in 957 is 21, which is divisible by 3 but not by 9, so 957 is divisible by 3 but not 9.

19. MULTIPLES OF 5 AND 10

An integer is divisible by 5 if the **last digit is 5 or 0**. An integer is divisible by 10 if the **last digit is 0**. The last digit of 665 is 5, so 665 is a multiple of 5 but not a multiple of 10.

20. REMAINDERS

The remainder is the whole number left over after division. 487 is 2 more than 485, which is a multiple of 5, so when 487 is divided by 5, the remainder will be 2.

FRACTIONS AND DECIMALS

21. REDUCING FRACTIONS

To reduce a fraction to lowest terms, **factor out and cancel** all factors the numerator and denominator have in common.

$$\frac{28}{36} = \frac{4 \times 7}{4 \times 9} = \frac{7}{9}$$

22. ADDING/SUBTRACTING FRACTIONS

To add or subtract fractions, first find a **common denominator**, and then add or subtract the numerators.

$$\frac{2}{15} + \frac{3}{10} = \frac{4}{30} + \frac{9}{30} = \frac{4+9}{30} = \frac{13}{30}$$

23. MULTIPLYING FRACTIONS

To multiply fractions, **multiply** the numerators and **multiply** the denominators.

$$\frac{5}{7} \times \frac{3}{4} = \frac{5 \times 3}{7 \times 4} = \frac{15}{28}$$

24. DIVIDING FRACTIONS

To divide fractions, **invert** the second one and **multiply**.

$$\frac{1}{2} \div \frac{3}{5} = \frac{1}{2} \times \frac{5}{3} = \frac{1 \times 5}{2 \times 3} = \frac{5}{6}$$

25. CONVERTING A MIXED NUMBER TO AN IMPROPER FRACTION

To convert a mixed number to an improper fraction, **multiply** the whole number part by the denominator, then **add** the numerator. The result is the new numerator (over the same denominator). To convert $7\frac{1}{3}$, first multiply 7 by 3, then add 1, to get the new numerator of 22. Put that over the same denominator, 3, to get $\frac{22}{3}$.

26. CONVERTING AN IMPROPER FRACTION TO A MIXED NUMBER

To convert an improper fraction to a mixed number, **divide** the denominator into the numerator to get a **whole number quotient with a remainder.** The quotient becomes the whole number part of the mixed number, and the remainder becomes the new numerator—with the same denominator. For example, to convert $\frac{108}{5,}$ first divide 5 into 108, which yields 21 with a remainder of 3. Therefore, $\frac{108}{5} = 21\frac{3.}{5}.$

27. RECIPROCAL

To find the reciprocal of a fraction, switch the numerator and the denominator. The reciprocal of $\frac{3}{7}$ is $\frac{7}{3}$. The reciprocal of 5 is $\frac{1}{5}$. The product of reciprocals is 1.

28. COMPARING FRACTIONS

One way to compare fractions is to re-express them with a **common denominator**.

$\frac{3}{4} = \frac{21}{28}$ and $\frac{5}{7} = \frac{20}{28}$, $\frac{21}{28}$ is greater than $\frac{20}{28}$, so $\frac{3}{4}$ is greater than $\frac{5}{7}$.

Another way to compare fractions is to convert them both to **decimals.** $\frac{3}{4}$ converts to .75, and $\frac{5}{7}$ converts to approximately .714.

29. CONVERTING FRACTIONS TO DECIMALS

To convert a fraction to a decimal, **divide the bottom into the top**. To convert $\frac{5}{8}$, divide 8 into 5, yielding .625.

30. REPEATING DECIMAL

To find a particular digit in a repeating decimal, note the **number of digits in the cluster that repeats.** If there are 2 digits in that cluster, then every 2nd digit is the same. If there are 3 digits in that cluster, then every 3rd digit is the same. And so on. For example, the decimal equivalent of $\frac{1}{27}$ is .037037037..., which is best written $.\overline{037}$.

There are 3 digits in the repeating cluster, so every 3rd digit is the same: 7. To find the 50th digit, look for the multiple of 3 just less than 50—that's 48. The 48th digit is 7, and with the 49th digit the pattern repeats with 0. The 50th digit is 3.

31. IDENTIFYING THE PARTS AND THE WHOLE

The key to solving most fractions and percents story problems is to identify the part and the whole. Usually you'll find the **part** associated with the verb ***is/are*** and the **whole** associated with the word ***of***. In the sentence, "Half of the boys are blonds," the whole is the boys ("*of* the boys), and the part is the blonds ("*are* blonds").

PERCENTS

32. PERCENT FORMULA

Whether you need to find the part, the whole, or the percent, use the same formula:

Part = Percent × Whole

Example: What is 12% of 25?
Setup: Part = .12 × 25

Example: 15 is 3% of what number?
Setup: 15 = .03 × Whole

Example: 45 is what percent of 9?
Setup: 45 = Percent × 9

33. PERCENT INCREASE AND DECREASE

To increase a number by a percent, **add the percent to 100%**, convert to a decimal, and multiply. To increase 40 by 25%, add 25% to 100%, convert 125% to 1.25, and multiply by 40. 1.25 × 40 = 50.

34. FINDING THE ORIGINAL WHOLE

To find the **original whole before a percent increase or decrease**, set up an equation. Think of a 15% increase over x as $1.15x$.

Example: After a 5% increase, the population was 59,346. What was the population *before* the increase?

Setup: $1.05x = 59{,}346$

35. COMBINED PERCENT INCREASE AND DECREASE

To determine the combined effect of multiple percents increase and/or decrease, **start with 100 and see what happens.**

Example: A price went up 10% one year, and the new price went up 20% the next year. What was the combined percent increase?

Setup: First year: 100 + (10% of 100) = 110. Second year: 110 + (20% of 110) = 132. That's a combined 32% increase.

RATIOS, PROPORTIONS, AND RATES

36. SETTING UP A RATIO

To find a ratio, put the number associated with the word ***of* on top** and the quantity associated with the word ***to* on the bottom** and reduce. The ratio of 20 oranges to 12 apples is $\frac{20}{12}$ which reduces to $\frac{5}{3}$.

37. PART-TO-PART AND PART-TO-WHOLE RATIOS

If the parts add up to the whole, a part-to-part ratio can be turned into two part-to-whole ratios by putting **each number in the original ratio over the sum of the numbers.** If the ratio of males to females is 1 to 2, then the males-to-people ratio is

$\frac{1}{1+2} = \frac{1}{3}$ and the females-to-people ratio is $\frac{2}{1+2} = \frac{2}{3}$. Or, $\frac{2}{3}$ of all the people are female.

38. SOLVING A PROPORTION

To solve a proportion, **cross multiply**:

$$\frac{x}{5} = \frac{3}{4}$$

$$4x = 5 \times 3$$

$$x = \frac{15}{4} = 3.75$$

39. RATE

To solve a rates problem, **use the units** to keep things straight.

Example: If snow is falling at the rate of 1 foot every 4 hours, how many inches of snow will fall in 7 hours?

Setup:

$$\frac{1 \text{ foot}}{4 \text{ hours}} = \frac{x \text{ inches}}{7 \text{ hours}}$$

$$\frac{12 \text{ inches}}{4 \text{ hours}} = \frac{x \text{ inches}}{7 \text{ hours}}$$

$$4x = 12 \times 7$$

$$x = 21$$

40. AVERAGE RATE

Average rate is *not* simply the average of the rates.

$$\text{Average } A \text{ per } B = \frac{\text{Total } A}{\text{Total } B}$$

$$\text{Average Speed} = \frac{\text{Total distance}}{\text{Total time}}$$

To find the average speed for 120 miles at 40 mph and 120 miles at 60 mph, **don't just average the two speeds**. First figure out the total distance and the total time. The total distance is 120 + 120 = 240 miles. The times are 3 hours for the first leg and 2 hours for the second leg, or 5 hours total. The average speed, then, is $\frac{240}{5}$ = 48 miles per hour.

AVERAGES

41. AVERAGE FORMULA

To find the average of a set of numbers, **add them up and divide by the number of numbers.**

$$\text{Average} = \frac{\text{Sum of the terms}}{\text{Number of terms}}$$

To find the average of the five numbers 12, 15, 23, 40, and 40, first add them: $12 + 15 + 23 + 40 + 40 = 130$. Then divide the sum by 5: $130 \div 5 = 26$.

42. AVERAGE OF EVENLY SPACED NUMBERS

To find the average of evenly spaced numbers, just **average the smallest and the largest**. The average of all the integers from 13 through 77 is the same as the average of 13 and 77. $\frac{13 + 77}{2} = \frac{90}{2} = 45$

43. USING THE AVERAGE TO FIND THE SUM

$$\text{Sum} = (\text{Average}) \times (\text{Number of terms})$$

If the average of ten numbers is 50, then they add up to 10×50, or 500.

44. FINDING THE MISSING NUMBER

To find a missing number when you're given the average, **use the sum**. If the average of four numbers is 7, then the sum of those four numbers is 4×7, or 28. Suppose that three of the numbers are 3, 5, and 8. These numbers add up to 16 of that 28, which leaves 12 for the fourth number.

POSSIBILITIES AND PROBABILITY

45. COUNTING THE POSSIBILITIES

The fundamental counting principle: if there are ***m* ways** one event can happen and ***n* ways** a second event can happen, then there are **$m \times n$ ways** for the two events to happen. For example, with 5 shirts and 7 pairs of pants to choose from, you can put together $5 \times 7 = 35$ different outfits.

46. PROBABILITY

$$\text{Probability} = \frac{\text{Favorable outcomes}}{\text{Total possible outcomes}}$$

If you have 12 shirts in a drawer and 9 of them are white, the probability of picking a white shirt at random is $\frac{9}{12} = \frac{3}{4}$. This probability can also be expressed as .75 or 75%.

POWERS AND ROOTS

47. MULTIPLYING AND DIVIDING POWERS

To multiply powers with the same base, **add the exponents:** $x^3 \cdot x^4 = x^{3+4} = x^7$. To divide powers with the same base, **subtract the exponents:** $y^{13} \div y^8 = y^{13-8} = y^5$.

48. RAISING POWERS TO POWERS

To raise a power to an exponent, **multiply the exponents.** $(x^3)^4 = x^{3 \times 4} = x^{12}$.

49. SIMPLIFYING SQUARE ROOTS

To simplify a square root, **factor out the perfect squares** under the radical, unsquare them and put the result in front. $\sqrt{12} = \sqrt{4 \times 3} = \sqrt{4} \times \sqrt{3} = 2\sqrt{3}$.

50. ADDING AND SUBTRACTING ROOTS

You can add or subtract radical expressions only if the part under the radicals is the same.

$$2\sqrt{3} + 3\sqrt{3} = 5\sqrt{3}$$

51. MULTIPLYING AND DIVIDING ROOTS

The product of square roots is equal to the square root of the product:

$\sqrt{3} \times \sqrt{5} = \sqrt{3 \times 5} = \sqrt{15}$. The quotient of square roots is equal to the **square root of the quotient:**

$\frac{\sqrt{6}}{\sqrt{3}} = \sqrt{\frac{6}{3}} = \sqrt{2}$.

ALGEBRAIC EXPRESSIONS

52. EVALUATING AN EXPRESSION

To evaluate an algebraic expression, **plug in** the given values for the unknowns and calculate according to PEMDAS. To find the value of $x^2 + 5x - 6$ when $x = -2$, plug in -2 for x :

$(-2)^2 + 5(-2) - 6 = 4 - 10 - 6 = -12$.

53. ADDING AND SUBTRACTING MONOMIALS

To combine like terms, **keep the variable part unchanged while adding or subtracting the coefficients.** $2a + 3a = (2 + 3)a = 5a$

54. ADDING AND SUBTRACTING POLYNOMIALS

To add or subtract polynomials, **combine like terms.**

$(3x^2 + 5x - 7) - (x^2 + 12) =$

$(3x^2 - x^2) + 5x + (-7 - 12) = 2x^2 + 5x - 19$

55. MULTIPLYING MONOMIALS

To multiply monomials, **multiply the coefficients and the variables separately.**

$2a \times 3a = (2 \times 3)(a \times a) = 6a^2$

56. MULTIPLYING BINOMIALS—FOIL

To multiply binomials, use **FOIL**. To multiply $(x + 3)$ by $(x + 4)$, first multiply the **F**irst terms: $x \cdot x = x^2$. Next the **O**uter terms: $x \cdot 4 = 4x$. Then the **I**nner terms: $3 \cdot x = 3x$. And finally the **L**ast terms: $3 \cdot 4 = 12$. Then add and combine like terms: $x^2 + 4x + 3x + 12 = x^2 + 7x + 12$.

57. MULTIPLYING OTHER POLYNOMIALS

FOIL works only when you want to multiply two binomials. If you want to multiply polynomials with more than two terms, make sure you **multiply each term in the first polynomial by each term in the second.**

$(x^2 + 3x + 4)(x + 5) =$

$x^2(x + 5) + 3x(x + 5) + 4(x + 5) =$

$x^3 + 5x^2 + 3x^2 + 15x + 4x + 20 =$

$x^3 + 8x^2 + 19x + 20$

FACTORING ALGEBRAIC EXPRESSIONS

58. FACTORING OUT A COMMON DIVISOR

A factor common to all terms of a polynomial can be **factored out**. All three terms in the polynomial $3x^3 + 12x^2 - 6x$ contain a factor of $3x$. Pulling out the common factor yields $3x(x^2 + 4x - 2)$.

59. FACTORING THE DIFFERENCE OF SQUARES

One of the test maker's favorite factorables is the **difference of squares.**

$$a^2 - b^2 = (a - b)(a + b)$$

$x^2 - 9$, for example, factors to $(x - 3)(x + 3)$.

60. FACTORING THE SQUARE OF A BINOMIAL

Learn to recognize polynomials that are squares of binomials:

$a^2 + 2ab + b^2 = (a + b)^2$

$a^2 - 2ab + b^2 = (a - b)^2$

For example, $4x^2 + 12x + 9$ factors to $(2x + 3)^2$, and $n^2 - 10n + 25$ factors to $(n - 5)^2$.

61. FACTORING OTHER POLYNOMIALS—FOIL IN REVERSE

To factor a quadratic expression, **think about what binomials you could use FOIL on to get that quadratic expression.** To factor $x^2 - 5x + 6$, think about what First terms will produce x^2, what Last terms will produce +6, and what Outer and Inner terms will produce $-5x$. Common sense—and trial and error—lead you to $(x - 2)(x - 3)$.

62. SIMPLIFYING AN ALGEBRAIC FRACTION

Simplifying an algebraic fraction is a lot like simplifying a numerical fraction. The general idea is to **find factors common to the numerator and denominator and cancel them.** Thus, simplifying an algebraic fraction begins with factoring.

To simplify $\frac{x^2 - x - 12}{x^2 - 9}$ first factor the numerator and denominator: $\frac{x^2 - x - 12}{x^2 - 9} = \frac{(x - 4)(x + 3)}{(x - 3)(x + 3)}$

Canceling $x + 3$ from the numerator and denominator leaves you with $\frac{x - 4}{x - 3}$.

SOLVING EQUATIONS

63. SOLVING A LINEAR EQUATION

To solve an equation, do whatever is necessary to both sides to **isolate the variable.** To solve $5x - 12 = -2x + 9$, first get all the x's on one side by adding $2x$ to both sides: $7x - 12 = 9$. Then add 12 to both sides: $7x = 21$, then divide both sides by 7 to get: $x = 3$.

64. SOLVING "IN TERMS OF"

To solve an equation for one variable **in terms of** another means to **isolate the one variable on one side of the equation**, leaving an expression containing the other variable on the other side. To solve $3x - 10y = -5x + 6y$ for x in terms of y, isolate x:

$$3x - 10y = -5x + 6y$$
$$3x + 5x = 6y + 10y$$
$$8x = 16y$$
$$x = 2y$$

65. TRANSLATING FROM ENGLISH INTO ALGEBRA

To translate from English into algebra, look for the key words and systematically turn phrases into algebraic expressions and sentences into equations. Be careful about order, especially when subtraction is called for.

Example: The charge for a phone call is r cents for the first 3 minutes and s cents for each minute thereafter. What is the cost, in cents, of a call lasting exactly t minutes? ($t > 3$)

Setup: The charge begins with r, and then something more is added, depending on the length of the call. The amount added is s times the number of minutes past 3 minutes. If the total number of minutes is t, then the number of minutes past 3 is $t - 3$. So the charge is $r + s(t - 3)$.

INTERMEDIATE ALGEBRA

66. SOLVING A QUADRATIC EQUATION

To solve a quadratic equation, put it in the $ax^2 + bx + c = 0$ form, **factor** the left side (if you can), and set each factor equal to 0 separately to get the two solutions. To solve $x^2 + 12 = 7x$, first rewrite it as $x^2 - 7x + 12 = 0$. Then factor the left side:

$$(x - 3)(x - 4) = 0$$
$$x - 3 = 0 \text{ or } x - 4 = 0$$
$$x = 3 \text{ or } 4$$

Sometimes the left side might not be obviously factorable. You can always use the **quadratic formula.** Just plug in the coefficients a, b, and c from $ax^2 + bx + c = 0$ into the formula:

$$\frac{-b \pm \sqrt{b^2 - 4ac}}{2a}$$

To solve $x^2 + 4x + 2 = 0$, plug $a = 1$, $b = 4$, and $c = 2$ into the formula:

$$x = \frac{-4 \pm \sqrt{4^2 - 4 \times 1 \times 2}}{2 \times 1}$$

$$= \frac{-4 \pm \sqrt{8}}{2} = -2 \pm \sqrt{2}$$

67. SOLVING A SYSTEM OF EQUATIONS

You can solve for two variables only if you have two distinct equations. Two forms of the same equation will not be adequate. **Combine the equations in such a way that one of the variables cancels out.** To solve the two equations $4x + 3y = 8$ and $x + y = 3$, multiply both sides of the second equation by -3 to get: $-3x - 3y = -9$. Now add the equations; the $3y$ and the $-3y$ cancel out, leaving: $x = -1$. Plug that back into either one of the original equations and you'll find that $y = 4$.

68. SOLVING AN EQUATION THAT INCLUDES ABSOLUTE VALUE SIGNS

To solve an equation that includes absolute value signs, **think about the two different cases**. For example, to solve the equation $|x-12| = 3$, think of it as two equations:

$$x - 12 = 3 \text{ or } x - 12 = -3$$
$$x = 15 \text{ or } 9$$

69. SOLVING AN INEQUALITY

To solve an inequality, do whatever is necessary to both sides to **isolate the variable**. Just remember that when you **multiply or divide both sides by a negative number**, you must **reverse the sign**. To solve $-5x + 7 < -3$, subtract 7 from both sides to get: $-5x < -10$. Now divide both sides by -5, remembering to reverse the sign: $x > 2$.

70. GRAPHING INEQUALITIES

To graph a range of values, use a thick, black line over the number line, and at the end(s) of the range, use a **solid circle** if the point ***is* included** or an **open circle** if the point is ***not* included**. The figure here shows the graph of $-3 < x \leq 5$.

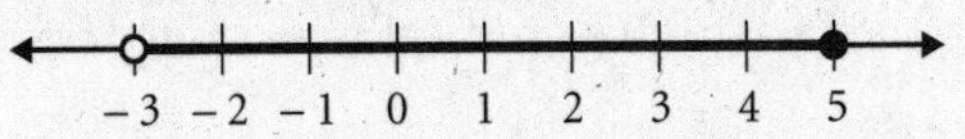

COORDINATE GEOMETRY

71. FINDING THE DISTANCE BETWEEN TWO POINTS

To find the distance between points, **use the Pythagorean theorem or special right triangles.** The difference between the x's is one leg and the difference between the y's is the other leg.

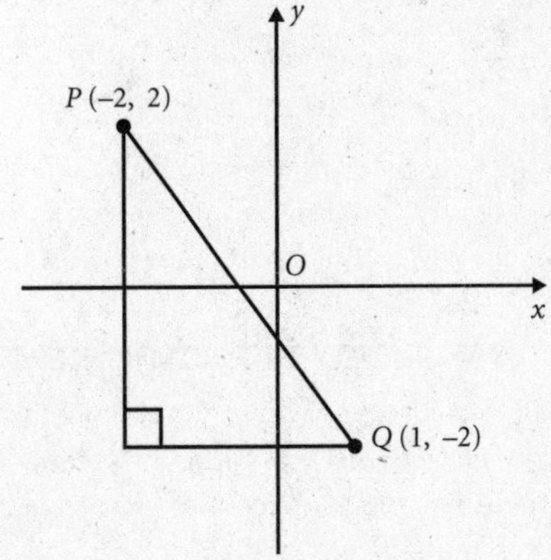

In the figure above, $\overline{PQ}$ is the hypotenuse of a 3-4-5 triangle, so $PQ = 5$.

You can also use the **distance formula:**

$$d = \sqrt{(x_2 - x_1)^2 + (y_2 - y_1)^2}$$

To find the distance between $R(3, 6)$ and $S(5, -2)$:

$$d = \sqrt{(5 - 3)^2 + (-2 - 6)^2}$$
$$= \sqrt{(2)^2 + (-8)^2}$$
$$= \sqrt{68} = 2\sqrt{17}$$

72. USING TWO POINTS TO FIND THE SLOPE

In mathematics, the slope of a line is often called m.

$$\text{Slope} = m = \frac{\text{Change in } y}{\text{Change in } x} = \frac{\text{Rise}}{\text{Run}}$$

The slope of the line that contains the points $A(2, 3)$ and $B(0, -1)$ is:

$$\frac{y_2 - y_1}{x_2 - x_1} = \frac{-1 - 3}{0 - 2} = \frac{-4}{-2} = 2$$

73. USING AN EQUATION TO FIND THE SLOPE

To find the slope of a line from an equation, put the equation into the **slope-intercept** form:

$y = mx + b$

The slope is m. To find the slope of the equation $3x + 2y = 4$, reexpress it:

$3x + 2y = 4$

$2y = -3x + 4$

$y = -\frac{3}{2}x + 2$

The slope is $-\frac{3}{2}$.

74. USING AN EQUATION TO FIND AN INTERCEPT

To find the y-intercept, you can either put the equation into $y = mx + b$ **(slope-intercept)** form—in which case b is the y-intercept—or you can just plug $x = 0$ into the equation and solve for y. To find the x-intercept, plug $y = 0$ into the equation and solve for x.

75. EQUATION FOR A CIRCLE

The equation for a circle of radius r and centered at (h, k) is

$$(x - h)^2 + (y - k)^2 = r^2$$

The figure below shows the graph of the equation $(x - 2)^2 + (y + 1)^2 = 25$:

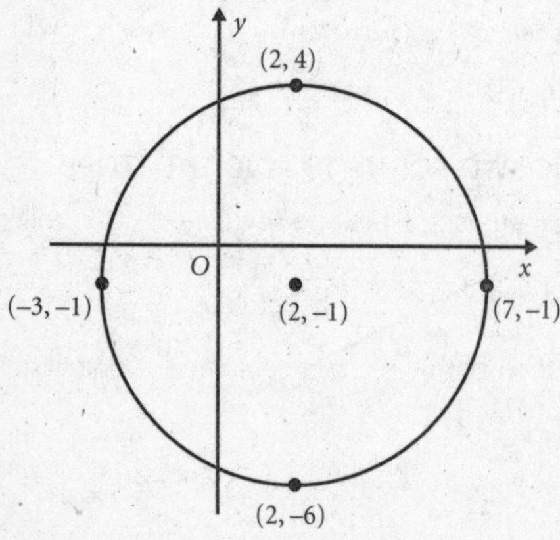

76. EQUATION FOR A PARABOLA

The graph of an equation in the form $y = ax^2 + bx + c$ is a parabola. The figure below shows the graph of seven pairs of numbers that satisfy the equation $y = x^2 - 4x + 3$:

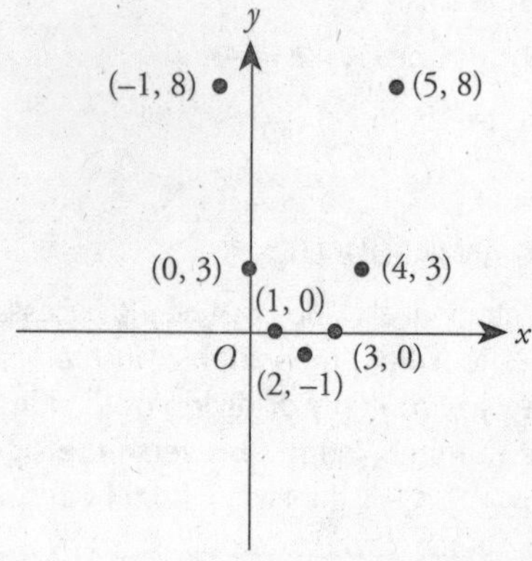

77. EQUATION FOR AN ELLIPSE

The graph of an equation in the form

$$\frac{x^2}{a^2} + \frac{y^2}{b^2} = 1$$

is an ellipse with $2a$ as the sum of the focal radii and with foci on the x-axis at $(0, -c)$ and $(0, c)$, where $c = \sqrt{a^2 - b^2}$. The figure below shows the graph of: $\frac{x^2}{25} + \frac{y^2}{16} = 1$

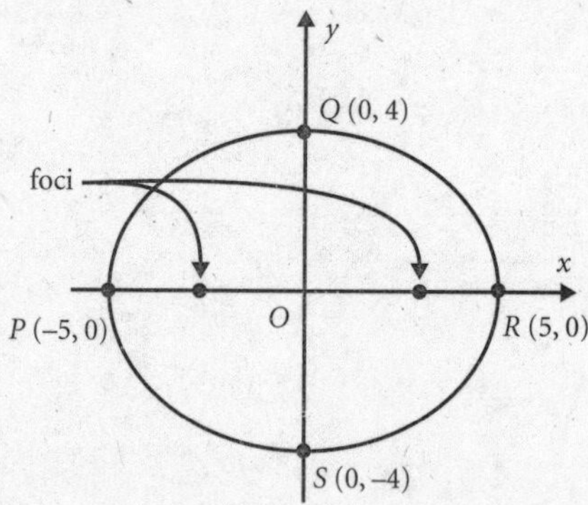

The foci are at (–3, 0) and (3, 0). $\overline{PR}$ is the **major axis**, and $\overline{QS}$ is the **minor axis**. This ellipse is symmetrical about both the x- and y-axes.

LINES AND ANGLES

78. INTERSECTING LINES

When two lines intersect, **adjacent angles are supplementary** and **vertical angles are equal**.

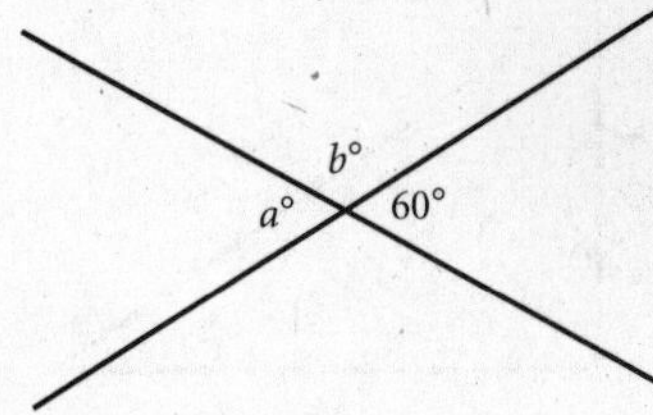

In the figure above, the angles marked $a°$ and $b°$ are adjacent and supplementary, so $a + b = 180$. Furthermore, the angles marked $a°$ and 60° are vertical and equal, so $a = 60$.

79. PARALLEL LINES AND TRANSVERSALS

A transversal across parallel lines forms **four equal acute angles and four equal obtuse angles.**

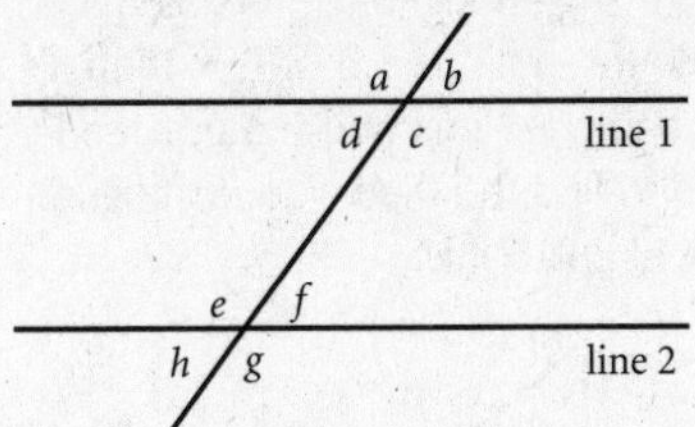

Here, line 1 is parallel to line 2. Angles a, c, e, and g are obtuse, so they are all equal. Angles b, d, f, and h are acute, so they are all equal.

Furthermore, **any of the acute angles is supplementary to any of the obtuse angles**. Angles a and h are supplementary, as are b and e, c and f, and so on.

TRIANGLES—GENERAL

80. INTERIOR ANGLES OF A TRIANGLE

The three angles of any triangle **add up to 180°**.

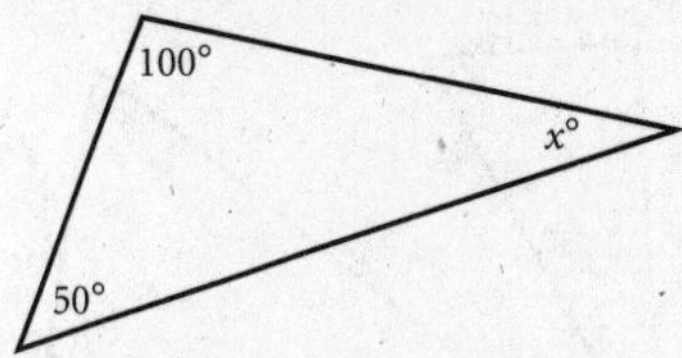

In the figure above, $x + 50 + 100 = 180$, so $x = 30$.

81. EXTERIOR ANGLES OF A TRIANGLE

An exterior angle of a triangle is equal to the **sum of the remote interior angles.**

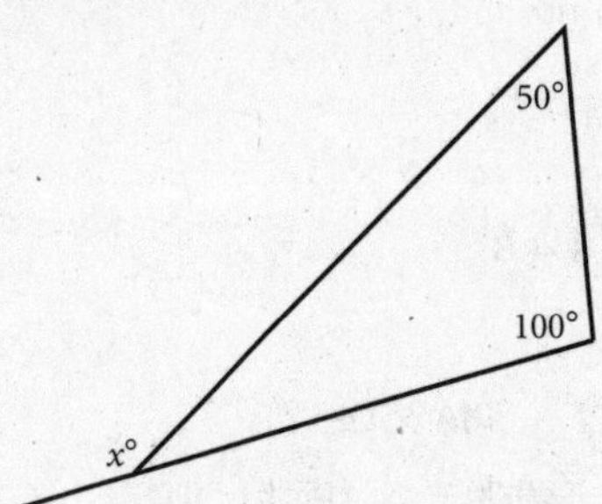

In the figure above, the exterior angle labeled $x°$ is equal to the sum of the remote interior angles:

$x = 50 + 100 = 150$.

The three exterior angles of any triangle add up to 360°.

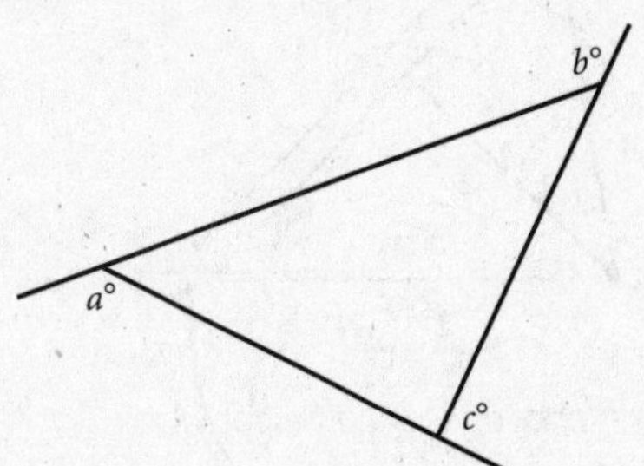

In the figure above, $a + b + c = 360$.

82. SIMILAR TRIANGLES

Similar triangles have the same shape: **corresponding angles are equal and corresponding sides are proportional.**

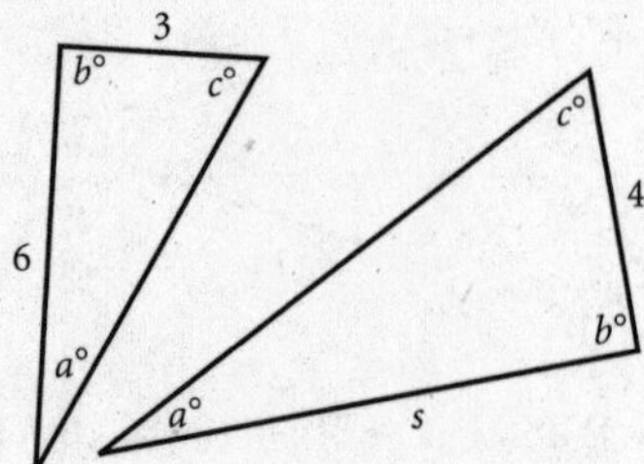

The triangles above are similar because they have the same angles. The 3 corresponds to the 4 and the 6 corresponds to the *s*.

$$\frac{3}{4} = \frac{6}{s}$$

$$3s = 24$$

$$s = 8$$

83. AREA OF A TRIANGLE

Area of Triangle $= \frac{1}{2}$ (base)(height)

The height is the perpendicular distance between the side that's chosen as the base and the opposite vertex.

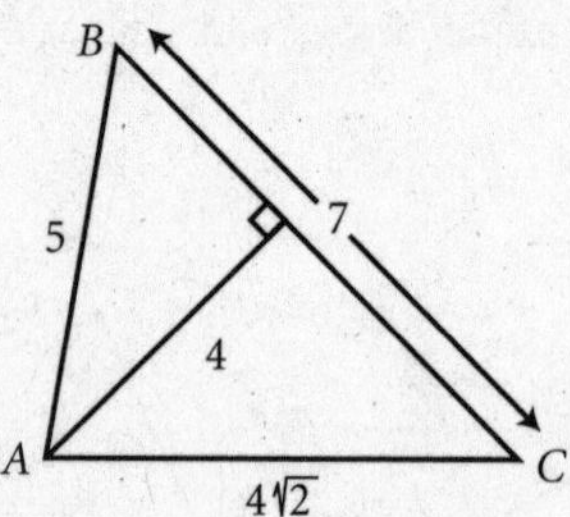

In the triangle above, 4 is the height when the 7 is chosen as the base.

Area $= \frac{1}{2}bh = \frac{1}{2}(7)(4) = 14$

RIGHT TRIANGLES

84. PYTHAGOREAN THEOREM

For all right triangles:

$(\text{leg}_1)^2 + (\text{leg}_2)^2 = (\text{hypotenuse})^2$

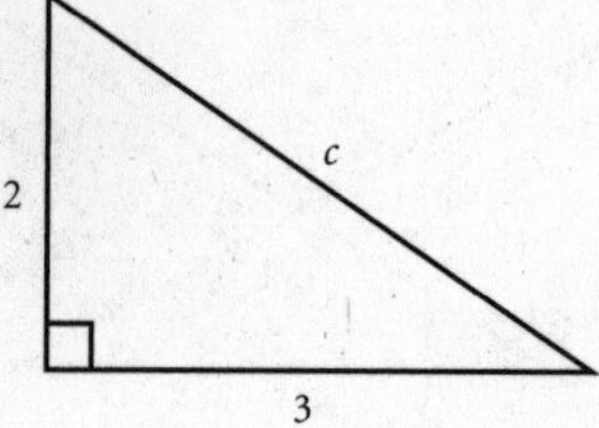

If one leg is 2 and the other leg is 3, then:

$$2^2 + 3^2 = c^2$$

$$c^2 = 4 + 9$$

$$c = \sqrt{13}$$

85. SPECIAL RIGHT TRIANGLES

• ***3-4-5***

If a right triangle's leg-to-leg ratio is 3:4, or if the leg-to-hypotenuse ratio is 3:5 or 4:5, then it's a 3-4-5 triangle and you don't need to use the Pythagorean theorem to find the third side. Just figure out what multiple of 3-4-5 it is.

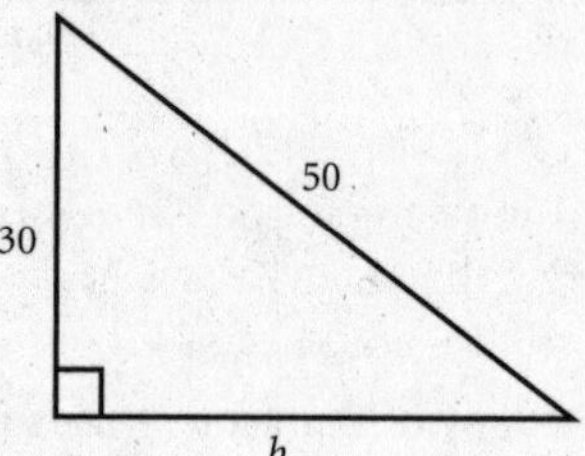

In the right triangle above, one leg is 30 and the hypotenuse is 50. This is 10 times 3-4-5. The other leg is 40.

• ***5-12-13***

If a right triangle's leg-to-leg ratio is 5:12, or if the leg-to-hypotenuse ratio is 5:13 or 12:13, then it's a 5-12-13 triangle and you don't need to use the Pythagorean theorem to find the third side. Just figure out what multiple of 5-12-13 it is.

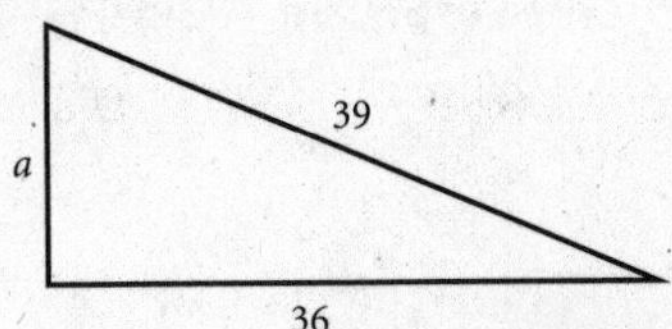

Here one leg is 36 and the hypotenuse is 39. This is 3 times 5-12-13. The other leg is 15.

• ***30°-60°-90°***

The sides of a 30°-60°-90° triangle are in a ratio of **$1 : \sqrt{3} : 2$**. You don't need to use the Pythagorean theorem.

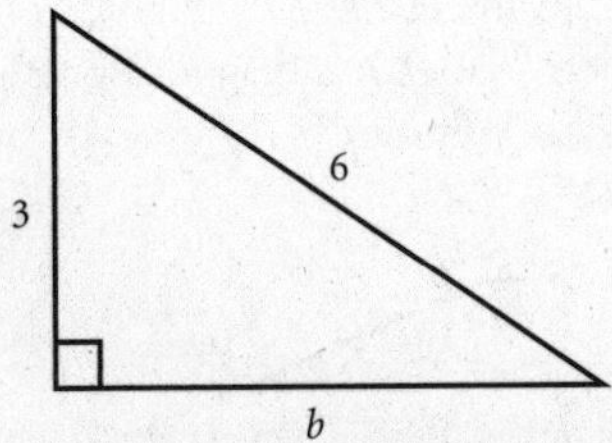

If the hypotenuse is 6, then the shorter leg is half that, or 3; and then the longer leg is equal to the short leg times $\sqrt{3}$, or $3\sqrt{3}$.

• ***45°-45°-90°***

The sides of a 45°-45°-90° triangle are in a ratio of **$1 : 1 : \sqrt{2}$.**

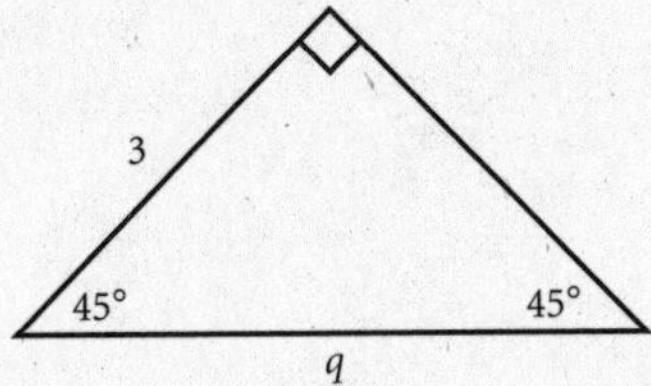

If one leg is 3, then the other leg is also 3, and the hypotenuse is equal to a leg times $\sqrt{2}$, or $3\sqrt{2}$.

OTHER POLYGONS

86. SPECIAL QUADRILATERALS

• ***Rectangle***

A rectangle is a **four-sided figure with four right angles**. Opposite sides are equal. Diagonals are equal.

Quadrilateral *ABCD* above is shown to have three right angles. The fourth angle therefore also measures 90°, and *ABCD* is a rectangle. The perimeter of a rectangle is equal to the sum of the lengths of the four sides, which is equivalent to 2(length + width).

• ***Parallelogram***

A parallelogram has **two pairs of parallel sides.** Opposite sides are equal. Opposite angles are equal. Consecutive angles add up to 180˚.

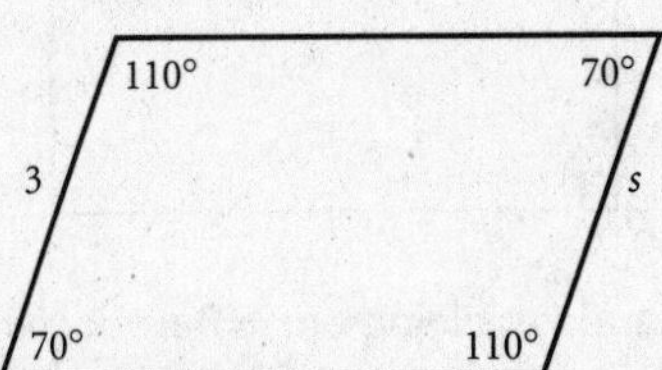

In the figure above, s is the length of the side opposite the 3, so $s = 3$.

• ***Square***

A square is a **rectangle with 4 equal sides.**

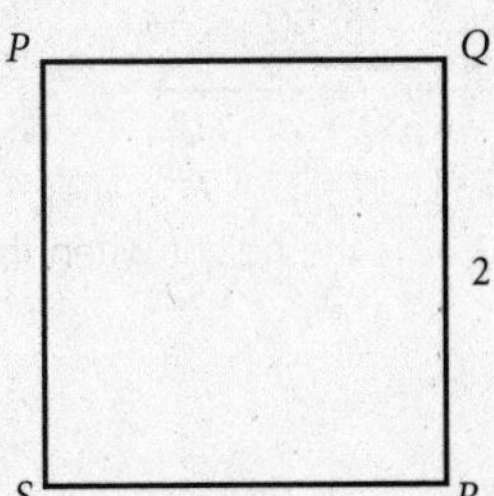

If *PQRS* is a square, all sides are the same length as *QR*. The perimeter of a square is equal to four times the length of one side.

- **Trapezoid**

A **trapezoid** is a quadrilateral with one pair of parallel sides and one pair of nonparallel sides.

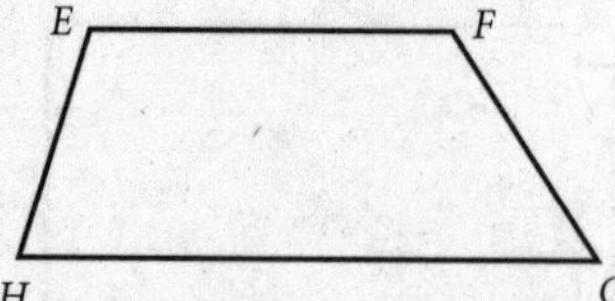

In the quadrilateral above, sides $\overline{EF}$ and $\overline{GH}$ are parallel, while sides $\overline{EH}$ and $\overline{FG}$ are not parallel. *EFGH* is therefore a trapezoid.

87. AREAS OF SPECIAL QUADRILATERALS

Area of Rectangle = Length × Width

The area of a 7-by-3 rectangle is $7 \times 3 = 21$.

Area of Parallelogram = Base × Height

The area of a parallelogram with a height of 4 and a base of 6 is $4 \times 6 = 24$.

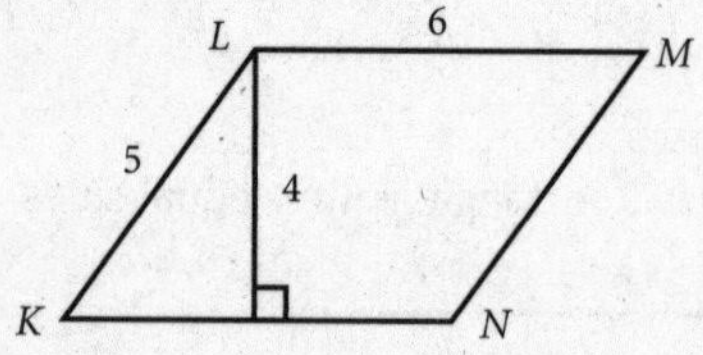

Area of Square = (Side)²

The area of a square with sides of length 5 is $5^2 = 25$.

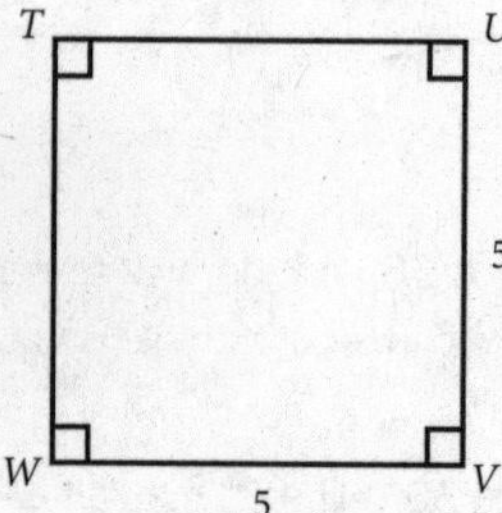

$$\textbf{Area of Trapezoid} = \left(\frac{\text{base}_1 + \text{base}_2}{2}\right) \times \textbf{height}$$

Think of it as the average of the bases (the two parallel sides) times the height (the length of the perpendicular altitude).

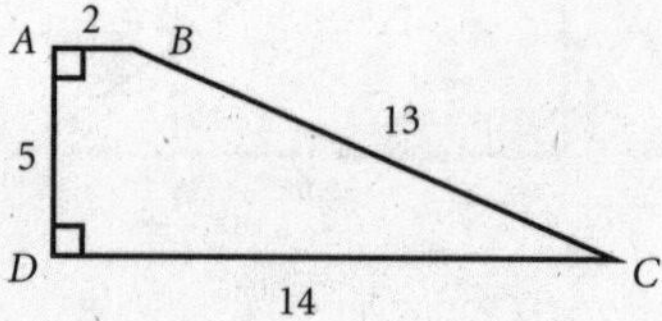

In the trapezoid *ABCD* above, you can use side $\overline{AD}$ for the height. The average of the bases is $\frac{2 + 14}{2} = 8$, so the area is 5×8, or 40.

88. INTERIOR ANGLES OF A POLYGON

The sum of the measures of the interior angles of a polygon is $(n - 2) \times 180$, where n is the number of sides.

Sum of the angles = $(n - 2) \times 180$ degrees

The eight angles of an octagon, for example, add up to $(8 - 2) \times 180 = 1{,}080$.

To find **one angle of a regular polygon**, divide the sum of the angles by the number of angles (which is the same as the number of sides). The formula, therefore, is:

$$\text{Interior angle} = \frac{(n-2) \times 180}{n}$$

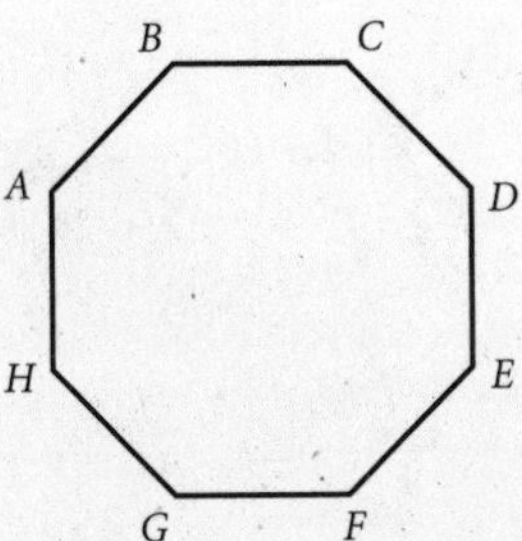

Angle A of the regular octagon above measures $\frac{1{,}080}{8}$ degrees.

CIRCLES

89. CIRCUMFERENCE OF A CIRCLE

Circumference of a circle = $2\pi r$

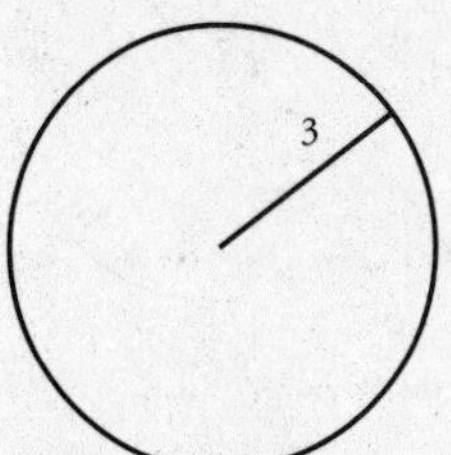

Here, the radius is 3, and so the circumference is $2\pi(3) = 6\pi$.

90. LENGTH OF AN ARC

An **arc** is a piece of the circumference. If n is the measure of the arc's central angle, then the formula is:

$$\text{Length of an Arc} = \frac{n}{360}(2\pi r)$$

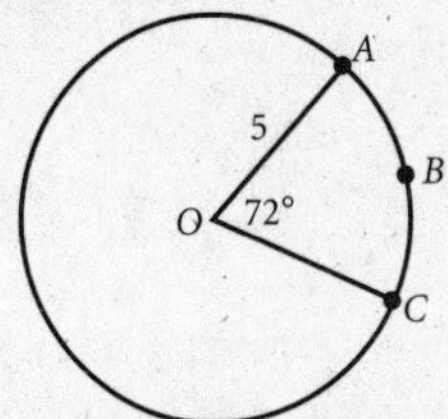

In the preceding figure, the radius is 5 and the measure of the central angle is 72°. The arc length is $\frac{72}{360}$ or $\frac{1}{5}$ of the circumference:

$$\left(\frac{72}{360}\right) 2\pi\,(5) = \left(\frac{1}{5}\right) 10\pi = 2\pi$$

91. AREA OF A CIRCLE

$$\text{Area of a circle} = \pi r^2$$

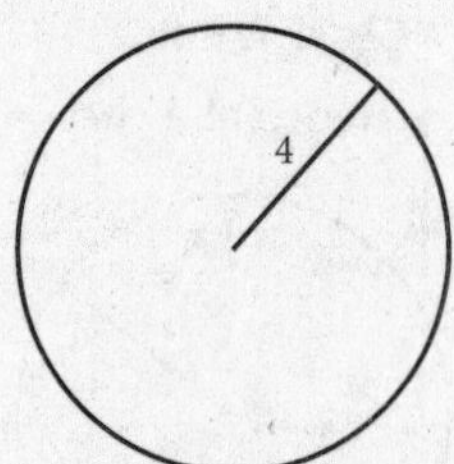

The area of the circle above is $\pi(4)^2 = 16\pi$.

92. AREA OF A SECTOR

A **sector** is a piece of the area of a circle. If n is the measure of the sector's central angle, then the formula is:

$$\text{Area of a Sector} = \left(\frac{n}{360}\right)(\pi r^2)$$

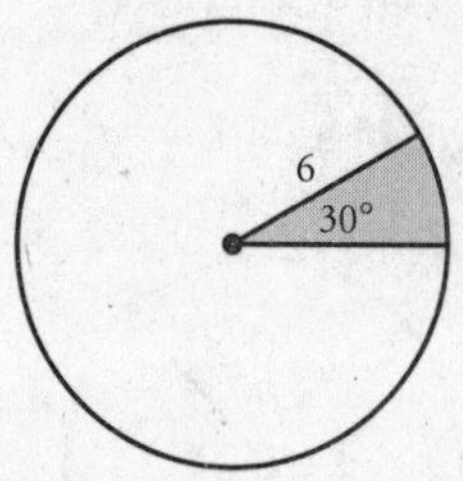

In the figure above, the radius is 6 and the measure of the sector's central angle is 30°. The sector has $\frac{30}{360}$ or $\frac{1}{12}$ of the area of the circle:

$$\left(\frac{30}{360}\right)(\pi)(6^2) = \left(\frac{1}{12}\right)(36\pi) = 3\pi$$

SOLIDS

93. SURFACE AREA OF A RECTANGULAR SOLID

The surface of a rectangular solid consists of 3 pairs of identical faces. To find the surface area, find the area of each face and add them up. If the length is l, the width is w, and the height is h, the formula is:

$$\text{Surface Area} = 2lw + 2wh + 2lh$$

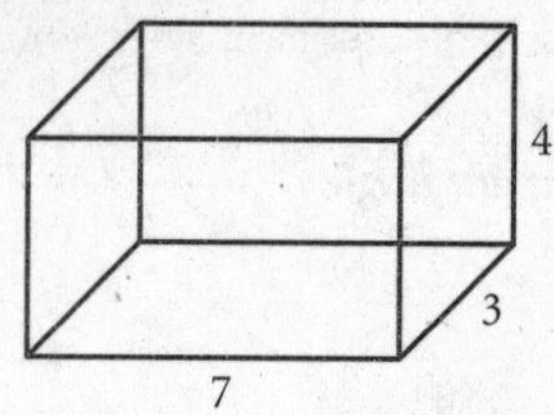

The surface area of the box above is:

$$2 \cdot 7 \cdot 3 + 2 \cdot 3 \cdot 4 + 2 \cdot 7 \cdot 4 = 42 + 24 + 56 = 122$$

94. VOLUME OF A RECTANGULAR SOLID

Volume of a Rectangular Solid = lwh

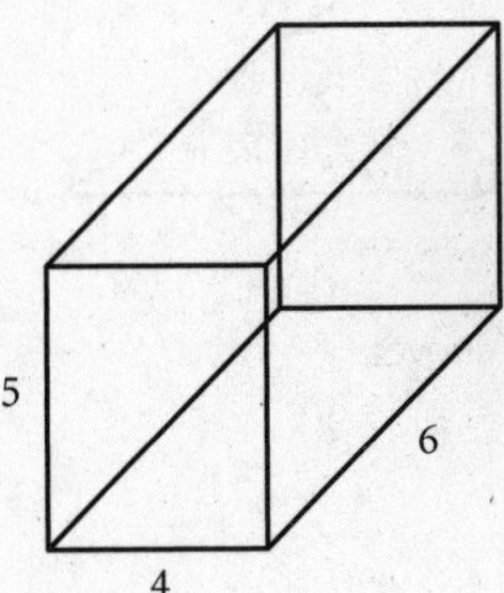

The volume of a 4-by-5-by-6 box is $4 \times 5 \times 6 = 120$

A cube is a rectangular solid with length, width, and height all equal. The volume formula is below, if e is the length of an edge of the cube.

Volume of a Cube = e^3

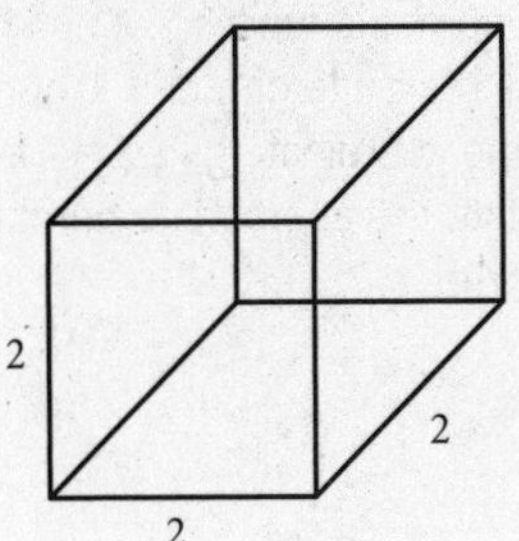

The volume of the cube above is $2^3 = 8$.

95. VOLUME OF OTHER SOLIDS

Volume of a Cylinder = $\pi r^2 h$

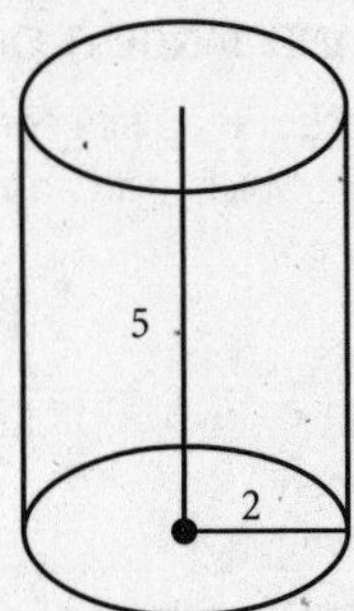

The volume of a cylinder where $r = 2$, and $h = 5$ is $\pi(2^2)(5) = 20\pi$

Volume of a Cone = $\frac{1}{3}\pi r^2 h$

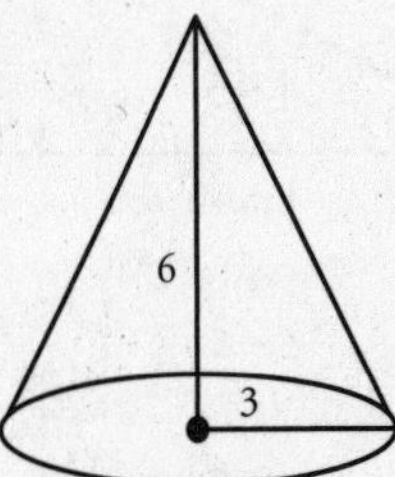

The volume of a cone where $r = 3$, and $h = 6$ is:

$$\text{Volume} = \frac{1}{3}\pi(3^2)(6) = 18$$

Volume of a Sphere = $\frac{4}{3}\pi r^3$

If the radius of a sphere is 3, then:

$$\text{Volume} = \frac{4}{3}\pi(3^3) = 36\pi$$

TRIGONOMETRY

96. SINE, COSINE, AND TANGENT OF ACUTE ANGLES

To find the sine, cosine, or tangent of an acute angle, use SOHCAHTOA, which is an abbreviation for the following definitions:

$$\textit{Sine} = \frac{\text{Opposite}}{\text{Hypotenuse}}$$

$$\textit{Cosine} = \frac{\text{Adjacent}}{\text{Hypotenuse}}$$

$$\textit{Tangent} = \frac{\text{Opposite}}{\text{Adjacent}}$$

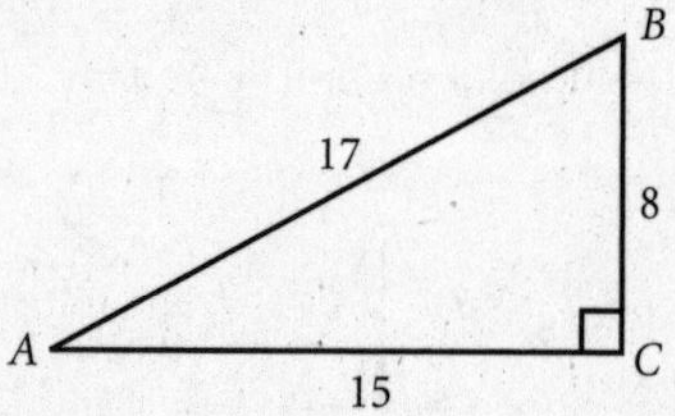

In the figure above:

$$\sin A = \frac{8}{17}$$

$$\cos A = \frac{15}{17}$$

$$\tan A = \frac{8}{15}$$

97. COTANGENT, SECANT, AND COSECANT OF ACUTE ANGLES

Think of the cotangent, secant, and cosecant as the reciprocals of the SOHCAHTOA functions:

$$\textit{Cotangent} = \frac{1}{\text{Tangent}} = \frac{\text{Adjacent}}{\text{Opposite}}$$

$$\textit{Secant} = \frac{1}{\text{Cosine}} = \frac{\text{Hypotenuse}}{\text{Adjacent}}$$

$$\textit{Cosecant} = \frac{1}{\text{Sine}} = \frac{\text{Hypotenuse}}{\text{Opposite}}$$

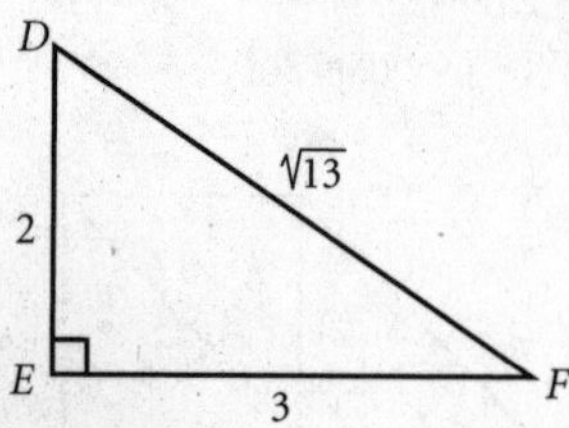

In the figure above:

$$\cot D = \frac{2}{3}$$

$$\sec D = \frac{\sqrt{13}}{2}$$

$$\csc D = \frac{\sqrt{13}}{3}$$

98. TRIGONOMETRIC FUNCTIONS OF OTHER ANGLES

To find a trigonometric function of an angle greater than 90°, sketch a circle of radius 1 and centered at the origin of the coordinate grid. Start from the point (1, 0) and rotate the appropriate number of degrees counterclockwise.

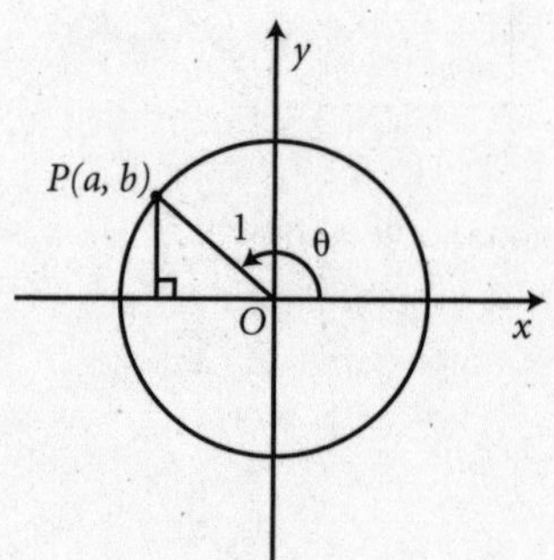

In the "unit circle" setup above, the basic trigonometric functions are defined in terms of the coordinates a and b:

$$\sin \theta = b$$

$$\cos \theta = a$$

$$\tan \theta = \frac{b}{a}$$

Example: $\sin 210° = ?$

Setup: Sketch a 210° angle in the coordinate plane:

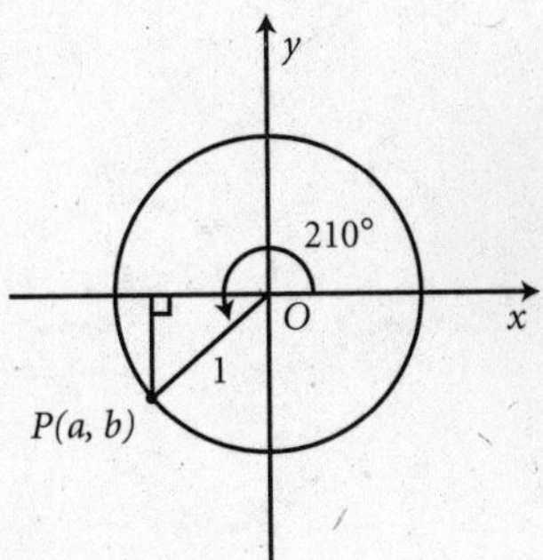

Because the triangle shown in the figure above is a 30°-60°-90° right triangle, we can determine that the coordinates of point P are $-\frac{\sqrt{3}}{2}, -\frac{1}{2}$. The sine is therefore $-\frac{1}{2}$.

99. SIMPLIFYING TRIGONOMETRIC EXPRESSIONS

To simplify trigonometric expressions, use the inverse function definitions along with the fundamental trigonometric identity:

$$\sin^2 x + \cos^2 x = 1$$

Example: $\frac{\sin^2 \theta + \cos^2 \theta}{\cos \theta} = ?$

Setup: The numerator equals 1, so:

$$\frac{\sin^2 \theta + \cos^2 \theta}{\cos \theta} = \frac{1}{\cos \theta} = \sec \theta$$

100. GRAPHING TRIGONOMETRIC FUNCTIONS

To graph trigonometric functions, use the x-axis for the angle and the y-axis for the value of the trigonometric function. Use special angles—0°, 30°, 45°, 60°, 90°, 120°, 135°, 150°, 180°, etc.—to plot key points.

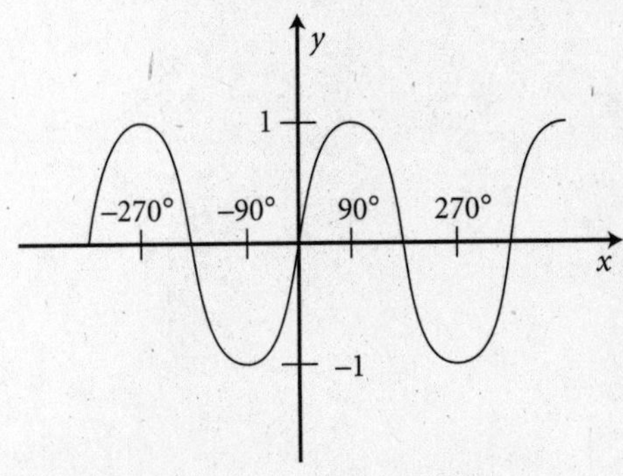

The figure above shows a portion of the graph of $y = \sin x$.

CD-ROM User's Guide

The CD-ROM you received with this book contains section-length practice tests for each question type on the ACT and two full-length practice tests. Once you've completed a test, the program scores and analyzes your results and offers comprehensive explanations to each question. We recommend alternating between the tests in your book and the tests on the CD-ROM.

SYSTEM REQUIREMENTS

Windows®:

Windows® 98SE, NT 4.0 (with Service Pack 6), 2000, ME, XP

Pentium®II 300 MHz or faster, 15 MB free hard disk space, 640 x 480–thousands of colors (millions recommended), SoundBlaster-compatible sound card, 4x CD-ROM or higher.

Note: An Internet connection is required for the web features of the program.

Macintosh®:

Macintosh® OS 8.6, OS 9.1, 9.2.2, OS 10.1.3, 10.1.5, 10.2.4, 10.2.8, 10.3, 10.3.7, 10.3.8, 10.4

400 MHz Power PC®, G3, G4 or faster, 15 MB free hard disk space, 640 x 480–thousands of colors (millions recommended), 4x CD-ROM or higher.

Note: An Internet connection is required for the web features of the program.

INSTALLATION INSTRUCTIONS

Windows®:

Exit out of all open applications; make sure you have no applications running.

Insert the Higher Score CD into your CD-ROM drive. The installation window opens automatically if Autorun is enabled on your system.

If you have Autorun disabled on your system, from the Start Menu, choose Run and type (or browse for) d:\setup.exe (where d: is your CD-ROM drive).

Press OK and follow the prompts.

You are now ready to use the software. You must have the CD-ROM in your computer when using the software, even though you have installed information on your hard drive. To launch the program, go to the Start Menu, choose Programs, then Kaplan and then Higher Score on the ACT or double-click the Higher Score on the ACT icon located on your desktop.

Macintosh®:

Exit out of all open applications; make sure you have no applications running.

Insert the Higher Score CD into your CD-ROM drive

Double-click the Kaplan install icon.

You will be presented with a dialog box that will let you choose where to install the program. Follow the prompts.

You are now ready to use the software. You must have the CD-ROM in your computer when using the software, even though you have installed information on your hard drive. To launch the program, double-click the Higher Score on the ACT icon.

User Tips:

You can skip over the introductory music by either hitting the **ESC** key or by going into the program Preferences and checking the box labeled "Skip Intro." You can use the **ESC** key to skip over most of the audio voice-overs or videos within the program. Please be sure to have your headphones plugged in or your speakers turned on before using the program. If you are experiencing any problems installing this program, please visit the Customer Service area of our website at kaptest.com/support.

GETTING STARTED

When you open the program, a dialogue box will ask if you would like to view Frequently Asked Questions on the ACT (see description below). Click "yes" or "no." If you choose to skip this, you then will be asked if you would like to take the Diagnostic Test. Clicking "no" will take you to the Home screen.

The Home screen has the following features.

Help: Click here for detailed instructions on all of the CD-ROM's features and on how to navigate through the different screens. This should be your first stop when using the software for the first time.

Test Center: The test center includes a full-length diagnostic test, two practice tests for each subject (English, Math, Reading, and Science), and two full-length practice tests.

My Test Scores: Get computerized feedback on your performance after you take a practice test.

Frequently Asked Questions: Here you can find anything and everything you'll need to know about the ACT. In the FAQ table of contents, click on a topic to get more information. When you choose a topic, you can use the arrow keys at the bottom of the page to navigate between topics.

kaptest.com: Click here to access the Kaplan website, where you'll find many more test-prep resources.

Quit: You probably can guess what clicking here will do.

Start by giving yourself a tour of the software using Help. Then take the Diagnostic Test to figure out where you need the most practice. My Test Scores will break down your results so that you know exactly where to focus your study, and each time you take a practice test you'll see where you have improved.

Good luck!

*Minimum System Requirements**

	Windows®	Macintosh®
Operating System:	Windows, 98SE, NT 4.0 (with Service Pack 6), 2000, ME, XP	Macintosh OS 8.6, OS 9, OS 10.1.3, 10.1.5, 10.2.4, 10.2.8, 10.3, 10.3.7, 10.3.8, 10.4
CPU Type and Speed:	Pentium II® 300 MHz or higher	400 MHz Power PC®, G3, G4, or higher
Hard Drive Space:	15 MB	15 MB
Graphics:	640x 480 thousands of colors (millions recommended)	640x 480 thousands of colors (millions recommended)
CD-ROM Speed:	4x CD-ROM or higher	4x CD-ROM or higher
	SoundBlaster compatible soundcard	
	Note: An Internet connection is required for the web features of this program.	Note: An Internet connection is required for the web features of this program.

Installation instructions are in the User's Guide.

If you need assistance with installations, need to request a replacement disk, or have any other software questions, please visit the "customer service" area of our website at www.kaptest.com.